LEGITIMACY AND LAW IN THE ROMAN WORLD

Greeks wrote mostly on papyrus, but the Romans wrote solemn religious, public, and legal documents on wooden tablets often coated with wax. This book investigates the historical significance of this resonant form of writing; its power to order the human realm and cosmos and to make documents efficacious; its role in court; the uneven spread – an aspect of Romanization – of this Roman form outside Italy, as provincials made different guesses as to what would please their Roman overlords; and its influence on the evolution of Roman law. An historical epoch of Roman legal transactions without writing is revealed as a juristic myth of origins. Roman legal documents on tablets are the ancestors of today's dispositive legal documents – the document as the act itself. In a world where knowledge of the Roman law was scarce – and enforcers scarcer – the Roman law drew its authority from a wider world of belief.

ELIZABETH A. MEYER is Associate Professor of History at the University of Virginia and has published articles on Roman history and epigraphy in several major journals.

LEGITIMACY AND LAW IN THE ROMAN WORLD

Tabulae *in Roman Belief and Practice*

ELIZABETH A. MEYER

University of Virginia

CAMBRIDGE UNIVERSITY PRESS
Cambridge, New York, Melbourne, Madrid, Cape Town, Singapore, São Paulo

Cambridge University Press
The Edinburgh Building, Cambridge CB2 8RU, UK

Published in the United States of America by Cambridge University Press, New York

www.cambridge.org
Information on this title: www.cambridge.org/9780521497015

© Elizabeth A. Meyer, 2004

This publication is in copyright. Subject to statutory exception
and to the provisions of relevant collective licensing agreements,
no reproduction of any part may take place without the written
permission of Cambridge University Press.

First published 2004
Third printing 2006

A catalogue record for this publication is available from the British Library

Library of Congress Cataloguing in Publication data
Meyer, Elizabeth A.
Legitimacy and law in the Roman world : tabulae in Roman belief and practice /
Elizabeth A. Meyer.
p.   cm.
Includes bibliographical references and index.
ISBN 0 521 49701 9 (hardback)
1. Legal documents (Roman law)   2. Roman law.   3. Wooden tablets – Rome – History.
I. Title.
KJA2170.L44M49   2004
340.5´4 – dc21   2003051532

ISBN 978-0-521-49701-5 hardback

Transferred to digital printing 2007

for my mother, and in memory of
my father (7.27.15–11.17.93)

Contents

List of illustrations	*page* viii
Acknowledgments	ix
List of abbreviations	xi
Introduction	1

PART ONE: THE WORLD OF BELIEF

1	The use and value of Greek legal documents	12
2	Roman perceptions of Roman tablets: aspects and associations	21
3	The Roman tablet: style and language	44
4	Recitation from tablets	73
5	Tablets and efficacy	91

PART TWO: THE EVOLUTION OF PRACTICE

6	Roman tablets in Italy (AD 15–79)	125
7	Roman tablets and related forms in the Roman provinces (30 BC–AD 260)	169
8	Tablets and other documents in court to AD 400	216
9	Documents, jurists, the emperor, and the law (AD 200–AD 535)	250
	Conclusion	294

References	299
Index	341

Illustrations

1	Phase 1 Campanian wooden document: simple diptych.	*page* 128
2	Phase 2 Campanian wooden document: doubled diptych.	129
3	Phase 3 Campanian wooden document: doubled diptych with *sulcus*.	130
4	Phase 4 Campanian wooden document: triptych.	131
5	Phase 5 Campanian wooden document: *pertusa* triptych.	132
6	Physical forms of formal procedural acts and official copies from first-century AD Campania.	147
7	Physical forms of formal financial documents from first-century AD Campania.	148
8	Physical forms of chirograph documents from first-century AD Campania.	153
9	Papyrus double-document.	189

Acknowledgments

The trunk, branches, and leaves of this book have their root in a Yale thesis of many years ago. Ramsay MacMullen and Gordon Williams supervised it, and in years after the one propped and guided the sapling, while the other watered it with a gardener's anxious patience, and kept the gnawing squirrels away. Richard Garner, too, guarded the shoot at its emergence, and subsequently encouraged its growth. J. E. Lendon – with much sweat and occasional good-natured swearing – repeatedly pruned over-luxuriance, those branches that drew off vitality from the major growth. Without their devoted care, weeds, drought, and beetles might long ago have doomed the tree.

Others, too, have been remarkably kind and generous with their time. The entire manuscript was read, at different stages, by Daniel Gargola, Joseph Kett, Melvyn Leffler, Diana Moses, T. F. X. Noble, Richard Saller, Michele Salzman, and David Snyder. Helpful *anonymi* read it as well, both for the Press and for the University of Virginia, and sent unsigned suggestions for improvement. (Keith Hopkins long ago, and David Johnston more recently, have unveiled themselves, and so it is my privilege to thank them by name.) Help with queries or specific chapters was generously given by Edward Courtney, Joe Day, Denis Feeney, Kenneth Harl, Ann Kuttner, David Martinez, and Elizabeth Tylawsky. Together all have helped to make this a far better book, although they are not, of course, responsible for its contents.

Fellowships from the Mrs. Giles Whiting Foundation, the American Council of Learned Societies, the National Endowment for the Humanities, and the University of Virginia all provided time to work on the project. As a junior fellow at the Center for Hellenic Studies, under the enlightened regime of Kurt Raaflaub and Deborah Boedeker, my understanding of Greek parallels in the Roman imperial context was much advanced. Friends and colleagues at the Center, at Yale (once upon a time), and now at the

x   *Acknowledgments*

University of Virginia – especially the art historian Christopher Johns – have all made me realize how fortunate I have been in my intellectual companions, and how necessary such companionship is in the creation of any scholarly work.

Pauline Hire accepted the book for publication by Cambridge, but its revision outlasted her reign, and as a consequence it appears under the able and protective editorship of Michael Sharp, who has also provided much helpful support in the years it has taken us to get this book to press. I am also grateful to Lew Purifoy and his peerless Interlibrary loan staff at Virginia, to Mike Powers, who checked references for me, and to Linda Woodward, who meticulously copy-edited a long and difficult typescript.

Unless indicated, translations are my own, but are often influenced by those of previous translators: to any I may have slighted of recognition, I offer my thanks here.

Abbreviations

Standard abbreviations (from H. G. Liddell and R. Scott, *A Greek–English Lexicon* [Oxford, 1968] or the *OLD*, sometimes expanded) are used for ancient authors and works cited in the notes. Abbreviations for papyri and tablets come from J. F. Oates *et al.*, *Checklist of Greek, Latin, Demotic and Coptic Papyri, Ostraca, and Tablets*, 5th edn. (*Bulletin of the American Society of Papyrologists* Supplement 9 [2001]); I have listed other abbreviations I use most frequently below, along with abbreviations for collections of Roman law books and inscriptions. Journal titles are written out in full in the bibliography.

AE	*L'Année épigraphique*, various editors (1888–). Paris.
ANRW	*Aufstieg und Niedergang der römischen Welt*, H. Temporini and W. Haase, eds. (1972–). Berlin and New York.
CAH²	*The Cambridge Ancient History*, 2nd edn., various editors (1961–). Cambridge.
CCSL	*Corpus christianorum series latina*, various editors (1956–). Turnhout.
CEL	*Corpus epistularum latinarum* (*Papyrologica florentina* 23), P. Cugusi, ed. (1992). Florence.
CGL	*Corpus glossariorum latinorum*, G. Goetz, ed. (1893–1901), seven volumes. Leipzig.
ChLA	*Chartae latinae antiquiores*, A. Bruckner and R. Marichal, eds. (1954–). Basel.
CIL	*Corpus inscriptionum latinarum*, various editors (1863–). Berlin.
CJ	*Codex Iustinianus* (*Corpus iuris civilis*, 3rd edn., II), P. Krueger, ed. (1884). Berlin.
CLE	*Carmina latina epigraphica*, F. Buecheler and E. Lommatzsch, eds. (1895–1926). Leipzig.

xii   *Abbreviations*

Coll.   *Mosaicarum et romanarum legum collatio*, J. Baviera,
                 ed., in *FIRA²* II.544–89.
Cons.   *Consultatio veteris cuiusdam iurisconsulti*, J. Baviera,
                 ed., in *FIRA²* II.591–613.
CPL   *Corpus papyrorum latinarum*, R. Cavanaile, ed.
                 (1958). Wiesbaden.
CT   *Theodosiani libri XVI cum constitutionibus
                 Sirmondianis et leges novellae ad Theodosianum
                 pertinentes I. Codex Theodosianus,* 2nd edn.,
                 T. Mommsen and P. Meyer, eds. (1905). Berlin.
D.   *Digesti Iustiniani Augusti*, T. Mommsen and
                 P. Krueger, eds. (1868). Berlin.
DJD 27   *Discoveries in the Judaean Desert XXVII: Aramaic,
                 Hebrew and Greek Documentary Texts from Naḥal
                 Ḥever and Other Sites*, H. M. Cotton and
                 A. Yardeni, eds. (1997). Oxford.
FGH   *Fragmente der griechischen Historiker*, F. Jacoby,
                 ed. (1923–). Berlin.
FIRA²   *Fontes iuris romani anteiustiniani*, 2nd edn.,
                 S. Riccobono *et al.*, eds., (1940–69), three volumes.
                 Florence.
FV   *Fragmenta quae dicuntur vaticana*, J. Baviera, ed., in
                 FIRA² II.464–540.
G.   *Gai institutionum commentarii quattuor*, E. Seckel
                 and B. Kübler, eds. (1935). Leipzig.
GL   *Grammatici latini*, H. Keil, ed. (1855–1923), eight
                 volumes. Leipzig.
IC   *Inscriptiones creticae*, M. Guarducci, ed. (1925–50),
                 four volumes. Rome.
IDR/TabCerD.   *Inscripţiile Daciei Romane* 1.165–264 (*Tablitele
                 Cerate Dacice*), I. Russu, ed. (1975).
                 Bucharest.
IG   *Inscriptiones graecae*, various editors (1873–). Berlin.
IGBulg.   *Inscriptiones graecae in Bulgaria repertae*,
                 H. Mikhailov, ed. (1958–70). Sofia.
IGLS   *Inscriptions grecques et latines de la Syrie*, L. Jalabert
                 et al., eds. (1911–86). Paris.
IGR   *Inscriptiones graecae ad res romanas pertinentes*,
                 R. Cagnat *et al.*, eds. (1906–27), three volumes.
                 Paris.

Abbreviations

IKEph.	*Inschriften griechischer Städte aus Kleinasien 11–17: Die Inschriften von Ephesos*, H. Wankel *et al.*, eds. (1979–84). Bonn.
IKSmyrna	*Inschriften griechischer Städte aus Kleinasien 23–24: Die Inschriften von Smyrna*, G. Petzl, ed. (1982–90). Bonn.
IKStrat.	*Inschriften griechischer Städte aus Kleinasien 21–22: Die Inschriften von Stratonikeia*, M. Çetin Şahin, ed. (1981–90). Bonn.
ILBelg.	*Les Inscriptions latines de Belgique*, A. Deman and M.-T. Raepsaet-Charlier, eds. (1985). Brussels.
ILLRP	*Inscriptiones latinae liberae rei publicae*, A. Degrassi, ed. (1963–5), two volumes. Florence.
ILS	*Inscriptiones latinae selectae*, H. Dessau, ed. (1892–1916), three volumes. Berlin.
Inscr.Ital.	*Inscriptiones Italiae*, various editors (1931/2–). Rome.
I.Priene	*Inschriften von Priene*, F. Hiller von Gaertringen, ed. (1906). Berlin.
Just. *Inst.*	*Iustiniani institutiones*, 2nd edn., P. Krueger, ed. (1899). Berlin.
Lex Irn.	"The *Lex Irnitana*: a New Copy of the Flavian Municipal Law," J. Gonzalez, *Journal of Roman Studies* 76 (1986): 147–243.
Leg. Vis.	*Leges visigothorum*, K. Zeumer, ed. (1902), in *Monumenta germaniae historica. Leges* (quarto series), *Sectio 1*, vol. 1. Hanover and Leipzig.
LRB	*Lex romana burgundiorum*, L. R. de Salis, ed. (1892), in *Monumenta germaniae historica. Leges* (quarto series), *Sectio 1*, vol. 11 part 1 (pp. 123–63). Hanover.
NMaj., NMarc., NT, N.Val.	*Theodosiani libri XVI cum constitutionibus Sirmondianis et leges novellae ad Theodosianum pertinentes* 11. *Leges novellae ad Theodosianum pertinentes*, 2nd edn., T. Mommsen and P. Meyer, eds. (1905). Berlin.
OGIS	*Orientis graeci inscriptiones selectae*, W. Dittenberger, ed. (1903–5), two volumes. Leipzig.
OLD	*The Oxford Latin Dictionary*, P. G. W. Glare *et al.*, eds. (1982). Oxford.
ORF[4]	*Oratorum romanorum fragmenta*, 4th edn., H. Malcovati, ed. (1967). Padua.

Paulus, *Sent.*	*Sententiarum receptarum libri quinque, qui vulgo Julio Paulo adhuc tribuuntur*, J. Baviera, ed., in *FIRA*² II.321–417.
P.Euphr.	1–5: D. Feissel and J. Gascou, "Documents d'archives romains inédits du moyen Euphrate (IIIe siècle après J.-C.) I. Les Pétitions (*P.Euphr.* 1 à 5)," *Journal des Savants* (no volume, 1989): 65–119. 6–10: D. Feissel, J. Gascou, and J. Teixidor, "Documents d'archives romains inédits du moyen Euphrate (IIIe siècle après J.-C.) II. Les Actes de vente–achat (*P.Euphr.* 6 à 10)," *Journal des Savants* (no volume, 1997): 3–57. 11–17: D. Feissel and J. Gascou, "Documents d'archives romains inédits du moyen Euphrate (IIIe siècle après J.-C.) III. Actes divers et lettres (*P.Euphr.* 11 à 17)," *Journal des Savants* (no volume, 2000): 157–208.
P.Euphr.Syr.	J. Teixidor, "Deux documents syriaques du IIIe siècle après J.-C, provenant du moyen Euphrate," *Comptes rendus de l'académie des inscriptions et belles-lettres* (no volume, 1990): 145–66.
PG	*Patrologiae graecae cursus completus, series graeca*, J. P. Migne, ed. (1844–91). Paris.
*PGM*²	*Papyri graecae magicae*, 2nd edn., K. Preisendanz and A. Henrichs, eds. (1973–4). Stuttgart.
P. Jericho	*Discoveries in the Judaean Desert* XXXVIII: *Miscellaneous Texts from the Judaean Desert*, J. Charlesworth *et al.*, eds. (2000). Oxford.
PL	*Patrologiae latinae cursus completus, series latina*, J. P. Migne, ed. (1844–91). Paris.
P. Mur.	*Discoveries in the Judaean Desert 2: les grottes de Murabba'ât*, P. Benoit *et al.*, eds. (1961). Oxford.
P.Yadin	*The Documents from the Bar Kokhba Period in the Cave of Letters 1: Greek Papyri*, N. Lewis, ed. (1989). Jerusalem. *The Documents from the Bar Kokhba Period in the Cave of Letters 2: Hebrew, Aramaic and Nabatean-Aramaic*, Y. Yadin *et al.*, eds. (2002). Jerusalem.

Abbreviations

RE	*Real-Encyclopädie der classischen Altertumswissenschaft*, A. F. von Pauly *et al.*, eds. (1894–). Stuttgart.
RIB	*The Roman Inscriptions of Britain* I, R. B. Collingwood and R. P. Wright, eds. (1965). Oxford. *The Roman Inscriptions of Britain* II, S. S. Frere and R. Tomlin, eds. (1992). Oxford.
RIJ	*Recueil des inscriptions juridiques grecques*, R. Dareste, B. Haussoullier, and T. Reinach, eds., (1891–4), three volumes. Paris.
SEG	*Supplementum epigraphicum graecum*, various editors (1923–). Leiden.
*SIG*³	*Sylloge inscriptionum graecarum*, 3rd edn., W. Dittenberger, ed. (1915–24). Leipzig.
T.Alb.	*Les Tablettes Albertini: actes privés de l'époque vandale*, C. Courtois *et al.*, eds. (1952). Paris.
TAM	*Tituli Asiae Minoris*, various editors (1901–). Vienna.
TH	1–12: G. Pugliese Carratelli, "*Tabulae Herculanenses* I," *Parola del Passato* 1 (1946): 379–85. 13–30: G. Pugliese Carratelli, "*Tabulae Herculanenses* II," *Parola del Passato* 3 (1948): 165–84. 31–58: G. Pugliese Carratelli, "*Tabulae Herculanenses* III," *Parola del Passato* 8 (1953): 454–63. 59–75: V. Arangio-Ruiz and G. Pugliese Carratelli, "*Tabulae Herculanenses* IV," *Parola del Passato* 9 (1954): 54–74. 76–87: V. Arangio-Ruiz and G. Pugliese Carratelli, "*Tabulae Herculanenses* V," *Parola del Passato* 10 (1955): 448–77. 88–102: V. Arangio-Ruiz and G. Pugliese Carratelli, "*Tabulae Herculanenses* VI," *Parola del Passato* 16 (1961): 66–73. those published and numbered (1–16) by M. Della Corte, "Tabelle cerate Ercolanesi," *Parola del Passato* 6 (1951): 224–30, are cited as Della Corte (1951) in the notes.
TPSulp.	*Tabulae Pompeianae Sulpiciorum (TPSulp.): edizione critica dell'archivio puteolano dei Sulpicii* (*Vetera* 12), G. Camodeca, ed. (1999). Naples.

xvi *Abbreviations*

T.Vindol. I	*Vindolanda: The Latin Writing Tablets* (*Britannia* monograph series no. 4), A. K. Bowman and J. D. Thomas, eds. (1983). London.
T.Vindol. II	*The Vindolanda Writing Tablets (Tabulae Vindolandenses II)*, A. K. Bowman and J. D. Thomas, eds. (1994). London.
Ulp. *Reg.*	*Tituli xxviii ex corpore Ulpiani qui vulgo Domitio Ulpiano adhuc tribuuntur*, J. Baviera, ed., in *FIRA*[2] II.262–301.

Introduction

With typically Roman prudence the emperor [Trajan], by a preliminary test of the trustworthiness of the oracle [of Apollo], took steps to thwart the possibility of hidden human trickery, and began by sending sealed tablets [*codicillos*] with a request for a written reply. To the surprise of the priests, who were, of course, unaware of the nature of the emperor's tablets, the god bade a sheet of papyrus [*chartam*] be brought and ordered it to be sealed, without any writing on it, and dispatched. When Trajan received the document he was filled with astonishment, since the tablets [*tabellis*] he had sent to the god also had had no writing on them; and he then wrote and sealed other tablets [*codicillis*], to ask whether he would return to Rome after the war was over. The god thereupon bade a centurion's vine branch be brought from among the dedicated offerings in the temple, broken in pieces, and the pieces wrapped and sent to the emperor. (Macrobius, *Saturnalia* 1.23.14–16)

To the god the emperor of the Romans sent tablets; to the emperor the god of the Greeks sent papyrus in reply. Apollo was far the more practical: Egyptian papyrus was the paper of the ancient world, inexpensive and, in the East, ubiquitous. In parts of the Roman Empire where papyrus could not be had cheaply, as in the cold camps on Hadrian's Wall, folk might write instead on the bark of trees. But for certain types of composition, Romans like Trajan – although their world rustled with papyrus – preferred to write instead on thick wooden boards, on *tabulae*, on tablets. Yet *tabulae* were objects of complex manufacture, and so expensive; writing on a tablet – usually with a stylus on a coating of wax set into a rectangular depression in the board – was more laborious than writing with a pen on papyrus; and *tabulae* were heavy to carry and awkward to store. So the frequent Roman choice of the tablet as a medium for writing is a curious one, and presents an appealing antiquarian mystery that would have delighted the kind of ancient sage who thrilled to ponder mysteries like "why the priest of Jupiter, whom they call the *flamen dialis*, is not allowed to touch either

2   *Introduction*

flour or yeast?" or why Greeks and Romans wore rings on the fourth finger of the left hand.[1]

Yet from the gnarled root of this apparently antiquarian puzzle ramifies a tree of historical questions and answers: they are the subject of this book. These are questions about the archaic Roman world-view, about ways of ordering the state and cosmos, about legitimate authority, about the interaction of conquerors and conquered and Roman government and its subjects, about Roman justice and its social context, and finally about the historical evolution of the Roman law. For the peculiar Roman practice of writing on tablets had a cultural resonance. Tracing its significance and history reveals something about what it meant to be Roman.

A Plutarch or an Aulus Gellius who asked questions about the *flamen dialis* could, and in Plutarch's case often did, propose multiple but not necessarily contradictory solutions to such delightful puzzles.[2] So too writing on tablets can have multiple justifications. As a medium for writing, tablets had practical attractions, especially for preserving important documents and preventing fraud: writing on wax showed evidence of tampering; folded together, wax tablets were hard to damage; sealed up with string they were difficult for malefactors to break into unnoticed. The crude physical and practical differences between tablets and papyri are the beginning of an explanation for the differences in how Romans used them. But not the entirety of it: this book's argument is that writing on tablets was perceived by Romans to have special powers. This belief was eventually incorporated into late-antique Roman law, where as a concept it is the ancestor of the modern document called, in lawyer's terms, "dispositive": the legal document as the legal act itself. That written documents have decisive force at law may strike a modern reader as uncontroversial, as a type of universal truth. At Rome, however, this status in legal commentary and written law was only achieved over centuries, and classical jurists did not espouse it. Tablets, their uses, and their efficacy form the link: they are part of a continuous tradition linking earliest and latest Roman thought and practice, Roman history and Roman law. Tablets were a special kind of writing with their own history, moving from a semi-religious, quasi-magical Republican world of ceremonial and public order to the highly rhetorical yet pragmatic world of late-antique imperial law.

It was legal documents that Romans most often wrote on tablets. Yet in a book of nine chapters only in the last are the views of the Roman

---

[1] Plut. *Mor.* 289E; Gel. 10.10.
[2] Feeney (1998) 129–30, on Plutarch.

Introduction 3

jurists and the evolution of the Roman law systematically discussed. This reverses the method of investigation that would be followed by Romanists, professional students of Roman law: their first resort would be to the clean and apparently definitive discussions of the classical jurists, and only after this might they glance at the world of what people actually did to see how well or ill shabby popular practices conformed with these juristic precepts.[3] The backwards structure of this book reflects both the chronological distribution of the evidence and my historian's prejudice that Roman law can be profitably approached historically. This demands, in turn, that before the written law itself is examined, tablets first be placed in their contexts: the wide realm of Roman justice – the far larger mass of behavior manifest in document and court, only a small part of which strict law touched – and the even wider world of Roman culture, without which Roman justice is itself incomprehensible.

An underlying aim of the book is to throw another rope bridge over the chasm between the study of Roman history and the study of Roman law, a crevasse that has been growing broader and more forbidding for nearly a century. In Mommsen's day the assumptions underlying the study of history and of law fitted well together, and the same men often studied both. But decades of independent evolution have left Romanist and historian inhabiting two nearly irreconcilable mental worlds. The Roman empire of the Romanist is still much the same orderly commonwealth that Mommsen imagined, a recognizably modern state grounded in the rule of law. But the Roman empire many contemporary Roman historians now imagine has evolved into something weaker, less rational, and more *ad hoc*: they see in Rome the deliberately arbitrary and enjoyably corrupt monarchies of the *ancien régime*, old Sicily rather than modern Zurich. And so the kind of question that can occupy the Romanist, like "What is the essential nature of Roman obligation?" seems at times almost surreal to the historian, who cannot imagine why, in a world without police and with a distant government, where not even judges were expected to have legal knowledge, anyone could or would pay close attention to this type of legal discussion. But the Romans also took their law very seriously, and thought it characteristic of themselves to do so: the law cannot safely be left out of an historical vision of their world. So why and how could law in fact work in this kind of world? Not because it was rigorously and minutely enforced by thousands of officials or revered in its details by a knowledgeable public, but because it was anchored fathoms deep in Roman culture. By anchoring the efficacy

---

[3] See Crook (1996) on the differences between Romanists and historians.

4 *Introduction*

of the law in Roman culture, and trying to understand not so much what the law was but why it commanded respect, this book instead offers a way of reintegrating law into the Roman world the historians see, and gives to the project and concerns of Romanists an historical justification they may not have known they needed. It charts practical Roman conceptions of legitimacy, not the law itself, in a Roman world whose commitment to the law was intermittent.

To the Romanist, this book also offers a contextual perspective on the thinkers they study. Roman jurists responded to and relied on long-lived traditional practices and expectations, and to some extent set themselves and their work beyond them. Understanding the cultural context of the law therefore casts into higher relief the originality of the juristic tradition and juristic methods of thought, and helps also to delineate just what was original. A study that proceeds from lay practitioners to jurists reveals that laymen – even those who went to court and drafted and valued legal documents – did not think in the same ways as jurists. The edifice the jurists built had its own units of measurement and building materials, as Romanists have long known, but this book offers them an opportunity also to stroll around the grounds and appreciate the Great House from the perspective of game park and tributary village. It also invites Romanists to contemplate the possibility, fundamental to anthropological studies of law and taken as true here,[4] that the Great House could not exist or speak effectively without a common basis of understanding with its villagers: that their practices and beliefs exercised a considerable influence over what the Great House could accomplish. Not necessarily over what it said, but whether it would be listened to, for if the villagers did not deem the law and the authority of those who spoke and wrote it legitimate it would not work.

To the historian of Rome, the classicist, or to anyone interested in Roman things, this book offers an understanding of what Romans thought were powerful ways of getting things done, and how these evolved over time. Study of how tablets were used in the Republic reveals that the ordering of state, religion, magic, legal procedure, and some legal acts all shared an ancient and ceremonial protocol in which writing on *tabulae* played an important part, a protocol that we shall call the "unitary act" because all of its many parts had to be accomplished if it was to work. When performed correctly a unitary act irrevocably changed some aspect of the visible or invisible world: it did not need human enforcers, but drew its

---

[4] Moore (1978) 1–31; see also Rosen (1989) 81–2.

Introduction 5

power and authority from the formal ritual of its own making. Another way of getting things done at Rome was through relations of reciprocity, either the familiar exchange of money for goods and services or the reciprocal exchange of favors. Since reciprocation was often not immediate, such social relations were underwritten by the good faith – *fides* – of the parties. This way of accomplishing one's ends also affects the appearance and use of *tabulae*, as *fides* and its real-world expressions – *bona fides* legal acts, sealing, subscribing, writing in one's own hand – migrated onto the tablet that had drawn its traditional power from the unitary act, as well as from its traditional ability to reveal fraud. *Fides* supplied the human protectors and enforcers that the unitary act traditionally had not needed: the absolute efficacy of the unitary act was bolstered by *fides*, *fides* itself was validated by the certain power of the unitary act, and the improved and protected *tabula* that resulted was authoritative, powerfully supported, and splendidly useful as proof. For centuries the combined power of ceremonial unitary acts and *fides* on legal *tabulae* was comfortably relied upon by laymen and assumed by at least some Roman jurists, who reverentially burnished and repaired its parts. But late-antique emperors – and those who drafted their laws – sometimes felt able to set aside traditionally authoritative forms, substituting for them the authority of the imperial will. What once magico-religious authority had established, what the *fides* of individuals had once fortified, what pragmatic imperatives had once embraced, now universal acceptance of the authority of the emperor was thought adequate to uphold. Understanding of legitimacy could change and develop: legitimacy did not depend merely on inert and conservative traditionalism, but could be shaped by the Romans' ability creatively to combine traditional forms of efficacy and new ways of thinking.

As the power of the Romans grew they took their characteristic ways of doing things – and so their tablets – with them out into the provinces of their empire and used them not only between each other but as the perceptible voice of government. Provincials who sought the ear of Roman officials in some places hastened to mimic this Roman form – even if only by writing on and folding their papyrus differently – and in others left it strictly alone. This significantly uneven pattern of cultural influence illuminates the process by which subjects were introduced to, and adopted, the ways of their Roman overlords, and so helps us understand the complex process of exchange and acculturation we have come to know as romanization. At the same time it allows insight into the impact of the Roman government in the provinces: Roman officials, for example, interested themselves acutely in the treatment and preservation of documents, an exception to the otherwise

6   *Introduction*

hands-off Roman style of ruling. And whatever the effect of their furious edicts it is possible to trace indirect influence out from Rome (what the emperor did) to the provinces (what the governors did) to the subject, in how he or she made his or her documents conform to Roman expectations. The true power of a weak, distant Roman government – how it changed the lives of its subjects most – may lie more in the consequences of government's passive expectations about how those who approached it should comport themselves than in its active decrees, more in the example it set than in its positive activities, more in legal practice than in the law itself.

Part I of this book is a synchronic analysis of the traditional power of the tablet in Roman society. After setting up a contrast through an initial chapter on Greek legal documents, it establishes the shared characteristics, significance, and common power of different types of *tabulae*. In each of its chapters, it reconnects Roman legal documents, which were always written on tablets, with this older world of thought and belief. Wooden *tabulae* were a very ancient special form. They were used in the context of special acts (mostly ceremonial and formal), shared antique language and style, were put to similar uses, and displayed certain performative, almost magical, powers. Their capacity to fix, preserve, and finish was proverbial, making them (for example) a conventional image for the power of memory. If you fix images to backgrounds like letters to wax tablets, said Cicero, you will have them in your mind forever.[5] The active participation of tablets in great ceremonial acts gave them a special importance to Romans, and a special resonance and power whenever they were used. Legal tablets – which were one essential part of the legal ceremonies that individuals performed between themselves, like contracts – drew their own socially approved worth from their membership in this larger family of tablets.

The weight of the evidence in Part I is chiefly Republican. Part II is a diachronic history of the legal tablet from the first century AD through the reign of Justinian. Two chapters survey archeological finds of tablets, first in Italy and then elsewhere in the empire, tracing the evolution of the physical form of the tablet and the legal acts written upon them through AD 300. Practice is the story here; *fides* and romanization are the themes. Then the story is carried forward by investigating how tablets were used in Roman courts and how they were treated by classical and late-antique jurists: here there is attention to the relationship of strict law to broader

---

[5] Cic. *de Orat.* 2.354 and *Part.* 7.26, *Rhet. Her.* 3.31; conventional, see (e.g.) Plat. *Theaet.* 194c or, later, Artem. *Oneir.* 2.45 and Eun. *VS* 495 (the orator Libanius).

Introduction 7

legal affairs and relations between subject and government in the Roman world.

The straddle this book attempts between Roman history and law means that, despite best efforts, it does not precisely conform to the standards of either field. Thus quotation of Latin (and Greek) is selective, and translations, especially of texts on tablets and legal texts – usually my own – often deliberately follow the Latin with agonizing closeness, to let the rough and often asyndetic syntax of tablets' Latin, as noticeable and characteristic to Romans as it is to us, come through clearly. The material cited in the notes is hardly stingy, but Romanists will feel the lack of a thorough review of scholarship, will feel that I have drawn back – perhaps unfairly – from overly explicit participation in the controversies into which my positions oblige me to plunge, and will feel that the argument lacks the elegant and economical decisiveness that argument from legal texts permits them to achieve. This is not least because the book attempts to shift the assumptions and the basis of argument and to make the positive, but often messily historical, case for itself. It aims to restore the context and traditions of Roman belief and practice to the study of Roman law, and to the study of writing in Roman law in particular. It seeks to draw together law and legal practice, religious and magical beliefs, Campanian wood *tabulae* and Egyptian papyrus double-documents. Above all, it aspires to yoke them into a coherent and interrelated entity, into a loosely governed but dynamic cosmos, into a broad empire of diversity and similarity – into a world like that the Romans ruled, when once they ruled a world.

PART ONE

The world of belief

In Roman legal affairs and other ceremonial acts with public implications, writing on wooden, wax, or bronze tablets was special and preferred. To Greeks, on the other hand, tablets were not particularly special, and they often chose papyrus for such acts. This was a distinction with a real difference. For the Romans, the form conveyed several fundamental messages. As a necessary part of a ceremonial act, a tablet could come to embody, in a final and authoritative way, the substance of that act, but as part of such an act, it also helped to create the new reality that such an act aimed at establishing. These three related aspects – ceremonial, authoritative, and active – all characterize the traditional Roman understanding of the importance of words written on tablets in manipulating and fixing both visible and unseen realities.

By "ceremonial" (or "ritual")[1] I mean patterns of behavior that are standardized and repeatable, and that are performed in a far more distinctive and self-conscious way than those that can be deemed habitual. Performing one's "morning ritual," for example, is merely habit for ninety-nine out of a hundred people. For Louis XIV, however, who rose every day at eight and was attended by his First Physician, First Surgeon, and wet-nurse, then, at eight-fifteen, by his Grand Chamberlain (who opened the bed-curtains, presented the king with holy water, and handed him the Book of the Office of the Holy Ghost) and those courtiers who had been granted the privilege of the *grandes entrées* or the second *entrées* (these last came in while the King was putting on his breeches, and every other day watched the king being shaved), it was a ceremony.[2] By "authoritative" I mean that tablets are the

---

[1] Gargola (1995) 5 and nn.7–8; he and I follow in part Goody's definition (1961) 159 of ceremonial as "a specific sequence of ritual acts," where "ritual" means "a category of standardized behavior." Cf. Goody (1977) and Bell (1992) for critiques of theories of ritual, and Muir (1997) 1–17 for a lively introduction to the possibilities offered by the historical study of ritual.

[2] Louis XIV: Saint-Simon (1985 [1714–16]) v.605. Humphrey and Laidlaw (1994) 3 emphasize that "ritual" signals a quality rather than a type of action; cf. 64–87, a refutation of more ambitious

9

The world of belief

final word (in the English sense of "authoritative") but can simultaneously exercise "authority" (in the Roman sense of *auctoritas*); *auctoritas* in Rome was not merely a passive concept, but a quality that commanded response or respect. Thus "authoritative" also implies "active," by which I mean that in the hands of human actors, tablets are sometimes understood to make something happen that otherwise would not happen.[3]

These terms give expression and lively consequence to ritual aspects of Roman culture whose significance and impact are only now coming to be appreciated in studies of Roman history and literature.[4] In understanding this significance and impact, studies of Roman religion have led the way.[5] In Roman legal studies, the magisterial compilation of Rudolph von Jhering in 1875 laid a broad foundation, but his extensive descriptions of formal words and gestures, and of the culture of Roman law in general, have inspired less analytical scholarship than they have deserved.[6] By building on this basis, by finding within Roman formalism and ceremony an early, active, and important role for writing on tablets, and by judging the weight that Romans attributed to these ceremonies, Part I of this book will argue for a larger interdependence between law, legal acts, and Roman society than is usually recognized. For since writing, speaking, and tablets functioned in legal matters much as they did in religious acts, state acts, and magical acts, traditional beliefs about their interrelationship and importance not only influenced, but also reinforced and supported the legal process, and thus help to explain why legal acts of all sorts would be accepted as legitimate and binding in Roman society. The methods followed in legal acts were the same as those followed by men attempting to shape other worlds they could not fully see or perfectly control, whether the imagined world of political community or the perceptible world of the divine.[7] They were, for centuries, the methods that best achieved the ends that citizens and

---

theories of ritual knowledge and communication. J. Smith (1987) 103 emphasizes that ritual "is a process for marking interest," and thus to be distinguished from the "equation . . . with blind and thoughtless habit."

[3] For *auctoritas*, see Hellegouarc'h (1963) 295–320, Lendon (1997) 30–106, 272–9. This simple definition of active does not stand in opposition to the "symbolic" – defined "in an anthropological context . . . as objects (signs) used to express . . . some abstract notion regarded as a value by the community," G. MacCormack (1969a) 458 – but subsumes it: tablets can symbolize something, but (to my mind) in the act of expression can also do more.

[4] Marshall (1984), Zorzetti (1990) 302; Hopkins (1991); Edmondson (1993) 180–2; Feeney (1998) is a wide-ranging cultural study that looks at religion, ritual, and literature.

[5] E.g., Jocelyn (1966); MacMullen (1981); North (1986), (1989); Beard (1992).

[6] Jhering (1891 [1875]), esp. 2.2.441–674 on formalism and form; these aspects of Roman law are frequently treated merely as primitive elements that were thankfully set aside, see G. MacCormack (1969a) 439 nn.1–2; Jhering is "too little used," R. Mitchell (1984) 555 n.59.

[7] Gargola (1995) 16 and 66, similar observations in different contexts.

The world of belief 11

jurists most wanted. By being both familiar and traditionally efficacious, such methods made law an "embedded" rather than a separate sphere of action, and engaged the immense power of a world of belief on the side of order in human affairs.

Part I begins with a contrast, a brief survey of Athenian and Hellenistic legal documents and acts – what can be known about them, how they were viewed, and how they were used (chapter one). It continues with an exploration of the ways in which Roman documents on tablets, by their characteristics and associations (chapter two) and language (chapter three), were by nature very different; examines the different ways in which these tablets were used and perceived to be efficacious; and concludes by arguing the same weight and efficacy for legal documents on *tabulae* (chapters four and five). Above all, it invites historians and scholars of Roman law to revisit the complex and multi-layered world of Roman ceremonial, and to contemplate some of its contributions in constituting the Romans' first great construction of how and why acts in their cosmos not only worked, but worked well.

CHAPTER I

The use and value of Greek legal documents

Greek legal documents provide an important contrast – in language, treatment, and consequence – to Roman legal documents, for in the Greek world, what can be known about the wording and style of legal documents, as well as what can be known about attitudes towards them, underlines their ambiguous status and lack of independent legal authority. The evidence is mixed and uneven: for classical Athens, legal documents themselves do not survive, and are instead only referred to by fourth-century orators, while for the later Hellenistic world, especially Ptolemaic Egypt, the legal documents themselves exist, but in no descriptive context that allows a direct understanding of their value and relationship to their legal act. This has left considerable room for scholarly disagreement over how Hellenistic documents in particular were conceived and valued. Only relatively recently has a consensus over the legal strengths and, especially, weaknesses of these documents been forged, led by J.-P. Lévy and H.-J. Wolff.[1] What is written here adds to what has already been done by giving particular emphasis to what is known about the generation of these documents, what can be deduced from the wording of the documents themselves, and what can be hypothesized from social attitudes about documents when these are known, components specifically chosen because of the contrast they will provide to a discussion of the same components in Roman documents on tablets that follows.

CLASSICAL ATHENS

The implications of the mixture of oral and literate forms of communication that characterized classical Athens have been much studied in the last thirty years, as have the technical complexities and social implications of the

---

[1] Lévy (1959a); Wolff (1978) 141–69; and see below nn.34–5.

12

The use and value of Greek legal documents

Athenian legal "system."[2] Even so, little is known about the context in which a legal document was generated, what it looked like, or what wording it used, although it is agreed that legal documents came to be used only in the fourth century BC.[3] Indeed, no attention appears to have been paid to the appearance or wording of these documents; they seem to have attracted no attention by virtue of having a physically distinctive form; and remarks of orators make clear that by themselves these documents carried little conviction in court. This all suggests only a most perfunctory fourth-century Athenian interest in developing and valuing legal documents.

When a document like a contract or a will was written down, the only convention followed by Athenians was the summoning of witnesses, who could be either carefully called ahead of time or rounded up at the last minute. These witnesses were given little to observe, for they were never assumed, after the fact, to know anything about the content of the document, and often testified only that a document had been made.[4] Thus the creation of such a document, as well as the legal act such a document might have embodied or expressed, was visually and audibly uninformative. This inexpressiveness suggests by its very lack of emphasis an unimportant, undistinctive process.[5]

These documents could be written on tablets (a γραμματεῖον or γραμματεῖδιον) or on papyrus, and were usually sealed.[6] Their wording, as far as

---

[2] Harris (1989) 65–115 put the study of functional Greek literacy on an entirely new basis, but since then Steiner (1994), and, especially, R. Thomas (1989) and (1992) – to be read with Sickinger (1994) and Boffo (1995) – have turned our attention to some of the implications of an interconnected oral-literate world. All give references to earlier scholarship; interested readers should start there, since further references in this chapter will be extremely selective. Legal: Todd (1993), a salutary contrast to Harrison (1968) and (1971) in its organization and sensitivity to extra-legal issues, with an extensive introduction (3–29) to questions of legal methodology and scholarship.

[3] R. Thomas (1989) 41 and n.83 (Isoc. 17.20 is the first reference to written contract, 400–390 BC); Rhodes (1980) 315; Garner (1987) 137.

[4] On context, see Thphr. fr. 21 on sale (Szegedy-Maszak [1981] 63–73), which lays out legal steps preliminary to the sale itself. Witnesses: Is. 3.18–19 and R. Bonner (1905) 39–40; their ignorance, Is. 4.12–14, Calhoun (1914) 136 n.4, and R. Bonner (1905) 40 (wills); Todd (1990) on witnesses as supporters of the defendant rather than as truth-tellers; *contra* Pringsheim (1950) 17–19 this need for witnesses is not "formalism," and their number varied.

[5] Little weight: Garner (1987) 137–8 on two rhetorical commonplaces, and see below n.12.

[6] Kußmaul (1969) 63–71 (list of συνθῆκαι: two written on γραμματεῖα, one on papyrus [Dem. 56.1], three on unknown medium); there is no indication of medium in the rhetors' citation of wills (cf. Harrison [1968] 153–5) except for Is. 6.29 (γραμματείου). For various uses of tablets in an Athenian court, Boegehold (1995) 240–1. Wooden or waxed tablets were not considered a particularly distinctive medium at Athens, cf. Wilhelm (1909) 240–9 for a selective list ("destinés à une publicité temporaire," 240), Harris (1989) 95 ("quite commonplace"), Sickinger (1999) 147–8 and 208 n.25, Rhodes (2001a) 34–6, and Fischer (2002); *contra*, Sharpe (1992) 128, who presumes the importance of what the Athenians wrote on wooden boards and tablets, and attributes excessive importance to Dziatzko, who noted (1900) 14–26 that writing on tablets was a part of how Athenians saw their own past, and that (138) the gods do not seem to use papyrus βίβλοι.

14 *The world of belief*

it can be deduced, is entirely consistent with everyday and informal usage both within and outside Athens,[7] even though inscribed examples are incomplete: pre-classical debt-markers are very brief ("To X, Y owes . . ."), while Athenian *horos*-stones marking obligation are similarly terse, and even seem incomplete by legal standards, as do Athenian lease-inscriptions.[8] The one συγγραφή (contract, in this case a maritime loan) quoted in a speech of Demosthenes lays out its terms in perfectly unexceptional Greek.[9] Even documents of the same legal "type" (like contracts or wills) are thought to have had no characteristic phrasing or style until the end of the fourth century, if then. There is nothing in the language and style of a classical Athenian legal document to suggest that it was not very informally conceived – as nothing more than an accessory to an action whose weight or essence was elsewhere.[10]

Fortunately, the fact that so much of the Athenian evidence about legal documents is embedded within the speeches of fourth-century orators does permit an assessment of contemporary reactions to them. Although it is clear, from the number of references to legal documents after mid-century, that they were increasingly used, and useful because they could fix some details that witnesses might forget or misremember (as was true also of written witnesses' statements),[11] from the ways in which they were presented it is also clear that they were never trusted.[12] How could they be, when they had come into existence – so Aeschines claimed – out of mutual suspicion? "We would all agree that we make agreements with one another through distrust, so that the man who sticks to the terms may get satisfaction from the man who disregards them," he said, making an explicitly wide

---

[7] Style of Athenian documents: Kußmaul (1969) 80–2 (on συγγραφαί) and Todd (1996) 121 (in general, "the language of law was the language of the street"). Little attention to appearance and language: Gneist (1845) 439–40, 468–82; Kußmaul (1969) 69–71; Harrison (1971) 153–4.

[8] Pre-classical: on lead tablets, *c.* 500 BC (Corcyra), with witnesses listed, Calligas (1971) 85–6 (he suggests bottomry loans); see also Wilson (1997–8) 43–53, who surveys the non-Athenian evidence and proposes "formalised or accepted language" in the various uses of the verb δίδωμι in a contract from fifth-century BC Gaul. *Horos*-stones, see Finley (1952) 118–93 and Millett (1982); also R. Thomas (1992) 90 on their incompleteness (lacking dates and one party's name). Lease inscriptions, Kußmaul (1969) 60 ("*formlos*").

[9] Dem. 35.10–13.

[10] Attic lease-documents, for example, came in several different forms: Behrend (1970) 114. Shared format: R. Thomas (1989) 42.

[11] Used after mid-century: Garner (1987) 137 (cf. Isoc. 17.20); Harris (1989) 68–71. Fixing details (but not trusted): Dem. 33.36 (depositing a contract to prevent alteration by either party). Witnesses' statements: Dem. 45.44 (no changes possible this way); cf. Harris (1989) 71–2 and n.31; on dating, Ruschenbusch (1989) 34–5.

[12] Not trusted: Is. 1.41–2 (weak and unimpressive form of evidence), 7.2 (sealed will weaker than adoption); see Soubie (1973) and (1974); Lentz (1989) 71–89; Harris (1989) 72–3 and 88–92; and Cohen (2003).

The use and value of Greek legal documents

(and therefore believable) claim while also reminding his audience of the extensive Greek tradition that equated writing with deceit or the intent to deceive.[13]

Such suspicion was clear in court. In at least twenty-two of thirty-one cases where a legal document is cited as evidence, it was either attacked as forged and unreliable, or preemptively vouched for by witnesses or depositary, the man with whom it had been deposited for safekeeping.[14] Moreover, when documents were attacked, the method preferred was an impugning of the witnesses' or (especially) the depositary's reliability.[15] This is a good sign that the strength of a document was contributed by the staunchness, standing, and oral testimony of the people around it, and not by any value inherent in the document itself. As Aristotle said, "for of whatever sort those may be who wrote their names or guarded [the contract], such is the trustworthiness of the contract."[16] By the end of the fourth century, a legal document was still considered, by its very nature, weak evidence, the witnesses to it or its depositaries the best guarantors of its value.[17]

This preference for reliable people over unreliable writing eventually promoted the habit of deposit with a *polis*-official, a practice attested outside Athens before the end of the fourth century, in Athens by (possibly) the end of that century.[18] That more documents, chiefly contracts and wills, came to be used over the course of the fourth century is thus not so much an index of the growing acceptance of writing as definitive proof as it is of the growing complexities of commercial life and the healthy suspicion in which parties continued to hold each other – or, in the exceptional case of maritime loans, as a result of a law (*c.* 350 BC) stipulating that only when

---

[13] Aeschines: 1.161 (τὰς συνθήκας... ποιούμεθα). Greek tradition: starting with Homer *Il.* 6.168–9 (tablets with writing condemn Bellerophon), continued in Plato's *Phaedrus*, etc.; cf. Detienne (1989), S. Lewis (1996) 142–6 (letters).

[14] Documents in court and forgeries: numbers arrived at by a comparison of R. Bonner (1905) 61–6 and Calhoun (1914) 135–9, cf. Lentz (1983) 248, 256–7 and Harris (1989) 72–3; Lentz (1989) 74 notes "over one hundred instances" of documents of some sort (including laws) cited in court.

[15] Calhoun (1914) gathers references; Kußmaul (1969) 76–80; Todd (1990), esp. 27–9 and n.15.

[16] Arist. *Rhet.* 1.1376b.

[17] The one example of unchallenged use of an unwitnessed contract in a court of the 320s (Hyp. 5.8), on which Pringsheim (1950) 46 n.1, (1955) 290 based his argument for a gradual shift in valuation away from witnessed documents to the document alone, is incomplete and exceptional: Finley (1952) 298 n.22, Kußmaul (1969) 80–2, and Maffi (1988) 203–10. Protection afforded documents used in court reflects not the high value placed on these documents (as argued by Préaux [1964] 181–3), but the determination of antagonists not to let the other gain an unwarranted advantage.

[18] Officialdom: [Arist.] *Oec.* 2.1347b (Chios, deposit in δημόσιον), cf. Steinacker (1927) 47–51; Arist. *Pol.* 1321b (official "supervising" public contracts, "sacred recorder" holding copies) – neither existed in Athens at the time of Aristotle's writing, Harris (1989) 70, but soon thereafter, a συνθήκη is deposited with θεσμοθέται (Finley [1952] 125 no. 17); cf. R. Thomas (1992) 133–4 (skeptical on Athens), Sickinger (1999) 134.

16 *The world of belief*

there was a written contract, a *syngraphe*, could a "maritime case," a δίκη ἐμπορική (*dike emporike*), be brought.[19] Thus even in a society where the oral and the literate mingled, the implications of the latter were at best ambiguous; as S. C. Todd has remarked, "the effects of literacy," even in the fourth century, "did not run very deep."[20]

THE HELLENISTIC GREEK WORLD

This ambivalence surrounding legal documents and their courtroom use almost certainly continued through the Hellenistic period, whether or not significant substantive continuities between Athenian and later Greek law can be postulated.[21] Here, the distribution of evidence is diametrically different from what it had been in classical Athens. Documents do survive, on papyri or stone, many but not all from Ptolemaic Egypt.[22] Yet this pleasing fact of survival tells us nothing about their inherent value, despite wishful scholarly thinking,[23] and there are few oratorical (or other) assessments of the value of these documents to help – neither endorsements of, nor attacks on, their reliability.[24] But some parallels with Athens would suggest that these documents, while proving themselves ever more useful in everyday life, did not develop any fundamentally new character or function.

As in classical Athens, so too in Ptolemaic Egypt the implications of legal documents are, in their form and language, neutral. Although it becomes possible to distinguish, by their form, specific types of legal documents in Ptolemaic Egypt, all written on papyrus, any one specific type of document

---

[19] Chiefly contracts and wills: see Arist. *Rhet.* 1375a, contracts were the only written form of inartificial proof in his list; bank-books also called on, Isoc. 17.2. συγγραφή required for δίκη ἐμπορική: Dem. 32.1, cf. Isager and Hansen (1975) 79 (precedent-setting for other contracts?), and note that one earlier in the century was written on a γραμματεῖον, Lys. 32.7; MacDowell (1978) 233–4; Todd (1993) 334–7.

[20] In general, Gernet (1955) 173–200, Préaux (1964) 180–1; quotation, Todd (1990) 33 n.23; cf. 29 n.15 ("in the field of literacy, at least, Athenian law seems to have been more static than is sometimes supposed").

[21] Finley (1952) vii–viii.

[22] For a collection, see *RIJ passim*. This gives the documents themselves, not references to documents, as, e.g., Durrbach and Roussel (1935) 178 no. 1449 Aab 11.29–31, 192 no. 1450 A 104–5 (Delos, second century BC), an inventory listing a γραμματεῖον δίπτυχον λελευκωμένον (whitened diptych tablet) containing a loan (restored) and a συγγραφή; it is identified by Vial (1988) 58–60 as a copy of a document made between 314 and 305 BC.

[23] Steinacker (1927) 37–8, papyri themselves remarkably unforthcoming about what their own value is.

[24] The only one known to me is *UPZ* 2.162 (117 BC), a petition and account of a trial (about property) in which numerous documents and quotations of law were adduced; the winning side does seem to have the better (more relevant) documents, but in the end the case was decided by a royal amnesty (7.15–17).

The use and value of Greek legal documents

cannot be associated with any one type of legal act. As H.-J. Wolff summarizes, "we come to the conclusion that the use of one or another . . . [of the many types of document] was to a high degree no more than a question of the local custom of the time."[25] In other words, the choice of document-type, such as a six-witness *syngraphe* or a *cheirographon*, did not correlate significantly with a specific legal act.[26] Moreover, lacking this fundamental connection to its legal act, the legal document also, as at Athens, conveys no sense of any ceremonial attendant upon its making. Similarly, the language used was not significant or marked, being either local dialect or, for legal acts whose participants came from widely separated parts of the Greek world, the *koine*.[27] This perceptible standardization of form, and the apparent transparency of language, are attributed not to any changed perception of what a legal document was, but to the growing influence of notaries.[28] That the impetus for this change in documentary habits came only from this quasi-official quarter is also argued by W. Harris, who judged that the people using these documents (both in Egypt and elsewhere) were "mainly from governments and . . . [were] senior government officials pursuing their own interests." That is, what was changing in the Hellenistic world was the level of fussy bureaucracy in government, not the internalized significance of a legal document.[29]

Moreover, parallel also to Athenian practice, the hunt for witnesses and depositaries of the most reliable kind continued, and found its logical bureaucratic conclusion in the securing of documents through "registration" with public officials.[30] In this way, privately generated documents could

---

[25] Wolff (1978) 136–9 at 137.

[26] Description of document types: Wolff (1978) 57–135. A six-witness συγγραφή was a dated, narrative document written in the third person ("x, son of y"); the names of six witnesses were listed at the bottom (57–8, 107); a cheirograph was phrased in the first person ("I"), and often given the standard prescript of a letter; it was supposed to be in the handwriting of the author, although professional writers also helped (107–8).

[27] *Koine*: Kußmaul (1969) 86 (in συγγραφαί); cf. *IG* 12.7.67–9 (Arkesine, on Amorgos), three συγγραφαί in *koine*. Widely separated: the first contract preserved from Egypt, *P.Eleph.* 1 (310 BC), has protagonists from Temnos and Cos, the witnesses from Gela, Temnos, Cyrene, and Cos (emphasized by Harris [1989] 118 n.6). Note also the contrast in the Nikareta loan documents (*IG* 7.3172): the συγγραφή with Nikareta (3172A) is in *koine*, but the headings, decrees, and agreements about this contract, preserved with it, are in Boeotian dialect.

[28] Standardization, notaries: Wolff (1978) 5–6 (stressing existence throughout Greek world), 8–15, 18–27.

[29] Harris (1989) 119–20; the number of these documents before the 130s BC is "remarkably small."

[30] Use of witnesses continues: Préaux (1964) 182; one of the witnesses of the six-witness συγγραφή was called the συγγραφοφύλαξ, a private depositary (Wolff [1978] 59 n.12); Boussac (1993) 682–4 and Auda and Boussac (1996) suggest that the thousands of seals found in a house in Delos (an Athenian dependency), burned in 67 BC, derived from legal documents kept by such a person. For a list of similar collections of seals in the Hellenistic and Roman eastern Mediterranean, Salzmann (1984) 164–6.

18 *The world of belief*

be witnessed and then deposited in an "official archive" of a city or even a village, becoming part of that entity's records and protected from tampering by the official in charge of the archive. Such archives are widely attested: in Paros, Priene, Andros, Tenos, Nikopolis, Seleucia, and at several levels in Egypt.[31] This process of registration, and the complex ways in which archives functioned and archive-officials worked to protect the documents deposited in them, demonstrate the perceived vulnerability of documents, and the need for unimpeachable, reliable witnesses to secure their value. A legal document standing by itself was still perceived as having only a limited value: it needed strengthening and protecting.

This is not a new conclusion: it was first suggested in 1845 by H. R. Gneist, who analyzed the form (or rather formlessness) of Greek legal documents.[32] But scholars subsequently challenged his rather negative assessment of legal value, driven not least by their suspicion that Gneist's conclusion was at best paradoxical, since he deemed of little significance documents whose everyday value, as evidenced by their survival, seemed to grow with every decade.[33] L. Mitteis in 1891 tipped the debate's scale decisively in this other direction, by suggesting that since Greeks accepted the idea of fictive loans, they had created or at least accepted the idea of "dispositive" documents – strong documents that embodied rather than simply documented the legal act undertaken – and, moreover, that Roman sources were aware of this, and recognized it as different from most Roman practice.[34]

---

[31] Paros: Lambrinudakis and Wörrle (1983), second century BC (many further references); Priene, *I.Priene* 1.114–16; Andros, *IG* 12.5.721; Tenos, Partsch (1921) 132; Nikopolis, Klose (1984), sixty-one seals from a public archive stretching back into the Hellenistic period; Seleucia, Invernizzi (1996); cf. Préaux (1964) 190–1 (equivalents attested in Crete, Sardis, Mesopotamia, etc.), and Berges (1996), Carthage. Egypt: regional (e.g., Tebtunis, Soknopaiou Nesos, Krokodilopolis), Wolff (1978) 34–46, Préaux (1964) 192–4; in general, R. Thomas (1992) 133 n.17, 140–4. The popularity of, and dependence on, registration are deemed to be the cause of the decay of the six-witness συγγραφή, Wolff (1978) 67–71, 81–105, 169–73; Amelotti and Migliardi Zingale (1989) 305 suggest that the addition of subscriptions also contributed.

[32] Gneist (1845) 413–18.

[33] Steinacker (1927) 26 (a generalization); he also pointed out that Gneist's argument was suspect on other levels, e.g., in the identification of one "Greek law" (27).

[34] Mitteis (1891) 469–72 on Nikareta's contract, *IG* 7.3172A = *RIJ* 275–311 (no. XIV) (*c.* 230–150 BC): a difficult case whose circumstances are not fully understood, cf. Hennig (1977) 131–8, with Brandileone (1920), (1932), and Lévy (1959a) 455, who sees no fiction (*mensonge*) here. Two Roman sources touch on the Greek συγγραφή, but contradict each other: *G.* 3.134 calls it a *genus obligationis proprium peregrinorum*, but he is uncertain of its juridical force, *litterarum obligatio fieri videtur chirographis et syngraphis* (emphasis mine; for the Roman *litterarum obligatio* referred to, see chapter 5 pp. 108–10); Ps.-Asc. on Cic. *2 Verr.* 1.91 (Orelli) contradicts by specifically excluding chirographs and claiming that only *in syngraphis etiam contra fidem veritatis pactio venit*. That συγγραφαί were fictive, binding contracts to be equated with the Roman *litterarum obligatio* seems, therefore, very tenuous. For clear summaries of the Mitteisian view, see Vinogradoff (1922) 240–5, Kunkel (1932), and Gröschler (1997) 303–6.

The use and value of Greek legal documents

More recently, however, the unnecessary extremeness of this view, and the extent to which it relied only on Mitteis's assumptions and Roman misperceptions, have been recognized, and a strong compromise position that conserves all the evidence has won widespread acceptance. As H.-J. Wolff makes clear, these legal documents could not have been considered "dispositive" because their internal forms were interchangeable and their value seems to vary by place and circumstance; but they *were* increasingly valued because their validity *as proof* of a transaction's occurrence was increasingly accepted. There is no need to make surviving legal documents into absolute exemplars of dispositive acts (a modern analytical category), especially when a simpler interpretation of any given document as leaner or plumper proof of a legal act is sufficient to explain the value apparently attributed to it.[35]

Hellenistic legal documents therefore took on no new "dispositive" role for themselves, nor were perceived to have done so by those who used them. Their growing value as proof merely continues the trend observed in Athens: to be anything at all, a legal document had to be protected and secured. Once it was – once there was greater dependence on, and faith in, city or village archives and their officials – then legal documents could assume a value commensurate with the public trust in those institutions.[36] Historical context and legal value, as in Athens, intermingled. The deliberately limited and unemphatic role allowed to Athenian legal documents in court points to a deeply felt ambivalence about the reliability of writing itself that was society-wide and not merely court-determined; an Athenian court was a microcosm of Athenian society, its standards of credibility what people in general felt, documents themselves a late and dubious entry into a well-established agonistic arena. In the Hellenistic world, by contrast, the greater security granted to documents by the improved methods of safekeeping practiced raised the value of such documents to a level of believable proof

---

[35] Wolff (1978) 141–69; at 141–4 nn.1–9, summary of the dispute over the value of Hellenistic legal documents, cf. Freundt (1910) 31–5 and Mélèze-Modrzejewski (1984). Note the distinction Wolff draws (144 n.9): that "Hellenistic documents could come close to having *the practical effects* [his italics] of what we understand as dispositive documents," but (as his following discussion makes clear) this kind of near-efficacy was the result of any given document's perceived strength *as proof.*

[36] That the use of, and apparent reliance on, documents could increase without a commensurate shift in their legal valuation can also be paralleled elsewhere: cf. Yemeni society before 1962, where "[i]n traditional legal practice there is no generalized reliance on the efficacy of a written instrument, while at the same time few people would consider transacting without using documents. Whether a transaction placed in written form holds firm depends nearly entirely on the nature of the social relationship between the transacting parties and the stature of the associated witnesses . . . there is a strong aversion to documentless transactions at the same time that the documents themselves are not thought to have decisive strength" Messick (1983) 48.

that would not have gone unchallenged in an Athenian court. In both cases, however, a legal document was part of everyday life, and partner to all of that life's uncertainties. Unmarked in language and unceremoniously created, Greek legal documents were no more reliable than the men who made them, witnessed them, and guarded them. Roman documents, as we shall see, were very different.

CHAPTER 2

Roman perceptions of Roman tablets: aspects and associations

Aeschines and Demosthenes saw Athenian legal documents as the physical consequences of human suspicion, and treated them accordingly. In striking contrast, it was at first rare (although not unknown) for a breath of suspicion to touch a Roman legal document, as it was at first rare (although eventually much better known) for suspicion of corruption to touch the Romans themselves. In legal and financial transactions, the Romans were considered astonishingly trustworthy, at least by a Greek observer. As Polybius in the second century BC said, with some admiration, "Among the Greeks, public men, if entrusted with a single talent, though protected by ten copyists, as many seals, and twice as many witnesses, cannot keep faith; but among the Romans, in their magistracies and embassies, men having the handling of a great amount of money do what is right because of the trust pledged by their oath."[1] Documents (with officials, seals, and witnesses) could not prevent Greek misbehavior, but were not even mentioned in an assessment of Roman good behavior, where the absolute quality of Roman *fides* struck the observer first. Yet at Rome these documents existed. Their uses there were different, for they were generated for entirely different purposes and through an entirely different, complex, and formal process. What they *were* was very important: attention was paid to their physical appearance (this chapter), and their style – form and phrasing – was notably different from that of any comparable Greek documents, as well as from everyday Latin (chapter 3). What they could *do* was, as will be seen, also very different (chapters 4 and 5). As a consequence of this, these documents, which were written on tablets, would for centuries be widely understood to stand in a special relationship to their legal acts.

Roman tablets and most things written on them belong to one large family, their shared traits as noticeable as Hapsburg jaws, and similarly traceable in word-portraits, over generations and through collateral groups.

[1] Polyb. 6.56.13–14.

21

22   *The world of belief*

In addition to sharing a generally rectangular physical form, these tablets are associated with acts that order the state and the household; they observe no clear distinction between public and private; and they are not temporary jottings, but authoritative and final embodiments of the new reality they help to create. That legal documents belong in this family, and deserve the respect granted to its other members, is shown by their display of these traits, as well as by their similarities of language, style, and efficacy that will be examined in subsequent chapters. Such resemblances mark out all its members, like members of other famous families, as inheritors of a claim to shape the world.

Roman-law documents written on *tabulae* were traditional creations far older than the imperial dates of the surviving examples would suggest. *Tabulae* were smallish rectangles, often of wood, itself usually (but not always) hollowed out and coated with wax into which letters were incised with a stylus.[2] They could be hung on walls, or two, three, or more of these could be folded together or stacked to form diptyches, triptychs, or polyptychs, and in these multiples could be called a *codex* or *codices*.[3] The material (or medium) could eventually shift from being wood and wax, or bronze, to parchment or papyrus, but even so these documents would continue to be called *tabulae*, and when necessary folded, bound with string, and sealed.[4] Sets of wooden tablets were also commonly called *tabellae*, *codicilli*, *pugillares*, and, at times, *libelli* ("little books").[5] By Horace's time, Roman schoolboys are depicted as possessing tablets of these sorts,

---

[2] Roman legal documents from Egypt are known through wooden tablets and papyrus copies, listed in Marichal (1950), (1955), and (1992a); tablets surviving from Roman Egypt, when not for (Greek) schoolroom use, were used by Roman citizens for legal, financial, and (very late) liturgical documents (Brashear and Hoogendijk [1990] give the list). Physical description: W. Smith *et al.* (1901) II.753–4, Bowman and J. D. Thomas (1983) 32–45, Wolf and Crook (1989) 10–14, and cf. *D.* 37.4.19 (Tryphonius), common opinion (*quod volgo dicitur*) called possession of property given contrary to a will possession *contra lignum*, "against the wood;" for bibliography on *tabulae*, Brashear and Hoogendijk (1990) 27–9 n.8; general overview, Sachers (1932), Cavallo (1992), Eck (1998), and Rhodes (2001b) 145–8.

[3] *Codices*, e.g., Sen. *Vit. Brev.* 13.4.

[4] These are papyrus double-documents (discussed chapter seven pp. 187–202): see Turner (1978) 28–44 (adding *P. Turner* 22 and Welles *et al.* [1959] 14), Wolff (1978) 79 n.117, N. Lewis (1989) 6–11, Amelotti and Migliardi Zingale (1989), Vandorpe (1995) 10–11. All eventually called *tabulae*: *D.* 37.11.1 (Ulpian); see also Paul. *Sent.* 4.7.6 and *FV* 249.6 for late legal equivalences similar to Ulpian's.

[5] *Liber* ("book"), strictly speaking, means "the bark of a tree"; from this *libellus* is derived. Both therefore imply wood, as in Cic. *de Orat.* 1.195.3 (*libellus* of *tabulae*) and various legal equivalences (*D.* 2.13.6 *passim* [Ulpian], esp. 2.13.6.6–7, physical format is referred to interchangeably as *tabulae, codices*, and *libelli*; *D.* 43.5.1.*pr.* [Ulpian]); see Premerstein (1926) cols. 27–8. Since *liber* and *libellus* can refer to the concept (a "book") as much as to the form in which, and materials from which, a book is made, and since those materials came to vary (cf. *D.* 32.52 [Ulpian] on what can comprise *libri*, as well as Catul. 1; Mart. *Ep.* 14.186 and 192, implied 14.184, 188), references to *libelli* (which occur in all the

Roman perceptions of Roman tablets

and it has been deduced that they learned to write on them.[6] Because of this, and because of the erasability of wax, it is commonly assumed that Romans had always learned to write this way; that *tabulae* were therefore, because a schoolroom material, disposable and cheap; and that the choice of a tablet for any task was therefore merely one of convenience.[7] Thus this physical form, although curious, possibly even awkward, and surprisingly long lasting, has never been one to which any particular significance has been attached.

But despite the vigor with which Plautus's schoolboy whacked his pedagogue on the head with a *tabula* in the *Bacchides*,[8] the first of these assumptions – that tablets were primarily or initially for schoolroom use – is probably wrong. For this scene is almost certainly only borrowed from the play's Greek original rather than characteristic Roman practice: the use of the *tabula* in education probably did not antedate the wholesale importation of Greek slaves in the second century BC, who brought with them not only entirely different forms of knowledge but also entirely different methods of learning it.[9] Yet even after its introduction, the schoolboy tablet in the Latin-speaking Roman world may be less common than supposed,[10] since only one of the more than 1,070 surviving Latin *tabulae* known to me

---

categories in which *tabulae* occur) have been used sparingly in what follows, and references to *libri* generally omitted.

[6] Schoolboys: Hor. *Sat.* 1.6.74, *Ep.* 1.1.56; Petr. *Sat.* 46.3 (bent over *tabula*, but no direct reference to writing); Juv. *Sat.* 14.191 (*ceras*); Isid. *Etym.* 6.9.1 (*parvulorum nutrices*); in images of boys and tablets they hold tablets but do not write, e.g., Nappo (1989) 86–8 no. 12 (fig. 8; Pompeii), Massow (1932) 132–42 no. 180 (Neumagen), Parássoglou (1979) 7 n.9 (Naples Museum), Bilkei (1980) 63 (Pécs), Merten (1983) 29–30 (Trier), Gonzenbach (1984) 251 (Kaiseraugst silver, fourth century AD). Quint. *Inst.* 1.1.27 suggests that wax tablets, although used when children learn to write, are not as good as a tracing-board; Mart. *Ep.* 4.86.11–12, *charta* (not wood tablets) used by schoolboys for exercises. *Tabulae* become common only in later schoolroom scenes, e.g., *CGL* 3.327.32 or Dionisotti (1982) 99 (line 22), 101 (line 45), 111 (on line 27), Amm. Marc. 28.4.13 (scribes with *pugillares tabulae*, for which the only thing lacking was a *magister ludi litterarii*), and also in Byzantine Egypt, Cribiore (1996) 68 and medieval Europe, e.g., Rouse and Rouse (1989) 176. Erasability: Quint. *Inst.* 10.3.31 (but for adults blocking out speeches, not children).

[7] Assumptions: e.g., Turner (1968) 6–7 (for "first drafts") or S. Bonner (1977) 127, but very common.

[8] *Bac.* 441.

[9] Borrowing from Greek original: Harris (1989) 159; tablets were used in Greek schools, see (e.g.) Beck (1975) 16–17. Greek pedagogues were probably known in Rome in the third century BC, but did not become numerous until the second century (S. Bonner [1977] 40).

[10] Schoolroom: even Egypt provides only forty-three published school-tablets before the fifth century AD, all in Greek (Brashear and Hoogendijk [1990], who 45 n.1 consider this a fluke; Cribiore [1996] 68 dates twenty-nine to the Roman and fifty-three to the Byzantine periods, none to the Ptolemaic), compared to sixty-three ostraka and seventy-six papyri for schoolroom use in the Roman period (Cribiore [1996] 73). Cribiore (1996) 55 also points out that tablets were often the possession of the teacher, not the student. Very wet (e.g., wells in Germany) or very dry conditions help tablets to survive, but conditions alone are not enough to explain the non-survival of Latin schoolboy tablets.

24 *The world of belief*

seems to have served this purpose.[11] And despite the *tabula's* appearance in the hands of scribes[12] and poets,[13] the second – related – assumption (that tablets were for rough drafts) is probably wrong as well: the *tabula* was not chiefly the Roman equivalent of a stenographer's pad or a spiral notebook. The primary context and implications of Roman *tabulae*, both non-legal and legal, were entirely different.

TABULAE IN GENERAL

The most basic meaning of *tabula* (and its diminutive, *tabella*) seems to be that of a wooden plank, such as would float across the waves to a man from his foundered ship, or (in a more Roman image) be laid out as flooring in an olive-shed: it has the requisite shape, substance, and texture at the heart of all but the latest meanings of *tabula* and *tabella*.[14] These planks were formally arranged and written upon early, in ways associated with the ceremonial actions of augurs, priests, magistrates, and *templa* – with men, space, and time associated with the state's ordered and divinely approved governance. The ceremony, the writing, and the physical object together helped to create order.

Tabulae were a basic part of the augurs' equipment in creating *templa*, areas marked off as in some way dedicated or sacred, within which auspices could be taken and in which, therefore, these men could perform their public functions. Lesser *templa*, according to Festus the dictionary-writer, were created by the augurs when "any places were separated off by *tabulae* or linens, so that they not gape open with more than one door, and were marked off with fixed words. Therefore a *templum* is a place thus spoken

---

[11] Schoolboy: only Wiegels (1982) 347–51 (Sulz am Neckar), although 185 tablets cannot be read. The earliest Italian tablet, from a seventh-century BC Etrurian tomb, has an alphabet incised around its edge, but (*contra* S. Bonner [1977] 36) this proves little about the contemporary or subsequent use of tablets: this ivory artifact is an import from the Near East, which if anything suggests that tablets were first used for commercial purposes, Bundgård (1965) 11–24.

[12] Scribes: Calpurnius Piso (in Gel. 7.9.2–4), story of Cn. Flavius, scribe (i.e., accountant: see Cic. 2 *Verr.* 3.183) turned curule aedile (cf. Liv. 9.46.2); Festus (333M), both poets and *librarii*, keepers of public accounts on *tabulae*, called *scribae* by *antiqui*; on *librarii*, see N. Lewis (1974) 50–1.

[13] Poets: Plaut. *Pseud.* 401; also, e.g., Catul. 42.11–12 (*codicillos*) and 50.2 (*tabellis*); Cic. *Arch.* 25 (bad epigram on a *libellus*, handed to Sulla); Hor. *Sat.* 1.4.15; Ov. (e.g.) *Pont.* 4.2.27, 4.12.25; Juv. *Sat.* 1.63 (filling up wax); see Bucher (1987 [1995]) 25 for some casual uses of *codicilli*.

[14] Ship planking, e.g., Cic. *Off.* 3.90; dry flooring in farm-buildings, e.g., Cato, *Agr.* 3.4 (*tabulata*). The major semantic difference between *tabula* and *tabella* is that although *tabella* is used for many of the meanings of *tabula* discussed below (albeit only once by jurists), *tabula* is rarely used to denote "letter" (Plaut. *Asin.* 763; Gel. 17.9.17; Apul. *Apol.* 85), as *tabella* can, although stylus tablets are frequently *re*-used as letters. Thus *tabellarii* are mailmen or couriers, while *tabularii* are accountants and keepers of records. I argue elsewhere (E. Meyer [2001]) that letter-*tabellae* can have some of the special resonances of *tabulae*. In general, see *OLD s.v. tabula* and *tabella*.

Roman perceptions of Roman tablets

forth or separated off, so that it lies open from (only) one side, and has angled posts fixed to the earth."[15] Planks as well as linen would be written on, and the linens eventually gathered together into books.[16]

Time, people, and actions could be similarly ordered, and special moments and categories separated off, through *tabula*-actions taken by priests, magistrates, and others. According to Cato the Elder, the *pontifex maximus* recorded on a *tabula* the events considered of religious importance for any given year – "how often grain was expensive, how often fog or whatever obscured the light of the moon or the sun."[17] Other authors indicated the listing on this tablet of magistrates' names, other prodigies and portents like fires, consular activities and campaigns, and reasons for special thanksgiving, in short things worthy of recall done "at home and abroad, on land and on sea."[18] The sacral calendar, in the keeping of the priests, was called simply the *tabula*, and published on a whitened tablet (*in albo*);[19] from *tabulae* could be read prayers pronounced by the priests and repeated by the magistrates (a process known as *praeire verba*);[20] on *tabulae* were recorded the ritual utterances of the censors as well as the results of their quinquennial census – land, buildings, and census-class of all the citizens,[21] along with any public contracts and public expenses and income[22] down to

---

[15] Lesser *templa*: quoted, Fest. 157M (*minora templa fiunt ab auguribus cum loca aliqua tabulis aut linteis sepiuntur, ne uno amplius ostio pateant, certis verbis definita. Itaque templum est locus ita effatus aut ita septus, ut ex una parte pateat, angulosque adfixos habeat ad terram*); see Serv. *in Aen.* 4.200, Weinstock (1934), and Gargola (1995) 27 on ritual inauguration.

[16] *Libri lintei*: Liv. 4.7.12 and 4.13.7. *Libri lintei* at Anagnia pertaining to *sacra*, Fro. *ad M. Caes.* 4.4.1; Sibylline books on linen, Symm. *Ep.* 4.34.3 and Claud. *Bell. Get.* 231–2 (*carbasus*); Etruscan linen book preserved at Zagreb, Brashear and Hoogendijk (1990) 7 n.4. Cf. Mourgues (1995b) 107–8 n.8, with Piccaluga (1994), who notes linen's sacred character, esp. in contrast to parchment and papyrus.

[17] Cato, quoted in Gel. 2.28.6 (*quod in tabula apud pontificem maximum est, quotiens annona cara, quotiens lunae aut solis lumine caligo aut quid obstiterit*).

[18] Other portents: Gel. 4.5.1–6, Dion. Hal. 8.56.1, Liv. 8.18.11–13 (dictators, ritual actions, the plebeian secession); "at home..." Serv. *in Aen.* 1.373; in general, Frier (1979) 83–93.

[19] Calendar: Cic. *Att.* 6.1.8; Cic. *Mur.* 25 (called *fasti*); Petr. *Sat.* 30.3, a private version nailed up (*defixae*) on doorposts.

[20] Priests: Val. Max. 4.1.10, a scribe *praeiret* the prayer from the *publicae tabulae*; see also chapter four n.8 on *praeire verba*.

[21] Ritual utterances of censors, Var. *L.* 6.86. Census itself: e.g., Liv. 6.27.6; Cic. *Mil.* 73, public memory *impressam* on *tabulis publicis* of the census (recording a list of beneficiaries of the grain dole, see Nicolet [1980] 64); Cic. *Har.* 30; Gel. 16.13.7, the *tabulae Caerites* were the tablets on which those deprived of their voting rights were listed by the censors; Div. 8 (Orelli), censor's tablet an *album*. Censorial tablets elsewhere: the twelve colonies (Liv. 29.37.7), Larinum (Cic. *Cluent.* 41.8), *CIL* I² 593.13–16 (= *FIRA²* 1.142–3 no. 13). For a third-century BC depiction of the census with *tabulae*, see Kuttner (1991).

[22] Contracts: assigned outside of Rome in *CIL* I² 593.34–40 (= *FIRA²* 1.144 no. 13) to *tabulae publicae* of urban quaestor or treasury official; Vitr. *Arch.* 2.8.8 (*locationes ex tabulis*, unclear whether the censors'). *CIL* I² 583.58 has quaestor "writing into the *taboleis popliceis*" the amount given to the praetor as surety by a man condemned under the *Lex Acilia*. State income: Liv. 26.36.11, private contributions

26   *The world of belief*

the number, size, and even posture of plundered statues.[23] Surveyors' maps, also associated with the censors, were incised on wood and bronze tablets.[24] The edict of the praetors (and, later, provincial governors) appeared each year on whitened tablets;[25] lists of members of the senate were kept on similar tablets.[26] Judges, decurions, and members of associations were also listed this way.[27] Treaties were recorded on *tabulae*,[28] as were the laws (*leges*) and plebiscites of the Roman people,[29] and decrees of the Senate.[30] All four

---

in publicis tabulis; Cic. *Agr.* 1.4, public land and buildings entered into *tabulis censoriis*; Plin. *NH* 18.11, all sources of revenue for Rome once in the censors' tablets; tax obligations for provincials to be πάν]των δέλτων προσοδικῶν, Reynolds (1982) 58 no. 8 line 31 (Aphrodisias).

[23] Statues: Cic. 2*Verr.* 1.57 (*in tabulas publicas ad aerarium*), with Ps.-Asc. (Orelli; *perscriptum in tabulis*, a sign of *diligentia*); cf. Liv. *Per.* 57, Scipio enters the gifts of Antiochus into *tabulae publicae*.

[24] Surveyors and censors, see, e.g., Nicolet (1980) 64 (map of *ager publicus* in Campania); bronze tablets, Dilke (1971) 112–14; cf. Siculus Flaccus, *de Cond. Agr.* L154 (*arbores finales alii in aenis, alii in membr<an>is*, the first two words emended to *<in> arbore<i>s tabulis*, Campbell [2000] 120); Hyginus Gromaticus L200–2 (Campbell [2000] 158); see Moatti (1993) 31–2, and Campbell (1996) 88–90.

[25] Praetor's edict: on whitened boards with red headings, rubrics (Quint. *Inst.* 12.3.11; *D.* 2.13.1.1 [Ulpian], *D.* 43.1.2.3 [Paulus]), referred to as *stipulatione quam . . . in albo propositam* in the *lex Rubria*, *CIL* 11.1146 lines 34–5. Provincial governor, Cic. 2*Verr.* 3.26 ("I wouldn't have dared to say it, if I could not have read these edicts from his own *tabulis* in so many words!"). Other edicts also posted on tablets: proscriptions, e.g., Cic. *S. Rosc.* 21, 26; Cass. Dio 30–35.109.12 (καινότητα . . . λελευκωμένον πίνακα) and 47.8–13; *CIL* 2.5041 (bronze tablet); for others, see Hinard (1985) 18–35; imperial parallels, e.g., Suet. *Gaius* 49.3 (two *libelli*); Herodian 1.17.1 (a hinged tablet of lime-wood) and 2.1.10; Cass. Dio 67.15.3 (σανίδιον); *HA Comm.* 9.3, men to be killed listed on a *tabula*. Herodian and Cassius Dio may be referring to *tabellae* of the leaf type, Haran (1996) 221 n.24. Other imperial edicts, e.g., Alföldy (2000) or *FIRA²* 1.420–2 no. 73, edict of Vespasian ἐν λε]υκώματι.

[26] Senators on *album*, Tac. *Ann.* 4.42.3 (name erased); Cass. Dio 55.3.3 (ἐς λεύκωμα; began with Augustus); *CT* 12.1.48; senators still called οἱ τοῦ λευκώματος in Procop. *Anecdota* 29.21.6.

[27] Judges, see the *lex Acilia*, *CIL* I² 583 lines 15, 18, 27 (*ioudices* and patrons), Suet. *Tib.* 51.1; decurions, members of associations see Schmidt (1893) cols. 1333–4, 1336 and Eck (1998) 213; also candidates for the consulship, in the *lex Valeria Aurelia* (Crawford [1996] 1.519–20 lines 20–1); a list of men freed from liturgies on λευκώματι, *P.Gen.* 2.91 lines 13, 20, and 30 (AD 50–1); lists of competitors in games on whitened tablets, Eck (1998) 214–15; lists of centurions, Eck (1998) 215 n.79 (unpublished).

[28] E.g., Cic. *Phil.* 5.12, Sen. Rhet. *Contr.* 10.5.3 (generalizing), or the three between Rome and Carthage, on bronze tablets (Polyb. 3.22.1–26.1), *SIG³* 732 (Rome and Thyrreion, on πίνακες, line 5), or that between Antiochus and Rome in 189 BC (App. *Syr.* 39), ἀναθέντες on the Capitol "where other treaties were customarily put." A *deditio* (Nörr [1989]) and a Roman arbitration (Richardson [1983]) on bronze tablets have also been found.

[29] *Leges*: the Twelve Tables (*tabulae*) themselves (*contra* R. Mitchell [1990] 124–5 and n.199), inscribed on bronze (Liv. 3.57.10; Dion. Hal. 10.57.7 calls them bronze *stelai*) and nailed to the rostra (Diod. Sic. 12.26.1), itself a *templum* (Liv. 8.14.12); *D.* 48.13.10 (Venuleius Saturninus), *tabulam aeream legis*; cf. (e.g.) Hor. *Ars* 399 or Cic. *Phil.* 1.3; custom believed very old, Dion. Hal. 3.36.4 (laws of Servius Tullius ἐν . . . σανίσιν); Cass. Dio 42.32.

[30] *Senatusconsulta*, see, e.g., *CIL* I² 581 (= *ILS* 18, and A. Gordon [1983] 83–5), lines 26–7, this *sc* is to be inscribed on a bronze tablet (*in tabolam ahenam*) and nailed up (*figier*) where it can most easily be read; also Cic. *Cat.* 1.4, mention of an *sc inclusum* (embodied) *in tabulis*; Val. Max. 6.4.3 (*tabellas*), and Suet. *Nero* 49.2 (*codicilli*); in Greek, called δέλτοι, e.g., *SIG³* 764 lines 8–10 (45 BC), *OGIS* 456 lines 48–53, Jos. *AJ* 14.219 and 319.

Roman perceptions of Roman tablets

were sometimes, the first three often, inscribed on tablets of bronze,[31] as were copies of the edicts that granted citizenship or legal privilege and were nailed up (*defigere*) in or on temples or *templa*.[32] By the end of Nero's reign, at least three thousand bronze *tabulae* (of senatorial decrees and plebiscites on matters of alliance, treaty, and privileges to individuals) hung on the Capitolium alone, *tabulae* which Vespasian thought had to be reconstituted (*restituenda*) after they had been destroyed in the great fire.[33]

This type of order, overseen or made possible by the proper actions of these priests and magistrates, characterized Romans' financial and religious lives outside the forum as well. Respectable men, bankers, and magistrates were all expected to keep their financial accounts on *tabulae* just as the censors "kept the books" of the Roman state and associations regulated their own financial affairs, and carefully preserved these tablets at home, in the room called the *tablinum*.[34] Therefore it was later reasoned that *tablinum* was so-called from *tabulae*, because "magistrates of old in their

---

[31] Bronze: Plin. *NH* 34.21.99, bronze to secure the perpetuity of monuments (and at 34.20.97–8 he gives the proper recipe for mixing bronze for tablets), and Dion. Hal. 3.36.4, with Williamson (1987a), whose important arguments will be extended in what follows, and Salway (2000) 121–3; cf. Pomponius Porphyrion's third-century AD commentary on Horace's *Ars* 399 (Pauly II.507), wooden predated bronze, and Poccetti (1999) 556–60, inscribing on bronze an Italic habit from at least the third century BC. Many imperial examples, e.g., *AE* 1976.677–8 (honorific), which make reference back to very early ones, and Plin. *Ep.* 8.6.13, Pallas's honors; Cyprian *ad Don.* 10 (*publico aere praefixo iura proscripta sint*); Corcoran (1996) 146 n.101 for early fourth-century examples; inscribing on tablets an honor and a privilege, *FIRA²* 1.331–2 no. 64 (edict *at perpetui[t]atis memoriam aera incisus*; Timgad, AD 361–3); see also *CT* 14.4.4 (AD 367) and *CJ* 11.24(23).2.1 (AD 424).

[32] *Diplomata* (copies of an edict conferring *beneficia*, see chapter seven n.4): Liv. 8.11.16 (Campanians), and numerous *diplomata* themselves state that they are copied off bronze originals, see *CIL* 16 *passim*; Roxan (1978), (1985), and (1994); Pollux 8.128, δέλτοι χαλκοί of Roman veterans; most discharge certificates (*honesta missio*) were probably on wood, only a few on bronze, Eck (1998) 203–4, who also notes that bronze diptychs were accurate physical copies of wood tablets. On choice of location for posting on or near Capitolium, see Dušanic (1984) and Roxan and Eck (1993) 73–4. Other gifts, e.g., *IG* 2–3² 3299, a Greek city "honored by gifts, as can be confirmed on the δέλτος on the Capitoline in Rome" (Athens, AD 132), or *SB* 4224 (second century AD), copy of a letter of Antony in which it is requested that privileges granted to victors in sacred games be recorded on a δέλτον χαλκῆν.

[33] Suet. *Vesp.* 8.5 (referred to collectively as *instrumentum imperii*); placement, Corbier (1987) 43–6.

[34] Respectable people: Cic. *2 Verr.* 1.128, 156, *Q. Rosc.* 1; richest farmers, Cic. *2 Verr.* 3.173, 189; Roman citizens in Gaul, Cic. *Font.* 11, 34; private folk, Cic. *Rab. Post.* 9. Bankers: Plaut. *Curc.* 410 (*ceras quattuor*), *Miles* 72–3 (with Gröschler [1997] 320), *Truc.* 71; Cic. *Caec.* 17, Quint. *Inst.* 11.2.24. Tax-collectors' associations: Cic. *2 Verr.* 2.182, 186, 187. Magistrates: Plut. *Ti. Gracch.* 6.2 (δέλτους of his transactions as quaestor); Reynolds (1982) 57 no. 8 line 2 (quaestorian tablets); quaestors customarily handed in their accounts *in tabulas publicas*, Ps.-Asc. on Cic. *2 Verr.* 1.11 (Orelli). The expectation that important people kept *tabulae* was occasionally confounded, Cic. *de Orat.* 2.97 (Sulpicius); if you did not keep them it was held against you, Cic. *2 Verr.* 3.112. For accounts in general, see Ste. Croix (1956) and Gröschler (1997) 246–97. Accounts depicted as *tabulae* visually, often along with rolls, so the continued use of tablets was deliberate choice: Birt (1976 [1907]) 66–7; for their depictions on high imperial monuments from Trier and elsewhere, Baltzer (1983) 46–60, 96–102.

28   *The world of belief*

magistracy were accustomed to have there a place made for the sake of public accounts, for the *tabulae* of accounts." The *tablinum* was one of the rooms of the Roman house in which public affairs, and especially trials and arbitrations, were regularly conducted even in the late first century AD.[35] Less substantial people, opined the architect Vitruvius, would of course have no need for such a room.[36]

Individuals of any rank and wealth could also make vows, and if what was wished for came to pass, could tie a vow (*votum*) written on a tablet to a god's statue or attach a *tabula* to a temple-wall or a tree within a sanctuary labelling or embodying payment of what had been promised.[37] Horace imagined himself doing so at the end of a tempestuous love-affair, as if saved from shipwreck.[38] Triumphing generals had earlier done the same, after surviving somewhat more serious events. "Nuncupated vows" were those, said Cincius the jurisconsult in the first century BC, "which consuls and praetors make when they depart for their province; these are repaid (*referuntur*) on *tabulae*, with many people present."[39] Livy provides several instances of the dedication of these *tabulae triumphatores* (and spoils of war, or temples) on the Capitolium and elsewhere, and preserves their inscriptions in the very archaic Saturnian verse.[40] Even curse-*tabulae*, created as

---

[35] *Tablinum*: quoted, Fest. 356M (*quod antiqui magistratus in suo imperio tabulis rationum ibi habebant publicarum rationum causa factum locum*); Plin. *NH* 35.7, filled *codicibus . . . et monumentis* of things done during office; *TH* 34 is an illegible documentary polyptych found in a *tablinum*, see Capasso (1997 [1990]); *tabulae publicae* containing question-and-answer in a trial before the senate were kept, "as is traditional" (*more maiorum*) says Cicero, in private hands (*Sull.* 42); keeping records in general, Liv. 6.1.2, Haensch (1992) 230, and note Sen. *Vit. Brev.* 13.4, *publicae tabulae codices dicuntur.* In the fourth century AD, magistrates were still taking records home (Opt. *App.* 2.3 = Maier [1987] 176 no. 22); true even in nineteenth-century Britain, when (e.g.) Lord Salisbury committed the state to actions documented only in the papers he kept at Hatfield house, Roberts (1999) 509–10. *Plurimae causae* conducted in *tabularia* in Tacitus's day, *Dial.* 39.1.

[36] Vitr. *Arch.* 6.5.1. "Legal home" later defined as where one has one's residence (*sedes*), keeps one's *tabulas*, and organizes one's affairs (*D.* 50.16.203 [Alfenus Varus]).

[37] To statues: Apul. *Apol.* 54, Juv. *Sat.* 10.55 ("it is *fas* to wax up the knees of the gods"), perhaps also indicated in 12.102–3 (*fixis vestitur tota libellis porticus*). Augustus in AD 14 plans to read vows from tablets, but he decides to have Tiberius read instead (Suet. *Aug.* 97.1).

[38] Horace: *Odes* 1.5.13–14. Vows for rescue from shipwreck *in tabulis* common "even today," i.e. the third century AD, see Pomponius Porphyrion's commentary on Hor. *Odes* 1.5 (Pauly 1.31), cf. Hor. *Sat.* 2.1.33, *votiva . . . tabella* and Wachsmuth (1967) 141–2 n.246. Tablets in sanctuaries in general: MacMullen (1981) 159 n.78. Walls or trees: Veyne (1983) 289–90, and the *tabula ansata* or eared tablet (an artistic stylization of the physical form) was a favorite Roman imperial form for votives, Fraser and Rönne (1957) 179–82, Albert (1972) 34, Pani (1986) and (1988), borrowed even at Sagalassos, Cormack (1997) 146.

[39] Cincius, quoted in Fest. 173M (*vota nuncupata dicuntur, quae consules, praetores, cum in provinciam profiscuntur, faciunt: ea in tabulas praesentibus multis referuntur*; cf. Liv. 45.39.11).

[40] Examples: Liv. 6.29.9 (*tabula* of Titus Quinctius); 40.52.5–7 (*tabula* of Regillus); 41.28.8–10 (*tabula* of Ti. Sempronius Gracchus); Saturnians, identified in a (probably) first-century AD treatise on meter, preserved in *GL* 6.265.8–21 and attributed to Caesius Bassus: "among us (i.e. the Romans) . . . on

Roman perceptions of Roman tablets

part of a complex ritual procedure, were intended by their authors not only to be out of the reach of the victim, but (often) to make their way to the *templa* of the gods of the underworld. They were buried in or by graves or dropped down wells throughout the Roman world, the two methods, like hand-delivery rather than mailing without a zip- or post-code, differing only in the speed of their arrival.[41]

This association of *tabulae* with careful action undertaken on behalf of the propitious or desired order of Rome and one's own household was believed by Romans to be early. Moreover, these two contexts were also often linked where *tabulae* were concerned. This suggests that state and household, public and private, were not – at the early age from which tablets may have derived, or on these later occasions when they were used – considered distinct. For example, King Servius's fifth-century BC institution of the census, "by which all distinctions of property, rank, age, employment, and office were written onto *tabulae*," was characterized by the second-century AD epitomator Florus as, "thus the greatest city-state was delineated with the exactitude of a small household."[42] This parallel was more than a happy literary conceit: the census indeed acknowledged no distinction between the public state and the private household, as a florid comparison by Dionysius of Halicarnassus made clear.[43] Private morals and the public weal were inseparable, as their combination on the censors' tablets reflected. Even the storage of these *publicae tabulae* was "private" as well as "public": they could later be found either in the temple of the Nymphs, the *atrium Libertatis*, or in the censors' own homes.[44]

---

the ancient *tabulae*, which *duces* about to triumph used to nail on the Capitolium and announce in the *titulum* their victory in Saturnian verses, I have found examples of such (i.e. this meter)." Cf. Vell. Pat. 2.25.4, Sulla fulfills his vow to Diana at Mt. Tifata with a bronze tablet.

[41] Curse-tablets: called *plumbeis tabulis*, e.g., Tac. *Ann.* 2.69.3; see in general Audollent (1904), e.g., 191–3 no. 135, where the author of the tablet refers to writing a curse *in as tabelas*. Graves and wells (and other bodies of water), Jordan (1985) 207 and Faraone (1991a) 3 with nn.6–8; intended for underworld, Heintz (1998); infernal regions as *templa*, Ennius in Var. *L.* 7.6 and Cic. *Tusc.* 1.48. They could be on wood as well as the more usual lead, a habit continued in Christian amulets: see Brashear (1992b); *tabulae ansatae* (above n.38) could also be drawn on late amulets, Kotansky (1983) 175–6.

[42] Florus 1.6.3 (*ut omnia patrimonii, dignitatis, aetatis, artium officiorumque discrimina in tabulas referrentur, ac sic maxima civitas minimae domus diligentia contineretur*); cf. Momigliano (1989) 109.

[43] Census: Dion. Hal. 20.13.2–3; see Greenidge (1977 [1894]) 63–74 on its documentable veracity, Nicolet (1980) 73–81, and Kuttner (1991) for its early date.

[44] *Tabulae census* in *aedes* of Nymphs, Cic. *Mil.* 73; in *atrium Libertatis*, Liv. 43.16.13; note Purcell's (1993) identification of the so-called *tabularium* in the Roman forum as the *atrium Libertatis*, which attaches this building – with its "storage" of census- and status-documents, as well as the *formae agrorum* (143 nn.68–9, 144 n.76), to the Capitoline hill and its numerous *tabulae*. Own homes, see Rawson (1985) 238–9.

30 *The world of belief*

This lack of distinction between public and private can also be seen in accounts, and is reflected in Cicero's imprecise use of the word *tabula*. *Tabulae*, sometimes specifically *publicae tabulae* or *privatae tabulae*, appear frequently in Cicero's works, and nowhere more frequently than in his denunciations of Verres. Both types of *tabulae* are used by Cicero to show the same thing, the *ratio* or financial accounting of a man's magistracy which assesses a man's handling of both public and private money. The looseness of Cicero's phrasing shows that he does not draw meaningful or substantive distinctions between *publicae* and *privatae tabulae*; they clearly contained much the same information.[45] The spheres of private and public are intermingled. Moreover, the eventual preservation of these *tabulae* was as public and as private as preservation of the census had been.[46]

Finally, *tabulae* of all these various sorts, with their lack of clear distinction between public and private, share a further quality: they were all made with conspicuous care and finality, their creation not a matter of haste. Cassiodorus, misconstruing this many centuries later, saw here a cause for reproof: "The sayings of the wise and the ideas of our ancestors were in danger," said he. "For how could you quickly record words which the resistant hardness of bark made it almost impossible to set down? No wonder that the heat of the mind suffered pointless delays, and genius was forced to cool as its words were retarded." Cassiodorus's notion of genius differed from an earlier era's. Such delay, rather than impeding talent, prompted careful thought and the winnowing of the unimportant.[47]

It was in this way, with care and discrimination, that pontifical *tabulae* were made. This care has been overlooked because of a confusion over the relationship between *acta* (*diurna, urbis, publica*), *tabulae*, and (*libri*) *commentarii*, a confusion compounded (I suspect) by the regular assumption that *tabulae* must be the first medium on which information is recorded because they seem so primitive. The first record was much more likely to be the *acta* themselves, literally "things done," which have been variously interpreted as, or as akin to, Rome's "city chronicle" or "Rome's daily

---

[45] *Tabulae* alone in Cicero occur frequently, *tabulae publicae* alone rather more rarely: Cic. 2*Verr.* 2.104, 2.105, 5.10, *Sull.* 40, 42, *Vat.* 34, and *Cluent.* 62 all contain information about legal hearings; *Font.* 2 (accounts); 2*Verr.* 3.83 (misentering what is received as tax); *Pis.* 36 (what has happened at a vote). Otherwise, *tabulae publicae* cited as such can be those of the municipalities pillaged by Verres or others, see chapter eight nn.41–2. Financial accounting of magistracy: e.g., Cic. *Font.* 5 (*ratio . . . publicis privatisque tabulis*). Bowman and Woolf (1994) 15 find parallels between the accounting system used at Vindolanda and "the way Republican aristocrats used writing to manage the complex finances of their *familiae*"; cf. Thilo (1980) 170–81.

[46] Hybrid nature, public and private storage: Culham (1984) and (1989).

[47] Cassiodorus: *Variae* 11.38.34; cf. Jerome *Ep.* 8.1 (primitive ancestors and writing on wood).

Roman perceptions of Roman tablets

gazette."[48] These were first "published" by Julius Caesar – what the term means is disputed – but there is no reason to suppose that they had not been kept, unpublished, long before.[49] There is much overlap of content between these *acta* and the *tabulae* of the pontifex maximus, which ceased to be set up before 91 BC.[50] Attested in the *acta* were prodigies, military victories, an attempt on Antony's life, the impeachment of Scaurus, the issuing of senatorial decrees, Caesar's refusal of the title of king, public salutations of dignitaries, and the births, divorces, and funerals of important people.[51] Moreover, a fragment of a sixteenth-century manuscript, long dismissed as a humanistic forgery, may preserve an authentic fragment of these *acta diurna*; it too lists the same sorts of things (prodigies, consular activities, funerals, etc.) and is dated to 168 BC.[52] It is therefore possible that the *acta* were chronologically contemporary with, as well as logically prior to, the tablets: that each year's *tabula* was written at the end of a year from these more informally kept *acta*. Indeed, that the year's *tabula* was written at the end of the year is specifically implied by Cicero, who claimed that the pontifex maximus committed to writing the events (*mandabat litteris*), copied them onto a whitened tablet (*referebat in album*), and set the *tabula* out at his house.[53] This statement is most naturally interpreted as a narrative sequence of actions in which the *tabulae* of the pontifex maximus were the formal compilation of the year's most important events, seen from the perspective of the end of the year, the *acta* the record of events more or less as they occurred.[54] A similar distinction exists in the records of the Arval brethren, which were kept through the year in preliminary form,

---

[48] Pre-Caesarian city chronicle (*acta urbis*), Croke (1990) 170–2; gazette (and distinct from *acta senatus*), Baldwin (1979).

[49] Publication of *tam senatus quam populi diurna acta*, perhaps meaning now "publicised or copied for wide circulation" (Croke [1990] 171), Suet. *Jul.* 20.1; but see White (1997), casting doubt on Suetonius and drawing a distinction between "news" and "newspaper."

[50] Before 91 BC: Cicero *de Orat.* 2.52 (perhaps as early as 130 BC, in association with P. Mucius Scaevola as pontifex), cf. Frier (1979) 83 and Drews (1988).

[51] Baldwin (1979); parallels in the news read to Trimalchio (Petr. *Sat.* 53.1–10) "as if from the *urbis acta.*"

[52] *Acta diurna*: see Lintott's (1986) cautious rehabilitation of *CIL* 6.5.3403*, embraced by Croke (1990) 170–2. Contents, using Lintott's numeration: raining stones (line 27), fire (line 46), consular sacrifices (line 3), consuls depart for province (lines 58–61), funeral (line 67); Plin. *NH* 2.147 also reports that a rain of milk and blood in 114 BC *relatum in monumenta est*; that *monumenta* could be the *acta* argued by Baldwin (1979) 190.

[53] Cic. *de Orat.* 2.52; *pace* Frier (1979) 89–90, who treats Cicero's remarks as a series of unlinked clauses, preferring to follow Servius's (*in Aen.* 1.373) much later account, which lists the existence of the whitened tablet first, and Bucher (1987 [1995]), who argues that the *album* and the *tabula* were not the same, and that the latter had to be bronze.

[54] Cf. a parallel in the *acta senatus*, recorded in direct discourse (Talbert [1988] 145), and also the differences between *acta, diarium, diurnum, ephemeridae*, and *annales* in Isid. *Etym.* 1.44.

32   The world of belief

then inscribed at the end of each year on stone *tabulae*.[55] Tacitus's scornful distinction between important events (*res inlustres*), fitting for annals, and contemptible items like praise for the foundations and beams of Nero's amphitheater, fit only for the *acta diurna*, is therefore a distinction based on style, tradition, and the fact that between *acta* and any subsequent stage that could be called *annales* information and events were to be winnowed on the basis of their importance.[56]

Such events, culled from ephemeral records and affirmed and set out on tablets in this way, could then be the subject of further literary treatment. *Libri commentarii*, sometimes called just *commentarii* and sometimes called just *libri*, were a stage beyond *acta* and *tabulae*.[57] It was from *tabulae* of the priests that "the ancients rendered (*retulerunt*) annual commentaries in 80 books" called the *annales maximi*.[58] "Commentaries" were, from their postulated etymology and actual usage, functional creations,[59] ranging from preparatory musings for speeches[60] to writings by grammarians and jurists[61] to farming advice[62] to reminiscences of your adventures as a magistrate[63] to useful collections of (with learned insights into) augural and priestly lore.[64] They were synthetic and analytical ruminations in continuous prose on facts and experiences, and not (as has been specifically

---

[55] Beard (1985) 119 and n.37, 126, and 131: the Arval inscriptions may also display a tendency to include on the tablets more of what had been in the *acta* (see docs. 133–6). See also Beard (1998) 82–3; Wilkins (1996) 140; and Beard *et al.* (1998) 195 n.100.

[56] Tac. *Ann.* 13.31.1.

[57] Rohde (1936) 14–15. The physical form of consular *commentarii* could be *tabulae*, but in multiples (i.e. bound together to make *libri*): *FIRA*² 1.260–6 no. 36 refers (line 30) to εἰς τὴν τῶν ὑπομνημάτων δέλτον (with Mommsen [1885] 280 and Culham [1996] 177).

[58] Eighty books: Serv. *in Aen.* 1.373. Sempronius Asellio says only that *annales . . . quasi qui diarium scribunt, quam Graeci* ἐφημερίδα *vocant* (fr. 1 [Peter]).

[59] See in general *OLD s.v.* "*commentarius,*" Premerstein (1900), Rüpke (1992) 201–10, and Mourgues (1998) 124–32; meaning firm by Isidore's time (*commentaria dicta, quasi cum mente. sunt enim interpretationes, ut commenta iuris, commenta Evangelii, Etym.* 6.5–6); etymology, see Bömer (1953) 212 on the -*arios* ending.

[60] Speeches: e.g., Servius Sulpicius's "notes (*commentarii*) of his speeches were so carefully drawn up that it seems to me that he was composing *in memoriam posteritatis,*" Quint. *Inst.* 10.7.30.

[61] Grammarians, cf. Quint. *Inst.* 1.8.19; jurists, e.g., Gel. 1.12.18 (Labeo).

[62] Col. 1.1.3.

[63] Magistrates: consular commentaries preserved the formulaic summoning of the centuriate assembly (Var. *L.* 6.88) and other information; cf. the contents of Julius Caesar's *commentarii* of his Gallic campaigns (Hirtius, *BG* 8.*pr.*2; and Williamson [1983] 240–2), and surveying results and decisions in boundary disputes, Moatti (1993) 52–3.

[64] Lore: augural commentaries, Linderski (1985); contents of priestly books, Rohde (1936) 14–50 and Frier (1979) 111 n.11, 121, 182–3 on *annales*. On special occasions, *commentarii* could be inscribed, see Scheid (1994) 177 n.19 and 183 on the inscribed *commentarium* of the secular games of 17 BC. The terminology is reversed only in Liv. 1.31.8, 1.32.2 (cf. Dion. Hal. 3.36.4), and 1.60.4, where the pontifex copies out onto a tablet entries from the *commentarii* of Servius; this may be a special case (Plut. *Marc.* 8.5 refers to the commentaries of Numa, Cic. *Rab. Perd.* 15 to *regum commentariis*).

Roman perceptions of Roman tablets

shown in the case of augural commentaries) mere listings of individual facts or "archival" documents themselves, although these might be included.[65] Cicero and later writers derived much of their pontifical and augural information from such books, and fixed prayers were read from them as well as from *tabulae* themselves.[66] Commentaries created links *between* specific pieces of information which existed in final form on *tabulae*. Consequently *acta*, pontifical tablets, and commentaries all record much the same information, but worked over to differing degrees, and only in the last stage, that of *commentarii*, subjected to literary treatment.[67] It is when they are seen in comparison with the more ephemeral and undifferentiated records from which they were made, as well as with the more sophisticated and continuous studies subsequently written to explain them, that the final, factual, unadorned nature of the priests' *tabulae* becomes particularly clear.

This emphasis on authoritative finality exists clearly in the way *tabulae* as financial records were viewed. *Tabulae* as final accounts are carefully distinguished from everyday financial records and daybooks (*ephemerides* or *adversaria*):[68] they were not kept by sons under *patria potestas*, and, as Cicero emphasized in his speech in defense of Roscius the comic poet, they were *grave* and *sanctum*, while *adversaria* were *leve* and *infirmum*. These *tabulae* were, moreover, preserved *sancte* (most commonly in a *tablinum*), while daybooks were destroyed virtually immediately, after their financial information had been transferred into the *tabulae*, an act that was to be performed (in this case) every month or so. Indeed, Cicero – his own client having *tabulae* that said one thing, the plaintiff having a set of daybooks that said another – hinted strongly that *tabulae* had *diligentia* and *auctoritas*, whereas daybooks did not. *Tabulae* embrace and refuse to let go

---

[65] Linderski (1985).

[66] Augural books/commentaries: Cic. *Div.* 2.42, augurs' prayers recorded in *commentarii*; called ἱερατικοῖς ὑπομνήμασιν by Fest. 317M and Plut. *Marc.* 5.1; the *antiquitatum libri* included prayers for sacrifices (Var. *L.* 6.18); Gel. 13.23.1 claimed that prayers could be found *in plerisque antiquis orationibus*. Priests: from *tabulae*, see above n.20; from books, see Cic. *Dom.* 139 (incorrect if *sine libris*); Gel. 13.23; and list and discussion in Rohde (1936) 14–70. Cf. Cic. *Rab. Perd.* 15 (*ex annalium monumentis*). Similarly, a *decretum* of Verres's read from his commentary (Cic. *2Verr.* 5.54).

[67] Magistrates' *acta* also called *hypomnemata* (cf. *CGL* 3.33.33), and in Egypt were made up after the fact, not day-by-day as ἐφημερίδες were, Wilcken (1894) 97 and Bickermann (1933) 350–1.

[68] *Ephemerides*: Nepos, *Att.* 13.6, Prop. 3.23.20, Sen. *Ep.* 123.10; Voigt (1888) 531; Jouanique (1968) 30; they can exist on ostraka too, Marichal (1992b) 49–56 (a military equivalent); *contra*, Thilo (1980) 181–7. See Birt (1976 [1907]) 66 for artistic examples of reading from rolls and copying into tablets; Ov. *Am.* 1.12.25 for a depiction of a niggardly man, surrounded by his *ephemerides* and *tabulae*; Pugliese Carratelli (1950) 274–5 and Camodeca and Del Mastro (2002) for accounts on wood and papyrus found together at Herculaneum; and Beard (1998) 90, on *AE* 1987.333, a *sevir* and *curator arcae* with scroll and codex on his tomb-relief. Daybooks could also be called *ephemerides*: e.g., Cic. *Quinct.* 57; *HA Gall.* 18.6. As raw records, diaries are thus parallel to *acta* and financial day-books.

34   *The world of belief*

of (*amplectuntur*) the *fides* and *religio* of a man's everlasting *existimatio*, while daybooks support only "the memory of a moment." The *tabulae publicae* of the praetor had a similar *auctoritas*. Because of these qualities, malefactors (Cicero insists) find that *tabulae* cannot "honestly" or with honor (*honeste*) be set aside, ignored, or lost.[69]

On the other hand, when inconveniently revelatory, tablets could be tampered with or "injured" – a significant and reprehensible act.[70] It is because *tabulae* are supposed to be finished and perfect that changing them once they are done has such serious implications. When a censor picked up a stylus in order to remove an entry from the census-tablet, it was a matter of painful gravity; yet it was only by imitating the upright censor (said Horace) and removing words that lacked splendor and weight that a poet would write proper (*legitimum*) verse.[71] Visible indications of change in tablets could be interpreted as signs not only of shame, but of fiddling and untrustworthiness, and even change based on an honest mistake therefore became a matter for explanation and apology.[72] In short, a tablet's wax serves to reveal change, not to facilitate it. A change is a blemish, a retrospective negative reassessment of a man's *existimatio*.[73] Perhaps from this source spring both the inclusion of erasure as part of the crime of forgery[74] and the special significance always attributed by Romans to what we call *damnatio memoriae*, the visible (even violent) removal of a man's name or a man's image from any public monument on which he might appear.[75] The visible

---

[69] *patria potestas*: Cic. *Cael.* 17. Characteristics of *tabulae*: Cic. *Q. Rosc.* 6 (*grave et sanctum*), 7 (preserved *sancte*), 8 (transfer), 6 (*diligentiam* and *auctoritatem*; cf. *Flacc.* 20, *auctoritatem* and *fidem*), 7 (*fidem* and *religionem*) with Thilo (1980) 162–70, 276–86. *Publicarum tabularum*, Cic. *Arch.* 9.5; *honeste*, Cic. *2Verr.* 2.186. After the victory of the Numantines, Tiberius Gracchus asked for the return of only his quaestorian δέλτους and frankincense for public sacrifice, Plut. *Ti. Gracch.* 6.2. Romans used wood tablets for accounts until the Late Empire, Andreau (1996) 427 and (1999) 45.

[70] Cic. *2Verr.* 2.187.

[71] Poet and censor: Hor. *Ep.* 2.2.109–10, cf. *Sat.* 1.10.72–3; the underlying challenge to Horace at *Sat.* 1.4.14–16 may well be, then, who can write a *perfect* first draft (hence the use of *tabulae*). In Suet. *Claud.* 16.1–2, Claudius agrees to remove a censorial *nota* by a man's name, but only as long as the *litura*, erasure, still shows: the signs of erasure were themselves significant.

[72] Erasures seized upon as sign of evil-doing: Cic. *2Verr.* 2.101–5 (in Sthenius's court case), *2Verr.* 2.187–91 (revenue-contractors' accounts clearly altered, to hide Verres's name); *Arch.* 9 (no erasures around Archias's name in the *tabulae* of Metellus). Apology: Cic. *Arch.* 9 (Metellus).

[73] Revealing changes: Erman (1905a) 118–24 demonstrated that forgery of documents on papyrus was easy, forgery of those on wax tablets difficult. Man's *existimatio*: Sen. *Vit. Beat.* 8.3, the good man is one whose *placita* last and whose decrees have no erasures, *nec ulla in decretis eius litura sit*.

[74] Legal definition of forgery: *D.* 48.10.1.4 (Marcian), *D.* 48.10.16.2 (Paulus) on the same penalty for forging sealed documents as for false entry in accounts, tablets, public records (all without a seal), or destruction of same; *D.* 48.10.23 (Paulus), forgery is imitating handwriting, tampering with or copying over *aut libellum vel rationes*.

[75] *Damnatio memoriae*: in general, see Vittinghoff (1936) 18–32 and 64–74 (later juristic concepts); cf. Kajava (1995), Eck *et al.* (1996) 197 n.560; Suet. *Dom.* 23.1 (*titulos eradendos*), *HA Comm.* 20.4–5

Roman perceptions of Roman tablets

indications of obliteration, the sense of the absent in the present, carried the greatest significance.

From the evidence of priestly records and financial accounts, therefore, *tabulae* were not only seen as distinctive and of great consequence for the health of the state and the household, but also as the product of considered thought, meant to be authoritative and final statements of what had happened or (in the case of prayers) the correct ways in which things had been done and should be done. Authoritative and final tablets can, however, exist in different varieties. Bronze tablets in particular conveyed a message of eternal existence and validity. This fact, however, does not mean that its converse was true, that tablets not of bronze must therefore have been intended to be, and were seen as, "only" temporary or less authoritative. Public inscriptions could be put on wood, with no self-consciousness of being temporary.[76] Wax, seemingly the most temporary of mediums, was (as has been said) intended to last – Romans with venerated wax masks of their ancestors in their *atria* would have been offended if you thought otherwise, as would emperors who sent images of themselves, painted on wax tablets, to the cities of the empire.[77] Forged wooden tablets with a "contemporary" history of the Trojan War on them fooled Nero precisely because he (and others) had no trouble believing that tablets could have lasted for 1,300 years. Wooden tablets, with or without a variety of coatings, were thought to last a very long time, even if only bronze tablets were believed eternal.[78]

Texture and material contributed only the relative degrees of physical longevity – lasting or more lasting – while the tablet shape itself contributed the authority. Thus what clearly distinguished whitened *tabulae*, the *alba*, was their particular quality of being authoritative and final *at that moment*. They were used for the year's events on priests' *tabulae*, which were considered discrete and definitive for that year; for the praetor's edict,

---

(*nomen . . . eradendum* from public and private monuments). Flower (1998) 160–2 suggests that removal rather than erasure of an inscription may have been more common.

[76] Eck (1998) 205–6 (a building inscription, *RIB* 1.1935; an honorary inscription from Dura-Europos; a very late dedicatory inscription from Jerusalem); the difference is merely that these survive very poorly.

[77] Thus some incorrectly argue that whitened tablets are intentionally temporary, see (e.g.) Wenger (1953) 55–9, Mommsen (1969 [1887]) III.419, Bucher (1987 [1995]) 21–2. Wax busts: Sall. *Jug.* 4.6, Ov. *Am.* 1.8.65, Juv. *Sat.* 8.19–20. Emperors: Kruse (1934) 49–50 (wax on wood), cf. *P.Oxy.* 3792 (fourth century AD), wax εἰς ἰκόνια τῶν Σεβαστῶν. The arrival of these official images was treated like an official visit of the emperor, Herod. 8.6.2, *HA Max. Duo.* 24.2, and S. MacCormack (1981) 67–73 (late antiquity).

[78] Trojan War (Dictys): L. Septimius's prologue to Dictys (ed. Eisenhut) tells the story, with Peruzzi (1973) II.129–30. By Symmachus's day, information was to be transferred to tablets to avoid the decay to which papyrus was subject (*Ep.* 4.34.3).

36   *The world of belief*

which was the authoritative statement of law for that year; for lists, like those of senators, judges, decurions, and members of associations, which were considered fixed and final at the time they were made.[79] All could change the next year, and were expected to, but even that knowledge did not change the fact that they mapped out that body's complete composition at one specific time. Tablets were done anew, not revised, when the new year came or the need arose. They were authoritative and final statements of what was true, and new *tabulae* would not necessarily make the old ones any less true for the time at which they had been made, since for a later time, the reality being established would naturally be different. New tablets simply made old ones irrelevant. Thus *novae tabulae* ("new tablets") permitted debtors to start anew: once, these debtors had owed, but with new tablets they did not. This phrase is usually translated as the "cancellation of debt," but this implies striking out something that, with a close look, you could see had once been there; with a new tablet the previous debt, because not recorded, simply did not exist. To reinforce this, agitators for debt reform had an understandable penchant for burning old *tabulae*.[80] Only if entities or actualities themselves were carried over from year to year was a new tablet conceived as having an effect on a previous one: thus the new census, which had *auctoritas*, was thought to make the mistakes of the old "disappear."[81] The Roman proverb *"manum de tabula!"* ("hands off your tablet!"), which means "enough!," probably therefore means "enough!" not in the sense "enough, you've revised it to death" but "it's done, it's finished" – you lift your hand from the last word and it's perfect.[82]

LEGAL *TABULAE* OF INDIVIDUALS

Tabulae thus record, in distinctive form, information significant for the orderly existence of Republican Rome and its inhabitants; were used in ways

---

[79] See Corbier (1987) 50: "photographiant à un moment précis la composition d'un groupe déterminé."

[80] *Novae tabulae*: common phrasing starting with Caesar, see *OLD s.v. tabula* 7b, and including Quint. *Decl.* 336; cf. Piazza (1980) 75–91. Debts that were repaid rather than forgiven had lines or *SOL(utum)* drawn through them: Pompeii, *TPSulp.* 62 (AD 42), 60 and 61 (AD 43), 82 (AD 44/5), 54 (AD 45), 99 (AD 44; Camodeca [1995b] 695), 64 (AD 53), 58 and 65 (no date); at Vindonissa, Speidel (1996) 98–101 no. 3 (AD 77–101); Vindolanda, *RIB* 2.2443.24 (AD 120–30); Vitudurum, Fellmann (1991) 23 and 34 no. H16 (mid-first century AD); Aristoboulias, *DJD* 27.69 (AD 130), cf. also *DJD* 27.27 (post-Herodian); in Egyptian papyri, Taubenschlag (1955) 420 and Maresch and Packman (1990) 76–7. In classical Athens, by contrast, repaid debt was erased, Sickinger (1999) 68–9. For burning, see chapter five n.80.

[81] Census: *auctoritas*, *D.* 10.1.11 (Papinian); disappear, *D.* 50.15.2 (Ulpian). The *forma* of the *gromaticus* was authoritative also, Moatti (1993) 32.

[82] *Manum de tabula*: Cic. *Fam.* 7.25.1 and Petr. *Sat.* 76.9; its later metaphorical meaning discussed by Benediktson (1995).

Roman perceptions of Roman tablets

that acknowledged no appreciable difference between public and private; and were considered authoritative and final. These characteristics all seem to reflect an older world, an early Roman world that created and preserved order through scrupulous and methodical ceremonial and religiosity of the sort Polybius referred to when he singled out as most remarkable the Romans' *deisidaimonia*, fear of the gods, and its concomitant ceremonial "in both public and private life" so great that "nothing could exceed it."[83] Legal documents of individuals written on *tabulae* were viewed as having these same characteristics, and were themselves almost certainly of similar age. This set of general correspondences is the first to suggest that the significance of legal tablets as part of a legal act should be assessed according to the value that other tablets – their historical parallels in a wider Roman world – had as part of *their* acts. Similar features such as these suggest a family relation, and family relation in turn will suggest parallel functions.

Although no conclusion about the actual rather than perceived uses of writing in the early and middle Republic will ever be uncontroversial,[84] a case can nonetheless be made for the antiquity, and traditional importance, of writing on tablets in the legal affairs of individuals.[85] From the fifth century BC there is no evidence of it. Indeed, the phrase from the Twelve Tables, "*cum ?faciet nexum ?mancipiumque, uti lingua nuncupassit, ita ius esto*" ("when he ?shall perform *nexum* and *mancipium*, as his tongue has pronounced, so is there to be a source of rights") would seem to exclude documents from being considered a necessary part of a legal process, although the fragmentary state of these early laws should not be forgotten.[86]

---

[83] Polyb. 6.56.7–8; Poseidonius (in Ath. *Deipnos.* 274a) notes εὐσέβεια . . . θαυμαστή; cf. Dion. Hal. 2.63.2, Liebeschuetz (1979) 4 (relation to ritual), Feeney (1998) 81–2 (fear of divine anger).

[84] Roman historians saw a large role for writing in their past: Livy and the annalists relied on many acts of writing by their ancestors, like the *tabulae* of the pontifex maximus, the Twelve Tables, treaties, laws, cult inscriptions, *libri lintei*; commentaries on religious and governmental practices; the consular *fasti*; and even histories, cf. Crake (1939), Poucet (1988) 294–8, and Degni (1998) 33–4 for Romans' belief that their use of tablets was very old. It was because they saw written records as valuable and characteristic that these historians could be – and were – often taken in by forgeries and fabrications. Modern studies of Republican literacy and its uses agonize over what was actually written down and what was subsequently fabricated, yet diametrically opposed opinions can be formed on any of these issues precisely because so much of this "evidence" was reported by, or believed to exist by, later Republican and early imperial historians; see Harris (1989) 149–59 with (e.g.) Timpe (1988).

[85] Date of introduction of writing into legal business disputed: the older view is that of Kaser (1971) 230–1 (introduced with Hellenistic culture); *contra* Schulz (1946) 25 (long known, but purely evidential; citing Mitteis [1908] 294); Weiß (1953) 53 finds it worthy of note that writing was widespread so early but legal acts maintained their oral character for so long; Albrecht (1997) 631 emphasizes that the vocabulary of legal acts points to practice "dominated by oral tradition and symbolic action." Wieacker's argument of early introduction (1988) 558–9 with n.34 has been followed and developed here.

[86] Twelve Tables: Table VI.1, discussed by Steinacker (1927) 70, trans. Crawford (1996) II.581.

38   *The world of belief*

Yet writing in legal affairs, if not in existence then, was probably not far distant. For there are notable affinities of phrasing and use between religious and legal writing – to be discussed in detail in chapters three through five – and similarities such as these should date back to a time when the *pontifices* held in their hands most of Roman jurisprudence. This should be an early time, before the third century BC.[87] Moreover, recent studies have emphasized the vitality and flexibility of formalism, and the antiquity and prominence of writing, in Roman religion. Whatever the use and date of writing in religion, so too most likely the use of writing in law and legal transactions.[88]

By the second century BC written paradigms for both religious and legal practice existed. In addition to providing written examples of prayers, Cato the Elder laid out written examples of the form to be followed in contracts for the gathering and milling of olives; in sales of olives and grapes; in the lease of winter pasturage, and in the sale of the increase of the flock.[89] He was followed in this by Varro, who at the end of the first century BC provided the "ancient formulae" for the warrantied sale or purchase of sheep, goats, swine, cattle, horses, and dogs, formulae which must have derived from legal acts he could observe or from earlier writers like Cato. Formulae like these, which had to be followed yet varied slightly in every case, promoted rather than discouraged both paradigmatic formularies and the use of writing on a case-by-case basis.[90]

By the Late Republic, although not mentioned by contemporary historians at all (who were themselves not in the slightest interested in social or legal history), legal practice had embraced documents heartily. As Cicero

---

[87] Affinities, e.g., between wills and treaties, *G.* 2.104 and Liv. 1.24.7; similarities of language – *prima postremaque* – in prayer and the *solutio per aes et libram, G.* 3.173; Plin. *NH* 13.69 claims that personal documents (*privata*) were written on linen and wax, the same materials used by augurs and pontiffs (above nn.15–16). In hands of *pontifices*, Kaser (1971) 27–9, Wieacker (1988) 310–30, 558–9, and R. Mitchell (1990) 170–9.

[88] Close association: pontifical commentaries on religious ritual and "religious law" parallel or provide models for pontifical commentaries on civil law, from which grow "secular" commentaries on civil law (Watson [1992], especially 63–79); forms of legal acts probably shaped by priests, Wieacker (1988) 326–40; Humbert (1993) finds parallels between formalism in law and ritualism in religion. Civil law has been correctly characterized as "in its nucleus not sacral, but still noticeably pontifical" (Kaser [1971] 27). See also Scheid (1984), R. Gordon (1990) 188–9, and R. Mitchell (1990) 69 (on the lack of distinction sacred/secular in early Rome). Role of writing: a "distinguishing mark of archaic Roman and Italic culture," Harris (1989) 154. Newer studies of religion: see North (1976), (1986), and (1989); Liebeschuetz (1979); Beard (1985).

[89] Cato (all but one, in *Agr.* 144, called a *lex*): *Agr.* 144–7, 149, and 150.

[90] Varro: *R.* 2.2.5–6, 2.3.5, 2.4.5, 2.5.10–11, 2.7.6, 2.9.7, and 2.10.4 (he notes six ways of selling or purchasing slaves also, but does not give formulae). On the possible relationship between "formalism" (i.e. *certa* or *concepta verba*, see below, chapter three n.51) and writing, see the suggestions of G. MacCormack (1969a) 441–7.

Roman perceptions of Roman tablets

said, "these things are part of the written (part of) law – on the public side *lex, senatusconsultum*, treaty; on the private side accounts, pact, agreement, stipulation." In another discussion he declared that in settling disputes, "controversies can arise as much from wills, stipulations, and all other things which are done through writing as from laws." In a third, the *pro Caecina*, he asserted that the meaning of the legal act itself would be sacrificed to words if the intention of the writers were not taken into account "in *lex, senatusconsultum*, magistrate's edict, treaty, or *pactio*; or, to return to private things, wills, judgments (*iudicia*), stipulations, pacts, and agreements done by formula" – a clear acknowledgment of a connection of writing and legal act.[91] A previous act of *sponsio* could be checked *ex . . . tabulis*, a *restipulatio* could be recited in court, Mucius Scaevola was jokingly encouraged to write wills for all Romans: everywhere Cicero looked he saw documents, even though he may have had his gaze firmly fixed on persons of his own lofty position.[92]

This sense of the importance of writing in legal affairs continued through the Empire. By the early third century AD, the jurist Paulus could imagine a record-room (*tabularium*) on an estate (*fundus*) in which were "the sales (*emptiones*) of many slaves, documents (*instrumenta*) of farms and various contracts and, moreover, the account-entries (*nomina*) of debtors," over the ownership of which there could be dispute in a case of an advance legacy. The existence of such documents, and even of rooms to store them in, could be casually taken for granted.[93] Documents, *tabulae*, were regularly and extensively used – and this was generally known – in legal affairs in the late Republic and Empire. The absence of actual legal documents surviving from the Republican period is not, therefore, very significant. It is likely that they were in existence by the third century BC, certain that they were extensively used by the first despite the fact that jurists – at

---

[91] Historians' lack of interest: Ogilvie and Drummond (1989) 23. Cicero quotations from *Part.* 130 (he has already made a distinction between the written things, *ea quae scripta sunt*, pertaining [*propria*] to law, and the unwritten; the written is subdivided into public and private, and *scriptorum autem privatum aliud est, publicum aliud: publicum lex, senatusconsultum, foedus, privatum tabulae pactum conventum, stipulatio* [*pactum conventum* here could also be taken as a phrase, "agreement-pact"]). The second quotation is from *Top.* 96, *non magis in legibus quam in testamentis, in stipulationibus, in reliquis rebus quae ex scripto aguntur* (cf. *Rhet. Her.* 2.13, *scirentne . . . adversarii id scriptum fuisse in lege aut testamento aut stipulatione aut quolibet scripto*); it is unclear from the context whether *aguntur* simply means "are accomplished through" or "are argued from" the writing. The third is from *Caec.* 51, *quae lex, quod senatus consultum quod magistratus edictum, quod foedus aut pactio, quod, ut ad privatas res redeam, testamentum, quae iudicia aut stipulationes aut pacti et conventi formula . . .*

[92] *Sponsio*: Cic. *Att.* 12.17; stipulation, Cic. *Att.* 16.11.7 (he plans to read them); restipulation, Cic. *Q. Rosc.* 37; Mucius Scaevola, Cic. *de Orat.* 2.24.

[93] *D.* 32.92.*pr.*; cf. Tomlin (1996a) 215 on a judicial tablet from London, which "implies what does *not* survive: records of the ownership of land, farm by farm, throughout the Roman province."

40 *The world of belief*

least Gaius, and in the earlier extracts that survive in the *Digest* – did not bother to mention them as important or regularly in use even at a later time.[94]

Legal documents specifically on *tabulae* seem to have been used especially in acts of mancipation – an archaic way of transferring property (itself known as *res mancipi*, generally property of great value), and the procedural basis of other legal acts like the mancipatory will – and contractual obligation, especially the specifically Roman form of it known as stipulation.[95] Cicero had mentioned both acts when touching on writing in legal affairs,[96] and other writers show a breezy familiarity with the use of *tabulae* in them as well. Pliny the Elder was fascinated with Lollia Paulina's sparkling emeralds and pearls, worth forty million sesterces, but also mentioned that she possessed their *tabula* of mancipation, and would show it as a voucher of ownership.[97] Declaimers could play with the terms commonly used in the warrantied mancipation of a slave, and in doing so mention tablets. Thus in a practice declamation on the set theme of, "Should a man who married his daughter to his manumitted slave be convicted of insanity by his son?" rhetoricians, striving to display their talents, introduced a slave's tablets of sale (*tabellae emptionis*) and their familiar formulae. One says, "a father accepts a son-in-law in mancipation," while another notes that the son-in-law "is not a runaway or a wanderer." Yet another: "'He is free from thefts and guilt.' Such is the praise of our son-in-law!" Yet another: "'he is no vagrant'; I add that he is not a runaway, I add that he is free of guilt and thefts. Have I taken away from the nobility of your son-in-law?" If a man has once been a slave, tablets of his mancipatory sale are assumed to exist, and these tablets will use familiar, formulaic phrases that can be manipulated to what clever speakers hope will be devastating effect.[98] Mancipatory wills – called *testamenta per aes et libram* after the props, the bronze and the scale, used in the ceremony – survive in even greater profusion, the result of a Roman inclination to inscribe chapters of them on stone, and they are also frequently referred to (225 separate wills, by one count) in literary

[94] No Republican examples: Kroell (1906) 19–26 and Mitteis (1908) 290–1.

[95] For a general list of legal documents on tablets, Wieacker (1988) 78–81 nn.81–8; for lists of occurrences in literature, Lévy (1952). Great value: mancipation was used for *res mancipi*, that is, slaves, horses, donkeys, mules, oxen, Italic land, and rustic praedial servitudes, perhaps some of the more valuable items in an agricultural society such as early Rome's was.

[96] Cicero: above n.91.

[97] Lollia Paulina: Plin. *NH* 9.117 (which suggests that the definition of *res mancipi* had broadened by his time); cf. other mancipations of sale, Apul. *Apol.* 92 and 101; *D.* 13.7.43.*pr.* (Scaevola), 19.1.13.6 (Ulpian), 20.6.8.15 (Marcian), and 47.2.52.23 (Ulpian).

[98] Sen. Rhet. *Contr.* 7.6.22–3.

Roman perceptions of Roman tablets

sources.[99] *Tabulae* that show debt, *tabulae* of *cautiones* (written stipulations), *cautiones*,[100] and *tabulae* that promise marriage or dowry (*dotales, matrimoniae,* or *nuptiales*)[101] can also be glimpsed out of the corner of one's eye in both literary and juristic authors. Romans were obsessed with property and "final judgments" of social and familial relationships, and sources reflecting that obsession can also reflect the accurate detail – the fine print, the tablet – as well.

These numerous acts and their *tabulae* were never considered in any substantive or legal way private, even though their contents might not be known to a wide public. Lollia Paulina was, after all, ready to demonstrate her lawful ownership of her famous emeralds and pearls "by tablets, at a moment's notice":[102] except in the case of wills, there was little shyness about reading the document out loud at any time, and even wills could be read, before the death of the testator, to an admiring and appreciative audience. Julius Caesar, his biographer claimed, habitually wrote Pompey into his will as heir, then read the will to the approving soldiery, while the fictional freedman Trimalchio indulged in a similar manipulation of the sobbing members of his household.[103] Pompeius Reginus opened his will and read it aloud in the senate in order to demonstrate that he, unlike

---

[99] References to wills, Champlin (1991) 187–93 (counting people, not actual references – some are mentioned more than once; he also lists five possibles); for Roman obsessions, *ibid.* 5–28.

[100] *Tabulae* showing debt: Cic. *2 Verr.* 1.137; Hor. *Sat.* 2.3.70; Apul. *Apol.* 75; *D.* 30.104.1 (Julian), and *D.* 35.1.40.3 (Iavolenus). *Tabulae* (or *tabellae*) and *cautiones* showing debt: *D.* 39.6.28 (Marcellus), 45.2.11.1–2 (Papinian), and 47.2.83(82).3 (Paulus; = Paul. *Sent.* 2.31.32); waiving obligations of freedmen, Sen. Rhet. *Contr.* 4.8 (only excerpts). *Tabulae* (or *cautiones*) of obligation and stipulation: *D.* 45.2.11.2 (Papinian; *cautum*) and *CJ* 8.40(41).6 (AD 214); note that *vadimonia* (promises to appear in court) are strengthened by written stipulations on tablets, Ov. *Rem.* 665–8 (*duplices... tabellae*). Plin. *NH* 7.183 (*tabellae* written in forum) and Hor. *Sat.* 2.3.69–70 (*tabulas*) both refer to either legal or financial (stipulations/contracts or accounts) documents. *Tabulae* of *cautio*: *D.* 26.10.5 (Ulpian). *Tabulae* of chirograph: *D.* 30.1.84.7 (Julian), *D.* 30.44.5 (Ulpian). The word *cautio*, "protection against danger," may refer to the danger of misspeaking (as in prayers); creating a *cautio* through writing may, therefore, have originally been a way of ensuring both fixed terms and the correct utterance of formulae, see *OLD s.v. cautio.*

[101] Tablets of dowries: Cic. *Att.* 15.21.2; Tac. *Ann.* 11.30; Suet. *Claud.* 29.3; Juv. *Sat.* 2.119, 6.200 (*tabellis*), 9.75; Quint. *Inst.* 5.11.32 (referring to Cic. *Top.* 15), Apul. *Met.* 4.26 (*pacto iugali... tabulis... maritus nuncupatus*) and *Apol.* 67, 68, 88, 91, 92, 102; *tabulas... de nuptiis* glossed in Greek as δέλτους, *CGL* 3.35.14; Serv. *in Aen.* 10.79 (before there were *tabulae matrimonii*, parties exchanged *cautiones* in which they *spondebant*); *D.* 23.4.29.*pr.* (Scaevola), 24.1.66.*pr.* (Scaevola), 33.4.12 (Scaevola), 38.16.16 (Papinian; *instrumento*), and 39.5.31.*pr.* (Papinian); *T.Alb.* 1 (AD 493, North Africa) refers to itself as a *tab. dotis.* The presence of an *auspex* at dowry-tablets' making (Juv. *Sat.* 10.336) suggests that these too were of Republican origin.

[102] Plin. *NH* 9.117.

[103] Contents of wills probably not generally known, *G.* 2.181 ("since of course in the testator's lifetime the contents of his will are unknown"); Plin. *NH* 14.141; *D.* 22.3.3 (Papinian); and the concupiscent curiosity that surrounded will-openings, cf. Champlin (1991) 18, 87–102 (*captatio*). Caesar, Suet. *Jul.* 83.1; Trimalchio, Petr. *Sat.* 71–2.

42   *The world of belief*

the brother who had disinherited him, was acting properly.[104] Jurisconsults indeed considered testamentary *tabulae* as legally belonging to the public. "The instrument of the tablets of the will," said Ulpian, "does not belong to one man, that is, the heir, but to all those in whose favor anything has been written in it; indeed, it is rather a public instrument," although public access to it could be delayed until after the death of the testator. Indeed, by the late Republic testaments could be placed in temples, as many other types of *tabulae* were, or left with friends or at home, as was true also of magistrates' tablets.[105]

As with other tablets, so here too legal *tabulae* and the acts they accompanied were also seen as final and authoritative, as long as they had been completed correctly. The effectiveness of mancipation was immediate, that is, the transfer it effected could not be put off to some future time; it was not in any way compromised by questions of intention, trickery, or fraud; and it was irrevocable.[106] Furthermore, the one giving in mancipation was known as the *auctor*, and the act "contained an inherent warranty against eviction" (i.e. as buyer you were protected against claims that you were not legally the new owner, in which defense the seller was required to assist).[107] This legal defense to which you were entitled, known as the *actio auctoritatis*, could not be set aside by agreement between the two parties, a fact that makes clear the derivation of *auctoritas* from the very nature of mancipation itself. The earliest meaning of *auctoritas* was, in fact, "right of ownership" or "title," precisely what mancipation conveyed. For this reason a tablet of sale is also referred to, casually, as a *tabella auctoritatis*, for it literally conveyed this type of authoritative ownership. The primary concern of mancipation and its tablets was *auctoritas*.[108]

---

[104] Pompeius Reginus: Val. Max. 7.8.4. For other examples of reading, Champlin (1991) 24.

[105] Ulpian, *D.* 29.3.2.*pr.* (*tabularum testamenti instrumentum non est unius homini, hoc est heredis, sed universorum, quibus quid illic adscriptum est: quin potius publicum est instrumentum*); cf. *D.* 10.2.4.3 (Ulpian); *D.* 28.4.4 (Papinian). Papinian's judgment in *D.* 28.1.3 that *testamenti factio non privati sed publici iuris est* is discussed by Leuregans (1975). Tablets of will once (*olim*) deposited *in publico* or with friends etc., cf. Fro. *ad M. Caes* 1.6.5; Champlin (1991) 76–7; Vidal (1965); Williamson (1987a) 175 n.59, keeping "all tablets" (especially laws and plebiscites) in temples.

[106] Mancipation's characteristics, see *D.* 50.17.77 (Papinian), Paul. *Sent.* 1.7.6, 8; J. A. C. Thomas (1976) 153, Buckland and Stein (1963) 332. An entirely different formal act had to be taken to undo a mancipation, called the *solutio per aes et libram*, see *G.* 3.173–4; Liebs (1970) argues convincingly that these so-called *contrarii actus* were early but "created" acts that followed the form of the formal mancipatory acts which legally they served to undo; Knütel (1971) dates them very early.

[107] *Auctor*: Prichard (1974) 391; cf. *OLD s.v.* (for additional meanings, e.g., the proposer of a law) and Brophy (1974) 208–9; quotation, Watson (1968) 16.

[108] *Actio auctoritatis*, *D.* 21.2.76 (Venuleius). Meaning of *auctoritas*, *OLD s.v. Tabella*: Sen. Rhet. *Contr.* 7.6.23; cf. *D.* 13.7.43.*pr.* (Scaevola), *instrumentum . . . auctoritatis* of land.

Roman perceptions of Roman tablets

Similarly, a mancipatory will with its tablets also passed on this type of authoritative ownership, but – even more important – was believed to be a final, judicious, uncompromising summation of what you really thought about people. It radiated social as well as legal authority.[109] Erasures caused suspicion of forgery, and therefore it was customary (*ut solet*) to add, "I myself made the corrections, emendments, and erasures"; and like a mancipation, a mancipatory will could not, theoretically, be revoked.[110] But its authority was not therefore eternal, for the making of a new will "broke" or made irrelevant an older will, just as many other types of tablets had made their predecessors irrelevant. A will's finality was therefore both absolute and limited, as was true also of other writing – writing that was not on bronze and therefore claiming eternal validity – on *tabulae*.[111]

The fact, then, that legal documents of individuals were written on *tabulae* and shared tablets' general characteristics associates such documents with an older world that did not clearly distinguish between public and private, one whose facts were given final existence and whose order was authoritatively created or reaffirmed by the *tabulae* on which they were set down. Such associations between legal and other tablets are further reinforced by the common technical vocabulary with which all such *tabulae*, legal or otherwise, were handled (*conficere*, "to set down carefully";[112] *figere* and *defigere*, "to nail up"[113] – curse-tablets, which cannot physically be nailed up on a temple or the person at which they are aimed, are frequently wrapped *around* a nail instead).[114] But such linguistic associations are not limited merely to the vocabulary of tablets' treatment: strong similarities also exist in the style and phrasing shared by all the seemingly various things written on *tabulae*, the subject of chapter three.

---

[109] Wills' social authority: Champlin (1991) 5–28; his is the phrase "final judgments" (above p. 41).

[110] Erasure, *D.* 28.4.1.1 (Ulpian); irrevocable, *G.* 2.151 (even if testator desires that will not stand).

[111] "Breaking" the will: *G.* 2.144 and esp. 151, *D.* 28.3.3.4 (Ulpian), 29.1.36.4 (Papinian), Ulp. *Reg.* 23.2, Just. *Inst.* 2.17.2, Buckland and Stein (1963) 332–3. This is a Roman characteristic, for Greek law administered by the *idios logos* in Egypt different, Kreller (1919) 389–95, El-Mosallamy (1970).

[112] *Conficere*: Cic. *Q. Rosc.* 8 (and many others), Plin. *Ep.* 1.10.9; cf. *OLD s.v.* for ritual meaning.

[113] *Defigere*: *tabulae* are *figuntur*, Cic. *Phil.* 1.3 (*tabula... Caesaris beneficii*), 2.91, 2.92, 2.97, 5.12, 12.12 (*figentur* and cancelling, *refigere*); *Fam.* 12.1.1; Tac. *Hist.* 4.40.2 (*figerent*); Serv. *in Aen.* 6.622 (because laws engraved on bronze tablets are nailed to walls); punishments for taking down, *D.* 48.13.10.8 (Venuleius Saturninus); calendars, Petr. *Sat.* 30.3; *tabula* of *pontifex maximus* affixed to exterior of *Regia*, Poucet (1988) 303 and n.54; votives, e.g., *GL* 6.265.8–21. Even most (Greek) schoolboy tablets and late liturgical texts from Egypt had holes for hanging, Brashear and Hoogendijk (1990) 25; cf. Eck *et al.* (1996) 267–8 on the difference between *figere* and *ponere*.

[114] Wrapped around a nail, see Audollent (1904) LV–LVI, Preisendanz (1972) cols. 5 and 19 (the primary purpose of Attic curse-tablets seems to be binding, Roman nailing, cf. Faraone [1991a] 4–10), and Jordan (1988). Some imperial curse-tablets (in imitation of their wood counterparts?) were folded, see Tomlin (1988) 84. On nails as instruments by which circumstances are fixed, see Foresti (1979) 145, Piccaluga (1983).

CHAPTER 3

The Roman tablet: style and language

In their various aspects and associations, Roman tablets can be seen to share a number of characteristics. This perceived resemblance can be reinforced and extended by an examination of the Latin written on these tablets, for all writing on tablets shares three unusual traits that separate it off from everyday Latin. First, its style and syntax are not those of the everyday: they correspond much more closely to the style and syntax of what philosophers of language call "formalized" language. The definition of this "voice of traditional authority" arrived at by the anthropologist Maurice Bloch is most applicable here: such language is an "impoverished language" in which "choice of form, of style, of words and of syntax is less than in ordinary language" – by consciously following certain patterns, others are excluded.[1] Second, this formulaic language was recognized as archaic or archaizing, its set forms (and spellings) redolent of the past but modifiable through general agreement or for particular circumstances as long as that old-time flavor was retained. Finally, all writing on tablets shared components that went by the same names, *formula*, *ordo*, and *nomen*, and was characteristically subject to extensive abbreviation and parody. In sum, what was written on tablets – prayers (of augurs, priests, magistrates, and individuals), treaties, *leges*, edicts, accounts, vows, curse-tablets, and individual legal acts – all displays a rhythmic formulaic quality that helps to identify these entities as formally related, a fact of relation also demonstrated by the ways in which Romans grouped them all into one conceptual category, that of the *carmen*.

[1] Bloch (1989 [1974]) 22–9 at 25 (note also chart); cf. ix–xi, where he defends himself against his critics and explains the relationship of his speech-act terminology to Searle's (1969); Irvine (1979) summarizes the anthropological definitions of formality. English legal language is also recognized as belonging to this group, cf. Charrow *et al.* (1982) 179–82, Odum (1992), on limitations of, and the retention of mistakes in, this language, and Tiersma (1999) 100–4; Roman legal language is too ("allgemein zeigen . . . auch die profanrechtlichen Formeln in Rhythmus, Syntax und Vokabular oft die gleiche Handschrift"), Wieacker (1988) 326; and Wilkins (1994) 164, who prefers the concept of "linguistic engineering" to "impoverishment."

The Roman tablet: style and language

STYLE AND SYNTAX

(a) Tabulae *in general.* The style and syntax of these documents is variously identified by scholars as "the *carmen*-style" or "legal etiquette."[2] This style is characterized by repetition; accumulated pleonastic synonyms (either nouns or verbs), often in asyndeton; detailed and precise identification of what is wanted or required; and the use of assonance and alliteration to create something that would sound rhythmical and impressive. The syntax is usually either that of a substantive clause of purpose ("I beg you that . . ."), subjunctive following an indirect command ("it is decreed that . . . "), or a future condition marked by *si* and the imperative or the jussive subjunctive ("if you are called, go").

Prayers with this style and syntax survive in great number. Cato the Elder presents one of the earliest known, the prayer to be used for the purification of fields. While the *suovetaurilia* (pig, ram, and bull) is being led around, say:[3]

Mars pater, te precor quaesoque uti sies volens propitius mihi domo familiaeque nostrae, quoius rei ergo agrum terram fundumque meum suovitaurilia circumagi iussi, uti tu morbos visos invisosque viduertatem vastitudinemque calamitates intemperiasque prohibessis defendas averruncesque; utique tu fruges frumenta vineta virgultaque grandire beneque evenire siris pastores pecuaque salva servassis duisque bonam salutem valetudinemque mihi domo familiaeque nostrae; harumce rerum ergo fundi terrae agrique mei lustrandi lustrique faciendi ergo sicuti dixi macte hisce suovitaurilibus lactentibus inmolandis esto; Mars pater, eiusdem rei ergo macte hisce suovitaurilibus lactentibus esto.

Father Mars, I pray and beg you that you be willing and propitious to me my house and my household, for the sake of which thing I have ordered *suovetaurilia* to be led around my field my earth and my farm, so that you forbid keep off and ward off sicknesses seen and unseen, dearth and devastation, ruins and intemperances (i.e. bad weather), that you make to become large and permit to come to good issue fruits grains vineyards and undergrowth, protect shepherds and the flocks in safety and give good safety and health to me my house and my household; for the sake of which things, for the sake of purifying and making purification of my farm my land and my fields, as I have spoken, be honored with these suckling *suovetaurilia* to be offered up; Father Mars, for the sake of this same thing, be honored with these suckling *suovetaurilia*.

---

[2] Norden (1939) 91–106; Ogilvie (1969) 35; North (1976) 6 and 10; G. Williams (1982) 54–5; Williamson (1983) 104–14; Timpanaro (1988), and Courtney (1999) 8–9; also Jhering (1891 [1875]) 2.2.560–625 ("formalism" of this sort a cultural-historical rather than juristic phenomenon), Magdelain (1995) 67–111 (religious and legal language); and chapter four n.2. On language of prayers in general, see Appel (1909), Hickson (1993) 1–15.

[3] Cato the Elder: *Agr.* 141.2 (text in Courtney [1999] 46–7).

46   *The world of belief*

The structure (*peto quaesoque uti sies*), the repetition, the synonyms, the specificity of what is desired (and not desired), the sounds – *viduertatem vastitudinemque* and *fruges frumenta vineta virgultaque* roll impressively off the tongue – and the end-rhymes all combine to create a typical example of a prayer, and of this style and syntax.[4]

Numerous small variations in prayer language abound, but the basic format remained the same for centuries. Although distant from Cato's prayer by hundreds of miles and 300 years, this prayer for the dedication of an altar (inscribed in Salona, in Dalmatia, in AD 137) is structurally and stylistically similar:[5]

... C. Domitius Valens IIvir i.d. praeeunte C. Iulio Severo pontif. | legem dixit in ea verba quae infra scripta sunt:|

Iuppiter optime maxime, quandoque tibi hodie hanc aram dabo dedicaboque ollis legib. | ollis regionibus dabo dedicaboque quas hic hodie palam dixero, uti infimum solum huius arae est: | si quis hic hostia sacrum faxit quod magmentum nec protollat, it circo tamen probe factum esto; ceterae | leges huic arae ea[e]dem sunto, quae arae Dianae sunt in Aventino monte dictae. hisce legibus hisce regionib. | sic uti dixi hanc tibi aram, Iuppiter optime maxime, do dico dedicoque uti sis volens propitius mihi collegisque | meis, decurionibus, colonis, incolis coloniae Martia[e] Iuliae Salonae coniugibus liberisque nostris.

... C. Domitius Valens the duumvir *i(ure) d(icundo)*, with C. Julius Severus the pontifex dictating, spoke the *lex* in these words which are written below:

O Iuppiter best greatest, at whatever time I shall give and I shall dedicate this altar to you today, with those *leg(es)* those boundary-lines I shall give and I shall dedicate, which here today I shall speak openly, such is the lowest extent of this altar: if anyone should make here a sacred place with a victim, although he does not hold forth the sacrifice, for that reason nevertheless let it be correctly done; the other *leges* for this altar let them be the same, (as those) which are of the altar called of Diana on the Aventine Mount. With these *leges* these boundary-li(nes) thus, as I have said, I give I speak and I dedicate this altar to you, Iuppiter best greatest, so that you might be willing and propitious to me and my colleagues, the decurions the farmers the inhabitants of the colony of Martia Julia Salona, to our wives and children.

Alliterative stacking of verbs (*do dico dedicaboque*) and intentional repetition (*ollis . . . ollis*) creates both an impressive effect and a rhythm,[6] as does the

---

[4] Style: see further De Meo (1986) 133–69 and Courtney (1999) 62–7.

[5] *ILS* 4907 (= *CIL* 3.1933); cf. Beard *et al.* (1998) 330. Note the use of *ollis*, for *illis* (archaic); the precise meaning of *magmentum* (entrails?) is disputed, see Latte (1960) 389 n.2.

[6] Especially if Dessau, in his note to *ILS* 4907, is correct in construing the meaning of the first lines as "with those *leges*, which here today I shall speak openly . . . and with those boundary-lines (that mark

The Roman tablet: style and language

specific list of those to whom Iuppiter Optimus Maximus is requested to be "willing and propitious" (as Cato had asked of Mars). Both a purpose clause ("I give so that you might be willing") and a conditional clause are present, and the entire thing is called a *lex*.

The same characteristic, and complicated, grammatical structures appear in Roman treaties, laws, and edicts. The Romans believed that their treaty with the people of Alba Longa was the first that memory had preserved. It laid out that each would abide by the consequences of the three-on-three battle of the Horatii and the Curatii, and ended (so Livy reports) as follows:[7]

Legibus deinde recitatis "Audi" inquit "Iuppiter audi pater patrate populi Albani; audi tu populus Albanus. ut illa palam prima postrema ex illis tabulis cerave recitata sunt sine dolo malo utique ea hic hodie rectissime intellecta sunt illis legibus populus Romanus prior non deficiet. si prior defexit publico consilio dolo malo, tum tu illo die Iuppiter populum Romanum sic ferito ut ego hunc porcum hic hodie feriam; tantoque magis ferito quanto magis potes pollesque." id ubi dixit, porcum saxo silice percussit.

When the *leges* had been recited, he said: "Listen Iuppiter listen father *patratus* of the Alban people; listen you Alban people. As those [terms] have been openly recited from first to last from those tablets or wax without malicious fraud and as these things here today have been most perfectly understood, from these *leges* the Roman people shall not be the first to fall away. If first it shall have fallen away by public counsel by malicious fraud, then you on that day Iuppiter thus strike the Roman people as I shall strike this pig here today, and by that much more may you strike as by that much more you are able and you are potent." When he said this, he struck the pig with a stone with a rock.

Technically, this could be a prayer or the sanctioning oath of the treaty: the two are difficult to distinguish. It employs the *hic hodie* found in the Dalmatian inscription, and repeats it (as *dolo malo* and *ferito* – in various forms – are repeated); it amasses alliterative synonyms (*potes pollesque*) and uses parallel structures (*tanto . . . quanto*); summons the god, and the Albans, with an imperative; and makes an agreement with Iuppiter in the form of a condition. In short, it all sounds very much like the other three examples examined so far.

---

that) this is the lowest extent of the altar": the prayer therefore rearranges word order to get the effect identified here.

[7] First treaty, Liv. 1.24.7–9 (reading *tum illo die Iuppiter* in the *OCT* app. crit. for the ms. *tum tu ille Diespiter*); Ogilvie (1965) 111–12 identifies the language used here as "pseudo-archaic," particularly the use of the nominative for the vocative and *defexit*, "a putatively ancient form of the future perfect." For Livy's generally accurate rendering of Rome's "highly formulaic liturgy," see Hickson (1993) 144–8, Beard *et al.* (1998) 9.

48   *The world of belief*

That this language and syntax are not, however, just the fruit of Livy's archaizing but literary imagination is shown by a fragmentary inscription from the late second century or early first century BC of an actual treaty, found on the west coast of the Black Sea:[8]

[—dolo ma]lo quo po[plus Ro|manus—]t b[e]llum face[re– | —p]equ[n]ia adiovanto [– | —po]plo Callatino bell[um| —poplo Rom]ano quei[ve] sub inperio | [eius erunt—po]plo Romano utei et | [—]prio[.] faxit [p]oplo [– | —pop]lus Romanus popl[– | —]o. sei quid ad hance [– | —]t[. . .] ad<d>ere exim[erev]e | [—] voluntate licet[o | —i]xe[. . . .]nt id societat[e | —in tabulam ahe]nam utei scriberetur [at]q[ue] | figeretur altera Romae in Capitolio loc]o optumo in faano Concor[d(iae), | altera Callati — proponeretur].

[Let the Roman Pe]ople [not consider it right to allow foes and enemies of the Callatinian People to cross over their own fields and (the fields of those) whom they command] with malicious fraud in order that they might be able to wage war against the Callatinian People [or those who shall be under their command, nor (let the Roman People consider it right to help) the enemies with arms nor] assistance-money [by the public will with malicious fraud . . . If anyone] shall have made war with the Callatinian [People (through) the Roman People, or the Roman People] or with those who shall be under their command, (then) [the Callatinian People let (each) help what will be allowed from the treaties] to the Roman People as also to [the Callatinian People, if anyone] shall have made war first [with the Callatinian People or the Roman People,] then let the Roman People the Callatinian People [the one help the other.] If they should wish, both being willing, to this [*lex* of alliance or from this *lex*] to add to subtract, [. . . by common] wish let it be permitted, [and that which they shall have added let this be added and] that which they shall have removed let this be removed from the alliance [. . . that this treaty] shall have been written on a bronze [tablet and nailed up the one at Rome on the Capitol] in the best place in the temple of Concordia [the other at Callatis . . .].

This inscription's fragmentary state necessitates the reconstruction of some of its passages from other treaties. This is not difficult or controversial, however, because treaties (others not as long as this one) display the same patterns and formulae. There is parallelism here in the recurring alternation between the Roman People and the Callatinian People; repetition (*dolo malo*); precision (it is important to distinguish between "if anyone shall have made war" and "if anyone shall have made war first"); and the *si* and imperative construction.

---

[8] Callatis, *ILLRP* 516, different text in Marin (1948); restorations are made by analogy with treaty with Cibyra (*OGIS* 762), and can vary slightly from editor to editor.

The Roman tablet: style and language

Both the prayer by which the altar in Salona was dedicated and the two treaties, or oath and treaty, make internal reference to the *lex*, law, that is at least part of the larger whole being preserved. Cicero claimed that treaties were distinguished from laws by the latter's imperative constructions, but some *leges* clearly made use of subjunctives as well.[9] What exactly *lex* is to refer to, either in these (or in many other) examples, has never been entirely or satisfactorily pinned down.[10] But the formal statements that the Romans named *leges*, written on tablets, have many of the characteristics hitherto described, and *leges* in treaties obviously do use imperatives (and are not only *preces*, as Cicero implies). Examples of *leges* abound, and can be drawn from a very wide chronological and geographical range. In quotations from the earliest, the *leges* of the Twelve Tables (in Rome), can be read, "if he (i.e. anyone) summons to a pre-trial, he (i.e. the defendant) is to ?go" (*si in ius vocat, ?ito?*; Tab. I); "when ?he shall perform *nexum?* and *mancipium*, as his tongue has pronounced, so is there to be a source of rights" (*cum ?faciet nexum? mancipiumque, uti lingua nuncupassit, ita ius esto*, Tab. VI.I); "if a slave shall have committed theft or shall have harmed a harm, «<he is to be given for the damage>»" (*si servus furtum faxit noxiamve no<x>it*, «<*noxiae datus esto*»>)" (Tab. XII) – even in these miserable fragments the by-now familiar structure (*si* and imperative) can be seen, along with alliteration, end-rhyme (*faxit . . . noxit*), and even *figura etymologica* (*noxiam noxit*), all of which were also seen above in the prayer-*lex* by which the altar in Salona was dedicated.[11]

A much later *lex* on a bronze tablet, conventionally called "that on the *imperium* of Vespasian" and drawn up in response to far different

---

[9] Cicero: *Balb.* 36.1. Imperatives and subjunctives: Crawford (1996) 1.14 notes that the subjunctives dependent on the *veleatis iubeatis ut* construction of the *rogatio*-phase of a law were not always converted into future imperatives in the final version of the law.

[10] *Lex* is used to describe many of the things discussed in this section, especially their specific terms: *ILLRP* 132 (*leigibus | ara Salutis*), 270 (*leege Albana dicata*), 508 (*ollis legibus*); *CIL* 6.30837, 9.3513; *lex censoria* (Plin. *NH* 8.209 on foods; 8.223 and 36.4, no shrews or dormice at banquets); for additions to original formula, Liv. 43.14.5; Cic. *Rab. Perd.* 15, restrictions on slave-executioners); *leges* of treaties (Liv. 30.16.10, 30.38.7, 30.43.10, 38.11.9, 38.45.1, 38.59.1); *leges* of contracts preserved in Cato, *Agr.* 144–9; Cic. *2Verr.* 1.109, praetor's edict as *lex annua*; Brophy (1974) 250–7, *lex* used of clauses in a variety of contracts in Plautus. Magdelain (1978) summarizes previous attempts to explain what (it was thought) the Romans believed all these forms had in common (12–22); he himself (*passim*) emphasizes as common to *leges* the importance of the act of reading from a written text, the lack of distinction between public and private, and the imperative form.

[11] Text, translation, and attribution to tablets: Crawford (1996) 11.578–83; general discussion, 11.555–721. He points out (11.571) that the language of the Twelve Tables reflects a "multiplicity of layers of modernisation," and that tense and mood in subordinate clauses can be very diverse, although the future imperative is "standard in main clauses."

The world of belief

circumstances, reads in part as follows (the first section of the inscription, with the verb on which all the clauses depend, is missing):[12]

utique ei senatum habere relationem facere remittere senatus consulta per relationem discessionemque facere liceat, ita uti licuit divo Aug(usto) Ti. Iulio Caesari Aug(usto) Ti. Claudio Caesari Germanico; utique cum ex voluntate auctoritateve iussu mandatuve eius praesenteve eo senatus habebitur omnium rerum ius perinde habeatur servetur, ac si e lege senatus edictus esset habereturque ... sanctio. si quis huiusce legis ergo adversus leges rogationes plebisve scita senatusve consulta fecit fecerit sive quod eum ex lege rogatione plebisve scito s(enatus)ve c(onsulto) facere oportebit non fecerit huius legis ergo id ei ne fraudi esto neve quit ob eam rem populo dare debeto neve cui de ea re actio neve iudicatio esto neve quis de ea re apud [s]e agi sinito.

[It is decreed] ... that it be lawful for him to hold a meeting of the senate to present a motion to refer to make a decree of the Senate through a motion and through a division thus, as it was lawful for the divine Aug(ustus) Tiberius Julius Caesar Aug(ustus) Tiberius Claudius Caesar Augustus Germanicus; that when by his wish or authority his order or mandate or him being present a meeting of the senate shall be convened, the *ius* in all matters should be maintained should be observed, as if the senate had been summoned and was being convened in accordance with *lex* ... Sanction. If anyone in implementation of this *lex* has acted or shall have acted contrary to *leges* rogations or plebiscites or decrees of the senate, or if he shall not have done in implementation of this law that which it shall be fitting for him to do according to law rogation or plebiscite or d(ecree) of the s(enate), that is not to be a matter of fraud to him, nor is he to owe as payment anything to the people on account of this matter, nor is there to be to anyone from this matter an action or judgment, nor is anyone to permit an action to be entered in his court concerning that matter.

Here the syntax is that of *uti*-clauses, but this time of an indirect command following a verb of decreeing, and that of conditions, the latter under the heading of "sanction." There is also the usual multiplication of related if not perfectly synonymous words, like "laws rogations or plebiscites or decrees of the senate" and "his will or authority his order or mandate." Rhythm is created here, as elsewhere, by the repetition of *uti* and end-rhyme (*habere ... facere remittere, habeatur servetur*) and by alliteration (*dare debeto*).

Although this document calls itself (in the sanction) a *lex*, in its body it actually follows the more polite formulations of a decree of the senate.

---

[12] *lex de imperio* 3–9, 34–9: see Crawford (1996) 1.549–53 (my trans. is based on his); except for the sanction it does not use the imperative (Tac. *Hist.* 4.3.3 reports that the senate decreed, or *censebant* at 4.6.3, "all the usual powers" to Vespasian), and Crawford notes (1.550) that its form is that of the *rogatio* of a law.

The Roman tablet: style and language

What this contrast in, and scholarly dispute over, form chiefly indicates is that, again, rhythm, internal structure, and style of *lex* and decree are in general similar, as they are also in plebiscites and edicts.[13] A plebiscite on weights and measures ran as follows:[14]

Ex ponderibus publicis, quibus hac tempestate populus oetier solet, uti +coaequetur+ se dolo malo: uti quadrantal vini octaginta pondo siet; congius vini decem pondo siet; sex sextari congius siet vini; duodequinquaginta sextari quadrantal siet vini; sextarius aequus +aequo cum librario siet; sex de quinque librae+ in modio sient. si quis magistratus adversus hac dolo malo pondera modiosque vasaque publica [modica] minora maiorave faxit iusseritve fieri, dolumve adduit qui ea fiant, eum quis volet magistratus multare, dum minoris partis familias taxat, liceto <?eiusque pecuniae petitio esto;> sive quis in sacrum iudicare voluerit, liceto.

That in conformity with the public weights, which at this time the people are accustomed to use [it is decreed]: that there +should be equality+ unto itself without malicious fraud, that a quadrantal of wine should be eighty in weight, that a congius of wine should be ten by weight; that a congius of wine should be six sextarii; that a quadrantal of wine should be forty-eight sextarii; that an exact sextarius +should be (equal) with an exact librarius; that sixteen librarii+ should be in a modius. If any magistrate in contravention of this shall with malicious fraud have made these weights and measures and public measuring vessels lesser or greater or shall have ordered (this) to be done or shall have employed fraud by which these things happen, whatever magistrate should wish to fine him, let it be allowed, as long as he assesses it at the lesser part of the *familia* (estate?), or if anyone shall have wished to adjudge (the money) to a sacred purpose, let it be allowed.

This is clearly repetitive, clearly attempting to be precise and exhaustive, and combines again indirect commands with *uti*-clauses and conditions.

A plebiscite on weights and measures is not, perhaps, the most important official act that can be studied. Far more famous and important was, for example, the praetor's edict, posted on tablets. This, like so much else, survives only in fragmentary quotations, of which many must be reconstructed, but even this much is enough to display the characteristic features. "If anyone shall not have obeyed the one speaking the law, for as much as the matter will be, I will give an action" (1); "let them not plead for another, except for parent patron patroness children and parents of patron patroness or their own children, for brother sister wife father-in-law mother-in-law

---

[13] Debate, A. Gordon (1983) 121.
[14] Plebiscite: Fest. 246M, under *publica pondera*; I have used the text of Cloud (1985) 414 and adapted his translation (414–15). He also notes (416) that "the spelling has been extensively updated," and that, although the text is "appallingly corrupt," genuine archaisms have survived: "*oetier* for *utier*, *adversus hac . . . quis* for *si quis* and the tmesis of '*dum. . .taxat*'."

52   *The world of belief*

son-in-law daughter-in-law stepfather stepmother stepson stepdaughter ward (male) ward (female) madman madwoman, to whom guardianship or curatorship of these people will have been given by the parent . . ." (16); "against him who from fire collapse shipwreck a boat a ship having been destroyed is said to have taken to have received anything with malicious fraud (*dolo malo*) or to have inflicted any damage in these matters I will give action . . ." (189).[15] Alliteration, asyndeton, precision, exhaustion, repeated sounds, a familiar structure – all are here. Elsewhere, phrases already familiar, like *dolo malo* (187, 188, 227) or "by laws plebiscites decrees of the senate edicts decrees of the emperors" (*per leges plebis scita senatus consulta edicta decreta principium*, 44) recur.[16]

Evidence of the style and syntax of Roman financial accounts is more exiguous, but what little survives seems to conform to the other examples. The only quoted example of them to survive – from Cicero's favorite criminal, Verres – has a discernible rhythm (*accepi . . . dedi . . . reliqui*), but this may be happenstance.[17] Vows are better preserved. Some of the most famous are of a specialized type, vows or *devotiones* of consuls to sacrifice themselves, along with the enemy; because they were famous, their language was either known or seen as archetypal, and displays the elements of the style delineated: "I pray and worship you I beg your favor and I perform (a sacrifice) that you make to prosper violence victory for the Roman people of the Quirites . . . Thus I have spoken aloud with words . . . thus do I devote the legions and auxiliaries of the enemy with myself to the infernal shades and to earth."[18] On other, more mundane occasions, after vows had

---

[15] Praetor's edict (Lenel [1956] = *FIRA*² 1.335–89 no. 65): *si quis ius dicenti non obtemperaverit, quanti ea res erit, iudicium dabo* (1); *pro alio ne postulent, praeterquam pro parente, patrono patrona liberis parentibusque patroni patronae, liberisve suis, fratre sorore, uxore, socero socru, genero nuru, vitrico noverca, privigno privigna, pupillo pupilla, furioso furiosa, cui eorum a parente . . . ea tutela curative data erit* (16); *in eum, qui ex incendio ruina naufragio rate nave expugnata quid rapuisse recepisse dolo malo damnive quid in his rebus dedisse dicetur . . . iudicium dabo* (189). Cf. Katzoff (1980) 820 on the similar style of the Egyptian prefect's edict; the aedilician edict uses the (older) future imperative rather than *ut* or *ne* + subjunctive, Jakab (1997) 144.

[16] I emphasize what *leges*, plebiscites, *senatusconsulta*, and edicts have in common; scholarship has mostly concentrated on understanding their differences, see Jhering (1891 [1875]) 2.2.603–31, Schulz (1946) 96–8, Kaser (1951), Daube (1956), Marouzeau (1959), and De Meo (1986) 67–131; summarized by Crawford (1988) 129–32, who also distinguishes two styles (the second characterized by doublets, repetition, and cumulation of tenses), and (135 n.12) expresses doubt whether the "cumulation of near synonyms or recurrence of the same word in successive phrases" is characteristic of either. The overall legalistic style is, however, Roman, cf. Lintott (1992) 59–65.

[17] Cic. *2Verr.* 1.36; it was common also that accounts have the date at their beginning: *D.* 2.13.6.6 (Ulpian). Thilo (1980) 53–70 notes that narrative accounts such as these become briefer over time.

[18] *Devotio*: Liv. 8.9.7–8 (*vos precor veneror veniam peto feroque uti populo Romano Quiritium vim victoriam prosperetis . . . sicut verbis nuncupavi, ita . . . legiones auxiliaque hostium mecum Deis Manibus Tellurique devoveo*); Livy emphasizes at 8.11.1 that he is repeating "the very words" of this *devotio*

The Roman tablet: style and language

been made and success has been granted, the vow was fulfilled through the offering of a temple or a statue or whatever else was promised, and the fact of fulfillment signalled through a posted tablet or an inscribed gift. The writing itself is the final step in the discharge of the obligation, linking agent, vow, and repayment, and can be attached to the vowed item. The earliest language used is very simple and, by its nature, indicative in mood rather than conditional, unlike the other examples so far. "L. Gemenio(s), son of Lucius, of Peltuinum, on behalf of himself and his own happily and in return for benefits received, gives as a gift to Hercules; by the same *leges* an altar of Safety." But even at this level of simplicity, the usual alliterations are present, as well as *figura etymologica* in *donum dedit*; *lubens merito* and *donum dedit* will appear regularly in dedications, i.e. vows fulfilled, for centuries, often abbreviated as *l.m.* and *d.d.*, as will *v.s.*, *votum solvit*.[19]

Such rhythmic regularity combined with simple syntax is presented in rather more extended form by the dedications couched in Saturnians. An example from around the middle of the second century BC:[20]

> M. P. Vertuleieis | C.f.
> quod re sua d[if]eidens asper | afleicta
> parens timens | heic vovit voto hoc | solut[o]
> [de]cuma facta | poloucta leibereis lube\<n\>|tes
> donu(m) danunt | Hercolei maxsume | mereto.
> semol te | orant se voti crebro | condemnes.

Marcus and Publius Vertuleius, sons of Gaius. That which, despairing for his shattered affairs, squalid, fearful, the father vowed here, the sons – when this vow was fulfilled by means of the tenth set aside and offered as a sacrifice – happily give as a gift to Hercules especially meritorious. Together they pray that you frequently condemn them (to the fulfillment) of a vow.

Brief quotations from the dedicatory *tabulae triumphatores*, boasting of achievement in war, show the same qualities. The *tabula* of Regillus read, "for finishing a great war, for subjugating kings"; Acilius's, "he routed, he set to flight, he overthrew the greatest legions."[21] What is particularly

---

(*verbis... ipsis, ut tradita nuncupataque sunt, referre*). This consul's son is depicted as making a similar (and now formulaic) *devotio, conceptis sollemnibus ac iam familiaribus verbis*, Sen. *Ep*. 67.9; cf. Macrob. *Sat*. 3.9.10–11 for another recorded *devotio* with *do devoveo*.

[19] Early metrical vow: *ILLRP* 132 (*L. Gemenio(s) L.f. Pelt*[—]. | *Hercole dono* | *dat lubs merto* | *pro sed sueq(ue)*. | *Edem* [= *isdem*] *leigibus ara Salutus*).

[20] Vow in Saturnians: *ILLRP* 136 (= *CLE* 4).

[21] *Triumphatores*: see Liv. 6.29.9, 40.52.5–7, 41.28.8–10; quotations in treatise on meter attributed to Caesius Bassus (*duello magno dirimendo regibus subigendis... fundit fugat prosternit maximas legiones*, *GL* 6.265.25 and 29).

54   *The world of belief*

interesting about these inscriptions is not just that they are clearly in the style, if not precisely the syntax, of all these other early documents, but that Saturnians are so congruent with this style and its contexts. Saturnians are not a quantitative meter *per se*. Rather, their bipartite structure is "often underlined by alliteration, assonance, and syntactic parallelism," and Saturnians were more clearly syllabic in character before they started to be modified according to Greek metrical principles in the second century BC. Servius in fact referred to Saturnians themselves as rhythmic, although by this he probably did not mean a non-quantitative meter.[22] Therefore in their form, as far as it can be recovered, Saturnians have a generic and recognized similarity to the structured and rhythmic prose of the many other texts preserved on tablets. Moreover, what the Romans most clearly understood about Saturnians was that they were very ancient – sung by fauns and seers (*vates*), said Varro, quoting Ennius – and that they had their origins in a religious context, in the archaic worship of Mars and the still obscure god Saturnus. One late source, Charisius, even claimed that examples of verses and hymns in Saturnians could be found on *libri lintei*. A classic study of Saturnians has concluded that Saturnus and Mars, when properly worshipped, marched into battle with the Romans and gave victory to them, and that from this came songs of military destruction and victory such as were inscribed as fulfilled vows on tablets and posted on the Capitolium. In other words, Saturnians are an integral part of this older public and private, religious and secular world of Rome under the Republic, their special qualities congruent with the language of significant acts in this world so often on tablets, and preserved and perpetuated in the language of fulfilled vows.[23]

Curse-tablets provide the penultimate example of this *carmen*-style, and utilize all the various forms of syntax seen so far. For they pray, they offer various inducements, they state facts, they lay out conditions, and they occasionally attempt, in a polite way, to compel. Two examples:[24]

Dea Ataecina Turibrig Proserpina per tuam maiestatem te rogo oro obsecro uti vindices quot mihi furti factum est quisquis mihi imudavit involavit minusve fecit eas [res] qiss tunicas VI[. . . pa]enula lintea II in[dus]ium cuius i c u . . . m ignoro ia [. . . . .]ius ui.

---

[22] Saturnians not quantitative: Cole (1969), quoted 20; 66, 72–3 (second-century modifications).

[23] Varro: *L.* 7.36 (*versibus quo<s> olim Fauni vatesque canebant*), quoting Ennius *Ann.* 207 (Skutsch; 214 Vahlen); cf. Fest. 325M on Saturnians. Charisius: *GL* 1.288–9; study: Palmer (1974) 184–5.

[24] Audollent (1904) 177 no. 122 (Emerita, no date); 248–51 no. 190 (Minturnae, no date; reading *femora* for *femena* in line 11 [the suggestion is M. Powers's]; I use here the marginally better text of *CIL* 10.8249, and the very end might have been rewritten by someone else).

The Roman tablet: style and language

O goddess Ataecina Proserpina of Turibriga by your *maiestas* I ask I beg I implore you that you take revenge because I have been victim of an act of thievery: whoever changed seized on or made less those things, w(hich) a(re) w(ritten) b(elow): six tunics, . . . two linen cloaks, an outer tunic of which . . . [paralyze him painfully, or something similar].

Dii i(n)feri vobis com(m)e(n)do si quic[q]ua(m) sa(n)citat[i]s h(a)bet[i]s, ac t(r)ad<r>o T[y]c(h)ene(m) Carisi quodqu[o]d a[g]at, quod i(n)cida(n)t omnia in adversa. Dii i(n)feri vobis com(m)e(n)do il(l)ius mem(b)ra colore(m) fi[g]ura(m) caput capill[os] umbra(m) cerebru(m) fru(n)te(m) supe[rcil]ia os nasu(m) me(n)tu(m) buc(c)as la[bra ve]rba (h)alitu(m) col(l)u(m) i[e]cur (h)umeros cor [p]ulmones i(n)testina<s> ve(n)tre(m) bra(ch)ia di[g]itos manus u(m)b(i)licu(m) v[e]sica(m) fem[or]<en>a [g]enua crura talos planta(s) [d]i[g]i[t]os. Dii i(n)feri si illa[m] videro tabesce(n)te(m) vobis sacrificiu(m) lub(e)ns ob an(n)uversariu(m) facere dibus parentibus il(l)iu[s] voveo peculiu(m) tabescas.

O gods of the underworld, I entrust to you, if you have any religious force, and I hand over to you Ticene (daughter of) Carisius, that whatever happens all of it turn out contrary to her wishes. O gods of the underworld, I entrust to you her limbs complexion appearance head hair shadow skull forehead eyebrows mouth nose chin cheeks lips speech breath neck liver shoulders heart lungs intestines stomach arms fingers hands navel bladder thighs knees shanks ankles soles toes. O gods of the underworld, if I might see (her) shrivelling away, to you I vow that I shall willingly perform a sacrifice on the anniversary of her parental gods. May you make her *peculium* shrivel.

The first prays and implores, while the second consigns and wishes. Curse-tablets can follow varied forms of syntax while using the same style; at times, when cursing and beseeching become desperate, they even become peremptory. As a fragmentary curse from Hadrumetum insists, "Don't ignore my utterances!"[25] In both, the alliterations and impressive sounds are present in full force, along with the exhaustive lists in asyndeton, and even language like *libens* more regularly seen in vows. The style and purpose of both are clearly the same – repetitive and precise impressiveness to curse the enemy in properly effective language.[26] This purpose is reinforced by these tablets' physical contexts. The second of the quoted curses is on a lead tablet, transfixed with a nail and found in a grave. The first, however, is a marble tablet found affixed to the retaining wall of an artificial lake.

---

[25] Hadrumetum: Audollent (1904) 402–3 no. 289, *noli meas [spern]ere v[oc]es*, in a curse upon four horses found in a Roman cemetery (second-to-third century AD).

[26] Style: cf. Tomlin (1988) 70–1, who describes the language of the curse-tablets from Bath as very much like "petitions in an under-policed world," displaying a "popular legalism"; see also 72–3 for redundancy, repetition, and synonyms. Elements of vow language exist but are rare in curse-tablets, Versnel (1991a) 95 n.19; note that (92) he identifies prayer and *defixio* as being on extreme ends of "spectrum of more or less hybrid forms."

56 *The world of belief*

This physical placement shows that cursing could have a public face, that a curse was not necessarily hidden in earth or water, although such privacy in general protected the curser and made success much more likely.[27]

In sum, these texts all have in common a desire to bring shape and consequence to this interrelated world of public and private, to a possibly disordered or obscure universe – obscure in the sense that human effort and actual result did not always exist in an immediately understandable relationship. The degree to which uncertainty was felt to play a role helps to explain the use of varying syntactic structures for expressing the same thought. The two major constructions, the *si*. . . imperative or jussive subjunctive form and the *precor*. . . *ut* form, exist along a continuum of thought: "I pray that you be. . . for the sake of which I have done," "I do this so that you will be. . . ," "if they do this, you be. . . ," "if he does this, let it be" or "let this happen," "they decree that it should be." Each does not mean exactly the same thing, but the same thought can be effectively expressed in any of these ways. The more the act was complete, the more indicative the tone ("he dedicates. . ."); the more the future relationship being shaped was one between humans, the more circumscribed the element of uncertainty ("if he. . . let him go"); the more the relationship between humans and gods, the more the active power of uncertainty can be sensed ("please. . .").[28]

(b) *Legal* tabulae *of individuals.* Legal documents on tablets involving individuals are all also characteristically phrased in this *carmen*-style, and can move along this same continuum of certainty and uncertainty. Take a second-century AD mancipation (which includes its customary stipulatory warranty-clause), from Dacia:[29]

Maximus Batonis puellam nomine | Passiam, sive ea quo alio nomine est an|norum sex [written above the line: circiter p(lus) m(inus) empta sportellaria] emit

---

[27] Some forms of cursing a legitimate form of prayer and not necessarily private, Faraone (1991a) 17–20, Versnel (1991a) 61–3; perhaps in the middle of this spectrum is Varro's spell against gout, *R.* 1.2.27 (*ego tui memini, medere meis pedibus, terra pestem teneto, salus his maneto in meis pedibus*).

[28] Cf. Momigliano (1989) 108: "[o]ne of the characteristics of Roman piety was to keep separate the spheres of gods and men, but to take *equal* precautions in both. This resulted in the use of very precise formal language for anything which affected either divine law (*fas*) or human law (*ius*)" (emphasis mine) – which I adjust because, with Beard (1992) 750, I see a "continuous spectrum" rather than a polarity "between the human and the divine," and therefore also a spectrum of appropriate syntax. The whole range of this syntax (as seen above) also in magical acts, Cagnat (1903–4) 152.

[29] Mancipation, *IDR/Tab.Cer.D.* no. 6 (= *CIL* 3 p. 937 no. VI, *FIRA*² 3.283–5 no. 87; AD 139); the meaning of *sportellaria* is disputed, cf. Macqueron (1982) 49 ("an extra?"), and *idem* 49 n.1 for the emendation of *eo* to *ea* in line 7; I have also restored the [o]-ending to *Kaviereti* in line 16, which *IDR* left off. See also *CIL* 4.3340.155 (= *FIRA*² 3.291–4 no. 91; Pompeii, AD 61): *sive ea mancipia alis nominib(us) sunt, sua esse seque possidere neque ea mancipia. . . ali ulli obligata esse neque sibi cum ul(l)o com[munia] esse eaque mancipia singula sestertis num[mis sin]gulis Dicidia Magaris emit ob seste[rtios n. . . . et] mancipio accepit de Popp<a>ea Prisc[i liberta Note] tutore auctore D. Caprasio A[mpliato].*

The Roman tablet: style and language 57

mancipioque accepit | de Dasio Verzonis Pirusta ex Kaviereti[o] | ✳ ducentis quinque. || iam puellam sanam esse a furtis noxisque | solutam, fugitivam erronem non esse | praestari. quot si quis eam puellaam | partemve quam ex e{a} quis evicerit, | quominus Maximum Batonis quo||ve ea res pertinebit habere possi|dereque recte liceat, tum quanti | ea puella empta est, tam pecuniam | et alterum tantum dari fide rogavit | Maximus Batonis, fide promisit Dasius || Verzonis Pirusta ex Kaviereti[o]. Proque ea puella, quae s(upra) s(cripta) est, ✳ ducen|tos quinque accepisse et habere | se dixit Dasius Verzonis a Maximo Batonis. (*Actum*-clause and subscriptions omitted.)

Maximus son of Bato has bought and accepted as a *mancipium* a girl by name Passia, or if she is (known) by any other name, m(ore or) l(ess) around six years old, having been bought as a foundling, for 205 (denarii), from Dasius son of Verzo, a Pirustian from Kavieretium. It is vouched for that she is a physically sound girl, not charged with theft and damage, is not a fugitive truant; but if anyone shall have claimed back this girl or any portion of her, as a result of which it is not legal for Maximus son of Bato or him to whom the affair will be relevant to hold and possess her rightfully, in that case Maximus son of Bato demanded that the exact sum and an equivalent amount be paid in good faith. Maximus the son of Bato asked to be given in faith, Dasius son of Verzo a Pirustian from Kavieretium promised in faith. Dasius son of Verzo said that he received and has for this girl, w(ho) i(s) w(ritten) a(bove), 250 denarii from Maximus son of Bato.

Here there is parallelism, in the required balancing of stipulatory clauses (*fide rogavit . . . fide promisit*), end-rhyme (puell*am* san*am* fort*is* nox*is*que solut*am* fugitiv*am* erron*em*) – striking even in a language given to end-rhyme; there is also the piling-up of verbs to express, precisely and exhaustively, what legal acts have taken place (*emit mancipioque accepit, habere possidereque*), and a careful conditional.

The same features appear in one of the best-known Roman mancipatory wills, from Egypt:[30]

Antonius Silvanus eq(ues) alae Ī Thracum Mauretanae stator praef(ecti), turma Valeri, testamentum fecit. omnium bonor[um meo]rum castrens[ium et d]omesticum M. Antonius Sat[ri]anus filius meus ex asse mihi heres esto: ceteri ali omnes exheredes sunto: cernitoque hereditatem meam in diebus C̄ proximis: ni ita creverit exheres esto. tunc secundo gradu [. .] Antonius R. .[. . . . .].[.].[.].lis frater meus mihi heres esto, cernitoque hereditatem meam in diebus L̄X̄ proximis: cui do lego, si mihi heres non erit, (denarios) argenteos septingentos quinquaginta. procuratorem bonorum meorum castrensium ad bona mea colligenda et

---

[30] This will (excerpted here) is sometimes known as the "tablettes Keimer;" text in *CPL* 221 (= *FIRA*² 3.129–32 no. 47; AD 142). Others, e.g., *CIL* 10.114 (= *ILS* 6468–9), can reflect even more complicated uncertainties, and therefore record even more repetitively precise arrangements to overcome them.

restituenda Antonia<e> Thermutha<e> matri heredi<s> mei s(upra) s(cripti) facio Hieracem Behecis dupl(icarium) alae eiusdem, turma Aebuti, ut et ipsa servet donec filius meus et heres suae tutelae fuerit et tunc ab ea recipiat: cui do lego (denarios) argenteos quinquaginta. do lego Antonia<e> Thermutha<e> matri heredi<s> mei s(upra) s(cripti) (denarios) argenteos quingentos. do lego praef(ecto) meo (denarios) arg(enteos) quinquaginta. Cronionem servom meum pos<t> mortem meam, si omnia recte tractaverit et trad<id>erit heredi meo s(upra) s(cripto) vel procuratori, tunc liberum volo esse vicesimamque pro eo ex bonis meis dari volo. h(oc) t(estamento) d(olus) m(alus) <<h>> <a>(besto). familiam pecuniamque t(estamenti) f(aciendi) c(ausa) e(mit) Nemonius dupl(icarius) tur(mae) Mari, libripende M. Iulio Tiberino sesq(uiplicario) tur(mae) Valeri, antetestatus est Turbinium sig(niferum) tur(mae) Proculi.

Antonius Silvanus horseman of the First Mauretanian squadron of Thracians, attendant to the prefect, in the unit of Valerius made the will. Of all my goods military and domestic let M. Antonius Sat[ri]anus my son be my heir by the *as*: let all others be disinherited: and let him accept my inheritance within the next 100 days: if he shall not thus have accepted (it) let him be disinherited. Then in the second grade let [. .] Antonius R. .[. . . . .].[.].[.].lis my brother be my heir, and let him accept my inheritance within the next 60 days: to him I give I give as a legacy if he will not be my heir 750 silver *denarii*. Agent of my military property, for collecting my goods and handing them over to Antonia Thermutha mother of my heir written above I make Hierax the son of Behex, *duplicarius* of the same squadron in the unit of Aebutius, so that she might preserve (it) until my son and heir shall be in his own tutelage and then might receive (it) from her: to him I give I give as a legacy 50 silver *denarii*. I give I give as a legacy to Antonia Thermutha mother of my heir written above 500 silver *denarii*. I give I give as a legacy to my prefect 50 silver *denarii*. If my slave Cronio shall have dealt with everything correctly and shall have handed over (all) to my heir written above or to the agent, then I wish him to be free and I wish the *vicesima* (twentieth-tax) for him to be given from my property. F(rom) this w(ill) let m(alicious) f(raud) be absent. Nemonius, *duplicarius* of the un(it) of Marius b(ought) the *familia* and the *pecunia* for the m(aking) of the w(ill), M. Julius Tiberinus *sesq(uiplicarius)* of the un(it) of Valerius was the *libripens*, Turbinius the *sig(nifer)* of the un(it) of Proculus was chief witness.

The repetition of imperatives (*heres esto . . . exheredes sunto . . . exheres esto . . . heres esto . . . heres esto*) creates rhythm, as does the repetition of *do lego*. At the same time this is a precise document: property is carefully disposed of, contingencies ("if he will not be my heir," "if he – slave – does right") carefully accounted for.

Surviving examples of stipulations also reveal the same characteristics. Some of the oldest and most formulaic derive from Varro:[31]

---

[31] Var. *R.* 2.2.6, bracketing *id est ventre glabro* as a later gloss.

The Roman tablet: style and language

illasce oves qua de re agitur sanas recte esse uti pecus ovillum quod recte sanum est extra luscam surdam minam [id est ventre glabro] neque de pecore morboso esse habereque recte licere haec sic recte fieri spondesne?

Do you promise that these sheep, about whom business is being transacted, are rightly sound, as (is) the flock of sheep which is rightly sound, excepting the blind in one eye the deaf the bare-bellied, that they are not from a diseased flock and that it is allowed to have them rightly, do you promise that these things thus will rightly be?

The repeating infinitives, all dependent on the final "*spondesne?*", the presentation of *luscam surdam minam* (three defects that must be specified as excluded) in asyndeton, and the regular, rhythmic reappearance of *recte* help to place this stipulation, and others like it,[32] in the same class and same conceptual world as the other acts written down on tablets examined here. Sometimes the verbal connections were, intentionally, even closer than that: the warranty clause in the mancipation ("it is vouched for . . .") was modelled on the aedilician edict, whose terms its clauses reasserted;[33] these stipulations that accompanied the sale of farm animals were modelled on the *leges* of Manilius (cos. 149 BC);[34] actions at law (in olden times, said Gaius) should be framed in the very words of *leges* and therefore could also be seen as immutable in the ways *leges* were;[35] in a similar way the formulae of later legal action, although in general form often drafted and posted by the praetor, also shared wording with sections of the praetor's edict itself.[36]

ARCHAIC AND ARCHAIZING LANGUAGE

What was written on tablets, from prayers to legal documents, maintained – as the chronological spread has shown – this syntax and style, this rhythmic prose, for centuries, and this was one of the ways it conveyed its authority.[37]

---

[32] See also Var. *R.* 2.3.5, *illasce capras hodie recte esse et bibere posse habereque recte licere, haec spondesne?*, and 2.5.11, *illosce iuvencos sanos recte deque pecore sano esse noxisque praestari spondesne?* Financial stipulations show this wording and these qualities as well, e.g., . . . *et usuras probas recte dari stipulatus est M. Carisianus Maximus spopondit L.* [–] (Marichal [1972–3] 378 no. C, from Vindonissa), as do those attached to transfers of property, e.g., *haec recte dari, fieri, praestarique stipulatus est M. Herennius Agricola, spepondit T. Flavius Artemidorus* (*CIL* 6.10241).

[33] Warranty clauses: compare above to aedile's edict, Gel. 4.2.1 (*quis fugitivus errove sit noxave solutus non sit*), and *D.* 21.1.1 (Ulpian).

[34] Stipulations: Var. *R.* 2.3.5, 2.5.11.

[35] Actions: *G.* 4.11; cf. Jhering (1891 [1875]) 2.2.631–74.

[36] Formula: Greenidge (1901) 150–61. General discussion of modelled acts, Rabel (1907).

[37] Cic. *Leg.* 2.18: *et tamen, quo plus auctoritatis habeant, paulo antiquiora quam hic sermo est*; conveying authority, Albrecht (1997) 625.

60   *The world of belief*

Such formalization of language, its "relative fixity . . . isolates it from the processes of historical linguistics," as Bloch says. This results in language and usage that were, and were recognized as, archaic,[38] and kept the language of most of these acts in Latin long after the citizen-body, or at least its elites, had become bilingual in Greek and Latin.[39] In AD 218, for example, the Arval brethren were still singing a prayer in this very antique style to Mars, the Lares, and the Senones;[40] in the dedication of a shrine to Liberty on Cicero's Palatine property the priest used *verba prisca*, and the *lex* of the prayer that dedicated the altar in second-century AD Salona (above p. 46) used *ollis* for *illis*;[41] Cicero referred in passing to an archaic locution "of the sort that the censors' tablets used," and these tablets in Pliny the Elder's day still listed all income under the ancient heading of *pascua* ("pastures"), "because for a long time this was the only form of income," and because for a longer time, most likely, this was the only acceptable way of referring to income of all types.[42] Through the first century BC (after which

---

[38] Bloch (1989 [1974]) 27 (quotation) and 22–3, among the Merina whom Bloch studied such speech was conceived as "speaking the words of the ancestors," at times through a form of direct possession. Archaic, understood as archaic: Twelve Tables, Sen. *Ep.* 114.13; Cic. *Leg.* 2.18, *de Orat.* 1.193 (*verborum prisca vetustas*, also encompassing the *libri* of the priests); Quint. *Inst.* 8.2.12 (go to commentaries of priests, oldest treaties, and obscure authors to find words "which are not understood"); Polyb. 3.22.3, language of first treaty between Rome and Carthage very far removed from anything contemporary; cf. Adams (1995) 89.

[39] Of *leges* and *senatusconsulta*, translations into Greek (never any other language) could be made, but the language of composition was Latin. *Leges* did not apply to non-citizen populations and were translated from the Latin outside Rome, see N. Lewis (1996) 209. *Senatusconsulta*, written in Latin but possibly applying to Greek non-citizen populations, were carefully translated by Romans at Rome, Sherk (1969) 7, 13–19. Treaties were also translated, and with a similar care and Latin legalism that suggests control of the language from Rome, Viereck (1888) xi. Roman edicts were most likely composed in Latin and translated, Mourgues (1995b) 120, *contra* W. Williams (1975) 52–3; Mourgues (1995b) 124 and n.50 emphasizes the literalism of Roman imperial chancery documents translated into Greek, deducing from it an "obsession romaine de l'absence d'altération du texte." The imperial (but not the provincial) census was in Latin until AD 212, Kaimio (1979) 123; legal decisions in court cases were given in Latin, Kaimio (1979) 122–3 (note, e.g., *CPL* 212, Latin decision of a *iudex datus*, and *P.Oxy.* 3016, decision of ξενοκριτῶν in Latin when all else in Greek); Roman-citizen legal acts of mancipation had to use Latin until the Severan period, when the linguistic requirements for mancipatory wills were relaxed (although perhaps only in Egypt?), *SB* 5294 (a will that refers to a ruling of Severus Alexander, AD 235; the first surviving imperial constitution on the subject is *CJ* 6.23.21.6 [AD 439]), cf. Kaimio (1979) 147–9; the third-century emancipation *CPL* 206 (= *FIRA* ² 3.31–3 no. 14; Oxyrhynchus) still uses Latin.

[40] Arval Hymn: see A. Gordon (1983) 160 for editions and date; *contra*, Piva (1993), who argues that the Arval Hymn is a third-century AD creation, incorporating magical names rather than archaisms. Cf. Apul. *Met.* 4.22, in imitation or parody robbers also sing *cantica* to Mars.

[41] Dedications: on Capitoline, Cic. *Dom.* 125; altar in Salona, *ILS* 4907; on archaisms in religion generally, De Meo (1986) 148–54; cf. Quint. *Inst.* 1.6.41, *sed illa mutari vetat religio.*

[42] Census, Cic. *Orator* 156, *ut censoriae tabulae locuntur fabrum et procum* rather than *fabrorum et procorum; pascua*, Plin. *NH* 18.11; cf. Gel. 2.10, learned discussion of *favisae*, found in censors' tablets. The banker and auctioneer Jucundus pays *pascua* in the mid-first century AD, *CIL* 4.3340.145.

The Roman tablet: style and language

these acts become much less common) treaties and laws maintained older spellings and formulae.[43] The plebiscite on weights and measures (above, p. 51) used *oetier* for *utier*, and the praetor's edict evolved in content while continuing to be promulgated in its ancestral and formulaic form until the reign of Hadrian.[44] The recently published *senatusconsultum de Cn. Pisone patre* (AD 20) contains archaisms like *manufestissuma* and *celeberruma* as well.[45] Indeed, Cicero noted that the archaic pronunciation *af* for *ab* or *a* could still be found in financial accounts of his own time, although "not . . . in all of them, and in regular speech it has changed."[46] Both Cicero and Quintilian recognized a category of archaic words (like *nuncupare* and *fari*, said Quintilian) that were both unavoidable and "acceptable to habitual usage," while Varro gives examples of such habitual usage in his description of the *antiqua formula* or *prisca formula* of a stipulation accompanying a sale of sheep.[47] Even a second-century AD stipulation for dowry on tablets from Egypt used *matrimonio(m)* in its introductory formula, and it has been suggested that some letter shapes imposed by the challenge of writing on wax were seen as archaisms.[48]

To say that language on tablets was thought to be archaic, however, is not to claim that the language used in all of these *tabulae* was exactly the same as it had been in, say, the third century BC. Some uses of archaic language were more precise repetitions of the distant past than others, while some language was archaizing rather than archaic. Thus while the prayer of the Arval brethren, although from AD 218, does appear to be genuinely early (and nonsensically garbled) Latin, repeated year after year and transcribed at a far later date,[49] other documents in archaic Latin were more consciously modernized, as has been suggested for the preserved remnants of both the Twelve Tables and the praetor's edict, and yet others were composed in

---

[43] Treaties: note the *faxit* in the treaty with Callatis (above p. 48). Laws: *ei* for *i* in *CIL* 1² 204 (70 BC) and *CIL* 1² 206 (45 BC). There are very few imperial examples of either treaties (Heuß [1934] 19 n.1) or laws (only two possible after Nerva, Rotondi [1922 (1912)] 471–2).

[44] Plebiscite, Cloud (1985) 416; praetor's edict, Kaser (1951); further on archaisms in law, De Meo (1986) 85–98; and note that magistrates were (it was said) required to pronounce penalties only in (units of) sheep or goats (Plin. *NH* 18.11; Gel. *NA* 11.1.4).

[45] Eck *et al.* (1996) 55–6.

[46] *Af*: Cic. *Orator* 158 (*af, quae nunc tantum in accepti tabulis manet ac ne his quidem omnium, in religio sermone mutata est*; summarized by Velius Longus's commentary, *GL* 7.60); Solin (1968) 10 suggests that the handwriting of a second-century AD curse-tablet is deliberately archaizing.

[47] Categories of words: Cicero (*de Orat.* 3.170, *aut vetustum verbum sit, quod tamen consuetudo ferre possit*) and Quint. *Inst.* 8.3.27 (*quaedam tamen adhuc vetera vetustate ipsa gratius nitent, quaedam et necessario interim sumuntur, ut nuncupare et fari*); sheep, Var. *R.* 2.2.5–6, above p. 59.

[48] *P.Mich.* 4703 (= *FIRA*² 3.41–3 no. 17). See also Adams (1990) 231 for "hypercorrect" archaizing in *TPSulp.* 15 (AD 37). Handwriting: Marichal (1992a) 177–8.

[49] Arval hymn earliest Latin: Schulz (1946) 27 (although see above n.40).

62   *The world of belief*

a deliberately archaizing style.[50] The results of this type of adjustment –
a modernization of spelling or verbal form (e.g. *fecit* for *faxit*), or even a
deviation from a pattern or form previously used – were called by the
Romans *concepta verba*, whereas the oldest, most fixed form was called *certa
verba*. Both formulations, however, were used to describe words, forms,
and phrasing within this archaic or deliberately archaizing style. Both were
accepted as characteristic of prayers, laws, vows, legal documents, and so
on; and the antonym to both was the "formless" (*incerta*) arrangement of
words.[51] Therefore the conscious use of archaic language did not absolutely
bind the user, year after year, to only certain words in only a certain order.
Change could be allowed and approved, as when Scipio Aemilianus changed
the traditional form of a vow and had the new form recorded on *tabulae
publicae*;[52] or when Varro believed he could detect permitted variations in
the deeds and words used by the consul to summon the *comitia centuriata*;[53]
or when Clodius thought he had correctly dedicated a shrine, even though
Cicero later with obvious exaggeration attacked him for being unable to
speak "one solemn word."[54]

Such *concepta verba*, formal but archaizing rather than archaic and thus
younger than *certa verba*, could also be the result of adjustment for place as
well as for time. *Templa* for augury were, according to Varro, created by the
speaking of *concepta verba* that were not the same for every place. He gave the
utterance by which *templa* were created on the Capitoline – it began "*templa
tescaque*, let them be to me thus, up to where I shall have named them
properly with my tongue" – but a variant for another place would not be
any less powerful. Variations and modulations could and did occur without
loss of efficacy.[55] It was the style and the ancient feel that were important;

---

[50] Modernizing: Kaser (1951) 32–4, but form still early, Drummond (1989) 115–16; see Courtney (1999)
13–26. Archaizing: Courtney (1999) 93–102 (on *senatusconsulta*) and 107 (on Livy).

[51] *Certa* and *concepta verba*: prayers, Plin. *NH* 28.11 (*certis*), Apul. *Met.* 11.22 (*concepti sermonis* in priests'
books), Macrob. *Sat.* 3.9.2 (*evocarent certo carmine*), Liv. 1.32.8 (*carminis concipiendique* of fetials);
census, Gel. 4.20.3 (*concepta*); legal procedure, Cic. *Inv.* 2.58; *G.* 4.37, 4.45, 4.139, 4.160; *D.* 4.6.43
(Africanus; *stipulatio*), *D.* 24.3.56 (Paulus; *stipulatio*), vows, e.g., Fest. 88M (dedication of a *fanum*
with *certa verba*); *D.* 48.19.9.5 (Ulpian), drawing up accusations referred to as *libellos concipiant* (also
D. 49.1.1.4 [Ulpian], *libelli* of appeals *concipiendi*); Amm. Marc. 28.1.20–1, drawing up *conceptae
praecationes*, to be performed *obsecrato ritu sacrorum sollemnium numine* (AD 371); contrast with
incerta, Liv. 31.9.7 (vowing for *incerta pecunia* rather than *certa* allowed for the first time, 200 BC).
On *certa* and *concepta*, see Gioffredi (1978), notion of solemnity retained.

[52] Scipio Aemilianus: Val. Max. 4.1.10; Marx (1884) 65–8 says fictional, but at very least an early imperial
audience could find it plausible; cf. Valette-Cagnac (1997) 289–90.

[53] Varro, *L.* 6.95.

[54] Cicero *Dom.* 141 (*neque verbum ullum sollemne potuit effari*).

[55] *Templa*: Var. *L.* 7.8, *tem<pla> tescaque me ita sunto quoad ego ea rite lingua nuncupavero*. Chronological distinction: e.g., *G.* 4.30, in pleas.

The Roman tablet: style and language

these, which the Romans saw as ancient and powerful wording, were not what most modern scholars have called "formalism," which they define as a strict adherence to a form that had never changed and never would. After judicious consideration, forms could and did change, and absolute-and-forever fixity was never part of the picture. Modern discussions that draw the line between formalism and agreed-upon form, deeming only the first of real antiquity and interest, miss the point: Romans saw archaic and archaizing, formalism and form, *certa* and *concepta verba* as distinct but different only in terms of chronological relationship or circumstance, not power.[56]

ELEMENTS, ABBREVIATION, AND PARODY

Finally, in addition to the various shared aspects of style and syntax and the archaic yet flexible quality of the Latin, there were several technical components which all writing on tablets was deemed to share, or to which it was subject, and which therefore link them all as well. First are the three elements of *formula*, *ordo*, and *nomen*; second is the regular abbreviation of this language; and third is the frequent parody to which this way of writing and speaking in Latin was subject. All characterize the language of tablets, and all help to link the different kinds of tablets yet more closely together.

(a) Elements and abbreviation. The *formula* is a pattern, a list, or a register. It can mean the way in which the census was to be taken, i.e. the words by which information was to be solicited from citizens; the provisions of a prayer or treaty or legal act; or the verbal patterns in which legal acts were performed or pleas, taken from the praetor's edict, were to be presented.[57] Moreover, such writing or even specifically its formula has

---

[56] Misdirected modern discussions: Mitteis (1908) 255–6 (formalistic or free), Watson (1992) 30–8, 79–80; better, Jhering (1891 [1875]) 2.2.441–9 (although as Nicholas [1992] 1606 points out, he creates too fine a distinction between what he calls "*Formel*" and "*Formular*," 2.2.577–93), Schulz (1946) 29 n.1, G. MacCormack (1969a) 441–2, who expressed skepticism over defining formality too rigidly; Nörr (1989) 28–38 (in *deditio*).

[57] Census, *formula census*, e.g., *CIL* I² 588 line 7, 585 line 21, 593 line 147; prayer, Cic. *Har.* 23 (aedile's dedication of Megalensia); treaty, Petr. *Sat.* 109.1 (joke); legal acts, e.g., *formulam sponsionis*, Cic. *Q. Rosc.* 12 or *testamentorum formulis*, Cic. *de Orat.* 1.180 and *Brut.* 195 (*antiquis formulis*); in stipulation, Var. *R.* 2.2.5–6; pleas from praetor, e.g., *CIL* I² 592.1 line 8, Cic. *Q. Rosc.* 25 ("You don't know the formula? It was very well known") or *Fam.* 13.27.1, cf. Cic. *Leg.* 1.14 ("What are you asking me to do? Compose *formulae* for stipulations and *iudicia*?"); Fest. 233M (of praetor); *G.* 4.34, 4.44, etc.; formula as list or register, especially of those eligible for military service: *CIL* I² 585 line 21 (*formula amicorum*). Cf. also Audollent (1904) CII–CIII and Martinez (1991) 1 n.2 for formulae identified in magic. What is written on tablets also develops formulae to mitigate the effects of possible omissions: e.g., Liv. 22.10 (in prayer) and M. Besnier (1920) 19–20 no. 33 lines 38–40 (a curse-tablet: *seive [plu]s, seive parvum scrip[tum fuerit], quomodo quicqu[id] legitim[e scripsit], mandavit seic*).

64   *The world of belief*

ordo, a correct sequence or order in which elements are to be presented;[58] and all such writing has at its heart a *nomen*, a name. This is true even in account-books, where any entry itself is called a *nomen*. Great care is taken to get names right, whether in prayers, treaties, vows, curses, or legal documents.[59] Names are solemnly "named," *nuncupare*.[60] Important entities, like money, gods, and vows were nuncupated,[61] as were census-status, augural boundaries and signs, certain parts of individual legal acts, and, by an eventual transference, the legal act itself or status that a legal act could confer – a husband is *nuncupatus* as such, as an heir can be.[62] Even the object of a medicinal spell for the cure of erysipelas is nuncupated.[63] Nuncupation was a serious, solemnly distinctive form of naming, done out loud as a form of "announcement."

The fact that these easily recognizable elements of *formula*, *ordo*, and *nomen* appeared so regularly, and the fact that formal language limited syntactical choice and vocabulary, helped to prepare the audiences of *tabulae* for another characteristic aspect of this language: the extent to which it was all regularly subject to abbreviation. This abbreviation is sporadically attested in prayers, most accounts of which are literary, but occurred regularly in laws and edicts, and surveyors' maps, for example, were annotated with "abbreviations in common use."[64] The abbreviation *A.F.P.R.*, used in accounts, could be made the subject of a joke in a trial in 116 BC, and

---

[58] *Ordo*: e.g., Cic. *Q. Rosc.* 6, *Dom.* 140 (dedication of shrine to Liberty *praeposteris verbis*), cf. Norden (1939) 91–2.

[59] *Nomina*: designation in the census, Nicolet (1980) 51; enrolling for a colony, R. E. Smith (1954) 19 n.15 and Piper (1987) 48–9; Cic. *S. Rosc.* 21 (proscription edicts), Frontin. *Aq.* 96 (*nomina* of those who are to care for the public water-supply to be entered in *tabulae publicae*); account-books, Cic. *Sest.* 72; vows, Beard (1991) 46–8; curse tablets, Ov. *Ibis* 93–4, Audollent (1904) XLIX–LIV and 270 no. 196 (*seive ea alio nomini est*), Jordan (1976), and Tomlin (1988) 95–8; legal documents, *CJ* 2.14(15).1 (AD 400; in general), *D.* 28.4.3 (Marcellus; in wills); see Huvelin (1904) 38–42.

[60] *Nuncupare* as "name," Varro, *L.* 6.60 (*nuncupare nominare valere apparet in legibus*); cf. Cincius the jurist, "nuncupated money is named, fixed, pronounced by its own names" (Fest. 173M, *nominata, certa, nominibus propriis pronuntiata*). *Nomen nuncupare* is a standard phrase, still found late, e.g., Apul. *Met.* 2.13 or Symm. *Ep.* 1.1.5.

[61] Money, see above n.60. Gods: e.g., Var. *Men.* 213.2 (= Nonius Marcellus 47M) or Apul. *de Deo Soc.* 153 and 177; cf. Ogilvie (1969) 24–9 on correct ways of addressing gods. Nuncupated vows: e.g., Caes. *BC* 1.6.6, Cic. *2 Verr.* 5.34, Liv. 36.2.3 (with pontifex maximus *praeeunte*), or Serv. *in Aen.* 7.471. Prayers (Liv. 40.46.9) and *deditiones* (Liv. 9.9.5) could also be nuncupated.

[62] Census class, Plin. *NH* 7.147 (figurative); augury, Var. *L.* 7.8, Serv. *in Aen.* 3.89. Nuncupations in legal acts: e.g., *G.* 2.104 (will); Serv. *in Aen.* 4.103 (marriage by *coemptio*). Nuncupated acts: Plin. *Ep.* 8.18.5 (will). Nuncupated husband: Apul. *Met.* 4.26 (in tablets); nuncupated heir, Suet. *Aug.* 17.1, *Gaius* 38.2, *Claud.* 4.7; *D.* 29.7.20 (Paulus).

[63] Plin. *NH* 22.38.

[64] Recognizable: Williamson (1983) 103, 116–19. Laws and edicts: see *FIRA*[2] 1 *passim*. Surveyors: Hyginus Gromaticus, *inscriptio singularum litterarum in usu fuerit* L202 (Campbell [2000] 158).

The Roman tablet: style and language 65

was still around in the second century AD.[65] *V.S.L.M.*, *votum solvit libens merito* – "he willingly paid his vow in return for benefits received" – can be found on vow-dedications throughout the Roman empire until the fourth century AD; and even curse-tablets occasionally used abbreviations.[66] Abbreviation was also very standard in legal texts and personal legal acts.[67] An astrological poem of the early Principate explained that the man born under the sign of Libra would come to know "the tablets of laws [the Twelve Tables], abstruse legal points, and words denoted by slight marks" – legal abbreviations – with the no doubt wearying result that "in his own house he is perpetual praetor."[68] Special glossaries were eventually created to provide explanations for these abbreviations. Valerius Probus's first-century glossary set out to explain "the ones that even now remain in *praenomina*, public laws, and the monuments of the pontiffs and the books of the civil law," called by him *publicae notationes*.[69] Such legal abbreviations were eventually forbidden entirely by the promulgators of the Justinianic code in the sixth century, perhaps because the tradition of a centuries-long familiarity with their meanings had finally snapped.[70]

Much of what was written, and abbreviated, in this older formulaic language appears on inscriptions. It has been generally assumed that it was the medium of bronze or stone, and the economies that the expense of inscribing imposed, that accounted for the very high degree of abbreviation to be found there. These factors may have contributed. But since the habit of abbreviation was not itself restricted to inscriptions, and is in fact not a Greek custom either (where the problems of medium and cost would have been virtually the same), it seems much more likely that abbreviation is a direct reflection of the special – and archaic, traditional, and

---

[65] *A.F.P.R.*: Cic. *de Orat.* 2.280 (it means "allocated formerly, posted up recently," trans. Rackham); the same phrase could also be abbreviated *A.G.P.R.* (*ante gestum post relatum*, for *ante factum*), Fro. *Ep. Ant. Imp.* 1.5.1.

[66] Vows: Eisenhut (1974) 971. Curse-tablets: see Audollent (1904) 146–7 no. 93, 149 no. 95, 151 no. 97, and 177–8 no. 122 (*qiss*; quoted above p. 54), but not very common.

[67] Legal texts, Isid. *Etym.* 1.23.1; personal legal acts, see *FIRA*² 3 *passim*; Pugliese Carratelli (1948) 166 (Herculaneum); Giovè Marchioli (1993) 104 notes early examples in legal texts; also Adams (1990) 246, a legal formula abbreviated into incomprehensibility on *TPSulp.* 51–2 (AD 37).

[68] Manilius 4.209–12, *hic etiam legum tabulas et condita iura | noverit atque notis levibus pendantia verba | . . . perpetuus populi privato in limine praetor.*

[69] Glossaries: quoted, the *de litteris singularibus fragmentum* 1.8–9 (*GL* 4.267–76 at 271, *quod [in] praenominibus legibus publicis pontificumque monumentis et in iuris civi[lis] etiamnunc manet*), and Valerius supplies a list, 3.1–24 (*GL* 4.272–3). See also the glossaries that follow Probus in *GL*, which show that the habit of legal abbreviation continued into the fourth and fifth centuries.

[70] Forbidden: *C. Deo Auct.* 13, *C. Omnem* 8, *C. Tanta* 22; Isid. *Etym.* 1.23.2; cf. *D.* 37.1.6.2 (Paulus, quoting Pedius), shorthand forbidden in wills. Cf. Bowman (1994) 116, abbreviations in some Vindolanda letters – but of words well known from epigraphic texts, like *noster*, *consulibus*, and the like.

66   *The world of belief*

familiar – quality of the material being written down.[71] Valerius himself attributes the beginnings of abbreviation to "common agreement."[72] Abbreviations do not necessarily distance an inscription or a piece of writing from its public, thereby signalling a restricted audience; they can just as well indicate phrases and words, or at least symbolize a concept, recognizable to a large number of people, like SCUBA, and NASA to Americans, or QUANGO to the British.[73]

(b) Parody. The familiarity of this kind of language is also demonstrated by the regularity with which it was parodied. For the common phrasing and appropriate details of all of these acts were sufficiently well known that parodies of these acts and their style and language were easily signalled and easily understood, and the concentration of parody on these acts in particular underlines again the fact that they are all, at some deep level, related. Such parodies began as early as Plautus, where they exist in great profusion and depend in particular on imitations of style and structure for their humor, while the content often veers dangerously away from what is standard or expected. The *lex Cornelia Baebia* is parodied in the prologue to the *Amphitruo*, the aedilician edict in *Captivi* and *Poenulus*, an edict assigning provinces in the *Pseudolus*. In *Asinaria*, a parasite draws up a contract between the young lover Diabolus, the young love-object Philaenium, and Cleareta, Philaenium's procuress, the terms of which are referred to as *leges* (and the author as *poeta*, no less), and which includes the familiar phrase *dedit dono* and terms like, "if she should look at another man, let her immediately become blind," "when she throws the dice, let her not say 'you' – let her name your name (*nomen nominet*)," and "let her not nod wink agree at another man."[74] According to Suetonius, upon Caesar's enrollment of "foreigners" in the Senate, a mock edict went up (*libellus propositus*): "May it be well done. Let no one wish to point out

---

[71] Abbreviation and inscriptions: e.g., Badian (1988) 203–4 or A. Gordon (1983) 15, where the origin of abbreviation is conjecturally, but with some reservations, attributed to the name-system and the desire to save space; see now Giovè Marchioli (1993) 103–25.

[72] Valerius Probus 1.7 (*ex communi consensu, GL* 4.271).

[73] No distancing effect: *contra*, Williamson (1983) 257–64, who sees abbreviation as deliberately elitist.

[74] Plautus: *lex Cornelia, Amph.* 64–74; aedilician edict, *Capt.* 813–23, *Poen.* 16–35 (with Jakab [1997] 123–5), edict assigning provinces, *Pseud.* 143–228 with Fraenkel (1960) 136–41; on other edicts, see Fraenkel (1960) 124–7, Dunn (1984) 42–66, and Slater (1992) 138; parodying the speech and actions of a land-surveyor, Plaut. *Poen.* 49–50 with Gargola (1995) 46–7. Diabolus: Plaut. *Asin.* 746–808; quotations 747 (*leges*), 748 (*poeta*), 752 (*dedit dono*); terms 770 (*si quem alium aspexit, caeca continuo siet*), 780 (*cum iaceat, "te" ne dicat: nomen nominet*), 784 (*neque illa ulli homini nutet nictet adnuat*); in general, see Costa (1890), Brophy (1974), and Dunn (1984); Kenney (1969) 250–1 points out that no use of legal metaphor (much less parody) can be paralleled in Greek poetry.

The Roman tablet: style and language 67

the senate-house to a new senator." Vitellius's edict against astrologers was mocked in the same way, through a *libellus propositus*: "May it be well done. Let Vitellius be no more, on the appointed date."[75] Taking parody even to the level of physical form, an early imperial inscription on a bronze tablet preserves part of the *lex Tappula*, a parody of a law, complete with correctly modelled prescript. Its subject is banqueting, and it depicts the people, appropriately enough, voting this law while meeting at the temple of Hercules, a notorious glutton.[76] In Trimalchio's household, a rule for servants – "whichever servant should pass outside without a master's order shall receive one hundred blows" – was inscribed on a *libellus* nailed (*fixus*) to the doorpost.[77]

Vows and treaties were also parodied in the *Satyricon*. "Venus, if I should have kissed this boy so that he does not feel it, tomorrow I shall give a pair of doves to him," vowed Eumolpus, followed the next two nights by increasingly lascivious requests and the promise of better gifts, in the same kind of language.[78] On another occasion, Eumolpus "sealed the tablets of a treaty" between the forces of Tryphaena and those of Lichas. The treaty's *formula* was stated in a series of *ut*-clauses, sometimes with *si*-clauses interspersed: Tryphaena must promise not to complain of any wrong done to her by Giton, nor steal any caresses from him without paying for them first, while Lichas is not to insult Encolpius, nor inquire as to where he has been sleeping at night.[79] Additionally, Trimalchio has his own will read aloud, complete with recognizable phrasing and what one trusts are exaggerations of usual bequests and requirements.[80]

---

[75] Edicts: Suet. *Jul.* 80.2 (*bonum factum ne quis senatori novo curiam monstrare velit*) and *Vit.* 14.4 (*bonum factum ne Vitellius Germanicus intra eundem kalendarum diem usquam esset*); the traditional heading of an edict was *bonum factum* (*sit*).

[76] *lex Tappula: ILS* 8761, its joke-qualities explained by Fest. 363M ("Valerius Valentinus wrote under a made-up name the convivial *lex Tappula* as a humorous *carmen*, of which Lucilius gave notice in this way: 'the rich laugh at the *lex Tappula*, and chew it [?] . . .' "); fragments translated by Crawford (1996) 1.32. See also Cic. *2 Verr.* 2.31, a joke made out of an action-formula by the substitution of an incorrect name; Maehler (1981) on Apuleius's parodies of Roman law; Cloud (1989) on satirists'; Grewe (1993) on Petronius; and Crawford (1988) 130–1, (1996) 1.27 on various "pastiches" (not parodies) in legal style.

[77] Petr. *Sat.* 28.7, *quisquis servus sine dominico iussu foras exierit, accipiet plangas centum.*

[78] Vows: Petr. *Sat.* 85–6 (*domina . . . Venus, si ego hunc puerum basiavero ita ut ille non sentiat, cras illi par columbarum donabo; si hunc . . . tractavero improba manu et ille non senserit . . . donabo; dii . . . immortales, si ego . . . abstulero coitum plenum et optabilem . . . donabo*). Prayers were also parodied: cf. Dunn (1984) 67–86 (in Plautus), Luc. *Icaromen.* 25, and (in general) Kleinknecht (1937) 157–210.

[79] Petr. *Sat.* 109.1–3 (*tabulas foederis signat, quis haec formula erat*).

[80] Petr. *Sat.* 71.

68   *The world of belief*

Wills were, in fact, easily parodied. A joke well known to Jerome and probably dating to the early fourth century AD, the *testamentum porcelli* or will of the piglet, implies that a will's formulae were very well known indeed. "Rows of chortling schoolboys recite the will of Grunnius Corocotta the piglet in school," wrote Jerome sourly, making a grumpy comparison with Cicero's account of having high-mindedly learned the Twelve Tables as a boy.[81]

Marcus Grunnius Corocotta porcellus testamentum fecit...patri meo Verrino Lardino do lego dari glandis modios XXX, et matri meae Veturinae Scrofae do lego dari Laconicae siliginis modios XL, et sorori meae Quirinae, in cuius votum interesse non potui, do lego dari hordei modios XXX. et de meis visceribus dabo donabo sutoribus saetas + rixoribus + capitinas, surdis auriculas, causidicis <et verbosis> linguam, bubulariis intestina, esiciariis femora, mulieribus lumbulos, pueris vesicam, puellis caudam, cinaedis musculos, cursoribus et venatoribus talos, latronibus ungulas. et nec nominando coco legato dimitto popiam et pistillum, quae mecum attuleram: de Thebeste usque ad Tergeste liget sibi collum de reste. et volo mihi fieri monumentum ex litteris aureis scriptum 'Marcus Grunnius Corocotta porcellus vixit annis DCCCC.XC.VIIII S, quod si semis vixisset, mille annos implesset.' optimi amatores mei vel consules vitae, rogo vos, ut cum corpore meo bene faciatis, bene condiatis de bonis condimentis nuclei, piperis et mellis, ut nomen meum in sempiternum nominetur. mei domini vel consobrini mei iubete signari.

M. Gruntius Beastie the piglet made the will...To my father Hoggius Lardinus I give and bequeath to be given thirty *modii* of acorns, and to my mother Veturina Sowa I give and bequeath forty *modii* of Laconian winter-wheat, and to my sister Squeala, at whose marriage I cannot be present, I give and bequeath thirty *modii* of barley. And of myself I will give and bestow to the cobblers my bristles to the brawlers my little heads (?) to the deaf my little ears to the pleaders <and the talkative> my tongue to the sausage-makers my intestines to the mincemeatmakers my shanks to the women my little loins to the boys my bladder to the girls my tail to the catamites my hams to the runners and hunters my ankles to the thieves my clawing hooves. And to the cook, not to be named, I give as a legacy the ladle and pestle, which I carried with me from Tebeste to Tergeste; may he bind his neck with a rope! And I wish a monument to be made for me, inscribed with golden letters: 'M. Gruntius Beastie, piglet, lived ninehundred-ninety-nine-and-a-half years; for if he had lived half a year more, he would have completed a thousand years.' My best friends, and counselors of my life, I beg you that you do well with my body, and that you garnish it with good condiments of nut, pepper,

---

[81] Jerome, *Comm. in Isaiam* XII pref. (*PL* 24.409–10), *testamentum...Grunnii Corocottae porcelli decantant in scholis puerorum agmina cachinnantium*; cf. *contra Ruf.* 1.17 (*PL* 23.412), "as if a crowd of the curly-locked did not recite Milesian fables in school, as if the testament of the piglet <of the Bessi> did not shake their limbs with laughter, as if trifles of this sort were not habitual at the banquets of the fops!"

The Roman tablet: style and language

and honey, so that my name may be uttered forever. My masters and cousins, you who are present at my will, see to it that it is sealed.[82]

Here certain regularly recurring features of a classical will are recognizable, such as the initial statement (*M. Grunnius Corocotta ... testamentum fecit*), the formula for legacies (*do lego dari*), and the insult of leaving out someone (here the cook, who is *nec nominando*).[83] In addition, there are several of the stylistic features already noted, like alliteration (*dabo et donabo, sutoribus saetas*) and an emphasis on names, including the testator's stately wish to perpetuate his own (*ut nomen meum ... nominetur*). Moreover, when the story of the piglet's capture by the cook was told (in prefatory material not included here), the piglet's prayer was thrown in for good measure, with the usual structure repeated three times for special emphasis (*si ... feci, si ... peccavi, si ... confregi, rogo ... peto, concede ...*).

One final example shows that the multiple uses, and implications, of *tabulae* (and the portentous drama of moments when they were used) were well understood and well parodied. In Apuleius's *Metamorphoses*, a man named Telephron tells the story of volunteering to guard a corpse, for a fee, against the nocturnal thievery of its body-parts by witches. With *verba concepta* taken down on *tabulis*, the grieving widow chronicled the appearance of the deceased: "Behold! Nose intact. Eyes unharmed. Ears undamaged. Lips immaculate. Chin unflawed. Do you, good fellow-citizens, bear witness hereunto." Dawn produced for her inspection an intact corpse, despite the fact that Telephron had gotten an exceptionally good night's sleep. But the dead man was made to speak, through the conjuring powers of Zatchlas the Egyptian magician. He revealed not only that he had been poisoned by his wife, but that witches had overnight stolen a nose and two ears – not his, but those of his nocturnal guardian Telephron. Why? Because witches had called on the corpse by name (*nomen*). But corpse and guardian were, coincidentally, both named Telephron, and the guard's limbs, being alive and warm, hadn't been quite as slow as the corpse's to respond to

---

[82] Text (excerpted), see Bott (1972). The date of the *testamentum porcelli* is disputed: see, e.g., Champlin (1987). The transfer of the opening to the middle and the bracketing of <and the talkative> as a gloss are thanks to G. Williams; I have capitalized "Scrofa" in line two. Other will-parodies known: Varro's Menippean satire called *Testamentum* (Gel. 3.16.13–14 and Buecheler [1871] 210), and Tac. *Ann.* 14.50.1, "Fabricius Veiento had composed many disgraceful things about senators and priests in those books to which he had given the name codicils," cf. D'Ors (1953) 74 and Aubert (1999) 311–13.

[83] Classical parallels: initial statements, e.g., *SB* 7630 (M. Aurelius and Commodus); legacies, e.g., *FIRA*² 3.132–42 no. 48 (AD 108, *do lego* only); *peto*, e.g., in a codicil, *FIRA*² 3.170 no. 56 (AD 175) or Amelotti (1966) 258 no. 4 (*rogo iubeoque*, second–third century AD); *iubeo*, e.g., *FIRA*² 3.169 no. 55d (*fieri iussit*, second century AD) or *CIL* 6.9405; insult of oversight, Apuleius *Apol.* 100; cf. D'Ors (1955) on the legal background.

70   *The world of belief*

the incantation. Telephron's horrified fingers fly to his nose and ears, and discover wax replacements: he has paid a very high price for not fulfilling an agreement.[84]

The audience's reaction to this terrifying tale? Laughter all around at Telephron's sad plight. *Concepta verba*, rhythmic and formulaic language, *tabulae*, and witnesses signalled that Telephron's night's work was formally (and legally) undertaken and very serious – a very serious joke – even though Telephron in his youthful jauntiness missed all the warnings. These elements also point to why the story is comprehensible on a deeper level: the widow's actions and phrasing, as well as the precision of the list of body-parts – an element of the city-sanctioned agreement between herself and Telephron – provide a clear reminder of the similarity between legal and magical style and language. As in a curse-tablet, noses and so forth are designated, and some are duly claimed, but from the wrong person, due to a most unfortunate confusion of *nomina*. What was done through Roman legalistic forms at the human level is subverted by parallel action in the realm of magic. How serious it all seems, yet how just the result, given both Telephron's youthful bravado and what *tabulae* are used for: what *excellent* entertainment!

This regular and sophisticated recourse to parody makes clear that actions associated with *tabulae* were extensively mocked as a group, and that the style and language of much that was written on tablets were so recognizable that centuries of successful imitation could not exhaust their easy appeal. It also makes clear that the archaic or archaizing language of these tablets was identified as such, but continued to be recognized, considered appropriate, adapted, and used for occasions that ranged from the very specific and personal to the grandly official. The style of tablets, the style of prayer and law, vow and curse, and even of careful accounts, was very much a living tradition, as ten minutes with Jerome's jolly schoolboys would have demonstrated.

All these similarities – of syntax and style, of language, of abbreviation, of parody – do not of course mean that a vow was considered the same thing as a prayer, or an edict the same thing as a will. Yet despite the differences that were always understood to have existed, the fact of underlying similarity,

---

[84] Telephron: Apul. *Met.* 2.24.5–7 (*verba concepta de industria quodam tabulis praenotante. "ecce" inquit "nasus integer, incolumes oculi, salvae aures, illibatae labiae, mentum solidum. vos in hanc rem, boni Quirites, testimonium perhibetote." et cum dicto consignatis illis tabulis facessit*); Zatchlas (2.28) is depicted as performing magical *postliminium*, and what the widow and Telephron agree upon is called a *placito* (2.24). On legal parody added by Apuleius to his donkey-novel prototype, see Maehler (1981).

The Roman tablet: style and language

of significant and ancient association, was never forgotten. Some unusual comparisons or metaphors used can help to demonstrate this: Catullus, for example, called marriage a *foedus*, and did not have some successful resolution of the battle of the sexes in mind.[85] Festus did not think twice about glossing a phrase in prayers according to its meaning in law, nor did Cicero, in drawing a parallel between *lex* and testament.[86] Both could depend on an interrelationship already perceived, the plausibility of which was already a matter of tradition. No chronological priority was assigned, and none needed to be, here or elsewhere. Whether Livy (in stating that the *leges* of the treaty between Rome and Alba Longa were read from wax tablets) was anachronistically assimilating the procedure for declaring war to the procedure for announcing a will, simply doesn't matter very much.[87] To him, the fact of similarity was uncontroversial.

The way in which this perception of shared distinctiveness was most clearly expressed was through the Roman tendency to group these word-acts together in one category, to call them all *carmina*, or sometimes both *carmina* and *leges* at the same time. Thus the Twelve Tables were to Cicero a *carmen necessarium* that he had learned to recite as a boy;[88] the praetor's edict was characterized by him as a *carmen magistri*;[89] Livy called the actual terms of the treaty between Rome and Alba Longa, not included in his history, *leges*, the last clause or oath a *carmen*;[90] priests, according to Seneca the Younger, framed "solemn words of a *carmen*" (*sollemnia pontificii carminis verba concepit*), an individual in a temple usually recited a carefully prepared *carmen*, and the Salians spoke or sung a *carmen*;[91] with *carmina* the spirits of the underworld were invoked, hailstorms could be averted, and splinted limbs made to heal.[92] Julius Caesar recited a *carmen* for a safe journey three

---

[85] Catullus, e.g., 64.335, 373; at 76.3, 87.3, and 109.6 he also refers to his own romantic relationship as a *foedus*; see Lyne (1980) 33–8 on Catullus's invention of the parallel.

[86] Festus, under *sub vos placo* (309M); Cicero, Cic. *Phil.* 2.109.

[87] Livy, 1.24.7; arguments over priority, Latte (1960) 5 n.1. See also Zon. 8.5 (= Cass. Dio 10), Pyrrhus refers to *devotio* as "incantation or magic" (ἐπῳδὴν ἢ μαγγανείαν). According to Crawford (1973) 2–3, first-century BC historians argued inappropriately over whether Rome's "treaty" with the Samnites after the Caudine Forks was a *foedus* or a *sponsio*; cf. Liv. 9.5.2–4 (and a similar mixing of terms in Stat. *Theb.* 8.629). No point in disputing the relative ages of religious and legal formula, since a parallel development, Latte (1960) 62; religious and magical practices once seen in the same mental category, Beard (1992) 759–60.

[88] Twelve Tables, Cic. *Leg.* 2.59 (cf. R. Mitchell [1990] 124 n.197).

[89] Praetor's edict: "*uti lingua nuncupassit . . . in magistri carmina scriptum videretur*," Cic. *de Orat.* 1.245.

[90] Liv. 1.24.3.

[91] Priests, Sen. *Cons. Marc.* 13.1 and Liv. 1.32.8 (*carmen* of fetials); individual's prayer, Plin. *Pan.* 3.1; Salians, Var. *L.* 5.110 (cf. Liv. 1.20.4).

[92] Underworld, Tac. *Ann.* 2.28.2, Verg. *Ecl.* 8.67–72, *CIL* 8.2756 (*carminibus defixa*; Lambaesis), and further references in Martinez (1991) 71–3. Hailstorms and splints, Plin. *NH* 17.267 (the words of the

72   *The world of belief*

times whenever he got in a carriage, "something which" – said Pliny the Elder – "we know many people to do today."[93] This perceived sameness of form and category at the heart of all of these transactions on tablets, this quality of being *carmen* and *lex* – being characterized by flexible but recognizably distinct style and language, and treated in ways that reflect this – prepares the way for understanding that the uses made of tablets and their distinctive language were parallel as well. This will be the subject of chapters four and five.

---

latter found in Cato, *Agr.* 160). The performance of these Roman healing-spells served as a parallel to Christian recitation of scripture: Orig. *Homilies on Joshua* 20.1 (Jaubert; trans. Lane Fox [1994] 140), "just as pagans have incantations with a healing or effective power, so much the more, when we recite scripture, even if we do not understand it, the angels will be present for us, as if called by some spell (*velut carmine quodam invitatae*)."

[93] Caesar, Plin. *NH* 28.21; cf. Amm. Marc. 29.2.26, an attempt to cure the malaria of the governor's daughter *carmine*. All in all, "la croyance à l'efficacité des *carmina* . . . tire son origine du vieux terroir italien . . . on peut lui assigner une vogue bien établie chez les anciens peuples latins," Tupet (1986) 2606.

CHAPTER 4

Recitation from tablets

The similar qualities attributed to tablets, their characteristic linguistic forms, and the parallel treatment accorded such forms all suggest that the underlying relationship the Romans themselves perceived, in calling these forms *carmina*, was no superficial one. Moreover, Roman *tabulae* not only displayed similarities. In the ceremonies with which they were associated, they were used in two similar, major ways, the subjects, respectively, of this chapter and the next: first, as templates for reading (itself performed in a distinct and powerful way, called *recitatio*),[1] and second, as the objects created in association with, and embodying the result of, that ceremony. In these ceremonies, tablets were not just useful but both significant and active. Their language, described in chapter three, is thus not only "formalized" but approaches what philosophers of language (following J. L. Austin and J. R. Searle) call "performative": "the issuing of the utterance is the performing of an action." Austin, Searle, and others have noted that defined circumstances (or "conventional procedure having a certain conventional effect") must exist for words to have performative effect, and that these procedures must be executed correctly and completely.[2] But the ways in which Roman *tabulae* are used demonstrate that, in this Roman context at least, performative language cannot be abstracted from physical form,

---

[1] *Recitatio*: U. Paoli (1922) established that *recitare* always denoted reading from a text; sometimes *praelego* and *perlego* are used, and in Greek ἀναγιγνώσκω "developed somewhat in the direction of reading aloud," Gavrilov (1997) 73; see now Valette-Cagnac (1997).

[2] Quoted, Austin (1962) 6, 14. Searle (1969) shifted the discussion of speech-acts and performative language towards intentionality, which I do not follow here. I emphasize also that the performative quality of tablets and their words is here to be argued from Roman evidence, not from the correlation of the Roman evidence to the tenets of speech-act theory, which I see as a suggestive parallel with no necessary probative value. Relevant applications of speech-act theory include Tambiah (1968) and (1985) on ritual, Frankfurter (1995) on ancient magic, and Ma (2000) on Hellenistic royal speech. For legal language as the classic performative language, see Charrow *et al.* (1982) 181, MacCormick and Bankowski (1986) 129, and Kurzon (1986); in Roman legal and religious acts, Wieacker (1988) 327, followed by Magdelain (1995) 67–111 and Valette-Cagnac (1997) 171–303; in Roman inscriptions, Wilkins (1996).

74 *The world of belief*

and that agreed-upon ceremonial completed correctly must be understood as far more than just a necessary "precondition" that allows performative language to have its effect. *Recitatio* of words from tablets, for example, will be shown to be an authoritative way of reading an authoritative document, and as such it does not merely make use of *tabulae*, but welds them into the ceremonies of which they are a part. A stylized form of reading like this, far from being some type of unfortunate "oral residue,"[3] is a deliberate choice that in other very different societies – among the Nukulaelae people of the central Pacific, for example[4] – reinforces the order, authority, and truth of the ceremonies of which they are a part.

Reading from tablets – the use of tablets as templates for speech – was characteristic of both Republican and imperial ceremonial practice. Here, three types of this use – prayers, curse-tablets, and the legal procedure of entering a charge (and having it accepted) in court – will be examined, followed by an analysis of what Romans believed such special reading would accomplish. Such high-profile *recitatio*, as easily imitable as the language of tablets had been, was embedded in larger acts of sacrifice, cursing, and the making or executing of the law, as well as in other acts (discussed in chapter five) like the making of the census, and of vows and dedications. The parallels will further illuminate the role of the tablet in legal procedure, thereby providing yet another reason for linking law and its pragmatic exercise and power to a world of traditional practices, and linking this particular kind of legal *tabula* to the world of all other tablets.

PRAYER

Reciting from *tabulae* was a way of getting through to and (one hoped) calling down power, and was a practice associated with occasions of high seriousness. A pedantic second-century AD grammarian, contemplating the differences between the prepositions *de* and *ex*, informs us in passing that "they who say what to say *de tabulis* ('from,' but in the sense of 'concerning tablets') exercise power poorly. For he speaks *de tabulis* ('concerning tablets') who praises or blames them; he speaks *ex tabulis* ('from,' in the sense of 'out of' tablets) who recites (*recitat*) what is written in them, and one ought

---

[3] Recitation as part of an "oral residue," Goody (1968) 13–14 and Ong (1982) 115–16.

[4] The Nukulaelae, and especially their practice of performing sermons from written texts (whereas political oratory is performed without a text), see N. Besnier (1995) 116–68, esp. 136 and 139 (orderliness), 141 (the seriousness of the occasion, and the preacher "cannot slip"), 163–4 (authority and truthfulness); see also 137 (the formal relationship of "notebooks" of sermons and "notebooks of traditional knowledge" with recipes, formulae, technological instruction, and magical techniques) and 166 (performance of sermons from a written text as a marked event in the islanders' lives).

Recitation from tablets

more correctly say 'reads' rather than 'says,' if one pronounces those things which one sees; for he who speaks, by contrast, does not look at the letters." Although this passage is confused, the grammarian is drawing a distinction not only between *de* and *ex* but also between uses of tablets, and in particular identifies a way of speaking that is actually a way of reading from them, a process labelled *recitat*.[5]

Indeed, formal recitation is usually signalled by *ex*, but not always: Pliny the Elder gives a vivid description of this use of recitation from writing in a ceremony of supplication (*obsecratio*), but uses *de* rather than *ex*.[6]

> quippe victimas caedi sine precatione non videtur referre aut deos rite consuli. praeterea alia sunt verba inpetritis, alia depulsoriis, alia commendationis, videmusque certis precationibus obsecrasse summos magistratus et, ne quod verborum praetereatur aut praeposterum dicatur, de scripto praeire aliquem rursusque alium custodem dari qui adtendat, alio vero praeponi qui favere linguis iubeat, tibicinem canere, ne quid aliud exaudiatur, utraque memoria insigni, quotiens ipsae dirae obstrepentes nocuerint quotiensve precatio erraverit . . .

> In fact, the sacrifice of victims without a prayer is supposed to be of no effect; without it too the gods are not thought to be properly consulted. Moreover, there is one form of words for getting favorable omens, another for averting evil, and yet another for a commendation. We see also that our chief magistrates have adopted fixed prayers; that to prevent a word's being omitted or out of order a reader dictates beforehand the prayer from (*de*) writing; that another attendant is appointed as a guard to keep watch, and yet another is put in charge to maintain a strict silence; that a piper plays so that nothing but the prayer is heard. Remarkable instances of both kinds of interference are on record: cases when the noise of actual ill omens has ruined the prayer, or when a mistake has been made in the prayer itself . . .

Here, the important action undertaken is a sacrifice, which is not believed to "count" (*referre*) without the prayer. This belief was still strong in the fourth century AD when the philosopher Iamblichus wrote, "prayers are not the least part of sacrifices: they in particular complete them, and through them the whole operation is made more powerful and complete . . . No religious ritual takes place without petitionary prayer."[7] The wording of the prayer is important, and in order to make sure it is spoken correctly magistrates have adopted, as Pliny says, "set prayers" (*certae precationes*)

---

[5] Grammarian: Terentius Scaurus, *de Orth.* (*GL* 7.31–2), *male imperant qui dicunt de tabulis quod dicere. de tabulis enim is dicit, qui eas laudat aut culpat: e tabulis is dicit, qui quod est in his scriptum recitat* †*scriptumque pronuntiatur si ea videt, et potius dici oportet 'legi' quam 'dici,' contra eas litteras non spectat*; I follow *GL*'s emendation of the word order at the end of the sentence, *scriptum recitat, et potius dici oportet 'legit' quam 'dicit,' si ea videt quae pronuntiat: nam qui dicit contra litteras non spectat.*

[6] Plin. *NH* 28.10–11 (trans. Jones).

[7] Iamblichus, *de Myst.* 5.26 (des Places 237.10–11), κρατύνεται . . . καὶ ἐπιτελεῖται.

76   *The world of belief*

which have been written down ahead of time and are dictated during the ceremony (*praeire verba*, the act of reading itself known as *recitatio*), with the magistrate repeating the words.[8] All this is set in a context of unspoken (and undescribed) ritual action which must also be performed correctly for the ceremony not to fail.[9] Thus the reading of the words in their correct order and the inclusion of every word that should be there are two of many crucial components to this ceremony. The prayer for the ceremony could be most certainly spoken correctly if repeated from a tablet. This is an "exercise of power," as our grammarian called it, perhaps because magistrates so frequently performed it, perhaps because it demonstrates an ability to gain access to power, an ability to call on the gods in correct and accepted ways whose very correctness implied that your prayer had been heard.

Although such recitation may not always have been performed, what evidence there is suggests that the more important the event, the more likely it was that there would have been recitation from tablets. Some literary accounts of prayers elide this conventional detail,[10] but it is noted on significant occasions, and there is an evident expectation that recitation would take place, and the concomitant sense that this was the best way to pray and sacrifice. For example, the dedication of Cicero's house on the Palatine as a shrine to Liberty was in part performed by an augur who was (Cicero claimed) supposed to do it with the help of a book but did not. He also stammered; these faults, Cicero argued, invalidated the dedication.[11] Cicero is probably right in insisting that the prayer should have been recited,

---

[8] *Praeire verba*: e.g., Liv. 39.18.3, in the rites of the Bacchanalia praying *ex carmine sacro, praeeunte verba sacerdote*; *ILS* 5050 (= *CIL* 6.32323) line 124, Agrippa is restored as the one who *praeit in haec verba* for Secular Games; see Wissowa (1902) 331 (includes gestures too) and Valette-Cagnac (1997) 247–91 (stressing that the written text does not merely serve as an aide-mémoire); about it, Harris (1989) 154 says, it "could well have been very old indeed." Precision was important: *in precibus nihil esse ambiguum debet*, Serv. *in Aen.* 7.120; cf. Arnobius *Adv. Nat.* 4.31 (perhaps citing Cic. *Har.* 23).

[9] Ritual actions involved, cf. Cato, *Orig.* fr. 18 (Peter), Var. *L.* 5.143, Plut. *Mor.* 266E, Ov. *Fasti* 4.821–8, all taken while prayer recited during foundation of a colony, discussed in Gargola (1995) 73–5; or in healing spells, Plin. *NH* 17.267 on *carmina* in Cato for sprained limb (*Agr.* 160, with Laughton [1938]) and for cutting down a sacred grove, and Var. *R.* 1.2.27 (for curing gout: chanting twenty-seven times, touching the earth, spitting, and fasting); Plut. *Mor.* 266D suggests that the ritual action of covering one's head during sacrifice is performed so as not to hear ill-omened sounds; cf. Cagnat (1903–4) 151–2.

[10] Prayers without mention of recitation, e.g., Liv. 4.27.1, 5.41.3, 8.9.4, 9.46.6, 10.28.14; Apul. *Met.* 11.2; cf. Appel (1909) 210; and perhaps supported by a narrow interpretation of the Pliny passage cited above (as being, e.g., limited to the first century AD, or to only the types of prayers mentioned there), e.g., Rohde (1936) 68. Silent prayer could also be performed, but was viewed with suspicion, Horst (1994).

[11] Cic. *Dom.* 139.

Recitation from tablets

for the antiquarian Varro noted that all dedications were made *pontifice prae<e>unte*.[12] The censors' prayer for the lustration was read from public tablets (*ex publicis tabulis... precationis carmen praeiret*),[13] prayers in the great Secular Games of 17 BC were read from *libri*,[14] and the Arval brethren read and spoke their famous archaic *carmen* from mini-tablets (*libelli*).[15] Sculptured images exist of people carrying *codicilli* (sometimes called *libri*) or *tabulae* in their hands while sacrificing.[16] The general perception seems to have been that Romans should recite their prayers, whether or not they always did so; this was the usual way of proceeding.[17] This is confirmed by the fact that someone like Marcus Aurelius was singled out as exceptional, for one of his noteworthy (and tediously characteristic) virtues was that as Salian priest no one read out prayers for him to recite (*nemine praeeunte*) since he had learned all the *carmina* himself.[18] Formulaic language prepared in advance and read from a tablet or a *liber* was an understood part of the action, used on important occasions, and *accepted* as traditional, while only superior individuals like Marcus Aurelius did without.

CURSE-TABLETS

A ceremonial setting like the one Pliny describes, with prayer-tablets used to call on otherworldly powers, also surrounds Roman curse-tablets. Ceremonial instructions in magical spells can be breathtakingly extensive, and suggest to J. Z. Smith and F. Graf an attempt to create around magical acts a space and a ritual that are parallel to, or a replacement for, the temples and rituals of religious acts, while D. Frankfurter has described the magicians of late-antique Egypt as the "central ritual specialists" of their towns, the

---

[12] Var. *L.* 6.61.

[13] Val. Max. 4.1.10a.

[14] *ILS* 5050 (= *CIL* 6.32323).

[15] See Beard's (1985) 159 text of the *acta* of AD 218.

[16] Sculptured images: Henig (1984) 87 fig. 32 (from Roman Britain); also Birt (1976 [1907]) 67–8 (where he suggests that the *libelli* might also be a sign of office); since magistrates while sacrificing also at times carry rolls, he sees the rolls as carrying the texts of prayers. The two should be reversed: since Marrou (1964) 209–57, Brein (1973), and Zanker (1995) 190–7, 268–84 have demonstrated that the carrying of a roll or *volumen* in art communicated literary talents and aspirations, this should point to high status (real or asserted), while *tabulae* and *codicilli*, if not specifically for prayer, are more likely to have conveyed a man's particular status as a magistrate, for they also announced appointment to office: cf. Suet. *Claud.* 29.1, Arr. Epict. *Diss* 3.7.30, *ChLA* 10.417 (= *CPL* 238, papyrus copy of *codicillorum*, first–second century AD), Mart. *Ep.* 14.4.2, Philostr. *VS* 2.590.4 (τὰς βασιλείους δέλτους appoint the sophist Hadrian imperial secretary, and he expires over them), *AE* 1962.183 = Pflaum (1971), from Bulla Regia (second century AD). For late-antique examples, see chapter nine n.142.

[17] North (1998) 52–3; other examples, see e.g., Gel. 13.23.1, prayers to gods in *libri*.

[18] *HA Marc.* 4.4.

78   *The world of belief*

"lector-priests" who were the sole "master[s] of the written word" in ritual magical matters.[19] The contrast with Athenian curse-tablets is instructive: while Attic curses or binding-songs could be sung, there is no hint that these Attic curse-tablets – consisting of only names in more than 75 percent of known cases – were used to establish ritual space or used as the basis for recitation or performance.[20] Even the earliest known Latin curse-tablet, on the other hand, is in the form of a diptych (a doubled tablet) and commands, on its left margin, *dic ilai* ("say that!"), suggesting an early use of recitation from writing on tablets as part of the action; another, difficult to read, enjoins *dicato* in its last line.[21]

Moreover, the involvement of a third party – the magician – in the performance of a curse is clear, his actions likely parallel to those of the priest who recited prayers for a magistrate to repeat. Roman tradition more securely records an association of magicians and curse-tablets, an association itself probably at least as early as the first century BC, when C. Vitrasi[us], identified as the magician, *literas perlegerit* on a curse-tablet from Cumae.[22] When a Roman magician was called upon for a curse, he could assist in two ways. First, he could simply write out the curse on a tablet. Some surviving Latin curse-tablets, and Greek tablets of the Roman period, suggest that the magician copied out the spell onto the tablet himself, since these tablets were found in caches, and in the same handwriting but with different intended victims.[23] Second, he may, like Vitrasius, have read out the curse himself, perhaps for the one cursing to repeat – an obvious necessity in a world where a wizard would have had many illiterate customers.[24] After

---

[19] J. Smith (1995) 24–5, Graf (1991) 195–6; cf. M. Meyer and R. Smith (1994) 4, for similar ceremony in Christian magical texts; Frankfurter (1997) 116, 119, 121.

[20] Attic tradition: little is known about what if any ceremony accompanied the deposit of Attic curse-tablets, which are themselves often just a list of names (Faraone [1991a] 4–5; statistics, 10); as summarized by Frankfurter (1994) 195, "the written spell essentially 'records' the ritual," which reflects the role of writing in the Greek tradition: "although magic could be written . . . writing itself was not magic."

[21] *Dic ilai*: *ILLRP* 1147 (second century BC, Pompeii); earliest Latin, see Preisendanz (1972) col. 19. *Dicato*: Audollent (1904) 187 no. 131 (= *CIL* 9.5575), from Picenum. *PGM*[2] 14.296–433 (Martinez [1991] 14–15), which enjoins writing and reciting (δίωκε), may be a late example of this tradition.

[22] C. Vitrasi[us]: Audollent (1904) 270–1 no. 197. This method of performing spells persists into late antiquity and Christianity: Aug. *Tract. in Iohann. evang.* 7.7 (= *PL* 35.1441) refers to *praecantatores* to whom the faithful resort for healing, and the *Conc. Aspasi episcopi Elusani* (= *CCSL* 148A.163–4) punishes *incantatoribus* and those who *praecantare* by expelling them from the Church, or by beatings.

[23] Magician writes tablets: Audollent (1904) XLIV–XLVII; Solin (1968) 7; Gager (1992) 4–5 and 123 n.11; Tomlin (1988) 98–101 and 118–19 no. 8 (clearly copied out). Caches with same handwriting: the Via Appia collection in Rome (second–third century AD, in Greek), Nock (1972) 177.

[24] Latin curse-tablets are usually couched in the first person, with instructions in imperatives, which implies that the one cursing was responsible for the writing and speaking; but curse-tablets are popular at every level of society, and thus necessarily among the illiterate, cf. Tomlin (1988) 98–101,

Recitation from tablets

all, magicians and priests could not easily be distinguished, as Apuleius reminded his second-century AD audience,[25] and it could well have been that acts of recitation and *praeire verba* provided the most visible links between the two: how people act is often more striking to observers than some more abstract sense of what they are. If the collaboration between magician and the one cursing was active rather than passive in nature, the heightened sense of the danger posed by the conjunction of magicians, books, and tablets hinted at in Roman sources would also make sense.[26] It is therefore likely not only that curses were intended to be written on tablets and recited, but that the action could parallel that of prayers, with the magician playing the role of dictating priest to the extent that this was necessary.[27]

LEGAL PROCEDURE

This use of tablets or books as providing correct formulae and therefore as playing an important role in a ceremony, tapping into power by (as it were) using the correct access code and (it was hoped) channelling the message correctly in a chosen direction, has direct parallels in Republican and later Roman civil (*legis actio* and formulary) and criminal procedure. Here, mastery of the correct formula was necessary for the case to move forward from the first stage of the proceeding, pled before a magistrate who would determine on the basis of what law or statute the case was being brought (and whether or not he would allow an action on this subject at all) to the second – what we would consider the trial proper. This second

---

Aune (1980) 1521 (perhaps even more popular with "the lower, uneducated classes"), and Hanson (1991) 181. Active collaboration between magus and client solves this large implicit problem; in the Egyptian tradition, the way around illiteracy was for spells to be "enacted, uttered, or simply washed off," but not recited and repeated (Frankfurter [1994] 196, [1995] 467).

[25] *Apol.* 25; priests and magicians were conflated in Pharaonic Egypt, and such conflation is part of a long tradition, Ritner (1995) 3354.

[26] Danger: of books and magicians, see Acts 19:19; magicians sent into exile, Cass. Dio 78.17.2; laws enforcing this (*CT* 9.16.4, 5, 7, 10 [AD 356–71]; *CJ* 9.17.4 [= *CT* 9.16.3. AD 317–19?], 9.19.9 [AD 389]); punishments, Paul. *Sent.* 5.23.17–18, 19; this could explain the (fictional) anxiety attributed to Domitian, who required Apollonius of Tyana to leave both book and tablet by the door when he entered, Philostr. *VA* 8.3.

[27] Books of magicians were probably a type of formulary book, parallel to *commentarii* written about, but including, ancient prayers (see chapter two nn.64 and 66): in Egypt, exist as *PGM*² (earlier collections may have been more scholarly than practical, Faraone [2000] 210–11); in North Africa, deduced from numerous similarities between tablets, Preisendanz (1972) col. 16; cf. Nock (1972) 177–80, Martinez (1991) 7, and Faraone (1991a) 4 and 23 n.11. Spelling on tablets varies widely and is a rich source of information about vulgar Latin (see, e.g., Garcia Ruiz [1967], Tomlin [1988] 74–9), so it is clear that recognizable patterns had to be written and spoken, but that absolute orthographic precision was not required.

80   *The world of belief*

stage, heard by a *iudex* rather than a magistrate, was, by contrast to the first, strikingly informal, concerned with nitty-gritty details of people and what they had done, not law. If this judge found against you, the legal result was predetermined, set by the magistrate who had remanded the case to the *iudex* in the first place. The magistrate was free to reject a case – not pass it on to the next phase – for any number of reasons even if correct words were used; correct language, read from a tablet, assured a hearing, not a result.

In the older type of procedure, *legis actio*, claims by a plaintiff had to be made in set words (*certa verba*) taken (in general) from the Twelve Tables, the defendant in some cases obliged to give a formulaic response;[28] the magistrate presiding over this initial stage of an action (in a formally arranged setting, with tribunal and spear) would then speak, also with set words.[29] The use of the right words was important. Gaius reported that a man who stated his claim using the wrong word ("vines" for "trees") destroyed his case (*rem perdidisse*). Why? "The answer" of the magistrate, said Gaius, "was that . . . [the plaintiff] lost his case, *because* the law of the Twelve Tables, from which arose the action for cutting down vines, spoke generally of trees being cut down," that is, Gaius's magistrate phrased his answer as a reaffirmation of the principle of formalism, the principle that correct words were most important. Magistrates punished, by refusal, those who did not use them.[30]

How would you know what actions were available, and how to phrase the words correctly? There were books made from tablets which could be consulted and possibly even taken along to that first hearing, although there is too little evidence for us to know for certain how they were used. The first to make such a collection available for general consumption was said to be Cn. Flavius who, the story went, stole a set of *legis actiones* made

[28] Formulaic exchanges between plaintiff and defendant in cases of litigation, but not cases of execution (in which only plaintiff speaks), see Greenidge (1901) 56–7 (compared to 69–75); Kaser and Hackl (1996) 97–8; Alföldi (1959) 9 argues that the *sollemnia verba* of the *vindicia* were exchanged in the presence of the praetor and his spear (Gel. 20.10.6–10), and Gargola (1995) 21–2 lays out other, non-verbal aspects of the praetor's ceremony.

[29] Magistrates' responses: cf. Sen. *Tranq.* 3.4 (quoting Athenodorus), the praetor "pronounces the words of his assessor" (*adsessoris verba pronuntiat*), which makes the assessor parallel to the the priest assisting a praying magistrate, cf. J. Paoli (1950) 281–9 and Valette-Cagnac (1997) 293–300; some formulae still used in the looser imperial *cognitiones*, see Lieberman (1944–5) 12 and n.73; but the praetor even announces that he will hear cases with formulae, Macrob. *Sat.* 1.16.14. In general on precision of wording of *actiones*, Jhering (1891 [1875]) 2.2.452–5; Ulpian *FV* 318 says that if anything is added to, or taken away from, the *certa verba* in the *datio* of a *cognitor, non valeat*.

[30] G. 4.11. *Contra*, Daube (1961) 4–5 and Watson (1992) 36–8, who argue that a legal defeat occurred because the plaintiff was *deliberately* using different language; the presiding magistrate in their view denied the claim because of this intent to deviate. But formalism with either *certa* or *concepta verba* is the use of agreed-upon words (see chapter three pp. 61–3), and actual deviation explains this story.

Recitation from tablets

by Ap. Claudius Caecus. He also "published" for the first time the sacral calendar of the priests, thereby revealing which days could be used for legal proceedings, and which not.[31] Further collections of *legis actiones* were subsequently published, indisputably by Sextus Aelius Paetus (cos. 198 BC) and probably by all the other important legal figures before the end of the second century BC mentioned by the jurist Pomponius in his brief sketch of the development of Roman law.[32] Collections of *legis actiones* also used abbreviations that Valerius Probus would later obligingly expand. Such "books," therefore, were probably much like those of prayer or even the books of magical spells, giving templates of the desired formulae for practitioners who had to get it right.[33]

This *legis actio* procedure came into *odium*, said Gaius, because of the "excessive *subtilitas* of the ancients who were then creating the law" – for "anyone who erred in the slightest destroyed his case (*litem perderet*)," meaning, most likely, that the case had to be brought all over again on another day.[34] Yet despite this odium, procedure by *legis actio* did not disappear entirely, for although much modified by the *lex Aebutia* (perhaps late second century BC) and the *leges Iuliae* (17 BC), cases before the centumviral court were still being initially heard by a *legis actio sacramento* in the second century AD.[35] But the procedure which scholars assume replaced – for the most part – the old system of *legis actiones* maintained its two procedural stages while allowing alteration in the language that could be used, now appropriately called *concepta* rather than *certa verba*. Instead of making his words conform precisely to set, traditional formulae, no matter how little

---

[31] Cn. Flavius: Liv. 9.46.5 (*civile ius . . . evolgavit*), Plin. *NH* 33.17 (calendar), Cic. *de Orat.* 1.186, *Att.* 6.1.8; since these *formulae* were not secret anyway (Schulz [1946] 10), Flavius probably compiled a set for handy public use.

[32] *D.* 1.2.2.7 and 38–9 (Pomponius; some are specifically writing *libelli*); the *Manilias venalium vendendorum leges* (Cic. *de Orat.* 1.246) and the (*Manili*) *actiones* (Var. *R.* 5.11) also belong in the second century BC; cf. Jolowicz and Nicholas (1972) 92, Wieacker (1988) 557 n.26. Paetus's compilation was in use through the end of the Republic, Schulz (1946) 35.

[33] Abbreviations: Valerius Probus 4.1–11 (*GL* 4.273–4).

[34] *Odium*: *G.* 4.30. In *Inst.* 4.11 and 4.30, Gaius makes clear that *res* and *lis* (not the *actio* itself, the right of an individual to sue, *D.* 45.1.51 [Ulpian]) are destroyed by wrong wording. *Lis* is *causa*, meaning "this pleading" or "this court case": *litis cecidisse* = *causam amisit*, Fest. 116M; see also Cic. *Inv.* 2.57; Cic. *Q. Rosc.* 10, Hor. *Sat.* 1.9.35–42 (at 37, *perdere litem*; cf. Cloud [1989] 65–6); and Quint. *Inst.* 7.3.17 (*causa cecidisse* by use of wrong word); all show that the cases failed *before* they went to *litis contestatio*, cf. Crook (1992) 545; only Plaut. *Cas.* 568 implies that everything was lost. The technical meaning of *res* is unclear. If it covers both *lis* and *actio*, then perhaps when a plaintiff used "vines" for "trees" he lost everything (*res*) because he had lost *lis* through using the wrong word, but *actio* because, if Daube is correct (above n.30), he had deliberately used the wrong word. *Actio* itself was extinguished by agreement of parties to go before *iudex*: *G.* 4.106–8.

[35] *Lex Aebutia*: J. A. C. Thomas (1976) 83 nn.2–3. Continuance of *legis actio sacramento*: Gel. 16.10.8, *G.* 4.31; Jolowicz and Nicholas (1972) 198.

82   *The world of belief*

they appeared to pertain to the case at hand, the plaintiff now had a much wider choice of formulae, and was himself responsible for the phrasing of the *demonstratio* (material specification of facts) and the *intentio* (statement of claim within it). This system has been called the formulary system.[36]

Much about formulary procedure resembled the procedure of *legis actio*, and therefore also the procedure followed in prayers and, I have argued, curses. Compilations of formulae and people to help you frame your formula were already in existence in the Late Republic.[37] Moreover, the magistrate, in this case the praetor, had to assent to a formula before it could be used, which meant that he maintained the same extensive control over legal language and activity that he had possessed under the *legis actio* system. Indeed, he controlled the legal language of action very closely, and laid out patterns of formulae and matters on which he would grant actions in his edict, these also abbreviated; the change was that now, because of the more flexible language, new and more specifically appropriate causes of action could be created more easily.[38] From the point of view of the plaintiff, the procedure still looked very much the same. The plaintiff initiated a suit by making the defendant aware of the charge, this time through "the making provision for copying, or the including and giving in a *libellus*, or dictating (the charge)."[39] It was also permissible to lead the adversary to the praetor's edict – set out on tablets – and point to the relevant formula. The charge, then, was generally written down on tablets or mini-tablets (*libelli*); when a case was dismissed, one phrase used was, "tablets shall be destroyed" (*solventur . . . tabulae*).[40] Armed with this charge, called the formula, the plaintiff then approached the praetor and asked for action to be granted. This *postulatio* was probably delivered verbally – but probably by being read out from a tablet, or read out and repeated, so that the proper form would be observed.[41] Cicero's description of the jurisconsult as "the herald of actions, the cantor of formulae, the bird-catcher of syllables"

---

[36] *Concepta verba*: G. 4.30. Formulary system: Kaser and Hackl (1996) 151–432 (cf. Cic. *Q. Rosc.* 24 on its breadth and flexibility – "to these claims the legal claims of the individual are adjusted").

[37] Formula-books: see above n.32, with later Republican additions of (e.g.) the *actiones Hostilianae* (Cic. *de Orat.* 1.245); drafters, Cic. *Leg.* 1.14 (a *humiliora* business); see Wieacker (1988) 560 n.41. They are postulated even for provincial Arabia in the second century AD, Biscardi (1972) 141–2, the Latin carefully translated into Greek. Abbreviations: Valerius Probus 4.1–5.24 (*GL* 4.273–5).

[38] Continuities in the role of the praetor also emphasized by Schiller (1978) 217.

[39] *D.* 2.13.1.1 (Ulpian), *edere est etiam copiam describendi facere: vel in libello complecti et dare; vel dictare.*

[40] Leading: *D.* 2.13.1.1 (Ulpian, but attributed to Labeo); destruction of tablets, Hor. *Sat.* 2.1.86 (meaning disputed, cf. Muecke [1993] 114); generated by the parties themselves, Jahr (1960) 5–58, esp. 29–37.

[41] *Postulatio*: cf. Greenidge (1901) 179. Kunkel (1973) 207 identifies *TPSulp.* 31 (AD 52) as precisely this kind of tablet, a formula as well as a nomination of a *iudex* drafted by the plaintiff.

Recitation from tablets

should refer to the jurisconsult's actions at this stage (the *postulatio*): the jurisconsult was performing by reading aloud, as a herald did, and virtually singing while keeping a very sharp eye on the words themselves.[42] Cicero's further characterization of these "bird-catchers of syllables" as being indecently obsessed with "insignificant things, almost with single letters and the interpunctuations of words,"[43] itself indicates the jurisconsults' continuing interest in the mechanics of reading aloud, a concern of both *legis actio* and formulary procedure.[44]

Formulary procedure was thus much like the earlier *legis actio* procedure, but made the latter more flexible. In formulary procedure writing on and reading from tablets were used to help the plaintiff avoid inadvertent error. Given the parallels with prayers and curses, this habit of reading and reciting seems to me more likely to have carried over a custom previously in existence than to have appeared *de novo*. In other words, given the existence of books of *legis actiones* and the need to approach the magistrate with extreme verbal accuracy in court, the chance that a charge was recited from a tablet when the *legis actio* procedure was followed, just as it seems to have been when the later formulary procedure was followed, seems, to me, quite high.

The overall continuities of practice between *legis actio* and formulary procedure also buttress and explain the fact that, despite the modulations of language – from *certa* to *concepta verba* – the emphasis on correct speech, the requirement of precision in legal language, remained alive in formulary procedure until the fourth century AD. The wording of judgments continued to be, necessarily, very careful: when the "supreme fine" (given according to the *mos maiorum* in terms of sheep and cattle even in Aulus Gellius's day) was pronounced, the gender of "sheep" (as in "*unum*" or

---

[42] Cic. *de Orat.* 1.236 (*iurisconsultus . . . leguleius quidam cautus et acutus, praeco actionum, cantor formularum, auceps syllabarum*).

[43] Obsessions of lawyers: Cic. *Mur.* 25, *res enim sunt parvae, prope in singulis litteris atque interpunctionibus verborum occupatae*; cf. Sen. *Ben.* 6.5.3 and Strabo 12.2.9, "the Mazakenoi use the laws of Charondas, choosing also a law-chanter (νομῳδόν), who, like the νομικός among the Romans, is the *exegetes* of the laws," with Svenbro (1993) 117–20 for the equivalence of ἐξηγεῖσθαι and *praeire verba* here.

[44] Mechanics of reading aloud helped by interpunctuation, a Roman, not a Greek, habit, cf. Sen. *Ep.* 40.11 (*nos etiam cum scribimus, interpungere adsuevimus*), the indentation of paragraphs, and a Latin orthographic system that distinguished between long and short vowels, seen in papyri, summarized by Anderson *et al.* (1979) 129–34; esp. useful for texts that had to be read aloud correctly, cf. Wingo (1972) 16 and Habinek (1985) 44 ("Roman punctuation was . . . aimed at guiding clear and effective delivery"), *contra* Small (1997) 22. The early appearance of these forms of punctuation is noted by Müller (1964) 6–54. In a continuation or development of this system, Jerome (*in Is.* 1.1. lines 94–9 [Gryson]) introduced punctuation for the correct reading of sacred texts; Cassiodorus (*Inst. Div. Litt.* 1 pref. 9 and 1.12.4) described this system as helping the *simplices fratres . . . pronuntiare lectiones inculpabiter*, see Petrucci (1984) 603–4.

84   *The world of belief*

"more than one" *ovem*) had to be masculine to be a legal (*iusta*) fine.[45]
Recognized formulae for beginning a suit were still in existence in AD 342,
when they, "with the pitfalls which they set by their minute observance of
syllables," were finally decreed "amputated."[46] Correct language correctly
performed, despite the differences between *certa* and *concepta verba*, between the outmoded precision of the *legis actiones* and the greater flexibility
of the formulary system, was clearly still important – or at least speaking
incorrectly was always thought to present dangers. The continuing requirement for precise language correctly uttered within a ritualized context –
whether absolutely fixed or of one's own and the praetor's composition –
suggests that the focus on language and text was at the heart of procedure,
and the use of both must be extended backwards in time, to a very early
date, as well.[47]

Legis actio and *formula* are both terms used to describe Roman civil
procedure, that is, the procedure that governed the citizen's pursuit of resti-
tution for wrongs done and covered by law, both the law of the Twelve
Tables and that created by public assemblies. So-called "criminal" procedure, however – in cases brought by citizens either before the *populus* or
before specially created courts, *quaestiones* – was also initiated in a similar
way. The first of the standing *quaestiones*, that *de repetundis* established in
149 BC, followed the *legis actio* procedure.[48] Then or sometime thereafter,
it became either required or customary for the person bringing the accusation, an act called *nomen deferre*, "to bring in the name," to write his
accusation on a tablet and submit it to the correct magistrate.[49] This is almost certainly what Domitius Ahenobarbus was doing when he produced
(*edidit*) a *tabellam* against Silanus in 104 BC, accusing him before the people
of having fought against the Cimbri without the people's authorization.[50]

As with the fixed or flexible formulae of civil procedure, so here too the
form of the accusation had to follow the wording (and the requirements)

---

[45] Gel. 11.1.4 (*M. Varro verba haec legitime . . . concepit*).

[46] *CJ* 2.57(58).1 (AD 342), *iuris formulae aucupatione syllabarum insidiantes cunctorum actibus radicitus amputentur*.

[47] Most scholars endorse this careful adherence to correct language in formulary procedure, cf. Biscardi (1965); *contra*, Arangio-Ruiz (1950), who believed there was insufficient evidence; see now Bove (1979) 95–9 on the widespread use of writing on *tabulae* in formulary procedure. Virtually necessary: Schlossman (1907) 49–50 and (1972 [1905]) 24–38 argues merely very, very useful but not required.

[48] Jolowicz and Nicholas (1972) 311.

[49] *nomen deferre*: seen (although not signalled as new) in the *lex Acilia* of 123 BC, *CIL* 1.2² 583 (= *FIRA²* 1.84–102 no. 7) chapters 3, 4 and others; cf. Greenidge (1901) 461, 465–6 (discusses written charge, also called *inscriptio* or *inscribtio*, for which see also *CT* 9.1.8, 11, 14, and 19 [AD 366–423]). For previous "criminal" courts, of which little is known, see discussion in Jones (1972) 1–39.

[50] Asc. on Cic. *Corn.* 80.

Recitation from tablets

of the *lex* that had brought the specific *quaestio* into existence. As the jurist Paulus, writing in the early third century AD, explained in the case of adultery:[51]

Libellorum inscriptionis conceptio talis est. "consul et dies. apud illum praetorem vel proconsulem Lucius Titius professus est se Maeviam lege Iulia de adulteriis ream deferre, quod dicat eam cum Gaio Seio in civitate illa, domo illius mense illo, consulibus illis adulterium commisisse." utique enim est locus designandus est, in quo adulterium commissum est, et persona, cum qua admissum dicitur, et mensis: hoc enim lege Iulia publicorum cavetur et generaliter praecipitur omnibus, qui reum aliquem deferunt . . . quod si libelli inscriptionum legitime ordinati non fuerint, rei nomen aboletur et ex integro repetendi reum potestas fiet.

The arrangement of the form of *libelli* is as follows: 'Consul and date. L. Titius announces in the presence of some praetor or proconsul that he is bringing Maevia as defendant under the *lex Iulia* on adultery, stating that she has committed adultery with C. Seius in the *civitas* of "A," at the house of "B," in the month of "C," in the consulship of "D" and "E."' For there must certainly be set out the place in which the adultery was committed, the person with whom it is said to have taken place, and the month; for this is laid down by the *lex Iulia* on criminal proceedings and is a general requirement for those who bring a charge against another. . . . But if the documents are not set out in legal form (*legitime*), the *nomen* of the one charged is deleted, and there shall be power to renew the charge all over again.

These formal requirements of the accusation are referred to by Modestinus as *sollemnia*, and if there are mistakes, the case is dismissed, although the accuser is allowed to "renew the charge."[52] As the words *tabella* and *libellus* in the examples above suggest, the physical form of this accusation (called a *postulatio*, as in non-criminal proceedings)[53] was a tablet, although its material may have changed.[54] The emphasis in the evidence is

---

[51] Paulus: *D.* 48.2.3.1, cf. 47.1.3, 48.2.7 (called *subscriptio*); *CJ* 9.1.3 (*inscriptionum pagina*, AD 222), 9.1.10 (*sollemnibus . . . inscriptionibus*, AD 239), *CJ* 9.2.13 (*subscriptionis*, AD 383), *CJ* 9.2.15 (*per inscriptionem*, AD 390); on the relationship of *libelli* and *tabulae* see chapter two n.5 and below n.54.

[52] *D.* 48.2.18.

[53] *Postulatio* crosses between civil and criminal procedure, especially as the two begin to overlap in the imperial *cognitiones*, cf. (e.g.) the cases in Tac. *Ann.* 1.74.1 (*postulavit subscribente*), 3.10.1 (*postulavit*); in formulary procedure the *postulatio* was the charge, but took the form of a "request" to the praetor for a *iudex*. It too has "usual formulae," *formulas usitatas* (Cic. 2*Verr.* 2.147); for a general discussion of the multiple terms used (*accusare, postulare, nomen deferre, inscriptio*), see Mommsen (1899) 381–6.

[54] Form a tablet: Cass. Dio 37.41.2-4 (L. Vettius's δελτίον of accusation against Catilinarian conspirators, which he was, exceptionally, allowed to emend orally), Philostr. *VA* 4.44 (γραμματεῖον), and, at the beginning of his own consulship, Cassius Dio (76[77].16) reports 3,000 names charged with adultery ἐν τῷ πίνακι; can still be on a γραμματεῖον in late antiquity, Soz. *HE* 2.25.7. *libellus* is the standard imperial name for accusations of both the civil and criminal sort, cf. (e.g.) Tac. *Ann.* 3.44.2 or *D.* 2.13.1.1 (Ulpian, quoted above); none to my knowledge survives, but the material from which

86   *The world of belief*

on their written form, but such accusations were "spoken" or "recited" as well.[55]

Prayers, curses, and charges were not only written utterances, but utterances read out or read out and repeated; and they were not the only ones. Other examples of recited tablets, or recitation of entities known to be listed on tablets, also exist. The roster of the senate was recited,[56] as were men listed as judges in 123 BC[57] and *senatusconsulta*, these last two in *contiones*;[58] the *leges* of Rome's earliest treaty, according to Livy, were read "from tablets or wax" (*ex illis tabulis cerave recitata sunt*),[59] Cicero was able to read out Verres's provincial edict from his tablets (*ex ipsius tabulis... recitare possem*),[60] laws from the Twelve Tables were recited,[61] Scipio Africanus had planned to recite his financial accounts of the Asiatic campaign to the Senate,[62] and a will when opened was recited, making the heir the *recitatus heres*: the recitation from the tablet here performed the words of the testator and made a person the heir.[63] All are certain types of writing, created in a particular way to be used for a particular reason; and all are recited.

they were made changed over time, so that although they could be wooden tablets, πιττάκια (see chapter five n.63 and chapter seven n.68) in the high empire, by late antiquity, they are regularly if not uniformly made out of papyrus (*charta*), as in (e.g.) Palladius *Vit. Ioann. Chrys.* 6.85–6 (Malingrey, χάρτην... τὸν λίβελλον) or *P.Oxy.* 902 (*c.* AD 465) and *P.Oxy.* 1033 (AD 392), and the procedure that relied on them is called "libellary procedure." Tablets and *libelli* are still linked in Diocletian's price edict, where 100 lines of *scriptura libelli vel tabularum* cost ten *denarii*, col. 7 lines 40–1 (Lauffer [1971] 120).

[55] Sen. Rhet. *Suas.* 7.14 (*diceret*) and *Contr.* 9.5.11 (*tabellis signatis denuntiare*), Quint. *Inst.* 11.3.150 (advice), and Quint. *Decl.* 322 (Ritter 268 line 6; imaginary; these also *recitentur*), make clear that *postulationes* were spoken, cf. *P.Hamb.* 1.29.23 (παρήγγειλα καὶ ταβέλλας ἐσφράγι[σα, AD 91–6); *SB* 7558.14 (ἀναγνωσθέντος... βιβλιδίου); Aug. *con. Cresc.* 3.56.62 (*dicta*), 4.4.5 (*recitavit*), *PL* 43.529 and 43.549; Soz. *HE* 2.25.7 (γραμματεῖον ἀνεγινώσκετο).

[56] Senate: Liv. 9.30.1 (*lectione*), 23.23.5 (*recitatio... senatu*), 29.37.1 (*senatum recitaverunt*), Cic. *Dom.* 84 (*in recitando senatu*); a task of the censors, but not considered part of the census (Suolahti [1963] 53–6).

[57] *CIL* I² 583 line 15 (= *FIRA*² 1.84–102 no. 7, *recitentur in contione*).

[58] *Senatusconsulta*, e.g., Liv. 39.17.1 (*recitari... senatusconsulta iusserunt*), cf. the indentations and *vacats* attributed to the original of the *sc de Cn. Pisone patre* (which would have helped with reading out loud), Eck *et al.* (1996) 123, and Valette-Cagnac (1997) 237–41.

[59] Liv. 1.24.7; cf. Liv. 42.21.4, tribunes *rogationem... recitarunt*, Cic. *2Verr.* 5.50, *recitentur foedera*.

[60] Cic. *2Verr.* 3.26; cf. *Lex Irn.* 63, 66, 73, and chapter C for recitation of decurions' decrees.

[61] Cic. *Tul.* 47.1; cf. Weiß (1912) 218–20 n.1 with 223–4, examples of *leges*, legal decisions, and imperial constitutions recited in trials, with the proper Greek analogue of *recitare*, ἀναγιγνώσκειν, used regularly only in Greek sources of the Roman period.

[62] Gel. 4.18.7–12 (*libro, rationes... recitarentur*).

[63] Recited heir: Cic. *Caec.* 54; see also Tac. *Ann.* 12.69.3 (Claudius's will not recited, which was unusual, but *invidia* was feared); *D.* 34.8.1 (Julian); *D.* 48.10.2 (Paulus), reciting a false will part of the crime of forgery. Reciting the will also marked the moment at which a slave was freed, *D.* 31.1.11.1 (Pomponius), see Valette-Cagnac (1997) 177–80.

Recitation from tablets

THE POWER OF RECITATION

This type of reading was not, however, merely flat or mumbled "reading." It was not thought of as simply useful, or just the best way to get divine, demonic, or magisterial attention: rather, straighten your tie, clear your throat, and adopt a properly portentous demeanor. Recitation was a marked mode of expression to be used on deeply serious occasions, probably closer to intoning or even singing,[64] therefore also on occasions when you wanted to be taken deeply seriously. It was a distinctive style of performance that paralleled well the distinctive language used, and conveyed the importance of the occasion by lifting it out of the everyday.

This distinctive seriousness was also conveyed by the authority of the tablets themselves, as is evident from several striking examples. Late in his short reign in the year AD 69, the emperor Vitellius contemplated abdication, and announced his decision to do so to the assembled soldiers, who protested so vehemently that he changed his mind. The next day, however, more flabbily determined than before, he returned to the rostra, this time wearing mourning, and in tears declared his abdication from a *libellus*. The soldiers still refused to let him abdicate, but clearly they were not meant to. Such a recitation from a written text was meant to impress upon them the seriousness of the occasion and, therefore, the strength and conclusiveness of the message – even, or perhaps especially, from someone as notoriously weak-willed as Vitellius. But they neither respected his – the emperor's! – wish, nor heeded the marked and solemn method he chose to convey it.[65]

Perhaps Vitellius was also harking back to the practice of Augustus who, when he finally denounced his adulterous daughter Julia publicly, did so through a *libellus* recited by a quaestor to the senate.[66] The expected seriousness of the acts of these emperors was well foreshadowed in a dramatic act of Tiberius Sempronius Gracchus, tribune himself and father of the famous tribune. Sometime in the 180s BC, he vetoed an action of his fellow-tribunes

---

[64] A musical component would also reinforce the analogy with formal language in other cultures, Bloch (1989 [1974]) 23; cf. Cicero's characterization of the jurisconsult (above n.42) as a *praeco* or *cantor*, and Polybius's characterization of Roman religious acts as declaimed or sung, ἐκτετραγῴδηται (6.56.8). Valette-Cagnac (1997) 158–9 draws a strong contrast between *recitatio* and *cantare*, but does not consider legal evidence.

[65] Suet. *Vit.* 15.2-3, *e libello testatus est*; Tiberius's testamentary dispositions read out in the Senate, but not heeded, Cass. Dio 59.1.3.

[66] Augustus's denunciation of Julia, Suet. *Aug.* 65.2.3. Cicero's exile had also been *recitaretur* in the Senate, although it is not clear what from (Cic. *Red. Sen.* 4); his speech after return *dicta de scripto est* (*Planc.* 74) "because it was so important" (Russell [1998] 35 and n.39); Russell also emphasizes that panegyrics and speeches on ceremonial occasions were read out.

88 *The world of belief*

arresting Lucius Scipio, brother of Africanus, by reciting a decree from a tablet (*ex tabula recitavit*). In doing so, he was acting against his own prejudices, for he was a violent personal enemy of Africanus and had sworn an oath to this effect right before reading. But Gracchus wanted to emphasize, in the most formal and solemn way possible, the final and implacable force of his opposition to Lucius Scipio's arrest. Coming from a man with religious scruples and an eye for correct procedure, this was a powerful way of delivering a powerful statement.[67]

Since a tablet was final and authoritative, and since reading from it was in itself final and authoritative, its recitation compelled, or was expected to compel, respect and silence, belief and obedience. For these reasons, recitation from tablets was the standard way of conveying a Roman governor's decision in a provincial court case, as can be seen in both Christian martyr-acts[68] and the inscribed resolutions of boundary disputes.[69] As Apuleius describes it: "the proconsul...speaks with moderate voice and, sitting, with frequent pauses often reads from a *tabella*. For the garrulous voice of the crier is the voice of a hired servant; the proconsular *tabella*, however, is a judgment (*sententia*) which, once read, may not have one letter added to it or taken away..."[70] In Seneca's *Pumpkinification of Claudius*, Augustus pronounces severe judgment on Claudius in a meeting of the senate of

---

[67] Reciting: Gel. 6.19.6–7. Ti. Sempronius Gracchus (*RE* 53) was responsible for invalidating his successors in the consulship, for he remembered after the fact that he had not taken one set of auspices when he recrossed the line of the *pomerium*, at the time of their election (Cic. *ND* 2.11): Cicero calls him *vir sapientissimus atque... omnium praestantissimus* for this.

[68] Musurillo (1972) 88, *Acta Scill. Mart.* 14; 162, *Acta Pion.* 20 (in Latin); 172, *Acta Cyp.* 4; 286 and 290–2, *Acta Agap. Iren. Chion.* 4, 6 (papyrus); 306, *Acta Crisp.* 4 (*de libello*), 318, *Acta Eup.* 3; several also have subsequent announcement by herald. Cf. *SB* 9016 (AD 160, from a *pinax*), Tert. *Apol.* 2.20, *de tabella recitatis*, Possidius *Vit. Aug.* 12 (pronounced by written judgment); *CT* 4.17.1–5 (AD 374–86) and *CJ* 7.44.1–3 (mid-third century to AD 374) link *libelli* and *recitare*, and *CT* 11.30.40 (AD 383), where it is now legally required that judges read written sentences from *libelli*; Agathias *Hist.* 4.11.2; *sententiam per tabellam*, Cic. 2*Verr.* 4.104.

[69] Boundary-decisions, *CIL* 3.567 (Domitianic) and 586 (Hadrianic), from Delphi and Lamia, *decreta ex tabellis recitata*, in 567 left off the Greek translation; *CIL* 2.4125 (AD 193), from Tarraco (*decretum ex tilia* [lime-tree wood] *recitavit*); early forerunners of this may be Polyb. 30.32.9, senate writing out *apokrisis* to appeal of Achaeans, and *CIL* 1² 584 (= *CIL* 5.7749, *FIRA*² 3.504–9 no. 163; 117 BC), the *sententia* of the Minucii in a boundary dispute, on a bronze tablet (as a result of the dispute *cognoverunt... composeiverunt... dixerunt*, then *sententiam ex senatus consulto dixerunt* [sic] in Rome); *CIL* 2827 (= *FIRA*² 3.509–10 no. 164; late first century AD), *sententiam dixit* in a *compromissum* over boundaries, also *CIL* 10.676 (Antoninus Pius), *sententia dicta*.

[70] Apul. *Flor.* 9.11–12 (Hunink), *proconsul ipse moderata voce... et sedens loquitur et plerumque de tabella legit, quippe praeconis vox garrula ministerium est, proconsulis autem tabella sententia est, quae semel lecta neque augeri littera una neque autem minui potest...*; according to Sen. Rhet. *Contr.* 7.8.7, a judge *tabellam* (of sentence) *revocare non potest*. This is in contrast to Greek practice, where even the conclusion that the magistrate pronounced the verdict has been challenged by Thür (1987).

Recitation from tablets 89

the gods by reciting from a tablet (*ex tabella recitavit*) in suitably formal, legalistic language, as Claudius himself had done in life.[71]

Such solemn authoritativeness granted to this form of reading from this type of physical object could and did prompt imitation in those looking to borrow authority for their words, or looking to graft a new tradition on to an old and prestigious one. Thus Cato the Elder had one of his speeches recorded on *tabulae* not because other forms of writing material were not available or because speeches were regularly recorded on tablets in his day, but because this speech was a contribution he wished to be understood as both perfect and permanent. He then had some parts of this speech recited when he was giving another speech (*On His Expenses*): he knew that his audience would attribute to those recited words a special significance. But he startled his audience: "ignore that," he said, of the recited account of his own actions, "they don't want to hear that." Another part – "erase that also, they don't want to hear that; keep going." Another – "erase that too – there's nothing they'd rather hear less than that." Yet more – "erase that down to the wood!" And so on. "You see to what pass the state has come, when I do not dare to mention my beneficent acts to the state, for which I wished to receive gratitude, lest it be a source of *invidia*?" Cato makes his grandstanding, self-serving point not only through the rhetorical device of *praeteritio*, but also by playing with his audience's expectation that *tabulae* were authoritative and untouchable, and that their recitation was to drive home authoritative points.[72]

Over three hundred years later, Marcus Aurelius *recitavit* his own *oratio* – most likely on a tablet, although this is not stated – to the praetorian guard, on whom he was conferring privileges.[73] What Cato the Elder did at least partly for self-dramatizing effect, this very serious emperor did as a matter of what was by now correctness, for preceding emperors since the time of Augustus had grafted all their words, not just those that followed the forms of accusations or magisterial edicts, on to this tradition of authoritative writing and recitation.[74] In the third and fourth centuries AD, imperial edicts or any type of *basilika grammata* were not only recited, but were to

---

[71] Sen. *Apoc.* 11; Claudius, Suet. *Claud.* 15.3 (*ex tabella pronuntiasse*).

[72] Cato, *ORF*⁴ 173 (*noli recitare* [following Query's conjecture] . . . *nihil <e>o minus volunt dici . . . ne invidiae siet*; from his speech on having made a *sponsio* with M. Cornelius), quoted as an example of παραλείψεως by Fro. *Ep. Ant. Imp.* 1.2.11; at 173.3, *recitavit*.

[73] Marcus Aurelius, *FV* 195, discussed as law by Ulpian; cf. Valette-Cagnac (1997) 213–16, 223–35.

[74] Augustus, Suet. *Aug.* 84.2 and above n.66. Although sources do not always make clear what imperial pronouncements are being read from, the subsequent treatment of such pronouncements identify them as *tabulae*: Augustus's *res gestae* on *aeneis tabulis* on his mausoleum, Suet. *Aug.* 101.4 (and note that the copy of the *res gestae* in Ankara has seven different types of punctuation, Wingo [1972] 29–49, 132; these assist with recitation, see above n.44); Claudius's speech affirming the civic rights

90   *The world of belief*

be listened to by an audience that had risen to its feet, uncovered its heads, become absolutely silent, and was feeling reverence, awe, and fear. John Chrysostom instructs that the Bible is to be listened to in the same way:

A profound silence reigns when those [imperial] rescripts are read. There is not the slightest noise; every one listens most attentively to the orders contained in them. Whoever makes the slightest noise, thereby interrupting the reading, runs the greatest danger. All the more should one stand with fear and trepidation . . . in order to understand the contents of what is read to you [from the Bible].

Imperial pronouncements were to be delivered much as prayer was, and holy writing was to be received with the reverence granted to both.[75] Recitation could please the divine ear or compel the humble one. By using tablets and recitation, these men asserted or implied *auctoritas* for forms of speaking that had traditionally not been considered authoritative, like mere speeches. And since, unlike Cato the Elder, emperors truly did "exceed all others in *auctoritas*,"[76] their use of this form of performance rapidly came to be seen as appropriate rather than merely a curious but crowd-pleasing rhetorical stunt. In this way, emperors inserted themselves into the ceremonial language, and the language of ceremonial, at Rome; and predictably enough, the popular reaction was to hear and read the emperors' words, in all its forms, as law.[77]

of Gallic Romans inscribed on bronze tablets and nailed up on the wall of their curia in Lyons, *CIL* 13.1668 (= *ILS* 212); Nero reads (ἀναγνούς) a speech written by Seneca to the praetorians and a similar one to the Senate (ἀνέγνω), and the senate votes that the latter be engraved ἐς ἀργυρᾶν στήλην and read out (ἀναγινώσκεσθαι) each time new consuls entered office, Cass. Dio 60(61).3.1. Plin. *Pan.* 75.2 notes that *orationes* of *principes* had customarily been *mandari aeternitati* by inscription on bronze; in early third century, "letters sealed in folded tablets" (κατασεσημασμένα γράμματα ἐν πτυκτοῖς πίναξι) were customarily used by emperors wishing to send private letters, Herod. 7.6.5; see Basil *contra Sab.* 22 (*PG* 31.608, βασιλέα λέγων τὸν ἐν τῷ πίνακι); and above n.16 for *codicilli* of appointment.

[75] Imperial γράμματα: John Chrys. *Homilia in Genesim* 14.2 (*PG* 53.112), quoted and trans. Lieberman (1944–5) 7–8, who adduces earlier parallels in Rabbinic writings (also 9–10, kissing the edicts); a veteran *recitasserit* an edict of Octavian's in *CPL* 103 (= *BGU* 2.628, AD 37–40), for what purpose and in what context, unclear; in Sen. Rhet. *Contr.* 10.pr.8 a rescript is *recitatum*; for other examples see Weiß (1912) 217–24, and Mourgues (1987) 80–1 n.17, 85 on the official character of the *recitatio* of the imperial subscript at the end of the *lex Irnitana*. This power of recitation may also be employed in the Christian habit of reciting miracle accounts from *libelli*, Aug. *Civ. Dei.* 22.8.20–1, *Serm.* 322 (*PL* 38. 1443–5).

[76] Augustus *Res Gestae* 34 (Brunt and Moore), *auctoritate omnibus praestiti*.

[77] Insertion into ritual: Laurence (1993) and Beard *et al.* (1998) 181–210. Words as law: see Mourgues (1987) 87 and Peachin (1996) 17–33, who makes clear that although in general the jurists did not explicitly include imperial *orationes*, *interlocutiones de plano*, *mandata*, and *sententiae* among the imperial *constitutiones* that were a source of law, popular (and some juristic opinion) did: "the opinion that an imperial pronouncement of any sort could be legally binding was held widely, and from early on, by experts and laymen alike" (18).

CHAPTER 5

Tablets and efficacy

Recitation from tablets was a distinctive and authoritative form of reading, as tablets themselves were a distinctive and authoritative form of writing. As was clear from the descriptions of prayers and curses, the contexts of recitation could be very distinctive too – complex, detailed, and ceremonial. Such was also true of a number of different acts not yet examined in detail, like the taking of the census, or the making of treaties, laws, and vows and dedications. All of these intricate ceremonial acts, interesting in themselves and for the way tablets are recited in them, also point to the most important aspect of tablets, that they were not merely used or useful but were considered to have an active role in establishing or changing something about the world, be it the composition of the citizen body or relations between states, men, or men and the supernatural: tablets, as will be seen, could be involved in the creation of, as well as embodiments of, a new, newly fixed reality. What these ceremonies were to achieve, their tablets were seen also to achieve, and this is the final characteristic that identifies tablets as members of the same family. Tablets and their words, and the human actions associated with them, are essential components of these multi-stage, complex, "unitary" rituals to be discussed here, rituals of a type found outside Roman culture as well;[1] their oral, gestured, and written aspects, performed in time and existing out of time, must all work together to make a desired action real.

The precise relationship of act to *tabula* is, in these cases, more difficult to grasp than the one described in the preceding chapter. To recite a prayer or curse from a tablet (or to have it repeated by a magistrate or magician's customer) is to use a tablet as a template for the spoken words of an action. On the other hand, if, instead of being already in existence, a tablet was generated or activated in the process of a ceremony, it was both result

---

[1] E.g., Indians' rituals for land possession and reclamation in Colombia, Digges and Rappaport (1993) 150: "... words, acts, and images all come together here to form a signifying system ... It is the unity of words, acts, and images in a particular context or event that gives ... meaning."

91

92   *The world of belief*

and part of it. Such a *tabula* was also not merely the memorandum of an action; rather, these *tabulae*, created or animated through ceremony, help to generate, express, and embody the achievement of that action's end. The creation of what the *tabula* represents, and thus also the *tabula* itself, is the point of the action. The tablet can be thought of as symbolizing the action, but only if action and tablet are understood to coexist.

This functional role taken by a tablet manifests itself in a number of different actions. Recitation from tablets, as described, was especially associated with acts – prayers, curse-tablets, Roman legal procedure – whose ultimate outcome would be determined by other parties, be they gods, demons, or magistrates. The creation of tablets as a significant act in itself was a crucial part of ceremonies of essentially human, or less petitionary, interaction (pages 92–107): the taking of the census; the establishment of treaties; the enactment of laws and edicts; the fulfillment of vows; and the successful cursing of another human. In two cases (pages 107–12), the drawing-up of accounts and the making of *senatusconsulta*, there was not even a clear ceremonial context: in these cases, the creation of the *tabula* completed and embodied the act itself.

Tablets themselves therefore come to exist in a spectrum that stretches from the actively participatory (recitation of a set formula in prayer) to the constitutive (accounts and *senatusconsulta*). Legal *tabulae* (pages 112–20) belong somewhere in the middle of this spectrum. Couched in performative language, they were created in and part of a multi-part ceremony, a "unitary" act in which all components (including the construction of the tablet) had to be correctly performed for the action to be valid. Here in these "unitary" acts, the similarities in how tablets work will again be demonstrated to suggest the membership of legal tablets in this larger group of *tabulae*. As a consequence, these tablets should be understood, as they were understood by contemporaries, not only as *being* like other tablets in form, character, language, and style, as has been demonstrated, but also as *being efficacious* – generative and symbolic – in the ways that these other tablets were. In chapter two, all tablets were described as special, as characteristically final and authoritative; this chapter describes why they could be so, by looking at their roles in "unitary" and constitutive acts.

"UNITARY" ACTS

(a) The Roman census. The Roman census existed only on tablets, creating and ordering the entity known as the citizen-body through the generation of *tabulae.* The census not only listed Roman citizens; it was the only regular

Tablets and efficacy 93

way in which a man's citizen-status could be established until the time of Augustus. By the censors' first looking over the earlier census and then making, on various tablets, a new list (through asking people a series of questions under oath, the *formula census*), a very special and powerful list was generated. It placed a man in a Roman hierarchy, based on not only property but also moral character, age, *familia*, and physical characteristics – based, in short, on the public opinion that the censors served and embodied. People's status, and thereby their very legal existence, depended on their being listed.[2] If you, although free, had refused to be registered in the census, the state could and would sell you as someone who had himself repudiated his free status; slaves listed in the census thereby gained their freedom.[3] Having a censorial *nota* put beside your name, or being erased from one *tabula* and moved to another, conferred *ignominia*, literally "a bad *nomen*,"[4] a mark of shame. Being moved to the tablet of the *aerarii* deprived you of the right to vote, itself referred to by Livy as the loss of *civitas* and *libertas*.[5] Your existence as a Roman of the Republic depended on your existence in the census.

When exactly the complex sequence of actions known as the census was complete, what marked the precise moment when status could be, or was, altered, was debated even in antiquity. The ceremony itself ended with a lustration (*lustrum*) and the driving of a nail into the wall of a temple.[6] Cicero asked whether the act of writing or the *lustrum* marked the moment when the census became real: "cannot there be controversy, when it is asked whether a slave is free when by the wish of his master he has been enrolled in the census (*census sit*), or when the *lustrum* has

---

[2] Census: Mommsen (1969 [1887]) II.359–415, Suolahti (1963) 32–52, Nicolet (1980) 48–88; "regular" way, Nicolet (1980) 65. Proof of citizen-status, Cic. *Arch.* 11 (arguing against, but clearly an uphill battle); oath, Gel. 4.20.3; criteria asked, Dion. Hal. 4.15.6, *CIL* 1.2² 593 lines 145–50 = *FIRA*² 1.140–52 no. 13 (provisions for census of Roman citizens outside of Rome, to be done with *publicas tabulas*). Importance of writing: Lemosse (1949) 177. General meaning of census, Nicolet (1980) 50, with Dumézil (1943) 188.

[3] Selling into slavery: paralleled in *lex Osca Tabulae Bantinae* chapter 4 (Vetter [1953] 13–28), a man beaten and his property confiscated; *G.*1.160; Dion. Hal. 4.15.6; slaves freed, Cic. *Caec.* 99, Daube (1946) 60.

[4] *Ignominia*: Pieri (1968) 113–22 (with further citations), *pace* Cicero, who protests too much against the importance of censorial *notae* (and censorial *subscriptiones*, which explained such *notae*), cf. *Cluent.* 119, 120–1, and 131; Asc. on Cic. *in Toga Cand.* 84, Gel. 4.20.6. Erasure: e.g., Zon. 8.6, Rufinus erased from list of senators for owning ten pounds of silver plate.

[5] Entered into the *tabulae Caerites* and made an *aerarius*, Ps.-Asc. on Cic. *Div. Caec.* 8 (Orelli); for *tabulae Caerites*, see Gel. 16.13.7, Hor. *Ep.* 1.6.62 (*Caerite cera*), Strabo 5.2.3 (εἰς τὰς δέλτους ... τὰς καιρετανῶν), Brunt (1971) 515–18; for meaning of *aerarius*, see Greenidge (1977 [1894]) 106–11. *Civitas* and *libertas*: Liv. 45.15.

[6] Complex ceremony described, Gargola (1995) 76–7; see 77–9 on the colonial census. Nail: Cass. Dio 55.10.4 (2 BC); Mommsen (1969 [1887]) II.413.

94 *The world of belief*

been completed?"[7] The question probably arose because, as Rome grew larger, entry onto tablets and the final ceremony came to be substantially separated in time.[8] Initially the two were not seen as separate enough to have their own identities: the so-called altar of Domitius Ahenobarbus, a late-second or first-century BC relief from the area of the Flaminian Circus in Rome, depicts these two elements of the census as equally important and as happening within one time frame, with emphasis on the entirety rather than on the elements. On the left, the citizen (with his own *tabulae* in hand) answers the questions put to him by the census-taker, who writes on his own (somewhat larger) *tabulae*; in the next group, to the right, the citizen is directed toward a census-class, thus actualizing artistically what had been done by tablets; to the right of these two groups, and occupying the rest of the panel, is the *lustrum* led by one of the censors. M. Torelli has called this type of arrangement paratactic rather than hypotactic, linked rather than narrated, with all the elements existing in asyndeton rather than subordination – despite the clear suitability of the subject for some sort of narrative depiction. All components exist together as a unity, and all are of equal weight.[9] Before Cicero, the census was a complex process, a process with multiple intertwined components, rather than one specific act or a series of specific acts. Moreover, the census in this relief is outside space and time: it is not depicted as any one particular census, but as *the* census.[10] At any given time there was only one in existence, correcting and replacing

---

[7] Cic. *de Orat.* 1.183 (*cum quaeritur, is, qui domini voluntate census sit, continuone, an ubi lustrum sit conditum, liber sit?*).

[8] Debate in antiquity: Liv. 1.44.1–2 (the census was *perfectus*, and then *censendo finis factus est* – the difference is obscure); Cass. Dio 54.28.4; Ps.-Dosithius 17 (*CGL* 3.55.48–56.24 and 3.107.27–46), restored in Mommsen (1969 [1887]) II.333 n.3 (*magna autem dissensio . . . utrum hoc tempore vires accipiunt omnia, in quo census [agitur] aut in eo tempore, in quo lustrum conditur: sunt enim qui existimant non alias vires accipere quae aguntur in censu nisi haec dies sequatur qua lustrum conditur; existimant enim censum descendere ad diem lustri, non lustrum [r]ecurrere ad diem census. quod ideo quaesitum est, quoniam omnia [quae] in censum aguntur lustro confirmantur*); cf. Mommsen (1969 [1887]) II.332–4, Pieri (1968) 82–6, and Wiseman (1969) 64–5.

[9] Altar: Torelli (1982) 5–16, esp. 11 ("the *census* and the *lustrum* . . . are . . . conceived and presented as contemporary actions"), 12–13 (gestures link two parts of relief together and *classis*-arrangement of the populace overlaps both parts, and "the relief signals only the difference in place and not the difference in time," 13), 126–8; see also Gruen (1992) 145–52 and Kuttner (1993). Kuttner (1991) has also identified a third-century predecessor that suggests a well-established visual tradition for the census. In the second-century AD province of Arabia, Babatha is still making her census-declaration on a tablet (πιτακίου, see below n.63) which, after being annotated in Latin, is posted on the basilica wall (*P.Yadin* 16, AD 127).

[10] The observation is Torelli's (1982) 128–9: even the armor that the figures wear appears "just as norms . . . and not as signs to orient the onlooker in time." Kuttner (1993) 212–13 argues that the "expressive 'awkwardness'" of its style was a stylistic analogue of the formal and archaizing language in which the census was performed, Gruen (1992) 152 that "the very archaic feel of the relief . . . gave the sense of a ceremony continuous with the antique past."

Tablets and efficacy

all others, created ceremonially on and through tablets, and embodied by them.

(b) Treaties. The creation of Roman treaties was another complex procedure, well established in the Republic, set but flexible: treaties "differ in their *leges*, but all are made the same way."[11] In the case that Livy wished to portray as being the earliest, between Rome and Alba Longa, fetial and king performed a ritual dialogue in which the king commanded the fetial to perform this task, provided him with the special herb or *sagmen*, and empowered him to speak for the Roman people. The terms (*leges*) of the treaty were read from "tablets or wax" and then an oath was sworn (making reference back to them) that "sanctioned the pact," in this case by the fetials, in other cases by magistrates (like consuls) on the spot. The Albans then did the same, according to their own customs. In some cases there was also question-and-answer oath, like "Do you bid me to make this pact?," with the appropriate acquiescent response.[12] At a later time, and when distance had become a problem, the senate and people would ratify the treaty that had been made before the oath was sworn.[13] A copy of the treaty would be engraved (often on a bronze tablet) and hung out on a temple in Rome and (usually) in some location important to the other party to the treaty as well.[14] Thus, again, a multi-step procedure, with writing on tablets used once or possibly twice – in the case of Rome's earliest treaty there is no mention of a final inscription, and in all but one other case there is no mention of a preliminary recitation, although some formal exchange of terms before oath and ratification is likely.[15]

---

[11] Quotation, Liv. 1.24.3 (*foedera alia aliis legibus, ceterum eodem modo omnia fiunt*); the antiquarian Claudius plays the role of fetial, Suet. *Claud.* 25.2; Wiedemann (1986) 484–90 (includes parallels to legal practice); and cf. *AE* 1948.241 (a fetial in a third-century AD epitaph). Procedure in general, e.g., Liv. 9.5.1–6 (ratification of people, fetials, and *caeremonia . . . sollemni* necessary), with Mommsen (1969 [1887]) 1.246–57, Alföldi (1959) 22 (spear), Walbank (1979) 116–17 (on oath and treaty).

[12] Earliest, Liv. 1.24.3–9 (*ex illis tabulis cerave*); cf. Magdelain (1990) 714–19, who distinguishes between the *foedus* of the fetials and the *sponsio* of the general. Making reference back to *leges* in oath, Heuß (1934) 22. *Sagmen* still being used in 201 BC in Africa, Liv. 30.43.9. Oaths sworn by magistrates: Polyb. 21.43, Liv. 38.39.1, *IGR* 4.33 (25 BC). Question-and-answer: Liv. 1.38.2, *G.* 3.92, Mommsen (1969 [1887]) 1.247. In AD 363, a treaty is still concluded *verbis . . . conceptis*, Amm. Marc. 25.9.11.

[13] Ratification (or its invalidating absence): Polyb. 1.17.1, 1.62.8–63.3, 6.14.10, 18.42.1–4, 21.17.9, 21.32.1 (then treaty quoted), 21.41.10–43.3 (treaty quoted); Liv. 9.5.1, 32.23.2.

[14] Engraving on bronze: Polyb. 3.26.1, Memnon *FGH* 3B 434 F18.16 (p. 350), Cic. *Balb.* 53, Liv. 2.33.9 (*columna aenea*; cf. Dion. Hal. 6.95.2), App. *Syr.* 39, Jos. *AJ* 14.188 (includes honors as well, still on Capitoline), 14.197; and see below n.16 for epigraphical examples. Who decided where (outside Rome) the treaty was to be posted is disputed, Edmondson (1993) 179–80.

[15] Exchange of terms, Polyb. 15.8.7 (203/2 BC) and 29.3.6. Ceremony also when treaty received, see *SIG*³ 694 = *IGR* 4.1692, prayers, sacrifice, holiday, and procession (129 BC). There are also parallels with *deditio*: cf. Nörr (1989) 28–9, and Liv. 1.38.2 (formulaic words), Val. Max. 6.5.1b (use of writing), Hölkeskamp (2000) 237–48 (gestures part of act); and Liv. 36.28.1–36.29.1 with Polyb. 20.9–10 and

96   *The world of belief*

Having a *foedus* written on tablets was, therefore, and was believed to be, a necessary and very ancient part of the making of a treaty. Of the nine epigraphically preserved treaties, four make in the text of the treaty itself provisions for inscribing on bronze tablets,[16] while three of these, and one other, stipulate in their terms that all later changes made needed to be written down to be valid. Instructions for inscribing are common in ancient treaties, but the clause that insists that any changes desired must be made in writing is not: this appears to be a Roman custom, and is phrased in the imperative.[17] Thus a treaty's inscription, although not its specific engraving on bronze, was integral to the fact of treaty itself; its terms could not change without the written instrument changing as well.[18]

The most important modern study of Greek and Roman treaties, A. Heuß's, asked two very legalistic questions: which elements of this process were actually necessary, and what was the role of the document? He concluded that only the oath was necessary, not inscription or even ratification; and as for the document, it was only, at best, proof. These answers were, for the Roman material, incorrect, because he used Greek evidence to draw conclusions about Roman practice; but he was also off the mark because he was pursuing the wrong train of thought. Like Cicero's question about the census, Heuß's questions about treaties attempted to dissect an act that, although occurring necessarily in and over time, was essentially a unity in which the creation of a tablet was important, and seen as complete only

---

Eckstein (1995), the Aetolian *deditio* of 191 BC, which the consul was persuaded to invalidate because of perceived formal defects.

[16] Astypalaea (*IGR* 4.1028), Callatis (above chapter three n.8), and Cibyra (*OGIS* 762) mention engraving in bronze, as do Maroneia (*SEG* 1985.823), *SIG*³ 694 = *IGR* 4.1692 (provisions for erecting bronze πίνακα of treaty in an Attalid city), and *IG* 4² 1.63 (provisions for erecting ἐν πίνακι χαλκέῳ at Epidaurus). The treaties with Methymna (*SIG*³ 693 = *IGR* 4.2), Aetolia (*IG* 9(1)² 241), the Thyrrienses (*SIG*³ 732), Cnidos (Täubler [1913] 450–1), and Mytilene (*IGR* 4.33) are all incomplete at the very end, where this provision occurs in the others. Bauman (1986) 89–91 notes that there are also no Greek parallels for significant aspects of Roman treaties like the *maiestas* clause.

[17] Writing down later changes in treaties is *sane contra Graecum morem* (*SIG*³ 693 n.4), found in Methymna, Astypalaea, Callatis, and Cibyra (see preceding note); also in literary accounts, e.g., Polyb. 21.42.27, Dion. Hal. 6.95.2 (possibly fictitious, but if so modelled clearly on Augustan practice); imperatives, e.g., ἐξέστω ... ἐκτὸς ἔστω (Methymna lines 19–20, Astypalaea, lines 46–7, Cibyra lines 10–12); *liceto* (Callatis line 11). It is not found in the early Roman/Carthaginian treaties, which are not quoted in their entirety and are cast in Carthaginian form, Walbank (1957) 338, 341, 346.

[18] Accompanying *senatusconsulta* instruct the persons who are to engrave, which implies that the formulae of a treaty (including that necessity for inscription) and therefore the definition of a treaty were fixed by tradition and could not be expanded to include additional instructions. Such *senatusconsulta* exist for Astypalaea and Mitylene, and are referred to in a decree of an Attalid city (*SIG*³ 694 = *IGR* 4.1692 lines 25–30); cf. also Reynolds (1982) 61, 90–1 no. 8 lines 90–2 and Jos. *AJ* 12.416–18, "the senate made a decree about this [the treaty with the Jews] and sent a copy to Judaea, while the original was engraved on bronze tablets and placed on the Capitol."

Tablets and efficacy

97

when that tablet was made and posted.[19] Peace or truce, or an informal alliance based on *amicitia*, or even joint action based on the same, you could have without a tablet, but not a formal treaty.[20] Thus, for example, in the case of the Romans' first treaty with the Aetolians in 211 BC, the inscribing of the treaty and its posting (in Rome, on the Capitol; for the Aetolians, at Olympia) occurred two years after the event. "This [delay] did not hinder active measures (*rebus gerendis*)" on the part of the allies against Philip V, said Livy, since they also had a friendly understanding, but clearly he felt that this act of inscribing had to be mentioned: it was part of what was understood to be the process, embodied its terms and therefore the entire notion of treaty, and brought that process of treaty-making to completion.[21]

(c) Laws. The creation of laws – public *leges* (including *plebiscita*), edicts of magistrates, and eventually *senatusconsulta* – although following an even more complicated procedure, also involved the creation of *tabulae* which formally determined, and gave concrete existence to, what had been decreed or decided. Here too, many steps needed to be performed correctly for a law to "be" a law. The procedure was as follows.[22] A magistrate wishing to introduce a law would draft it and post it on tablets for three *nundinae* (twenty-four days), during which time interested parties could copy it; this was called *promulgari*, "to make known." During this time the proposed law could be discussed in non-voting assemblies called *contiones*.[23] The law, depending on the office or inclination of the proposer, could be voted on in either the *comitia centuriata* or the *concilium plebis*.[24] Procedure in the *comitia centuriata* was the more complicated and ceremonial. Before this

---

[19] Heuß (1934); he argued that the absence of a consistent diplomatic vocabulary and signatures of parties ruled out the possibility that documents "were" the treaty, but the evidence for the first point is drawn only from Greek materials and the second point is an anachronistic importation. See also, against the conflation of Greek and Roman, Lonis (1980) and Bauman (1986) 85–91.

[20] Note that Fest. 113M on *inlitterata pax* does not apply, for *pax* not the same as *foedus*; the latter marked out people who had a "written peace" (εἰρήνη . . . ἔγγραπτος) with Rome, and whose status was more protected, in Rome's second treaty with Carthage (Polyb. 3.24.6). Military action on the basis of *amicitia* alone is well known, see (e.g.) Eckstein (1999) 403–4.

[21] Aetolians, Liv. 26.24.8–15; the treaty was posted on the Capitol at Rome *ut testata sacratis monumentis*. There are parallels in Roman declarations of war: "but if any of these things were omitted, neither the Senate nor the people had the power to vote for war," Dion. Hal. 2.72.9.

[22] For standard descriptions, see (e.g.) Mommsen (1969 [1887]) III.369–413; Rotondi (1922 [1912]) 137–48; Taylor (1966) *passim*.

[23] Posting on tablets: Cic. *Sest.* 72; Cass. Dio 42.32.3 (taken down, effectively bringing the process to an end); Augustus posts "laws" he wishes approved by the Senate ἐν λευκώμασι in the Senate house and allows senators to read them two at a time, in imitation of this procedure (Cass. Dio 55.4.1). Three *nundinae*: CIL 1.2² 581 line 15 = *FIRA*² 1.240–1 no. 30; debate over what this means, Rotondi (1922 [1912]) 125 n.3. Copy: Cic. *Agr.* 2.13, *Dom.* 41. *Promulgari*: Fest. 224M; Cic. *Leg.* 3.11; cf. Wesener (1962).

[24] Different assemblies: see Watson (1974) 6–20.

98   *The world of belief*

assembly was called, the auspices were taken; the assembly was announced
by the blowing of horns, by the *accensus* (clerk) of the magistrate calling
the people *in licium* (to the place of assembly) while walking around the
walls, and by the raising of a red flag on the Janiculum and the placement
of a guard there. There was then the reading of a *carmen precationis* and a
sacrifice.[25] Finally the law itself would be read by a herald, an act known
as *recitatio*.[26] The presiding magistrate then would ask the populace, *velitis
iubeatis, uti . . . vos Quirites rogo* ("do you wish do you order, that . . . I ask
you, Quirites"), to which the answer was *uti rogas* ("as you ask," i.e. "yes") or
antiquo ("I vote the previous," i.e. "I reject") – answers which after 131/30 BC
were determined by balloting (on *tabellae*) and announced by the herald.[27]
At this point, modern accounts of Republican law-making stop: at this
point, here and in the other assemblies (where procedure was simpler, but
still included the taking of auspices, the *carmen*, the reading, and the ritual
question-and-answer), a law is thought to be a law.[28]

To end the process here, however, is the result of looking at it from the
wrong perspective. No ancient source actually says what all the necessary
steps were to make a law, only that the omission of this or that step, or
this or that horrific occurrence, was ruinous: if a *lex* was being voted on
in the centuriate assembly but a bad portent was sighted, the red flag on
the Janiculum fell down, or a voter had an epileptic fit, the process was
ruined and no law ensued.[29] Moreover, a law that was not approved by

[25] Auspices: Cass. Dio 54.24.1; Var. *L.* 6.91; Fest. 113M. Horns: Var. *L.* 6.91–2. Flag: Liv. 39.15.11 (see
Rotondi (1922 [1912]) 138 n.4 for further references). *Carmen:* Liv. 39.15.1 (even for a *contio*); Rotondi
(1922 [1912]) 139 n.2.

[26] Announcement by herald: Mommsen (1969 [1887]) III.386 nn.3–5; Riepl (1913) 331. Recitation of
law: Dion. Hal. 7.17.4 (mythical times); Cic. *Leg.* 3.11; Asc. on Cic. *Corn.* 60–1 (tribune reading out
his own text, *codicem*, something never done before), cf. Cic. *Cluent.* 91 (quoted, Quint. *Inst.* 8.6.55)
and Quint. *Inst.* 5.13.18, praetor and tribune have *leges* in *codices*; App. *BC* 1.12 (reading forbidden),
Plut. *Cat. Min.* 28 (proposer himself reads, then when text taken away, starts to repeat by heart),
Cic. *Vat.* 5, *Phil.* 1.2–4, *Rab. Post.* 14, *Agr.* 2.10–13; Valette-Cagnac (1997) 181–208. Mommsen (1969
[1887]) III.391 and n.3 thought (on the basis of Asc. on Cic. *Corn.* 58: *praeco subiciente scriba verba
legis recitare populo coepit*) that a *scriba* read and the herald then recited; this is possible.

[27] Question-and-answer: Gel. 5.19.9; Mommsen (1969 [1887]) III.312 n.2 knows no other form. Ballots:
e.g., Cic. *Att.* 1.14.5; used also subsequently in provinces, *lex Malacitana* chapter 61 lines 47–50
(*CIL* 2.1964 = *FIRA*² 1.208–19 no. 24; Spain), and possibly Gaul, Williamson (1987b) 184, 186.
Announcement of voting results: *lex Malacitana* chapter 56 (by herald); Cic. *2Verr.* 5.15. Of elections:
Cic. *Mur.* 1 means that the herald announced on his, Cicero's, behalf; censors, Gel. 12.8.6; consuls,
Cic. *Agr.* 2.4; aediles, Var. *R.* 3.17.1.

[28] Procedure in other assemblies: Cic. *Fam.* 7.30.1 (auspices); Var. *R.* 3.2.1–3.17.10 *passim*; Cass.
Dio 54.24.1; Wieacker (1988) 406 and Gargola (1995) 53–4. End: Mommsen (1969 [1887]) III.413;
Frederiksen (1965) 184; Small (1997) 56; *contra*, Williamson (1983) 132.

[29] Invalidating factors: Wieacker (1988) 398 n.46. Auspices, Cic. *Phil.* 5.10 (and 5.7–8 generally); Asc.
on Cic. *Corn.* 69; Quint. *Inst.* 2.4.34. Flag: Cass. Dio 37.27.3–37.28.4, interpreted by Millar (1998) 16
as demonstrating that the flag was flown "at least until the third century AD." Epilepsy: Fest. 234M.

Tablets and efficacy 99

the senate was also no law, although after 339 BC senatorial approval was usually sought before the magistrate convened the assembly.[30] But there are two specific reasons to think that the process as properly conceived did not culminate merely in the herald's announcement of the voting results, but needed to proceed through to the inscribing and posting of the final version. First, the further stage of inscribing or posting is well attested, and most scholars would even go so far as to say that it was common;[31] second, destroying or taking down posted, inscribed tablets was believed to repeal the law. By taking down Clodius's tablet – the plebiscite that necessitated Cicero's exile – Cicero was believed to be enacting the repeal of Clodius's law. It took Cicero two tries, too – on the first occasion, Clodius's brother Gaius, a praetor, reclaimed them, but the second time Clodius was away, and Cicero was successful.[32] His defense was that it should be taken down because it (and others like them) was not law, because (he insisted) Clodius's holding of the tribunate had been illegal. This justification was not embraced, but the cancellation of the law was understood.[33] When edicts of citizenship came down on Caesar's orders in 45 BC, it was understood that the status they had conferred was cancelled.[34] Removal was concrete action and serious business.[35] The melting of bronze tablets by lightning was therefore an extremely dire portent, causing great alarm: the divine

[30] Senatorial approval: Wieacker (1988) 399 nn.52–4; Schiller (1978) 234–5, 240; Schwind (1973) 54 n.3; *contra*, Jolowicz and Nicholas (1972) 27.

[31] Inscribing and posting common: Jolowicz and Nicholas (1972) 28; Williamson (1987a) 173 ("regularly," even "routinely" after the second century BC); Crawford (1996) 1.25–7 gives references. This acknowledged in the *lex Licinia de legumlatione* of 62 BC, see *Schol. Bob.* on Cic. *Sest.* 135 (this does not refer to preliminary posting, cf. Schiller [1978] 241; also Cic. *Vat.* 33, *Att.* 2.9.1, 4.16.5, *Phil.* 5.8), and Sisenna fr. 117 (Peter), *perseveraverunt uti lex perveniret ad quaestorem* [at the aerarium] *ac iudices quos vellent instituerent*; Suet. *Jul.* 28.3 (*aerarium*). See also later law on taking down or tampering with posted tablets, *D.* 48.13.10 (Venuleius Saturninus). *Leges* could also be posted on the *atrium Libertatis*, where many burned in a fire (Fest. 241M); bronze *stelai* on Temple of Saturn and Temple of Castor and Pollux, Cass. Dio 45.17.3 and 45.17.6, and at *idem* crows also peck out names of Antony and Dolabella on a πινακίῳ in Temple of Castor and Pollux; Temple of *Fides*, Cic. *Div.* 1.19, 2.47, *Cat.* 3.19 (*in Capitolio*). The story of Pompey correcting a (major) mistake in a law between voting and posting (Suet. *Jul.* 28.3, with Williamson [1983] 202–5), and the fact that the inscribed version survived a serious challenge from Marcellus, also suggest that the posted version *was* the final version – although Rome in the fifties BC was sufficiently unsettled that we cannot know whether this is a story of traditional practice triumphant or subverted.

[32] Taking down, Cass. Dio 39.21.1–4 (Dio's language, as often, is imprecise: "στήλας about exile" were tablets with the plebiscite reviving the law exiling anyone who executed a citizen without trial).

[33] Cicero and Clodius: Plut. *Cic.* 34.1, *Cat. Min.* 40.1–2 (Cato challenges Cicero's interpretation); Cass. Dio 39.21. Similarly, Servilius orders Caelius's πινάκια annulling debt taken down, Cass. Dio 42.23.1–2, and the Antiochenes petition Titus physically to remove the bronze tablets (τὰς . . . χαλκᾶς . . . δέλτους ἀνελεῖν) granting privileges to the Jews, but he refuses, Jos. *BJ* 7.110.2.

[34] Cic. *Fam.* 13.36.

[35] Revoking a physical action: Williamson (1987a) 167–8; cf. the alleged treatment of the so-called "Laws of the Kings" (Liv. 1.7), Tarquinius Superbus abolished Tullius's laws but also ordered the

The world of belief

seemed to be rendering its low opinion of the laws it chose to liquefy, and to be changing reality back to what it had been before the law had come into being.[36] Indeed, seeing these tablets posted was more important for their legitimacy than reading what was on them.[37]

Edicts, also, were customarily written down, and here too, the understood life and force of an edict are tied to its inscription and posting.[38] This is perhaps best seen in a brief legal discussion of the praetor's edict. "If anyone should deface (*corruperit*)" the praetor's edict, said Ulpian, "while it is being put up or before it has been put up, the words of the edict itself will cease, but Pomponius says that the *sententia* of the edict should be extended to these cases." If damaged before posting, the edict cannot be said to apply strictly: damage the physical object, damage the applicability of the edict written on it. Only, it would seem, with Pomponius in the second century AD was a principle formulated that allowed jurists (and others) to apply the general tenor of the edict, which perhaps here means to allow cases which were – necessarily – formulated in the language of the spoiled sections.[39] Only this opinion allowed Romans to get around the clear difficulties damage would pose to the viability of the edict and, thus, to the traditional way in which cases were proposed to the praetor every day. Such an evaluation of the relationship between a written tablet and an edict is, even with all its ambiguities, rare; but here, at least, their interdependence is unmistakable. This inscribing of laws and edicts on tablets and their posting on buildings or structures was the last step in making these

tablets removed and destroyed; see also Cic. *2 Verr.* 2.101 and 106, Verres's tampering with *tabulae* is the destruction of what had happened.

[36] Melting: Cic. *Cat.* 3.19, *Div.* 1.19; Cass. Dio 45.17.3 (lightning strikes and scatters). All of the above, with further examples (especially from the *Philippics*) discussed by Williamson (1987a).

[37] A way of interpreting Suet. *Gaius* 41.1; cf. Riepl (1913) 347–8 and Cic. *Inv.* 2.162 (law is . . . *quod populo expositum est, ut observet* . . .). Williamson (1987a) 164 n.14 also argues (from Cic. *Rab. Post.* 14) that the general public's knowledge of the content of law was more likely to derive from public proclamation than from reading the posted version anyway.

[38] Edicts customarily written and posted, Cic. *Att.* 2.20.4 and 2.21.4; Mommsen (1969 [1887]) 1.205–7; Riepl (1913) 347; Schwind (1973) 49. See, e.g., censors' edicts (written, Suet. *Rhet.* 1, Gel. 15.11.2, Plin. *NH* 13.24, 14.95). Some Roman edicts and decrees in the East are referred to as δελτογραφήματα ("tablet-writings"), *OGIS* 458 line 62 (Priene, 9 BC) and Reynolds (1982) 159 no. 35 (Aphrodisias; restored), as is a decree of Julius Caesar's from Sardis, P. Herrmann (1989) 133 line 30 (who speculates, 157, that it comes from the *commentarii* of Caesar); cf. Robert (1966) 404–6. The fragmentary *IC* 1.29.1 may record the restoration of an ἐπίκριμα on a δέλτον (Rhytion, AD 120). According to Cassiodorus *Var.* 9.19–20, Athalaric was still posting edicts (for thirty days) in the sixth century; governors also order posting (προτεθήτω, *proponi iussi, propone, proponi volo*), examples in Eck *et al.* (1996) 127 n.294. As Katzoff (1982a) 209–10, 214 notes, the instructions for posting are never included in the edict itself, but are in an accompanying letter (as *senatusconsulta* accompanied treaties, see above n.18).

[39] Damage to praetor's edict, *D.* 2.1.7.2; for its historicity, see Palazzolo (1987); punishments still handed out late, for defacing and other forms of intentional damage, Paul. *Sent.* 1.13a.3.

Tablets and efficacy

enactments real, and represented the fact that some aspect of unseen reality had been authoritatively changed by this act; it was not undertaken for the dissemination of information or for memory's sake.[40]

(d) Vows and dedications. To undertake a vow resembled the act of prayer, but to pay it back after a wish had been fulfilled was more complicated – another intricate unitary act much like making a law, and often involving a tablet that helped the act to become complete.[41] Ulpian said, "if someone has vowed to dedicate something, he is bound by his vow. This binds the person who makes the vow, not the object which is vowed." This distinction between a person obligated by a divinity's fulfillment of a vow and the thing (or act) vowed makes clear why a tablet stating *V.S.L.M.* (or its equivalent) was so often necessary for a vow to be considered fulfilled. Although coming under the protection of the sanctuary, the promised object itself did not change its nature when delivered – "it does not become *sacer*," said Ulpian, unless the vow has been made by a magistrate.[42] Rather, the act of dedicating changed the person, who was set free, discharged of an unseen but very real obligation. The vow was repaid by the individual's act of dedication, not by the thing dedicated or even by its stashing in a temple, and therefore the object's special role as specifically fulfilling a vow had to be, somehow, indicated. The great number of altars labelled *V.S.L.M.* thus reflects not the direct vowing of altars but the vowing, and repayment, of sacrifices, which took place *on* altars. It was considerably more difficult to label the sacrificial animals, although these could (and did) march in processions with tablets around their necks.[43]

Vows and the physical embodiments of their repayment, tablets or inscribed objects, were very numerous in Republic and Empire, Rome and provinces, alike. How often the actual vow was written down is, as in the

---

[40] Therefore it matters little whether laws could be found, read, or understood, cf. Cic. *Leg.* 3.46, Williamson (1987a) 164 and (1995) 245–7 (emphasizing an aristocratic advantage in retrieving archived laws), Culham (1989) 112 and (1991) 126–8, and Matthews (1998) 256–7 on conventions of accessibility. Inscribing "so that the contents would be known" is found in documents Romans sent elsewhere (e.g., *CIL* I² 581 lines 28–9 = *FIRA*² 1.240–1 no. 30; Jos. *AJ* 14.319–22, 19.303–11 at 310; piracy law [*FIRA*² 1.121–31 no. 9 at lines B25–6]; *P.Lond.* 1914 line 4 [edict, AD 41]), but not in those in Rome itself. Later (third-century AD) interpretations (by those to whom law applied, e.g., in Midrash *Vayyikra Rabba* 1.10) noted that laws or edicts were not applicable until they were posted (displayed, "stretched out") in a public place of the city, Lieberman (1944–5) 6–7. *Memoria* appears in the publication instructions of imperial, not Republican, laws: Williamson (1983) 152.

[41] Vows, Wissowa (1902) 319–23 and Latte (1960) 46–7; ceremony involved, Gargola (1995) 22–3 (*votum, locatio, dedicatio*).

[42] Bound by vow and *sacer*: D. 50.12.2.pr. (Ulpian); protection of sanctuary (i.e. *res religiosa*) and different from *sacer*, Fest. 318M and 321M, *G.* 2.5, D. 1.8.6.3 (Marcian), and Wissowa (1902) 322–3.

[43] Altars, sacrifice, and animals, Veyne (1983) 286–8; on regularity of sacrifice in vows, Lucr. 5.1201–2. On dedication of vowed buildings with bronze letters, Volkmann (1967) 504 n.17.

102   *The world of belief*

case of prayers, open to question, although here too the pontifex maximus can be seen to read in advance (*praeire verba*) and there are scattered references to vows being written on tablets and read aloud, as Augustus planned to do at the census in the last year of his life.[44] Many literary accounts also make absolutely no mention of the ways in which a vow was repaid, merely that it was repaid; but inscribed objects and tablets indicating that a vow has been repaid became so common, and exist so early, that a form of actualization through writing must have rapidly become the only understood way of doing this.[45] Cn. Flavius, already mentioned for his publication of the pontifical calendar and early *legis actiones*, vowed a Temple to Concord at the end of the fourth century BC if he could settle a dispute between the *ordines* and the people. When he was successful, but no money was allotted for this purpose from public funds, he erected a bronze *aedicula* with a bronze tablet on it as repayment.[46] Bronze was, indeed, a favorite physical medium for the fulfillment of a vow.[47] If the pattern of bronze's exiguous survival from the Republic does not deceive, vows were the third most popular item (after laws and magistrates' pronouncements) inscribed on bronze.[48] The fact of inscribing, on tablets (or, here, on objects themselves) fulfilled the vow, while bronze (as in so many other cases) signalled expense undertaken and lasting gratitude. The act of inscribing could not be omitted if the extended ceremonial act of vowing and dedicating was to

---

[44] *Praeire verba*, e.g., Liv. 36.2.3; for writing as the actual vow, cf. Veyne (1983) 283–4, who adduces a relief in the Vatican as showing a vow on a "pancarte" or placard, and cf. Suet. *Gaius* 14.2, vows for emperor's health on *titulo proposito*; Augustus, Suet. *Aug.* 97.1 (the offering of this vow *mos*).

[45] How vow repaid not usually mentioned, Beard (1991) 45. Repaying frequent: of 1,323 inscriptions and inscribed objects in *ILLRP*, 317 (24 percent) are dedications and vows. Early: dedications without mention of vow are among earliest of Latin inscriptions found, e.g., *ILLRP* 1271a (sixth century BC); "*merto*" appears *c.* 250 BC (*ILLRP* 132: Geminius, quoted above p. 53) and specific mention of vowing in 218 BC (*ILLRP* 118, Minucius *vovit*); cf. Poucet (1988) 291 on early dedications. Actualization through writing: see Toutain (1900) 976, inscription "constituait tout l'ex-voto;" Veyne (1983) 290–1, every ex-voto accompanied by an inscription, with (among others) the example of the dagger dedicated by Caligula *addito elogio* (cf. Prop. 4.3.71–2). Note that every object dedicated in a sanctuary need not be the result of a formal vow, so that every object need not be inscribed or labelled.

[46] Plin. *NH* 33.19.

[47] Chance finds – e.g., fifty bronze *tabulae ansatae* from the shrine of Jupiter Peninus in the Alps (*Inscr. Ital.* 11.1.27–38 nos. 48–105 [fifty bronze, three marble]), or individual bronze letters from sanctuaries in Germany and Britain (*RIB* 1.305, 307–8) – suggest that the use of bronze in the written discharge of a vow's obligation was once a wide inscriptional habit, perhaps an inscriptional preference.

[48] Bronze, 37 of the 317 dedications (11.4%) are bronze: 61/317 are statue bases (19.2%), 31/317 are pieces of architecture (9.8%), 36/317 are objects (11.4%; 10 bronze); 22/317 are altars (6.9%), 48/317 are *tabulae* or *lamellae* (15.1%; 27 bronze; *lamminis* are also used in magic, Apul. *Met.* 3.17); and 119/317 are "rocks" or undifferentiated fragments (37.5%). Otherwise (and excluding laws and edicts), of bronze in *ILLRP* are six patronage tablets (1064–9), 19 *sortes* (1072–89), two curse-tablets (1149–50), six objects of unknown purpose (1197, 1204, 1206, 1251, 1254, and 1266); and two items that are probably dedications (578 and 593).

Tablets and efficacy

be completed, while its inscribing on a lasting material also fixed the validity of the act, as has been suggested for consecration *tabulae* from sanctuary sites.[49]

(e) Curse-tablets. Curse-tablets can be seen as compressing the extended ceremonial and unitary act of vowing and dedicating (or accusing and rendering final judgment) into a ceremony of one moment, and on to one *tabula.* These tablets and their relatives – the curses on marble tablets erected openly, or "judicial prayers" on tablets that resemble curses but evince a more supplicatory and prayer-like attitude, or even victory-charms written on gold tablets[50] – themselves not only wish or suggest or command, in performative language, an unpleasant fate for their object, but (as will be seen) often assume that what they enact has in fact come to pass. Their view is not only prospective, not only the one that commands, as in the earliest Latin curse-tablet (along the opposite margin from where it says "*dic ilai*"), "*ida fiat!*" – "let it be thus!"[51] They can also have a retrospective view of the act, and thus look back on a completed and complex action. By uniting these two views, the tablet brings together segments of sequential action and treats them as one act: it makes the presentation of a "unitary" act truly unitary. Recitation from curse-tablets has already been mentioned as a way of using tablets to gain access to other worlds and their powers; but curse-tablets also participated in, summarized, and symbolized the completion of their ceremonial action in the same way as census-tablets, laws, edicts, and vows.

What was believed to happen in the act of cursing, and what did tablets specifically do? Enemies, or at least some of their physical characteristics (like the shoulders and wrists of charioteers, or the tongues of courtroom opponents), were remanded into the keeping of a divinity, who was to paralyze rather than destroy them.[52] The "voodoo dolls" that can accompany curse-tablets usually enacted or represented this paralysis through very vivid binding or nailing, but the effective enactment of a curse is depicted as the result of a complex ceremony in which many things needed to be done and said correctly.[53] As Philostratus said, if men are not successful

---

[49] Wilkins (1996) 135–7.
[50] "Judicial prayers," Versnel (1991a) and (1991b) 191–2; victory-charms, cf. Kotansky (1991).
[51] Earliest: *ILLRP* 1147 (see above chapter four n.21).
[52] Shoulders and arms, Audollent (1904) 325–30 no. 242; tongue, *ILLRP* 1146. Paralyze rather than destroy: Faraone (1991a) 4–10.
[53] Voodoo dolls: Faraone (1991b), cf. Ov. *Her.* 6.89–92 (Hypsipyle *devovet* and makes *simulacraque cerea*), *Fast.* 2.575 (witch *cantata ligat cum fusco licia plumbo*; Martinez [1991] 9–10 n.40 interprets as binding the tablet itself). Drawing figures could also be part of this: Brashear (1992a) 50–1 notes that symbols and pictures as well as word-formulae can be traced to exemplars. Ritual unclear before late *PGM*[2]: Preisendanz (1972) col. 4; for a vivid late-antique example, see *PGM*[2] 4.296–433, ed. Martinez (1991) 8–20.

104 *The world of belief*

in procuring love through spells, "they blame it on some omission, saying they should have burned such-and-such an herb or offered such-and-such a sacrifice or melted such-and-such a substance, and that this was absolutely essential but hard to get."[54] Everything could be believed to be essential, even if at times necessity prompted the cutting of corners. Thus although it is true that it is the figure itself that is pierced, and true that in the only story from antiquity of escaping from a curse, it was the removal of nails from the hands and feet of a submerged statuette that loosened the paralysis of the victim,[55] nonetheless it was not just the dolls, or the dolls by themselves, that were efficacious. Being non-realistic representations, they required labelling.[56] Finding the tablets to which the dolls were attached, and which gave (among other things) the all-important name, could also loosen a curse, which indicates that they too were necessary for the curse to work.[57] Tablets specified the locus of punishment – person as well as limb or faculty – more precisely than a doll could, and could not be omitted. If the tablet were sunk or buried, safely out of reach of the victim, the curse would hold, and the new reality of pain or paralysis would be inalterable.

This efficacy was understood by the curser, who on occasion wrote tablets retrospectively – as if, by the action of cursing, reality had already been affected. In a number of tablets classified as "judicial prayers" by H. Versnel, the "consecration" of an unknown enemy creates a potentially dangerous situation for the one cursing: if the curser subsequently comes into contact with a cursed person, he or she faces danger of contagion. Therefore the prayer-curses add the proviso that the curser should be innocent of, and unpunished for, such contact. This second request assumes that the first action has been completed: precautions against unintended consequences are already being taken.[58] Thus although one part of the ceremonial act of

---

[54] Philostratus: *VA* 7.39 (trans. Luck); importance of all components for making a spell work, Gager (1992) 20.

[55] Escaping from curse, Sophronius *Narr. Mir. SS. Cyr. Ioan.* (*PG* 87.3. 3625), quoted in Faraone (1991a) 9; a nineteenth-century Greek parallel quoted by Fox (1912) 306–7.

[56] Labelling: Faraone (1991b) 190–6.

[57] An example: *CIL* 11.4639 (Tuder), the discovery of a *defixio* frees cursed decurions; cf. Versnel (1991a) 63.

[58] Contagion ("may I be free and innocent of any offenses against religion . . . if I drink and eat with him and come under the same roof with him"): Versnel (1991a) 72–5 at 72 and n.67 (best examples are in Greek of the late Hellenistic and Roman period – and one from third-century BC southern Italy, *IG* 14.644 – but the type of curse ["judicial prayers"] he is studying also has clear Latin parallels [81–93], and is now "the largest single subcategory of all curse tablets and binding spells," Gager [1992] 177); also, Fox (1912) 305 on Audollent (1904) 281 no. 210, the tablet serves to "remind the lower deities that the victim was already magically drowned."

Tablets and efficacy

cursing is to recite or repeat the words on the tablet, the language of the tablet itself presumes the efficacy of the act. The *tabula* helps to perform the act but also assumes successful performance. This retrospective quality suggests that the curse tablet not only participates in the act, but also has a summary perspective on that act; it has absorbed, and announces, the state that the act hopes to bring about, and therefore symbolizes the completed act much as the census or a dedication would.

The working of curse-tablets and their ilk thus parallels the way so many other actions with tablets work. They are unitary acts with many ceremonial parts, one of them the creation of a tablet that both expresses and fulfills the action. Yet it is harder to assert, in this case, something specifically Roman in why this was the proper method to be followed, as can be done for prayers, the census, treaties, laws, edicts, and vows. Sympathetic magic is a universal phenomenon; curse-tablets are thought to be a late (perhaps third-century BC) importation from Greece or Magna Graecia (in Sicily, they are known as early as the fifth century BC);[59] and most scholarly attention has been usefully focussed on what Egyptian, Greek, Jewish, and Roman traditions, and early and late magical tablets, have in common rather than on what might make them different. Moreover, curse-tablets and the rituals surrounding them are accretive.[60] Magpie-like, they gather up more and more traditions (like being phrased as both prayers and commands) and add more and more magical signs and names of divinities and demons over time. It is therefore very difficult to distinguish separate elements in the Greco-Roman-Egyptian-Jewish mishmash that is the result.[61]

Yet even in borrowing or importation, any society will transform what is borrowed into a thing that fits an understandable niche. There was much about a curse-tablet, about the active power of a written tablet, that would have looked familiar to Romans – much that was easily graspable by analogy with the way other acts on and with *tabulae* were performed. Hence, perhaps, a Roman contribution of ceremonial and recitation, on

---

[59] Sympathetic magic universal, Faraone (1991a) 8; imported, Liebeschuetz (1979) 138 (third century in Etruria, Audollent [1904] 182–4 no. 128); fifth century in Sicily, *SEG* 4.37.

[60] Accretive: survival and justification of retrograde writing, names of gods, Faraone (1991a) 5 and 8.

[61] Mishmash, e.g., Preisendanz (1972) cols. 11–14 and 21–2 (syncretism), Faraone (1991a) 15 ("hybrid flowering"), Frankfurter (1994) 199 (a synthesis of ritual approaches to power). Only with the "syncretism" of the late Hellenistic and early Roman periods do *defixiones* in Greek take on the fullness, and the stylistic markers, discussed above – repetition, rhythm, exhaustion, etc. (Preisendanz [1972] cols. 11–12); only in the Roman period does Greek writing assume sacred power, Frankfurter (1994) 211 (although he assumes that this could have come from an Egyptian tradition).

106 *The world of belief*

analogy with Roman prayers.[62] Hence also, perhaps, an intensification and specialization of the use of legal forms and language that made more explicit the perceived resemblance between a curse-tablet and a Roman *tabula* of accusation: some public curses in the third-century AD Phrygia are identified as τάβλας or πιττάκια,[63] like *libelli* small wooden or bronze tablets;[64] a Latin curse-tablet from Cumae announces that it carries a *nomen delatum*;[65] in another, from Britain, the curser *queritur* ("makes legal complaint before the court"); and so on.[66] A parallel "legalism" characterized vows as well.[67] Curse-tablets (and their more benign relatives) are more receptive to addition than all the other tablet-actions, so naturally they too borrow and combine within this world of *carmina* and legal formulae, and thereby affirm the notion of existing similarities and connections.

Other verbal links emphasize this perceived connection or consanguinity between the unitary ceremonial acts of cursing and vowing-and-dedicating, on the one hand, and going to court on the other, while also reaching out within the larger family of *tabulae* to the financial metaphors of accounts. To undertake a vow could be, for example, seen as incurring a debt, to discharge the vow a way of repaying, fulfilled and symbolized by a tablet. Until it was clear that the vow was to be paid back, the person was known as *voti reus* ("debtor of a vow"), which put him (or her) into a position parallel not only to that of the money-debtor but also to that of the defendant in a court case (also called a *reus*), one who had been accused in – written down

---

[62] The accretion of "hocus-pocus" in Egyptian magical texts, which created "the need for longer, more detailed formularies" and "constrained [a person] to conduct a whole ceremony, reproducing an entire incantation," was a phenomenon of the first century AD, Brashear (1995) 3414.

[63] πιττάκια: these are referred to in the so-called "confession inscriptions" from Lydia and Phrygia in *TAM* 5.1.251 (n.d.), and in another called τάβλας and attached to a βῆμα, P. Herrmann (1985) 251–4 AD 191–2 but identified by him as platters for ritual dining; Ricl (1995) 91–2 correctly identifies the τάβλας as πιττάκια. See also *TAM* 5.1.362 (AD 155–6), a π[ι]νακίδιον or small tablet used the same way; these "confession inscriptions" display other forms of Roman influence as well, e.g., in the transliteration of *exemplarium* into Greek (ἐξουπλάριον), Petzl (1994) 130–1 no. III lines 8–9. One bronze πιττάκιον has been found, Dunant (1978), with Ricl (1991) and Versnel (1991a) 74. The petitionary or accusational form of the curse follows the procedure of prayer or the law, entrusting the case to the god in writing, Versnel (1991a) 76 and 80–1 and Tomlin (1999) 558. A fourth- or fifth-century Coptic curse-tablet refers to itself as "bringing λίβελλος," Björck (1938) 52 no. 29. Note also Audollent (1904) 300–1 no. 228 (= *CIL* 8.12505, Carthage), a curse-tablet with interior and exterior writing, like sealed legal *tabulae* or double-documents.

[64] See below chapter seven n.68.

[65] *nomen delatum*, Audollent (1904) 270 no. 196.

[66] *queritur*, quoted in Versnel (1991a) 88; for legal language in general, Tomlin (1988) 70–1, Versnel (1991a) 71–2. Cf. also language of vows, e.g., *compotem* (M. Besnier [1920] 19 no. 33 line 18); vow language exists, but is less common, see above, chapter three n.26.

[67] General juristic flavor to vows, see Cic. *Leg.* 2.41 (*sponsio*), Juv. *Sat.* 13.232; Wieacker (1988) 318 n.45 calls them "streng sakralrechtlich;" Toutain (1900) 969 stresses that legal and contractual nature of Roman *vota* distinguishes them from Greek εὐχαί; see also Latte (1960) 46 and Watson (1992) 43.

Tablets and efficacy

on – tablets, and who remained bound over until the case was settled.[68] After the divinity had done its bit, the person became *voti damnatus*, "condemned to a vow" which he or she would then "pay" (*reddere* or *solvere*); curse-tablets also demanded that the cursed do this.[69] Sons *in potestate* could not be bound by vows, just as they could not keep accounts; the undertaking of vows was the serious act of a legally independent person.[70] Such perceived equivalences remind that, whatever the differences in the circumstances of their creation and the sphere of their ultimate application, vows and dedications, curses, *tabulae* of legal procedure, and accounts could still be understood to place their participants into the same bound states and under types of obligations that seemed, at heart, the same.

The census, treaties, *leges*, vows-and-dedications, and curses had in common the fact that their actions were distinguished by their ritual quality, not that they were necessarily performed through acts that were themselves the same. Moreover, these acts in each case were performed in sequence and could, with greater or lesser difficulty, be stretched over time, all the while maintaining the requirement that all parts be performed, and performed correctly: these were "unitary" acts in which the tablet that was made played an important part and, because it lasted beyond the end of the ceremonial act itself, symbolized and embodied the acts undertaken.

CONSTITUTIVE ACTS

This sense of rigorously observed ritual action of which the tablet was a part, and which was characteristic of acts in which tablets were recited as well as in the unitary acts (in which tablets could also be recited, as part of a larger ceremonial whole), is lacking in the next two types of tablets to be examined. Although the efficacy of these tablets, and their capacity to enact human resolutions, will be clear, the transactions embodied in Roman account-books and *senatusconsulta* of the Roman senate occurred without any particular ritual. Here there was no known ceremonial context to speak of, no act except implied intent or voted-on agreement beyond

---

[68] *voti reus*: Verg. *Aen*. 5.237, Macrob. *Sat*. 3.2.6 (*reus vocetur qui suscepto voto se numinibus obligat*), Serv. in *Aen*. 4.699, Hor. *Odes* 2.8.5–6; cf. Magdelain (1943) 113–20. Courts: Fest. 237M, Cic. *Cluent*. 86.

[69] *voti damnatus*: *ILLRP* 136, Verg. *Ecl*. 5.80, and see *OLD s.v. votum* 1.b. *reddere* and *solvere*: e.g., Plaut. *Rud*. 60, Verg. *Georg*. 1.436; in curses, e.g., Audollent (1904) 194–5 no. 137 (= *CIL* 15.6265 [Latium], *solvat*), or Wright (1958) 150 (*sangu(i)no suo solvat*), Audollent (1904) 330–2 no. 243 line 22 ([*so*]*lvite*). Athenian terminology for vows, in contrast, takes up the language of "being freed" from obligation (ἠλευθέρωσα [Plato *Ep*. 7.329b]) or "escaping" obligation (as one escaping a charge in a law-case, πέφευγας, Eur. *Hec*. 345).

[70] Sons: in vows, *D*. 50.12.2.1 (Ulpian); in accounts, see chapter two n.69.

108 *The world of belief*

the act of writing itself: these are constitutive acts, on tablets, and the making of or writing on the *tabula* is the most important part of the act itself. In a sense, the efficacy of the *tabula* is pure in these cases, since it brings about the desired act without contributions from gesture, speech, timing, or anything of the other variables that make the unitary act so complex.

(a) The contract litteris. One of the curiosities of Roman law, described in Gaius's *Institutes*, was the contract *litteris*, "by letters": "an obligation by letters comes into existence (*fit*) as, for example, in account entries (*nominibus transscripticiis*)" – that is, the writing of an entry into an account-book creates or re-creates the fact of debt and the legal obligation to repay. This, specifically distinguished by Gaius from an account entry that reflected the *actual* payment of money, has always been thought of as an odd transaction.[71] How can it have been permitted for X just to enter in his accounts that Y owed him money and thereby for Y to become liable to pay that money? How would Y guard against malicious thievery on the part of X? But that seems to have been how it worked. Given the nature of *tabulae* of accounts, what must be happening here is that the act of entering into accounts a *nomen* – the man keeping the accounts writes in his *tabula* (*scribere*)[72] that a certain sum has been paid to another person as a loan – itself alone creates the fact of the account-keeper's loan and thereby the legal obligation of the recipient to pay it back. Writing it down on a *tabula* makes a payment real. It can, in the examples Gaius gives, convert an obligation to repay based on an informal agreement into an obligation to repay based on the fact of a loan established by being written in an account-book, or convert an obligation of X to repay Y into an obligation of Z to repay Y. The mere entry – writing down *on tablets* – of a loan created the fact of payment and therefore the legal obligation to repay. The rapacious Otacilia relied on the understood workings of financial *tabulae* when she entered (into her own tablets) 300,000 sesterces as *expensum ferre*, "paid out as a loan" by her to her dying lover L. Visellius Varro, an entry that would compel repayment by his heirs. He had agreed to this, for by using her *tabulae* he would avoid the posthumous social indignity of leaving an

---

[71] *G.* 3.128, quotation; at 128–31 he describes the *nomina arcaria*, loans and the legal obligation to repay them established by the *actual* payment of money; see discussions in Zulueta (1953) 163–6; Buckland and Stein (1963) 459–61 (mechanism "obscure"); Watson (1965) 18–39 gives the Republican jurists' interpretation; cf. Thilo (1980) 290–5, 305–18. Liv. 35.7.2 depicts this way of creating obligation as common to both Romans and their Italian allies (*in socios . . . nomina transcriberent*); Liebs (1970) 148 n.157 argues for its antiquity, and the necessary antiquity of its use of writing.

[72] Language used, Voigt (1888) 537–8 and nn.25–8 (*nomen scribere, perscribere; acceptum, expensum ferre; rescribere, referre*).

Tablets and efficacy

inheritance to his married mistress while nonetheless providing for her.[73] In this case, and possibly also another related by Cicero,[74] an entry into *tabulae* of accounts alone created the fact of the loan that was the basis of the legal obligation to repay: at this time, a statement of a loan properly entered on a *tabula* had been as constitutive of a loan as an actual payment of a loan, and as instrumental in creating an obligation to repay.[75]

These Republican *nomina transscripticia*, as they were called, were not understood as fictitious, but as real and efficacious, which is why they could work. They were part of a world of financial transactions heavily dependent on tablets ("not a penny moves in Gaul without the *tabulae* of Roman citizens," said Cicero), although how great a part we cannot know;[76] they were part of the law that applied to citizens;[77] and an understanding of their nature also helps to explain Ulpian's determination of recompense in the theft of account-books. "He who steals *tabulae* or *cautiones* is liable in theft not only for what the tablets are worth in themselves, but for what is in them (*quod interfuit*), which means the amount of the sum contained."[78]

---

[73] Val. Max. 8.2.2 (Varro, alas, recovered, so Otacilia sued him for the money). Since this anecdote also confusingly stated that a jurist decreed that she had snared this money, or a claim to it, *inani stipulatione*, there has been much discussion of what actually happened here: see summary in Thilo (1980) 99–102.

[74] Cic. *Off.* 3.58–60, the story of Pythius, sly banker of Syracuse, who provoked through fraud the hasty purchase of a country property, achieved through entry in account tablets – *nomina facit, negotium conficit* – which held despite the deceptions revealed the next day; it was an example of what could happen before Aquilius introduced the formula *dolo malo* into sales. It is unlikely that Canius paid the money on the spot, since the estate was said not to be for sale, Canius had merely been invited for dinner, and the story emphasizes the speed of the transaction. On these two anecdotes, see Watson (1965) 29–36.

[75] This created problems of its own, reflected in Gaius's discussion, *G.* 3.131–2; the fact that the debtor did not seem to have to be present at time of entry (*G.* 3.138) also did not conform well with the later and more developed theory of contract (in Cic. *Off.* 3.58 the debtor was present, but this was fortuitous), nor did the possibility of fraudulent entry without the debtor's consent; Kunkel (1973) 214–18 argued that chirographs or attestations of entry were later sought by creditors as a way of demonstrating agreement and thereby strengthening the legal enforceability of a loan made in this way.

[76] Dependence on tablets: Cic. *Font.* 11 (this could also include what were later called *nomina arcaria* or *cautiones* of stipulations, of course), *Q. Rosc.* 13 and 15; the contract *litteris*, and *tabulae*, in use until late classical times, *FV* 329 (Papinian), and J. A. C. Thomas (1976) 268, but not into the fifth century, since Ps.-Asc. on Cic. *2Verr.* 2.60 (Orelli) does not understand what he is glossing, and says that the old habit of keeping account tablets had entirely ceased by his day.

[77] *Ius civile*: *G.* 3.132–3 (debated: perhaps peregrines could also be bound by an entry *a re in personam*); *D.* 15.1.4.1 (Pomponius), contract *litteris* does not apply between masters and slaves.

[78] Ulpian: *D.* 47.2.27.*pr.*, with an explanation for what should happen in "seemingly valueless" cases, like the recording of a payment already received: Ulpian suggests that the rule exists because creditor and debtor alike wish to avoid controversy (that these are account-*tabulae*, see Wieacker [1964] 564–6). In other words, he has no idea why *tabulae* of accounts receive special treatment, only that they do. See also *D.* 47.2.83.3 (Paulus), same view of stealing tablets and *cautiones*; paralleled in *D.* 32.59 (Julian), where bequeathing *tabula* of a chirograph equals bequeathing the *actio* that is contained in them; and Wieacker (1964), not an influence from post-classical law.

110   *The world of belief*

Only by the time of Justinian has this type of obligation – obligation "by
letters" – finally disappeared.[79] The reality of debts and credits was for
centuries determined by their being written into tablets, and travelled with
those tablets wherever they went and into whosoever's hands they fell. Such
debts and credits could be cancelled only by entries indicating that they had
been paid, or by tablets' physical destruction. Even Trajan's (or Hadrian's)
remission of back taxes, previously entered as owed on public account
tablets, was effected in its final phase through the burning of the *tabulae*,
as can be seen on a second-century AD relief from the Roman forum, the
so-called *anaglypha Traiani*. This was a depiction of more than just a joyous
public demonstration; such destruction was necessary, and far better than
the erasure of individual entries, which, although equally efficacious, might
incur suspicion of tampering. Better to destroy everything.[80]

   (b) Senatusconsulta. This relationship of writing and physical object is
even clearer in the case of *senatusconsulta*: there was no such thing as a *senatusconsultum* if it was not written down. A *senatusconsultum* was formulated
by chosen senators who summarized from memory what the opinion of the
senate on any given question had been, and this became the only opinion
that the senate expressed to the wider public.[81] It had to be written on tablets
to have any existence or strength whatsoever: a senatorial opinion of 44 BC
about the Jews could be depicted as not having been implemented – as not
achieving the status of *senatusconsultum* – because it had not been written
down and taken to the *aerarium*.[82] Similarly, in the year of Augustus's birth
(according to a story in Suetonius) a portent indicated that nature was to
bring forth a king for the Roman people, and a terrified senate judged
(*censuisse*, the usual term for the expression of a *senatusconsultum*) that no
male child born that year should be reared. Those with pregnant wives,
however, saw to it that the *senatusconsultum* was not taken (*deferretur*) to
the *aerarium*,[83] a preventive act whose point must have been understood as

---

[79] Just. *Inst.* 3.21.

[80] *Anaglypha Traiani*: Torelli (1982) 90 (the date is disputed). Other examples of the destruction of
tax-records (advantageous from either the Greek or the Roman view of documents): *SIG*[3] 684, letter
of cos. Q. Fabius Maximus on "the burning and destruction of archives and public records" (*c.* 139
BC); Suet. *Aug.* 32.2; Tac. *Ann.* 13.23.2; Jos. *BJ* 2.426–8 (AD 65), *BJ* 7.60 (AD 70); *HA Aurel.* 39.3;
Julian *Ep.* 204 (Bidez = Loeb no. 51; of disputed authenticity).

[81] Creation of *senatusconsulta*: Schwind (1973) 53–6, Sherk (1969) 7–10, Edmondson (1993) 161–3,
Coudry (1994), who notes that *senatusconsulta* were archived in the *aerarium* but also included in
the *commentarii* of the consuls; Frontin. *Aq.* 99–100.

[82] For an example written on *tabulae*, Val. Max. 6.4.3; 44 BC, Jos. *AJ* 14.221 (a later *senatusconsultum*
endorses the current consuls' decision on how to act in the previous, incomplete matter).

[83] King for Romans: Suet. *Aug.* 94.3. Strength of *senatusconsultum*: cf. Cic. *Pis.* 35–6 (a *senatus auctoritas
promulgassent* by magistrates then proposed, voted on, and passed as a *lex*, with the entire senate as
its *rogatores*); cf. Cic. *Sest.* 129.

Tablets and efficacy

leaving the *senatusconsultum* incomplete and without any strength. These anecdotes are not themselves necessarily true, but the process they depict is likely to be, for it is on this that the stories turn.

Moral force was, technically, all the strength a finished *senatusconsultum* had during the Republic, unless it was spoken to the people by edict of the magistrate to whom it was directed, or passed by the people as law. (Under the empire a *senatusconsultum* was granted the force of law.) In 63 BC Cicero had a *senatusconsultum ultimum* directing him to take action against Catiline "embodied in tablets" in his possession but, at the time of his first oration, had not yet announced it: the sword had been forged, but was still in its sheath.[84] But the senate's moral authority was very great, its opinions frequently expressed. Probably because of the sheer quantity of these tablets, more is known about how they were stored than is known for other tablets. They were put in (not on) the *aerarium*, the tablets themselves bundled into *codices* and numbered.[85] The vocabulary used in connection with them is therefore different from that used of laws: a *senatusconsultum* was *relatum in tabulas* and *deferretur in aerario*, whereas a *lex* was *conditur*.[86] On special occasions, *senatusconsulta* were engraved on bronze, sometimes in versions known to use abbreviations.[87] This somewhat different treatment – of storage, reference, and publication – may suggest that senators adopted the tablet form for *senatusconsulta* at an early date, precisely in order to extend tablets' pragmatic and symbolic authority to the prestige of their opinions,

---

[84] "Embodied in tablets:" *inclusum in tabulis* (rather than "inserted into the records"), Cic. *Cat.* 1.4 with *OLD s.v.* 8a.

[85] *Aerarium*: Liv. 39.4.8–9, Plut. *Cat. Min.* 17.3; Livy also claims (3.55.13) that plebeian aediles kept an extra set at the Temple of Ceres; Jos. *AJ* 14.188, 266–7 says that all δόγματα (i.e. *sc*) found engraved on bronze tablets on the Capitoline, but he likely means only those that accompanied treaties (above, n.18) or other special ones (e.g., those that had been made laws, or the early imperial *sc* about *asylia* engraved on bronze and *figere* to the temples of Asia Minor, Tac. *Ann.* 3.63.4). Method of retrieval seen in *CIL* 10.7852 (= *ILS* 5947, AD 69, Sardinia), Jos. *AJ* 14.219 (copied from public δέλτων of quaestors at *aerarium*), Reynolds (1982) 54–91 no. 8; Culham (1991) and (1996) 179–81 argues that these reference markers add claims to authenticity but are not in themselves necessarily accurate or true. Numbering: Gardthausen (1911) 13–15 with Sherk (1969) 7–10 and his index *s.v.* δέλτος.

[86] *relatum in tabulas*, Liv. 4.11.4, Cic. *Dom.* 50. *deferre* very standard for *senatusconsulta*, e.g., Liv. 39.4, Cic. *Fam.* 12.1.1, Plut. *Cat. Min.* 17.3 (κατέταξε). *Condere* for *leges*: Suet. *Jul.* 28.3, *Schol. Bob.* on Cic. *Sest.* 135, Amm. Marc. 16.12.70 (*condi[ta]* restored). The meaning of *condere* is difficult: since most citations indicate that tablets were posted, and usually posted out-of-doors (e.g., *CIL* 1² 2.1.587 lines 41–2 = *FIRA*² 1.131–4 no. 10, names to be posted *in pariete intra caulas proxume ante hanc legem*), it is unlikely that *condere* here has the specific meaning of "hide" or "store"; rather, I would prefer to take it in the sense of "uniting disparate elements in one place" (Ogilvie [1961] 32, on its meaning for the census) and "making" or "establishing"; see *OLD s.v.* Servius's *in Aen.* 8.322 *claud ebantur* is therefore almost certainly wrong, as Mommsen (1969 [1887]) 11.546 n.1 also thought.

[87] Bronze version not necessarily full version, Eck *et al.* (1996) 260–4.

112   *The world of belief*

and to assert quite firmly that *senatusconsulta* were indeed very close to *leges.*[88]

Contracts *litteris* and *senatusconsulta* show *tabulae* functioning at their most powerful, as actually creating, without the help of any surrounding ceremony, the entities they constituted. In most cases, however, tablets could claim or imply this power, but not exclusively: they were but a part, if the most lasting part, of what happened. Thus in these rituals spoken words, acts, gestures, the absence of invalidating interruption, and writing on tablets were *all* crucial. Tablets' active role was not merely the result of some need to keep records, to jot down reminders, to reinforce some oral announcements, to provide evidence, or in general "for memory's sake." In all these cases, ceremonial or not, writing on tablets was active and symbolic, as well as useful, all at once.[89]

LEGAL *TABULAE*

Constitutive acts, the contracts *litteris* on *tabulae* and *senatusconsulta*, exist at the furthest end of a wide spectrum of acts with tablets. The other end is anchored by the simpler acts in which the recitation of a prayer or the like is most of the action, and spanning a wide middle section are the unitary acts, which can recite from tablets or create them or both, under circumstances of great and necessary ceremonial complexity. The legal documents of individuals on *tabulae* belong in this wide middle category of unitary acts, for they were parts of larger ceremonies, and were important and powerful in the same ways that tablets in these unitary acts were – not only recited from, not purely constitutive of, but participating in the act and helping to complete it.

Such tablets, as noted before,[90] cluster around the two oldest Roman legal ceremonies, mancipation and stipulation, as well as being part (as already mentioned) of the contract "by letters," where the account tablet is itself

---

[88] Which others could imitate in turn: veterans in 41 BC ratified the agreement between Octavian and Antony and his partisans, inscribed their activities ἐς δέλτους, sealed them, and deposited them with the Vestals. For this action they were mockingly called "a hobnailed Senate," Cass. Dio 48.12.2–3.

[89] Memory: despite Cicero's claims at *de Orat.* 2.52 (on *tabulae* of pontifex maximus), *Sest.* 129 (about entering his own achievements on *tabulis publicis*), or *Phil.* 1.19.1 (*memoriae causa rettulit in libellum*), this is a new sensibility. Such a sensibility is attributed to an earlier age by Dion. Hal. 4.26.5; it appears in the acts of the Arval Brethren in 17 BC (*ad conservandam memoriam* and *ad futuram rei memoriam,* 58–63), cf. Scheid (1994) 177 n.19 (text) and 178 n.21, Eck (1999) 55–6, and above n.40.

[90] See chapter two nn.95–101.

Tablets and efficacy 113

the medium and embodiment of the legal act. No Republican discussions of legal tablets' use or efficacy survives, and previous assessments of their role have been based only on the neglect of them, or indifferent references to them, in the works of the imperial jurists; legal gestures are similarly neglected, if occasionally noted.[91] Tablets' functions have therefore often been misunderstood. For only by setting legal *tabulae* within the larger historical context of Roman tablets, as has now been done, it is possible to understand the belief of contemporaries in their efficacy.

(a) Mancipation. In the body of preserved Roman law, it is in the legal acts that involved *tabulae* that memories of the ritual context and the performance of the rituals themselves were preserved the longest: a distinctive form was used in a distinctive process. For a mancipation (in this case of a slave), the jurist Gaius in the second century AD provides the following description:[92]

Est autem mancipatio, ut supra quoque diximus, imaginaria quaedam venditio; quod et ipsum ius proprium civium Romanorum est. eaque res ita agitur: adhibitis non minus quam quinque testibus civibus Romanis puberibus et praeterea alio condicionis, qui libram aeneam teneat, qui appellatur libripens, is qui mancipio accipit, rem tenens ita dicit: HUNC EGO HOMINEM EX IURE QUIRITIUM MEUM ESSE AIO ISQUE MIHI EMPTUS ESTO HOC AERE AENEAQUE LIBRA; deinde aere percutit libram idque aes dat ei, a quo manicipio accipit, quasi pretii loco.

Now mancipation, as we have already said above, is a sort of imaginary sale, and it too is an institution peculiar to Roman citizens. And it is performed as follows: in the presence of no fewer than five Roman citizens of full age and also of a sixth person, having the same qualifications, known as the *libripens* (scale-holder), to hold a bronze scale, the party who is taking by the mancipation, holding the property, says: "I declare that this man is mine by Quiritary right, and be he conveyed to me with this bronze ingot and bronze scale." He then strikes the scale with the ingot and gives that as a symbolic price to him from whom he is receiving by the mancipation.

The first-century AD antiquarian Varro preserved the older language used for the physical act: "let him strike the scale with the rod."[93] This ceremony

---

[91] They are of more interest to scholars: cf. Sittl (1890) 129–47 (Greek and Roman both), Jhering (1891 [1875]) 2.2.568–77; Mor (1976), who traces also into early medieval practice; Wolf (1984).

[92] *G.* 1.119 (trans. shaped by arguments of Prichard [1960]); see also Ulp. *Reg.* 19.3.

[93] Varro: *L.* 163 (*raudusculo libram ferito*); the same in Fest. 265M. On the gestures, Mrsich (1979), summarizing extensive earlier work; on words, Buckland (1939) 19–20 (arguing that they are the public assertion of a right).

114   The world of belief

was also followed in other acts modelled on mancipation – the mancipatory will, emancipation or adoption of children, marriage or divorce by *coemptio*, noxal surrender of an erring child or slave, and *nexum*. These continued to make use of the rituals of mancipation until the time of Justinian, or at least as long as these legal acts themselves continued to be used.[94]

Gaius describes the will of his time, the *testamentum per aes et libram*, in sufficient detail to flesh out some of the complex action involved in the creation of a will. It involved witnesses, a bronze balance, *aes*, ceremonial actions and words, and – specifically noted – wax tablets:[95]

Eaque res ita agitur: qui facit <testamentum>, adhibitis sicut in ceteris mancipationibus V testibus civibus Romanis puberibus et libripende, postquam tabulas testamenti scripserit, mancipat alicui dicis gratia familiam suam. in qua re his verbis familiae emptor utitur: FAMILIAM PECUNIAMQUE TUAM ENDO MANDATELA CUSTODELAQUE MEA <ESSE AIO, EAQUE> QUO TU IURE TESTAMENTUM | FACERE POSSIS SECUNDUM LEGEM PUBLICAM, HOC AERE, et ut quidam adiciunt AENEAQUE LIBRA, ESTO MIHI EMPTA; deinde aere percutit libram idque aes dat testatori velut pretii loco. deinde testator tabulas testamenti manu tenens ita dicit: HAEC ITA UT IN HIS TABULIS CERISQUE SCRIPTA SUNT, ITA DO ITA LEGO ITA TESTOR ITAQUE VOS QUIRITES TESTIMONIUM MIHI PERHIBETOTE.

The proceedings are as follows: he who makes <the will>, as in other mancipations, takes five Roman citizens above puberty to witness and a scale-holder, and, having previously written his will on tablets, mancipates for form's sake his *familia* to someone. In this matter the *familiae emptor* makes use of these words: "I declare your *familia* and money to be within my mandates and in my custody, and be it conveyed to me with this bronze piece and" (as some add) "this bronze scale, to the end that you may be able to make a lawful will in accordance with the public statute." Then he strikes the scale with a bronze piece and gives that bronze to the testator as if in the place of the price. Then the testator, holding in his hand the tablets of his will, says as follows: "According as it is written in these tablets and on this wax, so do I give, so do I bequeath, so do I call to witness, and so, Quirites, do you bear me witness."

This was, like all mancipations, a ceremonial act. The "purchaser of the family" speaks certain words, strikes the balance with bronze, and gives the

---

[94] *Coemptio*, noxal surrender, and *nexum* appear to have died out before the other actions: *coemptio*, *G.* 1.113, 1.123 (different words used from a mancipation, so that the woman is not reduced to servile status; cf. Boethius's *Commentary* on Cic. *Top.* 2 [Orelli], *coemptio vero certis sollemnitatibus peragebatur . . . quam sollemnitatem in suis institutis Ulpianus exponit*); dying out, see Gardner (1986) 13. Noxal surrender: *G.* 4.75–9; dying out, cf. Just. *Inst.* 4.8.7 (only for slaves). *Nexum*: defined as all acts *per libram et aes*, Var. *L.* 7.105, Cic. *Rep.* 2.59, but already (supposedly) abolished by the *Lex Poetilia* (313 BC?), so they were speculating too. For the late-antique juristic treatment of the other acts, see chapter nine pp. 265–76, 291.

[95] *G.* 2.104.

Tablets and efficacy

bronze to the testator; the testator then holds his tablets and speaks a set of words in the legalistic *carmen*-style (words which themselves are written in the will, like "*do . . . lego*"). Gaius makes the tablets a clear part of the ceremony, just as they were in other unitary acts: the tablets were not just quietly present to record, conveniently, the details of the disposition of the testator's property; they were clutched during the ceremony and referred to (with *carmen*-style precision as "tablets and wax") in the ritual words. That tablets were ubiquitous in acts of mancipation is emphasized by the survival of several written formularies to guide the writing of tablets for mancipatory legal acts – templates to be followed when a particular act was to be undertaken.[96] They echo Gaius's insistence on a proper ceremonial order, *tabulae*, and formal *verba*: mancipation in all its forms was a unitary act.

(b) Stipulation. Stipulation, believed to have been the earliest form of Roman contract, was in one specific form, known as *sponsio*, limited to Roman citizens, as mancipatory acts were.[97] Gaius in the second century AD classified it as "verbal obligation," and described it as follows:[98]

verbis obligatio fit ex interrogatione et responsione, velut: DARI SPONDES? SPONDEO, DABIS? DABO, PROMITTIS? PROMITTO, FIDEPROMITTIS? FIDEPROMITTO, FIDEIUBES? FIDEIUBEO, FACIES? FACIAM. (93) Sed haec quidem verborum obligatio, DARI SPONDES? SPONDEO, propria civium Romanorum est; ceterae vero iuris gentium sunt, itaque inter omnes homines, sive cives Romanos sive peregrinos, valent. et quamvis ad Graecam vocem expressae fuerint, velut hoc modo: δώσεις; δώσω· ὁμολογεῖς; ὁμολογῶ· πίστει κελεύεις; πίστει κελεύω· ποιήσεις; ποιήσω, etiam hae tamen inter cives Romanos

---

[96] *CIL* 2.5042 (= *FIRA*[2] 3.295–7 no. 92, warranty clause omitted), *Dama L. Titi ser(vus) fundum Baianum, qui est in agro qui | Veneriensis vocatur, pago Olbensi, uti optumus maxumusq(ue) | esset, (sestertio) n(ummo) I et hominem Midam (sestertio) n(ummo) I fidi fiduciae causa man\cipio accepit ab L. Baiano, libripende antest(ato). adfines fundo | dixit L. Baianius L. Titium et C. Seium et populum et si quos dicere oportet*; note archaisms (e.g., *optumus maxumusq.*) and abbreviations. The second is a will-formulary, *P.Hamb.* 72 (Amelotti [1966] 266–7 no. 10), *siquid ego post h[o]c testamentum meum nuncupatu[m] | codicillis charta membrana aliove quo genere || scr[i]p[tum signatumque re]li[quero, quo non recto tes]|tament[i iure l]egum[v]e dari quid aut fieri iu[sse]|ro, [a]ut [si quid] vel vi[v]us dedi donavi deder[o] | donaver[o uel li]berum liberamve esse vetuer[o] | «au[t]» s«er[vum s]e[rvam]ve, ratum esto ac si in hoc t[es]||t[am]ento cau[tum] comprehensumve esset.\h(uic) t(estamento) d(olus) m(alus) abe[s]to. | Fam(iliam) pecuniam[q]ue testam(enti) f(aciendi) <c(ausa)> e(mit) quis [I] ISI, librip(endis) lo(co) quis, | ant(estatus est) qu[e]m;* note extensive final abbreviations.

[97] Oldest: e.g., Watson (1971) 117, *contra* Zulueta (1953) 152–3; it may be attested in the Twelve Tables, cf. *G.* 4.17a, where a *iudicis postulationem* is authorized for a case arising out of stipulation (the word quoted is *sponsione*). Whether *sponsio* and *stipulatio* were actually the same thing originally is debated; see summary in Jolowicz and Nicholas (1972) 280–1. Limited to citizens, *G.* 3.93 (*spondeo*), *G.* 1.119 (mancipations).

[98] Gaius (quotation): *G.* 3.92–3 (note that non-citizens are allowed to use *spondere* in acts of surrender, 3.94); cf. *D.* 44.7.1.7 (Gaius).

116   *The world of belief*

valent, si modo Graeci sermonis intellectum habeant. et e contrario, quamvis
Latine enuntientur, tamen etiam inter peregrinos valent, si modo Latini sermonis intellectum habeant. at illa verborum obligatio, DARI SPONDES? SPON-
DEO, adeo propria civium Romanorum est, ut ne quidem in Graecum sermonem
per interpretationem proprie transferri possit, quamvis dicatur a Graeca voce
figurata esse.

An obligation by words is created by question and answer in such forms as: "Do
you promise to give? I promise to give;" "Will you give? I will give;" "Do you
promise? I promise;" "Do you promise on your honor? I promise on my honor;"
"Do you guarantee on your honor? I guarantee on my honor;" "Will you do? I will
do." (93) Now this obligation of words in the form *dari spondes? spondeo* at any rate
is peculiar to Roman citizens; but the other forms belong to the *ius gentium* and
are consequently valid between all men, whether Roman citizens or peregrines.
And even though expressed in Greek, in such words as "will you give? I will give;"
"do you agree? I agree;" "do you promise on your honor? I promise on my honor;"
"will you do? I will do;" even these are valid nonetheless between Roman citizens,
provided they understand Greek. And conversely, though expressed in Latin, they
are still valid even between peregrines, provided they understand Latin. But the
verbal obligation *dari spondes? spondeo* is so far peculiar to Roman citizens that it
cannot properly be put into Greek, although the word *spondeo* is said to be derived
from a Greek word.

Aspects of this second-century view were recapitulated in the early third
century by Ulpian. According to him both parties had to be present, the
transaction had to be completed all at one time, and both parties had
to be able to speak and hear.[99] Moreover, it was required that the act be
a continuous one, that at most "some moment" might intervene between
question and answer, and that if anything else was begun after the question,
the stipulation was invalid "even if the reply is given in the same day."[100]
Such a requirement for continuous and virtually uninterrupted action also
existed for the mancipatory will: in requirements such as these, the idea of
the ceremonial unitary act lingered on in the juristic memory.[101]

---

[99] Ulpian and others: *D.* 45.1.*pr.* (the deaf or mute can enter into a stipulation through a slave),
D. 45.1.137.*pr.* (Venuleius), *continuus actus*; also G. 3.92–114, *D.* 44.7.1.13–15 (Gaius), *D.* 44.7.52.2
(Modestinus); *D.* 46.4.8.3 (Ulpian); Paul. *Sent.* 2.3; see Riccobono *et al.* (1957) 32–42.

[100] *D.* 45.1.137.*pr.* (Venuleius), *aliquod momentum . . . intervenire possit . . . ceterum si post interrogationem
aliud acceperit, nihil proderit, quamvis eadem die spopondisset.*

[101] Cf. *D.* 50.17.77 (Papinian) on the acceptance of no time limits or conditions in *actus legitimi*
(including emancipation, *acceptilatio, hereditatis aditio, datio tutoris,* etc.); this aspect noted by
Jhering (1891 [1875]) 2.2.589–90 and Bruck (1904) 3–4, 10–20 (where he attributes it to "form").
Also, *CJ* 6.23.28 (AD 530), "antiquity wished wills to be continuously executed," *antiquitas testamenta
fieri voluit nullo actu interveniente* (followed by a straight-faced explanation of what to do if testator
or witnesses are overcome by calls of nature); this requirement also transferred over into the so-called
tripartite will, *CJ* 6.23.21 (AD 439).

Tablets and efficacy

The jurists do not mention writing on tablets as part of stipulation, nor had Gaius mentioned them in his description of simple mancipation: as we shall see in chapter nine, their analytical world left much out, even factors essential for the validity of acts, as Gaius left out (for example) the requirement that stipulation be *continuus*. Scholars have suggested other actions that had once been part of stipulation: the pouring of libations (whence *spondeo*, σπένδω, derived),[102] offering the right hand as the symbol of *fides*,[103] combining the two by pouring a libation and extending the right hand,[104] or holding and breaking a reed or *stipula*.[105] To these possibilities should be added the presence and probable recitation of *tabulae*.[106] Gaius's description concentrates only on wording and omits all else. But witnessed *tabulae* of stipulation survive and are referred to in passing by jurists,[107] and non-juristic authors associate *tabulae* with stipulation and indicate clearly that tablets were expected to be a part of stipulation – especially, for example, in promises of dowry, where their existence was one item that helped to establish marriage in the eyes of participants and observers.[108] Juvenal

---

[102] Fest. 329M, citing Verrius Flaccus, gives a dubious etymology (*spondere . . . deinde oblitus inferiore capite sponsum et sponsam ex Graeco dicta[m] ait, quod i σπονδάς interpositis rebus divinis faciant*), while *Var. L.* 6.69–73 derives *spondere* from *sponte* with even greater implausibility; but Festus does also attest to the use of *spondere* in prayers (351M), *"bene sponsis, beneque volueris" in precatione augurali Messalla augur ait significare spoponderis, volueris*. Magdelain (1990) 719–23 argues that the formulaic exchange was not originally part of the act.

[103] Zulueta (1953) 152, stipulation "must be a verbalization of some ceremony of offering the right hand as a symbol of *fides*" – this in his discussion of the words *fidepromissio, promissio, fideiussio*.

[104] Huvelin (1904) 54 n.2.

[105] Isid. *Etym.* 5.24.30, *dicta autem stipulatio ab stipula: veteres enim, quando sibi aliquid promittebant, stipulam tenentes frangebant, quam iterum iungentes sponsiones suas agnoscebant*; Weiß (1929) cols. 2540–3 thinks a gesture with a *stipula* is the most likely because etymologically *stipulatio* is correctly derived from *stipula*. Less likely (to him) is Paulus's derivation of *stipulatio* from *stipulum*, "firm" (*Sent.* 5.7.1), or Varro's (*L.* 5.182) and Festus's (297M) derivation from *stips* ("coin"); see Kaser (1949) 267–70 and 333, Düll (1951), and Zimmermann (1996) 72.

[106] *Tabulae* of stipulation: see chapter two nn.100–1. Like the *tabulae* of the mancipatory will, they may have been made ahead of time: such is the implication of Cic. *Att.* 16.11.7, "though I have not yet read the stipulations (*etsi nondum stipulationes legeram*) . . . still I wish you would finish the business (*conficias*)" in the near future. Aug. *Serm.* 51.22 (*PL* 38.345) notes that at a wedding, *recitantur tabulae . . . in conspectu omnium attestantium . . . et vocantur tabulae matrimoniales*.

[107] Witnesses: *P.Mich.* 4703 (= *FIRA*² 3.41–3 no. 17), a Roman stipulation for dowry, preserves the subscriptions of six of the seven witnesses. They were kept: Cicero *Att.* 12.17 assumes that a twenty-five-year-old *sponsio* on tablets can be found; they are also regularly cited by jurists, cf. *D.* 45.2.11.1–2 (Papinian), *D.* 24.1.57 (Paulus), *D.* 45.1.122.1 (Scaevola), *D.* 45.1.126.2 (Paulus), *D.* 45.1.134 (Paulus), and *D.* 45.1.139.3 (Venuleius).

[108] Right way to proceed: cf. Suet. *Claud.* 29.3, even Messalina and Silius draw up *tabellas dotis*; Quint. *Inst.* 5.11.32 (quoting Cic. *Top.* 12.34) contrasts marriage tablets with the *mente coeuntium*, which implies two now competing definitions of marriage; in the imperial period, such tablets were sealed at the wedding itself, Apul. *Met.* 4.26, *Apol.* 68; see Treggiari (1991) 164–5. Sulpicius Rufus (Gel. 4.4) noted that in Latium a properly performed *sponsio* was a legally actionable marriage contract at least until the first century BC, which would have contributed to the sense that the stipulation

118   *The world of belief*

referred to such *tabellae* as *legitimae*, correctly made and legitimate.[109] Stipulation reached beyond the mere verbal exchange into ceremony, including *tabulae*: it too was once a unitary act, with proper order, gestures, *tabulae*, and formal *verba*.

Ritual gestures – breaking a reed, purchase with one sestertius, striking the scales held by the *libripens* – as well as formal language were existing or remembered parts of these legal acts. Although most of the ceremony surrounding stipulation had probably disappeared by the second century AD, participants were still performing ceremonial roles and words of some sort, and using *tabulae* as a significant part of the legal act. As long as ceremony with both words and gestures was performed and considered an essential part of the legal act, witnesses were there to observe the validity of the proceedings, as they were also in other ceremonial acts. Jurists like Gaius therefore dutifully record the requirement that mancipatory acts, especially wills, have Roman-citizen witnesses, but no longer specify that any were needed for stipulation by the beginning of the second century AD.[110] These *testes* or *superstites*, as they were called,[111] were not witnesses in our sense, expected later to testify to what they had seen or read, but judges, expected to stop an act at the time of its making if the performance were flawed. They are judges in particular of behavior and ritual correctness, as has been demonstrated in a discussion of the phrase *ego vos testor* in Roman declarations of war and *testes estote* in Roman legal procedure.[112] This is why the testator in performing the nuncupation of his mancipatory will "calls" upon the Quirites "to judge" (*testor*) as well as "to bear witness to me" (*testimonium mihi perhibetote*). Men watched individual legal acts

> "created" the marriage. Cicero's uncertainty (*de Orat.* 1.183) over whether a marriage was dissolved by communication of *certis . . . verbis* or by contracting a subsequent marriage also suggests that marriage in his time was seen as a kind of unitary act to be undone either by a specific reversing formula (like a mancipation) or by a new act (as was the case in the will or the census).

[109] Juv. *Sat.* 6.200–1, a wife *legitimis pactam iunctamque tabellis*, implies strongly that this was one of the ways of announcing and thus defining marriage; similarly at 2.119–20, where the four indicators of marriage are the *tabulae*, the good wishes of the guests, the bride reclining near the husband, and the crowd of banqueters.

[110] Gaius: 1.113 (*coemptio*), 1.119 (mancipation), 2.104 (mancipatory will, "as in other mancipations"). No witnesses: this probably not originally true, cf. Magdelain (1990) 739–40; and Cicero, making rhetorical points at *Q. Rosc.* 13–14 and 38, assumes that a stipulation would have witnesses and a *scriptor*.

[111] *Testes* and *superstites* the same, cf. Fest. 305M (*superstites . . . testes praesentes significat*), also Serv. *in Aen.* 3.339 and Isid. *Orig.* 18.15.8.

[112] *Testes* as judges: Watson (1993) 10–19, improving on Gallo (1957) and Biscardi (1971); *contra* Pringsheim (1961), who sees them as defendants and assistants. *Testes* are also required for marriage by *confarreatio*, formal marriage between patricians (*G.* 1.112); the *solutio per aes et libram* (*G.* 3.173–5); *vindicatio* (Fest. 305M); proving thievery in *furtum conceptum* (*G.* 3.186); and *cretio* (*G.* 2.164–73; Var. *L.* 6.81, Cic. *Att.* 13.46.3); the fetials' declaration of war (Liv. 1.32.5–14); in *litis contestatio*, Fest. 38M, 57M (on *contestari*). Two meanings of *testor* (*contra* Lévy [1954] 108 n.47 and [1964] 137 n.19), cf. *OLD s.v.*

Tablets and efficacy

and actors for flaws, as they watched law-making and the census, and as *custodes* were added on to public prayer to guard against interruption and disturbance.[113] Conversely, for *senatusconsulta* men not specifically called *testes* are noted as being "present at its writing," *scribendo adfuerunt*, since the writing of the *senatusconsultum* is the only ceremony a *senatusconsultum* has.[114] Thus legal tablets, like those of the census, of treaties, laws, and vows-and-dedications, were nested in a larger ceremonial context whose correct performance was scrutinized and judged; the presence of *testes* itself points back to unitary acts.

Legal *tabulae* were, therefore, like other tablets important contributors to the efficacy of their own unitary acts. Late legal sources can offer some confirmation of this. This evidence comes not from Gaius's *Institutes* or juristic monographs of the sort from which much of the *Digest* was compiled, but from the *Codex*, in the answers written in response to questions about the law posed by those who had to live with it. What the questions were can usually be surmised from the answers given, and the answers show what was on the petitioners', as well as the jurists', minds:[115]

Imp. Probus A. Fortunato. si vicinis vel aliis scientibus uxorem liberorum procreandorum causa domi habuisti et ex eo matrimonio filia suscepta est, quamvis neque nuptiales tabulae neque ad natam filiam pertinentes factae sunt, non ideo minus veritas matrimonii aut susceptae filiae suam habet potestatem.

Emperor Probus to Fortunatus. If, with neighbors or others knowing, you have had a wife at home for the purpose of procreating children and a daughter has been acknowledged from this marriage, then, although neither nuptial tablets nor (tablets) pertaining to the birth of the daughter have been made, the reality (*veritas*) of the marriage or of the acknowledged daughter has its own *potestas*.

The fact of a daughter's legitimacy and the fact of a marriage, called here "reality" or "truth," seem to Fortunatus in jeopardy without these all-important *tabulae* establishing legitimate birth and legitimate marriage. Without them, can there have been a marriage? And is the daughter legitimate? The emperor's jurists reassure Fortunatus that neighborly

---

[113] See chapter four n.6.

[114] In inscriptions, this is usually abbreviated as *scr. adfuerunt*, but literal Greek translations (γραφομένωι παρῆσαν) make clear that a gerundive (*scribendo*) and not a gerund is being translated, the Greek middle participle being regularly used in this way (see *FIRA*[2] 1.242–6 no. 31, 248–66 nos. 34–6, 269–72 no. 38); so it is the act of writing and not the person writing that is being judged. Cic. *Fam.* 15.6.2 also makes this usage clear. (My thanks to E. Courtney for the reference, and for discussion.)

[115] *CJ* 5.4.9. Worries about documents in general (usually called *instrumenta*), and their role in establishing states or facts, were very strong: cf. *CJ* 4.21.8 (AD 287; establishing ownership), *CJ* 6.23.2 (AD 225; a will), *CJ* 8.55(56).2 (AD 277; a donation), *CJ* 4.21.6 (AD 286; status), *CJ* 4.21.7 (AD 286; army discharge), and *CJ* 4.21.1 (AD 213; repayment of debt).

120   *The world of belief*

knowledge of an intent to enter into a marriage and of an acknowledgment of the daughter confirmed both marriage and legitimacy. Fortunatus's question, however, had been about tablets, not neighbors. He worried that tablets created the fact of marriage and the legitimacy or citizen status of his daughter, and in their absence these facts' existence was in question. The response reassured him that reality's existence, *veritas*, had other sources as well.[116]

Petitioners like Fortunatus worried about ruined validities and altered states. Documents with which they have been careless could (they think) by their absence exert real power and do real damage to *veritas*, an understandable fear in a world where the breaking of a slave's *tabula* of mancipatory sale was perceived to set him free.[117] Such fears are born not just when documents perish, but because of the role such documents are perceived to play in the legal act they symbolize: such legal documents were efficacious, both generative and symbolic as *tabulae* in the other unitary acts had been. As jurists would discover, extracting and isolating these tablets from their traditional ceremonial context was not an easy task, but far easier than wrenching them from the stubborn web of belief that doggedly continued to value them as part of the legal act itself and seemed impervious to juristic attempts at re-education. These strongly held beliefs, so often visible only as obstinate assumptions, spanned hundreds of years and covered areas of human activity that ranged from prayers and curses to census and treaty. This understanding of legal *tabulae* as part of their ceremonial unitary acts was tenacious because it was inseparable from an understanding of process that reached far beyond the legal act itself. Thus even if Lyco's much earlier statement in Plautus's *Curculio* – "I am not to put my trust in *tabellae*, through which *res publica et privata geritur*."[118] – is only a banker's exaggerated view of the world as so many account-books, it nonetheless accurately points to the true reach of acts with *tabulae* on that *veritas* which men could not see: things public and private (which could often not be distinguished), things extending to the divine or between humans, things for the present and for the future; things that had to be done right.

---

[116] This question had clearly been put to jurists before, cf. Papinian, *D.* 39.5.31.*pr.* ("I replied . . . since it is not *tabulae* that make a marriage," *respondi . . . neque enim tabulas facere matrimonium*).

[117] Slave's *tabula*: Aug. *Serm.* 21.6 (*PL* 38.145; metaphor), explained *Ep.* 185.15 (*PL* 33.799; *pessimorum servorum, ut liberi abscederent, tabulae frangebantur*) and *CJ* 7.6.1.1 and 11 (both AD 531); see Bellen (1965). *Tabulae* of manumission are clearly attested for earlier periods, and also (when done *vindicta*) part of a unitary act: cf. Mart. *Ep.* 9.87.3 (sealing a *tabella* of manumission), *BGU* 388 (a court-protocol, ταβέλ]λας τῆς ἐλευθερώ[σεως], second half second century AD), *SB* 5217 (a court-protocol, ταβέλλαν ἐλευθερώσε[ω]ς, AD 148), *M. Chr.* 362 (diptych, AD 211), John Lydus *de Mens.* 1.28 (Wünsch), τὰ ῥήματα τῆς ἐλευθερίας on limewood tablets.

[118] Plautus *Curc.* 552.

PART TWO

The evolution of practice

The Roman ceremonial acts described in Part I, those unitary acts legal and otherwise that with the help of tablets reshaped and fixed human *veritas*, were deeply rooted in a wider world of belief, their efficacy an entrenched part of Roman tradition. Yet the world around ceremony changed in the late Republic and empire: as Rome's dominion, so too the number of Roman citizens increased. In their actions and observations these new citizens both asserted the traditionalism of ceremony and changed it, relied upon it and questioned it, maintained it and undermined it. Pressures of time and space had already caused some delicate queries about the efficacy of traditional ceremony, as Cicero's investigation of the census in the first century BC had shown. But conservative adjustments, like those of language (*concepta verba* for *certa*), kept these ceremonial acts usable, while praetorian endorsements of informal legal acts (like consensual rather than stipulatory contracts) kept these formal acts distinct, and juristic commentary preserved both useability and distinctiveness. Such adjustment and parallel development allowed Rome's expansion into world empire to stretch or multiply many traditional Roman institutions, and permitted Romans of the late Republic and empire to adapt and assert, rather than lose, some fundamental sense of what it meant to be Roman in a rapidly changing world.

Even those Romans who might have questioned the point of ritual often performed it, for if nothing else – and ritual was frequently much else – the prestige of Roman citizen-status could be very usefully displayed in these traditional ceremonial acts reserved (when a matter of law) for Roman citizens. Consciousness of status could be a conservative force, prestige itself a bulwark against too much change. The social importance and legal privilege of Roman status helped to maintain the importance and distinctiveness of ceremonial acts, and of the tablets that were a part of them. In Campania in the first century AD, *tabulae* were not merely used by citizens, but can be seen to carry an increasing number of indicators of status-linked *fides* and may well have helped to establish a visible validity for informal, *bona*

122 *The evolution of practice*

fides acts. In the provinces, Roman citizens followed what they perceived to be Roman legal practices, and others who were not Roman citizens can be found at times imitating them, or at least imitating the physical form of their documents. A provincial elite distinguished in part by its adherence to strange and exclusive practices will support tradition in resolute if not necessarily accurate ways, reinforcing the received authority of *tabulae* with the anxious weight of their social pretension. All of this contributed to the continued use of tablets for certain kinds of legal acts: they can be found as late as the fifth century AD in Vandal North Africa.

Yet the assertive, even ferocious, competitiveness for Roman prestige, in itself so traditionally Roman, put pressure on Roman traditions at the same time. Thus the story of the *tabula* within the larger history of Roman legal documents is not simply that of its distinctive association with Roman-citizen acts, and its consequent spread into the provinces in the hands of Roman citizens. How a tablet was used subsequent to its generation – how it was valued and adduced as proof or attestation, whether of status or acts or character – moves it, in our perspective, from the sedate and careful world of Roman Republican ceremony into the lively, confrontational, and honor-drenched world of Roman imperial justice, and helps to explain how the dynamics of that world encouraged extensions of the *tabula*'s use and adjustments to its physical form and content. Moreover, Roman forensic realities make clear that while tablets' authority is, if anything, enhanced by the wary sensitivity to honor of the Roman courts, any claim to *exclusive* authority through tablets has been, by the third century AD, successfully undermined by the same sensitivity to honor and personal prestige, for other documents, especially holographic ones – written in one's own hand – came to be valued equally highly also. The influence of *fides* and prestige on traditional ceremonial form is thus both conservative and destabilizing, contributing simultaneously to its survival and to the creation of parallel channels eventually seen to possess similar value in practical application.

Roman judges (amateurs and gentlemen, in formulary procedure) were free to assess the value of all sorts of documents as they liked, and the continued but not exclusive importance of *tabulae* in their courts points to the fact that these men valued both formality and *fides*, as did their official counterparts in the provinces, Roman governors who presided over the inquisitorial procedure known as *cognitio*. But what to a Roman at Rome was a free system of proof through which his own traditional beliefs and social prejudices were expressed became, in a provincial setting, more of a trend-setting model, a paradigmatic if not perfectly predictable expression

The evolution of practice

of what the Romans wanted. By merely being himself, which meant being a Roman of a certain standing with a certain outlook, a governor could create a standard, as imperial behavior could set a standard for governors merely by example. By his very existence he could change how provincials, even Roman-citizen provincials, weighed documents or how they had them drafted in the first place. His authoritative presence and how he was to be approached similarly had an effect, over time, on the legal acts that were performed before him. By the third century AD, his endorsement of legal acts and his acceptance of legal documents is another factor, added to traditional formality and admired *fides*, that contributes to what a *tabula* is and how it can change.

Behind this governor stand emperor and jurists, who start to involve themselves authoritatively with these issues of legal acts, legal *tabulae*, and legal validity in the second century. The emperor is, increasingly, the ultimate official presence and official opinion, and by responding to petitions and answering questions jurists who have been given the *ius respondendi*, the right to give legal opinions that will be valid in court,[1] can change how people weigh and draft documents. They too become a party whose opinion on the questions of value and validity matters, as a praetor discovered when he had the jurist Ulpian out to the country villa for a weekend sometime before AD 208: when the praetor wished to manumit a slave but was not accompanied by his lictor whose presence was technically required, Ulpian, here the soul of congeniality, "allowed it."[2] The more the jurists' opinions are endorsed by the emperor, as they are in the fourth century AD and after, the more weight their opinions can have. By becoming authoritatively involved, emperors and jurists make the free system of proof less free, and help to establish a new societal standard for valid legal documents in which wooden *tabulae* are no longer dominant.

To combine what tablets were once believed to be (Part I) with what tablets were and how they were used both outside and within court, and in part shaped by that use (Part II), is to place what people believe about tradition (itself relatively stable and comparatively fixed) into the wider and more fluid world of what people actually did and why they did it. This juxtaposition therefore not only requires a shift in major focus from

---

[1] *D*.1.2.2.49 (Pomponius), a right conferred by Augustus "in order to increase the authority of the law" (*ut maior iuris auctoritas haberetur*); before this time jurists did not give sealed *responsa*, but rather wrote a letter to the judge or gave testimony. These were probably double-documents (debate, Wenger [1923] col. 2427, Katzoff [1982a], very few examples in Egypt; Frier [1996] 962–3), which demonstrates also that they were to be used in court.

[2] *Passus est*, *D*. 40.2.8, discussed by Honoré (1982) 18, who suggests the date and also points out that an earlier jurist in a similar situation had to persuade praetors to listen to him.

The evolution of practice

Republic to empire and from Rome to Italy and the provinces, but also gives a mandate to locate these beliefs and practices in time: instead of looking, synchronically, for characteristics and capacities that *tabulae* share over time and place, it is now both possible and necessary to look diachronically, to look for what happens to tablets as they are used, adduced in court, and weighed by the ultimate arbiters of value and validity over time. Bankers and businessmen, judges and officials, plaintiffs and defendants, the high and the low, emperors and jurists are the protagonists here.

Part II therefore traces expansions in the significance of *tabulae* that depend on both geographical and chronological changes. It is possible to start close to Rome, in the commercial Campanian cities of Pompeii and Herculaneum in the first century AD, where the many surviving *tabulae* preserve for the first time individual acts of both a legal and a financial nature, and show how the physical form of these *tabulae* was adapted and elaborated over time in response to concerns about how the tablets could be used subsequent to their creation (chapter six). Between the later first and the third centuries, it is the provinces, and especially Egypt, where *tabulae* are found, and where the dynamic of Roman example and provincial imitation and variation can best be traced (chapter seven). From all over – both Rome and provinces – comes the scattered evidence that stitches into a comprehensible picture of what happened in a Roman court, and what kind of pressures courtroom values put on litigants, on *tabulae*, and on the lighter papyrus documents, especially letters (chapter eight). Courts were not perfectly predictable, and practices not perfectly uniform. Yet the ways in which people wanted the *tabulae* to embody personal as well as ritual value, to continue to speak rather than merely to mark a finished and authoritative act, affected what they did and what happened in court. All this, as a consequence, affected the sorts of questions jurists were asked, and, along with the even more fundamental questions and problems that formal ceremonial acts themselves by their nature posed, shaped the arguments and decisions about legal acts, *tabulae*, and documents jurists and emperors arrived at in the centuries of the late Empire (chapter nine).

CHAPTER 6

Roman tablets in Italy (AD 15–79)

As a result of the eruption of Vesuvius, over four hundred legal and financial *tabulae* dating between AD 15 and AD 79 have been preserved in the Campanian region of Italy. Over these sixty-four years, several important changes in both the physical form and the internal formulation of these tablets can be observed, changes that are part of the larger transformation of the *tabula* from the authoritative embodiment of a ceremonial act into the embodiment of an act that drew its authority not only from the process of its making but also from the people who made it. These changes fall along three interrelated trajectories. First, there was a change in physical form, from diptych to triptych, that occurred at a different time and a different rate for documents of different types of act, reflecting not only the traditional linkage of type of legal act, style of writing, and physical form but also the conservative qualities of *tabulae* distantly or closely associated with ceremonial, unitary acts. Second, as physical forms changed so too did at least some of the acts themselves, the traditional association of act and form reinforced by the way change in both form and content took place: as a third tablet was hinged to the original two, so too were different acts added to but not coalesced with the original one, creating a multi-part combinational act on a triptych. The parallel is not exact, since the new tablet is not used for the texts of additional acts; instead, this third tablet protects seals. The development of the triptych form therefore also emphasizes a third change, the enhanced importance of sealing, an importance that itself reflects the way in which *fides*, faith, was increasingly added on to, and incorporated into, all wooden documents. This combining of formality and *fides* on the physical level, and of ceremonial acts and *bona fides* acts on the stylistic and conceptual level, had begun before AD 15 and would continue on after AD 79. Among the consequences visible before AD 79 is the incipient blending of the once-separate functions of *testes* and *signatores*, witness-judges and sealers, a melding acknowledged in a *senatusconsultum*

125

126   *The evolution of practice*

of AD 61 that marks the first certain and last known intervention of the state in the making of legal *tabulae* before the late antique period.

THE CAMPANIAN TABLETS

The collection of Roman wooden tablets known for the longest time came to light in July 1875, in the remains of a wooden chest carbonized by the flow of Mt. Vesuvius's eruption in AD 79. These are 153 documents of L. Caecilius Jucundus, a Pompeian banker who regularly extended credit at auctions, and are mostly *acceptilationes* (releases from obligation under *stipulatio*) for loans and rent-payments.[1] Two additional documents on *tabulae* were found (with a stash of gold and silver) in a Pompeian bath's furnace, in 1887: a (complete) mancipation of slaves as *fiducia* – to serve as surety – for a (fragmentary) loan secured by a stipulation.[2] Many more *tabulae* were subsequently discovered in wooden chests in different houses at Herculaneum between 1930 and 1940, and another 175 or so *tabulae* in a basket in a villa outside Pompeii's Stabian Gate in the so-called "Murecinian field," in 1959.[3] The Herculaneum tablets (*TH*) are financial, judicial, and property documents of a number of different people, while the Murecine tablets (*TPSulp.*) are the financial and legal transactions of three generations of freedmen Sulpicii, bankers active in Puteoli.[4] Jucundus's *tabulae* date between 15 and 62 (98 percent between 52 and 62), the Murecine tablets between 26 and 61 (87 percent between 35 and 55), and the Herculaneum tablets between 40 and 75 (60 percent after AD 61).[5]

No special significance can be attributed to the survival of these specific tablets, since they might have been merely awaiting cleaning-up and

---

[1] Finding of Jucundus's tablets (supplement one of *CIL* 4, hereafter referred to merely as *CIL* 4; nos. 3340.1–153) in his house: Andreau (1974) 13 n.1.

[2] These two (*CIL* 4.3340.154–5) date to AD 79 (Camodeca [1993d] 356), find-circumstances summarized by Zangemeister (1898) 406.

[3] The earliest finds of tablets in Herculaneum were in 1752 and 1754 (thirty illegible fragments, Del Mastro [1999]); most of the tablets were found, scattered through various buildings, when excavations recommenced in 1927, cf. Maiuri (1946); dates, Eck (1998) 209. There are approximately 160 legal acts from Herculaneum on an unspecified number of *tabulae* (Camodeca [2000] 54); it is unclear to me whether Camodeca is including Del Mastro's thirty fragments in his numbers; Camodeca (1999a) 18–20 estimates that at Murecine there were 173 or 185 tablets, and should have been about 350 tablets, combined as *c.* 130 diptychs and triptychs.

[4] Gröschler (1997) 57–66.

[5] Jucundus: limits set by *CIL* 4.3340.1 (AD 15) and *CIL* 4.3340.151 (AD 62); Murecine, *TPSulp.* 42 (AD 26 or 29) and *TPSulp.* 90–2 (AD 61), these dates and 87% from AD 35–55, Camodeca (1999a) 20; Herculaneum, Della Corte (1951) 228 no. 12 with Camodeca (1992) 19 n.44 (possibly AD 40, cf. Camodeca [1999b] 538) and *TH* 13–24 (AD 75), and 60% after AD 61, Camodeca (1995a) 73.

Roman tablets in Italy (AD 15–79) 127

reuse.[6] The tablets do not offer a comprehensive view of legal and financial documentation in the Campanian region, the type of document (e.g. mancipation or discharge of obligation) is frequently not the same from collection to collection, a substantial proportion of each collection cannot be securely dated,[7] many documents are not complete,[8] some are still unpublished,[9] and our understanding of the contents and the physical form of many of the documents has changed substantially upon re-editing, a project not yet finished.[10] The degree of speculation here is, therefore, high. The disadvantages are, however, offset by the richness of the materials and their closeness to practices in the city of Rome itself. Many of the region's great proprietors were Roman grandees, while some of the businessmen were themselves freedmen, or descendants of freedmen, of the Roman nobility;[11] and some of the legal cases were bound over to continue in Rome itself, in the forum of Augustus.[12] No one has ever doubted that the forms, materials, and law employed in Campania were identical to those in use at the same time in the city of Rome.

Given the constraints of the evidence, the changes in the physical form of these *tabulae*-documents are the most challenging to track. The earliest surviving document (*CIL* 4.3340.1, of AD 15) suggests that the first preserved stage was that of a simple diptych (**fig. 1**): a single text was written parallel

---

[6] Gröschler (1997) 26; Crook (1978) 238–9 suggests rejected drafts. Tablets from Pompeii show signs of reuse, e.g., *TPSulp.* 5, 10, 75, 83; *CIL* 4.3340.15, 17, 20, 22, 23, 30, 33, 39, 58, 126, 148, and 150.

[7] Murecine: 78 of 127 documents can be dated (60%), Camodeca (1999a) 20; *CIL*, 61 of 155 (39.4%; but most are dated before AD 62 by context); from Herculaneum no good statistics appear to be available yet.

[8] Jucundus's collection is 97% complete (Camodeca [1995a] 64), but Camodeca (1999a) 32 estimates that only 20% of the surviving documents from Murecine are complete; I know of no estimates for Herculaneum.

[9] From Herculaneum: since Camodeca (2000) 54 estimates that he has approximately 160 documents and the original editors published only 115, there are still at least forty left.

[10] Even fundamental facts like whether a *tabula* was written on with ink (making the writing exterior) or with a stylus (i.e. once on wax) can be misunderstood (*TH* 59, 60, and 63: Della Corte [1951] 225, 227, 229 compared with Arangio-Ruiz and Pugliese Carratelli [1954] 55 and 57); Della Corte used the term *pertusa* for notched rather than perforated tablets, thus misidentifying some as triptychs, Camodeca (1995a) 71; and even Arangio-Ruiz and Pugliese Carratelli were careless in claiming that tablets were *pertusae* (e.g., *TH* 4, 65, 89, 74 with Camodeca [1995a] 73). The physical descriptions of the unrevised *TH* documents must be considered less reliable than those of *CIL* and *TPSulp.*

[11] Proprietors, D'Arms (1970) 171–232 (late Republican and imperial) and (1981) 72–96; and Gardner (1999) 13–14 on Domitia Lepida (Nero's aunt) and Lollia Saturnina; relationship to Roman nobility, cf. (e.g.) Camodeca (1992) 28; note also the number of imperial freedmen active in Puteoli, Andreau (1994) 46–7. Even the dating, by *suffecti* rather than *ordinarii*, emphasizes the exceptional closeness to Rome, Rowe (2001) 228.

[12] *TPSulp.* 13–15, 19 (with Camodeca [1986]), and 27 (not a *vadimonium*, but makes mention of a *vadimonium . . . Romae*); *TH* 6 (undated), 13–15 (AD 75); 85 (AD 47) is a *sententia iudicis* handed down in Rome, Camodeca (1993c) 524–5 and (1999b) 532; cf. Cic. 2*Verr.* 5.34, people coming from municipalities to Rome *vadimonii causa*.

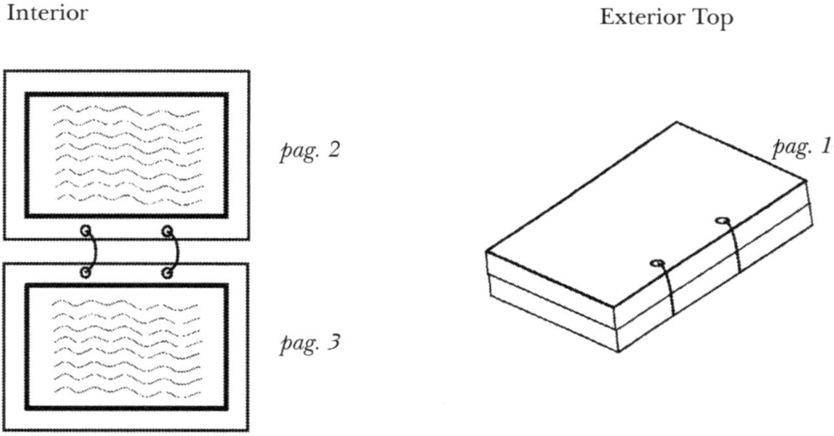

128 *The evolution of practice*

Interior   Exterior Top

pag. 2   *pag. 1*

pag. 3

Figure 1   Phase 1 Campanian wooden document.
Simple diptych with text of document written parallel to long sides of interior wax faces
(*pag.* 2 and 3). *Tabulae* hinged together but not sealed.

to the long side on the two interior wax faces (called *paginae*) of two *tabulae* that had been hinged together; these *tabulae* were then closed by having a string or *linum* wound around their middles for which the edges of these tablets are notched. In the second phase (**fig. 2**), this diptych comes to have a second, duplicate version of its text written in ink parallel to the short side (*transversa*) on the two outside faces of the two tablets, its string attached more securely to the wood by seals. The names of the sealers are written by a scribe to the right of a narrow groove or *stria* running down the middle of the exterior face of the second *tabula*, the *linum* then placed in this groove and seals placed over it. This form I call a doubled diptych. In the third phase (**fig. 3**), sometimes (but probably incorrectly) called "tripled writing," the *stria* is widened and deepened, and is now called a *sulcus*;[13]

---

[13] Because it is assumed that the seals are placed in the *sulcus so that* a third *tabula* can close up against the back of the second, the physical form of *any* document with a *sulcus* has been identified as a triptych. Phase-three *tabulae* have therefore been called "tripled writing" and assumed to be triptychs with *two* identical exterior texts, one running from *pagina* four to *pagina* one, as it would in a diptych, the second on the interior wax face of the third tablet. Yet *tabulae* identified as "tripled writing" are all fragmentary, the third tablet almost always missing, and none actually presents two identical exterior copies; Macqueron (1982) 7 cites *CIL* 4.3340.154 (Poppaea Note's *sponsio*) as the only example, but the exterior writing on *paginae* one, four, and five is so badly preserved (only *act. Pomp.* can be read on both *paginae* one and five) that it is uncertain that there were two exterior versions of the interior text (rather than one long exterior version, as is probably true of *CIL* 4.3340.155, Poppaea Note's *mancipatio*, see below pp. 140–2). Three of Jucundus's documents were thought by Zangemeister (1898) 418–20, 430–1 to be tripled, but as a *testatio*-style text, a copy of same, and then a version in chirograph style; this way of "tripling" a text is anomalous, is not usually what is meant when

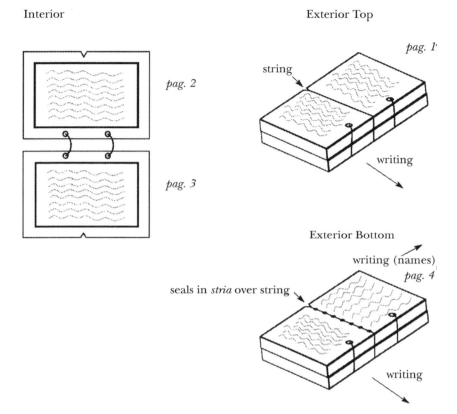

Figure 2 Phase 2 Campanian wooden document.
Doubled diptych closed with string (*linum*) and seals (*signa*). String and seals in shallow groove (*stria*) with names of sealers in ink to the right (*pag.* 4, right). First version of document written parallel to long sides of interior wax faces (*pag.* 2 and 3). Second version of document written in ink parallel to short side (*transversa*) on outside faces of tablets (*pag.* 1 and *pag.* 4, left).

in the fourth phase (**fig. 4**), a third *tabula* is added, making the entire document a triptych. In a triptych, it is still only the first two *tabulae* that are sealed shut, the seals placed over the *linum* in the *sulcus*; the deeper cut

scholars call a text "tripled," and is discussed below p. 143. I therefore doubt that "tripled writing on triptychs" ever existed, and find it more likely that the fragmentary phase-three documents are merely diptychs with a *sulcus*; as a way of noting that the question is not yet settled, I will keep this category distinct and call them "phase-three documents." See Arangio-Ruiz (1974 [1958]) 519 (noting the similarity to diptychs) and Camodeca (1992) 15 n.33 and (1995a) 63 n.10 and 76 (where he reserves judgment on tripling until he has finished re-editing *TH*; in [1999a] 33 and *passim* he regularly identifies documents with a *sulcus* as triptychs).

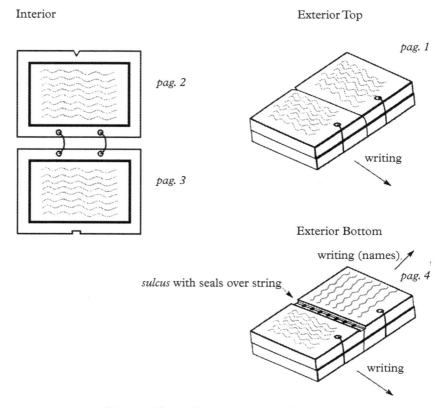

Figure 3 Phase 3 Campanian wooden document.
Doubled diptych with deep groove (*sulcus*) for seals.

of the *sulcus* allows the third tablet to lie against the second and protect the seals. This third *tabula* is hinged in with the other two but not sealed shut with them, and the only exterior text is now placed on its interior wax face. In the fifth stage (**fig. 5**) there is a different way of winding the *linum*: it is threaded through holes in the tablets near the top and bottom of the *sulcus* and then sealed over as before. This makes a tablet *pertusa* or "perforated," and is the consequence of a *senatusconsultum* passed in AD 61.[14] The pace of all these changes, visible between AD 15 and AD 79, is unhurried. Overall, *tabulae* clearly identified as diptychs (phases one–two) are clearly going out of use even before these Campanian tablets begin to survive – 27 percent of

---

[14] Discussed at greater length below, pp. 165–8; the date first identified by Zangemeister (1898) 278 as being between July 61 and June 62.

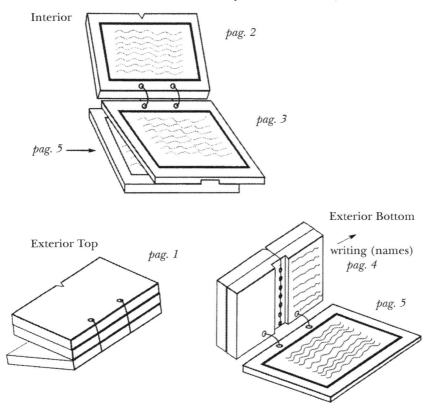

Figure 4 Phase 4 Campanian wooden document.
Triptych. First version of document written parallel to long sides of interior wax faces (*pag.* 2 and 3) of two sealed *tabulae*. Names of sealers in ink to the right of their seals (*pag.* 4, right). Second version of document written parallel to long sides of interior wax face of third *tabula* (*pag.* 5). Third *tabula* hinged to others but not sealed: when folded against the two sealed *tabulae* the seals in their *sulcus* (*pag.* 4) and the second text (*pag.* 5) are protected.

the tablets at Murecine are diptychs, but only 7 percent for Jucundus and 7 percent at Herculaneum[15] – and the *senatusconsultum* requiring change in the winding of the string took effect only gradually, the transition period being almost two years.[16]

---

[15] Camodeca (1992) 16 (Jucundus), and at 19 (Herculaneum) he also argues that this is not a matter of local variation; also Camodeca (1995a) 66–7, (1999a) 34 (Murecine).

[16] Camodeca (1995a) 74, mid-61 to May 63: the earliest was *CIL* 4.3340.152 (before Feb. 62), the last not to have it *TH* 61 (May 63); cf. Camodeca (1993d) 360, the change came more slowly to "small and residential" Herculaneum than to Puteoli.

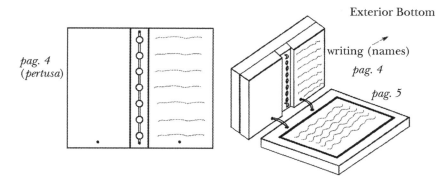

Figure 5 Phase 5 Campanian wooden document.
Triptych pierced (*pertusa*) obedient to the *sc* of AD 61. String with seals no longer passes around tablets but through holes drilled through them.

Why were these changes in physical form adopted? G. Camodeca has suggested that the shift from diptych to triptych was a trend of no particular significance.[17] Yet the fact that the documents of some types of act seem to have embraced this overall change less uniformly and less speedily than others permits a more nuanced interpretation. As will be seen, legal acts that were formal, especially procedural ones associated with *tabulae* and with using correct words and gestures, used the diptych form consistently before AD 50; financial acts (including mancipations) that made use of a *tabula* as part of their process appear as phase-three writing in the forties AD and survive as such as late as the early sixties. The triptych, on the other hand, is more uniformly associated with legal acts based on *bona fides* or trust, informal acts enforced by the praetorian edict, and begins to appear consistently for these acts as early as AD 35. All this suggests that the type of legal act undertaken determines, at least initially, the physical form chosen and the rate at which a different and newer form, the triptych, was adopted.

Type of act and the physical form of a document are associated with styles of composition and sealing as well. Although I suspect that there was once a time when a *tabula*-document associated with a unitary act was both unsealed and undoubled, by the early Empire in Campania there are no certain and few possible examples of this.[18] Instead, formal acts, all written as third-person narrations ("L. Sulpicius Cinnamus said that..."),

---

[17] Camodeca (1992) 19–20; (1995a) 66–7.
[18] I think *CIL* 4.3340.1 is a certain example: see below p. 143. Note also that most of the *tabulae* that were not legal tablets of individuals (like the census or curse-tablets, discussed in Part I) and even wills (which were), did not have doubled texts.

Roman tablets in Italy (AD 15–79)

are mostly sealed by multiple people (at least seven, but ranging up to eleven), while the acts based on *fides*, written as first-person narrations ("I have written that . . ."), are sealed by between three and six people, the author of the document usually sealing twice, at the top and the bottom of the *sulcus* where the string was most likely to pull away.[19] The first way of writing and sealing scholars call the *testatio*, since it sometimes claims to be "attesting," while the second calls itself the *chirographum*, the "handwritten," since although often and without controversy written by a third party,[20] it purports to be the personal writing of the chief actor involved. The two differ in the style of their formulation because this difference is dictated by the type of act they convey. That is, the *testatio style* is used for formal and procedural *acts* and holds on to the diptych *form* (or its derivative) longer, while the chirograph *style* is used for informal *acts* and agreements and embraces the triptych *form* more consistently at an earlier date.

The association of a certain style and a certain physical form with unitary acts is itself to be expected, as Part I has made clear. Modifications of form therefore suggest that modifications of style and act are also occurring. These are indeed found in some of the unitary acts, which expand by adding, in sequential fashion, other acts into the same document, making one large "combinational" act, at times in more than one style. People performing unitary legal acts with tablets in this sixty-five-year span of the first century AD thereby demonstrated their ability to make use of these acts' traditional capacity for careful flexibility and inclusion of the needful, even to the extent of incorporating very different types of acts – those based on *bona fides* – into this formal context. Simultaneously, a heightened empha-sis on *fides* is perceptible in the changes to each document's physical form, reflecting the ways in which documents were used and valued. This chapter will therefore look first at formal acts in *testatio* style (and the changes in their physical form, noting the ways other acts come to be added on); then chirograph-style acts and their close relationship to *fides* (and, surprisingly, to the formal act of *stipulatio*); and will then end with an assessment of how formality and *fides* entwined over time by tracing the ways in which witnesses who judged the correctness of a formal performance and sealers

---

[19] Sealing in *testatio*-style documents, see Zangemeister (1898) 432 and Camodeca (1992) 232, with *CIL* 4.3340.37, an example of eleven seals; sealing close to the edges of chirographs, Mommsen (1907 [1877]) 239, Erman (1899) 176–7.

[20] E.g., *TPSulp.* 78 (AD 38), *TPSulp.* 46 (AD 40), *TPSulp.* 98 (AD 43–5), *TPSulp.* 82 (AD 44–5?); *TH* 45 (AD 59, with Camodeca [2002a] 272–5); *CIL* 4.3340.17 (exterior), 22–5, 30, 34–5, 40, 46; cf. Camodeca (1992) 32–3 n.34; Marichal (1992a) 177 estimates that 54 percent of Jucundus's documents were written by third parties. Also, *D.* 20.1.26.1 (Modestinus), son writes chirograph for father.

134   *The evolution of practice*

who supported an act's protagonist with their *fides* were amalgamating their
once separate roles by the second century AD. None of this changes the fact
that a *tabula* was important for the act in which it participated, but points
to new types of attributed meaning and usefulness that will help to shift
our focus from a tablet's active role in the performance of a legal act to its
afterlife in the courts and the wider world of Roman justice.

FORMAL, PROCEDURAL, *TABULA*-BASED ACTS: THE "*TESTATIONES*" IN THE FIRST CENTURY AD

The purpose of this section is to demonstrate that in Pompeii and
Herculaneum, the surviving documents written in *testatio* style are the
old formal acts of Roman law or acts clearly related to them, and that
they change to triptych form slowly – more slowly than the documents in
chirograph style (pages 148–58) do. These *tabulae* are acts associated with
formulary procedure, like *vadimonia* (promises to appear for trial), *tabulae
sistendi* (attestations that one had, in fact, appeared), *interrogationes in iure*
(interrogations by the magistrate to determine liability) and *denuntiones*
(statements to that magistrate), formulae granting *iudices*, the giving of
cognitores (representatives), the performance of oaths, *testationes* (declarations), the formal passing (called the *intertium*) to the giving of the sentence,
and the sentence itself; the *nomina arcaria* (recently identified as attested
extracts from the account-*tabulae* of a bank or a freedman's patron)[21] and
other attested copies of *tabulae*; the conveyance of property through mancipation; and financial "receipts" modelled on *acceptilatio*, ceremonial release
from the obligation created by stipulation. Not every type of legal unitary
act leaves a record in Campania, and the spectrum represented is considerably wider than the simplifying categories of Part I would lead us to expect,
drawing in unsuspected subsets of related *tabulae*; but all documents in
testatio style have this common unitary-act background.

   (a) Vadimonia *and other procedural documents.* As the Campanian collections make clear, many stages and acts of formulary procedure – not
just that of bringing the charge to the praetor – made use of *tabulae*, the
early ones diptychs and the later triptychs. *Vadimonia*, given in response
to a summons or independently,[22] are agreements to meet to go to a legal

---

[21] Gröschler (1997) 372 (summary).
[22] Such agreements are made at moments when a defendant cannot come when he is summoned, when
a case is not completed in one day, or when it transpires that a case must be heard at Rome rather than
in a municipality, all discussed in detail in the praetor's edict, cf. *G.* 4.184–7, where the assumption is
that they are imposed by the magistrate. All surviving Campanian examples are actually agreements
between parties without any apparent intervention of the magistrate, see Kunkel (1973) 212–13 (on

Roman tablets in Italy (AD 15–79)

hearing in a variety of locations in different cities (Puteoli, Capua, Rome).[23] Of the twenty-one that survive, five are diptychs that can be dated to AD 52 or before; the earliest datable triptych is assigned to AD 48, while three others date to AD 75.[24] One *tabula sistendi*, a diptych, dates to AD 51, while two triptychs cannot be dated.[25] Two *interrogationes in iure* of AD 35 are diptychs and one *denuntiatio* a later triptych, while one *datio cognitoris* of AD 43 and two oaths of AD 49 are on diptychs, as are the notations of *intertium*.[26] Twelve datable declarations also confirm the early-diptych/late-triptych pattern, the earliest being two diptychs of AD 34 and AD 53, and eight of the other ten being triptychs dated after AD 70.[27] All in all, for twenty-seven of these fifty-eight procedural documents both form and date are known; all fourteen datable diptychs fall before AD 53, and all thirteen datable triptychs after AD 48.

One of the undated *vadimonia* and three of the declarations are phase-three documents. This seems to be a transitional option as documents evolve, probably still a diptych, with a second copy of the text beginning *transversa* on the back of *pagina* 4 (the outer face of the second *tabula*), but also with the deep *sulcus* of the triptych.[28] Phase-three writing is, like diptychs themselves, not uncommon among procedural acts written in *testatio* style, used not only for *vadimonia* and *testationes*, and for *compromissa* about a court case and for what appears to be some form of record of a case heard before a *iudex*,[29] but also for the agreements to abide by

---

SEG 18.555, a proconsular letter mentioning a *vadimonium*; Cyme, 27 BC) and Camodeca (1992) 43.

[23] *TPSulp.* 1bis, 1–15, 96; *CIL* 4.3340.33 (palimpsest); *TH* 6, 13–15; see also Cloud (2002).

[24] Diptychs: *TPSulp.* 1bis (AD 41, or 43–5), 12 (AD 40 or 43–4), 14 (after AD 44), 1 (AD 47), and 4 (AD 52); *TPSulp.* 15 cannot be dated. Triptychs: *TPSulp.* 3 (AD 48), *TH* 13–15 (AD 75); *TPSulp.* 6 and 10, and *TH* 6 (a phase-three document) cannot be dated. The other eight (see above n.23) are of uncertain physical form, since seven of them are only the first *tabula* (*TPSulp.* 11 may be a third *tabula*), and one is a palimpsest, i.e. existing only as traces on a tablet subsequently reused in a triptych.

[25] *Tabulae sistendi*: *TPSulp.* 16 (diptych); 18 and 21 cannot be dated; 19 (AD 40), 17 (AD 51) and 20 (no date) are of uncertain form.

[26] *Interrogationes in iure*: *TPSulp.* 23–4 (diptychs). *Denuntiationes*: *TPSulp.* 25 (triptych, AD 55); in *TPSulp.* 26 (AD 44) the form is unclear. *Datio cognitoris*: Della Corte (1951) 226 no. 5, republished by Camodeca (2002b) 230. Oaths: *TPSulp.* 28–9. *Intertium*: *TPSulp.* 32 (diptych, AD 48); the diptych *TPSulp.* 33 cannot be dated.

[27] Declarations (*testationes*): diptychs, *TPSulp.* 96 (AD 34) and 89 (AD 53); *TPSulp.* 116 cannot be dated. Three are phase-three documents: *TH* 87 (AD 70), 2 (AD 70–2), and 83 (no date). Triptychs: *TPSulp.* 87 (AD 51) and *TH* 16–20, 23–4 (all AD 75); for *TPSulp.* 41 (AD 39), 40 (AD 51), and 117 (no date) the form is uncertain. *TH* 21–2, 25–6, and 28 are probably triptychs of *testimonia* but cannot be dated, and may be a mixed form, since the language is that of a chirograph (*scripsi et iuravi*) but the sealing pattern that of a *testatio*; they are therefore not counted in the formal-act totals.

[28] *Vadimonium*, *TH* 6 (no date); declarations, see above n.27. No third *tabula* survives for any of these.

[29] *Compromissum*, *TPSulp.* 34 (AD 55?) and *TH* 82 (AD 52); in both cases, the governing verb is also missing); records, *TH* 86 (no date; this may be a record of a private agreement between disputants before trial, Kunkel [1973] 204).

136   *The evolution of practice*

the verdict of an arbiter, the *sententiae* or decisions he handed down, and records of a hearing before him, all dating between AD 62 and AD 69.[30] There are of course triptychs in these worlds of judicial or arbitral procedure as well, as was seen with *vadimonia* and witness statements: a formula granting a *iudex* dates from AD 52, a *sententia* of a *iudex* dates from AD 47, and two declarations in which an arbiter sets a day for a hearing date from AD 55.[31] Yet the impression given here too is one of a shift in the late forties: from diptychs to either triptychs (as in the preceding paragraph) or to phase-three writing. As diptychs change, they can take one of two forms; indisputable triptychs become dominant only in the seventies.

(b) Copies from tabulae *and the* nomina arcaria. This use of phase-three writing and its virtually simultaneous appearance with triptychs is shared by copies of *tabulae*, copies of account-book transactions (the *nomina arcaria*), and mancipations. Copies or extracts from official *tabulae* were always couched in *testatio* style and also written first on diptychs, then doubled with a *sulcus* (phase three), and finally recorded on triptychs. These documents often announce themselves as copies by beginning "*descriptum et recognitum ex . . . ,*" naming the *tabula*-document (or part of it) they were copying or extracting – frequently an edict – and the place where this *tabula* had been nailed up or found. These copies were copied again as exterior texts, the entirety sealed by seven or more people. Official Roman documents posted or accessible in Rome or elsewhere were copied with this language and sealed in this style,[32] and indeed the copies are commonly found in the provinces, most strikingly in the form of the military "diploma," a

---

[30] An arbiter was a man chosen instead of a *iudex* by the magistrate because of his greater specialized knowledge, and he would hear the second part of a civil case as a *iudex* would; records of his hearings would be parallel to records of a *iudex*'s hearings, Kunkel (1973) 203. Agreements, *TH* 84 (possibly *c.* AD 62) and 76 (AD 69); *sententiae, TH* 79 (AD 69) and 81 (no date); records of an arbitration, *TH* 77 + 78 + 80 + 53 + 92 (AD 69), with Camodeca (1994). The form of three other arbiter's declarations, *TPSulp.* 37 (AD 55–6), and 38–9 (no date), cannot be determined.

[31] *Formula, TPSulp.* 31; *sententia, TH* 85; declarations, *TPSulp.* 35–6. *TH* 91 (triptych), in which an agreement is forbidden (label: *pactos vetat*), is undated.

[32] E.g., a decree of a proconsul (*CIL* 10.7852 = *FIRA*² 1.322–4 no. 59, *ex codice ansato*, AD 69, with Haensch [1992] 222–3 n.36, Sardinia); *senatusconsultum* (*FIRA*² 1.291–3 no. 47, *ex libro sententiarum in senatu dictarum*, wooden diptych of AD 138, North Africa); imperial subscription (*IKSmyrna* 598 = *IGR* 4.1430 with W. Williams [1976] 235–40), [ἐκγεγ]ραμμέ[νον] καὶ ἀντιβεβλημ[ένον ἐκ τεύχους βιβλειδίων προτεθέντων ἐν ʽΡωμῃ ἐν τῷ] Παλατ[ί]ῳ ἱερῷ Ἀπόλλω[νος]; imperial grant (*AE* 1986.628, Kaygusuz [1986] 66–7 no. 3, *ex commen*]tari(*i*)*s . . . Lu*[*ci*(*i*)], Ainos); or edict of proconsul (Nollé [1982] 13 lines 20–1 with 32–40 and 55–6, ἐκ τεύχους χαρτίνου διαταγμάτων, AD 209, Mandragoreis); attested copies of subscribed petitions posted in Egypt and Palestine, cf. Hauken (1998) 98–105, 138–9 and chapter seven nn.114 and 133. Also, *D.* 10.2.5 (Gaius); cf. Erman (1905b) 457, W. Williams (1975) 63, and Cic. 2*Verr.* 2.189–190, the copying of the *tabulae* of the *societas* of the *publicani: exscribo . . . haec omnia . . . recognita et collata et ab hominibus honestissimis obsignata sunt.* Sealing, see below n.119.

Roman tablets in Italy (AD 15–79)   137

diptych copied from an original posted at Rome.[33] Campania provides three, possibly five, examples of this type of document in the later stage of its evolution. At Herculaneum, a triptych of AD 62 (*TH* 89) copies an edict of L. Servinius Gallus that bears in some way on the petitioned-for full (rather than Junian) Roman citizenship of L. Venidius Ennychus and his wife, while *TH* 5 (phase-three writing of AD 60) gives a *professio* of birth, and *TH* 88, the same from AD 66, the end of the nomination of a tutor – both acts which, if performed in Italian cities as they were by the Roman prefect or *iuridicus* in Egypt, were posted as an edict that included a list, from which individual copies of the relevant entry, like this one, could be made by interested parties.[34] Copies were also made of *libelli* – by legal requirement posted for thirty days – that announced the upcoming auction of encumbered property, with notation of dates of posting; nine of them survive, six on diptychs.[35] *Tabula*-originals, the embodiments of magisterial or procedural acts, prompt *tabella*- or *tabula*-copies, in *testatio* style and diptych form, changing only in some cases to phase-three writing or triptych copies after AD 60 (and thus even later than some of the conservative procedural documents); the style and form of military diplomas never changed at all.[36]

Tabulae of a bank or household were excerpted and copied in the same way, although here none in diptych form survive and the transition to other options must therefore have come earlier. The Campanian documents provide more than one example of what are called, for simplicity's sake, *nomina arcaria* or "cash entries" in accounts – which are, however, more than just account-book entries:[37]

Tabellae Titiniae A[ntracidis].
Exp.
Eupliae Theodori f(iliae) [HS ∞ DC] Meiliacae tutore aucto[re] Epichare Aphrodisi f(ilio) Athe[niensi] petiit et numeratos acce[pit] domo ex risco.

[33] Military diplomas and "discharge certificates" copy extracts from edicts, cf. (e.g.) *CPL* 104 = *W.Chr.* 463, *FIRA*[2] 1.424–7 no. 76 (AD 94), with Haensch (1992) 276 n.194; see Camodeca (1995a) 74–5 and Haensch (1996) 462–6.

[34] The name of the praetor in *TH* 89 is newly restored by Camodeca (1999b) 527–9. Della Corte (1951) 228 no. 13 (no date, form not known) may also be a nomination of a tutor, and the unpublished *datio bonorum possessionis* of the praetor from Herculaneum (Camodeca [1993c] 525) may be a text of this form and style. Egypt: see chapter seven nn.9 and 12.

[35] Six diptychs (some with only a single hole for hinging), *TPSulp.* 85 and 86 (both AD 51), 90–3 (all AD 61), and three of unknown form, *TPSulp.* 83–4 (both AD 51) and 88 (AD 53).

[36] Military *diplomata*, see Wenger (1923) cols. 2417–19 and (1953) 72–3.

[37] *Nomina arcaria*, G. 3.131 (the documents may be misnamed, given their complexity). Some fragments of actual account-*tabulae* or registers of loans themselves may have survived in *TPSulp.* 94 and 95 (both AD 42); Pugliese Carratelli (1950) 274 also published a fragment identified by Arangio-Ruiz (1974 [1964]) 678 n.7 as *rationes* or accounts, cf. Gröschler (1997) 72–3 n.18, but also Camodeca and Del Mastro (2002) 285.

138   *The evolution of practice*

Acp.

Risco. [HS ∞ DC] Eos HS ∞ DC nu[mmos qui s(upra) s(cripti) s(unt)] interrogant[e Titinia Antacide] fide sua esse ius[sit Epichares Aphrodisi] f(ilius) Atheniensis p[ro Euplia Theodori f(ilia)] Meliacae [sic] Ti[tiniae Antracidi.] Act[um Puteolis xiii k. Apr.] Sex. Palpellio [Histro L. Pedanio] Se[cundo cos.]

Tabellae of Titinia A[ntracis].

Pai(d out).

To Euplia the Melian, d(aughter) of Theodoros, with her tuto[r] Epichares s(on) of Aphrodisios, the Athe[nian], authorizing; she requested and received [1,600 sesterces] counted out from the cash-box at the *domus*.

Rec(eived).

From the cash-box [1,600 sesterces].

Those 1,600 s[esterces which are written above, Titinia Antracis ha]ving asked the question [Epichares the son of Aphrodisios] the Athenian promised faithfully on b[ehalf of Euplia] of Melos, [daughter of Theodoros], to Ti[tinia Antracis].

Don[e at Puteoli on the thirteenth day before the kalends of April, when] Sex. Palpellius Hister and L. Pedanius Secundus were consuls. (This is the copy on *pagina* 5; *TPSulp.* 60, AD 43)

What is happening here is a multi-step loan from one woman to another.[38] The obligation to repay, rooted in the handing-over of the money – a fact emphasized by the explicit *numeratos* in the text – is strengthened by a second act, a *fideiussio* (a form of stipulation used between non-citizens), making this a document in which two legal acts are used sequentially. The terminology employed, especially, *acp. risco*, is the same as that used in Roman account-*tabulae*,[39] and the *nomina arcaria* on *tabellae* that survive are therefore identified as extracts from these account-books, in the case of the Murecine tablets possibly from the *codex rationum* of the bank, in the case of the Herculaneum *tabellae* from the *rationes* kept between a patron and his freedmen.[40] These so-called *nomina arcaria* are thus individualized copies of entries made in account-*tabulae* joined to some type of stipulation, all in third-person *testatio* style; they are written as interior and exterior texts, and sealed by seven or more men. Six known cases (five between AD 43 and 62, and one undated) are in phase-three format, another eight (three between AD 43 and 53, one after AD 61, and four more undated) on triptychs.[41]

---

[38] On *numeratos* and *domo ex risco*, both of which emphasize the act of handing over the money (and which make this act different from Greek parallels), see Gröschler (1997) 340–1.

[39] Gröschler (1997) 199–246; summary of types of accounts kept by Romans, 246–80.

[40] Gröschler (1997) 279–80, 296–7; sometimes (*TH* 70 and 73) calling themselves *tabulae*. Cf. Rauh (1989) 72–5 for an overview of the various kinds of *tabulae*-transactions already in use by Cicero's time, and the ways in which banks could facilitate or effect transfers of money or obligation.

[41] Phase three, *TPSulp.* 62 (AD 42), 61 (AD 43); *TH* 70+71 (AD 59, with Camodeca [1993b]), 74 (with Camodeca [1993b], AD 62), and 73 (AD 62), and 72 (no date); triptychs, *TPSulp.* 60 (AD 43), 63 (AD 45), 64 (AD 53); *TH* 38 (after AD 61), and 67–9 and 75 (all undated); form unknown, *TPSulp.* 65 (no date) and *TH* unpublished (Camodeca [1993b] 198 n.8, label only).

Roman tablets in Italy (AD 15–79)

(c) Mancipations. The surviving mancipations – which convey a property into either the trust (*fiducia*) or ownership (through sale) of another – from Pompeii and Herculaneum are like the *nomina arcaria* on *tabellae* in several respects. They are, of course, written on *tabulae*; they too survive in phase-three form (and one diptych, too); and they are often also combinational, including more than one legal act or extract in one document. A sale from Herculaneum in which only the exterior text (on *paginae* four and one of a triptych) can be read here adds a stipulation of warranty to a mancipation:[42]

[–] quem [–] L. Comini [Primi –vendit]oris P. Corneli Pop[p]aei [Erasti –] Ofilli Eleupori emisse [m]an[cipioque accepisse se dixit L.] Cominius Primus HS ∞ IɔɔL [hominem – de] P. Cornelio Poppaeo Erasto [libri]pende L. M[ario] Chrys[e]rote. [hunc hominem sa]num furtis noxisque solutum esse [praestari et si qui]s eum hominem partemve quam eius evicerit quo [minus L. Comi]nium Primum herede mve eius habere [uti frui] possidere recte liceat, simplam pecuniam r[ect]e [dari, haec] ita uti adsolet recte praestari stipu[latus est L. Comin]ius Primus spopondit P. Cornelius Popp[a]eu[s Erastus].
A[ct]um in Pompeiano in figlinis Arrianis Poppaeae Aug(ustae) VIII Idus Maias C. Memmio Regulo L. Verginio Rufo cos. (Incomplete list of nine witnesses also on *pagina* four; *TH* 61, AD 63)

(pagina four, left)
–a man] whom [–] of L. Cominius [Primus–of the sell]er P. Cornelius Poppaeus [Erastus–] of Ofillius Eleuporius, [L.] Cominius Primus [said that he] bought and received as *mancipium* for 4,050 HS [the man–] from P. Cornelius Poppaeus Erastus L. M[arius] Chrys[e]ros was the *libripens*.
(pagina one)
[that this man] is guaranteed to be sound free from theft and *noxae*; [and that if anyone] makes eviction of this man or share (of him) [so that L. Comi]nius Primus or his heir shall be allowed that much the less [to have to use to enjoy] to possess him lawfully, simple value shall be l[awfully given]; that these things are lawfully guaranteed as is customary [L. Comin]ius Primus called for the promise P. Cornelius Poppaeus [Erastus] promised.
Done on the Pompeian estate in the Arrian pottery of Poppaea Aug(usta) on the eighth day before the Ides of May when C. Memmius Regulus and L. Verginius Rufus were consuls.

The document first records the sale of a slave through mancipation, then adds a stipulation that quotes – copies – the terminology about the punishable sale of defective slaves known to have been laid out in the aedilician edict.[43] Combinations like this, of the stipulation about defects

---

[42] Text in Camodeca (2000) 66–7 (the third tablet preserves no writing); trans. adapted from Crook (1967) 184.
[43] Punishment for defect was probably incorporated into the edict at least by Cicero's time, cf. Cic. *Off.* 3.71; full discussion at *D.* 21.2.31 (Ulpian); cf. Camodeca (1992) 144–51, (2000) 58–63, and Jakab (1997)

140   *The evolution of practice*

and the act of mancipation, were conceivable at least a generation before, in Seneca the Elder's time,[44] and we are therefore probably justified in restoring a mancipation in missing segments of a few other Campanian documents of sale where only this stipulation survives. These texts are otherwise parallel to the one quoted, with Roman-citizen protagonists (using *stipulatus est . . . spopondit* language) almost always selling slaves, and the lists of sealers, when preserved, crammed with Roman citizens.[45] In my judgment, then, eight documents of mancipatory sale and three documents of mancipation for *fiducia* survive.[46] With one exception[47] the changes in their physical form follow the pattern already seen: one early diptych, phase-three writing until at least AD 62, and the last two of the series are triptychs.[48]

This last surviving mancipation (for *fiducia*) reveals an unfamiliar new quality that will be discussed more fully later in this chapter. In the case of *nomina arcaria* and the other mancipations, we have already seen the tendency of formal acts to multiply on a tablet – so stipulations were, in both cases, added. In this last surviving mancipation from Campania a formal act (the mancipation), written in third-person *testatio* style, has added to it an agreement or *pactum*, an informal, *bona fides* act, written in first-person chirograph style:[49]

127–9, 171–96 (who doubts that the edict *required* individuals to give stipulations). According to Varro (*R.* 2.10.5), stipulations like these for slaves (but also for farm animals) were standard practice, but he implies that a stipulation (and especially a *stipulatio duplae*) was incompatible with or unnecessary in an act of mancipation, cf. Zulueta (1945) 51 and Arangio-Ruiz and Pugliese Carratelli (1954) 61. For this reason, Camodeca (1992) 144–58 at 152 identified any act with a *stipulatio duplae* as a *traditio* (transfer) or *emptio* (informal act of sale based on *bona fides*) rather than mancipation; but see Johnston (1999) 82 (later examples).

44 Seneca Rhet.: *Contr.* 7.6.22–4 (quoted chapter two p. 40), *mancipio accepit* as well as snide use of the terminology about defects.

45 Roman-citizen sealer-list, Arangio-Ruiz and Pugliese Carratelli (1954) 62.

46 Mancipation in sales, *TPSulp.* 42 (AD 26) and 43 (AD 38); 59–60 (both before AD 63, with Camodeca [2000] 55–66), 61 (before AD 63); *TPSulp.* 44 (no date); *TH* 64 (label only), and 63, a label that mentions *emptio facta est uti adsolet*, perhaps not a mancipation, cf. Arangio-Ruiz and Pugliese Carratelli (1954) 63. *fiducia*, *TH* 65 (AD 62), *TH* 66 (a *remancupatio,* so perhaps a kind of reverse *fiducia*; a label only, with witnesses, no date), and *CIL* 4.3340.155 (AD 79).

47 *TPSulp.* 42 (AD 26) is reported as having a *sulcus*, but nothing on *pagina* 4 can be read, not even the sealer-list that must have been there; so it is possible that there was also *transversa* writing on the left hand side of *pagina* 4; I therefore classify it as a phase-three document.

48 Diptych, *TPSulp.* 43 (AD 38); *TPSulp.* 44 cannot be dated. *TH* 65 (AD 62), 59 (before AD 63), and 60 (before AD 63) are all phase-three documents. Undated are *TH* 66 (triptych) and *TH* 63–4 (form unknown); last two are *TH* 61 (before AD 63) and *CIL* 4.3340.155 (AD 79).

49 Text is that of *FIRA*² 3.291–4 no. 91, restorations defended in Arangio-Ruiz (1974 [1942a]); remaining problems noted in Macqueron (1982) 151 (I have restored *antestatus* for *antestata* in *pag.* 2 line 10 and *eius* for *tuo* in *pag.* 2 line 13). The sum of the money lent is supplied from the chirograph-style loan document found along with this mancipation for *fiducia*, *CIL* 4.3340.154 = *FIRA*² 3.294–5 no. 91*bis.*

Roman tablets in Italy (AD 15–79)

Poppaea Prisci liberta Note iuravit pueros Simplicem et Petrinum, sive ea mancipia alis nominib[us] sunt sua esse seque possidere, neque ea mancipia [–] ali ulli obligata esse neque sibi cum ul<l>o com[munia] esse eaque mancipia singula sestertis nu[mmis sin]gulis Dicidia Margaris emit ob seste[rtios n(ummos) ∞LD et] mancipio accepit de Popp<a>ea Prisc[i liberta Note] tutore auctore D. Caprasio A[mpliato] libripende in si[ngu]la P. C[– an]testat{*us*} est in singula [–].
[Dicidia Margaris cum] Popp<a>ea Prisci li[b(erta) Note] pactum conventum fecit] uti<que> ea manc[ipia sumtu inpensa periculoque eius sint supra haec inter se convenerunt pactaeque ... inter se sunt.
Actum Pompeis ix Kal. ... L. Iunio Caesennio Paeto P. Caluisio Rusone cos.]
[Pactum conventum. quae mancipia hodie mihi ven]didi[sti ita tibi heredive tuo (?) restituentur ut antea pecunia quam] m[u]t[uam] pro duobu[s mancipiis tibi hodie (?) dedi o]mnis mihi <h>ere[dive meo solvatur vel ad me ut rede]at usu ve[ni]at. si ea pecu[nia omnis mihi heredive meo] kal(endis) Novem(bribus) primis solu[ta non erit ut mihi heredive meo liceat] ea mancip[ia q(uibus) d(e) a(gitur) i]dibus D[ecembr(ibus) primis pecunia praesenti] Pompeis in foro luce palam [vendere – neve] tibi eg[o] neve heres me[us teneamur nisi proptere]a si minus de dolo malo ea ve[nditione redactum esse ...]tatur.
Si quo minoris e[a] mancipia q(uibus) d(e) a(gitur) venie[rint in sortis vi]cem d[e]bebun[t]u[r] mihi heradiv[e meo quae reliqua erunt. quod si pluris] ea mancipia q(uibus) d(e) a(gitur) veni[erint id quod superfluum erit reddetur tibi h]ered[ive tuo –] ea pecunia [–]. utique ea mancipia sumtu inp[e]nsa peri[culoque tuo sint] id mihi tecum convenit e[t pacta tecum sum.
Dicidi]a Margaris Popp<a>ea [P]risci lib(erta) Note tuto[re D. Caprasio Ampliato] supra h<a>ec inter eas conveneru[nt pactaeque–] inter se sunt.
Ac[t(um)] Pompeis ix k[al. –] L. Iunio Caesennio [Paeto] P. Caluisio Rusone cos.
(On the edge of *tabula* I, *firmata* [*manc*]*ipiorum sumtio*, and at least three witnesses on *pagina* four; *CIL* 4.3340.155, AD 79)

Poppaea Note, freedwoman of Priscus, swore that the slaves Simplex and Petrinus, or if these *mancipia* are (known) by other names, are hers and that she possesses them and that these *mancipia* [–] are not claimed by any other person and that they are not (held) in common with anyone, and Dicidia Margaris bought these *mancipia* individually with a single sestertius for [1,450] *sestertii* and accepted (them) by mancipation from Poppaea [Note freedwoman] of Priscus, with her tutor D. Caprasius A[mpliatus] authorizing, P. C[–] (acting as) *libripens* for the single (nummus), [–] (acting as) *antetestatus* for the single (nummus) [–.
Dicidia Margaris made a *pactum conventum* with] Poppaea Note, fre[edwoman of Priscus,] that these *manc[ipia* would be at her assumed expense and danger, about these things they agreed amongst themselves and they made a pact ... among themselves.
Done at Pompeii on the ninth day before the kalends of – when L. Junius Caesennius Paetus and P. Calvisius Ruso were consuls.]
[*Pactum conventum.* Those *mancipia* which today you have s]old [to me thus, let them be restored to you or your heir when that previous money, which] today I gave to you as *mutuum* for the tw[o *mancipia* is a]ll [paid back to me or my heir]

142 *The evolution of practice*

or when it return[s to me or comes by *usus*]. If all that mon[ey shall not have been paid back] to me or my heir by the first kalends of November, [be it permitted to me or my heir] to sell for cash these *mancip[ia* whom this matter concerns o]n the first ides of December, [–] at Pompeii in the forum by day openly [–] and let neither me nor m[y heir be held unless on this account,] if less is returned from this sale on account of malicious fraud [–].

If these *mancipia* whom this matter concerns shall have sold for some lesser amount, let that [which shall be left over] be repaid to me or my heir in re[payment of (my) share. But if] these *mancipia* whom this matter concerns shall have sold for more, [let that which shall be extra be returned to you or your h]eir [–] this money [–]. And that these *mancipia* shall be at your assumed expense and dan[ger], this is agreed by me with you and I have made a p[act with you.

Dicidi]a Margaris Poppaea Note, freedwoman of Priscus with her tuto[r D. Caprasius Ampliatus] about these things they agreed amongst themselves and made a pact [–] between themselves.

Done at Pompeii on the ninth day before the kalends [of –] when L. Junius Caesennius [Paetus] and P. Calvisius Ruso were consuls.

The physical form of this mancipation-with-*pactum* is only mildly unusual; its exterior text runs from *pagina* one to *pagina* four (as in a phase-three diptych), but then continues – most likely[50] – on to *pagina* five. The third tablet of this triptych is thus being used for overflow: the interior combinational document was too long for only two sides. Other triptychs used the third tablet for a complete copy of the interior text, so this looks strange compared to them, but less strange when compared to the examples of phase-three writing for mancipations and other formal acts that had existed before.

(d) Acceptilationes. These will also develop into combinational documents written in two styles, like the mancipation-and-pact, while going through much the same sequence of interlocking physical, stylistic, and content-based changes to which the documents of unitary acts were subject in the first century AD. *CIL* 4.3340.1 of AD 15, the earliest of them, indeed the earliest wooden document from any of the Campanian collections, seems to be a simple diptych; it is a release given to Jucundus's father or patron, written in *testatio* style:

(Sestertios) n(ummos) DXX ob mulum venditum [M.] Pomponio M. l(iberto) Niconi, quam pequniam in stipulatum [L.] Caecili Felicis redegisse dicitur M. Cerrinius Eup<h>rates.

---

[50] Arangio-Ruiz (1974 [1942a]) 211, Macqueron (1982) 150, Amelotti and Migliardi Zingale (1989) 307 n.25. The overflow may have been necessitated by the fact that the exterior copy looks to have been written in a larger hand, and because one-quarter of the exterior of *pagina* four was taken up by the sealer-list.

Eam pequniam omnem, quae supra scripta est, [n]umeratam dixit se [a]ccepisse M. Cerrinius M. l(ibertus) [E]uphrates ab Philadelpho [C]aecili Felicis ser(vo). Actum Pompeis V. k. Iunias Druso Caesare C. Norbano Flacco cos.

M. Cerrinius Eup<h>rates is said to have realized 520 HS on account of the mule sold to [M.] Pomponius Nico, freedman of Marcus, which money was in the stipulation of [L.] Caecilius Felix.
All this money, which is written above, M. Cerrinius Euphrates, freedman of Marcus, said he had received, counted out, from Philadelphus, slave of Caecilius Felix.
Done at Pompeii on the fifth day before the kalends of June, when Drusus Caesar and C. Norbanus Flaccus were consuls.

Both outside faces of the diptych have been smoothed, but there is no trace of writing on the second outside face (*pagina* four). K. Zangemeister, the *CIL* editor, was loath to assume no exterior sealing, since the diptych was notched for a *linum*, but he did believe that the traces of writing he detected on the first outside face (*pagina* one) were at most an identificatory label. We should accept what he saw: a document in *testatio* style whose text, recording both the verbal release and the physical acceptance of counted-out money, was not doubled and whose seals (if there were any) were not identified on the tablet itself.

There are a number of other, fragmentary *testatio*-style documents like this in diptych form, all undated.[51] Next chronologically are three examples of triptychs with one original text and two more versions of it:[52] the first exterior text, running from *pagina* four to *pagina* one, duplicates the interior *testatio*-style text, but the second, on *pagina* five, does not properly duplicate it at all, giving instead a partial account of the acknowledgment of the receipt of money in chirograph style (to be discussed in the next section). In and after AD 54 this type of document settles into a double-document triptych, but with one *testatio*-style interior text and one chirograph-style exterior text, written on *pagina* five; thirty-seven of these survive.[53] An example:

(interior text)
HS n. IƆƆ∞ CCCCLVIS quae pecunia in stipulatum L. Caecili Iucundi venit ob auctionem Histriae Ichimadis mercede minus persoluta habere se dixit Histria Ichimas ab L. Caecilio Iucundo. Act(um) Pom(peis) non(is) Nove(mbribus) L. Duvio P. Clodio cos.

---

[51] *CIL* 4.3340.121 (only *pagina* two), 122–3 (*paginae* two–three), and 124 (only *pagina* two).
[52] *CIL* 4.3340.2 (AD 27), 5 (AD 54), and 49 (no date).
[53] *CIL* 4.3340.7–8 (AD 54), 10–15, 17 (all AD 55), 22, 25–7 (all AD 56), 28, 32, 34–5, 38–40 (all AD 57), 43 (AD 55–7?), 46 (AD 56?); 47–8, 51–7, 61, 65, 68–70, and 72 are undated. Additionally, *CIL* 4.3340.9, 18–19, 29, 31, 37, 59, 60, 62, 66, 67, and 73 preserve the inner *testatio*-style text but no exterior text, so these are probably but not certainly combinational documents.

144   *The evolution of practice*

(exterior text)
[L. Duvio P. Clo]dio cos. [non(is) Nove]mbr(ibus) [– sc]ripsi rogatu [Histriae Ichimadis ipsi] persoluta [esse ab L. Caecilio Iuc]undo HS n. [sex milia quadr]i(n)gentos quinqua[ginta sex semi]s ob auctionem, q[uam servus] eius fecit. [Act(um) Pom]peis. (*CIL* 4.3340.22, AD 56)

(interior text)   .
6456½ HS: money – which came into the stipulation of L. Caecilius Jucundus on account of the auction of Histria Ichimas's [goods], less the fee – Histria Ichimas said she has, paid back, from L. Caecilius Jucundus. Do(ne) at Pom(peii) on the non(es) of November, when L. Duvius and P. Clodius were consuls.

(exterior text)
When L. Duvius and P. Clodius were consuls, on the no(nes) of Novemb(er). [–] I wrote at the request [of Histria Ichimas that HS 6456½,] in coin had been paid back to her [by L. Caecilius Juc]undus on account of the auction, [which his slave] performed. Done at Pompeii.

Histria Ichimas said that she has in her possession paid-back money; another wrote (at her request), in first-person chirograph style, that the money has been paid back. Had Histria been male, the exterior version might simply have read, "I wrote that I accepted," *scripsi me accepisse*.

What these documents were was once disputed. Their *testatio* style, however – as preserved in the earliest example and in the interior text of the later combinational versions – points to the origin of this document in a formal act of some sort. Mommsen identified the interior *testatio*-style text as an *acceptilatio*, a ceremonial declaration (in response to a question) of the fulfillment of a stipulatory promise and thus a formal release from a stipulatory obligation rather than just a receipt for money repaid.[54] Although there is lack of scholarly agreement on this subject, given the absence of question-and-answer and correct terminology of an *acceptilatio* (both recorded in only one form in Gaius) in the interior text,[55] the congruences that remain are sufficiently numerous to suggest that the interior acknowledgment given in *testatio* style was indeed an older form, modelled closely on *acceptilatio* even if not perfectly embodying what

---

[54] Mommsen (1907 [1877]) 241–4 (citing *G*. 2.85 and 3.169, *D*. 46.4.6 [Ulpian]). *Acceptilatio* is a type of *contrarius actus* (discussed chapter two n.106) that "undid" formal acts like stipulation and mancipation; it was performed *sollemniter* and *unitas actus* was observed, Ankum (2001) 12.

[55] Summary of scholarship, Gröschler (1997) 312–3 n.50. The anti-*acceptilatio* views depend heavily on an exclusive application of Gaius's wording (3.169: *"quod tibi ego promisi, HABESNE ACCEPTUM?" et tu respondeas HABEO*), seeing the use of question-and-answer as necessary and the phrase *acceptum habeo* as the only possible answer. So Erman (1899) 192 considers no interior document reading *dixit se accepisse* or *habere numeratos* an *acceptilatio*; *contra*, Ankum (2001) 8–9, noting *D*. 46.4.8.4 (Ulpian), where (even) Greek is allowed in an *acceptilatio*. Watson (1991 [1960] 198–9) argued that *acceptilatio* was not a formal verbal act, but his view not accepted, Ankum (2001) 5.

Roman tablets in Italy (AD 15–79)　　　145

most scholars think it should be.[56] I think, therefore, that the interior text does grant release from an obligation to repay while simultaneously acknowledging, with *numerata, soluta,* or *persoluta,* that the money has been handed over:[57] the interior text combines *acceptilatio* or *persolutio* (release from obligation) and *apocha* (repayment), an act of speaking and an act of receiving, as a unitary act does.[58] The profusion of linguistic forms and the interesting mixture of styles in these interior *"acceptilatio"* documents imply that formal release from stipulatory obligation could exist in more various wording than Gaius's simple account of *acceptilatio* suggests, or that the *testatio*-style text is starting to record emended, expanded, and different versions of acts of release and repayment; and that – whatever the confusions were – a document of this type and in this style was valued.[59]

　　The exterior chirograph, in contrast, almost always uses only the simple phrase *scripsi me accepisse.* Since it neither uses *habere* nor acknowledges the physical act of handing over the money as the interior text does – *accepisse* seems to function as a general but verbally imprecise summary of what has occurred – the exterior text is not an exact if first-person legal equivalent of the interior text.[60] The entire document is again, therefore, a combinational one: the interior is a *testatio*-style *tabula*-document incorporating both acknowledgment of repayment and declaration of discharge, while the outside gives a first-person (chirograph-style) statement in writing that the act has taken place. This entire document has, therefore, moved from being an *acceptilatio*-type act in *testatio* style on a simple diptych to being a combinational act written in both styles on a triptych, all in the space of forty years. Many formal acts did not change so fast or so much, but all moved some distance along these intertwined trajectories.

---

[56] Older: Mommsen (1907 [1877]) 241–2, Thielmann (1961) 206–13, and Gröschler (1997) 312–13.

[57] This varying terminology, noted by Bruns (1878), perhaps reflects from what type of obligation release was being granted, but no good explanation has yet been offered; Andreau (1987) 575, 665 thinks *persolvere* refers to drawing on an account-book at a bank.

[58] Two parts of this often combinational act therefore continued to be distinguished: the words used in the act of speaking (*habeo* is the more important, cf. Sen. *Ben.* 7.14.5 [*omnia a te habeo*] and 7.16.1 [*habeo*]) and the entirety of the (often combinational) act itself, described as *acceptum facere,* Watson (1991 [1960]) 196–8. The multiple aspects of a unitary act, here still intertwined, are *later* separated by jurists, who emphasize that correct language clears the verbal obligation "as a type of imaginary *solutio*" (G. 3.169).

[59] This view is close to Mommsen's (1907 [1877]) 242–4. The variety may have caused confusion as well, perhaps prompting the mysterious formula *ex interrogatione facta tabellarum signatarum* found in nine or ten *persoluta habere* releases (*CIL* 4.3340.25–8, 32, 35, 40, and possibly 38; *TPSulp.* 82 [AD 44/45]), one *dixit se habere* release (*CIL* 4.3340.17), and one informal sale (*CPL* 193 = *SB* 6304, *FIRA*² 3.431–2 no. 134, Eger [1921]; possibly Hadrianic, Söllner [2001] 84).

[60] Erman (1899) 191–2 and Gröschler (1997) 311–12 n.47; *accepisse* is the exterior verb for all the different formulae discussed for the interior text, and the only interior verb used for the purely chirograph-style documents in Jucundus's collection.

146   *The evolution of practice*

(e) Summary. Procedural and other formal (and related) acts were always written in *testatio* style, began (in what survives) as diptychs, and changed only slowly – more slowly than chirograph-style texts, as the next section will make clear – to triptychs. Of the 144 from Pompeii and Herculaneum whose nature can be identified, and not including the combinational "*acceptilationes,*" dates and physical forms are known for eighty-nine. Twenty-three are diptychs,[61] dating as early as AD 15 and as late as AD 61; eighteen are in phase-three form, running from AD 26 to AD 70–2;[62] and the remaining forty-eight are triptychs, appearing first in AD 27 and continuing until the evidence runs out in AD 79.[63] In the documents related to procedure and copying, there are twenty diptychs between AD 34 and AD 63, but in that time only eight triptychs, which themselves start only in AD 47; the other ten occur later, in the year AD 75 (**fig. 6**). The same ten-to-fifteen year gap between earliest appearance of each type also occurs in the financial documents, but here earlier: the first diptych occurs in AD 15, the first triptych in AD 27. Triptychs are clearly dominant here in the fifties, although this is caused in large part by the contents of Jucundus's chest (**fig. 7**). Although the numbers are too small to be entirely probative, they are clearly suggestive. Diptychs were both the earlier form and the traditional form, and chosen steadily in all decades until the early sixties, when phase-three writing – which appears in the forties – became particularly prevalent. Of all the documents written in *testatio* style, those relating to money or property – the *nomina arcaria*, the mancipations, and the *acceptilationes* – were the ones to evolve towards phase-three writing and simple triptychs earliest, initially in the late twenties. The formal procedural acts that were simple rather than complex, by contrast, changed more slowly. The physical forms of the latter were under less pressure to change, while the *nomina arcaria*, the mancipatory acts, and the *acceptilationes* could in this century be simple but for the most part were not. They

---

[61] *CIL* 4.3340.1 (AD 15); *TPSulp.* 96 (AD 34), 23–4 (AD 35), 43 (AD 38), 12 (AD 40 or 43–4), 1*bis* (AD 41 or 43–5), Della Corte (1951) 226 no.5 (republished by Camodeca [2002b] 230, AD 43), *TPSulp.* 14 (after AD 44), 1 (AD 47), 32 (AD 48), 28–9 (AD 49), 16 and 85–6 (AD 51), 4 (AD 52), 89 (AD 53), 90–3 (AD 61), and including *TPSulp.* 99 (AD 44), an unidentified type of act in *testatio* style that includes a stipulation to repay part of a debt (included in totals as well, but not discussed above).

[62] *TPSulp.* 42 (AD 26), 62 (AD 42), 61 (AD 43), *TH* 82 (AD 52), *TPSulp.* 34 (AD 55?); *TH* 70+71 (AD 59), 5 (AD 60), 59 (after AD 61), 65 and 73–4 (all AD 62), 84 (AD 62?), 60 (before AD 63), 88+58 (AD 66, with Camodeca [2002a] 262), 79 (AD 69), 76 (AD 69?), 87 (AD 70), and 2 (AD 70–2).

[63] *CIL* 4.3340.2 (AD 27); *TPSulp.* 60 (AD 43), 63 (AD 45); *TH* 85 (AD 47); *TPSulp.* 3 (AD 48), 87 (AD 51), 31 (AD 52), 64 (AD 53); *CIL* 4.3340.5, 7, and 8 (AD 54) and all the other *acceptilationes* listed above n.53; *TPSulp.* 25, 35–6 (all AD 55); *TH* 38 (after AD 61), 89 (AD 62), 61 (before AD 63), 13–20, 23–4 (all AD 75), *CIL* 4.3340.155 (AD 79).

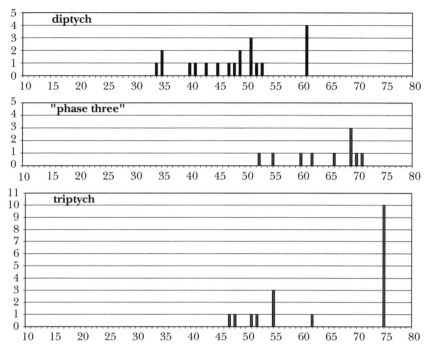

Figure 6 Physical forms of formal procedural acts and official copies from first-century AD Campania.
Formal procedural acts (*vadimonia* etc.) and official copies remain on diptychs and in "phase three" form (diptychs with *sulcus*) the longest, becoming predominantly triptychs only in the seventies AD.

developed instead into complex and combinational acts, their style still fundamentally conservative but at times allowing substantially different sorts of additions – additions in both the *testatio* and the chirograph style, with the latter, as will be seen, associated more clearly and consistently with the triptych rather than diptych form from the late twenties onward. *Nomina arcaria*, *mancipationes*, and *acceptilationes* were Roman acts performed in the fluid world of finance and (at times) foreigners rather than in the fixed world of duumvirs, arbiters, *iudices*, and praetors; their formal nature here served as the core from which they grew, not as a boundary they could not overcome. Form, act, and style were tenaciously linked, but all were added to – with a third tablet, with a second act, and with that second act at times in a different style.

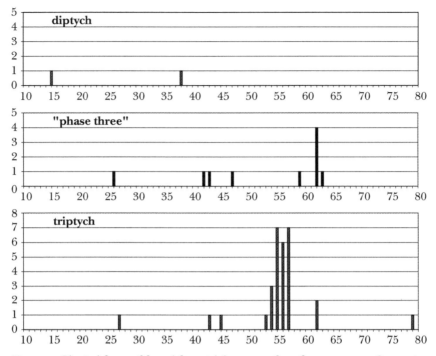

Figure 7 Physical forms of formal financial documents from first-century AD Campania. Formal financial documents (mancipations, *nomina arcaria*, and *acceptilationes*) become predominantly triptychs in the fifties AD, two decades before formal procedural acts and official copies, and two decades after chirographs.

CHIROGRAPHS IN THE FIRST CENTURY AD

The world of business is a world of trust. It is also a world of risk, of speedy decisions, of people not always known to you, and of appearances – and therefore also of people wearing twelve-hundred-dollar suits to establish that trust. Acts based on trust, on *bona fides* ("good faith") as the Romans called it, were in Rome developed, enforced, and thereby encouraged by the praetor's edict. Their pedigree was thus different from that of the old unitary acts, their age younger, their habits freer. Their style, when written, was that of the *chirographum*, using the first person; the document was one you sealed yourself, perhaps with a few friends. Although their physical form was early that of the diptych, *bona fides* acts take up the physical form of the simple triptych at least a decade before their elderly maiden-aunt *testatio*-style relatives do, and with a striking consistency. This difference in timing

Roman tablets in Italy (AD 15–79) 149

and commitment to the triptych form sets the physical documentation of the *bona fides* acts apart from that of the unitary acts, establishing that two traditions with not just two different documentary styles but also two different physical expressions are visible here, and only over time coming to affect each other.

Chirograph-style documents record many kinds of informal legal act. They invariably begin with a date (whereas texts in *testatio* style have their dates at the end), then give the names of the author-protagonists, who with two exceptions claim "*scripsi . . .*" followed by verbs that make clear which act has been undertaken.[64] "*scripsi me convenisse*" denotes an agreement,[65] "*scripsi me accepisse*" or "*scripsi me habere*" or even "*scripsi me percipere in solutum*" a discharge of obligation,[66] "*scripsi me accepisse mutua et debere*" or "*accepisse et debere*" (or other close variants) a loan called a *mutuum*,[67] "*scripsi me dedisse . . . pignori*" the giving of a *pignus* or pledge,[68] "*scripsi me locasse*" a lease,[69] "*scripsi me promisisse*" or "*repromisisse*" possibly a recasting in stipulatory form of an already existing obligation,[70] "*scripsi me mandasse*" a legal empowerment of another to do business for you,[71] "*scripsi et iuravi*" a form of sworn testimony.[72] Two informal sales, *emptiones*, survive from the Campanian region; one uses the phrase "*scripsi me emisse*," in this

---

[64] *CIL* 4.3340.138 (AD 53), the earliest in the series of receipts given by public slaves for tax payments (a diptych), uses as its main interior verb merely *accepi* (the exterior text reads *scripsi me accepisse*); the interior text in the sale of a cow from Holland similarly uses *emi*, not *scripsi* (Vollgraff [1917] = *FIRA*² 3.438–9 no. 137). Both may be relics of an earlier way of writing these chirograph-style documents, the official character of town-tax documents preserving this a little longer than in other documents. Pompeii's tax receipts are written *scripsi me accepisse*, and on triptychs, by AD 58 (*CIL* 4.3340.141), perhaps by AD 55 (*CIL* 4.3340.148: the interior text is fragmentary).

[65] *TPSulp.* 22 (AD 35), *TPSulp.* 27 (AD 48).

[66] *Scripsi me accepisse*, *TPSulp.* 70 (AD 41), 82 (AD 43–5), 71 (AD 46), 72 (AD 47), 73 (AD 48), 74 (AD 51), 75 (AD 52); *CIL* 4.3340.3 (AD 52), 6 (AD 54), 16 and 148 (AD 55), 20–1, 23–4, 45 (all AD 56), 30 and 33 (AD 57), 141–2, 145–6, and 150 (all AD 58), 143 and 147 (AD 59), 144 (AD 60), *TH* 40–1 and *CIL* 4.3340.151 (all AD 62), and *TPSulp.* 76, *CIL* 4.3340.50, 58, and 139 (no date); *scripsi me habere*, *TPSulp.* 77 (AD 48), *TH* 90+52 (AD 69), *TH* 90.4 (AD 70; *numerata*, by a slave), and *TH* 39 (no date); *scripsi me percipere in solutum*, *TH* 43 (AD 70; by a slave); *scripsi me habere in solutum*, *TH* 8 (AD 71, by a slave). *TPSulp.* 78 (AD 38) is written in Greek, by a Greek; he uses the phrase ἔγραψα ἀπέχιν; *CIL* 4.3340.138 (AD 53) used only *accepi*.

[67] *Scripsi me accepisse mutua et debere*, *TPSulp.* 51–2 (both AD 37), *TH* unnumbered (AD 40 or 41, Camodeca [2002a] 266–8), *TPSulp.* 54 (AD 45), 55 (AD 49), 56 (AD 52), and 57 (AD 50?); *scripsi me accepisse et debere*, *TPSulp.* 50 (AD 35), 53 (AD 40), and *TPSulp.* 59 (no date); *scripsi me debere*, *TPSulp.* 66 (AD 29), 67 (AD 38), 68 (AD 39), *TH* 42 (AD 67), and *TPSulp.* 69 (AD 51) (these last may be recasting *mutua* as stipulations); the governing verb is missing in *TPSulp.* 58 (no date).

[68] *TPSulp.* 55 (AD 49; also *mutua*) and 79 (AD 40).

[69] *TPSulp.* 45 (AD 37), 46 (AD 40); cf. Sen. *Ben.* 6.4.4, lease on *tabellae*.

[70] *TPSulp.* 81 (AD 45; incomplete promise for money *in stipulatum*) and *TH* 4 (AD 60).

[71] *TPSulp.* 48 (AD 48), and 49 (AD 49), both *scripsi me rogasse . . . eique mandasse*.

[72] *TH* 21–2, 25–6, 28, all AD 75 (?); the odd phrasing and late date may suggest a mixing of the traditional *testatio*-style witness statement and *chirographum*, see above n.27.

150   *The evolution of practice*

resembling the first-century AD purchase of a cow in Holland that merely uses the first-person verb *"emi,"* "I bought," more than it does one from Ravenna, which used *scripsi me accepisse* (written in Greek letters).[73] Three of these – sale, lease, and mandate – were already recognized as informal, *bona fides* agreements by the late second century BC, as was another not seen here, the *societas* or partnership;[74] the Campanian examples, obviously, show a healthy variety of other agreements as well. These informal acts are all paired with the first-person style, and also with a pattern of sealing in which the author-protagonist seals at least once and usually twice, at top and bottom of the *sulcus*. The exterior text is also regularly written in the first person, but in a different – often clearer and more correct – hand, usually attributed to a scribe.[75]

Thanks to Jucundus's collection of documents, it is chirograph discharges of obligation that are preserved in the greatest number (forty, of which twenty-four are his); loans (*mutua*) are the next most common (fifteen). Thereafter other types of documents are preserved in a numerically haphazard fashion: in seventy-three (of 114) documents in chirograph style, there is some clue as to what kind of act is at issue. Only in the case of the two litigational agreements, three documents tantalizingly labelled *"chirographum ex nomine facto"* (only the exterior label survives), the sworn testimony, and the combinational *acceptilationes* discussed above is there any sense that these chirograph-style documents venture into territory traditionally served by the older formal acts of Roman law.[76] Otherwise the acts are, as is to be expected, not just different in style but different in type and nature as well.

An informal act or contract has none of the history of the independent unitary act behind it, only the words of the praetor's edict and the promise of his enforcement. It was based on agreement, on faith, and on

---

[73] *TPSulp.* 101 (AD 48); *TH* 62 (AD 47, with Camodeca [2000] 70–3) preserves only a final stipulation but mentions the *traditio*, while *TH* 31 has only the label *chirographum fundi venditi* (no date), and *TH* 32 only the label, *HS millium [cen]tum Graniani fundi*. Holland: Vollgraff (1917) = *FIRA*² 3.438–9 no. 137. Ravenna: *CPL* 193 (= *SB* 6304, *FIRA*² 3.431–2 no. 134; possibly Hadrianic, Söllner [2001] 84), first published as Eger (1921).

[74] Cic. *Off.* 3.70, quoting from Q. Mucius; this is different from the date for the introduction of consensual agreements, about which there is greater controversy, see Rauh (1989) 50 n.20.

[75] *TPSulp.* 51 (AD 37), 52 (AD 37), 45 (AD 37), 68 (AD 39), and 27 (AD 48; with Camodeca [1992] 109), *TH* 19–20 (both AD 75?) and 27 (no date); all with Wolf and Crook (1989) 13. Despite the typical superiority of the outside text it was not used as a model to be followed, Powell (1992) 263; C. Seidl (1996) suggests dictation was given for the interior texts of some chirographs.

[76] Two *conventiones*, above n.65; chirographs mentioning *nomina*, *TH* 3 (AD 62, with Camodeca and Del Mastro [2002] 286), *TH* 10 (no date), and *TH* 36 (a *chirographum nominis facti*; no date); chirographs of oaths, above n.72; combinational receipts, above n.53.

Roman tablets in Italy (AD 15–79)

the threat of an appeal to the praetor. Your *fides* and your reputation were deeply intertwined, and your alacrity in defending these would hold you to your side of the agreement. (As Polybius had noted, two centuries earlier, "magistrates and legates" – who might be most tempted to skim from the large sums that passed through their hands – "consistently act properly because of the pledge of their faith.")[77] There is therefore no expectation of writing nor its necessary presence, yet a wide variety of *bona fides* acts are written, as here in Campania. The standard explanation is that these documents were drawn up to be proof of the agreement between the two parties, agreement that otherwise would be difficult to demonstrate in a later court of law; their purpose is therefore defensive, their nature sugges-tively Greek, as the Greek name *chirographum* broadly hints.[78] There can be no doubt that such proof of agreements was important; the need for such proof no doubt contributed to the use of secure wooden documents. But these Campanian chirograph-style documents – all but three of seventy-three[79] – have in common another interesting aspect that may imply another reason why they are written on tablets: they include a stipulation, a unitary act with which, as has been seen, the use of writing on tablets had been bound up for a very long time. Could it be that when simple *bona fides* agreements became complicated, when penalties for non-performance were desired, when an agreement was reformulated to include a third party, when a simple loan was to include interest, that terms were written down on tablets, *because* stipulations were employed?[80] Did the contractual ad-ditions to these consensual acts mandate the writing that in turn survives? Stipulations were easily combined with other acts by the mere addition of a phrase; but did that phrase from the familiar, orderly past, added to the insistent first-person world of *fides*, justify the use of the *tabula*-form with its formidable traditional authority? Were the "chirographs on *tabellae*" re-ferred to in *TPSulp.* 57 (AD 50) marked as different from other kinds of

---

[77] Polyb. 6.56.14–15 (τὸν ὅρκον πίστεως).

[78] *Graeculam . . . cautionem chirographi mei*, Cic. *Fam.* 7.18.1; standard account, e.g., Kaser (1955) 161; Amelotti and Migliardi Zingale (1990) 304 note that doubling the chirograph and sealing it was a Roman innovation.

[79] Only the two leases (*TPSulp.* 45 and 46) and a *pactum* giving a *pignus* (*TPSulp.* 79) have no stipulations included. The discharges of obligation of course also include no stipulation, since they release from, rather than create, obligation.

[80] As Kunkel (1973) 201 notes, citing the late-Republican *lex Rubria*, jurists separate stipulation and *bona fides* acts very decisively, but the record of what people do contradicts them, cf. Johnston (1999) 85 (Campania), 107 (Dacia), 111 (*bona fides* contracts regularly strengthened by stipulations); similarly stipulations added to *mutua* without the legal claims of either seemingly affected, despite later juristic opinion, Wolf and Crook (1989) 18 and Camodeca (1992) 173 n.29.

152   *The evolution of practice*

chirographs?[81] No matter. The traditional power and reliable resonances of tablets, as well as their capacity to show tampering, were such that it is easy to understand why Romans might find it attractive to place important documents of all sorts upon them.

The physical form of these *bona fides*, chirograph-style documents is preponderantly the triptych and preponderantly so from an early date – in contrast to the formal, *testatio*-style documents, which develop towards this (as has been seen) only slowly. Of the 114 documents in this style, seventy-three are triptychs, while thirteen are diptychs and ten are in the transitional phase-three format (for eighteen the physical form cannot be determined). The diptychs run from AD 35 (a *conventio* for a iudex) to AD 59 (an unknown type of act),[82] phase-three writing from AD 48 (a *conventio* about boundaries) to AD 70 (two discharges), with all but the first example of it, the *conventio*, falling after AD 60.[83] The association of the *conventiones* and the *compromissum* with the world of litigation might indeed help to explain their early diptych- or phase-three forms, both of which were otherwise uncommon choices for an informal act that was not a chirograph-style discharge of obligation.[84] The simple triptychs, in contrast, begin right away in AD 29, with twenty-three of them falling between that date and AD 51 alone, and another twenty-four between AD 52 and AD 62.[85] Chirograph-style documents thus appeared very consistently as simple triptychs from

---

[81] Also mentioned at *D.* 30.44.5 (Ulpian) and *D.*30.84.7 (Julian), *tabulas chirographi*; cf. Juv. *Sat.* 13.136–7, chirographs on wood. Some Roman chirographs from Egypt could be on papyrus, discussed in chapter seven n.159.

[82] Only nine datable: *TPSulp.* 22 (*conventio*, AD 35), 67 (loan, AD 38); *TH* unnumbered (loan, AD 40 or 41, Camodeca [2002a] 266–8); *TPSulp.* 55 (loan and *pignus*, AD 49), and 69 (loan, AD 51); *TH* 44 (unknown, AD 52, with Camodeca [2002a] 266–8), *CIL* 4.3340.138 (discharge, AD 53), *CIL* 4.3340.45 (receipt, AD 56), *TH* 45 (unknown, AD 59, with Camodeca [2002a] 272–5); and *CIL* 4.3340.50, 64, 139–40 (discharges, dates unknown).

[83] Only nine datable: *TPSulp.* 27 (*conventio*, AD 48), *TH* 4 (*repromissio*, AD 60), *TH* 40–1 (both discharges, both AD 62), *TH* 42 (loan, AD 67), *TH* 35 (label, *chirographum nomini facti*, AD 68), *TH* 90+52 (AD 69), *TH* 43 and 90.4 (both discharges, both AD 70), and *TH* 39 (discharge, no date).

[84] Twelve of twenty-two diptychs and phase-three documents are discharges of obligation (and three acts have not been identified), see above n.66.

[85] *TPSulp.* 66 (loan, AD 29), 50 (loan, AD 35), 51 (loan, AD 37), 45 (lease, AD 37), 52 (loan, AD 37), 78 (receipt, AD 38), 68 (loan, AD 39), 53 (loan, AD 40), 46 (lease, AD 40), 79 (*pactum* for *pignus*, AD 40), 82 (discharge, AD 43–5), 81 (*promissio*, AD 45), 54 (loans, AD 45), 100 (unknown, AD 47), 72 (discharge, AD 47), *TH* 62 (*emptio*, AD 47 with Camodeca [2000] 70–3), *TPSulp.* 77 (discharge, AD 48), 48 (*mandatum*, AD 48), 101 (sale, AD 48), 49 (*mandatum*, AD 49), 74 (discharge, AD 51), 103 (unknown, AD 51), 57 (loan, AD 50?), 56 (loan, AD 52), and 75 (discharge, AD 52); *CIL* 4.3340.6 (discharge, AD 54), 16 and 148 (discharges, both AD 55), 20–1, 23–4 (all discharges, all AD 56), 30 and 33 (discharges, AD 57), 141–2, 145–6, 150 (all discharges, all AD 58), 143 and 147 (discharges, AD 59), 144 (discharge, AD 60), 152 (discharge, AD 61–2), and 151 (discharge, AD 62); *TH* 7 (unknown, after AD 61), *TH* 3 (label: *chirographum ex nomine facto*, AD 62, with Camodeca and Del Mastro [2002] 286), and *TH* 8 (discharge, AD 71). Twenty-seven are undated: *TPSulp.* 58, 108, and 110–12 (acts unknown), *TH* 10 (label: *chirographum ex nomine facto*), *TH* 31

Roman tablets in Italy (AD 15–79) 153

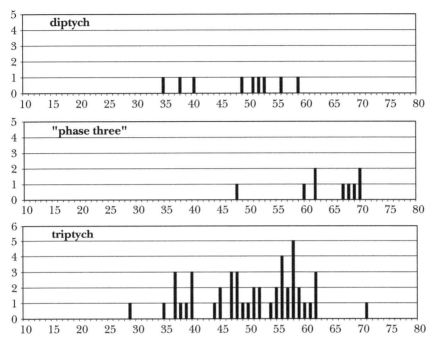

Figure 8 Physical forms of chirograph documents from first-century AD Campania. Chirograph documents of *bona fides* legal acts (leases, *pacta*, etc.) are predominantly triptychs starting in the late thirties AD.

an early date. Scattered diptychs remain, and the phase-three format is a momentarily popular choice in the sixties (as had been true for *testatio*-style documents as well, although in their case this use of doubled writing with a *sulcus* dated back to the forties), but the consistent commitment of chirograph-style informal acts, from AD 35 on, is to the triptych (**fig. 8**).

The fact that *testatio*-documents, those associated with the old unitary acts, are more conservative in physical form – migrate to triptychs more slowly than chirographs – confirms the special relationship between unitary acts and tablets argued from literary evidence in Part I. The use of *tabulae* for certain Roman legal acts is not simply a fashion, a convenience driven by a need for physical security or to prevent forgery: if it had been, the physical form of *testatio*-documents and chirographs would have evolved

(label: *chirographum . . . fundi venditi*), *TH* 32 (label: *chirographum . . . Graniani fundi*), *TH* 33–4, 36 (label: *chirographum nomini facti*), *TH* 37, 48, 51, 54–5, 57, and 95, Della Corte (1951) 225–6 no. 4, 226–7 no. 6, and 228 no. 11, and *CIL* 4.3340.58, 62, 97, 118, 126, and 153 (discharges).

154   *The evolution of practice*

at the same rate.[86] The comparative slowness of the physical evolution of *testatio*-documents indicates that the traditional tablet form conferred upon these documents a validity that made the addition of new types of physical security – *sulcus* to protect the seals, third *tabula* to protect the *sulcus* – less necessary than it was for the chirograph-documents that lacked this connection.

Foreigners, finance, flexibility, *fides*: can any of these explain the early interest in the triptych form? Some aspects of these chirograph-style documents do fit well with these factors. Anyone – man or woman, slave or free, citizen or peregrine – could perform an informal act under Roman law with proper authorization; it is speculated that *bona fides* acts and actions were originally acknowledged and accepted in part from a need to include commerce and foreigners in some kind of Roman jurisdiction,[87] and most of those acts preserved in writing do concern transactions with money and property. The documents that accompanied such acts could certainly be made quickly, since you always sealed them yourself. But what that had not been present in the diptych form did a triptych give to a document? On the physical level, only better protection of the seals, since the third *tabula* could close up against the second, with its seals snuggled in their *sulcus*, and thereby prevent their being knocked off by accident or design.[88] Nothing otherwise was different: a closed interior document, a doubled text (one readable without opening the document), and seals had all been present in earlier diptychs. This heightened interest in protecting seals in place suggests that the seal itself, rather than the need to keep the document shut, was coming to be seen as important; and it was with seals in particular that *fides* was expressed.

Romans were great users of personal seals, and thought they had been so for a long time.[89] Ateius Capito, the Augustan jurist, said, "the ancients

---

[86] The fact that they evolve at different rates is true whether or not I am correct in classifying "phase-three documents" as doubled writing on diptychs rather than "tripled writing" on triptychs (see above n.13). Were phase-three documents to be classified as triptychs, then eight more triptychs (all dating after AD 55) would be added to the chart of procedural documents and official copies, strengthening the impression of a late shift to triptychs in this category; nine triptychs would be added to the chart of financial documents, all but one after AD 40; and nine triptychs would be added to the chart of chirographs, all after AD 48 – but to a chart in which the early appearance of triptychs had already been strongly established.

[87] J. A. C. Thomas (1976) 279 (who notes "economic pressure" from non-Romans, because "... it may ... be noted that only those contracts ... essential to business life were ... introduced" as *bona fides* contracts); cf. *D.* 48.22.15.*pr.* (Marcian), after you lose citizenship can still buy and sell, lease and hire, etc.

[88] Camodeca (1995a) 76.

[89] Long history: Pliny, *NH* 33.9–12, 17–21 (initially of iron and expressed *virtus*, later gold; rings become important only in third century BC); cf. Erman (1905b) 457–61 and Kittel (1970) 82 (first surviving examples, engraved for sealing, from third century BC).

Roman tablets in Italy (AD 15–79)

customarily carried a ring around with them, for the sake of sealing, not ornament. For which reason it was not allowed to have more than one, nor for anyone except the free man to have one: (for) the *fides* that is contained in a little seal should adorn only (such) men, and slaves therefore used not to have the right to wear a ring."[90] A seal was yourself, a mark of your standing, and a summation of these: your *fides*. Cicero instructed his brother Quintus that his (Quintus's) ring was not to be considered a utensil, but "your very self, not the minister of another's will, but the witness-judge (*testis*) of your own."[91] The dying handed on their rings to their *heredes*, those who would take on the legal and familial persona of the dead in the next generation.[92] The regular act of *under*sealing a chirograph-style text – sealing at its end, not sealing it shut – preserved in Campanian documents shows sealing used in this way, as a device for a person in a world where the signature was not used, by men and women both.[93] Senator or equestrian, free or (eventually) slave, each came to be marked by the kind of ring he carried, although the extent of individual identification with a seal had its limits, since a man could use another's, with permission or, alas, sometimes without.[94] Slaves in Campanian chirograph-style documents do use sealing rings, although others usually underseal along with them; public slaves in Pompeii underseal documents but also have them sealed shut by others, often the *duumviri*, even though in one case the outer seals are provided only by the slave himself.[95] The *fides* of seals, whether derived from a master

---

[90] *Veteres . . . non ornatus, sed signandi causa anulum secum circumferebant. unde nec plus habere quam unum licebat, nec cuiquam nisi libero. quos solos fides deceret, quae signaculo continetur. ideo ius anulorum famuli non habebant*, quoted in Macrob. *Sat.* 7.13.12.

[91] Cic. *Q. fr.* 1.1.13 (*non minister alienae voluntatis, sed testis tuae*). Petronius (Tac. *Ann.* 16.19.3) destroyed his seal when he committed suicide, to prevent its misuse, but also, perhaps, as a companion act to his own death.

[92] Seyler (1894) 32 (examples).

[93] Sealing used in place of writing, Fest. 285M and 339M, *signare . . . antiqui eo pro scribe[re utebantur]*. Interior chirographs undersealed with a single seal in *CIL* 4.3340.1, 6, 30, 45, 50, 64, *TPSulp.* 51–3, 67–8, 45–6, 48, 77, 74, 58, and possibly 110 (with Wolf and Crook [1989] 12); exterior chirographs undersealed with a single seal in *CIL* 4.3340.10, 13–14, 26–8, 32, 39, 48–9, 52, 54, 63, 65, 68, 72, 78–9, 81, 83, 86–7, 101, 103–4, 106(?), 113–17; women sealing can be deduced from the fact that when another writes for her, there are two seals on *pag.* 5 (see below n.95), and that women could seal is demonstrated by *CIL* 4.3340.24 (sealed shut by a woman). Pompeian documents in chirograph style on both interior and exterior are undersealed only on the interior, see Zangemeister (1898) 433; in combinational *acceptilatio*-chirograph documents the exterior chirographs are undersealed, Erman (1899) 178, 182–3, 191.

[94] Plin. *NH* 33.29–33, Stat. *Silv.* 3.3.144. Using another's: the context of Cicero's advice to Quintus (above, n.91) is the need to restrain underlings, so the implication is that they can use Quintus's sealing ring; Augustus allowed Maecenas and Agrippa to use one of his two identical sealing rings (Cass. Dio 51.3.5–6). For some later incidences, *D.* 28.1.22.2 (Ulpian) and Just. *Inst.* 2.10.5.

[95] Slaves, e.g., *CIL* 4.3340.1, 6, 7, 25, 30; *TPSulp.* 45, 67–8, and 46, with Wolf and Crook (1989) 12–13; additional sealing also occurs when a slave or another has written for the protagonist, explicit in *CIL* 4.3340.7, 17, 25, and 34 (for women), and may be the case in more fragmentary *tabulae* with two

156   *The evolution of practice*

or your own, was at any rate happily distributed by status. Careful work with the lists of Campanian (and other) sealers has shown that *signatores* were arranged in a hierarchical order, with those of the highest social status first, freedmen (etc.) last, and the connections between sealing and status were implicitly or explicitly noted by Seneca, Pliny, Martial, and Juvenal.[96] If a seal was "your very self," in Cicero's words, your *fides*, then wielding it was a powerful pleasure and using a triptych to protect the seals, some of them explicitly your own, that closed a chirograph-style document was to protect yourself.

Authors of a *bona fides* act in a chirograph-style document on a triptych protected their texts with their seals, their seals with a third *tabula*. A person's *fides* was wrapped up and sealed in a bundle tied with string, all of which had to be preserved and defended. The stipulation may have been one reason for writing on a wooden tablet a *bona fides* act that in an age of uncomplicated agreements and pure faith need not have been written at all, but the change in the exterior treatment of the tablet's physical form – sealing and then the adoption of a triptych to protect the seals – is also a sign that the tablet itself has come to be seen as grasping and embodying not just a legal act but also *fides*. Moreover, in uncertain or unhappy times, the fashion in which you voluntarily display your *fides* can be demanded as a literal demonstration of it, as can its strengthening through the *fides* of others. Seneca the Younger in particular associates the *chirographum* (and *pacta* and *conventa*) and the *signatores* (and seals) when lamenting that *fides* was no longer pure and perfect, crying out that there was more trust in sealing rings than men's sterling consciences.[97] Sealing was by his time coming to be characteristic of all documents, but he thought his times were degenerate, and so in his hands sealing as a sign of *fides* was artfully twisted into sealing as a sign of no *fides*. Indeed, if your *fides* is bad, then sealed *tabulae* conveying *fides* are your means of committing a criminal

---

seals on *pag.* 5, *CIL* 4.3340.12 (woman), 38, 43, 51, 53, 55, 61, 74, 77, 98, and 110. Public slaves: interior (single) sealing in *CIL* 4.3340.138–9, 141–5, 147–8, 151; also sealed shut by *duumviri* 141–3, 145–7, 151. Sealed only by slave: *CIL* 4.3340.148.

[96] Andreau (1974) 170–95, 215–16; Jongman (1991) 226–73, noting corrections in *CIL* 4.3340.81 and 89 to get the order right; Camodeca (1992) 160, (1993a) 110 and 114, (1993e), (1999b) 534–5; the sealing of copies made in the *tabula Banasitana* (*AE* 1971.534) also followed status order, Haensch (1996) 463–4 n.70. Seneca: *Ep.* 8.6 (things people think important, and obviously are); Pliny, *Ep.* 1.9.2–3 (important persons like himself are called on to seal wills); Mart. *Ep.* 10.70 (I'm just so important), Juv. *Sat.* 3.81–2 (riffraff foreigners seal before *I* do!).

[97] Sen. *Ben.* 2.23.2, men unwilling to have *nomina* made of debt, to have guarantors (*pararios*), *nec signatores advocari, chirographum dare* are ashamed to admit that they have received benefactions; 3.15.1, *pacta conventaque* (both informal acts) *impressis signis custodirentur;* 3.15.3 *anulis* and *animis.*

Roman tablets in Italy (AD 15–79)

act: "a very great number of the crimes connected with money are carried out by means of rings," as Pliny the Elder observes.[98]

The demands of *fides* put pressure on other older documents as well; the use of a *chirographum* as the exterior text of an *acceptilatio* demonstrates this most clearly and vividly. The strong desire of creditors to hold debtors "by the hand" (*manu*) as well as *interrogatione*, "by the question-and-answer" (of, presumably, stipulation), itself observed and denounced by Seneca in book three of his *de Beneficiis* (AD 56–64), may also have been a manifestation of the same pressure.[99] The first certainly attested *acceptilatio* with a chirograph from Jucundus's collection (*CIL* 4.3340.7) is from AD 54. This pressure to strengthen, to "hold by one's hand," to demand a chirograph *even in a formal act*, both that of stipulation and the formal *acceptilatio* that "undid" the stipulation, may in fact be a new and notable phenomenon of the fifties. Pliny the Elder seems to offer a contemporary, if indirect, confirmation of the growing influence of *fides* as a component in all legal and financial documents. The growth of usury and the use of rings are related, he observes. An agreement for interest on a loan, which can only be exacted through stipulation, is secured by being written down and sealed, and it is "even the custom of the mob now" to use rings – the indicators of *fides* – when making *sponsiones*: first there was money, he says, then seals, and now (appalling) everybody does it. "The greater ordering (*ratio*) of life has begun to center around this *instrumentum*" – he has been talking about sealing rings, and here means *instrumentum* both in the sense of "useful object" and "legal document" – "although when this began is uncertain."[100] The transformation of wooden *tabulae* into sealed wooden tablets capturing and embodying both formal act and *fides* caught Seneca's disapproving eye in the fifties, and by the sixties and seventies Pliny notes their ubiquity and centrality. This is precisely the change that the Campanian documents themselves demonstrated.

The alteration of a traditional *tabula* in *testatio* style into a combinational hybrid with different kinds of acts written in both *testatio* and chirograph style is one of the more obvious signs of the influence of *fides* in the world

---

[98] Pliny, *NH* 33.26 (*denique vel plurima opum scelera anulis fiunt*); cf. Hor. *Sat.* 2.3.69–76, *tabulae* a way of binding a debtor, but did not work in this case, probably because of bad *fides*, Pers. *Sat.* 5.81 (seal of a person he loathes adds no *fides*), cf. Juv. *Sat.* 8.142.

[99] Sen. *Ben.* 3.15.2, *ille non est interrogatione contentus, nisi reum manu sua tenuit*; the latter should not refer to *manus iniectio* (seizure after failure to pay), since that technical term uses the verb *inicio*, cf. *OLD s.v.* 6b and *manus* 15b (including several examples in Seneca); this quotation is regularly associated with stipulation, see Erman (1899) 198.

[100] Plin. *NH* 33.28 (*... consuetudo volgi, ad sponsiones etiamnum anulo exiliente...*) and 33.27 (*...maiorque vitae ratio circa hoc instrumentum esse coepit, incertum a quo tempore*).

158 *The evolution of practice*

of formality. In consensual acts, *fides* had already shaped form with the change from diptych to triptych twenty years earlier; the eventual but later adoption of the triptych for formal and procedural acts was to be another sign of its influence. Not just a routine and pragmatic improvement, the shift to the triptych for the *testatio*-style documents of formal acts signalled here too a new emphasis on the sealers and on the *fides* – theirs as well as the protagonists', who can at times also be observed sealing[101] – that the wood now incorporated and protected. In this way, the strong influence of context on form, the way such documents were coming to be seen and used, begins to be perceptible.

THE EVOLUTION OF ROMAN DOCUMENTS: WITNESSES AND SEALERS

The Campanian documents offer a window into the changing world of Roman legal practice between AD 15 and AD 79. The association of sealing and *fides*, which illuminated this narrow window, also offers a useful way of looking at Roman legal *tabulae* and legal practice over a longer period of time. The trajectory of development that sees the addition of *fides* to formality in Campania can also be observed by following the initially distinct but gradually coalescing practices of witnessing and sealing, both before and after AD 15 to AD 79. This development was indirectly helped along, or at least reflected, by the official interest taken in protecting wills (pages 163–8), but otherwise was driven by the priorities of the practitioners themselves.

These practitioners frequently wore rings. The use of seals and sealing rings in the first century BC and later set Romans apart from others, and particularly from provincials in Egypt and the East. ". . . The greater part of the races of mankind, and even of the people who live under our empire and at the present day, possess no rings at all," wrote Pliny the Elder; "the East and Egypt do not seal documents even now, but are content with only writing."[102] Romans in contrast loved seals and rings, and never more so than in the first century AD, when seals were common and their rings

---

[101] *CIL* 4.3340.1 (slave), 14–15, 17–19 (17 questionable), 26, 28, 31, 34–5, 37–8, 40, 47–9 (in 48, two protagonists and both seal), 51, 54, 56, 65–6, 73–6, 80–1, 83, 85–7, 89, 99–101.

[102] . . . *nullosque omnino maior pars gentium hominumque, etiam qui sub imperio nostro degunt, hodieque habeat. non signat oriens aut Aegyptus etiam nunc litteris contenta solis, NH* 33.21, discussed Erman (1899) 179–81; surviving documents from Judaea, Arabia, and Mesopotamia do not use seals, see chapter seven nn.111 and 145. Greek testaments of the Roman period a notable exception, Wenger (1923) cols. 2403–4. In Egypt, undersealing is only a Roman-period practice, and "only the work of officials" (Vandorpe [1995] 25), e.g., orders for arrests.

Roman tablets in Italy (AD 15–79)

became luxury items, fantastic high art carved in precious stones, at times so precious that they were not even used for sealing, the fondness for their use parodied in an epitaph asking friends to "seal" an "edict" of the dead man's against urinating on the tomb.[103]

Yet the purpose for which they wielded these rings at the beginning of the first century AD is not as straightforward as has been assumed. For although a man using his seal to close another's document is regularly referred to by scholars as a "witness" and the legal efficacy of any legal documents (as simple proof) is regularly deemed to derive only from the "witness" given through this act of sealing,[104] witnessing and sealing were initially not the same function, and their uses have different histories. It was mostly formal acts that required independent citizen *testes*, "judges" of correctness,[105] while informal acts did not; witnessing was an ancient privilege of citizenship,[106] while the sealing of legal and financial documents is not attested before the first century BC;[107] and it was the earliest of the surviving formal acts, the *acceptilatio* from AD 15, that had no sealers, while all chirograph-style documents from Campania do. Moreover, women and slaves could not be *testes* in formal acts, but do appear as sealers of the chirograph-style texts: in the world of formality they have no independent standing, but in the world of *fides* they do.[108] In one case a document was sealed by the protagonist alone: in this case, as in the examples sealed by women

---

[103] Plin. *NH* 33.23 and 6.25; Roman rings and seals hard to classify and date, although most are first to third centuries AD, Spier (1992) 75–6 and 167. Epitaph: L. Herrmann (1958), dated (101) late Republican/early imperial: *adeste atque me favete, edicto huic obsignate* . . . (lines 47–8).

[104] E.g., Mitteis (1908) 295, Kaser (1934) cols. 1027–8, Talamanca (1964) 550–1, and Wolf and Crook (1989) 12; but very common.

[105] See above chapter five nn.111–12.

[106] Not only did you have to be a citizen to witness, but becoming *intestabilis* was a punishment (Twelve Tables VIII.11 [Gel. 15.13.11]: *qui se sierit testarier libripensve fuerit, ni testimonium fariatur, improbus intestabilisque esto*, Crawford [1996] II.582).

[107] The earliest evidence may be provided by what are believed to be seals of Italian traders on Delos, sometime before 69 BC, Boussac (1993) 687–9. Specific mention in the first century BC is made of a *tabula sistendi* (Cic. *Quinct.* 25), a declaration (*testatio*, Cic. *Quinct.* 66–7 and 2*Verr.* 5.102, metaphor at Cic. *Tusc.* 5.33), an arbitration (Cic. *Flacc.* 89), judges' *sententiae* (Cic. 1*Verr.* 40, 2.4.104), *syngraphae* (Cic. *Phil.* 5.12), and esp. wills: Cic. *Cluent.* 37, 38, 125, 162; *Mil.* 48; *Att.* 7.2.3 (will of M. Curius), 12.18a.2 (Cicero's own will), 14.14.5 (implied); *Q. fr.* 3.9.8 (testator sealing); Caes. *BG* 1.39.5. Sealing is referred to as characteristic of the praetor's court but applied to a money-mad courtesan's house in Cic. 2*Verr.* 1.137.

[108] No women as *testes*, Gel. 7.7.2–3, Plut. *Publ.* 8.4, *D.* 28.1.20.6 (Ulpian; a dispute, possibly arising from the different meanings of "witness" – in our sense, which women could do, and judging, which women could not), Just. *Inst.* 2.10.6; and Kaser (1934) cols. 1047–8, Wenger (1923) col. 2385; no slaves seal *testatio*-style documents at Murecine, Camodeca (1999a) 36. Slaves perhaps participate in the *fides* of their masters; women may have had *fides* of their own, but for whatever reason it was not usual for them to assert it extensively through sealing in the business world, Gardner (1999) 26–7 ("may be due to mere social convention").

160 *The evolution of practice*

and slaves, there was no objective observance of the act or the *tabula* by an acceptable person.[109] At least some of the *signatores* of chirograph-style texts in Campania cannot, therefore, be fulfilling the old-fashioned function of *testes* as judges of correctness. They are, rather, adding their *fides* to a document, and the act of sealing a chirograph-style text shut in these cases was analogous, rather, to the sealing of a personal letter, for which Plautus, Cicero, and others offer ample evidence (and which was both a Greek and a Roman habit): through it, some secrecy, protection, and verification that you were the author of that letter might be achieved, although even that was not assured.[110] Witnessing and sealing therefore once stood in a different relationship to the acts and documents with which they were associated: formal acts had to be "witnessed" (judged) but did not have to be sealed, while informal acts were customarily sealed but did not need to be "witnessed."[111]

An equivalence of *testis* and *signator* is established beyond doubt only when, for example, an author-protagonist calls on "those who are about to seal" to witness – which happens only when the protagonist is attesting,[112] or when the *antestatus* ("chief witness") in a mancipatory act is listed among the sealers.[113] Both are securely documented only outside Italy, and in the late first century AD and after. By that point, the *antestatus* wrote at the end of Antonius Silvanus's will in Egypt only "I sealed," not "I witnessed."[114]

---

[109] *CIL* 4.3340.21, a man seals his own document four times, with no other sealers, with Mommsen (1907 [1877]) 239 and Wolf and Crook (1989) 12–13. *TH* 48 brings in only one independent sealer.

[110] Some Roman chirographs from Egypt indeed take letter form, complete with opening salutation, e.g., *P.Fouad* 1.45 = *FIRA²* 3.391–3 no. 121 (AD 153); and *D.* 2.14.47.1 (Scaevola), a legally enforceable letter; Mitteis (1908) 293 n.8 notes that every letter can be called a chirograph ("handwritten") but every chirograph is not a letter. Sealed letters: e.g., Plautus, *Curc.* 422–3, *Pseud.* 988, 1000, but common; in general, Riepl (1913) 301–4 and Wenger (1923) cols. 2394–6. Greek as well as Roman habit, Erman (1899) 179; examples from Egypt, Vandorpe (1995) 12–15.

[111] *Contra* Kaser (1934) col. 1028.

[112] *Qui signaturi erant*: *CPL* 104 = *FIRA²* 1.424–7 no. 76 (a veteran *coram ac praesentibus eis, qui signaturi erant, testatus est*, AD 94); *CPL* 105 (AD 95); *CPL* 162 = *FIRA²* 3.9–11 no. 4 (AD 145), *ChLA* 47.1448 = *P.Col.* 8.221 (ἐπὶ τῶν παρόντων καὶ σφραγισάντων μαρτύρων, AD 147); *CPL* 213 = *PSI* 1027, *FIRA²* 3.179–80 no. 59 (AD 151), *ChLA* 3.216 = *CPL* 217, *P.Oxy.* 1114 (ἐμαρτύρατο τοὺς τόδε τὸ μαρτυροποίημα σφραγίζειν μέλλοντας, AD 237).

[113] *Antestatus*: in Campania, the one text mentioning an *antestatus* lacks a list of sealers (*CIL* 4.3340.155), and in general sealers are merely listed, with no verb given; second century AD, cf. (e.g.) the sealed will of Antonius Silvanus (*CPL* 221 = *FIRA²* 3.129–32 no. 47, AD 142), where the *antestatus* seals third, after the *familiae emptor* and the *libripens*; at the opening of the will of C. Longinus Castor (*BGU* 326 = *FIRA²* 3.146–53 no. 50, AD 191 and 194), the *antestatus* is present and acknowledges his seal; in a mancipatory donation from Rome (*CIL* 6.10239 = *FIRA²* 3.298–301 no. 94, second–third centuries), the *antestatus* is restored as sealing next-to-last.

[114] Antonius Silvanus, AD 142 (*CPL* 221 = *FIRA²* 3.129–32 no. 47, *signavi* and σιγνάουι); also true in documents from Dacia, the sale of a house, AD 159 (*IDR/TabCerD.* 9 = *CIL* 3 p. 945, *FIRA²* 3.289–91 no. 90, *signavi*), the sales of slaves, AD 160 (*IDR/TabCerD.* 8 = *CIL* 3 p. 959, *FIRA²* 3.287–8 no. 89,

Roman tablets in Italy (AD 15–79)

A mixture of the language of sealing and witnessing begins to appear in Roman legal documents in the second century, and is infrequent,[115] although some acts of copying are sealed by those who "are present" at this time as well.[116] Only over time, in other words, did the *testes* of unitary acts also become their *signatores*, and only later than that did the *signatores* feel themselves to be *testes*. Republican usage tended to keep the two separate;[117] only by the second century AD are the two verifiably starting to meld even in the minds of practitioners, and only then do juristic texts start to take their equivalence for granted.[118] The Campanian tablets lie within one segment along this slow trajectory of transition: their sealers cannot in every case be *testes*, but they do not express, with any verb, what they think they are doing.

Both *testatio-* and chirograph-style acts could stand on their own, but in the Roman world you always stood more sturdily in the comforting and supportive presence of your *amici*, men of standing and reputation. They would add their seals to yours on whatever type of document was being constructed, showing to the world an immediate public adherence

---

σεγνά<υ>ι); *tabulae nuptiales*, late second century AD (*CPL* 211 = *P.Mich.* 7.444), ἐσφρά[γισα. Sealing rather than witnessing is also referred to in epigraphical copies made of official edicts, the sealers' names merely listed at the end (W. Williams [1975] 68–70), although once an attempt was made to carve the seals, Wolters (1903) 333.

[115] *ChLA* 47.1448 = *P.Col.* 8.221 (ἐσφράγισα and *signavi* by those referred to as μαρτύρων in the text, AD 147); *testimonium* with an oath (*SB* 7523 = *FIRA²* 3.591–2 no. 188, ἐσφράγισα by those who are also the swearers, and are said to μαρτυροῦμεν, AD 153); a chirograph by a Roman from Egypt, AD 153 (*P.Fouad* 1.45 = *FIRA²* 3.391–3 no. 121, μαρτυρῶ and *adfui*). Clear use of witness – rather than sealing-language is found in the third century AD but in Greek-language documents, e.g., a chirograph-style donation, AD 247 (*P.Grenf.* 2.68 = *FIRA²* 3.305–7 no. 98, μαρτυρῶ); a double-document copy of a petition, AD 207 (*P.Oxy.* 2131), copied and sealed διὰ τῶν ὑπογεγραμμένων μαρτύρων; note that in *P.Dura* 26 = *FIRA²* 3.439–43 no. 138 (AD 227), the Romans use *signavi* but the Greek uses μ(α)ρ(τυρῶ). On late language, see Kaser (1934) col. 1040.

[116] *CPL* 104 (above n.112); in the dossier including the decision of a *iudex datus* in Chaeroneia (*IG* 9(1).61, AD 118), individuals who παρῆσαν each note ἐσφράγισα; a rescript of Antoninus to the Smyrnaeans (*IKSmyrna* 597 = *FIRA²* 1.435–6 no. 82, AD 139), ἐσφραγίσθη by seven, who παρῆσαν; and see *P.Fouad* 1.45 in preceding note. In Sahin and French (1987) 137 line 12 seven men were merely "present" (παρ]ῆσαν) at the copying of a rescript of Caracalla's. Those who "were present" may not have been "witnessing" in the old-fashioned sense, although Plin. *Ep.* 1.9.2–3 uses *interfui* of his attendance at a *toga-virilis*-donning ceremony, in a list of legal jobs he does in town.

[117] Cf. Sal. *Cat.* 16.2, *ex illis testes signatoresque falsos commodare*; Cic. *Att.* 16.16e, *decretis* of Caesar's *testibus et obsignatoribus*, *Div.* 1.87 (*testata consignataque*).

[118] *D.* 28.1.27, the famously rude answer of Celsus to a petitioner asking whether a man who wrote and sealed a will could also be a witness to it (the petitioner sees the difference explicated in the text, while Celsus collapses "witness" and "sealer" into one category in his reply); Venuleius (*D.* 22.5.22), in the second half of the second century AD (Kunkel [1967] 181–4) does still seem to make the distinction: local magistrates must be prepared to offer themselves and other *testes* or *signatores* to those wishing *testari*. Others amalgamate the two, like Celsus, cf. *D.* 43.5.3.9 (Ulpian), *D.* 28.1.22 (Ulpian – although note that at 22.4 an unidentified sealer is not considered a *testis*), and *CJ* 8.40.6 (AD 214), *tabulas obligationis ut testis adsignavit*.

162   *The evolution of practice*

to you, not (or not necessarily) a future promise of specific knowledge of a legal act and its execution.[119] *Tabulae* were written, some witnessed and some not; then *tabulae* came to be sealed shut, again, some witnessed and some not; then documents came to be written on triptychs, to protect the seals. Sometime after sealing began, then too began the slow process of assimilating witnesses and sealers, perhaps helped by the sense that acts of both witnessing and sealing could be understood as intertwined with a man's *fides*: as Sallust noted, to bear false witness *or* to seal falsely was to hold *fides* in contempt, and Cicero called Quintus's ring, so full of implications about *fides*, his *testis*.[120]

The *fides* of the sealers built a proud and self-satisfied rampart for a document that crumbled once those seals were broken, the *fides* leaking away through the breach.[121] Yet this grotesque offense was not frequently suffered by *signatores*, for Romans chose to avoid touching the *fides* of great men, and instead simply did not usually open sealed documents at all: when sealed legal documents were adduced in court, spectators and opponents were merely invited to inspect them, rarely to open them.[122] This could perhaps have been predicted, not just because of the touchy honor of Roman grandees, but because the sealing and the exterior doubling of a legal or financial text seem to have appeared simultaneously. Once a document is bound shut, its *linum* sealed down, and there are powerful reasons not to open it, how could you tell what it was? You can't simply rummage to find the one you want. A sealed document had to be marked on the outside as well. Indeed, if knowing the particulars – of an agreement, a receipt, a loan, anything – was useful, then having a summary or a text of the entire document on the outside would be very useful as well. For this reason, although sealing a document shut is the final expression of one set of

---

[119] Given the frequency with which some people sealed – P. Terentius Primus, in Jucundus's collection, sealed eighteen different documents (Erman [1899] 175 n.2; 190), numerous repeaters at Herculaneum are known (Camodeca [1993e] 343, more than ninety of the 300+ names of sealers known repeat at least once), the *signatores* of military *diplomata* repeated extensively starting in the Flavian period (Haensch [1996] 463–70), and fifteen of those who signed documents in the Babatha archive did so more than once (Ilan [2001]) – it is unlikely that a specific memory of the contents or even just of the documentation of a specific act could have been intended. Such repetition of names is also known for Roman *tabella*-copies in Egypt, Haensch (1996) 466. Sealers would presumably know the author-protagonist, as was true for *commilitiones* (outside of Rome) as *signatores* in military *diplomata* before the Flavian period, Dušanic (1984–5) 282.

[120] Sal. *Cat.* 16.2, *fidem, fortunas, pericula vilia habere . . .*; Cic. *Q. fr.* 1.1.13.

[121] Erman (1899) 185, (1905b) 474–5 (wills, but equally applicable to the sealing of other documents).

[122] Apul. *Apol.* 89, the examination of a profession of birth: *linum consideret, signa, quae impressa sunt, recognoscat, consules legat, annos computet*; cf. Weiß (1912) 230, no examples of sealed documents read out. The fact that two hinge-holes were at times reduced to merely one suggests that it was known that triptychs were not opened and therefore did not need working hinges, Chapman (1978) 400.

Roman tablets in Italy (AD 15–79) 163

beliefs about the efficacy of *tabulae* and the *fides* of the sealers, the addition of a second exterior copy or at least a summary, and sometimes also a label, to a document are never found separate from it.[123] A *tabula* had ceremonial associations and symbolic implications, but it was important to protect its contents untouched, useful to know its details, and crucial not to touch the *fides* of its *signatores* in a manner suggesting contumelious disbelief. Its physical form, with an exterior copy that made it possible to preserve the *fides* of the sealers indefinitely, reflected these apparently contradictory priorities well.

Witnessing and sealing were thus initially different, but both came to say something about an act and its *tabula*, the first carefully observing for flaws, the second supporting, with the *fides* of its sealers, the *fides* of the author-protagonist, as well as protecting the *tabula* against fraud and damage. As demonstrated *fides* grew more desirable and combinational acts grew more common, sealing (and with it the necessary doubling of the text) became standard. The Campanian documents let us see the trajectory, even if only one segment of it; but from that one segment, the rest can be extrapolated. Because some documents associated with ceremonial and formal acts seem to have been sealed even in Cicero's time,[124] the movement toward stamping a document with *fides* and finality must have been well underway even by then; the change to the triptych is, therefore, one of its last phases, complete by AD 70. The *tabula* gathers in an act, then multiple acts, then (or simultaneously) the *fides* of protagonists and sealers, then protects that *fides* (and the document) so spectacularly that the document itself need never be opened.

CONCLUSION: THE *SENATUSCONSULTUM
NERONIANUM* OF AD 61

For all of these changes, the intervention of the state, or even of jurists, was minimal. The desire to combine acts and give visible indicators of *fides* came from practitioners, and the evolution of documents in these directions should be seen as a trend – or even, Seneca the Younger might

---

[123] A label called an index can be found on the outside faces of diptychs (e.g., *TPSulp.* 23–4) and triptychs (*TPSulp.* 46–8, 50, 54, 56, 74; *TH* 66); where a label stops and a summary begins is at times hard to distinguish, as in *TPSulp.* 35–6. Labels can also be found on the edges of triptychs (*TH* 14, 16, 23, 26, 29, 42, 46, 64, 92–3; *TPSulp.* 51, 45, 52, 82, 56, and 25), running from one edge to the next as they would be stacked in order when sealed (both kinds of labelling are uncommon in the Murecine tablets, Camodeca [1995a] 63–4 nn.12–13). Labelling is also found at Vindolanda (Birley *et al.* [1993] 14, eight examples) and Cologne (Doppelfeld [1970] 13).

[124] See above n.107.

164   *The evolution of practice*

insist sourly, a contemptible fashion that seized people – that was driven by perceptions of the additional uses to which *tabulae* could simultaneously be put without changing their fundamental nature. Public interest as expressed by edicts or *senatusconsulta*, on the other hand, in general concerned itself only with the *tabulae* associated with one type of ceremonial act, the mancipatory will. Wills were of natural interest to every Roman, since they divided property and affected reputations, but one particular reason why they attracted the attention of lawmakers might have been that they by necessity had to use witnesses and sealers in ways that contradicted the logic of traditional practice. Only in the case of the mancipatory will did the observed efficacy of the act come to be stretched over time. The obligation on those who watched the ceremony for correctness did not end with the ceremony itself, as it would in (e.g.) the sale of a slave, for the transfer and settling of an estate, initially conceived as immediate when the *familiae emptor* "bought" the property, was increasingly delayed until after the testator died. Moreover, although a will was a public document, its terms in most cases came to be kept secret until the testator died, and that which Romans wanted to keep secret or private, like letters, they sealed. Like seals on letters but unlike seals on doubled documents, these seals were meant to be broken, but only after death. The ways Romans used mancipatory wills – to delay the distribution of property and to conceal the terms of that distribution – therefore extended a ceremonial formal act over time and put unnatural stress on the Republican concepts of witnessing and sealing. The high degree of *fides* desirable in will-witnesses, who were specifically asked by the testator to provide testimony but who did not (traditionally, or at least initially) seal, and the clear importance of the *signatores*, who protected the *tabulae* against unauthorized additions, might also have prompted the two roles to amalgamate in this type of document first.[125] Will *tabulae* (not acts or statements) were *testatae*; the only *testes* specifically glossed as "men who sealed" in the Republic were those of a will, according to Festus; and Cicero's usage suggests that here, the two were the same.[126]

---

[125] G. 2.104, *TESTIMONIUM MIHI PERHIBETOTE*, not noted for any other mancipatory act, but parodied in Apul. *Met.* 2.24; did not require witnesses to seal, Just. *Inst.* 2.10.2 (. . . *iure civili signa testium non erant necessaria*).

[126] *Testatas . . . tabulas*, Catul. 68.122; Festus (56M), "*classici testes* . . . are those who are summoned for the sealing of a testament;" Gel. 6.13 identifies *classici* as *cives* of the first class, which confirms the importance placed on standing and *fides* in witnesses and sealers, and suggests that especially high standing was desirable for wills. Cicero, see above n.107 on sealed wills. Even here, and into the third century AD, the *testes* were not expected to observe or know anything about the contents or trustworthiness of the *tabulae* themselves, Paul. *Sent.* 5.15.4.

Roman tablets in Italy (AD 15–79)

Delay and secrecy multiply the opportunities for malfeasance. Sulla's *lex Cornelia* laid down penalties for the forgery of wills, including tampering with a will's seals, and at some point before 70 BC, and indeed probably before Sulla's time, a *lex* had either recommended or required the sealing of wills.[127] By the middle of the first century BC the praetor had laid out the conditions under which he would grant *bonorum possessio* of property if a will had not been properly made. It had to be sealed by the "many seals the law required," later identified as seven, all from *testes*: the praetor implies that failures in formality were compensated for by the *fides* of the sealing witnesses.[128] The *lex Iulia de vicesima hereditatium* of AD 5 or 6 laid down the circumstances under which wills were to be opened, and since tax was collected in this way, this law also implies that all substantial property should or must pass through a written and sealed will.[129] Thus by the early imperial period, the state had attempted to regulate those aspects of mancipatory wills that practice had subverted, especially the way sealing shut preserved not a known act but one whose falsehoods or errors might become apparent only later, and the way witnesses needed to attest not only at a will's formal enactment but at its closing as well.

By agreeing to grant *bonorum possessio* for a sealed will, the praetor encouraged the sealing of wills, itself mentioned by an earlier *lex*; by laying down specific circumstances under which wills were to be opened, the *lex Iulia* required that wills be closed. In neither case, however, was there intervention in the technicalities of how a document was made or sealed, merely the suggestion or injunction that it was to be sealed. The only intervention of this technical sort known, for any document, is dated to AD 61. Suetonius, stressing its novelty, describes it and some associated measures:

It was then [in Nero's emperorship] for the first time (devised) against forgers that no *tabulae* should be sealed unless they were bored through and a string passed three times through the holes; and it was laid down for wills that the first two wax-tablets should be presented blank to the sealers with only the name of the

---

[127] Sulla, in Paul. *Sent.* 5.25.1, Sulla made punishable *qui . . . signum adulterinum sculpserit fecerit expresserit amoverit reseraverit* on a will, cf. Hitzig (1909) cols. 1973–4; Cic. 2*Verr.* 1.117 refers to *obsignatio* (of wills) *ex lege*, although the *lex* to which he refers is unknown; on forgery of wills in general, Champlin (1991) 82–7.

[128] Cic. 2*Verr.* 1.117, *si . . . tabulae testamenti obsignatae non minus multis signis, quam ex lege oportet, ad me proferentur*; cf. G. 2.147 and 119, *praetor si septem signis testium signatum sit testamentum . . . bonorum possessionem pollicetur.* The frequency of seven sealers in other later documents is often attributed to the example of wills as well, e.g., Bruns (1882 [1877]) and Mitteis (1908) 295 n.16.

[129] *Lex Iulia*, dated to either AD 5 or 6 (Cass. Dio 55.25), Nisoli (1949) 30–9. The circumstances of the opening were scripted, Nisoli (1949) 40–59 (at 51, he calls it "feierlich"); Vandorpe (1995) 16, with examples and language; *P.Oxy.* 3758 lines 134–55 (AD 325) gives a late account of the procedure.

166   *The evolution of practice*

testators written, and that no one who was the writer of a will for another should write in a legacy for himself . . .[130]

The circumstances that precipitated these related measures against forgers are probably as follows.[131] Tacitus describes a forgery scandal of the year AD 61, when a relative of the wealthy former praetor Domitius Balbus named Valerius Fabianus forged Domitius's will, drawing into his conspiracy two Roman *equites* and two senators, Antonius Primus (the future lieutenant of Vespasian) and Asinius Marcellus. They and other "less illustrious men" sealed this will, were discovered, and were all punished under the terms of the *lex Cornelia* except for Marcellus, who escaped punishment but not infamy because of the remembered distinction of his ancestors and the petition of the Caesar.[132] Senators must have labored mightily to credit what we can presume to have been Marcellus's defense – that he thought he was sealing Valerius Fabianus's own will, not Domitius's. To save face, they suggested a feeble measure about how wills were to be made, and could well have thrown in the measure about the boring-through of *tabulae* and the tripled *linum*, applicable apparently to all other documents, to look busy and responsible. Suetonius associates the two measures; so should we. Here as at other times the concern for wills was primary. The treatment of other documents was probably a fortuitous association or afterthought, as had been true also of the belated extension of the *lex Cornelia*'s penalties for forgery of wills to other documents in, most likely, AD 44, more than a hundred years after the original measure.[133] Suetonius was right to think that the *senatusconsultum* was one against forgers, since a loose *linum* could be slipped out of the notches of *stria* or *sulcus* but not out of a *tabula*'s bore-holes no matter how loose the *linum* was;[134] making *tabulae pertusae* may not have been a measure against any known incidence of forgery that exploited the weaknesses of a wound rather than bored-through *tabula* as much as a measure borrowed from military *diplomata* at a moment when it was important for the senate to be seen to be doing something.[135]

---

[130] Suet. *Nero* 17: *adversus falsarios tunc primum repertum ne tabulae nisi pertusae ac ter lino per foramina traiecto obsignarentur; cautum ut testamentis primae duae cerae testatorum modo nomine inscripto vacuae signaturis ostenderentur, ac ne qui alieni testamenti scriptor legatum sibi ascriberet . . .* For earlier bibliography, Nisoli (1949) 42 n.17.

[131] Erman (1905b) 469–70 separated (wrongly, I think) the measures against forgers and the measures about wills. Cicero *ND* 3.74 reports will forgery as common, and even the emperor Claudius was said to have sealed a forged will (Suet. *Claud.* 9.2), so what happened in AD 61 must have been truly scandalous.

[132] Tac. *Ann.* 14.40.2–5: *Valerius Fabianus . . . subdidit testamentum . . . igitur Fabianus tabulas <adhibitis> iis quos memoravi et aliis minus inlustribus obsignat.*

[133] *Coll.* 8.7.1 = *D.* 48.10.9.3 (Ulpian); cf. Mommsen (1899) 672, Talbert (1984) 441 no. 38, 451 no. 143.

[134] Mitteis (1908) 298–9.

[135] Camodeca (1993d) 355 and 359 (oldest *pertusa tabula* is *CIL* 16.1, 11 December AD 52).

Roman tablets in Italy (AD 15–79) 167

When Pliny spoke of crimes committed with rings, he meant bad faith, not subsequent tampering with seals of the enterprising sort Lucian would later describe.[136]

A late-antique text of an early third-century jurist, Paulus, described this *senatusconsultum* of AD 61 more extensively:

> The senate decreed that those *tabulae*, which contain the writing of either public or private *contractus*, are – once witnesses have been summoned – to be sealed in this way: the tablets, having been perforated on the top edge towards the middle, are bound around with a tripled string, and the seals of the wax placed on top of the string are impressed, so that the interior preserves the *fides* of the writing by means of the exterior. Tablets produced in another fashion have no value.[137]

Paulus's description of how legal documents in general (*contractus*) were to be treated matches Suetonius's. Paulus amplifies motive, suggesting that the new way of binding was undertaken "so that the interior preserves the *fides* of the writing by the exterior," and makes one final addition, that all *tabulae* not closed in this fashion were henceforth to be "of no moment." This last is unlikely as an immediate penalty in AD 61 since, as the Campanian documents show, the requirement of triple binding through specially bored holes was only taken up over the course of a leisurely two-year period; so this minatory phrasing is likely to be a late-antique gloss.[138] Paulus's language otherwise is more suggestive, reflecting changes in attitudes about tablets that were only coming to pass over the first century AD: that a *publicus* or *privatus contractus* would be written (this probably includes acts of all sorts, not just "contracts"); that people called to be present at the making of a document were witnesses who would seal; and that interior *scriptura*, and not just seals, preserved *fides*. If this version of Paulus is only a late-antique vision, then at least we know where we are by AD 300. But if it is (mostly) historically accurate, then the *senatusconsultum* of AD 61 took note of the trends that the Campanian *tabulae* themselves demonstrated – *bona fides* acts increasingly in writing, witnesses acting increasingly as sealers (or sealers as witnesses), and wood absorbing *fides* as well as being sealed

---

[136] Luc. *Alex.* 20–1; cf. Erman (1905a).

[137] Paul. *Sent.* 5.25.6, *amplissimus ordo decrevit eas tabulas, quae publici vel privati contractus scripturam continent, adhibitis testibus ita signari, ut in summa marginis ad mediam partem perforatae triplici lino constringantur atque impositae supra linum cerae signa imprimantur, ut exteriori scripturae fidem interior servet. aliter tabulae prolatae nihil momenti habent.* On the text, only Gerhard (1904) disagrees, emending the next-to-last sentence to *ut scripturae fidem integriorem servent*; cf. Erman (1905b) 467–8.

[138] Camodeca (1993d) 360 (and others suspected a lack of sanction also, cf. 364 n.41) ventures that the authoritarian tone and impulse of the last sentence are more appropriate to "late-imperial time of the compilers." For debates on this passage, see (e.g.) summary by Pólay (1971) 228–30.

168 *The evolution of practice*

with it – and thereby helped to fix them in place by making them not just legitimate and useful, but also required by law.

In any event, the evolution that his description marks is there; only the specific timing is at issue. Overall, a vast distance has been covered. Ceremonial acts, grounded in a ritual that made them part of an order greater than the mere human realm, were written on tablets, the entire act judged, that is, "witnessed." Informal acts, rooted only in the *fides* of those who undertook them and therefore constrained by the limits of the human, were not, but overcame this weakness by migrating on to *tabulae*. A single tablet or a simple diptych was, however, less satisfactory for demonstrating the personal *fides* that was so important for these legal transactions, and so *bona fides* acts came to be sealed, either undersealed or, eventually, sealed shut. As was seen here, with sealing shut the text was doubled, and gradually diptychs were replaced with triptychs, which could protect the seals better. The infiltration of *bona fides* into the world of unitary acts and *tabulae* put two very different kinds of act side by side and created the possibility of influence – which is what we then see, when protagonists and others start to secure the blackened wax of their acts' wooden tablet with the waxen *fides* of their seals.

This use of seals, so characteristic of letters and chirographs and so well emphasized by the form of the triptych, introduces *fides* into formal documents, and stamps authoritative ceremonial acts that have become increasingly complex and combinational with a new guarantee of untouchability. Witnesses of these acts become sealers only gradually, most likely first in mancipatory wills, in a process that runs from at least as early as the first century BC to at least as late as the second century AD. Public interest (and public scandal) focus on will-making, where a ceremonial act is extended over time and the uses of witnessing and sealing, because paradoxical, are subject to more regulation. This enthusiasm for regulating wills was only once driven, by circumstance, to extend itself to all legal and financial acts on *tabulae*, requiring them all to be *pertusae*. All *tabulae*, says Suetonius; all *contractus*, says Paulus; everything on tablets, Campanian practice seems to say, legal and financial, formal and informal together. No matter what the act is, if on *tabulae* – it need not be a triptych – there must be bore-holes, witnesses (although not in a specific number), seals, interior and exterior writing, and an assumption of *fides*. By AD 79, acts are combining and amalgamating, and *tabulae* are fixing and embodying new and complex, but authoritative, final, and useful acts that compel respect and have practical uses beyond the moment of their creation. These *tabulae*, and the status they convey, will be attractive and desired; they will be used, and imitated.

CHAPTER 7

Roman tablets and related forms in the Roman provinces (30 BC–AD 260)

Tabulae changed over time. Roman-law documents from the Roman provinces demonstrate close connections to Roman practice as it had developed in Italy in the first century AD, and through these connections, by the impact these documents have, and by the changes these documents themselves underwent, help to illuminate an administrative and legal dynamic in the complicated process of cultural change that characterized the first two-and-a-half centuries of the Roman empire. On these *tabulae*, and the behaviors and beliefs associated with them, there is perceptible influence from the center – not through laws or *senatusconsulta*, as had been the case with wills, but through authoritative example and Roman decisions taken for Roman reasons. This points to a mechanism of cultural change that is above all a mediated one, one in which – no matter what local practice a change may seem to mimic – the figure of the local Roman official or the distant emperor is the most important one, even as *fides* and formality continue to interleave and layer on the wood document. Social and legal hierarchies and the influence of their practices at the near-center, Campania, were visible but subtle and complicated, like a list of sealers from Pompeii; in the provinces, however, they are cruder and more obvious, and what appeared as smooth and subtle incremental evolutions in Roman legal *tabulae* in Campania as a consequence translate into much more jagged jumps and shifts in more distant parts of the Roman world. The result of this process is a legal *tabula* that survives and in most ways looks the same, but one also that is altered in some of its particulars, replaced in some of its applications, and keeping company in scandalously low ways with papyrus versions of itself. The basic form can stay, the material can change, but above all the governor or prefect will preside and determine, foreshadowing the imperial and juristic involvement in the construction and valuation of legal documents that will characterize Roman legal life in the third century AD and after.

169

The evolution of practice

It is from the provinces, and not from the center, that *tabulae* come after AD 79. This evidence, in the first three centuries of empire, is unevenly distributed, just as the evidence from Italy was, but with the added variable of differing geographic location. Dry or soggy circumstances often determined survival, and what survived outside Egypt very often reflects a military milieu, whether at Vindolanda in the far north-west or Dura in the far east. Within this unshapely body of material two patterns of use are apparent, one reflecting the administrative and legal habits followed by Romans (which changed in small ways over time), the other the responses these habits evoked in non-Romans. Officials' posting of Roman edicts and responses on *tabulae* in Rome and provincial cities prompted the practice of attested doubled copies on bronze and wood, while the observed devotion of Romans to Roman tablet-documents not only extended the geographical spread of wood documents but also prompted imitations in papyrus or parchment called *diplomata* or double-documents, efforts to conform to Roman expectations even when status, act, or object disqualified an actor from using a Roman-law form. Roman traditions and Roman citizens assumed that Roman documents would look a certain way, some non-Romans with a particular eye on a Roman context or court adjusted the way they drew up documents, and both together may have encouraged a dependence on specialized drafters and copyists who could also give legal advice. These last delivered not just accurate texts and attested copies but also documents that communicated and even advertised the Roman status or Roman hopes of their owners: Roman prestige made tangible in a world whose hierarchies made it valuable.

THE ROMAN WAY IN THE ROMAN PROVINCES

The period of Augustus's rule saw a number of carefully orchestrated benefactions and centrally mandated changes in administration and official record-keeping that help to explain some of the types of *tabulae* that survive outside Rome. The ways in which tablets were used had clear Republican precedents; the significant change now was the number of circumstances in which *tabulae* were required, which made tablets the by-products of policies (and thus usually of *leges* or *senatusconsulta*) that aimed at other results, such as the improvement of morals or the birth-rate among Roman citizens, or the collection of new taxes. The emperor now, for example, kept in his own *commentarii* the list of citizenship-grants he first gave on *tabulae*, not so much from any desire to centralize records as from a desire to monopolize

Roman tablets and related forms in the provinces   171

or at least control this type of highly valuable benefaction.[1] The emperor also granted immunities, citizenship, or *conubium* to the auxiliaries of his army and fleet, valuable benefactions of which it was necessary that he be seen as the only source, especially since the Republic offered legal but invidious examples of ambitious Roman generals enfranchising their own troops, for both glory and advantage.[2] These imperial grants – of citizenship, and privileges to soldiers – were listed on *tabulae* posted in Rome, as their Republican predecessors had been,[3] and the *tabella*-copies made from them found all over the Empire.[4] Benefaction, autocracy, and centralization are natural bedfellows, but it is autocracy that promotes benefaction and centralization, not an orderly impulse towards centralization that discovers the delights and snares of autocracy only too late.

(a) Egypt. In Egypt, the only province where the consequences of these and other tradition-dependent innovations in administration and their consequences for archival and documentary practices can be studied in any detail, the centralizing alterations undertaken by Augustus's prefect and his staff[5] perched atop an extensive structure of existing archives and practices like a penthouse on a pyramid, visible to most but accessible to few, and for a price. So a new Roman archive, a separate *tabularium* or *tablinum* of the prefect, was probably built in Alexandria.[6] So also Roman

---

[1] *Commentarii* going back to Augustus, see the *tabula Banasitana* (= *AE* 1971.534), lines 21–30 (*ex commentario civitate Romana donatorum divi Aug(usti)* and others), Mauretania Tingitana, AD 177; and Plin. *Ep.* 10.6–7, 10.105 with Sherwin-White (1973) 90. Cf. Mourgues (1998) 132–42, on the diplomatic form of the imperial *commentarii*.

[2] Republican predecessors: Marius, Plut. *Mar.* 28.2 (questioned as illegal); Pompey Strabo, *ILS* 8888 (= *FIRA*² 1.165–6 no.17, 89 BC, Rome), who grants citizenship *ex lege Iulia*; Octavian as triumvir, *IGLS* 3.718 (41 or 39 BC), κατὰ ν]όμον Μουνάτιον καὶ Αἰμίλιον, copied from a στήλη on the Capitoline in Rome. Cf. Roxan (1996) 251–3 on Vespasian's grants as *beneficia*.

[3] Veterans' copies of their grants of privilege locate the original tablet from which the copy was made, e.g., *ex tabula aenea, quae fixa est Romae in Capitolio ad aram gentis Iuliae de foras podio sinisteriore, tab(ula)I pag(ina) II loc(o) XXXXIIII* (*ILS* 1991, AD 71). Imperial viritane (individual) grants of citizenship were probably posted this way before the end of the second century AD: grants of citizenship were posted on tablets in the late Republic (cf. Cic. *Fam.* 13.36.1, a single tablet for multiple recipients), non-military individuals in the early empire also possessed (like soldiers) *diplomata* of citizenship (see below n.92), the procedure followed for all three should be congruent, and close reading of the *tabula Banasitana* also shows, *contra* Ando (2000) 82 n.28, that the grant with its entry on to *tabulae* was an act that took place before it was entered in the emperor's *commentarii*.

[4] First surviving copy of one of these *tabula*-entries, *ILS* 1986 (= *CIL* 16.1), AD 52; on these copies, called military *diplomata*, see *CIL* 16; Mann (1972); Roxan (1978), (1985), and (1994).

[5] For the breaks in continuity between Ptolemaic and Roman Egypt, N. Lewis (1970); effects of Augustan legislation, Modrzejewski (1970) 338–41 and Bagnall (1995) 66–8 (summary); an earlier assessment of archival changes, E. Seidl (1973) 71–9; Augustan Egypt in general, see *BGU* 2599.

[6] A Roman *tablinum* is clearly established by the second century AD (Cockle [1984] 118): *P.Oxy.* 34v col. 1 line 5 (AD 127) refers to a τακλεῖνον, i.e. a *tablinum*, in Alexandria (cf. *P.Oxy.* 1 p. 73); *P.Oxy.*

172   *The evolution of practice*

wills, subject now (by the Augustan *lex Iulia de vicesima hereditatium*)[7] to a 5 percent inheritance tax, were opened and read out – recited – in the forum or basilica of the emperor (where the *statio vicesimaria* could also be found, after the reign of Hadrian) in the presence of *strategos*, procurator (in the second century, the *procurator hereditatium*), or prefect.[8] So too Latin *tabulae* listing Roman newborns, their felicitous births announced by their parents before the prefect (or his deputy) within thirty days, were posted prominently in the *atrium magnum* or *forum Augusti* at Alexandria,[9] an honor-roll of infant privilege instituted or necessitated by the Augustan *leges Aelia Sentia* (AD 4) and *Papia Poppaea* (AD 9).[10] So too, if a Roman boy lived to fourteen and assumed the toga, his name would be listed on a *tabula* and posted again, and in the same *forum Augusti*, in obedience (I would speculate) to either Augustan precedent, or yet another Augustan law.[11] If a Roman woman needed a Roman tutor, a duty assigned to the prefect by the Augustan *lex Iulia Titia* and an otherwise unknown *senatusconsultum*, it is possible that the prefect posted this assignment on a *tabula* as well; certainly the grant was copied

---

1654 (*c.* AD 150) refers to the prefect's archive as ἡ ἡγεμονικὴ βιβλιοθήκη; *P.Oxy.* 2116 (AD 229) refers to an unidentified Ῥω]μαικὸν ταβουλάριον. All suggest that some (or one) archives were seen as specifically Roman. The *tablinum* kept the prefect's edicts (*SB* 11612, the prefect's *tablarii* copy one, AD 162) and *tabulae* of *honesta missio* of auxiliaries (see below n.23), attested to by two ταβουλάριοι in AD 103 (*P.Hamb.* 31) and AD 132–3 (*P.Diog.* 5), cf. Mann and Roxan (1988) 342 n.7; Haensch (1992) 275 and n.191 argues that they were kept in Rome. In τῷ ταβλαρίῳ in Caesarea (in Palestine), there was a μάτριξ (register, "of veterans" restored) in which a veteran's property claim could be confirmed (Maehler [1974] = *SB* 11043, AD 152); John Lydus (*de Mens.* 1.28, Wünsch) glosses ματρίκιον in the context of official Roman lists as τὸ πλατὺ καὶ παχὺ ξύλον. Ephesus had both the imperial *tabularium* for the province of Asia (*IKEph.* 1138) and the τῆς Ἀσίας δημόσιον ἀρχεῖον (Eus. *HE* 5.18), which suggests that a multiple layering of archives (Greek and Roman) existed here as well.

[7] See chapter six n.129.

[8] Opening and reading out, Nisoli (1949) 51–2 and Paul. *Sent.* 4.6.2: *testamenta in municipiis, coloniis, oppidis . . . in foro vel basilica . . . [aperiri] recitarique debebunt*, and the will-openings themselves preserve this language and the place of opening, cf. (e.g.) *CPL* 220 (*ape[r]t(um) et recitat(um) in Caesario* [. . . . .]*eo ante statione(m) XX he(reditatium)*), Arsinoe, AD 131), with Kreller (1919) 104–6, 395–406 and Amelotti (1947) 51–5.

[9] On the copies made of these Roman postings (*CPL* 148–58, 163–4 from AD 62 to AD 242) see Haensch (1992) 283–90. The *Atrium Magnum, CPL* 148, 150, 152–4, 156–7; *CPL* 151 names the *forum Augusti*. The *professiones* were spoken, and that act of speech taken down in a *kalendarium*, a papyrus daybook, from which the *tabulae* were subsequently made (cf. the formula *c. r. e. ad K., civem Romanum esse ad Kalendarium*, in the copies); *contra*, Pescani (1961) 135–40, the *kalendarium* as a separate archive.

[10] These laws (referred to in the copies, e.g., *e lege Pap(ia) [P]opp(aea) et Aelia Sentia, CPL* 148) concerned themselves with the status of *dediticii* and with marriage regulations and penalties respectively, but also (as a consequence) with Roman-citizen status and its registration; their importance for registrations of birth had been deduced from *D.* 22.3.16 and *D.* 50.16.147 (both Terentius Clemens), Schulz (1942) 80.

[11] See Lévy (1952) 463–4; Sanders (1947) 19 on *P.Mich.* 433 (a papyrus that calls itself *exemplum tabulae togipur[ae]*): this suggests "that the names of all youths taking the toga should be so posted."

Roman tablets and related forms in the provinces 173

on to a wooden tablet.[12] Even government permits for camels were granted on sealed *pittakia*,[13] although the *tabula*-documents associated with Roman formulary procedure do not appear in Egypt, since that procedure was never introduced here.[14] In contrast, Roman administrative and institutional innovations that did not directly affect the Roman-citizen population, such as the two new archives for Greek legal documents and Greek administrative reports in Alexandria (the Nanaion and the Patrica),[15] the introduction of the poll-tax and the institution of the fourteen-year census, both aimed at "the *laoi* of the *chora*,"[16] and the revising of the list of gymnasium members at Oxyrhynchus and Hermoupolis in AD 4–5 – the list that determined Greek citizen-standing when boys were accepted at age fourteen[17] – were supervised by local officials or liturgists,[18] who also used papyrus rather than wood and stored the results, for the most part when at the local level, in already existing Egyptian archives.[19] These various novelties instituted in the visible, and visibly recorded, public life of Egypt helped to reinforce the dramatically severe and hierarchical lines drawn between groups, especially

---

[12] Posting: one of the points at issue is the expansion of the abbreviation *b.d.e.r.e.e.t.s.s.s.* (*CPL* 200, AD 126–32) or *d.e.r.e.e.b.t.s.s* (*CPL* 202 = *SB* 6223; *FIRA²* 3.68–9 no. 25, AD 198); I suggest, for the first, *b(is) d(escriptum) e(t) r(ecognitum) e(x) e(xemplo) t(abulae) s(upra) s(criptae) s(unt)*; for the second, *d(escriptum) e(t) r(ecognitum) e(x) e(xemplo) b(is) t(abulae) s(upra) s(criptae)*; cf. Haensch (1996) 460 n.51. Both would thus have been copied from a posted *exemplum*, which (in the case of the nominations) could have been an *exemplum tabulae* (as was specifically true of the *tabula togipura*). The earlier nominations of tutors are: *CPL* 200–1 (on wood tablets; AD 126–32 to 150); *CPL* 202 (= *SB* 6223; *FIRA²* 3.68–9 no. 25; on wood tablet, AD 198). In *P.Oxy.* 273 (AD 95), a Roman woman refers to herself as "given a guardian by the *tabella* (ταβέλλη) of the prefect."

[13] Bernand (1984) 199–208 no. 67 lines 21–4 (= *OGIS* 674; AD 90).

[14] Modrzejewski (1970) 342; summons for *cognitio* procedure could be, however, on wood tablets, *P.Hamb.* 29 line 23 (= *FIRA²* 3.518–20 no. 169, AD 93).

[15] Nanaion, Burkhalter (1990) 211–12, later augmented in Alexandria by the library of Hadrian (*P.Oxy.* 1.34v, AD 127); Patrica, see Burkhalter (1990) 208–9 and n.72 (Augustan date), neither the same as the *tablinum* (*P.Oxy.* 1654). Documents stored in the Nanaion and the library (but not those for the Patrica) were first cleared through the καταλογεῖον, Cockle (1984) 116–17.

[16] Poll-tax an innovation, Bowman and Rathbone (1992) 112. Focus of Egypt's provincial census, Rathbone (1993) 89. The first census of which we have undisputed record is AD 33–4 (Bagnall and Frier [1994] 2–5), although a census-like document (a farmer reports his holdings in what is described as a ὑπόμνημα) survives from 19–18 BC (*P.Grenf.* 1.45–6).

[17] Gymnasium members, revised in AD 4–5, Nelson (1979) 35. On the Roman use of gymnasial groups as definers of Greek status, see Nelson (1979) 35, 56–9 and Bowman and Rathbone (1992) 121.

[18] Local officials or liturgists: for the archival systems that fed into the Nanaion and Patrica, Cockle (1984) 111–16; the census and gymnasium membership were supervised by the *strategos* and *basilicogrammateus* (N. Lewis [1983] 157; Nelson [1979] 27); a whole host of different officials were instrumental in the assessment and collection of taxes (Wallace [1938] 32–3, 292–335), including the *strategos*.

[19] The returns for the census on papyrus were eventually kept in the βιβλιοθῆκαι τῶν δημοσίων (Wallace [1938] 105). On procedures in the Greek archives of Egypt, Pierce (1968) 70–6, Husselman (1970), Burkhalter (1990) 195–6; on continuity of the system of registered private Greek documents (in Nanaion in the Roman period) with Ptolemaic practice, Burkhalter (1990) 211–12.

174   *The evolution of practice*

between Roman, Alexandrian Greek, metropolitan Greek, and Egyptian, and emphasized the exquisite separation of the Roman group at the very top.[20]

As the posting of these *tabulae* shows, the Roman prefect in the first and second centuries AD performed Roman acts and communicated Roman information to a Greco-Roman public in a traditionally Roman way. He followed Roman models in other ways as well, posting *tabulae* like those of imperial or prefectorial edicts,[21] and in a transcript of a court-hearing from AD 63 is heard instructing veterans – in Greek – to submit information to him on tablets, πιττάκια.[22] In the second century, he also handed out auxiliary discharges on wood tablets.[23] Roman habits and models for the day-to-day methods of governance were influential through the third and fourth centuries, when the Egyptian *metropoleis*, newly permitted to have *boulai* and grain-doles, would keep lists of bouleutic membership on waxed or whitened tablets.[24] In very late-antique Egypt, tax-lists are still referred to as ταβλία.[25]

This style or method of administration through posting and wooden tablets no doubt concorded with the expectations of the prefect's Roman-citizen audience, for in old-fashioned matters of family and the transmission

[20] For distinctions of status, see *BGU* 1210 (the *gnomon* of the *idios logos*) chapters 39, 42–5, 49, 53, 56 (on soldiers claiming Roman status without "legal discharge," νομίμην ἀπολύσιν); Reinhold (1971) 291–7; N. Lewis (1983) 18–19, 32–5; Alston (1995) 60–8, 141; N. Lewis (2000) 85, Romans will petition only the *epistrategos*.

[21] *CPL* 104 (= *FIRA²* 1.424–7 no. 76), copy of an edict of Domitian on a *tabula aenea* posted on the *Caesareum Magnum* in Alexandria (AD 88–9 or 94): the very specific description of where the tablet hung suggests that many more were also posted in the same area or on the same building. Prefects' edicts: listed, Katzoff (1980); they were then sent to *strategoi* with cover-letters commanding publication, Taubenschlag (1951), Katzoff (1982a). That they were to be copied on wood and posted is specified by *SB* 12144 (= Rea [1977], εἰς λε]ύκωμ[α] προθεῖναι, no provenance, AD 198–9) and *P.Lips.* 64 line 44 (= *W.Chr.* 281), ἐν ξυλίνοις δέλτοις ἐνχαράξ[ε]τ[α]ι τοῦτο τῷ δημοσίῳ προθεῖναι, AD 368), perhaps also suggested by *SB* 11346 line 18, γέγραπται ἐν δέλτ[ωι (Parássoglou [1974] 332–5, probably prefectorial, AD 41–54), and *BGU* 288 (a prefect's edict in which ἐκέλευσα τοῖς ἐν τῶι λευκώματι, Arsinoite nome, AD 138–61). There were Ptolemaic precedents for placing wooden boards in public, *P.Hib.* 29 (= *W.Chr.* 259, *c.* 265 BC), taxes on wooden boards (ὁ δὲ τελώνης το[ῦτο τὸ] γραμματ[εῖον] γράψας εἰς λεύκωμα μ[ε]γάλοις γράμμασιν ἐκτιθέτω) and *UPZ* 1.106, the king's words π[ρ]ο[θ]εῖν[α]ι [ἐν λ]ευκώμα[τ]ι (Memphis, 99 BC).

[22] Welles (1938) = Smallwood (1967) 82 no. 297b line 6. On πιττάκια, see below n.68.

[23] Auxiliary discharges (*honesta missio*), *CPL* 113 (= *ILS* 9060; Fayum, AD 122), subscribed *dedit* by the prefect of Egypt. Discharge certificates for legionaries were unusual, cf. *ChLA* 25.784 (= *PSI* 1026 line 15), *veterani ex legionibus instrumentum accipere non solent*, with Mann (2000) 160–1.

[24] Bouleutic lists, *SB* 7261 (λεύκωμα βουλευτικόν) and *P.Oxy.* 2407 (λεύκωμα ἀρχόντων), dated by Bowman (1971) 23–4, who notes also (22 n.1, 100) nomination to the βουλή from πιττάκια; "waxes" (κήρας) keeping lists of councillors up for special tasks, *P.Oxy.* 2110, lines 4 and 6 (AD 370). Parallels to Rome: list of senators on tablets, see above chapter two n.26. The only Greek parallel known to me for keeping (citizen?)-lists on tablets is *IKStrat.* 701, where Ti. Claudius Aristeas Menander and his wife give *sportulae* in the theater ἕκαστον δῆμον ἐκ τῶν δέλτων καλέσαντες.

[25] The examples are eighth century: *P.Lond.* 4.1420, 4.1421, 4.1423, 4.1428; *Stud.Pal.* 10.199, 10.298.

Roman tablets and related forms in the provinces

of property Roman citizens in Egypt kept to wooden tablets – although wood was expensive in Egypt – written in Latin, whatever their native language was. Thus in the second century attestations of the births of illegitimate but Roman children – births that specifically could not be announced to the prefect and posted in Alexandria, by the terms of the *lex Aelia Sentia* – were made, in Latin, on wooden tablets.[26] Mancipatory wills in the same century were written in Latin on wooden tablets, and acceptances of inheritances (*cretiones*) were submitted to the prefect on wooden tablets as well, and also in Latin.[27] In second-century *epikrisis* hearings, hearings on status, Roman slave manumissions (one specifically *vindicta*) are demonstrated through *tabellae*, and two such *tabellae* survive from the third century AD, one fragmentary, one using specifically Roman phrasing (*inter ami[c]os manumisit*).[28] From the third century also come a fragmentary copy of an emancipation of a Roman daughter which mentions *tabulae conligar[—]* and a Greek copy of a request for *bonorum possessio*, the original of which had also been on a tablet.[29] Although the numbers of these Roman-law or Roman-status wooden tablet-documents seem exiguous when compared to the great mass of Egyptian papyri from the first and second centuries, this probably reflects the Egyptian reality of relatively few Roman citizens, many of whom would have lived in Alexandria (whence little documentation survives), especially in the first century AD.[30] Yet although the numbers are few, the use of the tablet-form was clearly preferred or required, for all the acts so far described (attestations of Roman birth, nominations of tutors for Roman women, mancipatory wills, *cretiones*, Roman-law manumissions) do not exist (or at least survive) on papyrus in the first and second centuries.

---

[26] Illegitimate births: *CPL* 159–62 (AD 127–45), with Lévy (1952) 466–8; three out of four are from a military context. By the terms of the *lex*: Weiß (1948).

[27] Wills: *CPL* 221, 223–6 (AD 142 to late second century AD); *CPL* 222 (AD 147) is fragmentary, and likely a will-opening. *Cretiones*: *ChLA* 47.1439 (= *P.Wisc.* 2.50.2 line 30, AD 165; *tab[ulas?–] adi(isse) cr(evisseque)*; *CPL* 213–15 (AD 151–70; last two involving same heir), all from the Arsinoite nome.

[28] *Epikrisis* hearings: *P.Diog.* 6–7 (AD 142; *manumissio vindicta*) and *SB* 5217 (AD 148); see chapter eight pp. 232–4. Such *tabellae* are also one of the main concerns of a trial before the *idios logos* in the second half of the second century (*BGU* 388 = *M.Chr.* 91), see chapter eight pp. 235–6. Manumissions: the double-named manumittor of *Stud.Pap.* 48 (Severus, also known as Agathos Daimon; second century AD) could have received citizenship or some of its privileges, as his name shows (Taubenschlag [1955] 42, 98–9 misidentified him as peregrine); *CPL* 173 (AD 241), *CPL* 172 (*inter amicos*, AD 211).

[29] Emancipation: *ChLA* 12.251 (= *CPL* 206 line 2; *c.* AD 275?). *Bonorum possessio*, *P.Oxy.* 3108, ἀντίγρ(αφον) ταβέλλης διακα[τοχῆς], AD 240.

[30] Kunkel (1973) 195; outside Alexandria, many will have been veterans, estimated at less than 1 percent of the population of Egypt and concentrated in the villages of the Fayum like Philadelphia and Karanis, Alston (1995) 51.

176 *The evolution of practice*

(b) The western provinces. Evidence from western Roman provinces before AD 250 confirms this picture of Roman documentary practices on wood travelling with or followed by Romans, although the contrast is not as sharply illuminated by an indigenous documentary tradition in a different medium. The place of papyrus in the Roman hierarchy of writing materials – as the ephemeral medium for drafts and letters – was taken by "light" leaf-tablets made out of wood bark, now made famous by the finds at Vindolanda.[31] Moreover, most documents derive from a Roman military context, and as a consequence their distribution cannot compare perfectly with the Egyptian evidence which derives, when the protagonists can be identified, mostly from the milieu of Roman veterans who have married and settled among civilians.[32] Nonetheless, there are clear similarities. Provincial governance both West and East proceeded through the posting of *tabulae*,[33] the keeping of Roman records (not demonstrably a physical archive, and usually attested indirectly, through *tabularii*),[34] and through other administrative uses of *tabulae*,[35] even if some differed at times from practices in Egypt.[36]

[31] Leaf-tablets: Speidel (1996) 21 on the increasing cost of papyrus as it is transported west; one leaf-tablet letter (*P. Yadin* 54) has also been found in Judaea, Yadin (1978) 122–5; Tomlin (1998) 37 suggests that the "folded wooden strip in concertina format" is "the wooden equivalent of a short papyrus roll."

[32] Milieu: N. Lewis (1983) 20–5. Exceptions are *CPL* 159–61, professions of illegitimate Roman births made by fathers serving in the auxiliaries, and who therefore could not legitimately marry, and *CPL* 221, 223, and 226, wills of serving soldiers, citizens but still in the army.

[33] Note *B. Alex.* 56.6, Caesar *edictum tota provincia proposuerat*, and Cyprian *Ep.* 59.6, *edicto proposito* (both with Eck [1998] 214); the *lex Irn.* chapter 85, *formulas iudiciorum, sponsiones*, stipulations, *satis acceptiones, exceptiones, praescriptiones, interdicta* of the provincial governor are to be *proposita in albo*; in Arabia, Babatha has copies of petitions the governor has subscribed and posted, *P. Yadin* 33 (AD 125?) and 34 (AD 131), place of posting emended in Feissel and Gascou (1995) 78 n.45; on posting in general, Riepl (1913) 336–43 and 363–4; continues through late empire, Amm. Marc. 27.7.7 (*suspendi*) and Matthews (1993) 42; Johnston (1999) 10–11 (governor's application of Roman law too).

[34] Archives and *tabularii*, O. Hirschfeld (1975 [1905]) 58–64 (financial role of *tabularii* and storage of the census stressed); on provincial archives, see Burton (1975) 103, Raepsaet-Charlier (1986) 228 n.41, Rodríguez Neila (1991–2), Haensch (1992) and Moatti (1993) 73–8 (colonial *tabularia*).

[35] Prefects and governors outside of Egypt (in their roles as military commanders) handed out *tabulae* of *honesta missio* to auxiliaries (and at times legionaries) as one of their prerogatives, although technically discharge was granted by the emperor, Mann and Roxan (1988) 342, 346 and Mann (2000); examples, see Eck and Roxan (1998). *Coloni* in North Africa submit guarantees of crop-shares on *tabulae*, *CIL* 8.25902 (Henchir Mettich, AD 116); mining-privileges were copied onto *pittacia* from larger *tabulae* in Spain, *CIL* 2.5181 with D'Ors (1951); procurators and city- and customs-officials may have carried large *tabulae* (*RIB* 2.2443.1–2; *IDR /TabCerD.* no. 24 = *CIL* 3 p. 958 no. xxiii; France and Hesnard [1995]; Speidel [1996] 232–3 no. 65*bis*); inscribing on *tabulae* borrowed by Celtiberians from Romans, Beltrán Lloris (1999) 145–6. The *pittacium* is still found in the fifth- and sixth-century West, used as a kind of document transferring ownership; an extract from tax registers; a receipt; acknowledgment of debt by chirograph; *cautio*; or even "exit permits": see Goffart (1980) 101 (where also called *polyptycha*), 90–1 and n.63.

[36] Differences: the census in Arabia in AD 128 had landowners submitting a property declaration (Babatha's on a πιτακίου, *P. Yadin* 16 [AD 127]) that was then subscribed and posted by the governor;

Roman tablets and related forms in the provinces 177

Roman individuals, too, used *tabulae* as they had in Italy and Egypt. In Britain we find one *tabula* with a witness-statement and one with a record of an arbitration, and *tabulae* with acts that appear to involve debt or sale.[37] In Holland, an ox (a *res mancipi*) is purchased by tablet, but by a Roman from a non-Roman, and thus by chirograph, without a mancipation.[38] The Roman army camp at Vindonissa, in Switzerland, produced hundreds of fragments of *tabulae*, at least fifteen of which were certainly legal documents of some sort;[39] eighty-five more were letters of which only the address now survives, but in a high proportion of cases written over an original legal text now illegible.[40] There are also eleven examples of letters on *tabulae* from Britain (two clearly identified as reused), two from France, three from the camp of Valkenburg in Holland, and five from Germany.[41] One tablet from Rottweil appears to record the exercise of civil jurisdiction by a legionary legate, most likely also written over an earlier (legal?) text, while some of the over eighty (unpublished) fragmentary and virtually illegible *tabulae* from Cologne are said to be mancipatory wills and *vadimonia*, and a tablet from Hanau was reused as a receipt.[42] Wax-tablets from Alburnus Maior in Dacia preserve sales with mancipations, *bona fides* contracts with

---

in Egypt the local census was done through papyrus ἀπογραφή and subscribed by local officials in Greek. In Arabia, a petition to the governor also preceded one legal party's summons of another (Cotton [1993] 106), and one of Babatha's petitions was also written on a πιττάκιν (*P. Yadin* 25, AD 131); in Egypt, all surviving petitions are on papyrus.

[37] Witness statement, *RIB* 2.2443.11 (London, AD 84–96); arbitration, *RIB* 2.2443.19 (London, AD 118; fully published in Tomlin [1996a]). Debt or sale: *RIB* 2.2443.15 (London, AD 50–155); *AE* 1992.1139 (Carlisle, AD 83); *AE* 1992.1140b (unpublished; Carlisle, no date given but probably Flavian); Birley *et al.* (1993) pl. xxi inv. 974, unpublished sale of two slaves (Vindolanda, AD 97–103); *RIB* 2.2443.13 (Chew Stoke, late second or third century AD); probably *RIB* 2.2443.16 (London, no date). Wood of British *tabulae* imported, Frere and Tomlin (1992) 11.

[38] Vollgraff (1917) (= *FIRA²* 3.438–9 no. 137; Leeuwarden, date uncertain; with *emi*).

[39] Legal: Marichal (1972–3) 368 nos. H and I, and inv. 1942:13, 1942:48, 1942:203; Speidel (1996) 94–7 no. 2 (a pay-receipt), 98–101 no. 3, 102–5 no. 4, 148–9 no. 26, 234 nos. 66–8, 234–5 no. 72, 235–6 no. 79, 236 no. 82; the total numbers of fragments, mostly heavy or wax-tablets, Speidel (1996) 9 gives as 612, of which 102 were legible.

[40] Vindonissa: Speidel (1996), eighty-five fragments used for at least ninety-four letters; reused, Marichal (1972–3) 368–70 and Speidel (1996) 20. The same phenomenon of reuse for letters can be found elsewhere: Britain, *RIB* 2.2443.21, Tomlin (1992) 146–7 (stylus tablets from Carlisle); Germany, Wilmanns (1981) 16 (Rottweil), Galsterer (1986) 152 (Cologne, almost all reused, some three times), Körber (1900) 124 no. 206 (Mainz).

[41] England: *RIB* 2.2443.3–6, 10 (Carlisle, late Flavian); *RIB* 2.2443.7–9 (London, 2.2443.7 is before AD 155, the other two are not dated), *RIB* 2.2443.6 and 10 are reused; *AE* 1991.1155 and Caruana (1992) 69 no. 4 (Carlisle, no date); and Birley *et al.* (1993) pl. xix inv. 836 with Tomlin (1996b) 460 (reused twice for a letter?). France: Reze-les-Nantes, Aubin (1980) 404. Valkenburg: *CEL* 14–15 (no date and AD 40–2), and Glasbergen (1965–6) 111, 119 no. 35. Germany: Cologne, *AE* 1969–70.446 and Galsterer (1986) 153 (two); Mainz, Schillinger-Häfele (1980), and *CIL* 13.10033.7 may also be a letter; Wiesbaden, Nuber (1979–80) 656–8 no. 1.

[42] Rottweil, *AE* 1981.691 (Wilmanns [1981]); Cologne, Galsterer (1986) 153 (unpublished); possibly also *AE* 1969–70.445b; Hanau, Reuter (1999), AD 130.

178 *The evolution of practice*

stipulations, a discharge of obligation (*accepisse . . . se dixit*), an attested copy of a posted act dissolving a funerary *societas*, and two tablets of an account-book.[43] Many of these locations have also produced *tabulae* that can be identified as legal or financial from the existence of a *sulcus* alone.[44] At Carlisle, excavators also noted that the *tabulae* tended to cluster within forts, leaf-tablets outside them: letters travelled, but legal and financial documents stayed in good safe places, and presumably when possible with their owners.[45] The Latin, Roman-law, and thus Roman-status, orientation of wood *tabulae* from these sites, most of them camps, thus corresponds in general to that of the *tabulae* of Roman Egypt.[46]

(c) Form and content of tabulae *outside Italy.* An analysis of the physical form of these provincial *tabulae* is, if anything, even more challenging than the analysis of those from Campania. Few are complete, most cannot be read, and many are reused. Even so, their form evidently displays a sensitivity to practice at the center, following requirements and in particular keeping to the model of the document as it was constructed when it was introduced. For example, a very high percentage of those reused as letters in northern provinces are *tabulae* that are not *pertusae*, which is itself a strong indication that the requirements of the *senatusconsultum* of AD 61 were being followed. These *tabulae*, although of the wrong form, now, to be used as legal documents, were too useful to be thrown away. After the legal

[43] Mancipations: *IDR/TabCerD*. no. 6 (= *CIL* 3 p. 937 no. VI, *FIRA²* 3.283–5 no. 87, AD 139), *IDR/TabCerD*. no. 7 (= *CIL* 3 pp. 940–3 no. VII, *FIRA²* 3.285–7 no. 88, AD 142), *IDR/TabCerD*. no. 9 (= *CIL* 3 pp. 944–7 no. VIII, *FIRA²* 3.289–91 no. 90, AD 159), *IDR/TabCerD*. no. 8 (= *CIL* 3 p. 959 no. XXV, *FIRA²* 3.287–8 no. 89, AD 160). Stipulations: *IDR/TabCerD*. no. 3 (= *CIL* 3 pp. 930–2 no. III, *FIRA²* 3.394–5 no. 123, AD 162), *IDR/TabCerD*. no. 5 (= *CIL* 3 pp. 934–5 no. V, *FIRA²* 3.393–4 no. 122, AD 162), *IDR/TabCerD*. no. 14 (= *CIL* 3 pp. 950–1 no. XIII, *FIRA²* 3.481–2 no. 157, AD 167), *IDR/TabCerD*. no. 15 (= *CIL* 3 p. 952 no. XIV, *spopondit* restored, no date). Receipt: *IDR/TabCerD*. no. 13 (= *CIL* 3 p. 949 no. XII, *FIRA²* 3.391 no. 120, AD 167). Act dissolving a funerary association: *IDR/TabCerD*. no. 1 (= *CIL* 3. pp. 924–7 no. I, *FIRA²* 3.114–15 no. 41), the *collegium*'s two quaestors . . . *posito hoc libello . . . testantur*, and then a copy is made of this *libellus*, posted *ad statione<m> Resculi* (AD 167). Accounts: *IDR/TabCerD*. no. 16 (= *CIL* 3 p. 953 no. XV, no date).

[44] Britain: Collingwood (1930) 57 no. 10 (London); R. A. Smith (1934–5) 95–6 (London); *RIB* 2.2443.12 (Carlisle), 2.2443.17 and 18 (both London), 2.2443.27 and 31 (both Vindolanda); Chapman (1977) 67 no. 481 and (1978); Chapman and Straker (1986) describe four with *sulcus*; Tomlin (1991) 216–17 nos. 814–15, two (in addition to *RIB* 2.2443.12) described have *sulcus* (Carlisle), and (1992) 148 (two described have *sulcus*); Birley *et al.* (1993) pl. XXII inv. 689R and inv. 722A (both unpublished). Vindonissa: Speidel (1996) 25–7, 103 had a *sulcus* (fifteen listed above n.39). Nearby Vitudurum produced six *tabulae* with *sulcus*, one a complete triptych (Fellmann [1991] H10–12, 17, 33, 18, 27, and 28). Valkenburg: two fragments, Bogaers (1967 [1972]) 67–9 no. 1 and 74–6 no. 2; Mainz, *CIL* 13.10033.8 and 10, and Körber (1900) 123 no. 203. 137 *tabulae* are also not specifically identifiable as legal or financial.

[45] Caruana (1992) 68–9; cf. Marichal (1972–3) 378, letters at Vindonissa travelled, but mostly locally.

[46] Maloney (1987) 50, Latin as the "natural language" for business correspondence between two men with Celtic names (*RIB* 2.2443.7, London, AD 50–155, on a reused tablet).

Roman tablets and related forms in the provinces 179

act for which they had been used finally ceased to be of any importance, they could be pulled out again and have an address incised on one of their outside faces, a letter written on wax or in ink within. Notched *tabulae* could be employed in this second life for another sixty years before finally ending up in the great rubbish-tips of Vindonissa and Vindolanda, the scars of their long service making them both unfit for further use even as letters and particularly difficult to decipher now.

Other physical details of these provincial *tabulae* suggest a close connection between the construction of a legal *tabula* in a province and its construction closer to the center at the time it was introduced. Egyptian *tabulae*, for example, are notable in that, although all dutifully *pertusae* after AD 62, they simply never became triptychs.[47] They remained doubled and sealed diptychs for at least two hundred years, maintaining the physical form they had had when introduced into Egypt at the end of the first century BC, although occasionally running the exterior text from *pagina* one to *pagina* four rather than from *pagina* four to *pagina* one.[48] In Switzerland and England, on the other hand, where a Roman presence was established between twenty and sixty years later, we do find triptychs, although never in good enough condition to assess texts, seals, and sealers' names at the same time.[49] In Dacia, conquered by Trajan's legions in the early second century AD, we find (only) *pertusae* triptychs of both formal and informal acts as in Campania, their texts doubled in the way postulated for the latest of the Campanian documents, Poppaea Note's mancipation-and-*pactum*, running from *pagina* four to *pagina* five.[50] All are also sealed by four or seven sealers listed (apparently) by rank, who at times wrote their names next to their seals in their own hands, an occasional rather than common practice in Campania.[51] The sealers usually give their names in the genitive,

[47] The first surviving, from 23 July AD 62 (*CPL* 148 = *FIRA*² 3.5–7 no. 2), is not *pertusa*; the rest are, but remain diptychs, Camodeca (1993d) 359.
[48] Camodeca (1992) 22 n.51.
[49] Certain triptychs, Vitudurum, Fellmann (1991) 23 (H10–12); England (London), Chapman (1978).
[50] The Dacian tablets date between AD 131 and 167. Way of doubling observed by Camodeca (1995a) 61–2 n.8; only triptychs there, 67 and n.25.
[51] Seven sealers: *IDR/TabCerD.* no. 6 (= *CIL* 3 p. 937 no. VI, *FIRA*² 3.283–5 no. 87, AD 139, mancipary sale), the first a *princeps*, the second a *decurio*; *IDR/TabCerD.* no. 7 (= *CIL* 3 pp. 940–3 no. VII, *FIRA*² 3.285–7 no. 88, AD 142, mancipary sale), the first a veteran of *legio XIII Gemina*; *IDR/TabCerD.* no. 9 (= *CIL* 3 pp. 944–7 no. VIII, *FIRA*² 3.289–91 no. 90, AD 159, mancipary sale); *IDR/TabCerD.* no. 8 (= *CIL* 3 p. 959 no. XXV, *FIRA*² 3.287–8 no. 89, AD 160, mancipary sale), a veteran seals third; *IDR/TabCerD.* no. 3 (= *CIL* 3 pp. 930–2 no. III, *FIRA*² 3.394–5 no. 123, AD 162, loan with stipulation for interest); *IDR/TabCerD.* no. 1 (= *CIL* 3 pp. 924–7 no. I, *FIRA*² 3.114–15 no. 41, AD 167, attested copy); *IDR/TabCerD.* no. 21 (= *CIL* 3 p. 956 no. XX, no date, unknown act); *IDR/TabCerD.* no. 2 (= *CIL* 3 pp. 928–9 no. II, AD 159, unknown act) probably had seven sealers. Four sealers: *IDR/TabCerD.* no. 5 (= *CIL* 3 pp. 934–5 no. V, *FIRA*² 3.393–4 no. 122, AD 162, loan specifically

180   *The evolution of practice*

although very occasionally one will note *"signavi"* or have noted for him by a scribe *"agnovit"* ("he recognized" his seal).[52] The presence of one of the principals as a sealer, regularly seen in Campania, is standard also in the Dacian documents.[53] All of these practices that affect the physical form of the Dacian document can be seen as understandable extensions of the directions in which Campanian practice (as we last saw it in AD 79) was headed. The strengthening of the tablet of a formal act through *fides* continues, not just through sealing but through autograph notes next to the seal; autograph writing next to the seal was a way of putting yourself in or on a document that grew naturally out of the practice of sealing itself, and had occurred in Egypt as well.[54] Although there is no apparent conflation of the concepts of sealing and witnessing in these tablets, as was happening elsewhere in the second century, the use of the word *"agnovit"* for three sealers calls to mind the act undertaken by sealer-witnesses to a will, who were called upon to recognize their seals when it was opened. It therefore suggests not that these Dacian tablets were necessarily opened, but that the scribe who wrote "he recognized" was thinking of the sealers' responsibility toward their seals (on a different type of document) at a later point in time: the subsequent use of a tablet, rather than merely its current creation, was on *his* mind, just as the addition of the *fides* of seller or debtor looked to the continuing validity of an act as well as to its current completion.

As had been true in the Campanian documents, so in Dacia too acts continue to combine. Some combinations are just like the earlier ones, like an informal *conventio* for an association confirmed by a stipulation. Others show further development: a mancipation for the purpose of sale strengthened by a stipulation for defects that quotes from the aediles' edict

---

identified as a *mutuum*, with stipulation for interest). For autograph *adnotatio*, see Mommsen and Zangemeister (1873) 922; disputed by Bruns (1882 [1876]) 40 and Pólay (1971) 236. Campania, *CIL* 4.3340. 21 and 58; cf. also *FIRA*² 3.438–9 no. 137 (Leeuwarden), *CPL* 159 (AD 127), *CPL* 221 (= *FIRA*² 3.129–32 no. 47; AD 142), *CPL* 211 (= *P.Mich.* 7.444; late second century AD), and *CPL* 172 (= *FIRA*² 3.23–5 no. 11; AD 211 or 221).

[52] *Signavi, IDR/TabCerD.* no. 8 (= *CIL* 3 p. 959 no. xxv, *FIRA*² 3.287–8 no. 89) in Greek letters; *IDR/TabCerD.* no. 9 (= *CIL* 3 pp. 944–7 no. VIII, *FIRA*² 3.289–91 no. 90), *sig(navi)*. *Agnovit*: the first three sealers in *IDR/TabCerD.* no. 21 (= *CIL* 3 p. 956 no. xx) have this noted for them all in the same hand; this and the third-person form point to a scribe writing this for them.

[53] Campania, see chapter six n.101; *venditores* or *debitores* appear in the sealer-lists for all the acts listed above n.51 except *IDR/TabCerD.* no. 1 (= *CIL* 3 pp. 924–7 no. 1, *FIRA*² 3.114–15 no. 41, AD 167, attested copy). Mancipation required five witnesses and the *libripens* (*G.* 1.119 and 2.104, for wills), so the protagonist merely serves as an additional sealer, not as a substitute for a witness-sealer.

[54] For its growing use in Rome, see chapter eight n.79. In Egypt, see Greek wills like *P.Oxy.* 489 (AD 117), *BGU* 325 (AD 156–65), where autograph *adnotationes* or *adscriptiones* replace the scribe-written list of witnesses that had characterized Ptolemaic practice, Wenger (1953) 145; otherwise, in Roman Egypt witness adscriptions or subscriptions were rare, Kaser (1934) col. 1038, and *P.Oxy.* 1473 (AD 201) points them out as particularly noteworthy.

Roman tablets and related forms in the provinces

can (as in Campania) now be augmented by a statement of the *traditio* (delivery) of the slave and the acceptance of the purchase-price by the vendor.[55] In the last case it matters less whether the actual delivery of the slave was always considered to be part of a mancipatory sale, and more that the fact of *traditio* is included on the tablet as part of the process: the wording of the tablet is making explicit those steps and acts whose relationship to each other, if perhaps debatable by Romanists at an abstract level,[56] seemed a logical part of some larger whole. As these other elements are added, the space given in the document to the description of the details of the act of mancipation itself is reduced, for the phrase *nummo uno* is dropped,[57] and the *libripens* and the *antestatus* are not explicitly identified. The act of mancipation itself is thus shrunk down – although not necessarily degraded, denatured, or not performed[58] – into the words *mancipioque accepit*. The creation of combinational acts, in other words, continues, and in expanding imposes some economies in the language of their *tabulae*, but does not in actuality drop any part of what had been there before.

The details of the physical form and the content of the second-century Dacian documents thus continue trends or tendencies already visible in *tabulae* from first-century Campania, making it very likely that the Dacian examples took as their model tablets that picked up where the Campanian

---

[55] *Sanum traditum esse . . . pretium eius . . . accepisse et habere se dixit, IDR/TabCerD.* no. 7 (= *CIL* 3 pp. 940–3 no. VII, *FIRA²* 3.285–7 no. 88, AD 142) and *IDR/TabCerD.* no. 8 (= *CIL* 3 p. 959 no. XXV, *FIRA²* 3.287–8 no. 89, AD 160); (price) *accepisse et habere se dixit* only, *IDR/TabCerD.* no. 6 (= *CIL* 3 p. 937 no. VI, *FIRA²* 3.283–5 no. 87, AD 139) and *IDR/TabCerD.* no. 9 (= *CIL* 3 pp. 944–7 no. VIII, *FIRA²* 3.289–91 no. 90, AD 159). Acceptance of purchase-price: not present in the ox-sale from Holland (Vollgraff [1917] = *FIRA²* 3.438–9 no. 137; Leeuwarden, date uncertain), but Kunkel (1973) 219 n.44 suggests that the abbreviated formula *r.p.r.* should in part be expanded as *r(ecepit) pr(etium)*; yet also not present in *TH* 61 (end complete; AD 63); *pretium* restored, *traditio* only in *TH* 62 (*qui pretio accepto p]uellam . . . tradid[it]*, AD 47).

[56] Jahr (1963); Ciulei (1983) 25–6 also sees the use of *accepisse et habere* for the price as an indication that a formal act (whether or not part of the mancipation itself) had taken place.

[57] *IDR/TabCerD.* no. 7 (= *CIL* 3 pp. 940–3 no. VII, *FIRA²* 3.285–7 no. 88, AD 142) and *IDR/TabCerD.* no. 8 (= *CIL* 3 p. 959 no. XXV, *FIRA²* 3.287–8 no. 89, AD 160); that the phrase *apocatum pro uncis duabus* is substituted for *nummo uno* in two examples and referred to the current mancipation (not a previous one) first argued by Watson (1963), followed by Ciulei (1983) 22; cf. Macqueron (1982) 50–1.

[58] As argued by Pólay (1962) 391 and Kunkel (1928) col. 1001; cf. Camodeca (1992) 153 n.35. The inclusion of the *traditio* in the document, as well as the appearance of contradictions and mistakes (see below n.65), are not sufficient reason to categorize documents of mancipatory sale as designed to be only proof of their acts, as Kunkel (1973) 220 (*Eigentumsdokumente*) does; and it seems unwise to postulate the disappearance of the act of mancipation behind the phrase *mancipio accepit* when inscriptions of the second and third centuries AD in Rome make clear that the phrase is regularly used for a complete act of mancipation: *CIL* 6.10231 (= *FIRA²* 3.297–8 no. 93) and *CIL* 6.10239 (= *FIRA²* 3.298–301 no. 94), both second–third centuries, and *CIL* 6.10247 (= *FIRA²* 3.301–3 no. 95; AD 252) all mancipate property in Rome for the purpose of giving it as a gift and note that the property passes *nummo uno* (restored in 10239); the last two also name the *libripens* and the *antestatus*.

182   *The evolution of practice*

tablets had left off.[59] Yet were the protagonists actually Roman citizens (or at least possessors of the *ius commercii*),[60] and were these documents actually "correct" versions of the Roman acts they purported to represent? The names, especially of the protagonists, suggest less than full Roman status (Dasius Breucus, Maximus and Andueia Batonis, and so on), as does their regular use of the *fidepromissio* (rather than *sponsio*) form of stipulation, but they perform mancipations, and indeed do so in the presence of Romans, using Roman *tabulae* and meticulously following Roman forms. Nothing about these documents suggests major sloppiness or hasty imitations, children playing dress-up to indulgent, twinkly eyed parents. The most economical explanation is that these near-Romans exploiting the gold mines in Dacia, on their way to full Roman status as their names suggest, had received the *ius Latii* or one special dispensation – the capacity to mancipate, and indeed to mancipate not just slaves but also property that, because provincial, did not fall into the old categories (of Italic land, rustic praedial servitudes and the like).[61] Such an explanation seems preferable to postulating fundamental confusions on the part of more than sixty people, scribes, protagonists, and sealers alike.[62] The *tabulae* in both their internal and external aspects develop in ways that have deep roots in Roman practice and Roman concerns in Italy itself, whether or not they are used by some who have no right to perform some of the acts.

Provincial Roman practice was observant of details but conservative, taking as its model the form as it existed when the Romans had arrived.[63] This conservatism was at least in part a notarial conservatism, since scribal

[59] In terms of the development of legal ideas, Pólay (1980) 10–11 sees a modest development in the Dacian mancipations' guaranties: at Herculaneum they had been for the purchase price or its double, and here they are for *quantum id erit*, "the objective value of the merchandise."

[60] See Weiß (1916), Russu (1975) 183–6, Pólay (1980) 7–8, and Macqueron (1982) 47; cf. Ciulei (1983) 26–7, only two of the men in the mancipations, Claudius Julianus and Veturius Valens, may have been Roman citizens; if they were stipulating with non-citizens, both would use the *fidepromissio* form.

[61] A grant of *ius Latii* or merely of *ius commercii* gave people the capacity to mancipate, see Ulp. *Reg.* 19.4, *mancipatio locum habet inter cives Romanos et Latinos coloniarios Latinosque Iunianos eosque peregrinos, quibus commercium datum est*; in either case they would not be full Roman citizens and therefore not permitted to use the *sponsio* form of stipulation. A postulated special exemption (which might also explain that lack of alacrity in adopting the *tria nomina*) revives the hypothesis of Weiß (1916). Attempts have been made to prove Alburnus Maior *solum Italicum*, see Pólay (1980) 12, who also suggests that perhaps the definitions of what could be mancipated were wider than Gaius reports (1.120); for this see also chapter two n.97 (on Lollia Paulina's pearls).

[62] Confusion and infiltration of foreign law, e.g., Pólay (1980); another stance is to categorize the law represented here as "vulgar" or degraded, (e.g.) Tomulescu (1983).

[63] Arangio-Ruiz and Pugliese Carratelli (1954) 61 insisted that peripheral areas maintained Roman forms better, Camodeca (1992) 153 that practice there was worse: both views can be accommodated by understanding that provincial practice was conservative, but the model had been changing.

Roman tablets and related forms in the provinces   183

handwriting is regularly identified outside Italy, sometimes for both interior and exterior texts, while most documents from Campania are written
in two different hands (the interior written by scribal hands in the *acceptilationes*, the exterior by scribal hands in chirograph-style texts).[64] Surviving
templates for written acts come from these provincial contexts, and form-
books (for letters, and hypothesized for petitions) are rightly assumed to
have instructed scribes in the format desirable in Roman legal documents
as well, since scribes sometimes follow them too slavishly, without paying
proper attention to, say, the gender of the slave or the quantity of the object
sold.[65] Both scribes and practitioners most likely felt themselves to be in
no position to challenge the model – not in a position to amend or change
it, except inadvertently – and no doubt had no inclination to.[66] Tenacious
traditionalism of this sort is rooted in an admiring desire to conform, and
a strong desire to conform rests on a drive to belong, to be among the privileged and protected, which is exactly where a conformity to the accepted
practices of Roman law would put you. Romans displayed their superior
status in many ways, not least in the practice of their law and the day-to-
day legal business they performed, and Roman soldiers and provincials with
Roman citizenship or Roman privileges would do the same, as accurately
as they could. Over 500 heavy wooden *tabulae* surviving from the Roman
provinces were the result.

ROMANS AND OTHERS IN THE PROVINCES

Roman status and its privileges provided incentives, Roman legal practice
the model. In the western, and Latin-speaking, half of the empire, this

---

[64] See chapter six n.75.

[65] Templates: for mancipatory sale with guarantee against eviction, *CIL* 2.5042 (= *FIRA²* 3.295–7
no. 92) from Baetica (above chapter five n.96; first–second century AD); for a mancipatory will,
P.Hamb. 72 (Amelotti [1980] 393 n.24; second–third century AD). Form-books: for letters, [Libanius]
Char. Epist.; Cotton (1981) 8–9; for petitions, Feissel and Gascou (1995) 67 and Hauken (1998) 287–8;
for legal documents, Mommsen and Zangemeister (1873) 921; Biscardi (1972) 140–51 (a formulary
handbook?), Amelotti (1980) 396; Jakab (1997) 168; Söllner (2001) 91. Mistakes from following the
form too closely: applying noxality to the sale of a six-year-old slave-girl (and referring to *ex eo* rather
than *ex ea*, *IDR/TabCerD.* no. 6 [= *CIL* 3 p. 937 no. VI, *FIRA²* 3.283–5 no. 87, AD 139]); writing *eam
domum* when in fact it was only half of a house being sold, *IDR/TabCerD.* no. 9 (= *CIL* 3 pp. 944–7
no. VIII, *FIRA²* 3.289–91 no. 90, AD 159).

[66] "[E]s ist die Pflicht eines Notars, die Form zu respektieren," Amelotti (1980) 395. Scribes in Egypt and
the East, called νομικοί, also doubled as (Roman) legal advisors (see Amelotti [1947] 50 n.48, Katzoff
[1982a], and Crook [1995] 154–8), but perhaps not very good or daring ones, cf. Modrzejewski (1970)
346 n.187; in Latin-speaking provinces, *iuris studiosi*, *periti iuris*, or *testamentarii* (Amelotti [1980]
392–3) drafted documents (and do so into the late Empire, Amm. Marc. 28.4.26–7, and cf. Garnsey
and Humfress [2001] 69); these documents show striking continuities, as does the handwriting
(Cencetti [1950]). For their importance in romanization, Amelotti (1975) 15.

184 *The evolution of practice*

dynamic worked with a high degree of straightforward simplicity, facilitated by the spread of Roman citizenship and marked (as far as we can tell) by the unproblematic adoption of the concepts of Roman law as well as its visible display. In Greek- or indeed other-speaking eastern provinces, which always had fewer Roman citizens as well as their own cities and related archival and documentary practices and legal traditions, the dynamic worked as well, but more slowly and with interesting complications and variations. As the picture of Egypt has already shown, Roman and local documentary practices can merely coexist, dark wood silhouetted clearly against the creamy background of papyrus. But Roman administrators in the first and second centuries AD can also take exception to local archival practices, and use their power to create conformity to a Roman standard; and by the ways they choose to handle documents or change documentary forms – done, it will be argued, with a close eye on the habits of their imperial master and his staff – these Romans can also promote changes in the documentary habits of the peoples they govern without necessarily intending to do so. Thus, although complex, the dynamic in the East remains a Roman one, the changes in local archival and documentary practices either intended by Roman authorities and Roman citizens or inspired by imitation of them, and continuing trajectories of development already well underway in first-century AD Campania.

(a) Governors and local archives. Where Roman governors in the East encountered local archives they found much that displeased, and when they determined that documentary and archival practices, although well established, were defective, they did not hesitate to wade in and impose improvements. In Egypt (as mentioned above) this could even take the form of new central archives, first in Alexandria and later in the nomes. But what made a practice defective or inadequate? The sense that the physical treatment of documents was, in non-Roman hands, quite slovenly. In the newly established province of Lycia and Pamphylia (AD 43–8), the governor Q. Veranius rebuked and flogged a public slave for accepting into the city archives at Myra, contrary to previous edicts and threats, "*pittakia* with interpolations and erasures."[67] *Pittakion* at this date most likely refers to a tablet,[68] and use of *pittakia* here may suggest a muddled desire on the

---

[67] Wörrle (1975) 255 lines 9–10 (an inscription first published by Bean in 1960): παρευγραφὰς κ[αὶ ἀ]παλοιφὰς ἔχοντα πιττάκια.

[68] Although it is possible that πιττάκια are made out of papyrus, it seems to me more likely that, like the *tabulae* or *libelli* they imitated, they were mostly wood, and changed to the medium of papyrus only over time, and in previous chapters (chapter four n.54, chapter five n.63, above n.22) it has been assumed that they were wood. Wörrle (1975) 258 n.511, citing Wilhelm (1909) 243 and Preisigke

Roman tablets and related forms in the provinces

part of the local population to approximate an external Roman standard. In addition to threatening further punishment for public slaves who accepted such documents, Veranius decreed that any such document, "whether it is a covenant or a chirograph or a contract or a clarification or a set of specific instructions or an account rendered or a legal challenge or a disclosure about a legal situation or a decision of arbitrators or judges," legally invalid if written on a palimpsest or having erasures or interpolations.[69] Here, legal documents of the sort that had been important for the orderly public and private administration of cities long before the area became a Roman province had continued to be given their typical pre-Roman treatment, voluntary registration in the city's archives, but with insufficient care for their physical condition. That this was considered reprehensible by the new Roman governor is a reflection of what he thought the physical condition of a document should be. Given that Roman tablets were, ideally, perfectly inscribed, that any alteration was a cause for suspicion, and that the major problem in Rome was the counterfeiting of entire documents, it is not surprising that the governor took the step of imposing the same standard on Greek documents, and invalidating those that could not meet it.[70] Hypothetical counter-arguments of practicality and flexibility are dismissed: the knowledge of why emendations were made is evanescent, he says, and as a consequence such altered documents would inevitably appear

---

(1927) *s.v.*, argues that "very often" πιττάκια are made from papyrus, but most of the references gathered in these two authors give no hint of the material of πιττάκια. The ones that do – *SB* 4324 (n.d.), *P.Oxy.* 1063 (third century AD), *P.Oxy.* 1131 (fifth AD), *Stud.Pal.* 20.268B and 8.960 (sixth AD), *P.Oxy.* 142, 143, 145, 153, 1150 (all sixth AD), *P.Lond.* 780 (AD 535), *PSI* 474 (sixth AD), *SB* 4501 and 4843 (Byzantine), and *P.Ness.* 16 (AD 512) – are all very late, while in contrast examples like Reinach (1906) 243–8 no. 142, which refers (line 21) to the πιττάκιον of a will written by Attalos Adrastos, "of the Roman tribe," strongly suggest wood instead, as do the third-century AD consecrations of slaves to the goddess at Leukopetra, in which the πιττάκιον or γραμματεῖον was exhibited in a public place for at least ten days before being dedicated in the sanctuary, see Petsas *et al.* (2000) 57–8. This inscription from Myra is the best evidence for πιττάκια made of papyrus, since Greek legal documents were generally written on papyrus; the transition point may have been the third century AD (cf. *P.Euphr.* 5; Magdala, AD 243). Yet line 12 also forbids palimpsests, which are not common in papyrus (the only citations known to me are Cic. *Fam.* 7.18.2, *chartula*, and Plut. *Mor.* 779C, which in referring to a βιβλίον παλίμψηστον could be referring to a "palimpsest book" rather than to papyrus written on in palimpsest fashion), and apply more aptly to a medium (like parchment or wax) that retains previous imprints better (e.g., Catul. 22.5).

69 [ἐ]άν τε συμβόλαιον, ἐάν τε χειρόγρ[α]φον, ἐάν τ[ε σ]υνγρ[α]φή{ν}, ἐάν τε δήλ[ω]σις, ἐάν τε σημείωσ[ις], [ἐ]άν τε ἀπόλογος, ἐάν τε πρόκλησις, ἐάν τε περὶ δίκης ἐμφανισμός, ἐάν τε φερνιμαία, ἐάν τε διαιτητῶν ἢ δ[ικασ]τῶν ἀπόφασις (Wörrle [1975] 256 lines 30–4).

70 Attested problems at Rome, Plut. *Cat. Min.* 16–17; Cass. Dio 54.36.1 and 57.16.1–2. That Roman wills could have erasures without being invalidated is, *contra* Wörrle (1975) 284 n.706, no argument that Veranius was not bringing a Roman attitude to his work, for these corrections could only stand if explicitly attested by the testator (*D.* 28.4.1 [Ulpian]). Haensch (1992) 236 n.65 notes the various actions taken to improve documents and archives, both in Rome and the eastern provinces, in the mid-first century AD (between AD 37 and AD 61).

186   *The evolution of practice*

"open to suspicion" (ὑποψίας) and "without faith" (ἄ]πιστα) to "those who intend to review the documents."[71] In Egypt, problems of much the same sort seem to have been encountered in the handling of Greek documents, and were here handled by the creation of new archives[72] and the expression of new standards, particularly a hostility to erasures or additions. Indeed, a new Greek noun for "erasure" (ἀλειφάς) was coined at this time in Egypt, and as part of the phrase without "erasures or additions" probably translates a Latin legal phrase, without *"litura aut adiectio."*[73] By the middle of the second century AD, a debtor could postpone an action for the recovery of a debt by bringing a charge of πλαστὰ γράμματα, περιγραφή, or ῥᾳδιουργία against the creditor,[74] and by the late second century no altered document was accepted for registration in the Nanaion and the library of Hadrian, for unregistered documents assert that they have no erasures or interpolations, "just as those registered in the public archive."[75]

In each area Roman officials were trying to regulate or improve what was basically a system of Greek archives, archives which – to be sure – contributed to the orderly management of a Roman province, but which were supervised by locals and which exhibited the kinds of defects already acknowledged in Greek archives of the Hellenistic period; in one of these earlier cases, the improvements had even been paid for by a Roman.[76] The Roman solution in Egypt, the duplication of an entire archive to

---

[71] [τ]οῖς ἐπισκέπτεσθαι τὰ πιτ[τά]κια μέλλουσιν (Wörrle [1975] 256 lines 38–41).

[72] New archives for public documents in the nomes, called the "library of public acts," *c.* AD 53, which served to inspect the original and a copy, send the original on the Patrica, and keep the copy, cf. *P.Oxy.* 3332, *P.Mich.* 9.539–40, and *P.Fam.Tebt.* 15 (a prefect's edict about his displeasure at the slovenly state of the archive, AD 90), with Wolff (1978) 48–51, Cockle (1984) 113 nn.53–4, and esp. Burkhalter (1990). The same prefect was also displeased by the condition of the archive of property, and his measures were reinforced by an edict of Ser. Sulpicius Similis (AD 109), both in *P.Oxy.* 237. The Library of Hadrian was created in AD 127 as a repository for private Greek documents that had been registered, and "so that nothing done contrary to correctness (μηδὲν τῶν παρὰ τὸ προσῆκον) would go unnoticed" (*P.Oxy.* 34v); erasures and marginal additions were to be noted; and copies of the same were kept in the Nanaion, Burkhalter (1990).

[73] Quint. *Inst.* 11.2.32 and *D.* 28.4.1 (*lituras inductiones superductiones*, Ulpian), both cited by Bülow-Jacobsen *et al.* (2000) 177; at 180, they note that Veranius's ἀπαλοιφά was also a neologism.

[74] *P.Oxy.* 237 lines 14–15 (edict of prefect Valerius Eudaimon); the meaning of the terms is disputed. πλαστὰ γράμματα are "made" or "counterfeit" letters (probably referring to the entire document), περιγραφή is "fraud" in general (but could also refer to *circumscriptio*, the injury of a minor, Menkman [1946] 204), and ῥᾳδιουργία is "fraud" or "knavery." The last two need not specifically refer to tampering with documents, despite Hässler (1960) 33–5 and Menkman (1946) 204 n.34.

[75] Cf. *SB* 7197 (AD 170), *BGU* 666 (AD 177), *P.Tebt.* 396 (AD 188), *BGU* 578 (AD 189): these examples are cheirographs. *BGU* 171 (AD 149), among others, has the same formula about erasures and interpolations, but omits the comparison with the public archive.

[76] Supervised by Greeks: see above n.18. Already existing problems: Lambrinudakis and Wörrle (1983) 285 lines 8, 15–16 (Paros, second century BC).

Roman tablets and related forms in the provinces

prevent tampering and forgery, was not entirely unknown before.[77] What was more unusual was Veranius's disqualification of any documents with physical defects: erasures, interpolations, and palimpsest-writing had never invalidated a Greek legal document before.[78] This focus itself suggests an imported attitude, an application of Roman standards to a problem that Romans were finding distressingly prevalent in the East, and thus again a recognizably different attitude towards legal documents even when they were not your own.[79] Veranius thought to solve the problem only by publishing a Roman standard and flogging a slave, while the prefects of Egypt over time built up a more complicated, multi-step way of enforcing higher standards, but these standards were, at a later date, the same as Veranius's. In neither case were they, probably, entirely successful.[80]

(b) Indirect influence: double-documents. In first- and early second-century Egypt and Lycia, the actions of governors illuminate the nature of existing documentary and archival practices, both local and Roman, make some of the differences in traditions and attitudes clear, and have their own impact. In the second and third centuries, in provinces further to the east, there is less direct intervention to observe, and in these provinces the influence of Roman legal practice itself was much more indirect. Judaea, Arabia, Syria, and Mesopotamia together have turned up only one wood document before the seventh century[81] and few transactions unambiguously performed by two Roman citizens. Much of the papyrus documentation that does survive, however, seems to derive from a context best described as hopefully Roman, generated within the first thirty or forty years of an official Roman presence and written in the expectation of being accepted by a Roman official, as demonstrated by other signs of conformity, like the use of Greek rather than local languages (like Aramaic or Nabataean), and Roman dating formulae.[82] This expectant conformity also manifests itself through the papyrus or

---

[77] Duplication: Lambrinudakis and Wörrle (1983) 324–52 (Paros, second century BC). Roman: Aulus Aemilius Zosimos, son of Sextus honored for this at Priene, *I.Priene* 1.112–14 (after 84 BC).

[78] Lambrinudakis and Wörrle (1983) 308 n.131.

[79] Such attitudes were influential, and are found in Greek authors like Plut. *Mor.* 611A (proverbial).

[80] In Lycia, a second-century AD imperial edict noted "a prevalence of forgeries in the province," Bean (1960) 71 lines 11–13 (Oliver [1989] 390–1 no. 186 = *SEG* 19.854) from Zivint (Sibiunda) in Pisidia (part of the Roman province of Lycia and Pamphilia).

[81] *P.Dura* 53 (second or third century AD), accounts. Seventh century: *P.Ness.* 94, accounts. There are some references to *tabulae*, however: Luc. *Tim.* 21–2 mentions money moving from one man to another in a δέλτος, as well as the δέλτον of a will; and the borrowing of *tavla* in Jewish texts for lists and testaments (Sirat [1992] 57) is suggestive.

[82] Writing in Greek made the document "valid and enforceable in a Greek-speaking court, such as that of the governor of the province," Cotton and Yardeni (1997) 207; see also Cotton (1993) 101–2, (1997) on dating formulae, (1998) 169, (1999) 230–1, and Lewis (2001). This does not, however, necessitate that documents in other languages would not be accepted.

188   *The evolution of practice*

parchment "double-document" or *diploma* (δίπλωμα), which can be found in Egyptian documentary practice as well, where double-documents exist for different but related reasons. Thus these three areas will be treated together, but in chronologically coherent sequences and groups: Egypt and Judaea/Arabia first, since double-documents here appear most notably in the first and second centuries, then Mesopotamia/Syria, where most of the evidence dates to the third.

In a double-document, the legal act on the interior or recto side is written twice, each time transversely – perpendicular rather than parallel to the long sides of a papyrus – across (rather than with) the fibers, which is unusual.[83] It is "double" because it is written twice on the same piece of papyrus, the first (usually top or inner) version then rolled up and sealed shut, the second (usually lower or exterior) left visible, a format reminiscent of Roman wooden triptychs (**fig. 9**).[84] Double-documents had existed in Ptolemaic Egypt, but had decayed over time and had died out in the early first century BC (the last known dates to 77 BC), most likely because of the popularity of registration and archives.[85] In the last fifty years of use, these double-documents most closely approached being even a shadow of their former selves only in remote Egyptian villages with no archives of their own in which documents could be registered.[86] Further east, the same deterioration seems to have taken place, on a slower schedule: double-documents from first-century BC Avroman (Kurdistan)[87] and the first-century AD Judaean desert (coming from the Roman provinces of Judaea and Arabia)[88] have

---

[83] Recognized by Rea (1971) and Daly (1973: called a *rotulus*), developed by Turner (1978) 26–44. I am dependent on scholars' identification of the direction of the fibers when they choose to mention it. Every document written across the fibers is not necessarily a double-document, although every double-document is written across the fibers, see Cotton *et al.* (1995); writing across the fibers seems also to have been "preferred notarial practice in Jewish communities," about two-thirds of the Hebrew and Aramaic documents of the first and second centuries AD in *P.Mur.* being written across the fibers, N. Lewis (1989) 11 and n.17.

[84] Wolff (1937) 474; Sanders (1938) 108–9, N. Lewis (1989) 7; counselling caution about making the parallel too close, Benoit *et al.* (1961) 245.

[85] For a chronological list of Ptolemaic double-documents, see Bilabel (1924) and (1925), with updates in N. Lewis (1989) 7 n.6; decay through the attenuation of the interior text, N. Lewis (1989) 8. Last known: *P.Mert.* 1.6.

[86] Villages, Boswinkel and Pestman (1982) 24 (on its use at Akoris in the late second century BC).

[87] Avroman: Minns (1915) 28–30, two parchment or leather Greek documents of 23–22 BC and AD 44–5, and 23, "more or less duplicates" (for dates, cf. Bellinger and Welles [1935] 118 n.2); the first perhaps shows why doubling and sealing were necessary, since its exterior version changes "thirty" to "forty" and adds some obligations for "eatables" and "dues." A third double-document, in Pahlavi, was found with these two, published by Nyberg (1923). Minns (1915) 48–9 speculates that the Avroman documents survived for the same reason ("registration . . . had not penetrated into out-of-the-way places").

[88] There are four early Judaean desert documents in which inner and outer texts are approximately the same: *DJD* 27.9 (late Herodian, Aramaic); *P.Mur.* 19 (AD 72, Aramaic); *P.Yadin* 2 (AD 99,

Interior front : unrolled

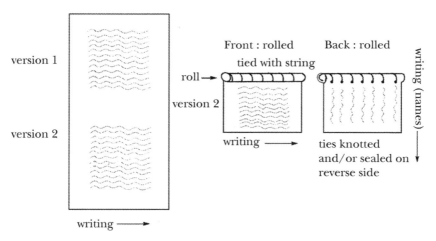

Figure 9 Papyrus double-document.
First version of document written across fibers of papyrus (*transversa charta*), rolled up, the roll tied with string, and the strings sealed or knotted. Second version of document, *transversa charta*, not closed. Names of sealers beside their seals, not *transversa charta*, on the back of the second version of the document.

basically identical interior and exterior writing, but some first- and second-century AD double-documents from the Judaean desert[89] begin to show the same decay, the same slide towards perfunctoriness and incompleteness in the interior version, as had occurred in second-century BC Egypt.

Aramaic), and *P.Yadin* 3 (AD 99, Aramaic). For fourteen or fifteen early documents, it is impossible to compare inner and outer texts: *P.Mur.* 20 (AD 51 or 65, with Cotton [1999] 224, Aramaic); *P.Mur.* 18 (AD 55–6, Aramaic); *P.Mur.* 21 (before AD 66?, Aramaic); *P.Mur.* 25 (AD 66–70, with Cotton [1994] 224, Aramaic); *P.Mur.* 29 (AD 66–70, with Cotton [1994] 224, Hebrew); *DJD* 27.21–2 (end Herodian, Aramaic); *DJD* 27.11 and 23 (AD 70–135, Aramaic); *DJD* 27.50+*P.Mur.* 26 (AD 70–135, Aramaic); *P.Yadin* 4 (AD 99, Aramaic); *Nahal Ṣe'elim* 2 (= Yardeni [2000a] 95, AD 100, Aramaic); *P.Jericho* 8 (first century AD, Aramaic); *P.Jericho* 9 and 10 (first century AD, Hebrew; these two may be the same document). The phrase "loans without διπλώματα," i.e. double-documents, in *P.Yadin* 5B2 (AD 110) suggests that the double-document form was still considered a significant one in early second-century Arabia.

[89] Interior texts are attenuated or compressed in six documents: *P.Yadin* 36 (AD 58–67, with Yardeni [2001] 125: "possibly much abridged"; Aramaic); *P.Mur.* 30 (AD 66–70, with Cotton [1999] 224, Hebrew); *P.Jericho* 7 (AD 84, Aramaic); *P.Yadin* 1 (AD 94, Aramaic); *P.Mur.* 23 (AD 132, with Cotton [1999] 224, Aramaic); *P.Mur.* 28 (first–second century AD, Aramaic). In only three, the inner and outer texts continue to be close: *P.Yadin* 7 (AD 120, Aramaic); *P.Mur.* 22 (AD 134, Hebrew), and *P.Mur.* 115 (AD 124, Aramaic). Inner and outer texts cannot be compared in at least three of the later Hebrew or Aramaic documents (as well as in a host of small fragments): *P.Yadin* 10 (AD 122–5, Aramaic); *DJD* 27.7 (AD 135, Aramaic, on leather); *DJD* 27.8 (AD 134 or 135, Aramaic/Hebrew); and *DJD* 27.23, 24, 24a, 25 (all fragments).

190   *The evolution of practice*

Then, however, come Roman armies, Roman officials, and Roman courts. In Egypt, double-document *diplomata* had been referred to again as early as 14 BC, in a legal settlement noting a Roman's abdication of a tutorship in "sealed διπλώματα."[90] The next known had been a Latin census-return (for the Roman, not local, census), and before the end of the century there would also be two Latin *testatio*-style documents by veterans making official declaration of their own status.[91] As tutorship, census, and status-attestation hint, they were oriented towards not just Roman law but Roman authorities, and were accepted by them for these acts. Roman officials were familiar with *diplomata* for certain types of business, and indeed Roman officials in the late Republic, and Julio-Claudian emperors, had used *diplomata* for postal passes and authorizations, state acts that in no way depended on the Roman status of the recipient or party affected.[92] Some of these official *diplomata* are found in Egypt, as requisitions, warrants, and certificates.[93] The way they and other *diplomata* were written across the fibers of the papyrus parallels the *transversa charta* way consuls and *duces* before Julius Caesar were said to have written reports to the senate, and which therefore, even in the papyrus medium, had some claims to being both an acceptable and an antique Roman practice.[94] Roman

---

[90] *BGU* 1113 (= *M.Chr.* 169; Alexandria, 14 BC), referring to τὸ συνσφραγισθ[ὲ]ν δίπλ[ωμα in which a Roman citizen named Canuleius abdicates his tutorship of L. Pomponius, assigned to him by "Roman will," so the abdication is probably in Latin.

[91] Census: *ChLA* 25.785 (= *CPL* 170, *PSI* 11.1183b, *FIRA²* 3.18–19 no. 8; Oxyrhynchus, AD 47–8), discussed in Rathbone (2001). The interior text was written in rustic capitals, the exterior in old Roman cursive, and both by different people; this may also be two copies of the same document, one folded and sealed, rather than a canonical double-document. Declarations: *ChLA* 4.248 (= *CPL* 176, *P.Ryl.* 4.611; Latin, Fayum, AD 87–8); *ChLA* 46.1364 (= *CPL* 102; Latin, Fayum, AD 92), with oath of sureties.

[92] The earliest and longest-lasting meaning of *diploma* in Latin sources is that of an officially issued pass to use the public post or to requisition transport, see Pflaum (1940) 122–48 and Plut. *Galba* 8.4, where the phrase τὰ καλούμενα διπλώματα indicates that *diploma* was a Roman technical term by the second century AD; S. Mitchell (1976) 125–7 discusses how the system changed in the late first century AD. Suetonius refers to some acts of first-century emperors as being done with *diplomata*, *Aug.* 50 (*in diplomatibus libellisque et epistulis*) and *Otho* 7.1, cf. Haensch (1996) 456–7; in *Gaius* 38.1 and *Nero* 12.1 *diplomata* refer to documentary proofs of citizenship (and *conubium*). In still later sources *diplomata* can be a general term for imperial document, e.g., Symm. *Ep.* 5.38 (*diplomatis sacri*) or *CIL* 9.2826 (*diplomatis annotationem exhibentis*, Buca, sixth century AD).

[93] The prefect authorized the requisition of transport through a δίπλωμα, e.g., *P.Lond.* 3.1171 (= *W.Chr.* 439, AD 42), or *OGIS* 665 line 25 (Hibis, AD 48), cf. *PSI* 446 line 12, ἀν[ε]υ διπλῆς, with διπλαῖ used in same sense as δίπλωμα (no provenance, AD 133–7); a warrant for arrests was issued as a δίπλωμα, e.g., *P.Oxy.* 3061 (Hibis, first century AD), with Turner (1978) 47; payment of certain sorts of tax gained the owner a δίπλωμα (e.g., *BGU* 213, δίπλωμα ὄνων [AD 112–13]; *O.Edfou* 2.272 [AD 109], or *P.Ryl.* 2.194 [AD 134–6], δίπλωμα ἵππων); cf. the purchase of monopolies indicated by δίπλωμα, Wallace (1938) 186–7 (e.g., *PSI* 7.787, bread-making; *P.Tebt.* 2.360, vegetable-selling).

[94] Suet. *Jul.* 56.6, *epistulae quoque eius ad senatum extant, quas primum videtur ad paginas et formam memorialis libelli convertisse, cum antea consules et duces non nisi transversa charta scriptas mitterent.* I

Roman tablets and related forms in the provinces 191

officials both used and accepted *diplomata* if they were properly executed, and in addition to being doubled, sealed, and witnessed documents that had a type of Roman pedigree and could show, at least externally, scribes' and protagonists' proper respect for the strange Roman insistence on the high physical standard of a document, papyrus *diplomata* in Egypt had the advantage of being convenient. Wood was understood to be better, and conveyed standing and (in Egypt) wealth, but under certain circumstances papyrus would do. Even so, papyrus double-documents generated in Egypt were always rare and more associated with the Roman community itself than with the hopefully Roman, no doubt because the status separations, so strictly enforced, limited the aspirations and therefore also the numbers of the latter.

In contrast, in Arabia and Judaea the double-document is revived in a non-Roman but aggressively conformist context, and the close causal relationship is well demonstrated by both chronology and usage. Arabia was organized as a new province in AD 106. Most of the early second-century double-documents in Arabia whose contents intersect with Roman spheres – when one of the parties is Roman, for example, or when summonses to the governor's court are exchanged[95] – again display a full interior text, while contemporary texts whose authors and scribes imagined no possible presentation to Roman authorities, as the fact that they were (e.g.) written in Aramaic indicates, continue to show the gentle decay characteristic of the aging double-document form. In other words, scribes perceived or were informed that a traditional form to which they had been increasingly indifferent could, with care, be resuscitated for certain acts and considered, in this revived state, more pleasing in Roman legal contexts.[96] For these acts, and when informed of a potential Roman audience, scribes therefore made the effort to write out the interior text in full; otherwise, business continued much as usual.

The most dramatic example of such eager conformity comes from the early second century. In the collection of Greek documents found in the

---

follow Turner (1978) 32–3: leaders wrote *transversa charta*, i.e. with the papyrus roll rotated ninety degrees, so that the writing ran perpendicular rather than parallel to the long sides of the papyrus roll, as was characteristic also of the δίπλωμα; *contra*, Cavallo (1992) 99–101.

[95] First postulations of connection, see Wolff (1937) 476 and Benoit *et al.* (1961) 244–7. The suggestion that the double-document originated in the east (e.g., Wenger [1953] 80–1 n.13) has been refuted by Kunkel (1933) and (1936), Wolff (1978) 61–3, Lévy (1982), and by the increasing body of actual documents.

[96] Sensitivity of the Arabian scribes to Roman prototypes, Cotton (1997); note also the texts' numerous Latinisms (N. Lewis [1989] 16–19), and the use of stipulation-clauses (*P.Yadin* 17, 18, 20–2, 37); *contra*, Rathbone (2001) 104 suggests that the interior writing of double-documents was often squashed because "a clearly legible outer hand" was more important in the Greek tradition.

192   *The evolution of practice*

Judaean wilderness, some of which the widow Babatha had taken with her
in AD 132 or 133, there were twenty-three double-documents confirming her
marital status, and documenting some financial transactions and her legal
struggle with the very superior and indubitably Roman Julia Crispina.[97]
In the collection were also two sets of two simple versions of the sale of
a date crop and seven Aramaic double-documents, all but one sales and
deeds of gift from her father's generation that helped to establish her claim
to some of her properties.[98] That Babatha would hoard documents such
as these comes as no surprise. That they were written in double-document
form, and indeed found along with some fragments of copied Roman
juristic texts,[99] is more surprising. The degree to which the woman and
the documents orient themselves towards Rome, like iron filings swiv-
elling in the presence of a strong magnet, is impressive. Babatha is no
Roman citizen and her documents are not on wood, but she is fearlessly
willing to meet the likes of Julia Crispina in the governor's court,[100] and
her extensive use of double-documents written in Greek is not coinciden-
tal. Like other provincials she seeks to curry favor and protect family and

[97] Four marriage contracts, *P.Yadin* 18 (AD 128; with stipulatory clause), 37 (AD 131, republished as
DJD 27.65, inner text only), and two others (*P.Mur.* 115 [AD 124] and *DJD* 27.69 [AD 130, from
Aristoboulias, little left of interior text; the last three are the marriage contracts of other women]);
five summonses, *P.Yadin* 14 (AD 125), 23 (AD 130), 25 (AD 131), 26 (AD 131; inner text badly abraded);
and 35 (AD 132?, fragment of outer text only); two witnessed declarations (μαρτυροποιήματα),
P.Yadin 15 (AD 125) and 24 (AD 130, outer text fragmentary); other contracts and deeds, *P.Yadin* 17
(AD 128); note also 31, very fragmentary but possibly a contract (after AD 125), 19, a deed of gift
(AD 128) – virtually contemporary with *DJD* 27.64 (AD 129), another deed of gift from the Judaean
desert, and both show some differences between the interior and exterior texts – and *P.Yadin* 20,
a concession of right (AD 130, inner text almost entirely lost); loan (on hypothec) of sixty denarii,
P.Yadin 11 (AD 124); three copies of land registrations for the Roman census, *P.Yadin* 16, the same in
style as *DJD* 27.61–2, all from AD 127; two copies of answered petitions, *P.Yadin* 33 (*c.* AD 125?), and
34 (AD 131, interior text never written) – note that *P.Yadin* 13 (AD 124), a copy of one of Babatha's
petitions to the governor (for her own use, because unsigned), is written with rather than across
the fibers and is not a double-document; copy of the nomination of a tutor for her son, from the
posted *acta* of Petra, *P.Yadin* 12 (AD 124), which N. Lewis (1989) 48 suggests translates a document
originally in Latin. *P.Yadin* 32 and 32a are fragmentary.
[98] Two sets of two versions of sale, *P.Yadin* 21 and 22 (AD 130, Greek; one the buyer's declaration, one the
seller's), and *P.Yadin* 47a-b (AD 134, Aramaic); the Hellenistic Greek practice was one text, not two,
Lewis (1989) 94. Nabataean Aramaic double-documents are *P.Yadin* 36 (acknowledgment of debt,
AD 58–76) and *P.Yadin* 1–4 (?dowry settlement and two sales, AD 94–9; with Yardeni [2001]); the
first two may have shorter interior texts, but in the second two the interior and exterior texts appear
to be the same, and in the last the interior text is not preserved; the Jewish Aramaic documents are
P.Yadin 7 (AD 120), full interior and exterior texts, and *P.Yadin* 10 (AD 122–5), Babatha's marriage
contract or *ketubbah*, for which only the outer text survives.
[99] *P.Yadin* 28–30 (AD 124–5).
[100] On the "remarkable rate of Romanization" displayed by the Babatha archive, Cotton (1993) 94; on
Babatha's (and others') readiness to use Roman courts, Cotton (1993) 106–7; on Julia Crispina's
powerful relations, Bowersock (1991) 341 and Ilan (1992).

Roman tablets and related forms in the provinces 193

property by adopting the forms she thinks most likely to win Roman approval.[101]

That the double-document became an eastern provincial's preferred form for interacting with Romans, or for performing or documenting non-Roman (or semi-Roman) legal acts whose validity a Roman court or a Roman official could be impressed into upholding, is further demonstrated by the pattern of language, origins, protagonists, and uses of double-documents mostly generated outside Egypt later in the second and third centuries AD, but found in Egypt. These Ἑλληνικὰ διπλώματα, doubled "documents belonging to the sphere of Roman law" but often written in Greek,[102] contained a debt,[103] an attested statement of receipt for a soldier's *deposita*,[104] declarations,[105] and marriage contracts (or dowry arrangements) in Latin;[106] and, in even greater number, sales of horses and slaves (*res mancipi*) in Latin and Greek.[107] All but one of the last originated outside

[101] On Babatha, Cotton (1993) 107; this kind of anticipatory conformity also identified at Cologne by Galsterer (1986) 154.

[102] They call themselves Ἑλληνικὰ διπλώματα, see ChLA 47.1448 (= P.Col. 8.221, AD 143), attestation of receipt for soldier's *deposita* (Thebaid); BGU 913. line 3 (Myra, AD 206). "Greek" probably refers to the language in which they were written in the second century AD, since all surviving examples from the first century AD are written in Latin; see Gilliam (1971) 67 and Wolff (1978) 78 n.110. Quotation, Wolff (1978) 79 (relying on Kunkel [1936] 426–7); cf. Wolff (1980) 782–4. Most of these acts can also be paralleled on tablets in Egypt: for attestation of debt, the τάβλα of BGU 1079, to be subscribed (mysteriously) "by Diodorus or the wife of the prefect" (= W.Chr. 60; see Wilcken [1908] 567–8, AD 41); for the *deposita*-document and the attestations of illegitimate birth, also drawn up in army camps – attestations that were called, in *epikrisis* hearings, "tablets of witness-acts" – see chapter 8 n.90.

[103] P.Wisc. 2.53 line 4 (AD 55): "I (Marcus Asclepius, cavalryman) hold a debt διὰ διπλώματος"; the debt was incurred by another, but the δίπλωμα has (somehow) passed on to M. Asclepius; the language of the document is unknown.

[104] ChLA 47.1448 (= P.Col. 8.221, Thebes, AD 143).

[105] Declarations: SB 7523 (= FIRA² 3.591–2 no. 188; Fayum, AD 153); it includes Latinisms, cf. Kortenbeutel (1932) 133. Acts in which the principal declares, attests, or "calls to witness" (using *testatus est*) are called μαρτυροποιήματα in Greek, P.Yadin 15 (AD 125) and 24 (AD 130?), P.Mich. 12.636. μαρτυροποίημα could also be used for an attested copy, as in IG 9(1).61 (Daulis, AD 118), two inscriptions made from copies of a decision (by a Roman judge) in land disputes, sealed by the judge and others; cf. double-document copies of petitions (BGU 970 + 525 = M.Chr. 242 [AD 177], PSI 1245 [AD 207]), and in SB 13059 (P.Mich. inv. 6554, AD 293), an [ἐκ]σφρα[γίσ]μα was thereby created. P.Jericho 16gr. has been identified as a μαρτυροποίημα (Haensch [2001]), but the writing is with the fibers rather than *transversa*, so possibly only a copy. In Egypt the μαρτυροποίημα is basically a third-century phenomenon, N. Lewis (1975) 163.

[106] ChLA 25.783 (= CPL 207, PSI 6.730; Latin, unknown provenance, first century AD); ChLA 4.249 (= CPL 208–9, P.Mich. 7.434 + P.Ryl. 4.612; Latin, unknown provenance, beginning second century AD); ChLA 5.295 (= CPL 210, P.Mich. 7.442, FIRA² 3.54–5 no. 20; Latin, Karanis, late second century AD, but drawn up at Caesarea in Mauretania).

[107] Horses, ChLA 25.782 (= CPL 186, PSI 6.729, FIRA² 3.436–7 no. 136; AD 77), two Romans using a *stipul(atus) est...spop(ondit)* clause (from Cappadocia); cf. P.Euphr. 10 (AD 250), a double-document sale of a horse brought from Carrhae to a village in the middle Euphrates valley (Feissel and Gascou [1989] 538). Slaves: P.Col. 8.219 (AD 140), reference to purchase of a slave by a Roman woman from a

194   *The evolution of practice*

Egypt, in cities of the East; most have one Roman-citizen protagonist (not two), and a few have no apparent connections to anything Roman at all. Romans and non-Romans, at times inside but especially outside Egypt, thus used *diplomata* in Latin and Greek with some regularity, if only as substitutes for wood in those acts that Roman citizens would have, but in these cases for some reason could not, write on their traditional *tabulae*. *Diplomata* seem to have been worth drawing up, from a provincial's point of view, only if the validity of the transaction was likely to face some Roman test: if it was an act that could be, by Roman tradition, embodied in a document (as sales of *res mancipi* were), and if you were likely to be challenged, as could well happen if you moved a slave or a horse from province to province. The small number of these double-documents may also imply that most of the day-to-day legal business in the eastern part of the empire was local, and expected to operate at a level far beneath that of any Roman interest.

Although double-documents are similar in how they were made and what they were used for both within and outside Egypt, differences in usage and drafting between Egypt and other eastern provinces before the middle of the third century again demonstrate the tight, or tighter, control exercised in Egypt over status-related behavior. These differences demonstrate not only that styles of Roman governance in different provinces could vary, which was to be expected, but that a difference in governing style (especially in what seems to have been permitted) affected some of the documentary styles adopted by the governed. Romans in Egypt used wood for documents that transferred property by will or marriage, and for documents or attested copies of official *tabulae* that demonstrated status and conferred

---

Greek man through a Greek δίπλωμα (origin possibly Alexandria, Gilliam [1971] 63 n.3); *P. Turner* 22 (AD 142), transaction between two Greeks, one with a Roman-citizen *fideiussor*, using a *fideiussio* stipulatory clause (Side, in Pamphylia); *BGU* 887 (= *FIRA*² 3.428–1 no. 133, AD 151), an Alexandrian buys a slave from L. Julius Protoktetos, using a *fideiussio* stipulatory clause (Side, in Pamphylia); *ChLA* 3.200 (= *CPL* 120, *FIRA*² 3.425–7 no. 132, AD 166), two Romans using a *stipulatus est . . . spopondit* clause (Seleucia-in-Pieria, in Syria); *BGU* 913 (AD 206), Gemella sells a slave to Simon (Myra, in Lycia); *SB* 7563 (AD 207), Ap[—] buys a slave from Petreius Antiochos (Pompeiopolis, in Paphlagonia); *P.Ross.Georg.* 3.27 (reign of Severus Alexander), reference to a slave purchased κατὰ δίπλωμα; *P.Vind.Bosw.* 7 (AD 225), reference to slave purchased ἐν τοῖς ἔξω τόποις κατὰ δίπλωμα Ἑλληνικόν; *P.Euphr.* 6–7 (AD 249, Osrhoene); *P.Euphr.* 8 (AD 251) and *P.Euphr.* 9 (AD 252), both Beth Phouraia; *P.Oxy.* 3053 (AD 252), slave purchased κατὰ δίπλωμα Ἑλληνικόν in Aurelia Tripolis (Phoenicia), now registered in Egypt; *P.Oxy.* 3054, same, in Bostra; *ChLA* 47.1415 (= *P.Oxy.* 2951; AD 267), two Romans using a *stipulatus est . . . spopondit* clause (Alexandria). *CPL* 193 (= *FIRA*² 3.431–2 no. 134, possibly Hadrianic, Söllner [2001] 84), a discharge of obligation in the sale of a slave by Aischines Flavianos, to T. Memmius Montanus, soldier, was drafted in Ravenna (in Latin written in Greek characters) but found in the Fayum and presumably came to Egypt with him; *P.Dura* 28 (AD 243), another double-document slave-sale, was drafted in Edessa but found in Dura.

Roman tablets and related forms in the provinces 195

tutelary authority; the only Roman-law papyrus double-documents certainly written for them by *nomikoi* or army-scribes before AD 212 were declarations or census-attestations and marriage contracts (which also appeared on wood).[108] Both wood and papyrus documents were regularly sealed, the act of sealing noted as often as not by the sealers.[109] Outside Egypt, wooden documents do not survive, and papyrus double-documents in Greek are not just declarations and marriage contracts, but also other kinds of contracts and sales (especially slave-sales), deeds of gift, concessions, and summonses, tied and knotted shut but rarely sealed,[110] with names of five or seven men who called themselves "witnesses" or *martyres* written next to the knots;[111] at times these acts are strengthened with stipulatory clauses and dated by Roman consuls, both not seen in Greek documents from Egypt until the 220s AD.[112] Such variety and imitative borrowing in other parts of the eastern Mediterranean, contrasted with the carefully bichrome picture in Egypt, suggests control and enforced limits there, of keeping what was Roman – at least in certain categories – separate and discouraging too much exuberant cross-fertilization and experimental imitation. There was no Egyptian Babatha, enthusiastically using local scribes to approximate a perceived Roman standard and riding a revival of the decaying double-document form in the process, and Egypt was neither Judaea (which turned only gradually and grudgingly towards Rome after AD 72)[113] nor Arabia (which reoriented with evident alacrity after the area became a province in AD 106). It would therefore seem that the governance of Egypt, conceived and carried out with a vigilant eye on the distinctions between citizens and others at the end of the first century BC, successfully maintained these distinctions over time, while the governance of Arabia (or even possibly Dacia, for that matter), beginning in the second century AD,

---

[108] *ChLA* 47.1439 (= *P.Wisc.* 2.50), if correctly identified as writing exercises by a νομικός, suggests that they specifically prepared for writing witness-attestations, marriage contracts, *cretiones*, and manumissions. Note also that a νομικὸς Ῥωμαικός translated C. Longinus Castor's will of AD 191 and 194 (*BGU* 326 = *FIRA²* 3.146–53 no. 50, at very end).

[109] E.g., sale of a slave in Seleucia Pieria, *ChLA* 3.200 (= *FIRA²* 3.425–7 no. 132, *signavi*, AD 166); *tabulae nuptiales*, *ChLA* 4.249 (= *CPL* 208–9, *P.Mich.* 7.434, ἐσφράγισα and ἐσφράγικα; AD 100); will-opening of C. Longinus Castor, *BGU* 326 (= *FIRA²* 3.146–53 no. 50, *signaverunt . . . signatores*; AD 191 and 194).

[110] Specifically noted as sealed, only *BGU* 913 (Myra, AD 206).

[111] Knotting but not sealing characteristic of the Judaean and Arabian double-documents in all languages, N. Lewis (1989) 10 and Cotton and Yardeni (1997) 11; five or seven witnesses in *P.Yadin*, N. Lewis (1989) 12. Identification as witnesses (both Greek and Aramaic): *DJD* 27.9, 62, 64, 69; *P.Mur.* 21, 29, 19; *P.Yadin* 11–12, 14–20, 23, 26, 31.

[112] Simon (1964) and E. Seidl (1973) 173–5; dating, N. Lewis *et al.* (1987) 234 and N. Lewis (1989) 27–8.

[113] Cotton (1999) 230–1 attributes the late introduction of Greek for legal documents in Judaea to the continued existence of Jewish courts.

196   *The evolution of practice*

was more relaxed in its enforcement of distinctions, and consequently (whether consciously or not) permitted more experimentation in the legal documents of non-citizens.

Another difference in the drafting of double-documents also suggests this difference in the governance of Egypt and that of her immediate eastern neighbors, with consequences again for documentary practice. In Judaea and Arabia in the first third of the second century AD, attested copies of official acts (approved land registrations, acts of a city council, answered petitions) were done in Greek double-document form. These attested copies in Arabia have no exact and contemporary Egyptian parallels. Attested copies in Egypt are of birth registrations and grants of tutorships, and are on wood with full inner texts; there are no attested copies of land registrations for the census, or of answered petitions, before AD 177, not least because Egyptian agricultural land was not registered for the census at all. Egyptian petitions in contrast existed, but inched uncopied as well as undoubled through variegated and diversifying papyrus channels like trickles of water over heat-cracked mud before the last quarter of the second century.[114] Registrations and the giving and answering of petitions were both treated as a part of the Greek administration of Egypt rather than as Roman business,[115] while the copies of answered Arabian petitions, in contrast, were Greek double-documents, a clear sign that in Arabia their business was categorized as Roman business. A distinction between the two provinces in the way the governor thought about his work resulted in a different way of

[114] Haensch (1994), previewed in Haensch (1992) 254–5, has laid out the four phases of treatment of petitions in Egypt (some first suggested in J. D. Thomas [1983]): (1) in the first and early second centuries, the prefect or official answered the petition with a letter (which recopied or attached the original petition); (2) in the second century, this method persisted for higher-status petitioners, but for the majority a system of subscription was now used (first attested in AD 131, cf. *P.Oxy.* 486 = *M.Chr.* 59 with Haensch [1992] 216, the last attested subscription of a single rather than duplicate petition that was not posted is *SB* 9340 of AD 198), and the official wrote the answer on the petition itself, and returned it to the petitioner; (3) *c.* AD 158, the petitioner handed in two copies of his petition and a lower official received one back, glued together with others deemed of similar type, with the prefect's instructions, while the other copy was subscribed and archived (for a newly discovered example of this type, see Serfass [2001]); (4) after AD 207 (two early examples, in AD 177 [*BGU* 970 + 525] and AD 179 [*P.Oxy.* 4481] are not seen as a significant trend) petitions were handed in singly again, the answers subscribed, but the petitions not returned to the petitioner; instead, these petitions were posted and petitioners, if they chose, could make copies for themselves. After posting, these glued-together, subscribed petitions were archived. *P.Yale* 61 (AD 208–10) makes provision for posting outside of Alexandria.

[115] Petitions in the east may once have been written on *tabulae*, since Herod Agrippa wrote a petition to Caligula on a δέλτον, Philo *Leg.* 276, but in Egypt they survive only on papyrus and are called *libelli* or βιβλίδια (in Greek sources λίβελλος appears first in the second century, as does λιβλάριος, see Bowersock [1991] 339); Greek equivalences (βιβλίδια) for *codicilli* or *libelli* are given in Greco-Latin schooltexts called *hermeneuta*, *CGL* 3.32.33 and 3.34.6.

Roman tablets and related forms in the provinces

answering petitions and affected whether or not copies were taken, and in what form. Again, Egypt rather than Arabia was probably the distinctive province.

A comparison of the unusual double-document copies of official acts from Arabia with their later analogues from Egypt also suggests that documentary practice could change in both provinces in response to a change in legal valuation whose origin must be the center of empire rather than its periphery. In the attested copies from Arabia, the interior texts are truncated to a laconic brevity not seen even in contemporary Aramaic legal documents: at best they are only two lines.[116] Within twenty-five years, however, a copy of a posted petition made in nearby Caesarea has full interior and exterior texts, as do the copies of answered petitions made in Egypt starting in AD 177. This initial difference, and the subsequent change, were demonstrably not a matter of mere scribal preference.[117] To have only a derisory interior text, as these Arabian texts between AD 124 and 131 do, suggests that Romans were keeping official records to which recourse could be had in times of difficulty.[118] At the same time it implies that official opinion attributed no importance to the interior text in attested copies of these acts in particular. Although no clear directive can be proved, a parallel at Rome suggests that practice in Palestine could well be responding to an official example recently set at home. Beginning in the reign of Trajan but accelerating during the reigns of Hadrian and (especially) Antoninus Pius, the military *diplomata* issued at Rome, copies of grants posted on *tabulae* there, start to show a decay of the inner text into carelessness and inadequacy.[119] It must have been true for military *diplomata* in particular that the exiguity of the interior text would never become known – and, therefore, that it was known that the *diploma* would never be opened.[120] Perhaps Arabian

---

[116] Copy of extract from council minutes appointing a guardian, *P.Yadin* 12; copies of registration of land, *P.Yadin* 16 and *DJD* 27.61–2; petitions, *P.Yadin* 33–4 (interior text of 34 never written); *P.Yadin* 13 is a copy of a petition made before submission, written with the fibers and not a double-document (parallels in *P.Euphr.* 2, AD 245–50, and *P.Euphr.* 3–4, AD 254 or 255, both copied with the fibers and not subscribed by the governor).

[117] Three scribes wrote fifteen of twenty-eight documents in *P.Yadin*, and Germanos, who wrote the truncated double-document *P.Yadin* 34, also wrote the full double-documents *P.Yadin* 23, 25, and 26.

[118] N. Lewis (1989) 9; *contra* Isaac (1994) 265, it cannot mean that the Romans kept no copies.

[119] Dating, Mommsen and Nesselhauf (1936) 150.

[120] Roxan (1996) 256; it cannot be because the grant could now be confirmed by inspection of the posted tablet at Rome, since this had always been the case. Cf. Eck (2000) 281–2, a late second-century AD diploma cut from an honorific bronze inscription still legible on the interior of the diploma: the recipient, because he never opened the diploma, would never have known.

198 *The evolution of practice*

copies of registrations of land for the census would also never be opened, the most crucially interested parties, those taking the census, being already in possession of the original subscribed *pittakion* anyway; and perhaps Arabian copies of subscribed petitions recorded only an order to take a petition elsewhere, attestation and "doubling" merely making the important point that the answer was indeed from the governor.[121] The same would hold true of the copy of the city's bestowal of guardianship. In all cases, as with military *diplomata*, the process of attesting through "doubling" communicates the authority of both the content of the document and the issuing body behind the scribe; it is this latter type of authority, buttressed by the *fides* of sealers, that is stressed when the interior text is treated desultorily. What the document looked like – that it was (apparently) doubled, closed, and finished with signatures or seals – conveyed, in these cases, the weight of act and message.

The change, from the truncated interior texts in Arabia in the 120s and 130s to full interior texts after mid-century in Caesarea and Egypt, probably indicates that the particular acts copied in Arabia were not (yet) perceived to have the specifically legal value that over the second century came to be attributed to them. Military *diplomata* and wooden copies of registrations of birth have legal value because the grant or registration itself is imperial or legally mandated, and in fact these documents do carry weight in court, where they help to establish status. But what the legal value of a copy of an answer to a petition was, in Arabia or elsewhere in AD 130, had not yet been established; only when that answer was also perceived to have legal value, carrying some legal weight in court, would a full double-document copy be taken.[122] The appearance of a full interior text in one doubled and attested copy of an answered petition in AD 150 therefore points to the changing – increased – legal weight of a prefect's subscription to a petition in both Palestine and Egypt, illuminates its relative weakness (especially in court, rather than among, say, other officials) before this time, and makes clear that petitioners were ultimately the ones responsible for taking advantage of this by securing a copy of the subscription in the kind of document that would

---

[121] *P.Yadin* 33–4 (both too fragmentary to surmise content).

[122] The first double-document copy of a subscribed petition clearly looks to a legal venue, for in *ChLA* 25.784 (= *PSI* 1026) veterans had petitioned the governor of Judaea for *subscriptio tua* and a validation of their status, and then had taken the copy to Egypt with them (where they will need it for the *epikrisis*-hearing). Attested copies earlier than AD 177 are generally of imperial edicts (whose legal value was unquestioned), but the copies are epigraphical (so we cannot tell whether they were doubled) and the purpose of copying and inscribing was probably honorific.

Roman tablets and related forms in the provinces   199

accurately communicate this legal weight, content and authority both.[123] In Egypt these copies were for a while hard to come by, since answered petitions may not have been regularly posted there before the early third century, but the archiving of an answered petition at this time, in mid-century, points to the subscription's new value as well.[124] The taking of double-document copies in different ways in these two provinces responds to a central model and a central valuation, the first (apparently) negative and the second positive, but both emphasizing the consequences when the authority of Authority, so to speak, changes over time.

The introduction of the subscription of petitions, the posting of sub-scribed petitions, and the taking of attested double-document copies of petitions in Egypt shows by its timing the surprisingly close connection between imperial action and provincial reaction and imitation in this con-servatively governed province. Subscription of petitions by the Egyptian prefect and his staff is first seen in AD 131, when Hadrian was emperor – the first emperor regularly to subscribe imperial petitions and to allow le-gal weight to be given to those subscriptions,[125] and a visitor to Egypt in AD 130, where he answered at least one petition with a subscription.[126] In Egypt, this introduction of subscription by the prefect had the effect of applying a Roman technique to a Greek document, and a desire to fol-low the imperial example even when it crossed over carefully maintained boundaries should surely be postulated, precisely because it crosses those boundaries.[127] Hadrian also seems to have posted his one subscribed peti-tion, but this may not have been regular imperial practice in the second

---

[123] Cf. Hauken (1998) 263 on petitioners and imperial subscription. Making an attested copy was a choice, not a requirement, see Hanson (1984) 193; it may have become more "professionalized" over time, with repeating witness-sealers like military *diplomata*, Haensch (1996) 466.

[124] Mid-century: see Haensch's (1994) phase three, above n.114.

[125] Hadrian and *subscriptiones*: Millar (1977) 243, Nörr (1981) 3; cf. Honoré (1998) 209. On the dating and weighting of imperial subscriptions, Haensch (1994) 488 nn.4–5; Hauken (1998). At most twelve epigraphical examples of imperial subscriptions are so far known, listed in W. Williams (1986), to which Şahin and French (1987; AD 212–13) and (perhaps) Shipley and Spawforth (1995) are to be added (they say of Claudian date; Hadrianic seems more likely to me).

[126] In Egypt, he gave a *subscriptio* to the priests of Soxis (*SB* 12509, with Lukaszewicz [1981]). He also directed (*D.* 39.4.4.1 [Paulus]) any governors buying property possibly subject to tax to send with the person making the purchase a *libello manu sua subscripto* and then send the *libellus* on to the *publicanus*.

[127] Ptolemaic petitions had also been subscribed, but differently, and no one postulates any continuities: see J. D. Thomas (1983) 370, citing Millar (1977) 241; only the prefect and the procurators subscribe, J. D. Thomas (1983) 371. Note also the language used in the prefect's subscription in *P.Oxy.* 4481 (AD 179), ἀντέγραφα (= *rescripsi*), previously thought to have been used only by emperors (see note *ad loc.*).

200 *The evolution of practice*

century[128] and Egyptian prefects did not post petitions for some time, the first known example being in AD 177.[129]

Regular posting of subscribed petitions belongs to the third century, and here too the imperial example is important. Septimius Severus visited Egypt in AD 199–200, and while there received, answered, and posted petitions, and heard court cases that involved Romans and non-Romans alike.[130] A. A. Schiller even thought that Septimius Severus actually took the prefect's place in court during his stay, and that his staff answered petitions that would usually have been answered by the prefect's staff.[131] Posting of petitions subscribed by the prefect, and even of some court decisions, followed, as did a special clerk – an ὀρθογράφῳ or "correct writer" – who could be hired to copy the subscribed petition for you.[132] That this is imitation rather than, say, a pragmatic decision is strongly hinted at by the practical problems involved. For although the numbers of petitions handed in to the prefect may have reached an all-time high in these years[133] and a switch to posting a petition no longer submitted in duplicate would have cut the subscribing

[128] Hadrian: *SB* 12509 says, προτεθήτω. Three early examples (posting indicated only by "PP") survive from the *CJ* (2.12[13].1, AD 150; 2.1.1, AD 155; and 5.25.3, AD 162), but indications of posting become much more regular and numerous after AD 200, Millar (1977) 244 n.28. Wilcken (1920) and (1930) first reconstructed *libellus*-and-subscription procedure from *IGBulg.* 4.2236 (= *SIG*³ 888); I separate subscription and regular posting, and see the latter as Severan; see also Mourgues (1995a) 269–71. Subscribed petitions were therefore among the *last* kinds of imperial communication to be posted, which helps to explain the uncertainty even among emperors over their usefulness or application beyond the one problem on which they commented (see Peachin [1996] 24, who argues for their increasing perceived usefulness precisely now, in the late second and early third centuries AD; Turpin [1991] 103–6). Cf. Katzoff (1981) 570 n.41, examples of imperial rescripts cited "as authority": only three from the second century, fifteen from the first half of the third.

[129] *BGU* 970 + 525 (= *M.Chr.* 242, AD 177); Haensch (1994) 498–9 suggests experimentation in the treatment of petitions in Egypt before the practice of posting is fully adopted under Septimius Severus.

[130] Severus on his visit posted up (προΰθησεν) his *decreta* (*SB* 7696, line 100), his *apokrimata* (*P.Col.* 6.123), and other communications not specifically identified but which are probably subscriptions (W. Williams [1974] 89–90); *apokrimata* were probably decisions of the emperor given in open court and not *subscriptiones* to *libelli*, Turpin (1981), and it is probably no coincidence that after the emperor's visit, even some court decisions of Roman officials in Egypt also start to be posted (see Turpin [1981] 156–7, *P.Paris* 69 [= *W.Chr.* 41, Severan]). Non-Romans: in *apokrimata*, Westermann and Schiller (1954) 47; "Egyptians" are referred to *P.Oxy.* 3019 (an extract from the emperor's legal proceedings, AD 200).

[131] Schiller, in Westermann and Schiller (1954) 46.

[132] *P.Oxy.* 3138 (mid-third century AD; cost, 600 drachmas). Roman-law drafter-lawyers, νομικοί, could write the petition itself, and charge (according to Diocletian's price edict, col. vii line 41 [Lauffer (1971) 120] the rather pricier ten *denarii* per 100 lines. In the third century, sealed and attested copies of other non-imperial subscriptions were also made elsewhere, e.g., Nollé (1982) 13 (lines 20–3 and 43–7), 32–8, 54–5, a subscribed petition from the governor (Mandragoreis, AD 209).

[133] Between 206 and 211, 1,804 petitions were handed in over three days during the prefect's *conventus* (*P.Yale* 61 with N. Lewis [1981] and Haensch [1997]), while column-entries in archives of petitions from the first half of the third century can range from one to 1,009 (Haensch [1994] 487 and 544–6); we have no comparable information from earlier periods.

Roman tablets and related forms in the provinces 201

time in half, posting papyrus is more difficult than is regularly assumed.[134] The one specific reference to how subscribed *libelli* were posted at Rome, in AD 238, refers to a copy made "from the book of *libelli* subscribed . . . and posted at Rome in the portico of the baths of Trajan,"[135] but does not specifically evoke the world of papyrus, even though the phrase is parallel to the one used in the Egyptian petitions (ἐκ τεύχους συγκολλησίμων βιβλειδίων ἐπιδοθήντων . . . προτεθέντων).[136] Posting in wood is easier than posting in papyrus, and hinging *tabulae* together makes posting a set of tablets as easy as posting one. If Septimius Severus posted *subscriptiones* this way, and brought this technique to Egypt, a practical and effective wooden prototype that builds upon a long Roman tradition has been *imitated* in papyrus. Here, the very unlikelihood and inconvenience of the process argues for strong imperial influence.

The varying uses of papyrus double-documents in Judaea, Arabia, and Egypt, and the differences in drafting they exhibit, both from area to area and over time, reflect a locally differentiated response to Roman authority and its known preferences for what a document should look like. There is no evidence to suggest that the Roman influence here was anything but indirect, a matter of reinforcing certain forms of behavior and setting certain types of example, the expression of a local response more restrained in Egypt than elsewhere. Yet there can be little doubt that the double-document and Roman authority were perceived to be associated, in Egypt and elsewhere. In the Book of Revelation, composed in the last quarter of the first century AD in western Asia Minor, a *biblion* of God's divine judgment not only is "written on the inside, and on the back" (as a scroll had been in Ezekiel 2:9–10), but also sealed with seven seals.[137] The addition of the seals to the image between the Old Testament and the New, the cry that no one was worthy to open the *biblion* and break its seals, and the execution of

---

[134] Cf. D'Ors and Martin (1979) 118; even W. Williams (1980) 293–4 admits the validity of their observation, while disputing their suggested solution. The posting of papyrus is not impossible, see Gleason (1986) 116 (quoting the *Life* of Joshua the Stylite, χάρτης).

[135] *IGBulg.* 4.2236 (= *SIG³* 888, Skaptopara in Thrace), *ex libro libellorum rescriptorum . . . et propositorum Romae in portico thermarum Traianarum*, the meaning of the phrase much disputed, cf. W. Williams (1986) 203; these subscriptions were not posted in the sacralized heart of the old city (as military *diplomata* were, for example, posted on the Capitolium), but in the portico of Trajan's baths, a sign of their different nature.

[136] *P.Oxy.* 2131 (AD 207); the Greek version must, however, add an extra word, "glued together," to make the meaning clear; the two earlier references to posted petitions (*BGU* 970 + 525, AD 177; *P.Oxy.* 4481, AD 179) do not mention συγκόλλησις. *PSI* 1026 (= *CPL* 117; Caesarea, AD 150) is also copied *ex libello proposito cum alis in portico Iuniae ba*[–]; *cum alis* (paralleled in *P.Yadin* 33–4 (μεθ' ἑτέρων) also does not imply glued rather than hinged together.

[137] For place and date, Collins (1992) 701; Rev. 5:1, βιβλίον γεγραμμένον ἔσωθεν καὶ ὄπισθεν κατεσφραγισμένον σφραγῖσιν ἑπτά; and Rev. 5:2, τίς ἄξιος;

202 *The evolution of practice*

God's will that commenced when the seals were broken and the document opened, all point to an image to which frightening weight is now being attributed. It is identified, surely correctly, as a double-document.[138] One powerful image in one influential book proves nothing, but combined with the revival of double-documents in Greek around this time points more convincingly to the significant if indirect impact of the way of drafting documents the Romans favored.

(c) Mesopotamia and Syria. Eighty years later and hundreds of miles further east, some of the same indirect influence – the same impulse to adjust documentary practice to a Roman model and a Roman standard – was also felt. The Romans took Dura Europos, on the Euphrates river, in AD 165, but left only a small garrison consisting mostly, or only, of Palmyrene archers. Even so, there was a response. By AD 180, there is a "considerable revival of Greco-Macedonian institutions," for example, and although the first two surviving legal documents after the Roman advent were still written on parchment, there are clear signs of an awareness of a different – Roman – standard. In the first, *P.Dura* 25 of AD 180, the parchment is no longer cut halfway across, between the inner and outer texts, before the inner (upper) text is rolled over and closed,[139] and in both this and the second, *P.Dura* 31 of AD 204, dating is by the old Seleucid system, by Roman consuls, *and* by the *imperium* of Roman emperors. In the first, the inner and outer texts are as similar as those of Babatha's legal documents had been: a phrase missing here or there ("his son," "living in the village Nabagath . . .," "the *katagraphe* is authoritative") on the inside, but basically exact copies, with the witnesses listed at the end of the outer text. The second, however, *P.Dura* 31 of AD 204 from the village of Ossa in Syria, shows a greater divergence between the two texts. Only in the outer text is the Roman-style dating given; only in the outer text is the stipulation given ("in good faith they questioned each other and have agreed with each other"); only in the outer text is the agreement to avoid quarrelling over written instruments specified. What would impress Romans is here, in the outer text. The scribe writing the interior version was pressed for space, to be sure, and he may just have enjoyed correcting the writer of the outer text,[140] but it looks as if some aspects of the text, although good to display openly, were quietly dispensed

---

[138] Sanders (1939) 590, defending the older reading of ὄπισθεν in Rev. 5:1; Turner (1978) 44.

[139] Cutting and rolling is characteristic of the early Ptolemaic (and pre-Roman Dura, Welles *et al.* [1959] 14) way of doubling a document, see Turner (1978) 38; interior texts in the later papyrus double-documents at Dura are merely rolled up and sealed.

[140] Scribal personality, cf. Welles *et al.* (1959) 129, 163 (making corrections), and 165 (improving the model); 164 lists all the changes made in *P.Dura* 31 in the inner text.

Roman tablets and related forms in the provinces 203

with on the inside. It may be that in the city of Dura itself, in other words, the physical form and the relation of inner and outer text more closely approximated a Roman standard, while in the village at least some Roman trappings were put on for show.

After AD 208, the Roman presence in Dura intensified, although by 265 the Romans would be gone, and one hundred years after that Ammianus Marcellinus, in an elegiac mood, noted that the abandoned city was overrun by deer.[141] In these sixty years, Roman soldiers appear more frequently in all the documents from Syria and Mesopotamia, which are now for the most part on papyrus[142] – rather than skins or parchment – and a good number of which are doubled, written in Greek with paleographic Latinisms and (translated or transliterated) Roman legal language, even if imperfectly used,[143] and witnessed by city decurions.[144] Documents drawn up in the city continue until mid century to have their witnesses sign at the bottom of the outer text, but in local villages and other cities of Mesopotamia witnesses sign on the verso, next to the knots that closed the document.[145] Moreover, in the surviving texts from the area after AD 225, the inner text is always dramatically shortened, a mere one-to-three-line summary of the exterior text, not an exact or even approximate copy.[146] This seems to be an abrupt change in direction after the two documents of AD 180 and 204, an intentional rather than inadvertent shortening of

---

[141] AD 208: Welles *et al.* (1959) 25; deer, 24.1.5 (AD 363).

[142] Others in addition to *P.Dura* are *P.Euphr.* 6–11, 13–17 (AD 232–52), and *P.Euphr.Syr.* A and B. Papyrus, Welles *et al.* (1959) 4 (it was especially used by the army, also); the use of papyrus in this part of the world, where skins and parchment were the norm, was a sign of Roman influence, Feissel and Gascou (1995) 66, Feissel *et al.* (1997) 4 n.3 (seen in Palmyra also); *P.Euphr.* 12 (AD 244, Beth Phouraia) is still written on leather, and has a Syriac subscription.

[143] Doubled, *P.Dura* 26–7, 29–30, and 32; *P.Euphr.* 6–10 (AD 249–52) and 12 (AD 244, on leather), and *P.Euphr.Syr.* A and B. Paleographic Latinisms, Feissel and Gascou (1995) 95, 107 (in *P.Euphr.* 3–5, petitions). Legal language: Welles *et al.* (1959) 21; Teixidor (1990) 165 (in Syriac documents), Feissel *et al.* (1997) 5.

[144] Welles *et al.* (1959) 6.

[145] Welles *et al.* (1959) 15–16. Bottom of exterior: *P.Dura* 27 (AD 225–40) and 29 (AD 251); verso: only *P.Dura* 32 (AD 254) from the city; *P.Dura* 26 (Sachare, AD 227) and 30 (Qatna, AD 232), *P.Euphr.Syr.* A (Marcoupolis Thera?, AD 240), *P.Euphr.Syr.* B (Marcoupolis Thera, AD 242), *P.Dura* 28 (Edessa, AD 243), *P.Euphr.* 6–7 (Marcoupolis Thera, AD 249), and *P.Euphr.* 10 (Carrhae, AD 250).

[146] *P.Dura* 26 (AD 227), deed of sale, the interior text "much reduced," although it "nevertheless contains all the essential details except the date"; *P.Dura* 30 (AD 232), marriage contract, inner text one line long; *P.Dura* 28 (AD 243), Syriac deed of sale, inner text "much abbreviated"; *P.Euphr.* 6–7, sale of slave (AD 249) and 10, sale of mare (AD 250), much abbreviated inner texts; *P.Dura* 29 (AD 251), deposit, interior text one line long; *P.Euphr.* 8 (AD 251) and 9 (AD 252), sales of slave, interior texts very brief; *P.Dura* 32 (AD 254), divorce agreement, upper text three lines long. *P.Dura* 27 (AD 225–40), deed of sale, is fragmentary. Two contemporary Syriac parchments (*P.Euphr.Syr.* A and B, from Marcoupolis Thera, AD 240 and 242), have more extensive interior texts, but are not true copies either.

204 *The evolution of practice*

the inner text going hand in hand with other more obviously Roman features. The inevitable conclusion is that at some point between AD 200 and 227, the treatment of the inner text of a doubled papyrus document came to be deemed unimportant by Romans themselves, and that fact was communicated through army scribes to other document writers.

There is only one highly idiosyncratic Italian parallel that is approximately contemporary, a "diploma" of a boxer demonstrating his membership in an athletic club in Naples from AD 194. In this document the interest has clearly shifted from the interior text to the exterior, which has eleven separate autograph subscriptions authorizing the payment of prize-money not included in the interior.[147] It is an honor-roll of a career in progress, not a certificate of a one-time achievement, and – in addition to proving the truth of the adage that to those who have, more shall be given – it demonstrates the never-ceasing achievements of the man and looks to the future rather than back to the point where he had started. This may be the significance of the change to legal documents in the third century as well: the denaturing of the interior text could be confirming the fact that documents were rarely opened, the *fides* of sealers or signers rarely challenged; that the process of the document's creation was authoritative, as was postulated for military diplomas; and that, above all, it was now context, how a document could be used after its generation, rather than what it was and the way it fixed what was done, that was now the overwhelming focus of interest. The Roman legal document no longer just finished the act, but assumed a future for itself that was looking more and more important. This influence of context on document had been part of the Roman story from the earliest appearance of *tabulae* in Campania, where formality was overlain with *fides*, but took various other forms in subsequent centuries, manifesting itself here with the dramatic reduction of the inner text of doubled documents but ending in the fourth century with the disappearance of doubling, whether in wood or papyrus, altogether.[148] Although some inhabitants of the province of Mesopotamia may have continued to depend on the Greek city-archives in Dura-Europus and elsewhere, and the denaturing of the interior texts

---

[147] *P.Lond.* 1178 (= *W.Chr.* 156), interior text sealed with three seals on the verso (Turner [1978] 28–9).

[148] Very few wooden legal documents survive from after the mid-third century, while contemporary wooden tablets for school- or copy-practice survive in elevated numbers, see Hoogendijk and van Minnen (1991) 101, who argue that even the (non-doubled) legal documents preserved on wood from late-antique Egypt were exercises of this sort; they are written not on wax, but directly onto the wood with ink. *ChLA* 5.282 (third century AD) preserves a fragmentary agreement (ὁμολογία) strengthened by stipulations in both Greek and Latin, δισσὴν γραφῖσαν, probably referring to the generation of two copies. Wooden documents from fifth-century AD North Africa are not doubled, Courtois *et al.* (1952) 9–11.

of their documents might be attributable to that and judged a part of the overall arc of what happens to Greek double-documents in Greek areas, if Romans had continued to insist on the first-century AD standard seen in Campania and elsewhere, these people would have followed. It was only because the Roman standard had changed that provincial practice, when it looked to Rome, did as well.

(d) Conclusion. When Romans established themselves, or settled, they brought their own documentary forms and attitudes with them. This is uncontroversial in the western provinces (where no other documentary habits are known to have existed) and notable in Egypt (where existing habits provide a clear contrast), but demonstrable also in eastern provinces in the second and third centuries, the evidence here provided mostly by the responses of the non-Roman population. Yet as the evolution of Campanian documents showed, and as the use of double-documents strikingly suggests, what was an acceptable documentary form diversified, and attitudes themselves underwent adjustment over time, making the existence and effect of a Roman "model" or standard more complex and more difficult to trace. The model itself was a moving target, as was true of the dynamic of romanization at any time, but an influential model, the prevailing style at the perceived center having a proponderant influence on the form adopted when Roman practice was introduced into a province. As one moves further East and later in time, away from the extremes of the enforced hierarchy and trumpeted exclusivity of early imperial Egypt and towards the looser jurisdictions of a post-212 border area, the sharp profile of Roman practice had softened. For the difference between the Arabia and Judaea of Babatha's time, or the great cities of the second-century Greek East, and the Syria and Mesopotamia of a subsequent century is not just that of the quality and the acumen of its scribes, although that must have been important; the clarity and definition with which the Romans conducted their own business must have been a factor as well. Amidst Greeks and Egyptians in the early empire, Romans adhered to a Roman (and clearly different) standard; amidst non-Greeks, a century later, Romans permitted an intermediate, Greek-looking standard as an acceptable substitute for Roman ways;[149] and sometime after AD 204, the most distinctive Roman features of even that hybrid type were gradually abandoned. What was done by the scribes used by Roman citizens and others in mid-third-century Dura, Beth Phouraia, Edessa, Marcopolis, or in the army camps of two different

---

[149] See, on Palestine, Rosén (1980); Millar (1995), and Cotton (1999) 228 for the tendency of Roman influence to express itself through Greek language and forms in the easternmost provinces and border areas of the empire.

206 *The evolution of practice*

Roman cohorts was careful, legitimate, and different from what had been done – carefully and legitimately – in first-century Vindonissa, Carlisle, or Oxyrhynchus; and by the end of the third century true double-documents in either wood or papyrus were rare.

WHY DOES ROMAN PRACTICE IN PROVINCIAL SETTINGS CHANGE?

The existence of a Roman standard and the importance of a Roman form, established above all at the time of its introduction, set many of the parameters of what a legal document for Romans or pleasing to a Roman audience should look like. Even so, within this Roman paradigm, change – visible only at the provincial level (since virtually nothing from Rome or Italy survives) and seemingly incorporating some local characteristics – did occur. "Seemingly" is an important word here, however: even in Egypt, where such adaptations are easiest (but not easy) to see, this change was not the result of direct influence from local documentary practice on Roman. Rather, Roman emperors and officials themselves demonstrated and thereby promoted at least some of these adjustments, giving an authoritative example to follow, as Hadrian had in the case of prefectural subscription. In Roman Egypt and the Roman East, two other significant changes in Roman documentary practice, in addition to the ones already described, occurred between AD 60 and AD 250. One was the second-century introduction of author-protagonist subscriptions for *tabulae* associated with formal acts; the other was the third-century displacement of wooden *tabulae* by papyrus for some Roman legal documents. In each case significant Roman imperial precedents can be found, and these changes therefore located within an evolution of Roman documents understood as driven above all by Roman reasons. These are not examples of the penetration of Roman practice by eastern ones, but the deliberate adjustment of Roman practice to Roman priorities and purposes.

All too often these two changes in Roman legal documents are depicted as invasive, as tendrils of local practice that strangled the purity of the Roman way, great if silent incursions that eventually led to oriental victory in the great *Kulturkampf* between East and West.[150] But legal change cannot be perfectly insidious, a virus insinuating itself silently into an unsuspecting host; it must be approved. Therefore, at its simplest, any change

---

[150] E.g., Amelotti (1980) 388 (specifically on subscription: "Eindringen"), or Arangio-Ruiz (1974 [1953]) 388, subscription "un uso ellenistico penetrato nei testamenti romani."

Roman tablets and related forms in the provinces   207

in acceptable Roman practice must also be a Roman change. As timing and context show, Romans, rather than being overwhelmed by the tsunami of foreign practice, instead fished happily and comfortably from the ocean, adapting and adjusting as they had once modulated their formulaic *certa verba* to maintain legitimacy and freedom of action all at once. For two centuries of empire, Roman legal practice had a sharp enough profile to know itself and be noticed and imitated by others, but also a notable capacity to change on its own terms, to absorb what it wanted from subjects and give the product back to them to be imitated in turn. Although this is merely one of the many dynamics of cultural change in the Roman empire, it is an important one.

Subscriptio, meaning the addition of a sentence (not merely a name) to a document, is found in documents of formal acts in Egypt (only), starting most likely in AD 131. This is the date of the copy of the first surviving Roman will with the Greek subscription, "I, Marcus Sempronius Priscus, have collated the will and it has been acknowledged by me as written."[151] Antonius Silvanus's will has a Greek subscription couched in very similar terms: "I, the above-written Antonius Silvanus, have collated my will as above, and it has been acknowledged and pleased me just as it is written," as do others.[152] This "collation" is reading through and checking the document, its Latin equivalent being *recognovi*, regularly found in attested copies and also in imperial subscripts; a third-century AD equivalent from Rome, added to a mancipation of property already strengthened by a stipulation, reads "just as it has been written above I have agreed, subscribed, and sealed."[153] Greek subscriptions to Latin texts are also found on two *testationes* of birth for illegitimate children, the first in AD 131: "I, the above-written Epimachus son of Longinus . . . have attested that the daughter Longinia was born as is set out [above]."[154] They also appear on three *cretiones*, statements of entry into an inheritance, in AD 151 and after; on a request for a tutor of AD 198; on a third-century manumission; and finally on a third-century profession of legitimate birth, subscribed once by the declarer and once by an unknown person, who writes, *recogn[ovi]* after the notation *exemplum*

---

[151] *ChLA* 10.412 (ἀντεβαλόμ[ην] . . . καὶ ἐπανεγνώσθη).

[152] Sentence, not name (and thus not conceptually the same as our signature), Bruns (1882 [1876]) 43–9 (an old debate even then). Antonius Silvanus, *CPL* 221 (= *FIRA²* 3.129–32 no. 47; AD 142); others, *P.Oxy.* 2857 (AD 134), *ChLA* 47.1403 (= *P.Coll.Youtie* 64; AD 211), *P.Oxy.* 2348 (AD 224).

[153] Copies, above n.132; imperial subscriptions, Mourgues (1995a) 267–300 (where the collation is often done by another, not the emperor himself). Mancipation: *CIL* 6.10247 (= *FIRA²* 3.301–3 no. 95; AD 252), Statia Irene gives away a monument, *sicut supra scriptum est consensi subscripsi et adsignavi*. In a contract: *D.* 44.7.61.*pr.* (Scaevola; ἐπέγνων . . . προγέγραπται).

[154] *CPL* 160 (= *BGU* 1690; *FIRA²* 3.11–12 no. 5); *CPL* 162 (= *P.Mich.* 3.169; *FIRA²* 3.9–11 no. 4, AD 145), ἐμαρτυροποιησάμην and written for her by another.

208 The evolution of practice

subscrip[tionis]. acc(eptum) and a date.[155] Five of the eight of these last are by or for women, the subscriptiones themselves written by a guardian or other male as a way (probably) of demonstrating approval of the woman's legal act.[156] All of these subscriptions are a form of adhésion personelle, as O. Guéraud called them,[157] but there are some differences. Those made for wills confirm a text and follow official and imperial language for doing so; those made for the other acts restate the verb of the act, which in the interior text was in the third person, and in Latin, in the first person in Greek. "She attested" becomes "I attested," "he freed" becomes "I freed," and "he professed" becomes "I registered." More extreme changes in language – in two of the cretiones, "she attested that she had entered into and made cretio for the inheritance" becomes "I entered into the inheritance" – show again that, just as in the combinational acceptilatio-discharges from Campania, the chirograph-style text was not intended as the precise legal equivalent of the interior text but an addition to it. Personal commitment is layered onto wooden double-documents, following either the official and imperial style or a simple chirograph style, but indeed is never required of any document or situation before very late antiquity.[158]

Chirograph-style endorsements of scribally generated documents, whether written in the first or the third person, were known in Egypt before AD 131. Romans had appended their subscriptions to financial documents there from an early date,[159] and locals had done so even in the Ptolemaic period.[160] This habit has therefore been all too readily identified

[155] Cretiones, CPL 213 (= PSI 1027; FIRA² 3.179–80 no. 59), her mother ἐμαρτυροποιησάμην and another wrote for her; CPL 214 (= FIRA² 3.181–2 no. 60) and 215, both AD 170, same woman προσῆλθον τῇ κληρονομίᾳ, written by her brother. Request for tutor, CPL 202 (= SB 6223; FIRA² 3.68–9 no. 25, AD 198), αἰτησάμη<ν κύριον> . . . Ἰούλιον; manumission, CPL 172 (= FIRA² 3.23–5 no. 11, AD 211 or 221), μεταξὺ φίλων ἠλευθέρωσα; professio, CPL 163 (= SB 9200; FIRA² 3.3–5 no. 1, AD 242), ἀπογράφ[ομαι.

[156] Approval, argued by Gardner (1999) 25 for Campanian documents; cf. P.Hamb. 101 (act unknown: a contract?), subscribed by M. Aurelius Severus, "I write as κύριος of my mother according to the customs of the Romans."

[157] Guéraud (1940) 28 (he assumes, p. 29, that professiones of birth had them, but they did not survive).

[158] Bruns (1882 [1876]) 77–111. Exceptions: if a testator wished to leave the writer of his will something, he had to indicate this with a subscriptio in his own hand (the example uses dictavi et recognovi, D. 48.10.1.8; Marcian); and codicils had to be handwritten.

[159] E.g., acknowledgments of debt written either as Roman or as Greek chirographs: ChLA 47.1340 (= SB 12609, AD 27), written in Latin by another (fateor me tibei debere) and subscribed ἔλαβον ὡς πρόκ(ειται); BGU 69 (AD 120), written in Greek by another (ὁμολογῶ ἔχιν παρά σου and subscribed ἔλαβον); ChLA 5.303 (= CPL 188, P.Mich. 7.438; AD 143), written first in Latin ([–] ac[c]ep[isse et de]bere with a stipulation, subscribed fragmentarily in Greek); ChLA 42.1207 (= CPL 189, P.Fouad 45; AD 153), written first in Latin (fateor me accepisse et debere, subscribed ἔλαβα [sic] καὶ ὀφίλω); SB 13030 (Priest [1983], AD 203) is subscribed by a cavalry signifer.

[160] Subscriptions may have begun in the late Ptolemaic times, although Mitteis (1912) 56 seems more certain than Kunkel (1933) 257; Mitteis notes that in Roman times it was "sogar die Regel" for

Roman tablets and related forms in the provinces

as merely a Greco-Egyptian intrusion into Roman ways of doing things,[161] but the slow pace at which this proceeds in *tabulae* of formal acts and the way in which it adds on to, rather than replaces, the interior and exterior Latin acts suggests that it was employed as an acceptable improvement to a traditional practice, one which indeed helped also to incorporate the necessary approval of a tutor. Imperial example was also probably important and helps to explain the timing of this improvement's appearance. Hadrian's subscription on the petition of the priests at the temple of Soxis in AD 131 had read, simply, "I have subscribed" (ὑπέγραψα);[162] there were no doubt others that have not survived, and all together provided an immediate model for those subscribing documents like wills or, as argued above, petitions. But his posting of a subscribed petition also conveyed the fact that subscribing a Roman document, even an official one doubled on a wooden diptych that would be inspected by a Roman authority, was not reprehensible. Because it was endorsed at the highest level, it could occur.

It is possible that this tight connection between Hadrian's subscription of a petition in Egypt and a change in Roman documentary practice will one day crumble when another, earlier Latin wood document is found that includes a Greek subscription. Arguing from limited bodies of evidence has its risks, including that of later embarrassment. But in that case it would also be appropriate to remember that subscription of *tabulae* was not an invention of the second century AD, but was practiced already in the late Republic, for example, when *tabulae* of accusations were subscribed by both the major accuser and any who joined the prosecution with him,[163] and censors making *notae* next to a man's name were sometimes said to

---

documents couched in the third person. Kreller (1919) 327 observes that testator-subscriptions become common *only* in Greek wills of the Roman period. The desire to subscribe sent customers to the ὑπογραφεύς "underwriter" (Youtie [1975]), who subscribed for others but was not the same person as the scribe writing the document; his counterpart in Arabia-Judaea was the χειροχρήστης "hand-user" (Cotton [1995]).

[161] E.g., Arangio-Ruiz (1974 [1942b]), on subscription, and (1974 [1948]), on the subscribed chirographs, above nn.159–60, in general reflecting both Egyptian practice and a Hellenistic origin; updated Camodeca (1992) 174 n.32. Here too, the two earliest chirographs with subscriptions are written by another rather than in the protagonist's own hand; the majority are from the mid-second century and after.

[162] See above n.128.

[163] Accusations, e.g., Cic. *Inv.* 2.58, *Q. fr.* 3.3.2, or *Apoc.* 14 (against Claudius); cf. *D.* 48.2.3.2 (Paulus), and 48.2.7.*pr.* (Ulpian), "so that no one should readily leap to an accusation since he knows that his accusation will not be brought without risk to himself," *ne facile quis prosiliat ad accusationem, cum sciat inultam sibi accusationem non futuram.* Cf. Paulus *Sent.* 5.16.14, *CJ* 9.1.3 (AD 222), Kübler (1931) col. 491, and Jones (1972) 64, 129 n.121.

210   *The evolution of practice*

have *subscripserunt*.[164] In these cases as in the legal examples above, the man (or woman and man) making the *subscriptio* is literally an "underwriter," a man who puts himself on the line for the act undertaken, asserting his responsibility for it through a statement. Here too subscription was a personal endorsement of a text that in itself was already authoritative, as was the case, for example, in the *subscriptio* of a city-founder on a surveyor's map or of a prefect on a *tabula* of *honesta missio*.[165] Value was always added, not created, by subscription. When emperors subscribed letters, they often add in their own hand only "*vale*" (as private citizens also did, for slaves or others did the actual work of writing),[166] but no one dared doubt that these letters were imperial letters; when they subscribed petitions, the same was true – the answer drafted by another was looked over by the emperor and then subscribed. This way of subscribing, of underwriting to commit yourself to the act as written, was and always had been a Roman rather than a Greek custom, especially in what J.-L. Mourgues has called the Roman "chancery" where official Roman documents of all sorts were generated.[167]

The last of the Egyptian examples given of a subscribed *tabulae* (above p. 207) also points to the second change occurring for some documents. This *professio* of legitimate birth, with a third-person Latin statement (*professus est*) followed by a subscription that uses the Greek verb ἀπογράφ[ομαι ("I register"), the standard verb used in the Egyptian census-return,[168] is then subscribed with *acceptum*, a date and the remark, "I have collated (this)," this second subscription noted as having been copied. The way in which this document is generated and handled has therefore changed quite notably: what had previously been copied at the behest of the parent from a *tabula* posted by the prefect is now, in AD 242, a declaration subscribed by the parent, handed in, and returned with an official's subscription – although since this last subscription is copied, there may well have been two copies of this declaration, one of which was subscribed but not returned. What has happened? This *professio* of birth is being treated like a kind of petition.[169] There has thus been a conceptual

---

[164] Cic. *Cluent.* 118, 126, 130, 132; Liv. 39.42.6 (*adscriberent notas*), Asc. on Cic. *in Toga Candida* 75, *titulos* specifically *subscripserunt*, as in Gel. 4.20.6 (a man had made *iocus scurrilis* before the censor).

[165] Founder, *manu conditoris subscriptum*, Hyg. grom. L203, 2–4L (Campbell [2000] 158), the *forma* here called an *instrumentum*; prefects only known to have subscribed discharge-*tabulae* in two cases, *AE* 1980.647 (AD 108) and *CPL* 113 (AD 122). As Mitteis (1908) 305 n.58 notes, text and subscription can be referred to as if two separate documents.

[166] Emperors, Mourgues (1995a) 271–3 (who sees here, however, an authenticating function); subscribing letters, e.g., Cicero and Pliny, Bruns (1882 [1876]) 70–1.

[167] Mourgues (1995b), esp. 122 (where he dismisses apparent Ptolemaic parallels).

[168] Bagnall and Frier (1994) 23.

[169] Noted by Guéraud (1940) 34.

Roman tablets and related forms in the provinces

change in what the *professio* is: from an act done in the presence of the praetor, posted on *tabulae*, and subsequently copied it has become a subscribed statement that asserts, at least, that a *professio* was made *apud praetorem*, a statement-and-subscription then read over or collated and approved. By becoming a petition, the *professio* of legitimate birth can also change in another way, seen in the three *professiones* that survive between AD 194/196 and 224. The earliest, very fragmentary, is on papyrus rather than wood, and seems to have the statement of the birth in Latin (written, as all its predecessors were, in the third person), followed by a one-line first-person subscription of the father in Greek.[170] Two from AD 224 are very similar, although the use of Greek is very limited (the papyri are damaged here); they are glued together, and perhaps were part of a longer roll of similar declarations.[171] Categorization as petition permits submission on papyrus; or submission on papyrus permits treatment and categorization as petition. It is marginally more likely that the first was the case, since the prefect controlled the practices of his own office, but at any rate, by the end of the second century, a "birth-certificate" could now be a document (of papyrus or wood) handed in (probably in duplicate), subscribed, and handed back to the parent, with one subscribed copy left in an archive.

The same happened to the process by which tutors for women were given, and at about the same time. In the subscribed wooden *tabula* of AD 198 mentioned above, the tutor is given, in response to a request written out twice as a Greek subscription, in the third person and in Latin. The whole document may in fact have been copied from a posted *exemplum*, as was traditional, right down to the subscriptions (although this last was surely new).[172] In contrast, the three nominations that follow (in AD 236, 245, and 247) are multi-handed documents on papyrus. They all have, in varying levels of completeness, the woman's request (in Latin: "*rogo, domine*"); her subscription in Greek ("I have handed in the petition, *bibl [idia]*") through someone who subscribes for her; the proposed tutor's Greek subscription of agreement; a first-person Latin statement from the prefect approving

---

[170] *ChLA* 3.214 (= *CPL* 158, *P.Oxy.* 894, *W.Chr.* 213). There is very little of the Greek subscription left, but what there is looks to be in a different hand from the Latin (so, cautiously, D. Martinez – with my thanks); this is, therefore, most likely an original, not a copy.

[171] *ChLA* 47.1412 (= *P.Oxy.* 2565; AD 224); the two are glued together side by side (not head to foot), the second not fully deciphered. The Greek of line 10, καὶ ὡς χ(ρηματίζει), is paralleled in another birth-certificate, *CPL* 164 line 6 (= *P.Michael.* 61, καὶ ὡς ἐχρ[ημάτιζε; this should date to the third century) and possibly part of a subscription like that of the νομικός in *SB* 9298 (below n.177), checking and approving the text.

[172] *CPL* 202 (= *SB* 6223; *FIRA*² 3.68–9 no. 25; includes formula *d.e.r.e.e.b.t.s.s*, see above n.12). The use of the third person, in contrast to the use of the first person in the two nominations that follow, was emphasized by Grenfell (1917–19) 260.

212   *The evolution of practice*

this (written by one of his secretaries, still noting *e lege Iulia et Titia et ex s.c.*); and, finally, the prefect's Latin subscription, "*legi*" or "*cepi*."[173] The nomination from AD 245 and another from AD 261 also call themselves "translations of the Romans," and give archival references to the τ(όμος) and κόλ(λημα) where they can be found.[174] In the third century, therefore, a request for a Roman tutor could be submitted in Latin on papyrus, with various Greek subscriptions, then annotated by the prefect's staff and the prefect himself, thereafter to be returned to the petitioner. Either two copies were submitted and one copy was archived,[175] or, after AD 247, one original was archived and it was from this archived copy that people were allowed to take copies. In either case, these requests for tutors were also being treated as petitions had been in the second or third centuries. Here also one further element in the transformation is known: "it is necessary," said the third-century jurist Modestinus, "for the woman to attest before the tribunal or otherwise in the *hypomnemata*; it is possible also to hand in *biblidia* extrajudicially, as the emperors themselves say."[176] These changes, couched as the widening of possible avenues, were "made possible" by the emperors themselves. The third-century examples of requests for *bonorum possessio* in cases of invalid wills or intestacy seem to suggest the same transformation: the amalgamation of the steps of request (*rogo, domine, des* . . .), subscription (by another, for an illiterate), and response into one papyrus document, akin to a petition, at the beginning of the third century.[177]

All of these cases involve acts that traditionally called for the direct intervention of the praetor, sometimes even his presence, as in declarations of birth. Over time, however, there was a subtle shift in the relationship of prefect and performer: what began as an act with a high-status audience in an

---

[173] *ChLA* 5.290 (= *CPL* 203, *P.Mich.* 3.165; a copy), *ChLA* 46.1361 (= *CPL* 204, *P.Oxy.* 1466; AD 245) and *ChLA* 4.269 (= *CPL* 205, *P.Oxy.* 720; an original).

[174] The second is *P.Oxy.* 2710 (AD 261): ἑρμηνεία τῶν Ῥωμαικῶν; *ChLA* 46.1361 has κόλ[λημα] ϙδ τ(όμος) εἷς, *P.Oxy.* 2710 τόμ(ος) α´.

[175] Modrzejewski (1974) 288 n.75; in the same note, he notes the similarities to what happens in declarations of birth.

[176] D. 27.1.13.10: χρῆ δέ μιᾷ μαρτύρασθαι πρὸ βήματος ἢ ἄλλως ἐπὶ ὑπομνημάτων· δύναται δὲ καὶ βιβλίδια ἐπιδοῦναι χαμᾶθεν, ὡς οἱ αὐτοί φασιν αὐτοκράτορες.

[177] See especially *ChLA* 28.865 (= *SB* 13610, *P.Daris* inv. 200 + *ChLA* 4.247 = *P.Ryl.* 610; AD 223), with Latin request, Greek subscription ("I have given βιβλίδια"), subscription and "*recognovi*," and marks of filing and reference to *exemplum testationis*; *ChLA* 11.486 (= *CPL* 216, *SB* 1010, *FIRA²* 3.182–4 no. 61, AD 249), which also has a Greek ἑρμηνεία, and *SB* 9298 is a Greek copy of the entirety with subscription of a νομικὸς Ῥωμαικός ("I have acted, χρηματίζω, and I translated"); *ChLA* 4.233 (= *P.Oxy.* 1201, AD 258), subscribed *ex edicto: legi*; followed by a "translation from the Latin" of the text of the petition; marks of filing; *PSI* 1101 (a copy; AD 271); and *P.Mich.* inv. 1946 (Gagos and Heilporn [2001], with Latin request; Greek subscription; *ex edicto*; *legi* restored; and marks of filing).

Roman tablets and related forms in the provinces 213

official setting completed by a tablet became a petitionary or supplicatory act to an authority often called *dominus*. The formal independence of an act was being lost as the presence of the granting authority loomed larger, as ceremony became petition, and as papyrus was allowed to substitute for wood. Not every act was drawn into the prefect's web, mummified, devoured, and regurgitated as petitionary activity or as an act preserved in his *hypomnemata* (to be discussed in the next chapter). Business that Romans transacted amongst themselves, like mancipatory wills, emancipations of children, and manumissions *inter amicos*, are in the third century AD still performed with tablets, although only a handful of examples or references survive.[178] Only by the fourth century do *tabulae*, doubled or not, seem to be truly gone, at least in Egypt.

The several hundred years in which first-person subscriptions and doubled wooden documents coexisted, and the similarly long tolerance for papyrus and wood at the same time in Egypt, have suggested to scholars that – moral judgments about the weakening of Roman legal fiber aside – the impact of one documentary practice on another was a direct one, an experiment performed in the laboratory of Egypt that foreshadowed the great mixing that was to take place in the centuries after AD 212.[179] It seems to me, rather, that the documentary history of Egypt shows much the opposite. Romans behaved differently, and this was known to be the case, but the responses or imitations this provoked in the local population seem to have been few: perhaps Greek wills started to be written *transversa* and sealed, for example, but other than that the difference between the responsiveness of the Egyptian population and that of other peoples in a position perforce to admire Roman peculiarity is more marked than the impact itself the Romans had before the third century, a fact that must be related at least in part to the legal separation of the various populations enforced by Roman authority. This has been noted before: the overall impact the Romans had

---

[178] Wills: Amelotti (1966) 54 believes that the ταβέλλας of *PSI* 293 (a fragmentary transcript of a court case) are tablets of a will. Emancipation: *ChLA* 12.251 (= *CPL* 206; Oxyrhynchus, third century AD), an *exemplum mancipation[is]* seemingly taken from *tabulae conligar[–]*; by AD 502 it too was an act whose "the fullest force" (*plenissimum robur*) could be achieved through the presentation of written "supplications" and *testificationes* to a competent judge, *CJ* 8.48(49).5 (AD 502). Manumissions: *CPL* 172 (Hermopolis, AD 211), *CPL* 173 (Oxyrhynchus, AD 241); only the *actum* formula survives in Latin, but the tablet is probably incomplete. Adoption – three emancipations and two manumissions – also provides an example of an act that once had to be performed, or performed before the magistrate, becoming petitionary, *CJ* 8.47(48).3 (AD 286); four years later, participants are reminded that "customarily" (*solet*) adoption is not performed on *tabulae* but *apud praesidem*, and clearly there was confusion about tablets, petitions, and performance here too, *CJ* 8.47(48).4 (AD 290).

[179] Perhaps most strongly stated by Taubenschlag (1955) 27–51.

214   *The evolution of practice*

in Egypt has not been deemed to be great.[180] None of this means, however, that the reverse is true, that Romans became saturated with Greco-Egyptian habits instead. They could and did enter into all manner of local financial transactions drawn up according to local law, in itself not surprising, since local enforcement must have been a concern of all the parties involved.[181] But otherwise the two most notable changes, the introduction of subscriptions into formal documents and the gradual substitution of papyrus for wood, suggest that local influence, if this is what it was, was mediated by authoritative example: that these changes would not have occurred had the procedures of the prefect not led the way, and that the prefect himself would not have changed his own practices, and what he would accept, had not the emperor's example inspired him to do so. We are again back at the principle that it is the model at the center that is decisive and influential, setting the paradigm for documentary practice both at the moment when a strong Roman presence is introduced into a province and subsequently, as when, in Egypt, the emperor comes to visit.

If true, at least for this narrow facet of the Roman experience, this suggests that the process of cultural adaptation and change in the Roman empire is above all a mediated experience. This is not a revolutionary concept for the study of the Roman impact, where the reception of Roman ideals, habits, and material culture is regularly understood to be tied to the political cooptation of a local elite.[182] The evidence of legal practice and habits gathered here shows that influences from her great empire on Rome were similarly mediated. When changes in documentary practices occurred, even those that through superficial similarity appear to be a local (Roman) response to a local (non-Roman) influence were actually mediated by authorities who by their example made a practice not only acceptable but Roman. Indeed, when looked at more closely, these changes have a long Roman back-story and a clear Roman motivation. The addition of witness- and actor-subscriptions to *tabulae* is part of the much larger story of the addition of *fides* to formal acts, which can also help to account for the attenuation of the interior text of a doubled act in the third century AD; a shift to papyrus for some wooden documents is part of the much larger

---

[180] The statements of Mitteis (1891) 109–10 are holding up well, despite challenges: see Modrzejewski (1970) 345–7; also, E. Seidl (1973) 49–55 (very few texts survive that suggest Roman law was even studied), and Youtie (1975) 203–4 (the Roman presence here did not express itself through Hellenization either, as in the east, above n.149).

[181] Taubenschlag (1955) 46–55; Modrzejewski (1970) 346.

[182] See Woolf (1998) for a careful recent version, and Edmondson (1993) 182–5 on the effects of legal practice; "Romanization" and the questions of identity it raises are now being rendered problematic, but these challenges are less relevant when legal questions are considered.

Roman tablets and related forms in the provinces 215

story of how papyrus had always played a role in Roman governance. There is of course constant cultural influence flowing in many different directions in Roman society, but hierarchy produces locks-keepers who will redefine Roman practice only if the result feels traditional at the same time. The Orontes may flow into the Tiber, but the Tiber then flows to the sea; none of its waters run uphill to the tops of Rome's seven hills without pumping, not even when the Tiber floods.

CHAPTER 8

Tablets and other documents in court to AD 400

Tabulae had their origins in ceremonial acts that, when performed correctly as ascertained by witnesses present and observing for flaws, were authoritative beyond the possibility of question. Only over time did the second life of tablets develop, the one in which *fides* sought to demonstrate its weight and proof of an act could be demanded – the life in which *tabulae*, rather than merely existing, were put to use in the business of daily life, as chapters six and seven have shown, but also, and perhaps especially, in court. Here *tabulae* in their various forms were quietly ubiquitous,[1] especially as peculiarly potent forms of proof, inducing Pompey-sized headaches in opposing counsel and inspiring some truly nimble argumentation in practitioners and theorists. But *fides* was aggressively important in this context too. Roman courts, as recent work has been showing, are not as familiar to us as we once thought: their dramas were less those in which truth was uncovered and more those in which carefully constructed plausibilities clashed, and in which, as a consequence, every fact had to be first embedded in the social standing that helped determine character, motive, and the limits of possibility.[2] *Fides* and prestige spoke powerfully and plausibly to judges and juries, telling them what people were like and what facts like those embodied by tablets actually meant; the conveyance or construction of *fides* and prestige was therefore the major frame taught by Roman rhetorical handbooks.[3]

---

[1] Ubiquity, shown by one of Trimalchio's dinner-party-gift riddles, gifts of meat and *tabulae* labelled with *pittacia* that read "dinner'd and forum'd" (*cenatoria et forensia*, Petr. *Sat.* 56.9), appropriate gifts for each occasion. In court settings: speeches can even be read from them, see (e.g.) Cic. *de Orat.* 1.174 (client's *tabellae*); Quint. *Inst.* 10.3.30 (*ceris*); Suet. *Claud.* 15.4 (defendant strikes Claudius with tablets and stylus he has with him); Mart. *Ep.* 5.51 (advocate whose left hand is weighted with *libelli* offered *codicilli* and *epistulae*); Philostr. *VA* 8.3, Apollonius is forbidden to take either a βιβλίον or γραμματεῖον into his trial. Not all agreed on whether one should recite written speeches, cf. Cic. *de Orat.* 1.150–5 and *Brut.* 91, and Plin. *Ep.* 1.20.9–25, but Cicero suggested, in *Planc.* 74, that his speech *Red. Sen. propter rei magnitudinem dicta de scripto est,* so here too the greater the occasion, the more likely the reading (as was seen also with reading from *tabulae* in chapter three).

[2] See (e.g.) Garnsey (1970) and Swarney (1993); I hope to do further work on this myself.

[3] E.g., *Rhet. Her.* 1.3 and Cic. *Inv.* 1.9 (*inventio* is devising of true or plausible); Cic. *Inv.* 1.27 says narrative is *rerum gestarum aut ut gestarum expositio*); *Inv.* 1.28, the narrative of a legal case should be

Although there were many reasons for *fides* and *tabulae* to intertwine over time in daily life, the two most often appeared together in the contested setting of the court, and this necessary propinquity must have laid at least some of the foundation for their subsequent layering. The fundamental nature of *tabulae* remained the same, while their value was augmented and qualitatively improved in the opinions both of those who made them and those who judged their value in court.

Yet over the centuries of Empire the context of the Roman court also helped to reduce the superior claims and absolute value of legal *tabulae* as *tabulae* – as wooden tablets of a certain shape, made in a certain way. Before the Late Empire there were no "rules of evidence" in Roman courts[4] – whether in the stage of formulary procedure that took place before judges or juries, or in the more authoritarian *cognitio* procedure followed by Roman governors – so judges, juries, and governors all followed their own instincts or prejudices about what made for good or better evidence. *Tabulae* are effective and important here, but at times judges could be tempted by wildflower-and-weed gardens of less formal documents whose attractions lay both in their easy practicality and in the rich color of their *fides*. Eventually these pragmatic blandishments had their effect, for between the time of Augustus and the time of Valentinian other written documents (like letters), especially when closely associated with an author by sealing or handwriting, inched into respectability alongside *tabulae*. Looked at from the wider perspective of the courts, personal *fides* thus improved not just *tabulae* themselves, but also the standing of these other documents, which as a consequence could at times even provide a challenge to the traditional authority *tabulae* were understood to possess. This *fides* so valued in court would also, eventually, help to ease the most difficult transition of all, the late-antique transformation of the *tabula*, a physical object believed to be imbued with authority, into a metaphor for authority, applicable to an official's archive even if the records of legal acts kept in it were not on real wooden *tabulae* but on papyrus. The *publicae tabulae* or *acta* of an official who heard court cases became an authoritative record in and of itself, and was cited with approval as significant evidence in later hearings. In this way the reorientation of so much legal business around Roman officials, noted

---

probabilis); *Inv.* 1.30, 46–7 (how to achieve verisimilitude and probability). Creating *fides*: *Part.* 5, 32, 35 (for an example, see *Schol. Bob.* on Cic. *Sull.* 37); speech must be adapted not just to truth but to listeners' opinions, *Part.* 90. The same found in Quint. *Inst.*: plausibility, 4.2.31, cf. 5.10.19, majority of arguments deal with what is credible; truth irrelevant, 4.2.34; how to make plausible, 4.2.52, 4.2.88 (same in untrue cases); things agreed (*constabit*) to be true, 4.2.90.

4 Commonly recognized, e.g., Honoré (1981) 174 (but argues against, 176–81), Buti (1982) 50, and Crook (1995) 17–21, 179.

218 *The evolution of practice*

in chapter seven as a growing phenomenon in the late second and early third centuries AD and responsible for the recasting of some *tabula*-documents on papyrus, becomes an even more established fact. There is with this, also, the glimmer of an ending. For this last and greatest melding of *tabulae* and *fides* takes place in a context that claims both for itself but in the end deems neither literally necessary. The emperor, and his officials, now make the rules; they are the authority, as what happens in court increasingly comes to show.

THE REPUBLIC

Tablets appear as standard in one of the very first accounts of what happens in a court, in a denunciation written *c.* 160 BC by C. Titius and preserved by Macrobius:[5]

> . . . describing men of prodigal habits going to the Forum full of drink, to act as judges, and what they were accustomed to say amongst themselves, he says: "They play at dice devotedly, drenched in scent, surrounded by a crowd of harlots . . . After [the tenth hour] . . . they make their way to the *comitium*, so as themselves not to become liable to law-suit. As they go, there is not an amphora in an alley that they don't fill, since they have each a bladder filled with wine. They arrive at the *comitium*; they gloomily bid proceedings begin; the parties state their case; the judge calls the witnesses; he himself goes and urinates; when he returns, he says that he has heard everything, calls for the *tabulae*, and glances at *litterae*; he can scarcely keep his eyes open because of wine. They retire to consultation (*in consilium*), and then they say to one another, 'Why should I be bothered with these worthless people, when rather we should drink mead mixed with Greek wine, we should eat a fat thrush and a fine fish . . .?'" There you have the actual words of Titius.

The activity here takes place in the second stage of formulary procedure, the miscreant judges those who hear the case after it has already been approved and sent on to them by the praetor. Although the protagonists are depicted as the judges' social inferiors, it is assumed to be plausible that the judges ask for *tabulae* and inspect *litterae*: these methods of proof (which may be one and the same thing, i.e. letters on tablets) cannot have been unusual even in the second century BC.

Why would judges have looked at such *tabulae*, even if, as in the above case, they could barely focus on them? They were written proof of

---

[5] C. Titius (a real person speaking in support of the Fannian law of 161 BC, not the judicial John Doe), quoted Macrob. *Sat.* 3.16.14–16: . . . *ubi redit, ait se omnia audivisse, tabulas poscit, litteras inspicit: vix prae vino sustinet palpebras.* By the first century BC, Roman courts had a *lector* or *recitator* for the reading of documents, Cic. *de Orat.* 2.223 and *Cluent.* 141.

Tablets and other documents in court to AD 400 219

something, of course, but proof of a particularly powerful kind. The treatment of *tabulae* in the late Republican rhetorical handbooks or discussions of rhetoric makes this clear: tablets could either nail a case or constitute one of the hardest obstacles an orator had to navigate his way around, for they had *auctoritas*.[6] "This *must* follow, for I recite *tabulae*," said Cicero at one point; cases involving *tabulae* were "difficult to get around."[7] As Greek orators had long before demonstrated, and as Cicero could have learned from them, impugning simple written proofs was child's play. There was something special about Roman *tabulae* that forced a different treatment of them in court, as Cicero himself recognized. For the most part, and because they support his case, Cicero (or other orators) will exult in the firm authority of tablets. Cicero is of course also as slippery as an eel, and when he needs to will try to undermine evidence that does not suit him; but even here his sinuous thrashings reveal the shape of the barrel in which he is confined, the architecture of expectation that his listeners bring to the valuation of documents. The arguments he developed to refute *tabulae* from necessity focussed not on the reliability of the document but on the interpretation of words and the intention of the author – itself in turn a reminder of the power of *tabulae*, since you only argue over the meaning of words when the fact of the words and their relevance to the case must be admitted.[8]

In later Republican anecdotes and speeches that survive, it was chiefly as financial accounts that *tabulae* are introduced.[9] If untruthful, it was

---

[6] Obstacles, *tabulae* and a person's firm *auctoritas* are the only things that restrict how much an orator can fabricate (*confingendum est*), *Rhet. Her.* 1.16; they have *auctoritas*, Cic. *Top.* 24.

[7] "This must follow": *hoc sequi necesse est*; *recito enim tabulas*, Cic. *de Orat.* 2.173; cases involving fact (*de re*), boundaries, inspection, *tabulae*, or *perscriptio* were *contortas res et saepe difficiles* (*de Orat.* 1.250). If there were no written document, Cicero would strive to get one, *Inv.* 2.134.

[8] See Cic. *Part.* 133–7; *Rhet. Her.* 2.13–14; Cic. *Part.* 2.128; Cic. *Inv.* 2. 122–14, and 141–2. For words in a law, a testament, the words of a trial itself, some stipulation or *cautio*, "it is not the type of writing but the interpretation of the word that is the source of the controversy," Cic. *Part.* 107. For a reported *controversia* over law vs. intent in will-making, see the famous *causa Curiana*, Quint. *Inst.* 7.6.9–11, and Quint. *Inst.* 3.6.95–103; on the very basic nature of the argument over letter vs. intent, see Schulz (1946) 76–7.

[9] (All dates and charges taken from appropriate entries in Alexander [1990]). Accounts: Val. Max. 6.5.6 (C. Papirius Carbo, 119 BC: nature of charge – *de repetundis* – makes it likely that accounts [on tablets] were a part of what was there); Cic. *de Orat.* 2.281 (Mucius Scaevola, 119 BC, *de repetundis*); Cic. *de Orat.* 2.280 (Rutilius, 116 BC, *de repetundis*); Cic. *Balb.* 11, Val. Max. 2.10.1 (Metellus Numidicus, *de repetundis*, 111 or 106 BC); Cic. *Scaur.* 40 (T. Albucius, *de repetundis*, 103 BC; *tabulis incorruptis*); Cic. *Quinct.* 17 (C. Quinctius's heirs; reclaiming debt; before 81 BC); Cic. *Font.* 2–3, 5, 11–12 (M. Fonteius, *de repetundis*, 69 BC?); Cic. *Flacc.* 44 and 48 (L. Valerius Flaccus, *de repetundis*, 59 BC); Cic. *Scaur.* 18 (M. Aemilius Scaurus, *de repetundis*, 54 BC). Account–*tabulae* from the *Verrines*: 2.1.28; 2.1.102; 2.1.128 and 2.4.31; 2.3.90 and 2.3.93; 2.4.12; cf. 2.2.182, financial *libellos* of Canuleius were the type of evidence Cicero "especially wanted to find"; Verres's own financial *tabulae*, 2.1.36, 61, 98, and 100–2

220   *The evolution of practice*

only because real villains, or Greeks, have made or tampered with them.[10] In general, they appeared as an unquestioned form of proof, and failure on the opposition's part to produce tablets of their own was seized upon as deeply suspicious.[11] This authoritative veracity was also characteristic of the other forms of *tabulae* adduced – census, wills, *leges, senatusconsulta,* a restipulation, and the *tabulae* or *codices* of the city praetors.[12]

Such *tabulae* could be imagined as animated proxies for their authors. "Your voice," Cicero called Fannius's *restipulatio* in the *pro Quinto Roscio,* and in the *Verrines* such voices "cry out"; in the *Verrines* tablets that did not belong to Verres were also referred to as "witnesses."[13] They could not be slighted without their author also feeling the sting. Albius, said Cicero, was pleased when Mucius Scaevola was acquitted by the testimony of Albius's accounts, but this was an indication of how clueless Albius was – for Albius's accounts, and thus Albius himself, were thereby proved to be the source of the problem, and had had "a verdict given against" them.[14] Author and tablet embody the same qualities. For this reason it was arrogance, Cicero claimed, to "recite one's own *codicem testis loco,*" a special kind of obnoxious self-replication on the witness-stand; but at least it was not insanity to bring them in, since tablets were recognized as an especially authoritative version

(Servilius's public accounts read as a positive example, 2.1.57). Fest. 274M noted that *iudices* thought highly of account *tabulae, quae publice data et accepta sint*; Nappo (1989) 88 no. 13 (fig. 9) may depict a court-scene in which such accounts (opened and displayed vertically) are used. Bankers' *tabulae* continued to have an "autorité particulière" in the courts of the empire, Andreau (1996) 432, and it was the judge's prerogative to demand them, *CJ* 2.1.1 (AD 155).

[10] Tampering: e.g., by Verres, Cic. *2 Verr.* 2.101–7, 187–91; Oppianicus fabricated an entire will and the town census, as well as *tabellae* taken at the torturing of slaves, with Sassia's help, Cic. *Cluent.* 41, 185; Cic. *Caec.* 71 (generalizing); Cic. *Flacc.* 20, 21.

[11] Unquestioned: *contra* (e.g.) Costa (1927) 163 and (1928) 145–6, who argued that the importance of witnesses mandates the negligible value of documents. Failure to produce: Cic. *2 Verr.* 3.112; *2 Verr.* 4.36; Cic. *Flacc.* 35; Cic. *Cael.* 17; Cic. *Font.* 11–12.

[12] Census: Cic. *Flacc.* 80 and 94. Will: see sources cited at Alexander (1990) 48–9 no. 93 (the *causa Curiana,* 94 or 93 BC); Cic. *Cluent.* 41, 124, 135; Cic. *Sull.* 54 (P. Cornelius Sulla, *vis,* 62 BC; reference to will only, not actually produced in court). *Leges:* Cic. *Cluent.* 148 and *2 Verr.* 1.143–8 (on *tabulae,* 2.1.144) and 2.3.83, cf. *de Orat.* 1.244; *senatusconsulta,* Cic. *Flacc.* 27 and 78; *restipulatio,* Cic. *Q. Rosc.* 37; city praetor's *codices* or *tabulae,* Cic. *2 Verr.* 1.157 (also called false *codicem*), 2.101–4, 3.41 (*codicem*), *Cluent.* 91 (Verres's), *Arch.* 9 and 31 (Metellus's); praetor's and provincial edicts, *2 Verr.* 1.104–18; edicts about tax-collecting, *2 Verr.* 3.25–6 (*ex ipsius tabulis,* also called *ex codice*), 2.3.36–7; decrees, *2 Verr.* 5.54 and 56; *tabulae* of sale, *2 Verr.* 4.43; treaty, *2 Verr.* 5.50; *tabulae* of testimony, *2 Verr.* 1.79 and 5.102–3; *condictio certae pecuniae,* Cic. *Q. Rosc.* 1–7 (Q. Roscius, between 76 and 68 BC); *sponsio, unde vi hominibus coactis armatisve,* Cic. *Caec.* 17 (S. Aebutius, 69 BC?; Cic. *Cluent.* 34, 40, 82 (66 BC).

[13] *tua vox*: Cic. *Q. Rosc.* 37; crying out, Cic. *2 Verr.* 2.104; witnesses, Cic. *2 Verr.* 5.10 (*tabulae publicae*); *tabulae* also *indicant* facts, cf. Cic. *Balb.* 19 and Cic. *Pis.* 36.

[14] Albius: Cic. *de Orat.* 2.281; cf. complaints about *tabulae* of praetor Gabinius, whose *levitas* and eventual condemnation "forfeited" (*resignasset*) the *fides* of his tablets, whereas Metellus's (*homo sanctissimus modestissimusque*) should be automatically believed, Cic. *Arch.* 9.

Tablets and other documents in court to AD 400

of one's self and one's business. No, insanity to Cicero was citing one's own day-books, which had no value at all.[15]

It was therefore but a distant possibility that *tabulae* could reveal malfeasance and their author still be innocent. The case of Metellus Numidicus, on trial *de repetundis* in 111 or 106 BC, showed this most clearly. When his (apparently suspicious) accounts were passed around – "as was customary" (*ut mos est*) – among the jury, these men averted their eyes, so that they would not be thought (said Cicero) to be doubting Metellus's honesty. Valerius Maximus added that they "were indignant that the honesty of so great a man hung on a little wax and small letters."[16] Rather than confront a possible contradiction between perceived greatness and its embodiment in physical form, the jury simply preferred not to look. If read, and if they made clear thieving or bad behavior, the *tabulae* would have exposed Metellus as a dishonest liar, and the jury would have been forced to condemn. Tablets' power could not be gainsaid, only avoided.

The association of a person with his tablets and the way in which his *tabula* grasped his *fides*, an occasional but powerful element in Cicero's depiction of *tabulae*,[17] show that – at least rhetorically – the concepts of *fides* and *tabulae* could cohabit happily as early as the seventies BC; jurists would later develop the concept that bankers' *tabulae* embodied *publica fides*, which is why the praetor could compel their submission to the courts.[18] It was not implausible to Cicero's audience that tablets had the capacity to seize, embody, and hold on to the protagonist's or principal's *fides*, but it was the courtroom setting that encouraged Cicero to point out the connection, at least when it worked in his client's favor or to his enemy's disadvantage. Quintus Roscius, for example, must be proved a solid and upright man, Verres a villain; so the accounts of the first (which also record facts that Cicero wishes to stress) show Roscius's sturdy honesty and attention to detail, while those of the second, full of inept erasures, show Verres up to his peculating snout in corruption.[19] The association will continue, the *fides* of others added on to *tabulae* and the *fides* of the protagonist made more emphatic through subscription, as has

---

[15] *arrogantia* and *amentia*: Cic. *Q. Rosc.* 5.

[16] Metellus: story, Cic. *Balb.* 11; *ut mos est*, Cic. *Att.* 1.16.4; indignation, Val. Max. 2.10.1.

[17] E.g., Q. Roscius's *tabulae* (see chapter two n. 69); cf. Cic. *Font.* 3.

[18] *D.* 2.13.10.1 (Gaius); even surveyors' bronze *tabulae* had *fides* by the (?) third century AD, Siculus Flaccus *de Cond. Agr.* T118.24 (Campbell [2000] 120), and in the fourth century it is imaginable that all *documenta* could, Amm. Marc. 29.2.27 (AD 372).

[19] Verres: *2 Verr.* 1.92–3 (Malleolus's), *2 Verr.* 1.158 (general indictment), and his own records as praetor, *2 Verr.* 2.101–4; *2 Verr.* 2.186–91 (of the *societas* of tax-collectors). Verres's praetor's edict indeed shows what sort of man he is, *2 Verr.* 1.104 (cf. 106, his *gravitas* and *auctoritas* revealed).

222 *The evolution of practice*

already been seen. But the simplest connection, making the very nature of the *tabula* serve the arguments thought most persuasive in the context, was made in speeches that came early in Cicero's career, including even the *Catilinarians*, where *tabellae* of Cethegus and the other conspirators, by which they had sent military instructions to the Allobroges, were a powerful sign of their *bad* faith, emphasized by the way Cicero forced the conspirators, also, to acknowledge their seals in public.[20] Almost two centuries later, Quintilian would extend this thought by claiming that *tabulae* captured *voluntas.*[21]

Early in Cicero's career, too, we can see a new type of talking *tabula* that embodies this connection. What will come to be called *testationes*, declarations or testimony written on *tabulae*, are referred to in speeches or appear in court at this time, defending, or speaking fact or praise in favor of, a defendant or plaintiff.[22] The first known instance of a *testatio* may have been in 81 BC in which Cicero defended Quinctius;[23] they were certainly in use eleven years later, when *tabulae* of how many sailors sea-captains had on duty were made. We later also see references to *tabellae* taken of an interrogation (*quaestio*) of a slave speaking under torture before men who had been called to witness; these too were statements of fact, made before witnesses, probably couched in the third person, and were read out (recited) in court, in 66 BC.[24] Declarations of fact such as these would have looked much like some of those from Pompeii and Herculaneum, in which men "attested" or "declared" (*testati sunt*) that this or that had occurred, or

---

[20] Cic. *Cat.* 3.10 (*tabellas*); these *litterae* were military dispatches, an unusual type of conclusive and authoritative letter on *tabellae*, E. Meyer (2001) 203; these *tabellae* were also autographs and included oaths, which added to the appearance of bad faith, Butler (2002) 88–90.

[21] *Decl.* 332 (Ritter 308 lines 6–7).

[22] *testationes* are written, not oral, despite some ambiguities in how they are used in later legal sources, e.g., *D.* 14.6.16.4 (Paulus), *D.* 26.7.5.10 (Ulpian), *D.* 50.16.238.1 (Gaius): see Lévy–Bruhl (1910) 93–104, Karabélias (1984) 601 (who cautiously allows for both) and Jahr (1965); cf. also the distinction made between *testationes* and *testimonium, D.* 48.10.1.*pr.* (Marcian), *D.* 48.10.9.3 (Ulpian); *testationes* are sealed, *D.* 48.19.9.5 (Ulpian) and therefore must be a physical object, either something written or, e.g., a picture, as in Apul. *Met.* 6.29 and Quint. *Inst.* 6.1.32, the parading of painted *tabulae* in court. A will can be called a *testatio* of judgment, *D.* 28.1.24 (Florentinus) and Gel. 7.12. *pr.*; Petr. *Sat.* 118.6 refers to "the *fides* of *religiosae* speech before witnesses."

[23] Cic. *Quinct.* 66–7, Alfenus the procurator of Quinctius's property states, on sealed tablets (*rei condicionisque tabellaes*), that he would defend Quinctius's interests, thus offering a kind of legal challenge to Naevius, Quinctius's opponent, and preventing Naevius's seizure of Quinctius's property; Cicero does not use these in court, only refers to them as demonstrating that Quinctius had acted properly.

[24] *tabulae* of sea-captains, Cic. 2*Verr.* 5.102–3; *tabellae quaestionis*, Cic. *Cluent.* 184 (*nam tabellae quaestionis plures proferuntur, quae recitatae vobisque editae sunt*; also *obsignatae*). Witnesses, *chirographis, quaestionibus* are threatened in Val. Max. 8.10.3. Cic. *Pis.* 69 uses *testificari, tabellas obsignare* as a metaphor for declaring something as true and certain – so true and certain that in *de Orat.* 1.174 they defeat the client without him, or his patron, understanding that this will happen; Cic. *Tusc.* 5.33 implies the same, your own words used to defeat you.

Tablets and other documents in court to AD 400

those from Egypt, which use the same third-person language as those from Campania.[25] Other witness-attestations from Herculaneum, however, use the first-person chirograph style, writing and swearing (for example) that they know a young woman, Petronia Justa, was born after the manumission of her mother, and thus was free-born.[26] *Tabulae* could therefore also fix a person's words in acts of writing, words that could then be read out in court as if the voice of the actual person. The style of this latter type of declaration was different, and it was probably a later creation than the first type.[27] The one was proclaiming before witness-judges that this or that had happened or was the case; by its process, by calling, declaring, and writing down on a tablet, it made a statement authoritative.[28] The other remained a subjective expression of a belief or an understanding, its force deriving from the *fides* of its sealers and its author, who sometimes strengthened what he (or she)[29] was saying with an oath, as L. Lucceius did in Caelius's trial, leading Cicero to claim that this *testimonium* too had *religio* and *auctoritas*.[30] By the 70s AD, however, a mingling of the two had occurred. Not only were both written on *tabulae*, but the seven witness-declarations in chirograph style collected for Petronia Justa's defense of her free-born status were sealed with a number of sealers more often seen with the third-person *testatio*-style documents, that is, with seven or more.[31] Differences in origin and nature had been smoothed out by the relentless pressures of the legal context where they were most valued, constantly flowing water reducing spiky and peculiar outcrops to softly similar profiles.

This current was already flowing in the middle of the first century BC, for personal opinion in the form of praise was already being proffered on *tabellae* then,[32] as well as praise merely going by the generic names

---

[25] *TPSulp.* 41 (AD 39), 87 (AD 51), 40 (AD 52), and 116 (no date); *TH* 5 (AD 60) and 2 (AD 70 or 72); Egypt, *CPL* 104 (= *W.Chr.* 463, AD 94), 159 (AD 127), 162 (a woman, AD 145); see also *RIB* 2.2443.19 (AD 118); and Cass. Dio 53.24.3, a man recording a denial on tablets, with witnesses.

[26] *TH* 16–20, 23–4 (AD 75); therefore witness-*testationes* were hard to classify, see chapter six n. 27.

[27] Kaser (1934) col. 1028; *Schol. Bob.* on Cic. *Flacc.* 37 also claimed that *tabulae* of accusation (type one) and *laudationes* (type two) were sealed with different materials, the first with wax and the second with white clay, *creta . . . candida*.

[28] Lévy–Bruhl (1910) 93–104 (depending mostly on late sources, however).

[29] Such expressions of belief paralleled by the language witnesses used when present: they scrupulously said "they thought" (*se arbitrari*), Greenidge (1901) 274 and 481. Women: they had *fides* and could appear as witnesses in court, cf. Greenidge (1901) 482–3 and Marshall (1989) 51 n.49.

[30] Cic. *Cael.* 55; cf. *SB* 7523 (= *FIRA²* 3.591–2 no. 188, AD 153). The style and form of the *testificatio* of Cic. *Mur.* 49 and the *testimonium* of Cic. *Q. Rosc.* 43 and *Mil.* 46 are unknown, although both are written. On oaths, see also Strachan-Davidson (1912) II.115–16 and Fordyce (1938).

[31] Listed above n.25.

[32] Cic. *2 Verr.* 1.128 (*virorum bonorum tabulis*), *2 Verr.* 1.156 (*honestissimorum tabulis*), *2 Verr.* 3.99 (*tabulae* of city of Thermae); *2 Verr.* 4.148 (*tabellas . . . commendaticias*); Val. Max. 6.2.5 (*tabellae* with praise from Pompey).

224　　　　　　　　*The evolution of practice*

of *laudationes* or *commendationes*, their physical form unknown.[33] From the late Republic onward, references to written testimony, conveying fact and praise both, only multiply. Ovid can play with the image, either by claiming to attest in his poetry, before witnesses who will seal, or by being the attentive scribe who takes down the statements of the gods on *tabulae*, in the *Fasti*.[34] By Quintilian's time, it was quite standard that "testimony is spoken either through *tabulae* or by those present."[35]

The making of *tabulae* and their submission to the court might be seen as a development that catered to the convenience of participants. Yet if developed for the convenience of the absent, it is strange how many authors of such *tabulae* nonetheless appeared, themselves, in court. Towns that sent laudations or supporting testimonials, for example, also sent substantial legations, who could be pointed out as present in the courtroom, and in the *pro Cluentio*, when the *testimonium* of Balbutius's father was recited by the clerk, he himself stood up and made himself known.[36] Written *testimonium* on tablets is challenged only once (because it directly contradicted another *tabula* on the exact same question; Cicero therefore claimed that it was sealed by a disreputable person),[37] and rather than being merely a matter of convenience seems to have set certain aspects of the case beyond the reach of advocates: it placed certain facts beyond dispute and presented the weight witnesses could bring to bear even more securely and impressively, to win quite decisively the approval of jury or judge. Tablets were chosen for witness-testimony and praise – even by those themselves present in court – because they could fix a statement and give it authority, making

---

[33] Cic. *Cluent.* 196 (a *laudatio*); Cic. *Fam.* 1.9.19 (Lentulus sends *laudationes*); Asc. 28 on Cic. *Scaur.* 46 ("most of" nine consulars "sent *tabellae*, since they were away from Rome"); *laudationes* given by Greeks (the physical form of which is not specified, although they were sealed) could (naturally) be forged, Cic. *Flacc.* 36. Use of *laudationes* was deemed excessive in the fifties, and Pompey attempted to limit their use, which led Cato to block the use of some of Pompey's own *laudationes*, Val. Max. 6.2.5; Plut. *Cat. Min.* 48.4 (ἔπαινον for Munatius Plancus), Cass. Dio 40.55.1–2 (βιβλίον ἔπαινόν τε for Milo).

[34] "This I confess; you may witness it; put your seal upon it, Quirites" (*confiteor: testere licet, signate Quirites*), *Pont.* 4.15.11; seemingly taking dictation, *Fasti* 1.93: he sits with *tabellis* in hand and the god Janus appears and speaks to him (as do many others in the course of the work, their words often taken down in the first person).

[35] Numbers increasing: Broggini (1964) 268; Quintilian, *Inst.* 5.7.1 (*testimonia . . . ea dicuntur aut per tabulas aut a praesentibus*), and cf. Tac. *Dial.* 36.7 (*per tabellam*).

[36] Praise, with legations present: Cic. *Cluent.* 196–7; Balbutius's father, Cic. *Cluent.* 168; cf. Cic. *2Verr.* 1.93, Malleolus's mother and grandmother. Had long-distance *testationes* been tolerated in any but the very great, the well-attested threat of *denuntiatio testimonii*, that is, compelling the attendance of a witness, would have been not only empty but also pointless; cf. Cic. *Flacc.* 14, with Kaser (1934) cols. 1059–60 and Greenidge (1901) 268 n.3, 485–8.

[37] Cic. *Cluent.* 185–6 (*tabellae* of a *quaestio* of a slave); Cicero savages the witness and denounces the woman responsible for it in lurid terms, and for all these reasons *in tabellis nihil est auctoritatis*.

Tablets and other documents in court to AD 400

(it was hoped) such a statement virtually irrefutable: the physical form took the everyday and made it authoritative. In these *tabulae* also inhered the *fides* of the author or protagonist, who felt dishonored and feared to incur *infamia* if his *testatio* was not believed,[38] and the additional *fides* of those who sealed, which was understood to support *testatio* and author in court, thereby creating danger (as Quintilian would later say) for the advocate who contemplated challenging such sealed *tabulae*.[39]

The kind of fixity tablets could offer in court was especially wonderful in a venue increasingly awash with different forms of documents, documents whose questionable evidential weight helps to demonstrate the strength of tablets. In the last century of the Republic, other forms of physically non-specific "letters" (*litterae*) were coming to be cited by advocates as well: speeches, jurists' works on law, financial day-books, and simple *epistolae* and *litterae*;[40] and decrees and *psephismata* from all over and the *litterae* and *publicae litterae* of the Greek cities of Sicily as well.[41] Unlike *tabulae*, these forms of writing had no intrinsic, or form-based, authority.[42] Sometimes,

---

[38] *D.* 3.2.21 (Paulus), *testes* who have made a *testatio* disbelieved, but should not *inter infames habentur* (for false witness) because they should not suffer for (adverse) judgment made against another.

[39] The standing of witnesses to *testationes* noted, cf. Cic. *Cluent.* 176–7 (*honesti* and *ornati*), 185–6 (lowly), Cic. *Flacc.* 37–8; see Wenger (1923) cols. 2378–448. Protection, Quint. *Inst.* 7.2.53 (summary); danger, *Inst.* 5.5.1 (claiming forgery multiplies the number of accused, i.e. the sealers count too).

[40] Speeches and legal writing: Cic. *Cluent.* 140–1; own speech, Cic. *Planc.* 74. *Ephemerides*: Cic. *Q. Rosc.* 1–8 (threatened), *Flacc.* 20 (*tributi confectio*, contrasted with *tabulae creditoris*). *Litterae* as letters: Cic. *Quinct.* 58 (Quinctius's *litterae*, a form of *ephemerides*, adduced to prove that he had not given *vadimonium* to appear, placed in the *argumentatio*, "where [Cicero] would have been taught to tuck away his weakest arguments," Butler [2002] 12); Cic. *Font.* 18; Cic. *Cluent.* 97 (Cosconius); Cic. *Sull.* 67 (Cicero's own *epistula* to Pompey); Cic. *Flacc.* 20 (*litterae* of Pompey), 78 (*litterae* of Cicero's brother), 90 (*epistulae* of Falcidius, at 93, forged); Cic. *Sest.* 11 (Cicero's *litterae* as consul to Sestius); from the *Verrines*, *litterae* to Nero, 2.1.83; to Segestans, 2.3.92; Metellus's letter, 2.3.45–6 and 122–8; Timarchides's letter, 2.3.154–7; Vettius's letter, 2.3.167–8 (*testatur*, 2.3.168). Val. Max. 4.2.7, Caelius *recitavit . . . epistulam* of Pompeius.

[41] *decreta*: Cic. *S. Rosc.* 25 (of decurions of Ameria); Cic. *Flacc.* 78; Cic. *Sest.* 10 (of decurions of Capua). *psephismata*: Cic. *Flacc.* 17 and 75. *litterae publicae* (recited, all from the *2 Verr.*): *2 Verr.* 3.74; 3.105–6; 4.91–2; 5.43; 5.147–8; 3.85; 3.89; 3.102; 3.120 (*litterae publicae* about land under cultivation); 3.175 (*rationes* and, at 171 and 173, *litterae publicae*); 4.79 (contract *ex publicis litteris*); 4.140 (temple-accounts as *litterae publicae*); their *testimoniis et litteris*, 1.10, 2.141, 2.155, 3.122, 3.175, 3.225, 4.91, 4.138, 5.43. *Tessera hospitalis*: offered, Cic. *Balb.* 41.

[42] Even Cicero cannot make Greek archives, *litterae*, better than they are: despite their importance to his case they often prove to be unreliable and he must find ways of excusing this, e.g., he claims Verres's tampering (2.1.88, 2.5.103; cf. 2.2.60, 2.2.90, 2.2.92–3, 2.2.105), others' tampering (2.2.107), or that they were incomplete because, uh, Greek cities would not want to record information they found disgraceful (2.4.134). In the *Verrines* he only refers to Sicilian city-archives as *tabulae publicae* three times, and then (in two cases) ironically: 2.4.134 (heightening the presumption that Greek cities would want to avoid entering disgraceful information), 2.4.146 (recording a eulogy to Verres), and 2.5.10 (Lilybaeum; where the incontestability of a court verdict is being emphasized); 2.5.48 is a reference to financial accounts (of the Mamertini) alone. The distinction (noted also by Butler

226   *The evolution of practice*

indeed, they were read out only for amusement value, as when Brutus quoted two contradictory speeches of Crassus, the opposing counsel, and Crassus in return cited legal works of Brutus's father which were set on various family estates, all of which Crassus sought to prove had passed out of the family through Brutus's profligacy.[43]

At other times, these documents were used in an attempt to establish facts, but even here were most helpful – like documents in Athenian courts – only when corroborated by sealers, or by other testimony or types of evidence.[44] Failing those, dare your opponent to disagree: Cicero's two favorite sources of letters in the sixties and fifties were Pompey and himself. Who would openly question the validity of letters written by the great Pompey, or by Cicero, or even by Cicero's brother, when Cicero was before you, looking you in the eye? Because of their form they could be challenged, but there was risk to the challenger if the author was an important man, or if important witnesses corroborated what these *litterae* claimed.

Weaker than tablets even when used positively by a friendly advocate, these other forms of document could also be, and were, argued against quite forcefully. *Tabulae* could be tampered with, it is true, but it was very unusual; Cicero can more than once be found offering to give up a case if only the opposition could demonstrate this or that in *tabulae*.[45] Letters, on the other hand, could in his opinion easily be fabricated, while day-books were the equivalent of jottings on napkins,[46] and *psephismata* – well, how ridiculous to consider such a Greek concoction the equivalent of a Roman *lex*, or even evidence. A *psephisma* was not *proposita* and *cognita* like a Roman law; the result was not a considered resolution but easy to represent as "the vagaries of the mob," "the howl of the needy."[47] Similarly, appearing with your testimony written on a papyrus *volumen* instead of

---

[2002] 36–9) between reliable (and usually Roman) *tabulae* and malleable (often Greek) *litterae* is generally adhered to; there are four exceptions, two of which (2.1.57 and 2.2.105–6) may be intended to set up the equivalence between Verres's tampering with his own *tabulae* as praetor (also called *publicae litterae*) and his corrupt condemnation of Sthenius for falsifying city archives (*publicae litterae*). At 2.4.37 Verres offers *litterae* in proof of a sale, to which Cicero replied, *id factum non oportuit* – perhaps because a statue of Apollo *should* not sell for 1,000 HS, or perhaps because *litterae* are not *proper* demonstration of sale (*oportuit* is ambiguous).

[43] Cic. *Cluent.* 140–1.

[44] The *litterae* of Cosconius were also supported by witnesses, Cic. *Cluent.* 97; Calidius proved a case of poisoning with chirographs, *quaestiones*, *indicia* (circumstantial evidence), and testimony, Cic. *Brut.* 277 and Val. Max. 8.10.3 (*testibus, chirographis, quaestionibus*); *litterae* in these cases are of indistinct physical form – *tabulae* are the marked category – and thus are probably not on tablets.

[45] Cic. *Q. Rosc.* 2–3, 2*Verr.* 1.61, 4.35–6; in *Arch.* 9 he attributes this opinion to his opponents.

[46] Forged letters: Cic. *Flacc.* 90–3 ("should this person, whom no one would believe if he swore an oath, prove this *by a letter*?"). Worthlessness of day-books: Cic. *Q. Rosc.* 5–7.

[47] Cic. *Flacc.* 17–23 (quotations 19, 23): decrees from two different Greek towns being attacked.

Tablets and other documents in court to AD 400 227

a tablet was a red-flag invitation to lawyerly abuse: Cicero will be happy to prove that what was written – which its author offered *pro testimonio* – is a fiction, was in fact written by somebody else.[48] Physical form was vitally important. Testimonial *tabulae* put their facts and evidence virtually beyond the everyday brawl of the courtroom, and this fact allowed other forms of written "evidence" to be subject to dispute in ways that observed very few rules. One only Cicero tells us explicitly: too much reading of his own speeches "would seem to accord better with my own studies than with the usage of these courts."[49] Thank goodness.

In the end *testimonia* and *tabulae*, or *testes* and *tabulae*, were the most directly effective forms of proof, and said to be so.[50] Truth was embodied in *tabulae*; the other forms of document were bitterly contested ground; and even a Cicero could not entirely overcome their differing implications.

THE EMPIRE

Just as in the Republic, so too in the Empire *tabulae* retained a special power in court, reflected in both advice given and strategies followed. Quintilian noted that "lightening" the impact of *tabulae* (and you must argue against them *saepe*) or refuting them requires "the greatest power of eloquence," all the energy and cleverness an orator can muster. Indeed, the only effective argument against them is that it could not have been so – the person was dead at the time, or some other demonstrable impossibility.[51] No, it is in the presentation and treatment of documents not on *tabulae* that the change in advocates' strategies between trials of the Republic and trials of the Empire and Late Empire is most clearly perceptible – trials for which the evidence is also considerably less rich, and more often than not written in Greek. Here, although physical distinctions between types of document are still perceptible, they are downplayed – especially in trials at Rome or which involved Roman principals – while associations with authors and

---

[48] *volumen*: Cic. *S. Rosc.* 101 (all written by Erucius, for Capito).

[49] Cicero's unaccustomed diffidence: *Planc.* 74 (*quod meis studiis aptius quam consuetudini iudiciorum esse videatur*). On customary rather than legal rules, Lévy (1959b) 191–2.

[50] *testimonia, tabulae, testes*: Cic. *de Orat.* 2.100 and 2.116 (*tabulae* and *testimonia* first); Cic. *Flacc.* 40; Cic. *Caec.* 71–2 (*testes* and *tabulae*); *Schol. Bob.* on Cic. *Flacc.* 39, by this time, *quando tabulae causis tantum et probationibus instrumento sint*, bandits wouldn't want to steal; Quint. *Inst.* 5.13.37 (*communes loci de testibus, de tabulis, de argumentis*) and 7.10.13 (*testimonia tabulaeve*, both recited); Ps.-Asc. arg. to Cic. *Div. Caec.* (Orelli), some think it's called a *divinatio* – "intuition" – because it's performed *sine testibus et sine tabulis*; continues into late antiquity, cf. Ambrose *Ep.* 5.11= *PL* 16. 895 (*veritatis documenta et testimonia*), Martianus Capella 5.474 (*tabulae, testimonia, quaestiones*) and especially 5.498 (*in scriptura, ut tabularum, in auctoritate, ut testium, in necessitate, ut tormentorum*).

[51] Quint. *Inst.* 5.1.2; arguing *saepe*, or that the person dead, etc., 5.5.1–2.

228   *The evolution of practice*

participants, and thereby documents' prestige, are stressed. *Tabulae* still retain their ancient authority, but claims of prestige clamor and cannot be ignored, and thereby help to bring other cheaper and more convenient forms of writing into a respectability that becomes harder to attack publicly. The gradual advance of *fides*-documents can be seen in provincial settings as well, although there the trump card through the second century AD still remained the *tabula*.

In the few court cases at Rome or before the emperor for which there is any indication of the type of proof used – cases in which more is known than merely, for example, that "the fourth day was given over to examination of the proofs," as Pliny remarked in his account of the *repetundis* trial of Julius Bassus[52] – a scattering of tablets and a wider variety of other documents were introduced, the latter without apparent apology. In Albucilla's trial for *impietas* and adultery, for example, *commentarii* (with examinations of the witnesses and slaves, done in Macro's presence) were sent to the Senate;[53] a different *repetundis* trial in the early second century brought the usual demand for accounts, but was then ended by production of a Bithynian decree dropping the charge;[54] and *tabulae* were demanded but not produced in a trial before Aulus Gellius and in a (municipal?) trial about a woman's property, to the discredit of those not producing them.[55] The use of all of these documents, of types usually on *tabulae*, should have been unexceptionable, and probably was – except for the *commentarii*, which the Senate in this case preferred to believe were forged, since Macro hated one of the adulterers and Tiberius had not sent letters (*litterae*) along with them, condemning the accused.[56] Witness-*testationes* were also used. Yet if the author of a *testatio* himself was not present in court, this absence could be seized on with relief as a way of undermining the difficult invincibility of *tabulae*, for absence reflected badly on a person, especially when combined with the obvious hostility that a willingness to testify against someone clearly signalled – and provable personal animosity was one way of "lightening" a witness who spoke against you and reducing his impact.[57]

---

[52] Plin. *Ep.* 4.9.15; cf. 2.11.18, *probationes* extended into the third day.

[53] Tac. *Ann.* 6.47.2–3 (cf. Cass. Dio 58.27.2–4, defendants' testimony and testimony taken under torture disagreed).

[54] Plin. *Ep.* 7.6 (Varenus), cf. Philostr. *VS* 561 for another decree read out in court.

[55] Gel. 14.2.7 (*expensi latione, mensae rationibus, chirographi exhibitione, tabularum obsignatione, testium intercessione* all not forthcoming); woman's property, *apud magistratus de plano* (*tabulae signatae* were wanted), *FV* 112.

[56] Tac. *Ann.* 6.47.3, *nullaeque in eos imperatoris litterae suspicionem dabant.*

[57] Absence reflects badly, Quint. *Inst.* 5.7.1–2; cf. *Schol. Bob.* on Cic. *Planc.* 27, *haberetur atque si adesset is, cuius validior esset auctoritas;* provable personal animosity a reproach, Quint. *Inst.* 5.7.33 (and 5.7.33–37 on ways to discredit witnesses).

Testimonium is what makes advocates sweat the most; one must do what one can do to diminish its effects when necessary.[58]

In a matter in which the emperor was consulted or was personally concerned, his opinion – however expressed and in whatever medium – would of course be taken very seriously by those making the judgment, overruling even other inherited presumptions about evidence, proper procedure, and the value of *testationes*.[59] As Juvenal sarcastically said about the fall of Sejanus, "Who was the accuser, with what proofs, proved with which witness? None of those things; a wordy and great *epistola* came from Capri."[60] It was no wonder that the Senate found the absence of *litterae* from Tiberius in Albucilla's case (noted above) significant, or that it desperately wanted the correspondence between Calpurnius Piso and Tiberius, at Piso's trial, for a *libellus* in Piso's possession was said to have contained *litteras et mandata* from Tiberius about Germanicus. This correspondence would have settled the issue of Piso's behavior, but also the more important question of the emperor's attitude and involvement, definitively.[61] These examples show that communication from an emperor in any form – rescript, letter, *tabula* – was exceedingly powerful in court, much prized by anyone who could claim it[62] and demanding deference from the judges who saw or heard it. Long before its legal value – its ability to make law – was established, the power of the emperor's mere words in court was overwhelming; his laws and edicts themselves were of course unassailable in court.[63] This accounts for imperial caution in issuing communications, and imperial attempts to restrict their application once issued.[64] Such writings were not so much orders as "helpful to us when we are in need," as one prefect

---

[58] Quint. *Inst.* 5.7.1.

[59] See, e.g., consultations of Hadrian on witnesses and *testationes*, D. 22.5.3.3–4 (Callistratus).

[60] Juv. *Sat.* 10.69–72.

[61] Tac. *Ann.* 3.10–17 (*scripsissent expostulantes, libellum, litteras, mandata, codicillos*; Piso committed suicide).

[62] Imperial writings used: Plin. *Ep.* 10.58.3 (*libellum a se Domitiano datum et epistulas eius ad honorem suum pertinentes*) and 10.65 (edict of Augustus, *epistulae* of Vespasian, Titus, and Domitian offered by Bithynians; they are copies, and Pliny is mistrustful); Philostr. *VA* 8.7 (imagined; letter from Vespasian); *P.Oxy.* 3820 (AD 340?); Agathias *Hist.* 4.2.2–6; *P.Oxy.* 3611 (AD 253–7) is an apparent example of an imperial rescript in private hands, cf. *Cons.* 6.4.

[63] Quint. *Inst.* 5.2.5 (best to hope for the law or edicts contradicting previous laws or edicts); the invincibility was part of what made other documents on *tabulae* hard to argue against, for *tabula*-documents are the types most readily cited as necessitating argument to get around, *Rhet. Her.* 2.13–18, Cic. *Inv.* 2.116 and 122 (wills), 137 and 149 (law or will), 140 (law); Cic. *Top.* 95–6.

[64] Emperors try to control, e.g., Garnsey (1970) 68 (generally unwilling to comment on substantive rather than administrative matters); see (e.g.) the later *CT* 1.2.2 (AD 315), 1.2.3 (AD 316), 11.12.3 (AD 365), and others; *CJ* 7.62.2 (Severus Alexander), 7.50.3 (AD 319), and 7.39.3 (AD 424) are explicit about the use of rescripts in court.

230   *The evolution of practice*

put it, guidelines that had to be followed rather than commands that had
to be obeyed.[65] It was accepted that they were "to be held in awe and
reverence";[66] "to transgress the edicts is of the same gravity as to commit
violence or homicide."[67] The reverence extended to the emperor's words
and writings was eventually offered to the writings of his officials as well.[68]
One advocate in third-century Egypt did attempt to argue that the current situation and the decisions of previous Egyptian prefects modified
the applicability of imperial constitutions somewhat, but he was clearly
propounding a losing case.[69] By the fourth century, a *prostagma* (ordinance) of the prefect of Egypt inspired in the *logistes* hearing a case such
"fear of the Nobility of so great an official" that he hastened to do the
prefect's bidding.[70] An Egyptian advocate even attempted to intimidate a
curator by introducing a *prostagma* of the prefect relevant to *other* defendants, not those currently on trial – a fact pointed out by their indignant
advocate.[71]

Emperors – and, eventually, their officials – are just the most extreme
example of the way in which prestige and power could give exceptional
value to non-specific written forms previously of less probative weight.
Moreover, as the reaction to the Egyptian prefect's *prostagma* suggests, this
phenomenon was probably exerting some influence on a less exalted level as
well, the ungainsayable example of imperial documents making it harder
to argue against the letters and papers of the non-imperial but mighty.
Fides and status did not undermine the independent authority of the tablet
form, only its implicit claim to exclusive authority; they competed rather
than destroyed. As a consequence, a variety of other documents were taken
rather more seriously in court. In yet another *repetundis* trial from the early

[65] *SB* 9016 (AD 160), Lysimachus makes two decisions, one based on "the attached imperial decrees
and the decisions of consuls," another "on the observations of emperors and consuls."
[66] Awe and reverence (θαυμαστοί . . . καὶ προσκυνητοί), *SB* 7696 line 86 (AD 250), a *nomos* of Severus
read, considered decisive by prefect; cf. *P.Tebt.* 286 (AD 121–38), rescript of Hadrian cited, "we must
revere (προσκυνεῖν) the judgments of Trajan and Hadrian that have been read," and for further
examples, see Ando (2000) 106–8; authority of rescript confirmed only by subscription of emperor,
CJ 1.23.3 (AD 292). Mourgues (1995a) 273 and 277 stresses the oral aspects of imperial decisions (*sacra
vox, oraculum, sacri adfatus*), while noting that imperial subscription to these decisions was a type
of performative act that complemented the imperial voice.
[67] *SB* 10967 (= Pearl [1970] 277, AD 186).
[68] Opt. *App.* 2.1 (= Maier [1987] 176 no. 22), *iussionem* of prefect considered *sacram*, attitude taken
toward it is one of *devotio* (*devotus sum*).
[69] *SB* 7696 (AD 250).
[70] *P.Oxy.* 3757 = *P.Oxy.* 3758 lines 78–97 (AD 325), where this πρόσταγμα induces the *logistes* to
summon the parties to the case and make them agree (cf. also *P.Oxy.* 3758 lines 5–38, pressure again
put on *logistes* by γράμματα of prefect).
[71] *P.Oxy.* 3759 (AD 325).

Tablets and other documents in court to AD 400   231

second century AD, probably at Rome, γράμματα were brought in showing
that unfortunate provincials had had to pay interest before they had even
received a loan, as well as a ὑπομνημα[τ]ισμός showing the governor's
inordinate affection for a boy whom he took along with him on assizes.[72]
Alexander Severus, citing Hadrian, enforced a condition (of sale) that a
female slave not be reduced to prostitution, and if she were, she was to be
freed, even though the condition was not in the *tabulas venditionis*, for he
deemed the condition valid if it could be proved through an *epistula*, or
even if it wasn't written at all.[73] The point here is not why he did this, but
the hierarchies of evidence this constitution acknowledges and deliberately
overrides.

Sometimes the reason for a document's valuation is directly observable.
In Libo's trial for subversive plotting under Tiberius, a written consultation
with an astrologer (about the possibility of future wealth) was presented,
as well as other *libelli* that Tacitus contemptuously labelled "preposter-
ous" (*vaecordes*), but the only *libellus* that made an impact was a list of
names from the imperial family and senate, with "mysterious and sinis-
ter marks" alleged to be in Libo's hand, recognizable to his slaves, next to
them.[74] Gaius executed conspirators against his family out of malice, but
also on the strength of γράμματα that were αὐτόχειρα.[75] In Classicus's
trial for *repetundis* a *scriptum* in his own hand about taking money, as well
as letters to his *amicula* in Rome rejoicing over this fact, were read out.[76]
Their own writings condemned these victims. The fact that the documents
were holographs – in the author's own handwriting – contributed to the
tight association of these writings with their authors and their *fides*. As *fides*-
documents advanced, so too could the importance of handwriting, perhaps
surprising in a world where most writing was as a matter of course done
for you (usually by slaves), and where once it had been so legally unimportant that Julius Caesar had repelled an attack based on an incriminating
letter in his own handwriting by appealing merely to the *testimonium* of
Cicero.[77] By the second century AD in Rome, however, handwriting documents was seen as a way of conveying yourself and your *fides*, and therefore

---

[72] *Repetundis* and γράμματα, *Acta Max.* ii line 4 (and at ii lines 16–17, ὑπομνημα[τ]ισμός; Musurillo
     [1954] 33). Stolen *libelli* read in court are mentioned at *D.* 47.2.73 (Modestinus); their weight is
     argued, but the answer unhelpful ("theft was committed!").
[73] *CJ* 4.56.2 (AD 223).
[74] Tac. *Ann.* 2.27–31 (*libellos* and *atroces vel occultas notas* at 2.30.1–2).
[75] Cass. Dio 59.4 (he claimed to have forgiven them and burned the letters, but burned only copies).
[76] Plin. *Ep.* 3.9 (*sua manu . . . scriptum*, and *epistolas*, at 3.9.13: "Hooray, hooray, I come to you a free
     man – having sold some of the Baetici I've recouped four million sesterces!").
[77] Suet. *Jul.* 17.1–2.

232   *The evolution of practice*

deeply implicating the writer (sometimes with gruesome consequences)[78] but highly honorific to receive.[79] Handwriting demonstrated a connection, as seals once had, but a better one, since seals could be borrowed or stolen.

Under the empire the special qualities of *tabulae* that permitted them to define and fix reality were now no longer exclusively prized, nor were *tabulae* the only written "voices" listened to. Associations and connections, proved by imperial interest or handwriting, were perceptibly widening the potential field of acceptable types of written evidence.[80] The same is also true in provincial settings, where many non-tablet documents come to be introduced without defense or apology, but here *tabulae* are more clearly of first importance through the second century AD. Their privileged valuation can be seen most directly in that most controlled and specialized of Roman venues, *epikrisis*-hearings under the prefect's jurisdiction, where the official himself acted as inquisitor. The prefect's *epikrisis* in Egypt served to determine the status of (especially) Romans settling in Egypt or those moving within Egypt, as well as cases of disputed status, and was particularly focussed on those who mattered: Alexandrians, army veterans, Roman freedmen, and Roman slaves – those who had in common their claims to privileged status or were being claimed as the property of such people.[81]

In these hearings, documentary evidence is most important. Most extracts include the formula "those documents (δικαιώματα) that they

---

[78] Note that the writers in nn.74–6 were all forced to commit suicide; also Cass. Dio 56 fr.3 (Augustus sacks a governor who made a mistake in a handwritten report), Amm. Marc. 28.1.20 (Hymetius incurs imperial disfavor in AD 372 for a handwritten letter asking the emperor to be milder), or Sid. *Ep.* 1.7.5 (Arvandus convicted on the basis of a letter written by a secretary which he insisted on claiming as his own); see also Theodoret *Ep.* 79.831.

[79] In the Republic you wrote your own letters as a matter of politeness to social superiors or intimates, or if you were aiming for extraordinary confidentiality (McDonnell [1996] 474–6); autograph letters were written and noted at this time and through the first century AD (cf. Quint. *Inst.* 6.3.100, a feeble witticism about a chirograph "in one's own hand"), but attention to their personal and honorific qualities grew only gradually, Millar (1977) 215. Handwritten imperial letters were a sign of great favor, Millar (1977) 221 n.62, their loss complained of, Philostr. *VS* 562–3 (Herodes Atticus); and Fronto desires Marcus to write to him in his own hand (*ad M. Caes.* 3.3.4); for later examples, Lendon (1997) 49 n.92. Since it was always known that personal handwriting had its own characteristics (cf. e.g., Cic. *Att.* 11.16.1; Gal. 6:11; Suet. *Aug* 64.3 [Augustus wants grandsons to imitate his handwriting]; Achtemeier [1990] 14–15 and Youtie [1975] 211–12), the slow shift to writing autograph *adnotationes* or even *subscriptiones* (chapter seven pp. 179–80, 207–10) was not motivated by a heightened desire to prove identity or prevent fraud.

[80] In the fourth century, even personal charms and love spells, *incantamenta . . . anilia* and *ludibriosa . . . amatoria*, are recited in court, Amm. Marc. 29.2.3.

[81] *P.Oxy.* 1451 lines 12–13 (and others); see Nelson (1979) 40–6 (cf. 3–9 on the changing interpretations of the *epikrisis*); also, Alston (1995) 49, 61, 215–16 n.23; other people were of course subject to *epikrisis* under different officials.

Tablets and other documents in court to AD 400

supplied (to the presiding official) are listed in each entry,"[82] and indeed they are so listed, with *tabulae* predominating. Veterans offer the δέλτος χαλκῆ, the bronze *tabula*, copied from the bronze originals in Rome, in all but one case specified as sealed;[83] legitimate Roman citizens (and often the children of veterans), the sealed δέλτος προφεσσίωνος or tablet of the *professio* of a child's birth made before the prefect;[84] illegitimate Roman citizens, the sealed δέλτος μαρτυροποιήσεως,[85] tablet of attestation or *testatio*, indicating that a child had been born from an unlawful marriage; freedmen (or -women), the sealed ταβέλλα ἐλευθερώσεως or *tabula* of freedom;[86] the masters of slaves, a document called an οἰκογένεια, attesting that these slaves were home-born, and a (local) census-registration (ἀπογραφή).[87] In two cases, length of army service and honorable discharge were also attested through documents generated by *tabularii*, one called an ἀπογραφή and one called a λί[βελλον].[88] By the mid-second century, it becomes more common to see a copy of an earlier *epikrisis* adduced as well.[89] And whenever an *epikrisis* extract is complete, it is clear that the person undergoing *epikrisis* has also brought in three witnesses, called γνωστῆρας, who swear or attest in writing, formulaically, that the person "used no other," i.e. used no false evidence.[90] Throughout, *tabulae* of Roman status and privilege – veteran or citizen, military diploma or profession of birth, tablet of manumission or witness-attestation – are fundamental, and were known to be so by the second century AD, when the *testatio* for M. Lucretius Clemens's illegitimate child Serenus states that it was made "so that he [Clemens] could prove, at his *epikrisis* after his honorable discharge, that he [Serenus] was his natural son."[91]

---

[82] ἃ δὲ παρέθεντο δικαιώματα . . . ἑκάστῳ ὀνόματι παράκειται, in *BGU* 1033 (AD 113–17); *BGU* 113 (= *W.Chr.* 458, AD 140); *BGU* 265 (= *W.Chr.* 459, AD 148); *SB* 5217 (AD 148); *BGU* 780 (AD 158–9); *SB* 9228 (after AD 160); *PSI* 5.447 (AD 167); *P.Oxy.* 1451 (AD 175).

[83] *P.Hamb.* 31 (AD 103; sealing not specified), *P.Diog.* 5 (AD 132–3), *P.Diog.* 113 (= *W.Chr.* 458; AD 148); *BGU* 780 (AD 158–9); *SB* 9228 (after AD 160); *BGU* 847 (= *W.Chr.* 460, AD 182–3).

[84] *P.Diog.* 6–7 (AD 142); *SB* 9228 (after AD 160); *BGU* 1032 (after AD 173); *P.Oxy.* 1451 (AD 175).

[85] *SB* 5217 (AD 148); *BGU* 1032 (after AD 173); *P.Oxy.* 1451 (AD 175).

[86] *P.Diog.* 6–7 (AD 142, demonstrates manumission *vindicta*); *SB* 5217 (AD 148).

[87] *BGU* 1033 (AD 113–17, κατ᾿ οἰκίαν ἀπο[γρα]φήν); *PSI* 5.447 (AD 167, both); *P.Oxy.* 1451 (AD 175, both).

[88] *P.Hamb.* 31 (AD 103, ἀπογραφή); *P.Diog.* 5 (AD 132–3, λί[βελλον]).

[89] *P.Diog.* 6–7 (AD 142); *SB* 5217 (AD 148); *PSI* 5.447 (AD 167).

[90] συγχειρογραφοῦντας . . . μηδενὶ ἀλλοτρίῳ κεχρῆσθαι, found in *P.Diog.* 5 (AD 132–3), *P.Diog.* 6–7 (AD 142), *SB* 5217 (AD 148), *PSI* 5.447 (AD 167), *BGU* 1032 (after AD 173), *P.Oxy.* 1451 (AD 175), *SB* 7362 (AD 188).

[91] *ut possit post honestam missionem suam ad epicrisin suam adprobare filium suum naturalem esse*, *CPL* 149 (= *P.Diog.* 1, AD 127) lines 11–13. *HA Marc.* 9.8 claims that Marcus modified the provincial system of birth-registration for a similar motive, discussed by Haensch (1992) 283–90.

234   *The evolution of practice*

Rarely do other forms of documentation come up, and then mostly for slaves. The category of "veterans without bronze" was also known to exist, although how their claims were judged we do not know.[92] They may have been like the man confirmed in his status because he presented an ἐπιστολὴ Ῥωμαϊκή from a former prefect attesting his honorable discharge.[93] Certainly the sailors-turned-legionaries who petitioned their prefect in Judaea for an *instrumentum* of honorable discharge before returning to Egypt must have thought that he could generate something that could help them – and since they brought only a double-document copy of their subscribed and posted petition to Egypt, they must also have expected that a *diploma* of this sort would be accepted by the Egyptian prefect too.[94] But the routine way, the accepted way, of demonstrating what needed demonstrating was by using your own *tabulae*, and this is what most people in these circumstances did. And although there is no evidence of an *epikrisis* anywhere else in the Roman provinces, the very ubiquity of Roman military diplomas suggests that veterans both wanted the *tabula* that copied and proved in an irrefutable way the lasting honor of their grants of status and privilege, and may have anticipated official or legal challenges to status of some sort in every province of the empire.[95]

The extent to which *tabulae* were adduced in other kinds of Egyptian court cases is unknown, for the evidence is scanty and unsatisfactory, but the overall picture suggests that here too *tabulae* were a special class of evidence superior to others. At the end of the second century AD, for example, a landowner in the Oxyrhynchite nome "thinks it fitting that his *tabellae* are read out," and in the next lacunose line the word Ῥωμαϊκά tantalizingly floats by,[96] but not even the subject of this dispute is known. A contemporary dispute over an estate (possibly over a guardianship, probably over an inheritance) in Alexandria, before the *idios logos*, is rather more extensive, and again involves proof of status. This hearing investigated not just the fate of the flocks and the silver plate, but whether or not slaves had been freed

---

[92] Mentioned in, e.g., *BGU* 113 and 265 (= *W.Chr.* 458–9): οὐετρανοὶ οἱ χωρὶς χαλκῶν. Seston (1933) identified these men as legionaries (and they did not receive *conubium*, Alston [1995] 215 n.23), but cf. Degrassi (1934) and Cavenaile (1953); they could also have been auxiliaries who did not pay for having a bronze diploma drawn up, if Roxan (1986) is correct.

[93] "Roman letter," *SB* 7362 (AD 188).

[94] *CPL* 117 (= *PSI* 9.1026), with Alston (1995) 216 n.23 (iii).

[95] They were copied from posted *tabulae* at Rome, see above chapter seven n. 1.

[96] *PSI* 4.293 (Oxyrhynchus, late second century AD), ἀξιώσα[ντος τὰς] ταβέλλας [α]ὐτοῦ ἀναγνωσθῆναι [–]ᾳ ἀναγνωσθέντο[ς. . . . .]οτε.[. . . . .] Ῥωμαϊκά μετα.[–]. Amelotti (1966) 173 n.2 interpreted these as will-*tabellae*.

Tablets and other documents in court to AD 400   235

before or after the murder of the Roman master, Sempronius Gemellus. *Tabellae* of manumission were key, and were carefully examined.[97]

Smaragdos [one of the former slaves] said: "I have returned, so that . . . the inheritance . . . the *vicesima* [twentieth-tax] . . . so that I might pay (it) on behalf of myself and my children."
Postumus said: "The *tabellae* were drawn up twelve years ago, and *now* you have remembered the twentieth-tax? At least you can seek out and fetch Eutyches [who had Smaragdos's tablets], taking the *beneficiarius* [the soldier seconded to assist a magistrate], and furnish the *tabellae*."
Smaragdos said: "I will look for him."
After a little while, Smaragdos returned and furnished three *tabellae*, and said that he could not find Eutyches. Postumus said: "From where, then, have you brought the *tabellae*?"
Smaragdos said: "I brought them having asked the slave who is in charge of the inn where Eutyches is staying."
Postumus said: "Two *tabellae* of manumission for the same name with different dates have been adduced, and I doubt that they were written by the hand of the deceased. How can this man [he is referring to yet another slave, named Eukairos] have been freed twice? Because of this, therefore, I am suspicious about all the other *tabellae* [i.e. including yours, Smaragdos], and many things therefore prove to me that (although) they [the tablets] were written up many years ago, the twentieth-tax was not paid, and that after some years that man [Gemellus], when he was making a census-return, there having been an *epikrisis*, entered these same men as his slaves in the census. But even they [the slaves] agree that they were never acknowledged as having been free, and that Gemellus was killed by treachery, and (that) after his death the *tabellae* were given to the slaves as a sign of [[his]] goodwill." And he ordered the *nomikos* who appeared to have written the tablets, Julius also known as Sarapion, to be brought in.
Diogenes the bailiff (?) said: "If you will examine, you will find by means of the *epikrisis* which took place . . . slaves registered in the census . . . of tablets."

Another participant, named Kasianos, insists – albeit in *lacunae* here, but at greater length later – that the *tabellae* have been altered. Clothing, flocks, and silver plate are discussed.

When the sought-for *nomikos* Flavius Julius, also known as Sarapion, arrived, Postumus said: "Did you know Sempronius [Gemellus]?"
He answered: "For many years . . . I was . . . and I wrote for him both *tabellae* of manumission(s) and *diplomata* of marriage and I have copies of them."
Postumus ordered the *tabellae* lodged with Gemellus the document-keeper [*bibliophylax*] to be produced, and when he gave one to him [Julius known as Sarapion], he asked whether the letters were familiar to him; which thing having

---

[97] *BGU* 388 (= *M.Chr.* 91) 1 lines 7–29, 2 lines 30–41, discussed, Mommsen (1905 [1895]); see also Haensch (1995) 272 and n.35 on Diogenes the bailiff or προσοδοποιός.

236 *The evolution of practice*

been agreed to, Postumus said: "How can it be that two *tabellae* of freedom for Eukairos are found?"
Julius known as Sarapion said: "They are customarily written in two copies."[98]
Postumus said: "If, as you say, you wrote two copies, how is it that the same date is not given in them, nor are the sealers the same?"
Kasianos said: "As I told you, Ptolemais, having filched Eukairos's *tabella* with the true entries, in which (tablet), when Auxon was dying, she entered the name of this man, in which forgery the name is still present now throughout the entire *tabella*."
Serenos [yet another advocate] said: "Eukairos said who gave him the *tabella*."

Kasianos's intrusions seem to be irrelevant and hostile distractions, since they claim erasure and rewriting of the name in the *tabella* of manumission, whereas the *idios logos* has noted that the two *tabellae* are for the same person, but with different dates and different sealers. Unfortunately, the *nomikos*'s answer to the very pertinent question of how two such tablets could have been generated is not preserved – if he did indeed answer it, and was not (perhaps to his relief) forgotten in the general mêlée of what appears to have been a very raucous hearing. By the end, however, the suspicions of the *idios logos* were not allayed, for he took all five *tabellae* – the three presented by Smaragdos, and the two contradictory ones of Eukairos he already had in his possession when this extract began – and sealed them (as a way of securing them in their present state; it is not clear from this that they had actually been opened), handing them over to the *bibliophylax*. He also ordered Smaragdos and Eukairos to be taken into custody and the *nomikos* to provide surety for them, while an underling went to make further inquiries.[99] It is noteworthy that the *idios logos* expects *tabellae* to be offered up when freed status is asserted (for he sends Smaragdos back to get his from Eutyches); that he is perturbed by the lack of congruence in two *tabellae* that should have been exactly the same; that he takes handwriting into consideration; and that he is not stampeded by the pushy Kasianos into proclaiming forgery when the *tabellae* do not agree. Indeed, the judge's scenario of what might have happened is more complicated precisely because he is trying to conserve the evidence: is it possible that a man was freed twice, but not informed of this fact the first time, and then re-registered as a slave? Postumus would clearly like to believe that this is true. He clearly also therefore presumes the truthfulness of *tabellae*.

---

[98] *Contra* Crook (1995) 65, the νομικός is not "giving evidence as to the Roman . . . rule about *tabellai*," but merely answering questions about notarial practice very carefully.
[99] *BGU* 388 (= *M.Chr.* 91) 3.7–10.

Tablets and other documents in court to AD 400   237

In the other rich and varied materials from Egyptian trials and legal hearings, neither tablets nor *diplomata* specifically appear. Instead, *testationes* and related terms are found, as well as written testimony read aloud,[100] and from the legal literature *testationes* specifically attesting to betrothal, marriage, or the taking of a freeborn woman into a state of concubinage are known, although not one survives.[101] There is also a bewildering array of catch-all non-specific terms: γράμματα, as well as letters from important people;[102] sometimes unspecified βίβλια;[103] sometimes βιβλίδια (which generally seem to refer to summonses or petitions).[104] In a case over a disputed inheritance heard in an army camp between AD 41 and 68,[105] *cautiones* (*cavitionibus*, here) were read out after the pleadings (*causam*) had been made. In other Egyptian cases cheirographs, agreements, and wills are all read aloud, and many other documents are referred to;[106] judges here no

---

[100] *testationes* and ἐκμαρτυρία, above chapter seven n.105; also, *SB* 7696 (AD 250) or *P.Oxy.* 1502 (AD 260–1, προσφώνησις . . . ἔγγραφος of a doctor).

[101] *testationes* of marriage (not the same as *tabulae nuptiales*): Karabélias (1984), based on *D.* 25.7.3 (Marcian) and *D.* 20.1.4 = *D.* 22.4.4 (Gaius); *testationes* of betrothal, *D.* 23.1.7.*pr.* (Paulus), *D.* 25.7.3.*pr.* (Marcian; is not allowed without a *testatio* "making this manifest"); other *testationes* in legal sources, *D.* 48.3.14.6 (Herennius Modestinus), *D.* 4.6.22.1 (Paulus), *D.* 22.2.2 (Pomponius, quoting Labeo); *testationes* of unknown nature imagined as being used in court, *D.* 6.1.27.*pr.* (Paulus); before an arbiter, *D.* 4.8.32.14 (Paulus).

[102] γράμματα: *BGU* 19 (AD 130/1), proving through γράμματα; *SB* 9213 (AD 215); *BGU* 1567, γράμματα referred to twice (third century AD). Letters: in governors' courts, *Acta Ath.* ii line 60 (Musurillo [1954] 63), *BGU* 19 (AD 135); others: *SB* 15 and 16 (AD 155/6; whose court in Egypt is unknown); *Acta Scill. Mart.* 12, *libri et epistolae* (Musurillo [1972] 88); *Acta Marc.* 3–4 (Musurillo [1972] 252 and 256), letter from prefect, also called *acta praesidis* and *acta praesidialia*; *P.Ryl.* 2.77 (AD 192), letter from *archontes* to *strategos* read out; *P.Fay.* 203 (second century AD), letter of the prefect (summary only); *BGU* 245, *strategos* gives decision on basis of ὑπομνήματα and ἐπιστολαί (second century); *SB* 12555 (letters to *strategos*); *SB* 12692 (AD 339), letter from prefect.

[103] *P.Hamb.* 29 (AD 89); *P.Oxy.* 3117 (third century AD).

[104] *SB* 8261 (AD 154–8), 7558 (AD 173), 5693 (AD 186), 11170 (second century), *P.Stras.* 21+*P.Lips.* 32 (= *M.Chr.* 93, *c.* AD 250), *BGU* 168 (second–third century), and *SB* 8246 (AD 340), all βιβλίδιον or βίβλια = *libellus*.

[105] *P.Mich.* 3.159 lines 9 and 12.

[106] Cheirographs, *P.Oxy.* 706 (AD 115; decisive in case of master vs. freedman), *P.Mil.Vogl.* 25 (AD 127); also called γράμματα of deposit), *P.Oxy.* 1408 (AD 210–14), *P.Amh.* 67 (AD 232); agreements, *P.Oxy.* 3757 = *P.Oxy.* 3758 lines 78–97 (AD 325); wills, *CPR* 1.18 (AD 124), *BGU* 361 (AD 184), *M.Chr.* 372 col. iv (second century), *P.Stras.* 21+*P.Lips.* 32 (= *M.Chr.* 93, AD 250), *P.Oxy.* 3758 (AD 325; three examples); orders, *W.Chr.* 27 (AD 159; before senate of Antinoopolis), *P.Oxy.* 3759 (AD 325) and *SB* 11223 (AD 332); *libellus*, *P.Stras.* 21+*P.Lips.* 32 (= *M.Chr.* 93, AD 250), *SB* 12692 (AD 339); receipt, *P.Flor.* 61 (= *M.Chr.* 80, destroyed by order of prefect after reading, AD 85); see also *M.Chr.* 372 col. 3 (διαγράμματα of debt) and col. 4 (sale; second century AD). Cases where documents are clearly at issue: *P.Oxy.* 37 (= *M.Chr.* 79, AD 49); *P.Oxy.* 1420 (AD 129, accounts); *P.Oxy.* 707 (AD 136, written rental agreement); *P.Tebt.* 286 (AD 121–38, purchase-agreements); *SB* 15–16 (AD 155–6, birth attestation); *BGU* 361 (AD 184, Roman will); *M.Chr.* 372 (document of slave birth, second century AD); *SB* 5676 (AD 232, συμβόλαιον, ὑποθήκη, cheirograph); *P.Oxy.* 1502 (AD 260–1, will); *P.Lond.* 1650 (AD 373, farming contract); *SB* 12581 (fourth century, *codicilli*); *P.Oxy.* 3757 = *P.Oxy.* 3758 lines 78–97 (AD 325, γραμματεῖα of discharge and debt); *P.Oxy.* 3758 (AD 325, proofs of ownership); *SB* 12692 (AD 339, deed of cession).

238 *The evolution of practice*

doubt followed the custom of the country, and saw no need to intervene and stop the use of these documents as evidence.[107] Elsewhere in the east, we also find offhand references to letters or other non-specific *grammata* in court settings or circumstances leading thereto, even anxiety-dreams about losing the *grammata* that would vindicate a defendant.[108]

In the province of North Africa in the second century AD, we find *tabulae* still dominant, other types of letters and documents gaining ground. Or at least we think we do: Apuleius's defense of himself against a charge of magic, his *Apology*, is so masterful, and makes every form of evidence to hand work so entirely in his favor, that by the end it is hard to make distinctions, even between more and most irrefutable types of documents. Indeed, everything proves not just that Apuleius is innocent of the charges, but also an Important Person, and cleverer than everyone else. Letters from Pudentilla and Aemilianus (Apuleius's wife and her brother-in-law from her first marriage) to Pontianus (a step-son, now deceased) demonstrate, with Apuleius's expert help, not only that Pudentilla wished to remarry (which Aemilianus had denied), but that Aemilianus knew this. Handwriting is used to establish the truthfulness of a mere letter, as well as the fact that it was Aemilianus's, and when Apuleius called on Aemilianus to recognize his own *subscriptio*, he turned pale, and was thereby "convicted" by his own testimony.[109] Point for Apuleius, working with a letter. Moreover, Apuleius refuted the prosecution's apparent trump, a letter in which Pudentilla accused Apuleius of being a magician. For after making a copy of the letter in the presence of witnesses, with Aemilianus countersigning the copy, Apuleius had this read out in court. This reading made clear that the letter had been misleadingly excerpted, and that the crucial sentence should read, "But now that certain ill-natured persons have brought accusations against us and attempt to dissuade you, Apuleius has suddenly become a magician and I have been bewitched by him and I love him," rather than just the last

---

[107] On the general importance of documents in Egyptian courts, E. Seidl (1973) 120–1.

[108] See, e.g., the case of Aelius Aristides (Behr). *Or.* 50.75–6, 78 (first hearing), 84 (additional letter from Rufinus read to governor), 90 (second hearing), 96 (more letters to a different governor), 98 (decision reversed), with Lendon (1997) 202–22; Fro. *ad Am.* 1.1.1 deems the direct writing of praise *to* the judge a harmless offshoot of the practice of writing laudations (as here) for court, and Aristides's case shows how close the two practices can be. For (later) examples of such letters, see Greg. Naz. *Ep.* 150 and 207, Sid. *Ep.* 4.6.4; Syn. *Ep.* 50 (Garzya) refers to this practice. Other cases, D. Chr. 43.6 (γράμματα stolen by kinsmen), *Acta Scill. Mar.* 12 (Musurillo [1972] 88); Frend (1956); Maraval (1990) 70 line 72r; even in novels, Heliodorus, *Aeth.* 10.12.4 (τάς τε ἐγγράφους πίστεις καὶ τὰς ἐκ μαρτύρων βεβαιώσεις), this a long-lasting platitude, cf. Greg. of Tours *Vit. Patr.* 17.pr., "some things confirmed by written account, by testimony of other writers, by our own eyes." Letters in court in late antiquity too, e.g., Amm. Marc. 14.9.8 (AD 354) and 15.5.3–4 (AD 355); in general, Harries (1999) 99–110. Anxiety-dream: Artem. *Oneir.* 5.10.

[109] Aemilianus's *subscribtio, Apol.* 69; "convicted" by his own testimony, *Apol.* 70.

Tablets and other documents in court to AD *400*   239

clause, which was all that the prosecution had reported. What was presented as a damning statement thereby became a metaphor and a statement of an accusation rather than a statement of fact.[110] Ten more points to Apuleius, from a letter. "You challenged me with Pudentilla's letter; with the letter I win the day,"[111] he crows, for Pudentilla not only denied that Apuleius was a magician, but later in the same letter denied the existence of magic itself. The opposition, country bumpkins that they are, cannot even read a letter correctly; what they presented as killer proof was proof only of their malice or stupidity. Having successfully turned the prosecution's evidence into his own, and having thereby set himself up as an expert in how to use letters, Apuleius then found it easy to dismiss in passing another letter adduced by the opposition, one claiming to show that Apuleius had won his wife through flattery (*blanditiis*): because it was written in barbarous Greek, it was clearly a forgery, for Apuleius (naturally) wrote superb Greek.[112] So much for the prosecution's documentary evidence, all of it letters. Apuleius needed to disqualify only one, and allowed the others since (as he brilliantly demonstrated) they spoke in his defense; because they are useful to him they have value, although they are dismissable when they do not.

Apuleius finds other letters useful too, specifically very fulsome letters from Very Important People,[113] but makes clear that he has on his side a form of truth superior even to these. Even if Pudentilla's letter had been correctly excerpted, he says, would her word in a letter prove Apuleius to be something he was not – like a consul, a painter, a doctor? Surely not. "And how much greater weight should that, which is subscribed *in iudicio*, have than that which is written *in epistola!*"[114] Yet even a trial cannot not prove Apuleius a magician; a letter certainly should not. Letters are still considered informal and somehow protean, and can be argued against with both facility and success. Never fear: there are more trustworthy forms of evidence, and they are at hand. When Apuleius finally turns to positive proof of his own points, he makes use of legal documents on *tabulae* that are themselves subscribed, and brings them in with a confidence that itself confirms their superiority to mere letters. Pudentilla is proved to be a little

---

[110] Pudentilla's letter, *Apol.* 78–83 (Ἀπολέιος μάγος, καὶ ἐγὼ ὑπ' αὐτοῦ μεμάγευμαι καὶ ἐρῶ); correct quotation, *Apol.* 83.
[111] *Apol.* 84 (*ad litteras Pudentillae provocastis: litteris vinco*).
[112] *Apol.* 87.
[113] *Apol.* 95–6.
[114] *Apol.* 79, *et quanto tandem gravis habendum est quod in iudicio subscribitur quam quod in epistola scribitur*; *quod in iudicio subscribitur* can refer to the indictment, and thus (by metonymy) to the case as a whole, and in the context of the argument about Pudentilla's letter seems to be used this way.

240   *The evolution of practice*

over forty (not sixty, as the opposition claimed) by the tablets of her birth-declaration, made "as is customarily done" (*more ceterum*) and preserved in part in the public *tabularium* and in part at home. The *linum* that ties the tablets together and the seals impressed upon it are examined, the consuls' names identified. Maximus the judge himself calculates how many consuls there have been since then; there are no questions, there can be no doubt, and the *tabulae* are not even opened.[115]

Apuleius then moves on to the question of motive, to prove that he did not marry (as well as would not have married) Pudentilla for her money. This too is chiefly accomplished through tablets. The *tabulae* of the marriage agreement speak "more eloquently" than Apuleius to the charge that he robbed her of her dowry: they show that the dowry was only 300,000 HS (a "trivial sum"), that it was made over to Apuleius as a trust and not a gift, and that if the marriage were childless the money was all to revert to Pontianus and Pudens. "Take them into your own hands, give them to Rufinus": the tablets show all.[116] Furthermore, Apuleius worked tirelessly to reconcile mother and estranged sons rather than to enrich himself. That this was achieved with the elder son, Pontianus, is demonstrated by numerous letters written by Pontianus shortly before his death, and also by his will, "unfinished though it may be," in which Apuleius is dutifully and respectfully mentioned.[117] It is, however, especially well demonstrated by Pudentilla's sealed will, which leaves her property to her sole surviving son, Pudens.[118]

Order the tablets to be broken open, Maximus. You will find that her son is the heir, that I get nothing save some trifling legacy for honor's sake lest my name, the husband's name . . . in my wife's will, not be mentioned . . . If she ever wrote anything while not in her right mind, you will find it here, nor will you have to go far to find it. "Let Sicinius Pudens, my son, be my heir." I admit it! He who reads this will think it insanity . . .

Pudentilla is still alive and could presumably testify to her own change of heart about her son; but this is not nearly as effective as breaking open her

---

[115] *Apol.* 89; he had previously also read *testimonium* from *libelli*, *Apol.* 57, which the opposition had presented (*Apol.* 59), reading it out because – Apuleius argues (following Quintilian's advice!) – the witness, who was possibly snoring drunk or sweating out impurities to prepare for another round of debauch, could not speak directly to the judge without blushing.

[116] *Apol.* 91–2 (*multo disertius ipsae tabulae loquantur*); *cape sis ipse tu manibus tuis tabulas istas, da impulsori tuo Rufino, Apol.* 92.

[117] *Apol.* 96–7.

[118] *Apol.* 99–101; quotation at 100–1: *rumpi tabulas istas iube, Maxime: invenies filium heredem, mihi vero tenue nescio quid honoris gratia legatum, ne . . . nomen maritus in uxoris tabulis non haberem . . . si quid quasi insana scripsit, hic reperies et quidem mox a principio: "Sicinius Pudens filius meus mihi heres esto." fateor, qui ho<c> legerit insanum putabit . . .*

Tablets and other documents in court to AD 400   241

sealed will and reading her intention to the court – so unusual, so contrary to what was proper! As Apuleius – who claimed credit for Pudentilla's change of heart – knew only too well, intentions can change; but writing them on tablets fixes them and makes them authoritative. Tablets are truthful, and under these circumstances testify even better than the people themselves. As a final touch, Apuleius rebuts the charge that he bought an excellent, large farm with Pudentilla's money by supplying witnesses and the *tabula* of sale: the property is proved to be minor, Apuleius's name unmentioned on the *tabula*.[119] Apuleius has not profited financially from this marriage. As he concludes, "Did he covet her wealth? The marriage settlement denies it, the deed of gift denies it, the will denies it! It shows not only that I did not court the generosity of my wife, but that I even repulsed it with some severity."[120] Case closed. Letters have been cited and re-read, handwriting examined, but *tabulae* were particularly effective in bringing about victory.

LATE ANTIQUITY

In the Late Empire, this wider variety of documents apparently acceptable in court, or at least appearing there, broadens to include one last type: records of former trials. These help to reconcile the perceived disparities between *tabulae* and other kinds of documents that could still be exploited by provincial lawyers, since reading these other types of documents into "the *tabulae*" fixed and established value with a certainty and durability that a man's *fides* could not. Only the emperor's *fides* and prestige were established, even quasi-objective values; those of other men were attributed qualities and were subject to the twists of fortune over time, much as they would hope, or attempt, to deny it. The *tabulae* of governors, while still personal, had greater and more stable prestige, and were powerful and authoritative in court; by adding value and giving protection to individual legal documents of all sorts they also made such documents (or even performed acts, like declarations) authoritative; and in the end they could even make an ephemeral medium like papyrus authoritative as well.

Records of former trials had been used in court in Cicero's time, although their effect is unclear.[121] In the first century AD Quintilian listed *praeiudicia*, previous legal decisions, as a type of inartificial proof, that is

---

[119] *Apol.* 101 (referred to first as *tabulis*, then as *emptio*).

[120] *Apol.* 102 (*tabula* of donation refers to a gift narrated at 93–4, but not brought into court).

[121] First century BC: see Greenidge (1901) 394–5, 487, and Cic. *Cluent.* 62, a challenge – *testium dicta recita* in a different trial (may be from *tabulae publicae*, but not conclusive), Cic. 2 *Verr.* 1.78–9, 84 (*testimonium* Verres had given in Cicero's possession).

242 *The evolution of practice*

something already in existence (rather than created by the orator) that could be adduced in court.[122] In Roman Egypt when court-records are cited it was usually only this decision, often recorded word for word (*kata lexin*) and in *oratio recta*, that was read out subsequently.[123] There may not have been much more in those records that could have been read out. Verres's *tabulae* had recorded the name of the defendant, whether or not the defendant was present, who spoke (or was to speak) for and against (*reus* and *accusator*), the substance of the cross-examination, and the result, and such information at Rome was generally recorded in the *publicae tabulae* of the praetor.[124] High imperial court-records – descendants of the *tabulae* such as Verres's, and called *hypomnemata* or *hypomnematismoi* in Egypt – were usually meticulous in recording the comments, actions, and decisions of the officials involved; who the parties were; any imperial writings cited as pertinent to the question; what arguments and evidence were used, although the actual content of these was omitted or, at best, skimpily recorded; witness-testimony, before the fourth century, was only briefly summarized in the record, sometimes so briefly that it is impossible to understand what was actually said.[125] Records were being kept not for their own sake, but to display the official's performance, which meant that their applicability to subsequent trials – unless of the official himself – was limited. They were *his* records, even when (in Egypt) deposited in a type of record-office, and

[122] Quint. *Inst.* 5.2; for their embedding in court-protocols, see below n.123.

[123] Reading decisions (a Roman habit, Jolowicz [1937] 12–15), *SB* 9252 (AD 118); *BGU* 19 (= *M.Chr.* 85, AD 135); *SB* 7601 (AD 135); *P.Mert.* 3.117 (after AD 141); *BGU* 329 (AD 152); *SB* 9016 (AD 160); *BGU* 970 (= *M.Chr.* 242, AD 177); *SB* 12555 (second century); *P.Fay.* 203 (second century); *SB* 7696 (AD 250); see indignation at *SB* 9213 (how can you be sure without reading the ὑπομνήματα? AD 215); *P.Oxy.* 1204 (AD 299); *P.Oxy.* 3117 (third century); *P.Oxy.* 3767 (AD 329 or 330); *SB* 12629 (AD 329–31); *SB* 11223 (AD 332); *CIL* 10.7852, a judicial decision copied from the *codex* of the proconsul and inscribed. For protocols in other provinces, Burton (1975) 103–4, Haensch (1992) 221–9 (on verdicts in particular; *n.b.* Ael. Aristid. *Or.* 50.78 [Behr], Apul. *Flor.* 9, *provinciae instrumento refertur*; Eus. *HE* 5.18, *acta* of trial of Alexander in the δημόσιον ἀρχεῖον of Asia). Decisions recorded word-for-word, see *SB* 9016 (AD 160, decision read κατὰ λέξιν, from a πίναξ); *SB* 12555 (second century); *BGU* 245 (second century); *BGU* 592 (second century, κατὰ λέξιν); *P.Stras.* 60 (= *W.Chr.* 77, letter of *strategos* κατὰ λέξιν in records of high priest, second century).

[124] Verres (as praetor): Cic. 2*Verr.* 1.157, 2.2.101–4, 2.3.41 (*codicis*), 2.5.102 (cross-exam); *reus* and *accusator* in the *tabulis publicis* also in Cic. *Cluent.* 86. Cross-exam: Cic. *Sull.* 40 ("what was said") and 41 (*dicta, interrogata, responsa*). Results: Plaut. *Rudens* 21; verdict of consul and sixteen senators entered εἰς τὴν τῶν ὑπομνημάτων δέλτον, *IG* 7.413 (= *FIRA²* 1.260–6 no. 36, 73 BC). Praetor's *tabulae publicae*: Cic. *Fam.* 8.8.3 (praetor did not enter Servilius as acquitted of extortion); cf. Cic. *Cluent.* 91 (Verres's *codex* as city praetor did not record a *subsortio*) and 2*Verr.* 1.119 (Verres's fellow-praetor filled *codices* with overturned decisions of Verres's). See also David (1999) on records of Republican *iudicia publica* (names of accusers and *subscriptores*, advocates, witnesses and *laudatores*).

[125] Contents of Egyptian court-records: see Coles (1966) and Crook (1995) 59–62, with Luc. *Apol.* 12. Other material not usually read back later, Skeat and Wegener (1935) 226 on *SB* 7696. Private *commentarii* were still kept on *tabulae* in the second century AD, Philostr. *VA* 1.3, τὰς δέλτους ὑπομνημάτων, keeping his words, γνώμας, etc.

Tablets and other documents in court to AD 400

it was *his* prestige and power, therefore, that enhanced their standing when his decisions were subsequently cited in court.[126]

Over time, and especially after AD 284, these court-records came to include fuller (if not entirely complete) accounts of everything that went on and what the protagonists and witnesses said.[127] This trend reflects not only the capacity of *tabulae*, with their formal powers and personal associations, to incorporate authoritatively what was done and said, as well as the *fides* of their principal, but also the increasing importance of the principal, the official, in personal legal acts and as a generator of verdicts and information that had a legal as well as an administrative impact.[128] Large segments of court-records came to be regularly reread in subsequent cases, as a way of accurately reconstructing what had happened, and of checking current testimony against previous acts or words.[129] Concomitantly, court-records became a regularly referred-to type of "proof" in non-legal settings[130] and the substratum of a literary "docudrama" genre, Christian martyr-acts;[131] they were becoming sufficiently valuable to others that money (which went to the official's staff) could be made from the generation of copies,[132] and the ways in which they were taken down came to be used for other types of disputes, particularly religious ones.[133] *Acta* or *gesta* (as they are usually

---

[126] Lévy (1998) 249; this made Roman court–records different from Ptolemaic records, Jolowicz (1937) 2.

[127] Bickermann (1933) 346–8 for changes in the fourth century, especially the sense that records now memorialize what happened (*gesta*) rather than only what the presiding official did, which (to his mind) makes the record substantially less his. Compare also *IG* 14.830 (= *OGIS* 595, AD 174), letter summarized in *acta* of senate of Puteoli with Opt. *App.* 1.17–21 (six letters read out and preserved in *acta*) or the *Coll. Carth.* (*PL* 11.1231–1420), where many documents – imperial *sanctio*, magisterial edict, *acta*, *mandata* – were read into record.

[128] The growing importance of the official, see chapter seven pp. 197–201, 210–15; Harries (1999) 70–6 on the authority of late-antique *acta*.

[129] A rescript of AD 194 notes an official's capacity to use these records, *CJ* 2.1.2. What happened: *SB* 11223 (AD 332, "I shall read what happened then," and the ὑπομνήματα were read); Symm. *Rel.* 19.9 (*gesta*); Opt. *App.* 1.17b (AD 320).

[130] Cyprian *Ep.* 67.6; *P.Oxy.* 1204 (AD 299), copy of ὑπομνήματα sent with a petition; canon 14 of the Council of Arles (*traditores* detected *ex actis publicis*, AD 314); Palladius *Vit. Ioann. Chrys.* 15.42 (Malingrey); Aug. *con. Cresc.* 3.28, 33, 56, 62, 70, and 80 (*PL* 43.509, 512–14, 527, 529–30, 534–5, 539–40), with Haensch (1992) 228–9. Possibly as early as the first century AD, Cass. Dio 59.16 (γράμματα from trials); in *FV* 112 and *D.* 28.4.3 (Marcellus) jurists are quoting court records; *CIL* 6.266 (= *FIRA²* 3.510–13 no. 165) dedicates trial-excerpts to Hercules (AD 226–44).

[131] See (e.g.) Niedermeyer (1918); Bisbee (1988) 4–17 (there is a flourishing literature that attempts to distinguish between authentic and inauthentic, of less interest to me here); Bowersock (1995) 23–5, 36–9; Eus. *HE* 7.11 tries to generate this feeling of authenticity by noting ὡς ὑπεμνηματίσθη.

[132] *CIL* 8.17896 (Thamugadi), line 34 sets payment to *exceptores*, and for paper, probably to prevent free-market gouging (AD 361–3); *P.Cair.* 67031 (summarized by Garnsey and Humfress [2001] 55) sets *sportulae* in trials where no written record was made at "half the 'going rate'."

[133] Ways in which they were taken down, described Teitler (1985) 5–18, Mourgues (1995a) 289–300 (all dependent on the *Collatio Carthageniensis*); see also below pp. 247–8. "The Church . . . transferred

244   *The evolution of practice*

called)[134] were an excellent way of demonstrating "what happened," for they fixed and made retrievably real, as *tabulae* in general always had, the official's days in court. Such archives themselves *testantur*, "attested," and "showed."[135]

Thus in AD 314, when bishop Felix of Aptunga was accused before Aelian, proconsul of Africa, of having handed over Scripture (according to imperial order in the Great Persecution of AD 303), the former magistrate Alfius Caecilian was required to bring himself, his secretary, and his *tabularius* to the trial so that both Felix's and Caecilian's actions could be replayed and understood. Since the *tabularius* was dead, Caecilian was instructed to bring the *acta* of his year in office, during which time the imperial order to sacrifice and hand over Scripture had been received, and during which time Felix had purportedly responded in ways for which he was currently on trial.[136] These *acta* – referred to, in a textually vexed passage, as *cera*, "the wax" – Caecilian had taken home with him, as magistrates (outside Egypt) often did.[137] He and Miccius, his secretary, were having trouble finding them; but either Caecilian or his *acta* were required, for the *acta* would demonstrate the *actus* (activities) and *fides* of Caecilian and others on that fateful occasion.[138] Eventually the court made do with Caecilian himself, although the presiding proconsul offered up some (unknown) *acta* of his own. "Both my questions and the replies of various persons are contained in the acts," said the proconsul; to his mind they would settle the issue.[139] Such *acta*, as was traditional, belonged to both the person and the office; the *fides* and status of the person and the office supported them; they were presumed to be true; and attempts to make *acta* authentic and to protect them against forgery, which in at least one case (which might have

> to the religious realm the method of preparing proceedings," Steinwenter (1915) 12, 27, Bickermann (1933) 345–7; Posner (1972) 214–15 (summary), for the use of synodal records in subsequent synods, and in church courts the same standard of proof applied as in secular courts, *N. Val.* 35.*pr.* (AD 452). Cf. verbatim record of acclamations in the Roman Senate upon the promulgation of the Theodosian Code (preface to *CT*), with Harries (1999) 65–7 (stressing acclamation and *acta* as creators of legitimacy); when *acta senatus* began to be taken down and what they included are debated, cf. Mommsen (1904) and Talbert (1984) 309–37; for references to surviving examples, Mourgues (1995a) 279–80 n.67.

[134] On terminology (including also *monumenta, charta,* etc.) see Steinwenter (1915) 5–10.

[135] Aug. *con. Cresc.* 3.58–61, 67 (*PL* 43.527–9, 532–3), *proconsularia testantur archiva*; Symm. *Rel.* 19.9, *ut gesta monstrabunt.*

[136] Opt. *App.* 2.1 (Maier [1987] 174–6 no. 22): Caecilian's presence, with *acta*, required; the hearing's records were to be sent on to another hearing.

[137] Opt. *App.* 2.3, wax; 2.2 (at home), both Maier (1987) 176 no. 22; the imperial official presiding over the *Coll. Carth.* in AD 411 also seems to have taken his home, for only after his death are they filed in the *publica monumenta, CT* 16.5.55 (AD 414).

[138] *Actus* and *fides*, Opt. *App.* 2.4 (Maier [1987] 178 no. 22); in *Coll. Carth.* 1.2, 1.217, 3.240, 3.272 (*PL* 11.1259, 1351, 1405, 1416), physical movement in the court is recorded.

[139] Opt. *App.* 2.3 (Maier [1987] 176 no. 22).

Tablets and other documents in court to AD 400   245

been hyper-careful) took the form of reading through, recopying, subscribing, and even sealing,[140] made them look much like old-fashioned *tabulae* or *diplomata* of individuals. Once, when those at Carthage were being consulted, a bishop remarked in amazement, "That's how testaments, not *gesta*, are customarily opened!"[141]

By the end of the fourth century, *acta* have become sufficiently important that when something has not been recited into them – as a *mandatum*, a deed of agency, was not in a long-running case that came before Symmachus as urban prefect in AD 384 – the opposition could claim that the agent had no legal standing, and that in fact there had been no deed of agency.[142] By this point, when they could be used to check witnesses' consistency in court or to determine whether or not other acts had taken place, *acta* were not only assumed to be accurate, but assumed to be inclusively accurate, and as authoritative as other *tabulae* had been.

Since an official's *fides* was linked to his *tabulae*, the inclusion of other types of evidence in them improved the quality and unassailability of that evidence by accepting it and protecting it. Caecilian's letter in AD 315 was examined as it was read into the record, with him pointing out the forged bits, because once in it would be harder to challenge.[143] The same validation seems to be imagined as true for witness-testimony, which is now frequently depicted as given by the serious act of "entering into" the *hypomnemata* or the *acta*.[144] "Depose what you did," a curator instructs four peasants in

---

[140] Accusations of, or incidents of, forgery: Cic. *ND* 3.74, imitating the handwriting of clerks; Philo *Flacc.* 131–4; the crooked εἰσαγωγεύς (i.e. *commentariensis*, Haensch [1995] 275–6) Lampon; governor's *commentarii* also tampered with records at Plin. *Ep.* 6.22.4 (*interceperat*); Opt. *App.* 2.10 (Maier [1987] 186 no. 22), a trick of the Donatists'. One hyper-careful case: Marcellinus at Carthage in the *Coll. Carth.* 2.53–4 (*PL* 11.1360); he also had four bishops supervise the recording process, *Coll. Carth.* 1.10 (*PL* 11.1265); the unfamiliarity of the Donatist bishops with the procedure could indicate either that it was exceptional or that they were inexperienced rustics. Another supposed case of forgery was the *acta* of the Synod of Constantinople in AD 448, see Teitler (1985) 100–3.

[141] *Coll. Carth.* 2.54 (*PL* 11.1360), *sic solent testamenta, non gesta reserari*.

[142] *Rel.* 19.3 (objection collapsed because the deed of appointment had been "read aloud and declared valid" in praetor's court, yet a third venue).

[143] A grave matter: Maximus uses the phrase "since the reading of his letter . . . has been placed upon the *acta*, we ask that his words should remain upon the acts" twice (*quoniam eius epistolae tenor etiam apud acta recitatus est quam ipse agnovit se mississe, quae dixit quaesumus actis tuis haereant*), Opt. *App.* 2.5 and 2.9 (Maier [1987] 180 and 184 no. 22); in Opt. *App.* 1 six letters were read in, more in *App.* 2.4 (Maier [1987] 177–9 no. 22); Pelagius had read letters in at his own hearing, Aug. *gest. Pel.* 45 (*PL* 44.346, laudations), and Augustine in turn had letters read in, *gest. Pel.* 48 and 54 (*PL* 44.347–8, 350–1). In *CJ* 4.21.3 (AD 226), Severus Alexander notes that a document whose validity had already been questioned *apud acta praesidis provinciae* in a previous trial will not be used in the next one.

[144] Cf. Opt. *App.* 2.4 (Maier [1987] 178 no. 22), Caecilian asked to listen to testimony *deposita* in the *acta*. On the reading of testimony into the *acta* to create *instrumenta publica*, see Bickermann (1933) 340–2 (a late-antique culmination of earlier trends).

246   *The evolution of practice*

AD 329, which he then formally summarizes for the record as, the testimonies "have been entered into the *hypomnemata*."[145] When Caecilian had declared that Ingentius had forged a part of the letter being read into the *acta*, the proconsul had said, threateningly, "your statement is set down in the *acta*," literally "your answer clings to the acts," as a duumvir of Cirta had also said in 303 to grave-diggers, ordered to bring forth Christian books, who claimed that there were no more.[146] The menace is implicit: it is a serious matter to give testimony that will become a part of an official's record, and trouble will follow if you are lying, for it will be preserved as truth.[147] Finally, in addition to letters and testimony, declarations[148] and some new-ish or quasi-legal acts themselves, like donations, sales, and estate-inventories, even Symmachus's contested *mandatum*,[149] can be performed for or entered into the record as a way of dignifying them, making them legally enforceable, and witnessing them.[150]

This way of making all elements of a hearing part of *acta* or *hypomnemata*, part of what was called of old the official's *tabulae*, is therefore a final if

---

[145] *P.Oxy.* 3767 (AD 329 or 330), ἐμφέρεται τοῖς ὑπομνημάτοις.

[146] *professio vestras actis haeret*, Opt. *App.* 2.9 (Maier [1987] 184 no. 22), Caecilian; cf. *FV* 112 (*sermo vester in actis erit*), and a similar phrase earlier, *SB* 7558 (= Boak [1932] 71 line 27, "what you have said has been written," AD 172/3?).

[147] This had been made clear earlier for other documents kept in or as *tabulae publicae*: there was *auctoritas* in *publicae tabulae*, Cic. *Arch.* 9; census and *monumenta publica* had preferential status, strengthened when *senatus censuit*, *D.* 22.3.10 (Marcellus); it was treason to write or recite a knowing falsehood on to *tabulis publicis*, *D.* 48.4.2 (Ulpian), *D.* 48.13.10 (Venuleius), or to make additions to, or deletions in, *tabulae publicae*, *D.* 48.13.12.*pr.* (Marcian).

[148] Most references are to various statements (at times called *professiones*) made in the *acta* (a selection): a *professio donationis* (*FV* 266a, AD 229; *FV* 249, AD 316; *CT* 8.12.3, AD 316 [*contestationem* of gift] and *CT* 8.12.8, AD 415); *D.* 27.7.4.3 (Ulpian), *fideiussores* entered in *acta publica* without demur are liable; *D.* 2.4.17 (Paulus), declaration *apud acta* to produce a person; declarations about status, *CJ* 7.16.24 (Diocletian and Maximian); Paul. *Sent.* 5.1.4; *CT* 7.2.2 (AD 385); *CJ* 7.6.1.10 (AD 531); *CT* 2.8.1 (manumissions and emancipations in *acta*, AD 321); adoptions may also have become *professiones* in the acts, cf. *CJ* 47(48).11 (AD 530) with Just. *Inst.* 1.12.8 (*actis intervenientibus*). Also, *CJ* 5.35.2 (widows who wish to act as guardian must state in *actis* that they will not marry again, AD 390); *CJ* 6.23.19 (spoken will, AD 413; followed by *CT* 4.4.7, AD 424, *NTh.* 16, AD 439, and *N.Val.* 21.1.2, AD 446); *CT* 10.22.6 (declaration proving status and lack of obligation, AD 412); *CT* 7.16.3 (sailing-masters and merchants declare their destination, AD 420). See also, earlier, *CIL* 8.14427 (*ob honorem duumviratus . . . sicut apud acta pollicitus est*, Marcus Aurelius; Mommsen restoration) and *Ephemeris Epigraphica* 5.1060 (*quam pollicitus est secundum acta publica*).

[149] Donations and sales, see chapter nine pp. 280–7; note that purely spoken donations continue, *CT* 8.12.8 (AD 415), and depositing in *actis* obviates any need for witnesses, *CJ* 8.53.31 (AD 478); see B. Hirschfeld (1904) 33–49 and Steinwenter (1915) 58–65, 70–4. Inventories of pupils' estates, *CT* 3.30.6 (AD 396?); *mandata*, also *Cons.* 3.1, 3.4. Steinwenter (1915) 87–92 argues that these were the only legal documents insinuated into the *acta*; the other legally enforceable acts done *apud acta* were all *professiones*. Amelotti (1985) 128 sees here the birth of *instrumenta publica*.

[150] Steinwenter (1915) 56–7 and Saradi-Mendelovici (1988) 120–1 stress the witnessing aspect (these acts now have *publica fides*), which the deposition of documents in Greek archives had also provided, D. Chr. 31.51; Bickermann (1933) 340–1 stresses the proof *acta* provide.

Tablets and other documents in court to AD 400   247

indirect way of asserting and making use of the age-old superior authority of tablets. If something was entered into the *publicae tabulae*, it could only be questioned with difficulty, and became worth citing later in court if need be. This was as true for documents read into these *acta* in the fourth and fifth centuries as it had been for evidence and testimony written onto *tabulae* in the first century BC. Thus the fact of this traditional superiority of tablets was, in general, acknowledged and extended by the way that tablets, and even other documents, were viewed in court. Tablets continued to be seen, and were treated, as presumptively and authoritatively true. The development of the magistrate's, and eventually the city's, *tabulae publicae* into the late-antique *acta* that fixed speech and protected and validated writing is, again, a Roman evolution that could not have occurred but for the substratum of Roman belief about what *tabulae* were and how they worked.[151]

One of the most notable aspects of this development is the strength of this belief even when separated from a literal reality. For here, in late antiquity, the special qualities of physical *tabulae* have become metaphorical and transferrable: papyrus can be granted the traditional authority of wood-and-wax *tabulae*. *Acta* in the late Republic and early Empire were papyrus documents of no particular value, from which the important information was culled and copied onto *tabulae*; magisterial and civic *acta* in the late Empire were also on papyrus,[152] and increasingly extensive, but have also acquired, or in some cases have been granted by imperial *fiat*, the fixing and authoritative qualities of the earlier wood-and-wax *tabulae*.[153] In these last centuries of Empire, the wooden tablet itself is still important and can still be used, but in the making of records it is used for the very first step of recording. The shorthand writers who were so important in the creation of verbatim transcripts of hearings, church councils, and other public events took their notes on wax *tabulae* despite tablets' unsuitability for fast writing.[154] Translations from these were made onto papyrus or

---

[151] Cf. Steinwenter (1915) 2, 26–7, 66–70, roots not to be sought in Greek documentary and archival practice; this was argued out between Wilcken (1894) and Mommsen (1899) 515–17, debates summarized by Steinwenter (1915) 11–12 and Saradi-Mendelovici (1988) 119.

[152] See Jolowicz's (1937) 4 discussion of the referencing system (volume and page).

[153] The privilege (if you were not one of the traditional magistrates), called the *ius actorum conficiendorum*, had to be petitioned for (e.g., *CJ* 1.56.2 [AD 366], to municipal magistrates), see B. Hirschfeld (1904) 23–32 and 50–65, Steinwenter (1915) 30–8, Steinacker (1927) 76–7; the persistence of archives that had this *ius* in the early Middle Ages, Steinacker (1902).

[154] Hearings or trials, cf. Amm. Marc. 14.9.3 (AD 354, interrogation of Gallus), Agathias *Hist.* 4.1–11, stenographers (brought from Constantinople) present at a trial in AD 555 in the Caucasus, discussed Suolahti (1975); other public events, Prohaeresius orates in Athens, with the recorders from the lawcourts (who can read back his speech), Eunapius *VS* 489–90. *Codices* and *tabulae* (e.g., *Coll.*

248   *The evolution of practice*

parchment (called "the authentic *scheda*," τὸ αὐθεντικὸν σχεδάριον), read over, subscribed, and (in some cases) deposited, but the *tabulae* were also kept, to be called on in cases of conflict.[155] What the papyrus or parchment *scheda* therefore had was a type of conferred authenticity created by the agreement of the parties concerned. The physical *tabulae* of wood and wax were the authoritative record, but could not be understood by the participants because they were written in shorthand (as was persistently remarked upon in AD 411).[156] It was the development of shorthand that created a gap between the traditional authority of the wooden form and the comprehensibility required by the uses to which some wished these records to be put. This gap was bridged by the agreement of magistrate and participants, who needed the comprehensible papyrus version also to be authoritative; even so, however, the papyrus record of the *scheda* could not be called *tabulae*. They could, however, assert their own *securitas* and *firmitas*, their capacities to grasp and hold, and did so.[157]

The authority of the magistrate (and, behind him, the emperor) could therefore grant validity to those acts that had existed through witnessing and recording in the past, specifically declarations, or to acts that had not been acknowledged as legal acts before. Older legal acts on *tabulae* – mancipations, stipulations, *bona fides* acts – are not known to have been made *apud acta* before the early sixth century AD,[158] probably because they did not need to be: the process by which they were made had long imparted its own validity. The previously ephemeral and insignificant could be invested with an authority approximate to that of the traditional and the formal when there were good Roman-looking reasons for it, like the place that *fides*, prestige, and power had given to great men in court and outside it, and as long as the emperor, or his officials, or his jurists, approved. So letters, once inferior to *tabulae*, are valued much more like them; so *acta*, once preliminary to *tabulae*, become much more like them; so papyrus and

---

Carth. 2.32, 2.35, 2.43–4 and 2.53 (*PL* 11.1357–8, 1360c), or a δέλτον (at Constantinople in AD 448, cf. Teitler [1985] 102–3); they are sealed daily (*Coll. Carth.* 1.133 [*PL* 11.1299]). Not good for fast writing, noted by Cassiodorus (above chapter two n.47) and Tengström (1962) 15. On the development of shorthand in general, see Coles (1966) 9–27.

[155] *Scheda*, see Tengström (1962) 35–49 and Teitler (1985) 102–3 (the latter also discusses the conflict over the record of AD 448); subscribing also at Arles in AD 314 (see the *acta*).

[156] *Notas non novimus*, they say (or *in codicibus legere non possumus*): *Coll. Carth.* 2.43 (*PL* 11.1358).

[157] Development of shorthand, cf. Mourgues (1998) 162–8. Firmness: *CJ* 6.23.19.1 (AD 413), a will insinuated into the *actis* will be *securus*; *CT* 16.5.55 (AD 414) grants the *gesta* of the *Coll. Carth. perpetuam firmitatem* upon their being *translata* into *publica monumenta*; *CJ* 8.53(54).30.2 (AD 459) notes that donations in the *acta* obtain *inconcussam ac perpetuam firmitatem*; *Nov.* 73.8.3 (AD 538), *perpetua firmitas*.

[158] The Ravenna papyri (Tjäder [1955] and [1982]) include documents of sale and lease, and *cautiones*.

parchment, once the ephemeral opposite to wood, are said, by Ulpian, to be able to constitute *tabulae* themselves – because Ulpian declared it to be so.[159] Romans in these very late centuries define for themselves not what *tabulae* are but what can be *tabulae* or their virtual equivalents, adding on rather than reducing. The larger cosmos and the actions of ritual that harness its forces no longer shape the Roman world; Romans, increasingly over time, shape their world themselves, although never without looking over their shoulders.

[159] *D.* 37.11.1; cf. Paul. *Sent.* 4.7.6 and *FV* 249.6.

CHAPTER 9

Documents, jurists, the emperor, and the law
(AD 200–AD 535)

In the centuries from the late Republic to the reign of the emperor Septimius Severus, Romans – as far as we know – laid down no written rules for themselves about what did or did not prove an act had taken place, nor any strict guidelines for judges or juries to follow when evaluating evidence in court. One of the great benefits of such a system, or such an absence of system, was that it permitted *fides* to make its case unconstrained by rigid and petty matters of proof, which if codified might be applied with no concern for the quality of the participants. Yet within this freedom, it was nonetheless possible to see paradigms for the proper weighting of *fides* and the authoritative use of *tabulae*. Together they made their own kind of system, one that melded a traditional belief in the efficacy of ceremony with the social certainties that privilege imparted to the privileged. The marriage of *fides* and formality in a free system of proof constructed not just a new and improved *tabula* but also a new kind of legitimacy, one much like the old because based in its traditions, but also glitteringly and solidly appropriate for its day, appealing to fundamentals that all Romans of the Right Sort would understand and that others could learn, even if sometimes the hard way.

The period of time between the third century AD and the age of Justinian sees the initial construction of precisely the kind of clear system of proof that the high Empire had avoided, rooted in a discussion of the essence, performance, and validity of formal and ceremonial legal acts that itself began in the high Empire. By being a part of these acts, the tablet was also a part of the traditional ceremonial formality or *sollemnitas* that jurists saw as characterizing these acts, and juristic attempts to mitigate the absolute consequences of defects in formality without diminishing the efficacy of formality often touch on writing as well as ritual words and gestures. The careful way in which remedies for errors in formality are proposed – almost always in the form of suggestions that these (gestures, words, order, writing *materia*) are no long necessary – illuminates

250

Documents, jurists, the emperor, and the law 251

the deferential position taken by both classical and post-classical jurists to the traditions of their own past and the practices of their own present, while the arguments offered in justification of this position, particularly those of abstract essence and compensation, are especially well-conceived responses to the peculiar problems and imperatives of formal ceremonial acts. Despite the fact that most of the body of Roman law as it survives today was edited in antiquity[1] and that some of this editing was specifically devoted to taking out references to formal gestures, words, and materials finally decreed unnecessary in the fifth and sixth centuries AD,[2] the influence of formality and its problems on legal thinking can be felt and was important.

The need to respond to ceremonial unitary acts and to the place of writing within them imposed a strong element of continuity between the classical (i.e. imperial, Augustus to Diocletian) and post-classical (Diocletian through Justinian) jurists. Despite the fact that their training,[3] employment,[4] and writings look very different – the florid style of late-antique pronouncements inspiring particular horror in legal scholars[5] – there are nonetheless fundamental continuities of approach, as a look at the juristic histories of stipulation, mancipation (to the extent that this can be

---

[1] Justinian's *Corpus Iuris Civilis* excerpted the opinions of the classical (second-century BC to third-century AD) jurists in the *Digest*; edited and selectively collected some imperial constitutions (including edicts, called *leges generales* in late antiquity, mandates, rescripts, and decrees) in the *Codex*; updated Gaius's *Institutes* as Justinian's *Institutes*; we now, as an unofficial fourth part, include Justinian's *Novellae*, laws passed after the compilations were made. The *CT*, or *Theodosian Code*, was a selective compilation of edited *leges generales* as well, and not a part of the *Corpus Iuris Civilis*; on its making, Honoré (1998) 123–53 and Matthews (2000).

[2] Taking out: Just. *Inst.* 2.10.10, *CJ* 7.25.1 (AD 530–1), *Inst.* 2.1.40, and *CJ* 7.31.1 (AD 531); it is generally agreed (Wieacker [1988] 157) that references to institutions considered antique by Justinian's time, like *mancipatio* and *sponsio*, were removed. Since Ulpian stated that *tabulae* of wills could be of papyrus and parchment (*D.* 37.11.1), and the need to write on wood was specifically relaxed by Constantine (below pp. 271–2), references to *tabulae* in formal acts have usually, but not always, been replaced with generic nouns, particularly *instrumenta*, that make no comment on form or *materia*. Excision and substitution are part of the study of "interpolations" in Roman law, on which I am generally conservative, as many scholars now are (cf. Kaser [1972] and Millar [1986] 275–6) – a contrast with the earlier generations (cf. Schiller [1978] 284–91 and Corcoran [1996] 14–19).

[3] Classical, Schulz (1946) 57–8 (systematic teaching beneath jurisconsults' *dignitas*), Watson (1974) 108–10, Schiller (1978) 397–401, Frier (1985) 144 n.21; post-classical jurists went to schools that had a set syllabus, an established mode of study, and granted a *testificatio* at the end; see Collinet (1925).

[4] Pre-classical (Republican) jurisconsults gave legal advice as *beneficia*, Cic. *Off.* 2.65, with Bauman (1983) 3 and Frier (1985) 140–1. Classical jurists probably did much the same, and were still gentlemen getting together to discuss legal matters, sometimes offering advice to the emperor himself, Kunkel (1967) and Jolowicz and Nicholas (1972) 378–80; their working habits (some drafting, still), Honoré (1979) and (1994), summarized Turpin (1991) 101 nn.1–4. The post-classical jurists are often officials employed in the emperor's bureaus and called "bureaucratic," see Schiller (1949).

[5] Honig (1960), Bauman (1980), Voß (1982); Honoré (1998) 21–2.

252   *The evolution of practice*

discovered, chiefly by looking at the mancipatory will), and other acts once performed with *tabulae* will show. The major difference between classical and post-classical jurists is not in their background or training, or even in their legal acumen, but in precisely the degree of deference they display to traditional categories, institutions, and ways of getting things done. Here the fact that post-classical jurists were employed by emperors does make a difference, for at a time when central power was becoming more influential, drawing more acts into its presence through petitions and *acta*, it was also becoming more willing to assert its power to shape law and legal practice openly, and jurists and law-drafting officials called quaestors[6] were in the enviable position of drafting the laws through which the emperor's impact was felt. The attitude towards antique formal behavior becomes less deferential than it once was, especially in the fourth century and after. The "it is no longer necessary" wording is still characteristic but occasionally slips like "we hereby amputate"[7] are also seen: the emperor can now, by his presence and his word, bestow efficacy by imperial grant, official *acta*, and imperial constitution. Jurists and emperors decree what makes an act legitimate, sometimes incorporating elements of the old formality in their definitions but sometimes not: for that above all is the late-antique imperial prerogative, to keep or discard from traditions as it wills. It was in this spirit that the Justinianic Corpus was itself constructed: "The fact is," said one of Justinian's preambles to the *Digest*, "that the men who conducted legal actions in days gone by, in spite of the large number of laws that had been laid down, nevertheless made use of only a few of them in litigation, either because of a lack of books, which it was impossible for them to procure, or because of ignorance itself; and lawsuits were decided according to the will of the judges rather than *legitima auctoritas*."[8] This was to stop: what the emperor and his jurists decided was "*legitima auctoritas*" was to be followed by others, and this applied to legal acts as well as to legal reasoning and courtroom decisions. The emperor was the source not just of law, but also of legal authority and legitimacy.

---

[6] On the procedures by which laws were drafted, see the work of Honoré, especially (1994); on the rhetorical contributions of the quaestor, Voß (1982); Honoré (1984), (1986) 136–61 (174–5 presumes legal training, but unnecessarily), (1998) 11–20, and Harries (1988) 169, in the fourth century the "prime requirement for the office was a sense of style," although in later centuries its "legal character" seems to have grown; for warnings about deductions from style alone, Classen (1977) 68–91.

[7] E.g., *CJ* 2.57(58).1 (AD 342; *amputentur*), *CJ* 6.30.17 (AD 407; *amputari decernimus*), *CJ* 6.23.26 (AD 528; *amputamus*).

[8] *C. Tanta* 17, *homines etenim, qui antea lites agebant, licet multae leges fuerant positae, tamen ex paucis lites perferebant vel propter inopiam librorum, quos conparare eis inpossibile erat, vel propter ipsam inscientiam, et voluntate iudicum magis quam legitima auctoritate lites dirimebantur.*

Documents, jurists, the emperor, and the law

STIPULATION

Stipulation (as was argued in chapter five) was a legal act that was once unitary and ceremonial, and one with which writing on *tabulae* was firmly associated from an early date. Its depiction in the legal sources is not much like this picture, and indeed even the discussions in classical and post-classical juristic sources are different from each other, which has contributed to a standard history of stipulation that sees it progressing from a purely oral form to a form largely converted into writing.[9] Restoration of the context of belief and practice around the jurists, however, as well as a look at some of their forms of argumentation suggest that jurists' emphasis on orality or writing in defining stipulation was a choice. A sensitivity to context and argument therefore also assists in the proper weighting of the significance of these emphases.

If classical and post-classical jurists are only compared with each other, the differences seem huge: there would appear to be no greater volte-face than the shift from stipulation defined as obligation created by the formal question-and-answer exchange of matching words to stipulation defined as obligation created by a document written in virtually non-specific language, and commensurately earth-shaking meteor-destroys-dinosaurs theories have been developed to explain this.[10] Set against their broader context, however, the changes, while still significant, are not so fundamental: they are, rather, the result of choices made from a set of options that had long existed rather than anything as dramatic as the triumph of the purely written over the purely oral. Both classical and post-classical jurists could and did rely on the unitary and formal nature of stipulation even when attempting to identify the essential nature of the act more clearly and striving to resolve, with arguments of compensation that reached from one part of the act to another, the problems that the formality of the act could pose. Their differing understandings and solutions produced strikingly dissimilar results, but behind problems and results there were underlying and fundamental continuities of both context and approach.

---

[9] Full treatments of stipulation abound, cf. Zulueta (1953) 154–6 (the traditional view), Riccobono *et al.* (1957) 26–85 (exaggerating the differences between classical and post-classical), or (most recently) Zimmermann (1996) 68–94, esp. 79 n.68 for the oral–written question.

[10] These take the form of "invasion" of classical law by Greek or "vulgar" elements: e.g., Levy (1929) 253–8 (summarizing earlier bibliography), (1943), (1951) 70, and (1956); Riccobono *et al.* (1957) 18–23 ("oriental character"), 49, 76–82; Pringsheim (1960) 13–14; Jolowicz and Nicholas (1972) 407–8, 469–77; and "vulgar" (from practice) as well, Collinet (1912); Wieacker (1955) 29–34; or Köhn (1977); Móra (1968) 140 cautiously appraises "vulgar" law as rooted in the classical period; *contra*, Stühff (1966) and Honoré (1989) 149–52.

254   *The evolution of practice*

(a) *The classical jurists.* The abstract conceptualization of legal terms and concepts was one of these approaches, and was one of the important tools developed by the pre-classical (Republican) and classical jurists.[11] This identification of essence, looking for the core value in the confusion of multiple experience, is not a statement of fact but an argument without an argument, as all debaters (and readers of Socratic dialogues) know, and may promote rather than stifle discussion. Cicero had asked a similar question about the Roman census and what its core was, because he wanted to know when it was properly over, and needed to know what "it" was before he could answer the question that particularly exercised him.[12] An answer to the question "what is stipulation?" that wished to convey the unitary quality of an act like stipulation, where several things (I have argued) had to happen for the act to be valid, would require description rather than an essentializing statement: you would walk through all the steps and narrate a process, tell the inquirer what you do rather than what it was. Statements of the sort seen among jurists are fundamentally different in nature and intent. Thus, saying "a stipulation is a *conceptio* in words, in which (words) he who is asked replies that he will give or do that which he has been asked," as the jurist Pomponius did, probably summarizing the Tiberian jurist Sabinus,[13] aims not at comprehensiveness but at clarity. This is a juristic verdict on the act's essential nature. For this reason there was no mention of possible gestures, or witness-judges, or writing, or the continuity of the act, or indeed of anything else, merely *verba* and the noun *conceptio*, itself pointing to a formula that had already modulated away from the fixed or *certa verba* postulated as the earliest way of speaking in formal acts.[14] For this reason too, juristic essentializing was also an especially powerful way to approach acts that existed in multiple forms, like marriage, and acts with multiple parts, like the ceremonial unitary acts. When poked with the stick of a normal question, a ceremonial unitary act rolled up like an armadillo in a ball, defying conceptual dismemberment by the smooth interconnectedness of its exterior defenses. A different approach, one that

---

[11] Schulz (1946) 66–7, definition and abstract conceptualization close to each other, but jurists practiced more of the latter than the former. "Definition" in English is simpler than Roman *definitio*, which examined cases and isolated common elements, Stein (1971) 760, Schiller (1978) 291–7, and Wieacker (1988) 630–3 – and implied consensus as to meaning, which varying abstract conceptualizations do not.

[12] See chapter five n.7.

[13] Pomponius (second century AD), *D.* 45.1.5.1: *stipulatio autem est verborum conceptio, quibus is qui interrogatur daturum facturumve se quod interrogatus est responderit.*

[14] For *certa* and *concepta verba*, above chapter three n.51; the original *certum* in stipulation must have been *sponsio*, the verb restricted in its use to Roman citizens, *G.* 3.93.

Documents, jurists, the emperor, and the law

contemplated the act in its entirety as an eagle observes an armadillo from afar, and looked for what all parts had in common rather than for what tail or claws did, was (in other words) not only likely to be more productive, but probably also necessary.

Pomponius-Sabinus's statement is, of course, only one sentence, excerpted in the *Digest* out of its context. But more of its context would not necessarily alter this assessment of it as an unexpressed argument about essence, as a look at the treatment given to stipulation in the mid-second-century jurist Gaius's lectures shows.[15] Gaius discusses stipulation in terms much like Pomponius-Sabinus's, with the adjustment that in his *Institutes* he starts not with stipulation but with obligation itself. He first lays out four different categories of obligation, then looks at *obligationes verbis* as the second of the four.[16] For him *verbis obligatio* "comes into being (*fit*) from question and answer, as with 'do you solemnly promise to give?' 'I promise',", a set of matching words characteristic of stipulation, although he does not specifically call it that here.[17] In stipulation there had to be this question and answer, and the words in the question and answer had to correspond, as they do in his examples, although – again – he does not say so specifically here. He then devotes his attention to listing what sorts of stipulations – stipulations for what sorts of things or acts – were "of no effect" (*inutilis*), and who could and could not stipulate. He later notes, in the middle of a discussion of consensual obligation, that those incurring a *verborum obligatio* cannot be *absentes*, that is, physically apart from each other.[18] Although regularly taken as a complete description of stipulation and its necessary components, *Institutes* 3.92–115 cannot be that, since Gaius does not claim that (or *fit* must carry a lot of weight), nor does he discuss faults in the performance of stipulation that made it invalid, nor does he mention that stipulation had to be a virtually continuous act, a *continuus actus*, as other jurists do.[19] This is, rather, an identification of essence

---

[15] For assessments of Gaius, see Honoré (1962) 59, not a textbook written for publication but lectures or lecture-notes, and Stanojević (1989); Schiller (1978) 344–8 for debates over Gaius.

[16] G. 3.88–9.

[17] *Verbis obligatio fit ex interrogatione et responsione, velut DARI SPONDES*, G. 3.92. Five other word-pairs are also given; whether his list is a restrictive one or not (only these words, and no others) is debated by Nicholas ([1953] 64–79: yes) and Winkler (1958: no), an argument revolving in part around the translation of *velut*. Best is probably Zulueta's (1953) 154 suggestion (variable within limits), endorsed by Nicholas (1992); then perhaps even forms not in Gaius discussed in Nicholas (1953) 73–7 can be included.

[18] No effect, G. 3.97–103; ineligible people, G. 3.104–9; *absentes*, G. 3.136.

[19] The only example he gives of an answer failing to match the question (G. 3.102) concerns what the stipulation was about (10,000 vs. 5,000), the verbs themselves being the same; he deemed that this lack of congruence invalidated the stipulation, whereas Ulpian (*D.* 45.1.1.4) will decide that the

256   *The evolution of practice*

masquerading as a description, Gaius's legal assessment of the core nature of an act stated as fact, following a technique and a tradition at least one hundred years old by his time. What he would think of the need for a time frame, or for witnesses, or for writing cannot be known for certain, since he does not mention them. He might have thought of them as unnecessary; he might have thought of them as necessary, but in striving for clarity wanted to convey what he deemed the simplest and most fundamental element; or, since people who performed stipulations did use witnesses and writing, all within a tight time frame, he might have been giving a statement of apparent fact that was covertly argumentative, that stipulation was this *and only this* despite what others might think. His way of writing permits rather than prevents speculation, and it cannot be said for certain that his account claims that stipulation was oral *rather than* written.

Ulpian and others, excerpted in the *Digest*, did concern themselves with many of the issues that Gaius had passed over or had mentioned but left unexplored, like what had to occur in a stipulation ("a stipulation cannot be effected unless . . .", "a stipulation is not valid if . . ."), which elaborations would invalidate it (insertion of conditions that were not agreed upon by one party, for example), and what kinds of stipulations could or could not be made (e.g. about another's property or acts), by whom.[20] Many of their statements reflect the kinds of problems that can arise in practice, pointing to the ways in which people must have used, or tried to elaborate, and extend the use of, stipulations. The *Digest* passages, although in some ways just as essentializing or, indeed, fanciful as those in Gaius's *Institutes* (both works do, for example, contemplate stipulations involving hippocentaurs), therefore should be seen as more responsive to problems a jurist might encounter than Gaius's lectures were – lectures whose point, after all, was to teach the author's conception of the fundamentals of law and legal acts, not of how the law might apply.

Two of the issues discussed by jurists in the *Digest* were particularly related to problems that arose from the formality of the act, specifically over which words had to correspond in the formulaic exchange, and what to do when something identified as essential was missing. Celsus and Florentinus, second-century AD jurists, claimed that impossible conditions or a word *extrinsecus* or irrelevant to the stipulation would be considered superfluous

stipulation is good for the amount that both sides of the exchange can reasonably be said to have in common. *Continuus actus*, *D.* 45.2.6.3 (Julian, called *modicus*); *D.* 45.1.137.*pr.* (Venuleius); *D.* 45.1.1 (Ulpian, permitting an *intervallum . . . medium* but no more), and Riccobono *et al.* (1957) 32–42.

[20] Ulpian and others, excerpted throughout *D.* 45; see also *D.* 44.7.1.7 and 44.7.1.12–15 (Gaius), *D.* 44.7.52.2 (Modestinus), and *D.* 46.4.8.3 (Ulpian).

Documents, jurists, the emperor, and the law

and (therefore) would not vitiate the obligation: so if you ask another to stipulate, "will you appear – (and) if you do not appear, you will deliver a hippocentaur?" Celsus will consider that you have merely said, "will you appear?" Florentinus, speaking for the other side of the formulaic exchange, decides that if you are asked to stipulate ("do you promise?"), you can show off your knowledge of Vergil and answer, "arms and the man I sing I promise," and the stipulation will nonetheless be valid. Florentinus also notes that if there is variation in what is promised or in the way in which parties are named, "it is agreed that this does not tell against it."[21] This is an extension of the essentializing approach: not only have these two followed the existing juristic conceptualizations of what stipulation is, they are asking what within that *conceptio* of words truly has to correspond and what can be ignored as "extrinsic." The strict formal correspondence of *all* spoken parts in fact need not be followed. As Pomponius-Sabinus, using the tool of abstract conceptualization, had isolated what he deemed to be the fundamental (but not necessarily *only*) component within the act of stipulation itself, so here Celsus and Florentinus isolate what could be ignored (and, therefore, what was fundamental) at the level of words themselves. Pomponius had also noted that a stipulatory question asked with a singular verb ("do you promise?") could be answered by two people with a plural verb, and this form of argumentation continued into the third century, when Ulpian, going even farther, would say that a man answering "why not?" to the question ("do you . . . ?") would be bound by the stipulation, as would a man answering in Greek to a Latin question (as long as the response is made "congruently").[22]

At times, however, when contemplating the problems caused by the formal nature of stipulation, Ulpian and Paulus would also call on those aspects of the act that were being left aside in the process of identifying essence. In three controversial passages, these two jurists seem to assert that writing alone can be valid as a stipulation, but they do so in a way that assumes not

---

[21] D.45.1.97.pr. (Celsus), "*te sisti? nisi steteris, hippocentaurum dari?*" . . . "*te sisti*" *solummodo stipulatus essem* (the trans. for hippocentaur in Watson [1985] is "heffalump"); D. 45.1.65 (Florentinus): *extrinsecus et nihil ad praesentem actum pertinentia . . . pro supervacuis habebuntur nec vitiabunt obligationem . . . sed et si in rei quae promittitur aut personae appellatione varietur, non obesse placet*); cf. D. 45.1.136 (Paulus), two parties calling the same object of stipulation by different names is acceptable.

[22] D. 45.1.5.1 (Pomponius-Sabinus), D.45.2.4 (Pomponius). Ulpian: D. 45.1.1.1 ("why not?"), 6 (Latin and Greek, *congruenter*); the "why not?" comment often thought interpolated because, e.g., Zimmermann (1996) 74, it is not thought "credible." Paulus is quoted as having said that agreement was the basis of stipulation (D. 45.1.83.1), but this (for once) should be ruled an interpolation because in Justinian's *Inst.* 3.19.13 this concept is identified as current, i.e. recently formulated in the sixth century AD (*iam dictum est*).

258   *The evolution of practice*

a tension or competition between writing and speech, but that writing and speech – which both convey the *verba* of the obligation – are complementary parts of the larger ceremony in which validity inheres.[23] They are both using a form of presumptive or compensatory reasoning, arguing from one part of the unitary act to another.[24] At *Digest* 45.1.30, Ulpian said that "it is to be generally understood that if a man has written that he has guaranteed (*fideiussisse*), then all things are seen as having been formally transacted (*sollemniter acta*)." *Fideiussisse* being one of Gaius's permitted words for stipulation, it would appear that the respondent in the exchange of words writing "that he has guaranteed" was sufficient to complete, and therefore to imply, the entire act of a formal stipulation. Two passages of Paulus's suggest much the same. In the passage excerpted at *Digest* 45.1.134.2 he stated that when "Septicius promised in letters (*in litteris . . . caverat*) . . . it must be understood, if the parties were present together, that words (*verba*) of stipulation on the part of Lucius Titius had preceded": a stipulation written by the respondent allows the legal presumption that the questioner had spoken *even if he hadn't*. And at *Digest* 44.7.38 Paulus stated that

> Non figura litterarum, sed oratione, quam exprimunt litterae, obligamur, quatenus placuit non minus valere, quod scriptura, quam quod vocibus lingua figuratis significaretur.

> We are not obligated by the physical expression (*figura*) of the letters but by the utterance or meaning (*oratio*) which such letters express, since it is agreed that that which is written is no less powerful than that which is indicated through voices expressed by the tongue.

In the second part of this awkwardly phrased opinion, writing is no less powerful in conveying the *oratio* that is the essence of the obligation than the voice: either is sufficient for the conclusion of a stipulation.[25] All three of these opinions suggest the same thing, that writing and speech, which both

---

[23] This argument also implicit elsewhere, see passages gathered together by Riccobono *et al.* (1957) 3 nn.8–10 from both *Digest* and *CJ*, dating to the second century and after: *cautiones, instrumenta*, and *chirographa* of stipulation all considered equivalent to (and therefore, he argues pp. 29–85, *all* interpolated for) the stipulation itself, and themselves the source of obligation; he also considers all of the classical passages discussed here interpolated, (1957) 68–9 (claiming that Ulpian would have mentioned this elsewhere had it been true), 72–3, 146–50, 59–64.

[24] "Presumptive" is Nicholas's ([1953] 233–52) term; he argues that presumptions arise from the fact of an evidentiary document and therefore from the practice of the courts. But why would a document otherwise considered weak and unimportant (in this type of argument) allow such a strong legal argument? By calling this argument "compensatory" I am going one step further, trying to explain why a presumption could arise: from the nature of the act itself.

[25] Watson (1985) and I both translate *quatenus* as "since" here; its possible translation as "to the extent that," which would give the opinion a much more limited and concessive flavor ("we are [only] obligated by the *figura* of letters to the extent that it is agreed that . . .") is made highly unlikely by

Documents, jurists, the emperor, and the law

convey *verba* but might shape them differently, express the same essence of the legal act of stipulation, the one implying the other and therefore confirming that the other exists.[26] The tradition of the unitary act permits Ulpian and Paulus to say, here where it is useful to them in the larger point they are making, that writing *and* speech express words and, therefore, the stipulation as well. The logic of finding the essence in one part and presuming the existence of the entirety from one part means that they can accept the document not only as excellent proof but can imagine the document standing in for the entirety of the act.

Paulus's second passage (44.7.38) also confirms, in another way, that in juristic thinking two essential components of the unitary act, writing and speech, are presumed to be complementary rather than contradictory, and points to the particular usefulness of compensatory arguments in remedying defects in formal expression or performance. Even in the first clause of this passage, quoted above, there is no contrast intended between *litterae* and *oratio*, for "letters" express *oratio*, a word which itself could signify both "utterance" and "meaning."[27] Letters, meaning, and speech are all presumed to congrue. Rather, the contradiction in this case exists between the *figura* of letters and the *oratio* that letters express, and Paulus notes that it is *oratio* that is to create the obligation. *Figura* means the physical shape of the letters, their appearance, their physical outline, their inflexions or spellings. The conflict that required Paulus's opinion was therefore between what was meant, what the letters "express," and misspellings or miswritings that deformed but did not obscure that meaning. The controversy that Paulus has solved – within the assumed framework of a unitary act, within an assumed congruence of writing, meaning, and speech – was the old one of the specific binding power of formal but incorrectly expressed words when their correct intent can be discerned. Paulus

---

the absence of a concessive like "only" in the first clause and the very strong *non minus valere* of the second: the author did not intend a concessive meaning here.

[26] *verba*: cf. *OLD s.v.*, as "words" rather than specifically "spoken words" (and as such throughout the *Digest* too); this broad definition (as "words") works also in Gaius's *Institutes*, where despite an apparent contrast arising or intended from putting the contracts *verbis* and *litteris* side by side, the actual contrast was that stipulation used *verba*, both spoken and written words, while the contract *litteris*, entering a sum in an account-*tabula* as owed without money changing hands, had no spoken component.

[27] *figura*: see *OLD s.v.* The second half of the excerpt, reinforcing the equal validity of writing and speech, makes the translation of *oratio* as "meaning" or "content" more likely. The same kind of problem may also be discussed in *D.* 50.17.92, where (Cervidius) Scaevola (second century AD) notes that defendant (*reus*) and *fideiussor* were bound even if a mistake was made in transcribing the *verbis* of the stipulation.

260   *The evolution of practice*

was not, rather incoherently, setting writing against speech and then contradicting himself, but addressing a problem that affected all other acts on tablets, and many other areas of the law, the problem of defects in formality.

In these passages, therefore, Ulpian and Paulus were not implying that stipulation was written *rather than* oral or oral *rather than* written. The two third-century jurists are instead tackling a difficult problem by implicitly reminding their audience that *verba* could be both written and spoken, and clearly stating that one could compensate for defects in, or the absence of, the other. Since stipulation was a legal act that combined and was believed to require several components done all at one time, you could borrow from one component to repair the other. The same kind of problem had been solved in the same way in a rescript of Antoninus Pius given in *CJ* 4.32.1: "if a *promissio* of interest given *interrogatione praecedente* is proved to have been given, although not written in *instrumenta*, by the best law [monies] are owed." If you can prove (through witnesses?) that the formulaic exchange took place, then money is owed, even if there was no document: here the fact of the exchange compensates for the absence of a document. Although no doubt intended to allay the anxieties of a petitioner who did not have, or no longer had, a written *instrumentum*, the rescript does so by pointing him to other related sources for the validity of the act, as can be seen also in *CJ* 8.37(38).1 of AD 200 or 201.[28]

The advantage that a broad construction of *verba* gave to Ulpian and Paulus parallels the advantage in argument that a more abstract concept, like "*conceptio verbis*" or "*obligatio verbis*" for the unitary act of stipulation, gave to jurists overall. It permitted the more abstract essence or quality they were identifying as central to be found in more than one part of a multi-part act, and was thus a very useful logical weapon with which to attack the practical problems caused by formalism. Although jurists used this form of reasoning to remove defective elements as irrelevant (because not essential), what was significant about the rescript from Antoninus Pius and the passages of Ulpian, Paulus, and *CJ* 8.37(38).1 is that they also used its very abstraction to repair defects by looking to other parts of the act to compensate. This tool of abstract conceptualization and its corollary tool, compensation,

---

[28] A rescript attributed to Papinian, Honoré (1994) 76–81: "if the transaction [it was a *cautio*] took place between parties who were present, it must be believed that it was with a stipulation preceding that the word of the promissor followed" (*tamen si res inter praesentes gesta est, credendum est praecedente stipulatione vocem spondentis secutam*); here "it must be believed" that the meeting and half the exchange imply the whole act.

Documents, jurists, the emperor, and the law

were therefore doubly powerful and appropriate when the context was that of the ceremonial unitary act and when jurists were looking not to discard, but to preserve, the formal and ceremonial qualities of those unitary acts. The embracing of these tools, and their use by jurists to redefine an act from the sum of its parts to a concept and to seek that concept in an act's parts, might also therefore have been a response specifically *to* the intertwined ceremonial and formal qualities of the older acts of Roman law, as well as a useful way to reduce the impact of formal defects in them. Arguments of essence and compensation do not intentionally or necessarily undermine formal and ceremonial unitary acts; they allow formality, ceremony, and unity to survive without placing an undue burden on the people who must perform acts characterized above all by those qualities.

(b) The post-classical jurists. Post-classical jurists continued to use abstract conceptualization and compensatory reasoning in tandem. The *Sententiae* attributed to Paulus, in fact a "pocket encyclopedia" dating to *c.* AD 300, gives its own apparently self-contradictory definition of stipulation. "Stipulations, which are formulated through a certain solemnity of *verba*, were introduced for the sake of making obligations valid," he says; a meeting is necessary for a valid stipulation; and – nonetheless? – a stipulation is valid even when the spoken exchange itself may not have taken place, for "if it should be written in a document that someone promised, then it is considered as if there had been an answer with *interrogatio* preceding."[29] As for Ulpian and (the real) Paulus, meeting and written answer imply the question; surviving parts stand in for missing parts, and allow the act to be considered complete. If *verba* are interpreted as only oral, then this definition is one with internal contradictions. But if *verba* are understood in their wider sense, then one part of the act, the writing, can imply the rest. This statement therefore continues to depend on the unitary nature of the act of stipulation, and the compensatory arguments that assume it, for its coherence.

This logic is extended in the sixth century. In Justinian's *Institutes* 3.19.12, an *instrumentum* that stated the existence of a meeting was now to be presumed true unless it could be proved that no meeting had taken place, as Justinian had also instructed in a constitution of AD 531,[30] but a little later,

---

[29] Date, characterization, and discussion in Schiller (1978) 46–8; Paul. *Sent.* 5.7.1–2, *obligationum firmandarum gratia stipulationes inductae sunt, quae quadam verborum sollemnitate concipiuntur . . . quod si scriptum fuerit instrumento promississe aliquem, perinde habetur atque si interrogatione praecedente responsum sit.*

[30] Just. *Inst.* 3.19.12 (meeting and litigation); AD 531, *CJ* 8.37(38).14.

262 *The evolution of practice*

it is announced quite forthrightly that promise in a document presupposes that everything has been done correctly:[31]

In stipulationibus fideiussorum sciendum est generaliter hoc accipi, ut, quodcumque scriptum sit quasi actum, videatur etiam actum: ideo constat, si quis se scripserit fideiussisse, videri omnia sollemniter acta.

It should be understood that when stipulations are taken from guarantors, generally whatever is written as done should be seen as having been done; therefore it is agreed that if someone should write that he has guaranteed, all things should be seen as having been solemnly transacted.

This is all part of a discussion in which the same seeming contradiction comes up again. "It is obvious" (*palam est*), says *Inst.* 3.19.7, that the deaf and dumb cannot be party to a stipulation (so an exchange that is spoken and heard is important); a verbal obligation *concepta* among absent persons is *inutilis*, says *Inst.* 3.19.12 (so a face-to-face meeting is important); but "whatever is written as done should be seen as having been done"? The compensatory logic is the same, but the weight has shifted. As scholarly wrangling shows, it is difficult to claim that this is a clear statement that a stipulation is (still) oral or (now only) written.[32] Gaius's *Institutes* had appeared to privilege *verba* in an oral exchange, while Justinian's *Institutes* appears to favor written, not spoken, *verba*, but neither gives a picture that is both clear and comprehensive because the authors have chosen different aspects of the unitary act to emphasize, one more obviously and forcefully than the other. The tradition was one in which all these aspects of speech, presence, and writing were not just intertwined but were seen, thanks to the good work of the classical jurists, to compensate for each other, and it is this tradition that Justinian's *Institutes* maintains. Speech never entirely excluded writing, nor did writing ever entirely exclude speech, despite appearances: one was always being called on to rescue the other.

In late antiquity, abstract conceptualization was also developed further – Paulus and others had only begun the process – as a tool to remedy defects in

---

[31] Presupposing question, 3.19.17 (same words as Paulus); *scriptum sit quasi actum*, 3.20.8 (last clause same as Ulpian, *D.* 45.1.30); G. MacCormack (1983) argues that it is the meeting of the parties (discussed below) that is being referred to here.

[32] These *Institutes* passages, and *CJ* 8.37(38).14 (AD 531, above n.30) are mostly interpreted as collapsing the stipulation down into only writing, but this is a long debate: see Buckland and Stein (1963) 461 n.4, also Knütel (1976) and Evans-Jones and G. MacCormack (1998) 134–8 (who note also that documents must be written in a certain way if they are to demonstrate the stipulation, so they too must follow a certain formality). G. MacCormack (1983) has also argued that despite *CJ* 8.37(38).14, the stipulation in Justinian's time was still understood by jurists as contracted through oral question and answer; Zimmermann (1996) 82 finds the discussion of stipulation in Justinian's *Institutes* "discordant."

Documents, jurists, the emperor, and the law

formalism and, eventually, much of formalism itself. Justinian's constitution to the advocates of Caesarea in AD 531 had decreed that the document implied the face-to-face presence of the two parties, but said nothing about question-and-answer, the matching *verba*, for those *verba* had been declared unnecessary eighty years earlier. A complete shift away from matching utterance of only specific words to the use of any words whatsoever in a question-and-answer was permitted in the middle of the fifth century by the emperor Leo:[33]

omnes stipulationes, etiamsi non sollemnibus vel directis, sed quibuscumque verbis pro consensu contrahentium compositae sint, legibus cognitae suam habeant firmitatem.

All stipulations, even if they are not composed with solemn or strict words, but in any words whatsoever, with the consent of the contracting parties, in conformity with the laws, shall have their own *firmitas*.

Sollemne, "habitual, formal, and ceremonial," should refer to how the words were performed in the ceremony, that is, that the verb of the question was to be matched by (i.e. equal to) the word of the answer.[34] *Directus* ("strict"), on the other hand, refers to the specific words themselves rather than how they were used; here these also will no longer be required. Justinian's *Institutes* summarizes this as, "the constitution of Leo ... requires only that the understanding of the meaning of words be mutual and that there be agreement between the parties, whatever the words in which it was expressed."[35] Problems of formalism that had concerned the classical jurists – permitted words, matching words, and mistakes that threatened to invalidate the act despite the fact that its intent could be discerned – were now simply declared solved, because the words that had caused these problems were no longer necessary. It was now agreement on the contract and the meaning of the words actually exchanged that was most important. Justinian's

---

[33] *CJ* 8.37(38).10 (AD 472), cf. Riccobono *et al.* (1957) 51–2, 56–7. In *CJ* 5.11.6 = *CT* 3.13.4 (AD 428), Theodosius and Valentinian had judged that *qualiacumque ... verba* would suffice for the constitution of dowry; the rule to which this is supposed to be the exception had been stated in the same year – it is now "clearly evident ... by what words a stipulation may be drawn up" (*quibus verbis stipulatio colligatur, NT* 1.1) – but this constitution does not survive.

[34] Ulpian, declaring in *D.* 45.1.30 that all things were *sollemniter acta* when a man wrote *fideiussisse*, was not commenting on the choice of that specific word, already known to be correct from Gaius, but larger deficiencies of performance that the writing repaired; Nicholas (1953) 77–8 thinks *sollemne* refers to the words themselves, but then cannot explain *directus* except as a pleonasm.

[35] Just. *Inst.* 3.15.1: *constitutio ... quae sollemnitate verborum sublata sensum et consonantem intellectum ab utraque parte solum desiderat.* At Just. *Inst.* 3.19.13 stipulation is also referred to "as is now said ... [as] valid because it is based on the agreement of those making the contract," *ut iam dictum est, ex consensu contrahentium stipulationes valent.*

264 *The evolution of practice*

summary therefore sees Leo's constitution as declaring parts of the formal act unimportant by reconceptualizing the nature of the act as agreement.[36]

Justinian himself also desired to lessen formality: "even if the customary words" and the "subtle, or rather, more properly, superfluous punctiliousness" of stipulations were allowed, why, he asks in *CJ* 2.56.4.7 (AD 529), should he not "amputate all the dread" (*formido*) imposed by ancient law from writing of this sort?[37] Yet he did not do so; nor had Leo (or others) ever *forbidden* any aspect of the traditional performance of the act of stipulation. All were merely adjusting for the impact that a flawed performance could have on the validity of the act itself. By noting that the formal and ceremonial requirements for an act of stipulation still inspired a dread of error and deeming that this dread must be removed, Justinian is acknowledging that despite hundreds of years of juristic reconceptualizations of the act and permitted relaxations of its formalities, stipulation was still being performed in a way that recognized and used customary words and could be characterized by both *observatio* and *formido*, punctiliousness and fear. Wooden *tabulae* from the last decade of the fifth century AD in North Africa, with their regular use of *spopondit*, point to a similar conclusion: the formal and ceremonial unitary act of stipulation was still being performed.[38]

The late-antique jurists writing imperial constitutions thus were working within the same context, and working to solve some of the problems with the same methods, as their classical predecessors. They too perceived stipulation as a unitary act with multiple parts, and accepted and extended the classical arguments that allowed existing parts to compensate for devastating deficiencies. Conceptualization too they extended, looking for the abstraction behind the concept of obligation by words, finding it in consent, and using it to justify a further reduction in the requirements of ceremonial performance. The eventual post-classical identification of stipulation as consensual is one major difference between them and their predecessors; another was the post-classical preference for writing as the part of the unitary act of stipulation that could best imply the entire act. Here, they made

---

[36] Van Oven (1958) 415–17, the stipulation is not "denatured" but merely "simplified" – possible, since the requirement for a meeting and for some exchange of *verba* still set it apart from consensual contracts.

[37] *CJ* 2.55(56).4.7 (AD 529): *si enim verba consueta stipulationum et subtilis, immo magis supervacua observatio ab aula concessa est, nos . . . cur non et in huiusmodi scriptura totam formidinem veteris iuris amputamus . . . ? Formido* is specifically religious dread (*OLD s.v.*). Justinian elsewhere modified content and applicability of the stipulation, *CJ* 6.23.25 (AD 528), 8.37(38).11 (AD 528), 5.13.1 (AD 530).

[38] *T.Alb.* 3–15, 22, 25–9, 31–2; cf. Diósdi (1971) and (1981) 51–68, it is illogical to assume, when the language in stipulatory documents is the same, that parties to stipulation in the classical period spoke the words but those later did not.

Documents, jurists, the emperor, and the law

their choice among alternatives that had always been present, so the distance between classical and post-classical was rather smaller than it might at first appear.

MANCIPATION AND THE ROMAN WILL

The history of mancipation can be largely written according to the same principles, but with one difference. Both stipulation and mancipation were processes, the first establishing obligation and the second conveying property, and both were added on to, or made parts of, other acts so regularly that in their documentary forms their separate legal identities were compressed. The difference is that for a very long time stipulation remained an independent type of obligation in the minds of the jurists (although perhaps not so clearly to its users, cf. chapter six), and thus continued to be discussed in textbooks and imperial constitutions through the post-classical period; mancipation, on the other hand, was a process that to them became conceptually part of any larger legal act whose purpose it served. In the first century AD it is still possible to speak of mancipation for the purpose of sale or mancipation for the purpose of bestowing a gift; but in the post-classical period those legal acts have become sale and donation, and mancipation is no longer discussed separately. Mancipation nonetheless leaves its traces here, as it does in the acts that were modelled specifically on it and survived into the post-classical period, like emancipation and adoption. Where the continued understanding of mancipatory acts can best be seen, however, is in the Roman mancipatory will, itself a complex unitary act. Jurists also looked for its essence and reconceptualized it over time, making regular use of compensatory arguments to lessen the effects of a botched ceremonial performance. The development of the mancipatory will, however, took a turn in late antiquity different from that of stipulation. Here, the compensatory principle that the essence of the will, identified now as *voluntas* or intent, inhered in each of its parts was dramatically enacted in the splitting of the mancipatory will into five different kinds of will acknowledged as valid by imperial jurists, each one a facet of what the unitary mancipatory will had once been.

(a) The classical jurists. Gaius, who in his *Institutes* gave the extensive description of the mancipatory will quoted in chapter five, actually nests his discussion of the mancipatory will within the larger category of "how we acquire property," just as he had placed stipulation within the larger category of "obligation." With the will, as with stipulation, Gaius does not overtly attempt to make an abstract formulation; instead he starts by saying,

266   *The evolution of practice*

eaque res ita agitur, "the thing itself is done this way," and the description that follows is as lengthy as one would expect for a ceremonial unitary act.[39] Even so, he attempts to identify one part of the will as more important than another. After giving the testator's nuncupation ("according as is written in these tablets and on this wax, so do I give, so do I bequeath, so do I call to witness, and so, Quirites, do you bear me witness"), Gaius notes that "by this general speech, obviously (*sane*), the testator is seen to name and confirm those things which he has written specifically on the tablets of the will." Gaius reports a general opinion here (*videtur*), which he sees as pretty obvious (*sane*) and which he therefore endorses: the nuncupation refers to, includes, and validates (in advance) these tablets. He is here looking to elevate the oral component above the others, understressing both *tabulae* and the ritual gestures (he had said earlier, "of course" – *scilicet* – "the will is done by mancipation") along the way.[40]

Later in his discussion, Gaius identified a different part of the act as crucial. "The formal punctiliousness (*observatio*)," he wrote, "which we have laid out above – selling of the *familia*, the witnesses, and the nuncupation – is not, however, sufficient for the validity of the will at civil law; before everything else it must be ascertained whether there has been an institution of an heir made in solemn form (*sollemni more*); for if an institution has been made otherwise, (all that) is unavailing (*nihil proficit*)." He gives one form of the *institutio heredis* as *sollemnis*, one form that is approved, and three that are (mostly) disapproved. "Wills take their efficacy (*vim*)," he says in summary, "from the institution of the heir, and because of this the institution of the heir is understood as the source and foundation (*caput et fundamentum*) of the entire will";[41] this language and logic calls to mind earlier imperial jurists examining what made a *lex* a *lex*, as well as Gaius's own treatment of that subject.[42] Since even in his own description the

---

[39] *G.* 2.104 (see chapter five p. 114); cf. Kübler (1934) cols. 985–1010; Zulueta (1953) 87–90; Tjäder (1955) 190–6; and Amelotti (1966) 111–90.

[40] *G.* 2.104, *et sane quae testator specialiter in tabulis testamenti scripserit, ea videtur generali sermone nominare atque confirmare*; mancipation itself, *G.* 2.102: it is called a will *per aes et libram, scilicet quia per mancipationem peragitur*. Modern scholarship cannot decide how to value tablet and utterance: Arangio-Ruiz (1953), Guarino (1955) and (1956), Archi (1956), and Champlin (1991) 5–6 (e.g.) deem *tabulae* subordinate; others deemed mancipation subordinate to *tabulae*, e.g., Nicholas (1987) 254 and 256; still others, e.g., Buckland and Stein (1963) 284, saw "the contents of the document [as] the true will"; and Serangeli (1982) 39–111 saw a strong contrast between law and reality.

[41] Institution of the heir, quoted *G.* 2.115–16; wording, *G.* 2.117, confirmed by *D.*28.5.1.3 (Ulpian); *vim*, *G.* 2.229; discussed Maschi (1937).

[42] Ateius Capito identified the *rogatio* as the *caput . . . et origo et quasi fons* of *lex*, Gel. 10.20.7–8 (*totius huius rei iurisque, sive cum populus sive cum plebs rogatur . . . caput ipsum et origo et quasi fons*

Documents, jurists, the emperor, and the law   267

nuncupation did not include the institution of the heir, this statement was not an attempt to privilege the oral component of the mancipatory will over all else;[43] by emphasizing the institution of the heir as *caput et fundamentum*, he was not saying that other elements were not also crucial. To him they were merely insufficient by themselves but still crucial as well, as were a host of other considerations brought out by various jurists.[44] As Gaius was discovering, disentangling a unitary act was a complicated business, and in the absence of a powerful abstract concept, the danger of self-contradiction was very great.

As Gaius's struggles would suggest, the achievement of a conceptualization of a mancipatory will was late in coming, much later than a conceptualization of stipulation had been: the making and evaluation of wills were more conservative undertakings than the making of even formal contracts, as the flexible usage of stipulation (seen in chapter six) and stipulation's own early loss of ritual gestures, internal development toward *concepta verba*, and open applicability to non-citizens had shown. But come it did: "a testament is the just expression (*sententia*) of our will (*voluntatis*) about that which someone wishes to happen after his death," said the third-century jurist Modestinus, echoed by other late-classical jurists.[45] This conceptualization would once have been controversial, since *voluntas* was not defined and rhetorical debate over the testator's "intent" (*voluntas*) when apparently contradicted by his "words" (*verba*) had been known since the early first century BC. Although the implications of these arguments are said to have been resolutely ignored by Republican jurists, by Quintilian's time they were at least discussing the problems such contradictions posed.[46] Only

---

rogatio est . . . nam, nisi populus aut plebs rogetur, nullum plebis aut populi iussum fieri potest); Papinian identified the essence of *lex* as a *sponsio*, *D.* 1.3.1 (believed to be very late by Schiller [1978] 222), all anachronistic impositions on earlier notion of *lex*, Magdelain (1978) 11, 42. Gaius: *G.* 1.3.

43 Many elements were possible in nuncupation: institution of heirs, *D.* 28.1.21.*pr.* (Ulpian; thinks they *should* be nuncupated in a way that they can be heard, but they can also be written), 28.1.25 (Javolenus), 28.5.1.1 and 5 (Ulpian), 28.5.9.2 and 5 (Ulpian), 28.5.59 (58).*pr.* (Paulus), 29.7.20 (Paulus); substitute heirs, *D.* 28.1.25 (Javolenus), 37.11.8.4 (Julian); legacies, *D.* 28.1.21.1 (Ulpian), 33.8.14 (Alfenus Varus). Buckland and Stein (1963) 282 see Gaius 2.229 as a definition of the Roman will.

44 Other elements still crucial, e.g., *testamenti factionem*, *G.* 2.114 and *D.* 28.1.4 (Gaius); institution of children as heirs or their disherison (*D.* 28.2.30 [Gaius], *necessario desiderantur*); cf. general requirements like *sollemnia* or no additions of *sui heredes* to agnatic family, *D.* 28.3.1 (Papinian).

45 *sententia voluntatis*: *D.* 28.1.1 (Modestinus); others, e.g., *D.* 29.3.2.2 (Ulpian), as long as it contains the *voluntatem*, it is called a *testamentum*.

46 Discussed in the *causa Curiana* of 94 or 93 BC (see Alexander [1990] 48); ignored, Schulz (1946) 79–80; Quintilian's time, cf. *Inst.* 7.6.1, "the jurists very frequently raise the question of written words and *voluntas*," not only (7.5.6) in the discussion of statutes, but also of "testaments, agreements, stipulations, and what is the case for all written documents, so too is the case for oral declarations."

268 *The evolution of practice*

sometime thereafter did *voluntas* achieve some common currency as the conceptualization of a "will."[47]

Such an abstract conceptualization was powerful, and accompanying it can be seen the same sorts of compensatory arguments that had also characterized the juristic history of stipulation. Such compensatory arguments had previously been infrequent; it was the praetor himself who had provided compensation for defect by creating an entirely new way to hold property (*bonorum possessio*), inferior to complete *dominium*, to compensate for formal defects in the construction of the mancipatory will. The compensatory arguments the jurists subsequently employed could therefore have two outcomes: they could restore a will to give either full *hereditas*, or restore it to give merely *bonorum possessio* (although the latter, after an imperial constitution of the mid-second century AD, was virtually the same as the former).[48] The application of this principle of *voluntas* corrected deficiencies in the writing by appealing to the nuncupation,[49] overcame the absence of the nuncupation by appealing to the writing and the absence of mancipation and writing by appealing to the nuncupation,[50] and was even used to overcome the absence of the institution of the heir.[51] This, when all the while the necessity that the testator be able to speak and hear was maintained, as were the requirements that there be something a witness could perceive by his senses (*sensu percipiat*) that told him he was observing a will even if he did not understand Latin; that approved formal language be used; that the will be made with *sollemnia*; and that

[47] Possibly sometime after the beginning of the second century AD, when the concept first appears with soldiers' wills, cf. *D.* 29.1.1.*pr.* (Ulpian), according to Trajan the bare *voluntas* of soldier was sufficient for his will (formalities were relaxed for soldiers as a special *beneficium*).

[48] A rescript of Antoninus Pius (*G.* 2.120) granted grounds for lawsuit (an *exceptionem doli mali*) to the *bonorum possessor* by will if he was confronted with a true (civil-law, i.e. intestate) heir; this required the heir rather than the possessor to prove the case, and left the possessor with the property; see Kaser (1955) 570.

[49] *D.* 28.5.1.5 (Ulpian: "we believe that more was nuncupated and less written," *credimus plus nuncupatum, minus scriptum*), in the case of defective language in the institution of the heir; since in Gaius's example the nuncupation did not include the institution of the heir, the remedy here is compensating on the basis of something that may not have been said. Same language and reasoning in *D.* 28.5.9.2 (where Ulpian is quoting Celsus, and "this *sententia* is supported by general rescripts"); cf. 28.5.1.6, Antoninus confirms even if word "heir" and an imperative verb lacking.

[50] Absence of act or *sollemnia*, *G.* 2.119 (specifically if *familia* not sold or testator did not utter nuncupation), 121, 149a, considered valid as a praetorian will; *D.* 29.7.20 (Paulus; valid as codicils and not technically to be called *tabulae testamenti*), cf. also Ulp. *Reg.* 23.6, 28.6; absence of mancipation and writing, *CJ* 6.11.2 (AD 242; grants *bonorum possessionem*).

[51] Intent stronger than requirement for institution of heirs and the emperor lets the legacies stand, *D.* 28.4.3 (Marcellus); intention of testator restores a person believed dead as heiress, *D.* 28.6.41 (Papinian); testator himself writes less but intended more, *D.* 28.5.9.2 (Ulpian), or writes more but intended less, *D.* 28.5.9.3 (Ulpian; much more here too); to be preferred to *verba*, *D.* 35.1.101.*pr.* (Papinian); affects how to understand visible changes in *tabulae*, *D.* 28.4.1 and 28.4.2 (both Ulpian).

Documents, jurists, the emperor, and the law

the whole be an act seamlessly performed.[52] Given that the compensatory arguments from the nuncupation (for defects in writing) seem to restore full *hereditas* while those from the writing (for defects in nuncupation or performance) seem only to enable the praetor to grant *bonorum possessio*, there is a clear inclination among the jurists to privilege speech as the most significant component; but all components are so intertwined that even this preference is a muted and incomplete one. Ulpian was happiest when the institution of the heir was announced in the nuncupation, for that was where he and other jurists thought it should be; but even he could only suggest this, not require it, given what most people believed about the interrelationship of mancipation, nuncupation, and *tabula* – and about the need for secrecy.[53]

The late conceptualization of a will as *voluntas* was in particular a strong weapon against any defects in the formal performance of a mancipatory will. Earlier jurists had also been assisted by statutes like the *senatusconsultum Neronianum*, by which legacies "invalid at civil law by reason of defective expression (*verborum vitio*)" were declared, nonetheless, valid,[54] but the adjustments and remedies they had particularly favored earlier resembled those employed for stipulation. Thus there were modulations in language, from *certa* to *concepta verba*, as in the institution of the heir (Gaius's list had included only one form that was *sollemnis*, but one other was *conprobata* or "approved"). They also created and applied categories of extrinsic and essential components of a will: legacies were superfluous to the validity of a will, as was incomprehensible wording not a part of the institution of the heir (or the disherison of others); so too, impossible conditions were "to be considered *pro nullis*," "as if they had never been written," "as if they were not in writing," for "what is expressed harms, what is not expressed does not harm."[55] Defects in these parts could simply be ignored, like adding "arms and the man I sing" to, or requesting hippocentaurs in, stipulations.

---

[52] Deaf or dumb, e.g., *D.* 28.1.6.1 (Gaius), *D.* 28.1.7 (Macer), *D.* 28.1.25 (Javolenus); Ulp. *Reg.* 20.13. *sensu percipiat*, *D.* 28.1.20.9 (Ulpian). Jurists' disapproval of language: *G.* 2.117 (quoted above); approved language for other parts of will, e.g., institution of heir (Ulp. *Reg.* 25.9), disherison (*G.* 2.127–8, 132), *cretio* (*G.* 2.165), substitution of heirs (*G.* 2.174), legation by vindication (*G.* 2.193), legation by damnation (*G.* 2.201, 203), legation by permission (*G.* 2.209), legation by preception (*G.* 2.216, 221), *fideicommissa* (*G.* 2.249–50, 277), freeing slaves (*G.* 2.267), appointing tutors (*G.* 2.289). *sollemnia* required for a will to be *iure factum*, *D.* 28.3.1 (Papinian); *sollemnia testamenti* necessary, *D.* 28.1.20.8 (Ulpian; an opinion attributed to *veteres*); one continuous act, *D.* 28.1.21.3 (Ulpian, *uno contextu actus testari oportet*).

[53] *D.* 28.1.21.*pr.* (Ulpian), instituted heirs should be nuncupated (*nuncupandi sint*).

[54] Discussed at *G.* 2.218.

[55] Legacies, e.g., *D.* 34.8.3.2 (Marcian); incomprehensible bits of wills – *reliqua autem per se ipsa valent*, *D.* 34.8.2 (Alfenus Varus); "impossible conditions," *D.* 35.1.3 (Ulpian), *D.* 34.8.3.2 (Marcian); harming, *D.* 35.1.52 (Modestinus; *expressa nocent, non expressa non nocent*).

270   *The evolution of practice*

Errors in the performance of stipulation, although serious, usually produced argument and litigation between two parties who were still alive; errors in the performance of a mancipatory will damaged the good work and good reputation of the deceased, and deprived the living of their rightful due. Remedies for formal defects in wills were therefore extremely important, perhaps more so than in stipulations, but had to be pursued with extreme caution and conservatism. There was much more juristic commentary on wills (if it is fair to generalize from a comparison of Gaius's treatment of the two subjects, or from how much was excerpted in the *Digest*), but it changed the understanding of the mancipatory will in the classical period of Roman law much more slowly. The same will not be as true in the post-classical period.

(*b*) *The post-classical jurists.* Post-classical jurists followed the late-classical conceptualization of a will as the *voluntas* of the testator, perceptible in all parts of the will, and continued to use it to remedy formal defects of execution. The priority of the testator's intention is regularly referred to, either in support of or in opposition to testamentary dispositions,[56] and defects in written wills, for example, can be repaired by reference to the nuncupation.[57]

Idem AA. Rufinae. Errore scribentis testamentum iuris sollemnitas mutilari nequaquam potest, quando minus scriptum plus nuncupatum videtur. et ideo recto testamento facto, quamquam desit "heres esto," consequens est existente herede legata sive fideicommissa iuxta voluntatem testatoris oportere dari.

The Emperors Diocletian and Maximian Augusti to Rufina. The solemnity of the law can never be mangled by the error of the one writing a testament, since it is regarded as less written and more nuncupated. And indeed where a will has been made correctly, even though "let him be my heir" is lacking, it follows that, since an heir exists, legacies or *fideicommissa* must be paid according to the *voluntas* of the testator.

The *voluntas* of the testator is apparent, the nuncupation again is assumed to have provided the important institution of the heir, and the principle *minus scriptum, plus nuncupatum* is enunciated yet again. Classical conceptions and maxims of interpretation still apply.[58] This concept of nuncupation and writing as complementary and capable of compensating for each other, and

---

[56] Intention: *CJ* 6.44.1 (intent of testator to discharge a debt, AD 213); *CJ* 6.42.7 (in *fideicommissa*, AD 225); *CJ* 6.42.17–18 (AD 286 and 290); *CT* 2.24.1 (AD 321/324); *CJ* 6.43.2 (AD 531); *CJ* 6.28.3 (intention overcoming *verba*, AD 531); *contra* Schulz (1946) 295, not interpolated from this later period into the earlier classical texts.

[57] *CJ* 6.23.7 (AD 290); on this rescript see also Tellegen-Couperus (1982) 23–6.

[58] Above, n.49.

Documents, jurists, the emperor, and the law

of the act as essentially unitary, would last for another hundred years – until at least, probably, AD 389. In this year, the emperors announced their rejection of bequests through codicils and letters, but professed themselves willing to accept them through "the legitimate writing or nuncupation of the will" (*testamenti vero scripturam legitimam vel nuncupationem*), and by their phrasing (and their use of the singular *testamenti*) may be indicating that nuncupation and writing were still considered alternatively acceptable parts of the same will.[59]

On the other hand, the relaxation of requirements for solemn or approved words, and their presentation in a certain order, came earlier, as had allowances for mistakes in names or lists of names.[60] The issue of special words themselves – whether specific words were necessary – and much else were settled decisively in AD 320/326:[61]

> Quoniam indignum est ob inanem observationem irritas fieri tabulas et iudicia mortuorum, placuit ademptis his, quorum imaginarius usus est, institutioni heredis verborum non esse necessariam observantiam, utrum imperativis et directis verbis fiat an inflex<is>. nec enim interest, si dicatur "heredem facio" vel "instituo" vel "volo" vel "mando" vel "cupio" vel "esto" vel "erit," sed quibuslibet confecta sententiis, quolibet loquendi genere formata institutio valeat, si modo per eam liquebit voluntatis intentio, nec necessaria sint momenta verborum, quae forte seminecis et balbutiens lingua profudit. et in postremis ergo iudiciis ordinandis amota erit sollemnium sermonum necessitas, ut, qui facultates proprias cupiunt ordinare, in quacumque instrumenti materia conscribere et quibuscumque verbis uti liberam habeant facultatem . . . in legatis vel fideicommissis verborum necessaria non sit observantia, ita ut nihil prorsus intersit, quis talem voluntatem verborum casus exceperit aut quis loquendi usus effuderit.

For the reason that it is unworthy that the last wills and dispositions of estates by persons who are deceased should become void on account of the failure to observe a vain *observatio*, it has been decided that those (things, unspecified) shall be removed whose use is only imaginary, and that, in the institution of an heir, an *observatio* of words is not required, whether this be done by imperative and strict words, or by terms that have been modulated. For it makes no difference whether the terms "I make you my heir" or "I appoint you my heir" or "I wish" or "I desire you to be my heir" or "be my heir" or "so-and-so shall be my heir," are employed; but

---

[59] *CT* 4.4.2 (AD 389); it is also possible that this phrase should be translated "the legitimate writing of the will, or the nuncupation," in which case the division into various types of will, attributed below (nn. 66–9) to the fifth century, belongs to the late fourth instead.

[60] E.g., *CJ* 6.23.4 (AD 239); *CJ* 6.23.17 = *CT* 4.4.3 (*testamentum . . . quod diversis hoc deficiens nominibus appellavit*, but this no reason to invalidate it, since *superflua non noceant*; AD 396?).

[61] *CJ* 6.23.15 + 6.37.21 + 6.9.9, split and inserted under different headings in the *Codex*, as was not uncommon (cf. *CT Min.* 4, C. *De Emend.* 2 [to *CJ*]); discussion of (disputed) date, Johnston (1988) 213–14, confirmed in Eusebius *VC* 4.26 (*PG* 20.1173).

272   *The evolution of practice*

no matter in what words the institution is made, or in what form of speech it is
stated, it shall be valid, provided the intention of the will is clearly shown by the
language used, nor is the weight of words required that the half-dead tongue of
a person pours out. Therefore, in the execution of last wills, the requirement of
formal speech is hereby removed, and those who desire to dispose of their own
property can write their wills upon any kind of material whatsoever, and are freely
permitted to use any words which they may desire ... No *observantia* of words is
required for the bequest of legacies, or the creation of *fideicommissa*, and it makes
no difference whatever what grammatical forms of verbs indicate his will, or what
way of speaking pours it out.

This constitution, addressed to the people, dispenses with the need for a
great deal. *Observatio*, also a term of Gaius's for the solemnities of a will,
is deemed "empty" and cannot be allowed to ruin a will; the necessity for
it is removed, and with it go special verbs in the institution of the heir,
the nuncupation itself (the "weight of words" poured out by the dying),
special writing *materia* (wooden *tabulae* must be meant),[62] and (presumably special) words in legacies and *fideicommissa*. Whether it also included
mancipation itself is unknown, since Justinian's compilers systematically
removed all references to it as they excerpted materials for both *Digest* and
Codex, but the survival of a will from AD 335–45 that still has a *libripens* and
a *familiae emptor* suggests that mancipation was still being practiced, and
therefore still part of *observatio*.[63] Only the particular wording of the institution of the heir is identified as *sermo sollemnis*, but all others are at least
included here as part of *observatio*, even though legacies and *fideicommissa*
had been specifically left out by the classical jurists.[64] With the removal of
the specific performance of special acts and words disappear also the *tabulae*
of the will itself: one last reminder that the three have all been intertwined
as bearers of legitimacy for a very long time. As long as intention is clear, say
Constantine's jurists now, any way of expressing it, on any type of material,
will do. That the component parts of the document or utterance itself had
to follow a certain order, which a ceremonial unitary act demanded and

---

[62] Suggested also by a retrospective view in Just. *Inst.* 2.10.12, *nihil autem interest, testamentum in tabulis
an in chartis membranisve vel in alia materia fiat*.

[63] Mancipation (in wills) deliberately removed from *Digest* and *CJ*, Just. *Inst.* 2.10.10, cf. J. A. C.
Thomas (1976) 152 n.9; will with *libripens* and a *familiae emptor*, *P. NYU* 2.15 (= Amelotti [1966]
280–2; AD 335–45, probably from the Fayum in Egypt).

[64] Forerunners, e.g., legacies, *CJ* 6.37.7 (mistake in name does not affect a legacy; AD 215); *fideicommissa*,
CJ 6.42.16 (intention of testator greater than language of a *fideicommissum*; AD 283); *CJ* 3.36.26
(AD 321), granting very limited validity to an unfinished will lacking *sollemnitas legum*, also *CT* 2.24.1
(AD 321 [324]), which granted a very limited validity to a will begun in writing but never "perfected"
and writing lacking *utilitate verborum vel sollemnitate iurum*, as long as intention of testator revealed.
The related institution of *cretio* was also relieved of the necessity for o[bser]vantiam in AD 339, *CT*
8.18.4, its need for *scrupulosam sollemnitatem* in AD 407, *CT* 8.18.8 = *CJ* 6.30.17 (AD 407).

Documents, jurists, the emperor, and the law 273

classical jurists had upheld, also came to be no longer required, but much later, under Justinian. This dispensation was again justified by reference to the intention, here called *mens*, of the testator; so too other unnamed failures of *observatio* that could be attributed to the work of the *tabellio* or scribe were deemed no longer harmful.[65]

As with stipulation, so too with wills the post-classical jurists were assiduous in their removal of the requirement for formalities – of special words, of words in a certain order, of gestures, of special writing materials. The definition of a will as an expression of *voluntas* or *mens* provided regular justification for the relaxation of these necessities, and the trajectory seems very much one of a formal, ceremonial act becoming form free. Yet wills after AD 339 could still be distinguished from other types of legal documents – if not as characteristically ceremonial acts using special language in a rigorously prescribed order, then by content, and by the ways imperial constitutions defined them. Post-classical jurists in the fifth century AD made distinctions between types of will based on how they were made: on the way they were sealed or the physical ways in which the *voluntas* of the testator was expressed. They imposed these distinctions, and because their opinions appeared as imperial constitutions, the post-classical jurists actually made new kinds of testaments rather than merely commenting on the validity of the existing one and adjusting requirements for its *observatio*.

In defining types of will and making these new ones, they looked to both past and present. They looked to the past when they declared that one will, the one "made by civil law," required five witnesses, while another, that "made by praetorian law," needed seven. The Roman civil-law will was the mancipatory will, for which the praetor granted *bonorum possessio* if sealed by seven witnesses but having some defect in the way it was made; civil and praetorian had not been two different wills for some time.[66] These two wills were both written; another, the wholly oral "nuncupative will" was established in AD 416 by separating the nuncupation from the *testamentum* and giving it an independent existence,[67] while a fourth will recombined the

---

[65] *CJ* 6.23.24 (AD 528), specifically also removing the requirement that anything appearing before the institution of the heir was invalid, which the classical jurists had held to: *G.* 2.229–30 and *D.* 28.5.1.1 (Ulpian); cf. Hor. *Sat.* 2.5.51–5 (can see by quick glance at first lines whether one is heir or partial heir). Justinian also removed the need for order in wills, stipulations, and contracts, *CJ* 6.23.25 (AD 528; in dotal instruments too, specifically attributed to Leo).

[66] *CT* 4.4.7 (AD 424); *CJ* 6.23.21 (AD 439), *N. Val.* 21.1.2 (AD 446), and Just. *Inst.* 2.10.2; cf. Archi (1956).

[67] *CJ* 6.36.8 (AD 424; *ex testamento quolibet modo sive scripto sive sine scriptura confecto*). Only one "oral" will is known before AD 300, that of the poet Horace, who was seized by a sudden illness and could not seal tablets: Suet. *Vita Horatii* 75 (Rostagni), *herede Augusto palam nuncupato, cum urgente vi valetudinis non sufficeret ad obsignandas testamenti tabulas*. *P. Vind. Gr.* 25819, cited by Amelotti (1966) 112 (for a description, 59) as an oral will, is probably not one.

274 *The evolution of practice*

older civil and praetorian "types" to create the "tripartite" will of AD 439/446, which the testator could offer, closed, to seven witnesses, before whom he must subscribe the document itself. The witnesses were expected to seal and subscribe, the entire act of will-making to be completed "on one and the same day and at one and the same time."[68] The fifth kind was the holographic will, which was written out personally by the testator and required no witnesses. Only the authenticity of the handwriting had to be proved, and "the agreement of the other circumstances which the sanctions of the ancient Emperors as well as Our own sanctions command to be observed in testaments."[69] Each of these late-antique wills was a refraction, one facet of the classical mancipatory will: the oral nuncupation itself; the *tabulae testamenti* witnessed by five; the *tabulae testamenti* sealed by seven; a handwritten version that carried so much more of the *fides* and prestige of the testator, the handwriting itself serving as witness; and, their own creation, the one that recombined so many of these new distinctions, the tripartite will. The conceptual definition of the will as *voluntas* remained the same, but imperial constitutions granted independent existence to five different versions of it. Aristotles following upon Platos, post-classical jurists created empirical classifications within one well-established conception and kept very few requirements overall, that of unbroken making being one of them, subscribing and witnessing the other.

Within these fifth-century classifications, the separation of writing and nuncupation was pronounced, and the writing itself increasingly stressed as authoritative. A constitution of AD 439, by making reference to *testamenta scripta*, written wills, and *testamenta per nuncupationem*, nuncupative wills, reinforced the distinction that the classificational scheme was creating.[70] In AD 446, testators were given a choice between *testamenta* made by civil

---

[68] Tripartite will, quoted *NT* 16.2 (AD 439), *quo facto et testibus uno eodemque die ac tempore subscribentibus et + signantibus + valere testamentum*; it was named "tripartite" in Just. *Inst.* 2.10.3, because the requirement of "the witnesses and their presence at one occasion for the sake of the ceremonial making of a will comes from the *ius civile*; subscriptions of testator and witnesses have been added by the *observatione* of sacred (= imperial) constitutions; seals and number of witnesses from the edict of the praetor"; it was adopted in the West by *N.Val.* 21.2 (AD 446), which relaxes some of the standards for simultaneity.

[69] *N.Val.* 21.2.1 (AD 446, *reliqua congruere demonstret, quae in testamentis debere servari tam veterum principum quam nostrae praecipiunt sanctiones*); a possible forerunner is writing left by the dead man in which "he is understood . . . only to have made plans concerning his testament" for distributing his property only among *sui heredes*, *CT* 2.24.1 (AD 321 [324]), deemed valid only among *sui heredes*; this much more restrictive principle of remedy reasserted in *NT* 16.5 (AD 439); reconfirmed in *CJ* 6.23.28 (AD 530), a handwritten will obviates the need for testator's subscription, but five witness subscriptions are necessary.

[70] *NT* 16.2, 16.6 and *passim* (AD 439). The separation may have occurred earlier, but the evidence for it is scanty and the secondary literature (see Kaser [1959] 341–5) is in favor of this date or later.

Documents, jurists, the emperor, and the law

and praetorian law, on the one hand, and disposing of their property *per nuncupationem* on the other.[71] *Testamentum*, once the general word for will, in this *novella* of AD 446 now meant written will, while *nuncupatio* meant an oral disposition of property which to be considered a will had to be listened to by seven witnesses, who were to hear a testator "manifestly making a testament without writing," not a man "announcing his decision, as is customarily done" (which must mean that with a written will, a man calls together his witnesses by telling them that he *has made* his will).[72] Simple unwritten declarations had no validity, especially in comparison to a written will. This had been decreed in a constitution of AD 416: "no person shall rob written documents of their proper force and bestow validity on unwritten declarations" – even if a testamentary declaration had named the emperor.[73] The contrast with the holographic will is striking. The favored medium for the expression of authoritative *voluntas* is now considered writing, not utterance. In Justinian's time the nuncupative will made by a blind man receives "full authority" (*plenum ... robur*) only after a notary draws up the instrument and it is properly subscribed and sealed, while the deaf and dumb are allowed to make wills if they can read and write.[74]

The post-classical jurists of the fourth century AD thus found themselves working in a context of traditional beliefs about the mancipatory will – beliefs about its unitary nature and the necessity for formal, ceremonial performance – that were assumed also by the body of juristic opinion they inherited, and especially by its definitions and methods of argumentation. For a century, these post-classical jurists too assumed the unitary nature of a will and allowed one element to substitute for another, but in the fifth century AD they proposed new categories of definition elegantly and logically dependent on the old understandings. Since each separate element of a multi-part unitary act contained intent, defined as the essence of a will, each element could be considered a will in and of itself. The result was five types of will, each derived from an aspect of the unitary act or a combination of some of them. Distinctions between categories were created by how each was made, which the jurists now laid out; in the preceding century, much of the ceremonial action, formal wording, and set *materia* that had once characterized them all before they were split apart had been

---

[71] *N.Val.* 21.1.2 (AD 446): *nam cum liceat cunctis iure civili atque praetorio, liceat per nuncupationem ... iudicia suprema componere.*

[72] *NT* 16.6 (AD 439), *simul uno eodemque tempore collecti testatoris voluntatem ut testamentum sine scriptura facientis audierint, non ut suum, ut adsolet fieri, narrantis arbitrium.*

[73] *CT* 4.4.5 (*nemo scriptis proprium auferat robur et non scriptis ... ingerat firmamentum*) = *CJ* 6.23.20 (AD 416); cf. *CJ* 6.23.3 (AD 232), even the emperor cannot claim under a will made *imperfecto.*

[74] Blind, *CJ* 6.22.8 (AD 521); deaf and/or dumb, *CJ* 6.22.10 (AD 531).

276   *The evolution of practice*

decreed unnecessary. Four of the five new fifth-century types of will required or assumed writing, although no longer specifically writing on tablets.

In the fields of both stipulations and testaments, complex ceremonial acts for centuries encouraged the development and application of the tool of abstract conceptualization and prompted efforts to soften the negative impact of defects in formalism without destroying formalism itself. These efforts were successful because of what I have called "compensatory arguments," in which the new conceptualizations and the existing understanding that an act was unitary (and included within it act, speech, and writing) together allowed the jurists to borrow from one part of the act to another when defects of gesture, writing, or speech were diagnosed. No major question or approach was predicated on a tension between oral and written by jurists of either period, despite modern scholars' attempts to write the history of these acts in these terms; rather the opposite, as the moderns' deadlocked wrangling over the mancipatory will in the classical period and stipulation in the post-classical period shows. Authoritative speech and authoritative writing were parts of the ceremonial tradition for both sets of jurists. The classical preference for speech and the post-classical preference for writing as carriers of validity did not arise *ex nihilo*; they were choices made among options within the wider unitary act.

OTHER, RELATED ACTS

Just as unitary acts on *tabulae* continued to influence the juristic discussions of stipulation and the mancipatory will, so too the emphasis given to writing elsewhere in post-classical juristic thinking is found only, or at least initially, in legal acts that were descended from (or modelled on) the old formal acts on *tabulae*. In these cases, this emphasis may also arise from the fact that these documents had been, for centuries, also better protected and harder to forge (a consideration that might have been important for stipulation and mancipation as well); but here too the jurists regularly point to other elements of an act that can compensate for defects. So we find writing emphasized not only in pure stipulation, but in marriage contracts and dowries; not only in mancipatory wills, but also in the emancipation of children; and writing emphasized also in the acts that traditionally had established status and privilege, like birth-registrations and benefits associated with army discharge, on wood. Finally, the emphatic role given to writing in establishing the validity of an act is also found in two acts that developed, as their form shows, out of a combination of stipulation and

Documents, jurists, the emperor, and the law

(at times) mancipation: donation and sale. How these last two were to be categorized – property transfers or consensual contracts? – was debated, and attitudes towards the place of writing in the act as a consequence varied in juristic thinking over time. Overall, however, the fault-line in the valuation of documents in the later law is the same as the earlier fault-line between formal acts on *tabulae* and acts that could be evidenced on a variety of other materials: earlier beliefs and practices have left clear and perceptible traces in post-classical juristic thought.

In this large family of formal legal acts once on *tabulae*, compensatory arguments are again used as petitioners, fearful that loss of, or damage to, a document meant the invalidation of an act, write in for help. Sometimes the answers were harsh, suggesting that even here there were no proper compensations that could be hoped for, as in earlier third-century answers on matters of establishing status through birth-registration and manumission.[75] More often petitioners were regularly reassured by third-century jurists that the act did not exist on account of the document alone, and therefore that the act had occurred and its existence could be demonstrated in other ways. Thus a father's missing subscription on a "document pertaining to marriage" did not invalidate it (as long as he gave his consent); the absence of a nuptial tablet did not invalidate a marriage (as long as neighbors were aware that you had taken a wife for the purpose of procreation, one of the definitions of marriage).[76] *Dominium*, the type of ownership conveyed through mancipation, exists and can be proved when documents are lost, and persons or "the uncorrupted faith" of instruments can prove an emancipation for which the *acta* are damaged.[77] The *fides* of a published testament is valid even if its *materia* are proved to have been

[75] Birth status, in the third century to be proved through *instrumenta* and *argumenta*, for witnesses insufficient, *CJ* 4.20.2 (AD 223), cf. *D.* 4.2.8.1 (Paulus); this may have relaxed a little later. Manumission, "just as a man cannot take away the liberty given to the manumitted, so he is compelled to provide an *instrumentum* of manumission," *CJ* 7.16.26 (AD 294).

[76] Marriage document: *CJ* 5.4.2 (Severus and Caracalla); marriage, *CJ* 5.4.9 (Probus), cf. *CJ* 5.4.22 (AD 428; confirms even in the absence of formalities, based on consent). The fragmentary *FV* 113 appears to rely more exclusively on writing: "the affection of parents persuades us, that obligation concerning the dowry arises from the sole giving of the *libellus*" (*nobis . . . parentium affectus persuasit, ut in sola libelli datione de dote obligatio gigneretur*). By the fourth century AD, there could be as many as three different kinds of legal acts on *tabulae* associated with marriage, the *tabellae sponsaliciae, dotales*, and *nuptiales*, the last referred to by Augustine's mother Monica as *instrumenta emptionis*; see Castello (1938).

[77] *dominium: CJ* 4.19.4 (AD 222), *instrumento emptionis* contrasted with *quibuscumque aliis legitimis probationibus*; same in *CJ* 10.3.3 (AD 239); *proprietatem* not compromised by *amissionem instrumentorum* in *CJ* 4.21.8 (AD 287), but no reasoning given; in *CJ* 4.19.21 (AD 294) these *instrumenta* are useful *ad probationem . . . dominii*. Emancipation: *CJ* 4.21.11 (AD 294); *CJ* 8.48(49).3 (AD 293) reminds that emancipation is done *actu sollemni*.

278　　The evolution of practice

destroyed.[78] Proofs or demonstrations (*indicia*) "which law does not spurn" did not have less *fides probationis* than *instrumenta* in a dispute over property; loss of *professio* of free birth did not destroy a man's free birth (nor should its absence or falsification prevent other evidence from proving the same); a badly drafted instrument had no adverse effect on status; and privileges of veteran status could be enjoyed if you could prove by other means what was in the lost documents of honorable discharge.[79] Missing or superfluous clauses, as well as wrong names and wrong facts, are not allowed to compromise the validity of acts of sale, so sales said to be gifts are sales only, and even if a clause forbidding the prostitution of a slave was not inserted into her *tabulas venditionis*, nonetheless she cannot be prostituted.[80] What is clear is that – in addition to the fact that petitioners knew perfectly well where *they* would place the greatest emphasis – several of these legal opinions attempt to allay the anxiety of questioners by assuring them that documents and the acts of which they were a part existed in an easy symbiosis. The gentle efforts to downplay the importance of documents offer other methods of proof and thereby redirect petitioners to the idea behind a complex act and away from an over-emphasis on what was only one aspect of it, even if that aspect was (as the purport of the questions themselves demonstrates) its only tangible and lasting one.

Juristic answers to questions about acts that were not, traditionally, formal acts involving *tabulae* took a subtly different approach. Here, in debts, *bona fides* agreements for dowries, divisions of property, pacts, and compromises, merely finding "other reasons" or "other proofs" if a document is lost or was never made is enjoined.[81] In these and other acts like them,[82]

---

[78] *CJ* 6.23.2 (AD 225), *publicati semel testamenti fides, quamvis ipsa materia, in qua primum a testatore scriptum relictum fuit ... intercidit, nihilo minus valet.*

[79] *indicia, CJ* 3.32.19 (AD 293); loss of *professione* of birth, *CJ* 4.21.6 (AD 286), and note that in *CJ* 2.42(43).1 (AD 223) they are still referred to as *tabulis*; should be able (*debeat*) to prove by other means, in a case of *omissa professio, CJ* 7.16.15 (AD 293); *instrumenti male concepti, D.* 1.5.8 (Papinian; a rescript of Antoninus); discharge, *CJ* 4.21.7 (AD 286).

[80] *CJ* 5.16.2 (AD 213; words inserted into *instrumentum emptionis* do not bind you); *CJ* 4.50.3 (AD 228; saying your mother paid); *CJ* 4.50.4 (Valerian and Gallienus; with, incorrectly, name of your mother-in-law); *CJ* 4.50.5 (AD 290; wife's name); *CJ* 4.50.6 (AD 293); no prostitution, *CJ* 4.56.2 (AD 223).

[81] Debts, *CJ* 4.21.1 (AD 213), *CJ* 4.21.5 (AD 240), *CJ* 8.42(43).15 (AD 293), and *CJ* 8.42(43).22 (AD 294); dowry, *CJ* 5.12.15 (AD 293); division of property, *CJ* 3.36.12 (AD 252); *pactum, CJ* 2.3.17 (AD 286); compromise (*transactio*), *CJ* 2.4.5 (AD 227). Documents not needed: possession, *CJ* 3.32.15 (AD 293; by sale) and *CJ* 4.21.12 (AD 294; by donation); sale, *CJ* 4.21.10 (AD 294) and *CJ* 4.52.5 (Diocletian and Maximian); lease, *CJ* 4.65.24 (AD 293); division of property, *CJ* 2.45(46).1 (AD 293), *CJ* 4.21.9 (AD 293), and *CJ* 3.37.4 (AD 294). See also *CJ* 3.32.10 (AD 290), when no *instrumenta* for home-born slaves, must be proved through *aliis probationibus* or interrogation of slaves themselves.

[82] Contracts, *CJ* 4.31.13 (Diocletian and Maximian), *CJ* 4.34.6 (AD 293), *CJ* 2.19(20).7 (AD 293), *CT* 2.4.3 (AD 371), *CT* 2.27.1 (AD 421), *CT* 2.13.1 = *CJ* 2.13.2 (AD 422), *N. Val.* 12.1 (AD 443), *N. Val.* 13.11

Documents, jurists, the emperor, and the law

writing was deemed "to pertain to" or "to contain" proof only,[83] "vanished" when the act (based on *fides*) was fulfilled,[84] and if something was missing in it, like a clause allowing suit against a creditor in a document of *pignus*, or a right of action in a compromise, nonetheless legal action on the basis of the legal act could proceed.[85] Compensatory reasoning is used, if writing is deficient or absent, only by making reference to "what happened" (*res gestae*)[86] or to "reality" or "the truth" (*veritas*), the latter a particular speciality of Diocletianic jurists, perhaps even Hermogenianus himself.[87] *Veritas* is to Diocletian's jurists an all-powerful concept that can animate any legal act and free it from its earthly imperfections, and so is at times used for the family of ceremonial acts as well. *Veritas* is one of the last and greatest abstractions proposed by the jurists, of whom Diocletian's were some of the finest.

The general distinction between formal acts once on *tabulae*, whose documents were indeed significant and whose unfortunate loss could be remedied by appeal to the other parts of the unitary act, and acts written in other forms, whose *scriptura* had at best evidentiary value, is maintained also in fourth- and fifth-century advice about what was important in court.[88] The ideal, of course, was a case proved "by reliable witnesses, the most evident documents, and undoubted demonstrations," as was said in 382.[89]

(AD 445), *N.Val.* 22.3 (AD 446), *N.Marc.* 2.2 (AD 450), and *N.Maj.* 2.1 (AD 458); lease, *CJ* 4.65.32 (Zeno); *pignus/pactum* to pay interest, *CJ* 4.32.4 (Severus and Caracalla).

[83] Transfer of property by *fideicommissum*, *CJ* 6.42.24 (AD 293, documents *ad probationem originis eorum pertinent*); compromise (*transactio*), *CJ* 2.4.5 (AD 227, *scriptura, quae probationem rei gestae solet continere, necessaria non est*).

[84] *CJ* 4.65.26 (AD 294; *evanuit*).

[85] *pignus: CJ* 8.13(14).12 (AD 293), cf. compromise (*transactio*), *CJ* 2.4.31 (AD 294).

[86] *CJ* 4.50.6 (AD 293; *res gesta potior quam scriptura*), and *CJ* 4.22.3 (AD 294; look at *quod gestum*, not *quod scriptum*); *CJ* 4.22.4 (AD 294), "if you have written in documents that what you have done was done by another, *plus actum quam scriptum valet*," act unspecified.

[87] *scriptura* and *veritas* at odds: contracts, *CJ* 2.5.1 (AD 293) and *CJ* 8.42(43).13 (AD 293); marriage document, *CJ* 5.4.13 (Diocletian and Maximian); sale, *CJ* 4.50.5 (AD 290), *CJ* 4.21.10 (AD 294), and *CJ* 8.53(54).10 (AD 293); birth documents, *CJ* 7.16.15 (AD 293); and cf. *CJ* 8.48(49).2 (AD 291), emancipations and donations. On *res gestae* and *veritas*, see Honoré (1981) 180. *Veritas* is the highest level of reference, better even than *res gestae*, cf. *CJ* 4.22.2 (AD 294), *CJ* 4.29.17 (AD 294). Writing is not always in conflict with *veritas*, for documents can establish it, *CJ* 2.4.19 (AD 293) and *CJ* 2.1.7 (AD 225), as can *acta publica*, *CJ* 2.1.2 (AD 194). Hermogenianus: Honoré (1994) 177–80; *veritas* not unknown before, *CJ* 4.31.6 (AD 229), *CJ* 8.32(33).2 (AD 197), and *CJ* 4.22.1 (AD 259).

[88] On proof in late antiquity in general, see Archi (1964), especially 404–13; Wieacker (1964) 575 explains this trend towards documents as a desire to bind a judge to their probative value.

[89] *CJ* 4.19.25 (AD 382, *testibus idoneis vel . . . apertissimis documentis vel indiciis . . . indubitati*); cf. *CT* 16.2.41, cases against clerics must be proved "by proofs and documents" (AD 412; *docenda probationibus, monstranda documentis*); *instrumenta vel testes*, *CT* 2.7.1 = *CJ* 3.11.2 (AD 314), *CJ* 2.44(45).2.1 (AD 321, *testibus vel instrumentis*), *CT* 1.22.2 = *CJ* 3.14.1 (AD 334; *testes vel instrumenta*), and *CT* 9.37.3 = *CJ* 9.46.9 (AD 382; *testibus . . . documentis*). This is a world where people can even imagine

280   *The evolution of practice*

Although worries about the forgery of documents had by no means been left behind, the authority of even a document suspected of forgery could confer temporary possession of property,[90] and the emperor Julian cautiously pronounced in 362 that γραμμάτια had "great strength" (μεγάλην ἰσχύν) as long as there was no disputed point that needed to be supported "by others" (ἐξ ἄλλων).[91] In AD 443, the emperor granted that if your necessary papers (*necessariis instructionibus*) were in a province to which you could not travel at the moment, because of a small problem with barbarians, then there would be no suit against you.[92] In contrast, letters (*epistulae*) do not provide good corroboration of legal acts, *pacta* had to be stipulated to have *firmitas*, and informal notes to yourself about money people owed you – called a *brevis* or a *chartula*, once *rationes* – simply were not enough to establish a legal debt, "for we do not think it appropriate that a man become a debtor through an *adnotatio*," nor, as a rescript adds, through a *subnotatio*.[93] It is not writing *per se* that defines the framework within which jurists are working, but writing as embodied, or once embodied and probably better protected, in a specific form. There, and there most reliably, was worth and weight.

Ancient significance, legal weight in establishing an act, and high probative value are all associated with the documents of formal acts once written on *tabulae*. Documents in two combinational acts, donation and sale, are valued in less-clear and sometimes contradictory ways, in itself a notable demonstration of how these two acts could be defined, redefined, and recategorized over time as a consequence of their hybrid background. Donation,

---

having documentary evidence of descent (Amm. Marc. 31.12.15; its absence noted at 28.1.30); Buti (1982) 50 concludes that documents predominate in the legal process.

[90] Conferring possession: *CT* 9.19.2 = *CJ* 9.22.22 (AD 326 [320]), type of document unclear. Worries about forgery continue, *CT* 11.39.6 (AD 369), *CT* 9.19.4.1 = *CJ* 9.22.23 (AD 376; list of forgeable items includes *tabulae testamenti*, chirographs, *testationes*, *rationes privatas vel publicas*, *pacta, et epistulas vel ultimas voluntates, donationes venditiones*, and others), and *CT* 11.39.7 = *CJ* 4.19.24 (AD 378).

[91] *CT* 11.39.5 (AD 362; in a court protocol).

[92] *N.Val.* 12.2 (AD 443).

[93] Letters, *CJ* 4.19.13 (AD 293, about birth status) and above n.28 (stipulations and other acts). *Pacta*: *CT* 2.9.2 = *CJ* 2.4.40 (AD 381). Accounts: quoted, *CT* 10.16.3 = *CJ* 10.2.5 (AD 377; *nomina* in an account-book called *chartulas*... *brevis* not confirmed by witnesses or *cautiones* to be rejected as worthless, because it is too easy to make another your debtor through your own notation); cf. *CJ* 4.19.7 (AD 262; *adnotationes* and *subnotationes* insufficient proof of debt) and *CJ* 4.19.6 (AD 245), *rationes* also inadequate. Precisely these problems were recognized in ἐφημερίδες centuries earlier, cf. Plut. *Mor.* 829D, and these sorts of problems may even have contributed to the demise of the account-*tabula* (and the literal contract) itself – the debtor nowhere signalled his acceptance of the obligation: see Ps.-Asc. on Cic. *2 Verr.* 1.60 (Orelli), *haec vetus consuetudo cessavit*, with Gröschler (1997) 74–5. The *adnotatio* is grouped with *instrumenta domestica* and *privata testatio* in *CJ* 4.19.5 (AD 245) as items insufficient even for proof; cf. *CJ* 4.21.19 (AD 529), similarly severe on unwitnessed *apochis*.

Documents, jurists, the emperor, and the law 281

the act of giving a gift, transferred property freely. Was its essential nature in the reason for giving – the *liberalitas* that led to the gift – or in the property transfer? The classical jurists, in *Digest* 39.5, concentrated on the first (which they subdivided into three types), and when thinking about any technicalities of transfer mostly seem to have imagined the conveyance of the gift as informal or as promised in the present for the future and secured by a stipulation.[94] In donations taking place in the present, documents could be used,[95] and the use of documents in gifts may have begun simply as a gift of the documents of (mancipatory?) sale themselves, as occurred in an imperial constitution of AD 210.[96] Diocletian's jurists followed the classical jurists in seeing donation as a reason for an act rather than an act, and petitions and answers show gifts given informally, occurring between absent parties, between three parties rather than two, and in *epistulae*; they judged that the documents (*instrumenta*) were in general incapable of binding a person to give what she had not intended to give, the force of the *veritas* of the act greater than that of writing – unless the giver had "subscribed specially,"[97] which would embody the intent to give freely.

Under Constantine, however, there was a change. Although the language of his constitution (*FV* 249) is cagey, the act of donation is stated to require three acts: first, a document (implied but not clearly stated as necessary here, more explicit in a specific case in AD 415),[98] the law listing what was to be included in it as a matter of *observatio*, the document itself not to be written secretly or privately, "but on *tabulae* or whatever other *materia* that the occasion will afford"; second, once the terms of the gift have been discussed and either accepted or rejected, *traditio* (informal conveyance)

---

[94] *liberalitas*, *D*. 39.5.19.2 (Ulpian); three types, *D*. 39.5.1 (Julian); stipulation, *D*. 39.5.2.4 (Julian), *D*. 39.5.33.*pr.* (Hermogenianus); see Buckland and Stein (1963) 253–8.

[95] E.g., *CJ* 8.53(54).23 (AD 294), first document of donation does not annul a second act of donation of same property; *CJ* 8.55(56).2 (AD 279), the loss of the document of donation did not invalidate the gift.

[96] *CJ* 8.53(54).1 (AD 210), if the *instrumentis* of sale of slaves (*emptionum mancipiorum*) handed over as gifts (*donatis et traditis*), then it is understood that *traditionem* of the slaves (which gave *bonorum possessio*) has been made; regularly thought interpolated, see Levy (1951) 146–7; but see also *CJ* 5.16.5 (AD 227), it is imaginable that an *instrumentum debitoris* can be given as a donation, although in this case the gift was invalid because it was between people who could not give each other gifts.

[97] *CJ* 8.53(54).6 (AD 286, *inter absentes*). Third parties, *CJ* 8.53(54).20 (AD 294). *epistulae*: *CJ* 8.53(54).5 (AD 284) contemplates the possibility that a donation could have been made *per epistulam*; in this case no *epistula* existed, but the *verba . . . testamenti* confirmed *liberalitas* and contained a *fideicommissum*; *CJ* 8.53(54).13 (AD 293) allows donations by letter, even a short one (refers to the *brevitas chartulae*), as long as it was *recte facta* (undefined). *CJ* 8.53(54).10 (AD 293; *instrumento, maiores veritate rei quam scriptura vires obtineat intellegis, de quo . . . nec specialiter subscripsisti*).

[98] *CT* 8.12.8 (AD 415), in a case of donors who wish to retain usufruct: an *instrumentum* must be made and that *instrumentum* also registered in the *acta* either before or after the *traditio*. *Omne ius compleat instrumentis* is also mentioned, but no valuation given, in *CJ* 8.53(54).26 (AD 316).

282   *The evolution of practice*

must follow, before witnesses who by their *fides* can later attest that the property was delivered; and third, *acta* before judge or magistrate must be drawn up and attached to the document of gift, or can be drawn up and attached "where the laws demand this."[99] Three other constitutions, one only three years later, make clear that, where appropriate, mancipation was expected to precede or substitute for *traditio*, for gifts between parents and children were specifically exempted from this general expectation. Gifts between them were instead valid "even if the formal words of mancipation" had not been spoken and "the formality of mancipation" not performed; other gifts, not between parents and children, were not.[100] In AD 323, however, Constantine does deny "that anything of the fixed form of words is required . . . those words have been abolished which previously were necessary in the making of donations."[101] Registration in *acta* was an act of *testificatio*, attestation, and the need for this, later also called an *observatio*, remains a constant, even for parents and children;[102] the other requirements in the next hundred or so years (as the special dispensations for gifts between parents and children showed) can sometimes be omitted, as was true even with the document (*scriptum*) itself, as long as the other requirements (*documenta*) were performed appropriately.[103]

Then, with the emperors Leo and Zeno, the pendulum swings back again: donation is again defined as "dependent on the intention of the donor,"

---

[99] *CT* 8.12.1 = *CJ* 8.53(54).25 = *FV* 249.5–6 and 8 (AD 323 [Mommsen] or February 316 [manuscript]), *in conscribendis autem donationibus nomen donatoris, ius ac rem notari oportet, neque id occulte [aut per inperitos (CT)] aut privatim, sed ut tabulae aut quodcumque aliud materiae tempus dabit; CJ* 8.53(54).25 has, at the end, *actis . . . quae apud iudicem vel magistratus conficienda sunt, ubi hoc leges expostulant*, which suggests some flexibility, but this ruled out by *CT* 8.12.3 (AD 316?), which stated that donations "could be valid in no other way unless testimony of them was made in the public records." This constitution also required that people could only give donations where they were domiciled, a specific requirement then repealed by *CT* 8.12.5 = *CJ* 8.53.27 (AD 333); need for *acta* repeated in *CT* 8.12.6 (AD 341), *CT* 8.12.8 (AD 415).

[100] *CT* 8.12.4 (AD 319), claiming to go back to Antoninus Pius; *CT* 8.12.5 (AD 333), the requirement of *traditio*, delivery, as well as mancipation waived, but not requirement for *instrumenta* and *acta*; that this was a special privilege reinforced by *CT* 8.12.7 (AD 355), everyone else must still perform *mancipatio* and *traditio*.

[101] *FV* 249.10 (*negamus certae formae verborum deinde esse quicquam requirendum . . . verba et ipsa abolita sunt antea necessaria in donationibus faciendis*: what this refers to is unclear, but probably some statement of the intent to give).

[102] *CT* 8.12.5 = *CJ* 8.53.27 (AD 333, *statuimus, ut donationes interveniente actorum testificatione conficiantur*); *NT* 22.1.9 (AD 442; implies that a man *actorum fide constituat* a gift); *observatione monumentorum*, *CJ* 8.53(54).34.3 (AD 529).

[103] *CJ* 8.53(54).29 (AD 428), *sine scripto*; *CT* 3.5.13 (AD 428), same emperors also decreed that if a donation before marriage has been validated in the *acta*, it is immaterial whether or not *traditio* took place (*donatio ante nuptias* had been considered an immediate gift rather than a promise of one by the classical jurists as well, cf. *D.* 39.5.1.1 [Julian]). References to documents of donation continue, see *CT* 16.2.27 = *CJ* 1.3.9 (AD 390; *conscribtum* of letter, codicil, gift, testament), *NT* 22.2.11 (AD 443, *donationis titulo*).

Documents, jurists, the emperor, and the law

the need for the expression of this intention in *acta* reaffirmed, and the requirements of witnesses to the *traditio* and a document are dropped.[104] Justinian himself removes the "superfluous verbiage" which customarily appears in donations, and with them, the last verbal traces of the act of mancipation:[105]

Verba superflua, quae in donationibus poni solebant, id est sestertii nummi unius assium quattuor, penitus esse reicienda censemus. quid enim verbis opus est, quae rerum effectus nullus sequitur? sancimus itaque nullo modo eorum mentionem vel in imperialibus donationibus vel in aliis omnibus de cetero fieri, sed et si quisquam per verbositatem aliquid tale inscripserit sive remiserit, nulla differentia sit.

Superfluous words, which are customarily put in donations, like "one sestertius" "one *nummus*" "four *asses*," we decree should absolutely be discarded. For what need is there of words which have no real effect? Therefore we order that no mention at all of these (words) should be made, whether in imperial donations or in all others pertinent, but if anyone should write in or omit such a word through long-windedness, it should make no difference.

You should not use these words; but it will not matter if you do. They are not necessary; mancipation itself may not be not necessary; *traditio* and witnesses are not necessary, even a document is not necessary; only a statement of intent in the *acta*, a kind of *professio*, is required.[106]

What jurists of the third, fifth, and sixth centuries thought about donation helps to highlight how unusual Constantine's three-fold requirements for donation were. Indeed, in comparison Constantine and his jurists looked to do something very different: not only did they focus on the giving of a gift and make it considerably more complicated, they sought to reconceptualize donation, transforming it into a new multi-part ceremonial act, complete with mancipation and/or *traditio*, witnessing of two sorts (observers and *acta*), and a document on a *tabula* (or other material) that affirmed the identity and intent of the donor, any conditions applicable to the gift, the property in question, and the *ius* by which it could be given. They aimed at tightening up lax and deceptive practices by making the

---

[104] *CJ* 8.53(54).30 (AD 459, *ipsa donatio sita est in voluntate donantis*; in *acta* such donations *obtineant inconcussam ac perpetuam firmitatem*) and 31 (AD 478, a document without the *subnotatione* of witnesses fine if subscribed by the donor *secundum solitam observationem*, but even so donations without writing have *suam firmitatem*); cf. *CJ* 4.21.17 (AD 528), donor expected to subscribe if there is a *contractus* of donation.

[105] *CJ* 8.53(54).37 (AD 531).

[106] And this possibly only for certain more valuable donations under specified circumstances, *CJ* 8.53(54).34 (AD 529), 36 (AD 531).

284   *The evolution of practice*

act more, not less, ceremonial[107] – characterized by new requirements that made clear when the act was finished and were in part based on traditional behaviors. An imperial constitution could decree ceremony and formality, just as it could also suggest that neither was needed, and the value of the document and other forms of *observatio* for establishing the validity of the donation went up and down accordingly.

Constantine seems to have attempted the same in the transaction that came to be known as sale. Sale has two components, an agreement that generates obligation and an exchange for money, and the classical Roman jurists for centuries saw these as two separate acts, contract (often the consensual *emptio-venditio* contract) and conveyance.[108] Even the first-century AD Campanian *tabulae*, however, show that combination of the two in one document was not unusual: documents recording mancipation, for example, include the price of the object and stipulatory warranties about its defects or value. Consensual, *bona fides* contracts required no writing (but usually had it); mancipation (but not *traditio*) as a form of conveyance, I have argued, did. The coalescence of contract and conveyance into first a single document and then a single act – a sale that began with a contract that created obligations and ended when the property changed hands officially – also provoked discussion among jurists about what the act was, and as a consequence they also disagreed about the value of a document in it. Diocletian's jurists were quite firm: sale (*emptio*) does not take place through documents, *non instrumentis gerantur*, and such a document should be imagined to be more like an *instrumentum testationis*, a declaration.[109]

Here too Constantine seems to have made a decisive contribution, although in a constitution of unsurpassed vagueness. In AD 337 he denounced tax-cheats, insisted that the buyer acknowledge the tax liability on the land, and decreed that there was to be a "public or fiscal inspection" at the time it was sold to guarantee this; required that sales which occurred *sollemniter* were to include a demonstration of the "certain and true" ownership of the

---

[107] *CT* 8.12.3 (AD 316?), more extensively in *FV* 249.5–6 (from which *CT* 8.12.3 was excerpted), many lawsuits suffered because of "the things written and done which are incomplete and written over . . . (and miscreant defrauders) pretending that what has been done has not been done and that what was written was inserted," *clandestina fraus, et quae facta sunt infecta et inducta quae scripta sunt simulans aliisque ac dehinc aliis*; see also *FV* 249.1 for further complaint. In *FV* 249.1 he claims to have established *voluntas omni libera sollemnitate* by a *dicta lex*, but this not entirely borne out by what he does, and he may be referring to a different *lex*.

[108] Zulueta (1945) 1–2.

[109] *CJ* 4.19.12 (AD 293; *res non instrumentis gerantur*, in a case of sale); cf. *CJ* 7.32.2 (Alexander Severus), *CJ* 4.21.10 (AD 294, *substantiam veritatis* of sale not affected by absence of documents), and Paul. *Sent.* 2.17.13. *instrumentum testationis, CJ* 4.38.12 (Diocletian and Maximian).

Documents, jurists, the emperor, and the law

land by the neighbors (the proper seller confirmed "by the shouts of the people"); demanded, in short, that "*sollemnitas* was to be observed in every sale."[110] Since cheaters had been rushing into sales performed solemnly "in whatever ways and whatever channels," however, there was something, even if inept, that had been *sollemniter*, formal and habitual, about sale even before Constantine undertook to reshape it.[111] At the end of the century these requirements were summarized as writing and registration: rustic or urban property could not be given to pay off a debt unless there was a *scriptura* "which transfers it," *traditio*, and registration in *acta* (as testimony), "for otherwise such property cannot pass to a new owner or quit the old ownership."[112] Another constitution in AD 444–5 decreed that sales of immovable property (land) were to be registered in municipal *acta* (and not just the registers of the census) as well, while movable goods could be sold without registration as before, as long as documents specifically called *pittaciis* were generated. Six years later, Valentinian generalized: those in public office were allowed to buy and sell, as long as it was according to "the common law," which was thereupon explained as "the price that has been defined and stated in writing shall be paid to the person who wishes to sell. The writer of instruments shall see, those persons shall know with whom it is necessary that the *documentum* of sale shall be filed," with *documentum* shortly thereafter – in the same law – referred to as *tabulis*.[113] If the constitutions of the later fourth and fifth centuries followed and extended Constantine's law, as their use of registration suggests, then it would seem that Constantine introduced an important change, amalgamating contract of sale and conveyance of land and laying out new *sollemnia* for this new act, including a witnessed test of ownership, a stated price, a public acknowledgment of the tax burden, registration, probably also a document, and, as implied, *continuus actus*. Constantine, in other words, has here again constructed

---

[110] *FV* 35 (AD 337), excerpted in *CT* 3.1.2 (AD 337), *ut omnino qui comparat rei comparatae ius cognoscat et censum, neque liceat alicui rem sine censu vel comparare vel vendere. inspectio autem publica vel fiscalis esse debebit hac lege* (35.3); *nisi eo tempore quo inter venditorem et emptorem contractus sollemniter explicatur, certa et vera proprietas vicinis praesentibus demonstretur* (35.4); *sub clamationibus populi* (35.5); *ita ergo venditionum omnium est tractanda sollemnitas* (35.7). On this constitution, Levy (1951) 128–31 (sale and conveyance are, here, simultaneous); and Honoré (1989) 142–9 (mancipation is here still the required mode of conveyance if the land is Italic).

[111] *FV* 35.5 (*ut quoque modo cuniculis nescio quibus inter emptorem et venditorem sollemnia celebrentur*); a sale of land was made *sollemniter*, with *sollemnes praestationes*, previously, *CJ* 4.46.2 (Diocletian and Maximian).

[112] *CT* 2.29.2 = *CJ* 4.3.1 (AD 394; movables like gold do not require registration).

[113] Valentinian III, *N. Val.* 15.3 (AD 444–5); quoted, *N. Val.* 32.*pr.* (AD 451; *iure communi . . . volenti vendere definitam et conscriptam pecuniam oportet inferri. videat instrumentorum scriptor, sciant ii, apud quos venditionis documentum necesse est adlegari*); *tabulis,* 32.1.

286 *The evolution of practice*

the externals of a new act, with the implication of the act's new nature and the requirement for new *sollemnia*.[114]

Justinian turned the clock back, restoring the consensual *emptio-venditio* contract, which, his *Institutes* claimed, existed *sine scriptura*, "for we have not innovated in sales."[115] It could, however, also exist in writing, in which case it was incomplete until reduced to writing.[116] It was indeed more common for sale to be in writing, for Justinian notes it as one of the contracts "accomplished in writing," *in scriptis fieri placuit*.[117] In either case, however, Justinian's stated understanding of sale is much closer to that of the classical jurists, for he marks the moment when it comes into being as the moment when the price is agreed upon. In this he was, as in donations, undoing the amalgamation decreed by Constantine and followed by others, and returning, at least in his thinking, to the contractual definition of sale prevalent hundreds of years earlier.

The imperial pronouncements of the post-classical jurists about the validity of acts, and their explorations of which components contributed most heavily to that validity, are very much in keeping with the opinions of classical jurists, despite the obvious difference of favoring writing as the most comprehensive locus of the act's authority. They follow many of the same types of argumentation even when examining acts of less importance, and exhibit the same prejudice against the merely evidentiary documents in acts that once had no claim to ceremonial performance. They can change their minds, but their shifts in direction particularly gather around two acts, donation and sale, whose amalgamations out of earlier ceremonial and informal acts were controversial in themselves and whose conceptualization therefore invited lively dispute. All the while, they are working within well-established traditions of both approach and practice, and the

---

[114] Honoré (1989) 150 thinks Constantine continued to keep contract and conveyance separate, since *FV* 35 requires that conveyance be performed on the land itself, while contracts can be made away from it. I am suggesting that only for the sale of land was an amalgamation proposed, and that even this was not perfectly maintained by his successors.

[115] Just. *Inst.* 3.23.*pr.* (*nihil a nobis . . . innovatum est*), 3.

[116] Just. *Inst.* 3.23.*pr.*

[117] Contracts: note language of *CJ* 4.21.17 (AD 528), "contracts for sale or exchange or donation . . . or for giving of deposit or for whatever other cause – those contracts, which it is agreed are accomplished in writing, and even (contracts) of compromises, which it is agreed are taken into an instrument, We decree will not otherwise have *vires*, unless the instruments, received into the world, are confirmed by the subscriptions of the parties" (*contractus venditionum vel permutationum vel donationum . . . dationis etiam arrarum vel alterius cuiuscumque causae, illos tamen, quos in scriptis fieri placuit, transactionum etiam, quas instrumento recipi convenit, non aliter vires habere sancimus, nisi instrumenta in mundum recepta subscriptionibusque partium confirmata*; cf. Kübler [1931] cols. 495–6); and *CJ* 4.38.15 (AD 530), *conventio* of sale when *in scriptis . . . redactum . . . completum et absolutum sit*, recapitulated Just. *Inst.* 3.23.*pr.*

Documents, jurists, the emperor, and the law

fact that they are reacting to the age-old distinctions between formal and informal acts can be seen even after the compilers and editors had done their work clearing out all the specific discussion of antique non-necessaries. They may have been working in a universe where unobserved moons were pulling them into elliptical deviations even as they tried to plot straight and true paths; but more likely they were sailing on a sea whose tides and shallows presented known dangers whose effects they were still, after centuries, trying to navigate safely, in boats of the same design.

EMPERORS AND *SOLLEMNITAS*

The two emperors, Constantine and Justinian – meaning their jurists as well, of course – are outstanding examples of the confidence with which law-makers of late antiquity approached their tasks. They were not afraid to construct new legal acts out of old ones, nor to give them a practical, visible existence by drawing on traditional elements in how the separate parts had been performed, nor to decree what would give an act *firmitas* or validity. One of the ancestors of both donation and sale was a formal act, while another was a *bona fides* act, so both donation and sale employed written elements that could be interpreted as demonstrating an abstract essential quality like *liberalitas*, as well as some of the gestures or motions that helped to convey property, all of it witnessed by the official's own *acta*. Constantine and Justinian create the present out of the past, the *sollemnia* of the new act out of the ceremonials of the old, and use their respective judgments to decide how much of the efficacy of the old *tabulae* they want in the new.

Emperors and their jurists are, in fact, in charge. Not only by deciding what makes an act valid and what is unnecessary in it, which the classical jurists had also done, cautiously; not only by insisting on the kind of validity performance in official *acta* can give to *professiones* or a newly constructed act;[118] not only by constructing new acts to begin with;[119] but also by going against traditional classifications and valuations when they so chose. Although the choice to emphasize the value and importance of documents is seen, generally, only in those formal acts once performed with *tabulae*, the

---

[118] See chapter eight n.148.

[119] Manumission in churches may be another constructed act, cf. *CJ* 1.13.1 (AD 316; must take place *adspectu plebis adsistentibus Christianorum antistitibus* and have *qualiscumque scriptura* made for the memory of the deed in place of *acta*; this is created in imitation of manumission before Roman officials in the *acta*, see chapter eight n.148); this called equivalent to what the Roman state did "with solemn gestures" (*sollemnitatibus decursis*) in AD 321, *CJ* 1.13.2.

288   *The evolution of practice*

emperor's jurists can also eventually overturn these traditional distinctions when it suits them. A constitution of Leo's insists on the importance of *scripturas* in consensual (and some other unspecified) contracts, defined as those made "secretly" (i.e. "in the presence of friends") for the sake of sale, compromise, loan of money with interest, forming a partnership, or for any other reasons: by being written these are now to be considered *publice scriptas*, having the force (*robur*) of "public documents," whether subscribed, witnessed, or conditional, and action brought on their account shall have full strength.[120] In the same way, Zeno decrees that *emphyteusis*, a long-term contract like a perpetual lease, should be its own type of contract, a *ius tertium* with its own *conceptionem definitionemque*, and, when written, would be valid and have *firma* and *perpetua stabilitate*.[121] The later in time, it would seem, the more this kind of drastic re-evaluation – especially the bringing up of previously unimportant writing in informal acts to full strength – is likely to occur.

The emperor Justinian was particularly rigorous when it came to the re-evaluation of documents because he imposed a set of common requirements on all sorts of written acts, developing and systematizing the concept of the "public document," giving that type of document a greater validity than the private document, and imposing requirements on all sorts of documents of whatever pedigree. The requirements were usually that documents, often drawn up by *tabularii* or *tabelliones*, be always subscribed by witnesses and often subscribed by the protagonist himself, and he imposed these requirements on many of the documents whose histories have been examined here, from wills to sales, consensual contracts to *emphyteuseis* to manumissions (which with these new safeguards can be performed through *epistulae*).[122] Those not drawn up by *tabelliones* had to be subscribed by at least three men.[123] All these documents will have *vis* because they will be made as the emperor decrees they should be, not because they are performed in traditionally authoritative ways that derive from the nature of the act itself. The emperor decides; others must follow, and do: the results

---

[120] *CJ* 8.17(18).11 (AD 472; *secrete . . . intervenientibus amicis*); see Saradi-Mendelovici (1988).

[121] *CJ* 4.66.1 (AD 476–84).

[122] *CJ* 6.23.28 (AD 530), *CJ* 6.23.31 (AD 534), wills. *CJ* 4.21.17 (AD 528), sales, exchanges, donations, giving of deposit, even compromises must have the *subscriptiones* of the parties (cf. Just. *Inst.* 3.23.*pr.*, need for sales to receive subscriptions and *completiones*), reinforced by *Nov.* 44 (AD 537) and *Nov.* 73 (AD 538); *CJ* 4.29.23 (AD 530; *instrumento intercessionis* made *publice* and sealed by three witnesses must be believed), *CJ* 4.66.3 (AD 530; *emphyteuticum instrumentum*); *CJ* 7.6.1.1–2 (AD 531), manumission can also be achieved by an autograph letter; cf. *CJ* 6.30.22.2 (AD 531, subscribing of an estate inventory). *Tabularii* made *instrumenta publica*, while *tabelliones* made *instrumenta publice confecta* (*tabelliones* first seen in *D.* 48.19.9.4 [Ulpian]); see also Pfaff (1905) and E. Seidl (1973) 83.

[123] *CJ* 4.21.20 (AD 530); referred to in *Nov.* 13 (AD 535; holographic document subscribed by three).

Documents, jurists, the emperor, and the law

in documents can be traced, as people did what he said and gave the weight he wanted to acts performed as he prescribed.[124]

Leo, Zeno, and Justinian undertake their systematic reclassification of legal documents as an act of imperial *auctoritas*, and it will be their decree that determines what makes a document valid and unquestionable, what gives it *robur*, what makes it believable. Here again, however, they are accomplishing their ends by choosing from their own traditions. The traditions they choose come from the ways *fides* has been added to documents for centuries, ways indeed that had been extending themselves in the third and fourth centuries to implicate witnesses and protagonists ever more deeply in the acts they performed. Witness-sealers first had their names written next to their seals, then wrote their names in their own hands, and then wrote a subscription that stated their presence and the fact that they had sealed; and for a will, the jurists Ulpian and Paulus decided, speaking for general agreement, that witnesses had to note in their own hand that they have sealed, and whose will they were sealing.[125] The more witnesses subscribed, as they were required to in wills during the reign of Constantine, the more anxious they became about their responsibilities for an act whose terms they might not even know; clearly, they felt that by subscribing a document they were becoming part of it, rather than judging its ritual as they once, long ago, had.[126] Protagonists added their own *fides* through subscription rather more comfortably, since it was their own act and their responsibility for it was not likely to be as troublesome to them,[127] and emperors subscribed their own acts as well.[128] Testator-subscriptions were required in the

[124] Tjäder (1985); Amelotti (1985) 132–7 (all effects well seen in the Ravenna papyri).

[125] Activities of witness-sealers, above chapter seven n.54; Ulpian, *D.* 28.1.22.4; *proprio chirographo adnotare convenit*, *D.* 28.1.30 (Paulus); cf. *CJ* 6.23.12 (AD 293), seven witnesses must seal in the same place in the presence of the testator, or *iure deficiat testamentum*.

[126] Constantine: referred to in *CT* 4.4.3 = *CJ* 6.23.17 (AD 396?/402), "provided that five witnesses, with full knowledge of their act, should subscribe their names to the testament, even though the contents of the testament had not been recounted to them" (*cum quinque huic non ignari subscripserint testamento, licet non eisdem series fuerit recensita*). Anxiety, because *tabulas . . . obligationis adsignavit*, *CJ* 8.40(41).6 (AD 214); *CJ* 5.37.15 (AD 287), if you have not subscribed as a *fideiussor*, do not fear – even though *signasti ut curator*). Jurists: *D.* 2.13.6.1 (Ulpian), subscribing to authenticate accounts and be implicated yourself; *D.* 15.3.20 (Scaevola), *D.* 18.5.8 (Scaevola); in others, *D.* 23.3.9.3 (Ulpian), *D.* 44.1.11 (Modestinus), *D.* 48.10.15.3 (Callistratus); *CJ* 7.16.32 (AD 294). Witnesses are rebuked for demanding to know contents in *N.Th.* 16.1. (AD 439), and the fact that they are to remain ignorant but that ignorance did not harm the validity of the will stressed in *N.Val.* 21.2.5 (AD 446).

[127] Subscribing seen as a form of *testatio*, *CT* 5.9.2 (AD 412; bishop), cf. *CT* 12.12.15 = *CJ* 10.65(68).6 (AD 416; decurions subscribe), *N.Th.* 7.4.3 (441; a *magister militum subnotare*), in a sale, *N.Val.* 32.5 (451; *primores . . . curiae . . . subscribant*).

[128] Constantine subscribes a proclamation, Eusebius *VC* 2.23 ("adds truth to what I say," *PG* 20. 1001); for imperial subscriptions to letters and imitative papal parallels in late antiquity, Mathisen (1998) 244–51; of church fathers, Dekkers (1952); God answers petition on tablet (*pittacium*), erasing the petition, in Leontius's *Vit. Ioann.* 96–9 (*PL* 93. 1656–8).

290 *The evolution of practice*

tripartite will after AD 439, and the ones that survive make clear that the protagonists themselves thought they were thereby confirming, or adding to, the validity of their own documents.[129] Slave-sales were to be subscribed by five important ("first") men, starting in AD 458.[130] Justinian took from these two traditions in particular, and made them one of the foundations of his own definition of validity, an imperially sponsored transformation, finally, of *fides* into formality.

His way of understanding what he was doing, as Constantine's had been, was as a redefinition of habitual formality or *sollemnitas*. What had once been a quality, "ceremoniousness," rooted in the performed act itself, and thus in the necessity for the performance that gave legitimacy to the act, became what emperors and post-classical jurists deemed it to be. Elements of the old *sollemnitas* blended with the new *observationes* and *sollemnitates* the emperor's jurists defined and required. As a consequence, the old ceremonial unitary acts never lost their "solemnity" or formality, only the necessity for specific older formal components, and at times had new elements added. Stipulation, Leo decreed, need no longer have *sollemnis vel directis . . . verbis*, but it did keep a verbal exchange and a document and was still characterized by *observatio* in AD 529.[131] Mancipation, which had used formal words (in donations) and the ritual gesture with the bronze balance (in wills) in the middle of the fourth century, was still using at least the first in AD 531, when Justinian decreed them no longer necessary (in donations).[132] Mancipatory wills, freed "from the necessity of solemn speech" by Constantine's constitution of AD 339, were still characterized by *sollemnitas* in AD 413 and "strict *observatio*" in AD 528, 530, and 534.[133] In

---

[129] Required by law (AD 439), *NT* 16; reaching west in 448 (*N.Val.* 21.1 (AD 446); for date, see Kübler [1934] col. 999). In wills, e.g., *P.Ant.* 1 (= *FIRA*² 3.159–63 no. 52; AD 460), "I have made it to be valid and secure by my subscription and (those) of the same seven lawful witnesses gathered at the same time and sealing, according to the divine command," or similar in *P.Vat.Aphrod.* 7 (AD 546–7) and *P.Cair.Masp.* 67324 (sixth century AD); also in western empire, e.g., Tjäder (1955) 204–17 P4–5 no. 3 (AD 480) and 204–17 P4–5 no. 2 (end fifth century).

[130] *N.Maj.* 7.10.

[131] Leo, *CJ* 8.37(38).10 (AD 472), above p. 263; *CJ* 2.55(56).4.7 (AD 529). The closely akin dowries were *sollemniter aut data aut dicta aut promissa* in AD 396 (*CT* 3.12.3 = *CJ* 5.5.6), but freedom of expression given *CT* 3.13.4 = *CJ* 5.11.6 (AD 428), and marriages (the constitution insists) are still contracted by consent, not by *instrumenta*, solemn processions, or wedding ceremonies, *CT* 3.7.3 = *CJ* 5.4.22 (AD 428).

[132] Customary formal words of mancipation in donation, *CT* 8.12.4–5, 7 (AD 319, 333, 355); bronze balance, above n.63; necessity for words removed, above p. 283.

[133] Wills: traditionally characterized by *sollemnitas* and *observatio*, *CJ* 6.23.8–9 (AD 290); necessity of solemn speech removed, *CJ* 6.23.15 (AD 339), above pp. 271–2; also in *CJ* 6.9.9 (AD 339, we have already excluded the *verborum inanium . . . captiones*, but decree the following *observari*); see Albanese (1984–5). Even in *CJ* 6.38.4 (AD 531), however, Justinian is still ruling on uncertainties in the interpretation of a will's formulaic expressions. *Sollemnitatem* in AD 413, *CJ* 6.23.19, also AD 530, *CJ*

Documents, jurists, the emperor, and the law

the sixth century, the act of mancipation in emancipation still used formal words, and the act of manumission in emancipation still used ritual blows.[134] "Since we have observed in emancipations that empty *observatio* has been retained, and fictitious sales of free persons and incomprehensible detours and injurious blows, for which no rational result can be found, we order that – *circuitus* of this sort lying quiet for the future – the one wishing to emancipate should have freedom to do so" before a magistrate, ". . . the empty *observatio* having been removed."[135] Donations were still considered to have *observatio* in AD 417 and to be *celebrata* in AD 426.[136] What helped all of these acts retain this quality of *sollemnitas* when specific components of it were removed, and before emperors added any new aspects that they would name "solemn," was the writing itself, which was done *sollemniter* and also helped to convey to what was written the quality of *sollemnitas*.[137]

Justinian and others, when they added as they took away, called their additional requirements *sollemnitates* and *observationes*. So the necessity for subscription, which Justinian took from a centuries-long incorporation of *fides* into documents, was when introduced called an *observatio*, that of

---

6.23.28; *observatio* in AD 528, *CJ* 6.23.24 and *CJ* 6.23.26 (*formalem observationem* in testaments *sine scriptis . . . amputamus*); AD 530 and 534, *CJ* 6.22.9 (*legitima observatio*) and *CJ* 6.23.31 (*subtilitatibus stricta observatio*, many of them *remissa* by previous emperors).

[134] Emancipation in the late third century was performed with *tabulae* (*CPL* 206 = *FIRA*² 3.31–3 no. 14), had *scriptura* (*CJ* 8.48[49].2, AD 291), was performed *actu sollemni*, *CJ* 8.48(49).3 (AD 293), and was *sollemnis*, *CJ* 8.47(48).9 (AD 294); it was an institution regularly used in the late Empire, Arjava (1998) 161–5. Manumission was performed *sollemnitatibus decursis*, "with solemn maneuvers," perhaps referring to gesture of using the rod (*vindicta*), performed in front of magistrate, *CT* 4.7.1 = *CJ* 1.13.2 (AD 321); when decreed by the emperor in the circus, it was spoken *lege*, Amm. Marc. 22.7.2. Adoption, which combined emancipation and manumission, was also considered solemn (*CJ* 4.19.14, AD 293, *adoptione sollemni . . . civili iure* and *CJ* 8.47(48).4, AD 290, *sollemni iuris ordine*), but may not have been performed with a *tabula*, see Wieacker (1956) and chapter seven n.178.

[135] *CJ* 8.48(49).6 (AD 531, *vanam observationem . . . venditiones in liberas personas figuratas et circumductiones inextricabiles et iniuriosa rhapismata, quorum nullus rationabilis invenitur exitus, iubemus huiusmodi circuitu in posterum quiescente licentiam esse ei, qui emancipare vult . . . vana . . . observatione sublata*); summarized as "an act that proceeded by antique *observatio* of the law . . . *per imaginarias venditiones et intercedentes manumissiones celebrabatur*," Just. *Inst.* 1.12.6. To register *testificatione* with a judge was done in AD 502, *CJ* 8.48(49).5. Adoption too Justinian says he frees of "the ancient *observatio* of emancipations and manumissions," *sine vetere observatione emancipationum et manumissionum*, *CJ* 8.47(48).11 (AD 530).

[136] *observatio*, *CT* 8.12.9 = *CJ* 8.53(54).28 (AD 417); *celebrata*, *CT* 8.13.6 = *CJ* 8.55(56).9 (AD 426); *traditio a sollemnitas*, *CT* 8.12.7 (AD 355).

[137] Writing of a will done *iure ac sollemniter*, *CT* 4.4.5 = *CJ* 6.23.20 (AD 416); a *tabula* of privileges is inscribed *debita sollemnitate* in AD 365, and tablets of patronage are still posted in Roman houses in the fourth century AD, MacMullen (1988) 82; accusations are solemn, *CJ* 3.42.6 (AD 244), *CT* 9.3.4 (AD 365), and *CT* 10.20.3 = *CJ* 11.8(7).3 (AD 365); Levy (1951) 129 and Kaser (1959) 199 n.27 thought the *sollemnitas* of Constantine's law about sale referred to writing. See also the interpretation to *CT* 3.5.2 (AD 319): betrothal gifts *iure celebrantur* become, in the interpretation written to explain the law, "when he has confirmed this betrothal gift with the solemnity of writing."

292   *The evolution of practice*

registration similarly an *observatio* or a *sollemnitas*.[138] Neither was new in practice, nor an *observatio* until an emperor said it was. Autograph additions to a will – the requirement that the testator write in an institution of the heir and money amounts in his own hand – were also not innovations, but required by Justinian as a new *observatio*.[139] The emperor and his jurists decreed the form of documents, and augmented the authority of the *tabelliones* assigned to write them; decreed the nature and higher status of the "public" document, incorporating into it *sollemnitas* and *observatio* as they chose to define them; and enhanced the solemnity and *firmitas* conferred by municipal or official *tabulae* by decreeing that some acts be performed there.[140] They did all this through constitutions and *ius* that themselves had *sollemnitas* and *observatio*.[141] Indeed, the imperial presence itself permitted a person to dispense with other forms of *sollemnitas* altogether: the emperor himself became, literally, an embodiment of ceremonial legitimacy. Through his constitutions he could reshape the existing component of *sollemnitas*, enhance the profile of institutions like *acta* that could confer it, and embody it himself. The legitimacy of a legal act could still be based on traditional ceremonial acts and formalities, but these survived (where they did) only when they had not yet been scrutinized for "result" or "effect," or not dismissed because "empty." The validity of documentary acts depended on what the emperor chose to value, and he chose to retain much that the past had bequeathed to him, as he retained as part of his visual vocabulary an archaizing style of "celestial letters" for his official documents and the use of *tabulae* for the honorific display of appointment to office or for the publication of imperial constitutions.[142]

---

[138] Subscription performed by *solitam observationem, CJ* 8.53(54).31 (AD 478); registration a *sollemnitas* (*CT* 3.5.13, AD 428, specifically of a betrothal gift) and a *monumentorum observatione, CJ* 8.53(54).34.3 (AD 529).

[139] *CJ* 6.23.29 (AD 531), reconfirmed in *CJ* 6.23.30 (AD 531); referred to also in Just. *Inst.* 2.10.4.

[140] Governor's proceedings already had *sollemnitas* of their own, *CJ* 7.16.15 (AD 293), hearing on status.

[141] Sacred constitutions have *observatio,* Just. *Inst.* 2.10.3; ius has *sollemnitas, CJ* 6.23.3 (AD 232, *sollemnibus iuris*), 6.23.7 (AD 290), 6.23.12 (AD 293). Dispensing with *sollemnitas*: *CJ* 6.23.19, not needed because no dispute arises over heirs appointed in Our presence by Our laws: so heirs can even be appointed by petition, AD 413). So much *sollemnitas* may have contributed to its ironic use as a word for a bribe, cf. Anon. *de Reb. Bell.* 4.1, *CT* 6.30.11 (AD 386), with MacMullen (1997) 127.

[142] Celestial letters, Marichal (1952) and Matthews (1998) 262–3. *Codicilli* of appointment are common in the late Empire, e.g., Himerius *Ecl.* 36.11 (χρυσᾶ . . . δέλτοι), Themistius *Or.* 18.224b, 23.292–3b, 31.353a (trope for office), Syn. *Ep.* 127 (Garzya), τὰς πινακίδας; or (e.g.) *CT* 6.22.1 (mentioning inner and outer writing; AD 321 or 325/6), with others in *CT*; cf. Seeck (1900) cols. 179–83 for additional references to them in Greek (γραμματεῖα and δέλτοι), Löhken (1982) 78–9 (references to them in the *Not. Dig.*), Cameron (1998) 399 on late-antique presentation *codices* as commemorative ivory diptychs; and R. R. R. Smith (1999) 178 n.74 on a scene of codicil presentation, the Theodosian missorium in Madrid. *Tabulae* as form of laws: *CT* 11.27.1 (AD 315), *CT* 12.5.2 (AD 337), *CT* 14.13.1 (AD 370 or 373?), *CT* 14.4.4 (AD 367), *CJ* 11.24.2 (AD 434).

Documents, jurists, the emperor, and the law   293

Above all, it was his choice to retain, amalgamate, or discard. As his treatment of acts once embodied in *tabulae* as well as newly constructed acts and the concepts of *sollemnitas* and *observatio* all show, the emperor himself was, in the third century and after, the ultimate source of legitimacy.

Conclusion

In China, in the nineteenth century, charms in the countryside invoking the help of the gods frequently employed the physical form and formulae of bureaucratic orders issued by the imperial government, complete with phrases used in official decrees and Chinese characters of command at the top, all written on yellow paper (the imperial color) in cinnibar ink (a red that signalled a decree's authenticity), and marked with an official seal.[1] In a bureaucratic empire – very intensely governed, by Roman standards – it was efficacious to compel even the supernatural with the external forms utilized by the bureaucracy. The puzzle the Romans present is the reverse of this: in an empire with hardly any machinery of enforcement – a handful of officials, a minute bureaucracy, no real police[2] – how could law have force? How can law have any power in the absence of the rule of law?

To be effective Roman law initially drew its authority from outside government and outside itself, from the wider world of belief in which it was embedded. Interpretations of early Roman law as in some way "magical" are therefore not as wrongheaded as their critics have thought.[3] For magic and law travel the same road (indeed, a wide road, travelled also by religious and other acts), aim at many of the same ends, and use many of the same techniques. This is not to say that law *was* magic, as has quite rightly been pointed out, any more than a *lex* was a *sponsio* or a marriage was a treaty. Roman poets or antiquaries who asserted such equivalences have, time and again, been shown to be, technically, wrong. Yet in repeatedly framing these equivalences, they were trying to express their own sense that some quality was shared, just as those who in AD 371 burned the libraries

---

[1] Ahern (1979) 3, this produces "the most powerful kind of mandate from the most powerful office in the land," and (1981) 16–30, 41 (what they have in common is "logic").

[2] Lendon (1997) 3–7 luridly depicts the weakness of Roman imperial government.

[3] Magic and law: see Kaser (1971) 28 n.36, 39–49 (summary of the debate); and especially Huvelin (1904) and Hägerström (1929), the latter attacked by G. MacCormack (1969a) and (1969b). Kinds of parallelism seen and debated, e.g., Dahlheim (1968) 20–2, on *deditiones* and *sponsiones*, or Watson (1993) 10–30, on declarations of war and legal procedure.

Conclusion

of the ouija-board conspirators against Valens did so in the firm conviction that they were burning books of magic and divination, although in fact the majority of those books were of "the liberal disciplines or law."[4] Something – and not just ignorance – kept encouraging Romans to see similarities. This similarity was not in fundamental essence but in performative power, not in interior but in exterior, not in the *what* but in the *how*. For the more ways in which legal acts followed widely accepted, formalized techniques of transfer, request, promise, or compulsion, the more likely their users were to believe in their efficacy and, therefore, the more believable and efficacious legal practice in general would be.[5]

Yet if the efficacy of law is a manifestation of social consensus, the sources of that efficacy will necessarily change as that consensus evolves. The most ancient sanction of the power of the *tabula* lay in its association with ancient unitary acts that ordered cosmos, state, and household. Physical form and special language connected individual legal documents with other well-known, venerable acts performed by Romans: the wooden *tabula*, along with its customarily rhythmic and formulaic language, was characteristic not only of political acts like the creation of treaties, magisterial edicts, *leges*, *senatusconsulta*, or the census, but also of religious acts like vows and prayers and important household acts like the entering of accounts, the making of a will, or the sending of a curse. These acts relied on tablets' understood capacity – as part of a protocol in which each step had to be performed and performed correctly – to bring an act to completion and to make it perceptibly real. Unitary acts on *tabulae* needed, and shared, the process and efficacy that a tablet contributed. Legal documents on tablets derived unquestioned strength and reliability from this shared background, and for this reason Roman documents on *tabulae* were very different from weak and suspected Athenian or Hellenistic documents.

The original power of *tabulae* was based on a belief in their association with an efficacy that extended beyond, and was independent of, the human realm. But in the self-assertive world of the late Republic and early Empire this original sanction came to be overlaid by another, the *fides* of individuals – manifested in *bona fides* legal acts, and conveyed by seal, subscription, and writing in one's own hand – which the inherited fixing

---

[4] Ouija-board: Amm. Marc. 29.1.41, *innumeri codices et acervi voluminum multi . . . cum essent plerique liberalium disciplinarum indices variarum et iuris*; cf. Pliny *NH* 30.12 (there were "traces of magic in the Twelve Tables" – always assumed to refer to content, e.g., *carmina*, but vague enough that he could well be describing an entire thought world).

[5] This corresponds in legal philosophy and speech-act theory to the observation that there must be some social rules about what constitutes validity for a valid act to take place, MacCormick and Bankowski (1986) 122 (paraphrasing Hart), 130–3.

qualities of tablets were found to be able to convey. The layering of *fides* over formality on a tablet created a document that was not only authoritative and efficacious in a cosmic sense but also splendidly powerful as proof in the immediate and contentious present, as advocates from Cicero to Apuleius acknowledged. As the imperial centuries passed, and the place of the emperor in the imaginations of his subjects – always bigger than in their practical lives – grew, so the sanction granted documents came to derive from the super-human realm, the realm of human *fides*, and the authority of the emperor all together. The emperor's rulings on the legitimacy of documents were accepted because they did not overturn or directly contradict traditional belief and traditional practice – and then, ultimately, because the rulings came from the emperor. The empire was the opposite of a constitutional monarchy: rather than the monarch taking his legitimacy from the laws, late-antique law borrowed its legitimacy in society at large from an acceptance of the authority of the emperor. So powerful was this late-imperial sanction that the old solemnities of the unitary act – the odd ceremonies and strange old words – could mostly be, eventually, dispensed with, although the sanctions of *fides* never were.

That the legitimacy of the law the emperor created was a belief held across the Empire is a testament to the ease of cultural transmission around the Empire, a tribute to the power of Romanization. Roman authorities could impose Roman ways, as that aching public slave in Lycia who kept documents in a fashion that a Roman governor thought slovenly had reason to remember. But the Roman example exerted far greater force indirectly. When people came to Roman government and asked officials for help they did so – in some places, at some times – in terms carefully comprehensible to their overlords, and on forms of documents they thought would strike their masters as familiar and persuasive. Yet in Egypt they did not imitate Roman ways: Roman authority seems not to have encouraged Roman-like documents from many of its non-Roman subjects there. Here we see one of the brakes on Romanization: just as a Roman preference could encourage outsiders to do things the Roman way, a hard Roman attitude could discourage outsiders as well – if the Romans found the aping of Roman manners under certain conditions impertinent.

The law whose absolute authority was increasingly accepted over time was not, of course, the work of the Roman emperor alone. Much was drafted, and would have been discussed, by jurists, whose influence became greater as they were drawn more closely into the imperial circle. The relationship of the jurists to traditional beliefs is a complex one, but perhaps can be best imagined as similar to that existing between wise men

Conclusion 297

and everyone else in the matter of *carmina*, described by Pliny the Elder. He asked, "Do the words and incantations of *carmina* effect anything?" and answered, "Individually, the wisest men reject belief in this, *but as a group and at all times people believe (in this) and don't think about it* ... It is believed today that our Vestal Virgins by a spell root to the spot runaway slaves, provided they have not left the city bounds, and yet, if this view is once admitted, that the gods hear certain prayers, or are moved by any form of words, the whole question must be answered in the affirmative."[6] Jurists were wise men; but so too was Pliny. The attitude of both to what people "as a group and at all times" thought seemed to aim, for centuries or pages, at the careful preservation rather than destruction of what was adhered to in belief and practice. Pliny gave examples; the jurists developed tools to remedy defects in the performance of formal, ceremonial acts.

At the same time it is in contrast to the worlds of lay thought and practice that the genius and intellectual ability of the classical Roman jurists reveals itself most strikingly. Their ambitions to establish legal science as a prestigious and independent discipline prompted them at times to distance the activity of legal interpretation – in both phrasing and methods – from the everyday world in which it was to work, a development paralleled by the high degree of conceptualization they achieved in the interpretations of law they produced. Yet while juristic writing strove for, and often achieved, a self-conscious distance from its living context of belief and practice, the influence of that context can at all times be felt. Post-classical jurists transformed an object in a context – the *tabula* – into a legally viable idea, the legal instrument that in some acts was dispositive in all but name: by stripping it of what had once been signs of its efficacy, its particularity of language and form, they gave it a wider, and juristically defined, applicability. Yet since this apparently new intellectual creation continued to derive meaning and strength from traditional belief as well as traditional practice, it also points to the ways the Romans never left their past behind even when they acted to free themselves from it.

In legal instruments (and official *acta*) the concepts and categories of the traditional past continued to live on in the post-classical present, just as *instrumenta* written on wooden *tabulae* (complete with the words *stipulatus ... spopondit*) can be found in late fifth-century Vandal North

---

[6] Words and incantations: Pliny *NH* 28.10–13 (my italics; trans. Jones, modified), *polleantne aliquid verba et incantamenta carminum ... sed viritim sapientissimi cuiusque respuit fides, in universum vero omnibus horis credit vita nec sentit ... vestales nostras hodie credimus nondum egressa urbe mancipia fugitiva retinere in loco precatione, cum, si semel recipiatur ea ratio et deos preces aliquas exaudire aut ullis moveri verbis, confitendum sit de tota coniectatione*; cf. Cic. *Har.* 23.

Africa while late-antique Egypt produces mostly papyrus, or as emperors continued to use *tabulae* as part of their own ceremonial language.[7] Objects lived on in ideas and religiously tinged, old-fashioned, and efficacious procedures were never completely banished from imperially sanctioned acts. The center of a Roman understanding of what constitutes a source of legitimacy similarly changed over time, and similarly never left its past entirely behind – as is only to be expected from a people who so approved tradition and traditional behavior, so admired their own past, and nonetheless proved so capable of doing, always, what they perceived as required and efficacious.

[7] Courtois *et al.* (1952) 7–11, 85; see also Santifaller (1953) 55 no. 17, transfer of property on *tabula antiqua ex papyro*, before AD 489); this language (and habit?) still traceable in some early Germanic law, e.g., *Leg. Vis.* 12.2.13 (polyptychs for tax), or *LRB* 3 (manumission through tablets).

References

Ancient texts are cited with standard numerations in standard editions that I assume readers have access to, like the Loeb Classical Library. Where specific or difficult-to-identify editions are used, I have indicated this in the note in (parentheses), except in the following cases, which appear too often to use this system: Fronto, *Epistulae* (ed. Van den Hout; Teubner, 1988); Livy, *Ab Urbe Condita* (ed. Ogilvie; OCT, 1974); Petronius, *Satyricon* (ed. Mueller; Teubner, 1995); Suetonius, *Lives* (ed. Ihm; Teubner, 1993); Tacitus, *Annales* (ed. Heubner; Teubner, 1994), *Historiae* (ed. Heubner; Teubner, 1978), and *Opera Minora* (eds. Winterbottom and Ogilvie; OCT, 1992).

Achtemeier, P. (1990) "*Omne verbum sonat*: The New Testament and the Oral Environment of Late Western Antiquity," *Journal of Biblical Literature* 109: 3–27.

Adams, J. N. (1990) "The Latinity of C. Novius Eunus," *Zeitschrift für Papyrologie und Epigraphik* 82: 227–47.

(1995) "The Language of the Vindolanda Writing Tablets: An Interim Report," *Journal of Roman Studies* 85: 86–134.

Ahern, E. (1979) "The Problem of Efficacy: Strong and Weak Illocutionary Acts," *Man* n.s. 14: 1–17.

(1981) *Chinese Ritual and Politics*. Cambridge.

Albanese, B. (1984–5) "L'abolizione postclassica delle forme solenni nei negozi testamentari," in (no editor) *Sodalitas: scritti in onore di Antonio Guarino* (*Biblioteca di Labeo* 8) II: 777–92. Naples.

Albert, W.-D. (1972) "Die *tabulae ansatae* aus Pergamon," *Pergamon: Gesammelte Aufsätze* (*Deutsches archäologisches Institut, Pergamenische Forschungen* I), 1–42. Berlin.

Albrecht, M. von (1997) *A History of Roman Literature from Livius Andronicus to Boethius* I. Leiden.

Alexander, M. (1990) *Trials in the Late Roman Republic, 149 BC to 50 BC*. Toronto.

Alföldi, A. (1959) "*Hasta – Summa Imperii*: The Spear as Embodiment of Sovereignty in Rome," *American Journal of Archaeology* 63: 1–27.

Alföldy, G. (2000) "Das neue Edikt des Augustus aus El Bierzo in Hispanien," *Zeitschrift für Papyrologie und Epigraphik* 131: 177–205.

References

Alston, R. (1995) *Soldier and Society in Roman Egypt*. London and New York.

Amelotti, M. (1947) "Un nuovo testamento *per aes et libram,*" *Studia et Documenta Historiae et Iuris* 15: 34–59.

(1966) *Il testamento romano attraverso la prassi documentale I. Le forme classiche di testamento*. Florence.

(1975) "L'età Romana," in M. Amelotti and G. Costamagna, eds., *Alle origini del notariato italiano*, 5–144. Rome.

(1980) "Notariat und Urkundenwesen," *ANRW* 2.13: 386–99.

(1985) "Il documento nel diritto giustinianeo: prassi e legislazione," in G. G. Archi, ed., *Il mondo del diritto nell'epoca giustinianea: caratteri e problematiche*, 125–37. Bologna and Ravenna.

Amelotti, M. and L. Migliardi Zingale (1989) "Osservazioni sulla duplice scritturazione nei documenti," in G. Thür, ed., *Symposion 1985: Vorträge zur griechischen und hellenistischen Rechtsgeschichte (Ringberg)*, 299–309. Cologne.

(1990) "Συγγραφή, χειρόγραφον – *testatio, chirographum.* Osservazioni in tema di tipologie documentali," in G. Nenci and G. Thür, eds., *Symposion 1988: Vorträge zur griechischen und hellenistischen Rechtsgeschichte (Siena–Pisa)*, 297–304. Cologne.

Anderson, R. D., P. J. Parsons, and R. G. M. Nisbet (1979) "Elegiacs by Gallus from Qasr Ibrîm," *Journal of Roman Studies* 69: 125–55.

Ando, C. (2000) *Imperial Ideology and Provincial Loyalty in the Roman Empire*. Berkeley.

Andreau, J. (1974) *Les Affaires de Monsieur Jucundus*. Rome.

(1987) *La Vie financière dans le monde romain: les métiers de manieurs d'argent (ive siècle av. J.-C. – iiie siècle ap. J.-C.)*. Rome.

(1994) "Affaires financières à Pouzzoles au Ier siècle ap. J.-C.: les tablettes de Murecine," *Revue des études latines* 72: 39–55.

(1996) "Les Archives des banquiers romains et leur conservation," in M.-F. Boussac and A. Invernizzi, eds., *Archives et sceaux du monde hellénistique/Archivi e sigilli nel mondo ellenistico: Torino, Villa Gualino (Bulletin de correspondance hellénique* supplément 29), 423–37. Paris.

(1999) *Banking and Business in the Roman World*. Cambridge.

Ankum, H. (2001) "Was *Acceptilatio* an Informal Act in Classical Roman Law?" in J. W. Cairns and O. F. Robinson, eds., *Critical Studies in Ancient Law, Comparative Law and Legal History*, 3–13. Oxford and Portland, OR.

Appel, G. (1909) *De Romanorum Precationibus (Religionsgeschichtliche Versuche und Vorarbeiten* 7.2). Giessen.

Arangio-Ruiz, V. (1950) "Sulla scrittura della formula nel processo romano," *Iura* 1: 15–20.

(1953) "Intorno alla forma scritta del «testamentum *per aes et libram*»," in G. Moschetti, ed., *Atti del congresso internazionale di diritto romano e di storia del diritto, Verona*, III: 81–90. Milan.

(1974 [1942a]) "'Firmata Mancipiorum Sumtio,'" in L. Bove, ed., *Studi Epigrafici e Papirologici*, 208–18 (first published in *Atti della accademia pontaniana* 61: 299–311). Naples.

References

301

(1974 [1942b]) "Documenti soggetivi e sottoscrizioni: a proposito della *donatio Statiae Irenes*," in L. Bove, ed., *Studi Epigrafici e Papirologici*, 200–8 (first published in *Atti della accademia pontaniana* 61: 287–99). Naples.

(1974 [1948]) "Chirografi di soldati," in L. Bove, ed., *Studi Epigrafici e Papirologici*, 315–26 (first published in [no editor] *Studi in onore di Siro Solazzi nel cinquantesimo anniversario del suo insegnamento universitario* [Naples], 251–63). Naples.

(1974 [1953]) "Il testamento di Antonio Silvano e il senatusconsulto di Nerone," in L. Bove, ed., *Studi Epigrafici e Papirologici*, 382–9 (first published in [no editor] *Studi in memoria di Emilio Albertario* [Milan], 1: 203–12). Naples.

(1974 [1958]) "Tavolette ercolanesi: debiti di denaro," in L. Bove, ed., *Studi Epigrafici e Papirologici*, 518–34 (first published in *Bolletino dell' instituto di diritto romano* n.s. 20: 293–310). Naples.

(1974 [1964]) "Le tavolette cerate di Ercolano e i 'nomina arcaria'," in L. Bove, ed., *Studi Epigrafici e Papirologici*, 673–85 (first published in [no editor] *Mélanges Eugène Tisserant* [*Studi e testi* 231–7, Vatican City], 9–23). Naples.

Arangio-Ruiz, V. and G. Pugliese Carratelli (1954) "*Tabulae Herculanenses* IV," *Parola del Passato* 9: 54–74.

Archi, G. G. (1956) "Oralità e scrittura nel testamento *per aes et libram*," in (no editor) *Studi in onore di Pietro de Francisci* IV: 287–318. Milan.

(1964) "Les Preuves dans le droit du Bas-Empire," in (no editor) *La Preuve I^e partie: antiquité* (*Recueils de la société Jean Bodin pour l'histoire comparative des institutions* 16), 389–414. Brussels.

Arjava, A. (1998) "Paternal Power in Late Antiquity," *Journal of Roman Studies* 88: 147–65.

Aubert, J.-J. (1999) "Du Lard on du cochon? Une lecture à rebrousse-soies du *testamentum porcelli*," in J. U. Kalms, ed., *Internationales Josephus-Kolloquium Aarhus 1999* (*Münsteraner Judaistische Studien* 6), 302–36.

Aubin, G. (1980) "Informations archéologiques," *Gallia* 38: 381–406.

Auda, Y. and M.-F. Boussac (1996) "Étude statistique d'un dépôt d'archives à Délos," in M.-F. Boussac and A. Invernizzi, eds., *Archives et sceaux du monde hellénistique/Archivi e sigilli nel mondo ellenistico: Torino, Villa Gualino* (*Bulletin de correspondance hellénique* supplément 29), 511–23. Paris.

Audollent, A. (1904) *Defixionum tabellae quotquot innotuerunt tam in graecis orientis quam in totius occidentis partibus praeter Atticas* in Corpore Inscriptionum Atticarum *editas*. Paris.

Aune, D. (1980) "Magic in Early Christianity," *ANRW* 2.23.2: 1507–57.

Austin, J. L. (1962) *How To Do Things With Words*. Cambridge, MA.

Badian, E. (1988) "E.H.L.N.R.," *Museum Helveticum* 45: 203–18.

Bagnall, R. S. (1995) *Reading Papyri, Writing Ancient History*. London and New York.

Bagnall, R. S. and B. W. Frier (1994) *The Demography of Roman Egypt*. Cambridge.

Baldwin, B. (1979) "The *Acta Diurna*," *Chiron* 9: 189–203.

Baltzer, M. (1983) "Die Alltagsdarstellungen der treverischen Grabdenkmäler," *Trierer Zeitschrift* 46: 7–151.

Bauman, R. A. (1980) "The 'Leges Iudicorum Publicorum' and their Interpretation in the Republic, Principate and Later Empire," *ANRW* 2.13: 103–233.

(1983) *Lawyers in Roman Republican Politics: A Study of the Roman Jurists in their Political Setting 316–82 BC (Münchener Beiträge zur Papyrusforschung und antiken Rechtsgeschichte 75).* Munich.

(1986) "Rome and the Greeks: Apropos of a Recent Work," *Acta Classica* 29: 85–97.

Bean, G. E. (1960) "Notes and Inscriptions from Pisidia: Part II," *Anatolian Studies* 10: 43–82.

Beard, M. (1985) "Writing and Ritual: A Study of Diversity and Expansion in the Arval *Acta*," *Papers of the British School at Rome* 53: 114–62.

(1991) "Ancient Literacy and the Function of the Written Word in Roman Religion," in M. Beard *et al.*, eds., *Literacy in the Roman World (Journal of Roman Archaeology* supplement 3), 35–58. Ann Arbor.

(1992) "Religion," *CAH*² IX: 729–68.

(1998) "Documenting Roman Religion," in (no editor) *La Mémoire perdue: recherches sur l'administration romaine (Collection de l'école française de Rome* 243), 75–101. Paris and Rome.

Beard, M., J. North, and S. Price (1998) *Religions of Rome: Volume I. A History.* Cambridge.

Beck, F. A. G. (1975) *Album of Greek Education.* Sydney.

Behrend, D. (1970) *Attische Pachturkunden (Vestigia* 12). Munich.

Bell, C. (1992) *Ritual Theory, Ritual Practice.* Oxford.

Bellen, H. (1965) "*Ut manumittas servum tuum, frangis tabulas eius*," *Zeitschrift der Savigny-Stiftung für Rechtsgeschichte, romanistische Abteilung* 82: 320–3.

Bellinger, A. R. and C. B. Welles (1935) "A Third-Century Contract of Sale from Edessa in Osrhoene," *Yale Classical Studies* 5: 93–154.

Beltrán Lloris, F. (1999) "Writing, Language and Society: Iberians, Celts and Romans in Northeastern Spain in the 2nd and 1st Centuries BC," *Bulletin of the Institute of Classical Studies* 43: 131–51.

Benediktson, D. T. (1995) "*Manum de tabula*: Petronius *Satyricon* 76.9," *Classical Philology* 90: 343–5.

Benoit, P., J. T. Milik, and R. de Vaux (1961) *Discoveries in the Judaean Desert 2: les grottes de Murabba'ât.* Oxford.

Berges, D. (1996) "Der Fundkomplex griechischer Siegelabdrücke aus Karthago," in M.-F. Boussac and A. Invernizzi, eds., *Archives et sceaux du monde hellénistique/Archivi e sigilli nel mondo ellenistico: Torino, Villa Gualino (Bulletin de correspondance hellénique* supplément 29), 341–8. Paris.

Bernand, A. (1984) *Les Portes du désert.* Paris.

Besnier, M. (1920) "Récents travaux sur les *defixionum tabellae* latines 1904–1914," *Revue de Philologie* 44: 5–30.

Besnier, N. (1995) *Literacy, Emotion and Authority: Reading and Writing on a Polynesian Atoll.* Cambridge.

Bickermann, E. (1933) "*Testificatio Actorum*: Eine Untersuchung über antike Niederschriften 'zu Protokoll'," *Aegyptus* 13: 333–55.

References

303

Bilabel, F. (1924) and (1925) "Zur Doppelausfertigung ägyptischer Urkunden," *Aegyptus* 5: 153–73 and 6: 93–113.

Bilkei, I. (1980) "Römische Schreibgeräte aus Pannonien," *Alba Regia* 18: 61–90.

Birley, E., R. Birley, and A. Birley (1993) *Vindolanda Research Reports (n.s.) 2: The Early Wooden Forts: Reports on the Auxiliaries, the Writing Tablets, Inscriptions, Brands, and Graffiti.* Hexham.

Birt, T. (1976 [1907]) *Die Buchrolle in der Kunst: Archäologisch-antiquarische Untersuchungen zum antiken Buchwesen.* Hildesheim and New York (Leipzig).

Bisbee, G. (1988) *Pre-Decian Acts of Martyrs and Commentarii* (Harvard Dissertations in Religion 22). Philadelphia.

Biscardi, A. (1965) "Contra la oralità della formula processuale classica," in (no editor) *Studi in onore di Biondo Biondi* 1: 649–66. Milan.

(1971) "'Testes estote': Contribution à l'étude du témoignage en droit romain," *Revue historique de droit français et étranger* 49: 386–411.

(1972) "Nuove testimonianze di un papiro arabo-giudaico per la storia del processo provinciale romano," in (no editor) *Studi in onore di G. Scherillo* 1: 111–52. Milan.

Björck, G. (1938) *Der Fluch des Christen Sabinus: Papyrus Upsaliensis 8 (Vilhelm Ekmans Universitetsfond* 47). Uppsala.

Bloch, M. (1989 [1974]) "Symbols, Song, Dance and Features of Articulation: Is Religion an Extreme Form of Traditional Authority?" in his *Ritual, History and Power: Selected Papers in Anthropology (London School of Economics Monographs on Social Anthropology* 58), 19–45 (first published in *Archives européenes de sociologie* 15: 55–81). London.

Boak, A. E. R. (1932) "A Petition for Relief from a Guardianship: *P.Mich.* Inv. No. 2922," *Journal of Egyptian Archaeology* 18: 69–76.

Boegehold, A. L. (1995) *The Lawcourts at Athens: Sites, Buildings, Equipment, Procedure, and Testimonia (The Athenian Agora* 28). Princeton.

Boffo, L. (1995) "Ancora una volta sugli 'archivi' nel mondo greco: conservazione e 'pubblicazione' epigrafica," *Athenaeum* 83: 91–130.

Bogaers, J. E. (1967 [1972]) "*Tabulae Ceratae,*" in W. Glasbergen, ed., *De Romeinse Castella te Valkenburg Z.H.,* 67–76. Groningen.

(1976) "Zweimal Valkenburg (Prov. Zuid-Holland)," in H. D. Tjeenk Willink and F. van Dishoek, eds., *Festoen: Opgedragen aan A. N. Zadoks-Josephus Jitta bij haar zeventigste verjaarday,* 123–35. Groningen.

Bömer, F. (1953) "Der *Commentarius*: Zur Vorgeschichte und literarischen Form der Schriften Caesars," *Hermes* 81: 210–50.

Bonner, R. J. (1905) *Evidence in Athenian Courts.* Chicago.

Bonner, S. F. (1977) *Education in Ancient Rome: From the Elder Cato to the Younger Pliny.* Berkeley.

Boswinkel, E. and P. W. Pestman (1982) *Les Archives privées de Dionysios, fils de Kephalas (P.L. Bat.* 22). Leiden.

Bott, N. A. (1972) *Testamentum Porcelli: Text, Übersetzung und Kommentar.* Zürich.

Boussac, M.-F. (1993) "Archives personelles à Délos," *Comptes rendus de l'académie des inscriptions et belles-lettres* (no volume): 677–93.

References

Bove, L. (1979) *Documenti processuali dalle* Tabulae Pompeianae *di Murecine*. Naples.

Bowersock, G. W. (1991) "The Babatha Papyri, Masada, and Rome," *Journal of Roman Archaeology* 4: 336–44.

(1995) *Martyrdom and Rome*. Cambridge.

Bowman, A. K. (1971) *The Town Councils of Roman Egypt* (*American Studies in Papyrology* 11). Toronto.

(1994) "The Roman Imperial Army: Letters and Literacy on the Northern Frontier," in A. K. Bowman and G. Woolf, eds., *Literacy and Power in the Ancient World*, 109–25. Cambridge.

Bowman, A. K. and D. Rathbone (1992) "Cities and Administration in Roman Egypt," *Journal of Roman Studies* 82: 107–27.

Bowman, A. K. and J. D. Thomas (1983) *Vindolanda: The Latin Writing-Tablets* (*Britannia* Monograph series no. 4). London.

Bowman, A. K. and G. Woolf (1994) "Literacy and Power in the Ancient World," in A. K. Bowman and G. Woolf, eds., *Literacy and Power in the Ancient World*, 1–16. Cambridge.

Brandileone, F. (1920) *Sulla supposta obligatio litterarum nell'antico diritto greco*. Bologna.

(1932) "Note a recenti difese del contratto letterale nell'antico diritto greco," *Rendiconti della classe di scienze morali e storiche (Roma)* 32: 105–29.

Brashear, W. (1992a) "Magical Papyri: Magic in Bookform," in P. Ganz, ed., *Das Buch als magisches und als Repräsentationsobjekt*, 25–57. Wiesbaden.

(1992b) "À propos des tablettes magiques," in É. Lalou, ed., *Les Tablettes à écrire de l'antiquité à l'époque moderne* (*Bibliologia* 12), 149–58. Turnhout.

(1995) "The Greek Magical Papyri: An Introduction and Survey; Annotated Bibliography (1928–1994)," *ANRW* 2.18.5: 3380–684.

Brashear, W. and F. A. J. Hoogendijk (1990) "*Corpus Tabularum Lignearum Ceratarumque Aegyptiarum*," *Enchoria* 17: 21–54.

Brein, F. (1973) "Bücher auf Grabsteinen," *Römisches Österreich* 1: 1–5.

Broggini, G. (1964) "La Preuve dans l'ancien droit romain," in (no editor) *La Preuve 1ᵉ partie: antiquité* (*Recueils de la société Jean Bodin pour l'histoire comparative des institutions* 16), 223–76. Brussels.

Brophy, R. H. III. (1974) "*Mancupium* and *Mancipatio* in Plautus: One Specimen of Plautine Legal Humor and Metaphor" (unpublished dissertation, University of Michigan).

Bruck, E. F. (1904) *Bedingungsfeindliche Rechtsgeschäfte: Ein Beitrag zur Lehre von der Unzulässigkeit von Bedingung und Zeitbestimmung*. Breslau.

Bruns, C. G. (1878) "Die pompejanischen Wachstafeln," *Zeitschrift für Rechtsgeschichte* 13: 360–72.

(1882 [1876]) "Die Unterschriften in den römischen Rechtsurkunden," in his *Kleine Schriften* II: 37–118 (first published in *Abhandlungen der Berliner Akademie* [no volume], 41–138). Weimar.

(1882 [1877]) "Die Sieben Zeugen des römischen Rechts," in his *Kleine Schriften* II: 119–38 (first published in [no editor] *Commentationes Philologae in honorem Mommseni scripserunt amici* [Berlin], 489–506). Weimar.

References

Brunt, P. A. (1971) *Italian Manpower 225 BC–AD 14*. Oxford.

Bucher, G. S. (1987 [1995]) "The *Annales Maximi* in the Light of Roman Methods of Keeping Records," *American Journal of Ancient History* 12: 2–61.

Buckland, W. W. (1939) "Ritual Acts and Words in Roman Law," in (no editor) *Festschrift Paul Koschaker zum 60. Geburtstag überreicht von seinem Fachgenossen* 1: 16–28. Weimar.

Buckland, W. W. and Stein, P. (1963) *A Textbook of Roman Law from Augustus to Justinian*, 3rd edn. Cambridge.

Buecheler, F. (1871) *Petronii Satirae et Liber Priapeorum*. Berlin.

Bülow-Jacobsen, A., H. Cuvigny, and K. A. Worp (2000) "*Litura*: ἀλειφάς, not ἄλειφαρ, and Other Words for 'Erasure'," *Zeitschrift für Papyrologie und Epigraphik* 130: 175–82.

Bundgård, J. A. (1965) "Why Did the Art of Writing Spread to the West? Reflexions on the Alphabet of Marsiliana," *Analecta Romana* 3: 11–72.

Burkhalter, F. (1990) "Archives locales et archives centrales en Egypte romaine," *Chiron* 20: 191–216.

Burton, G. P. (1975) "Proconsuls, Assizes and the Administration of Justice under the Empire," *Journal of Roman Studies* 65: 92–106.

Buti, I. (1982) "La 'cognitio extra ordinem': da Augusto a Diocleziano," *ANRW* 2.14: 29–59.

Butler, S. (2002) *The Hand of Cicero*. London and New York.

Cagnat, M. R. (1903–4) "La Sorcellerie et les sorciers chez les romains," *Annales de Musée Guimet* (no volume): 134–75. Paris.

Calhoun, G. M. (1914) "Documentary Frauds in Litigation at Athens," *Classical Philology* 9: 134–44.

Calligas, P. (1971) "An Inscribed Lead Plaque from Korkyra," *Annual of the British School at Athens* 66: 79–93.

Cameron, A. (1998) "Consular Diptychs in their Social Context: New Eastern Evidence," *Journal of Roman Archaeology* 11: 384–403.

Camodeca, G. (1986) "Una nuova fonte sulla topografia del foro d'Augusto (*TP-Sulp.* 19 = *TP* 84 = 102)," *Athenaeum* 64: 505–8.

(1992) *L'archivio puteolano dei Sulpicii* 1. Naples.

(1993a) "Per una riedizione delle *Tabulae Herculanenses* 1," *Cronache Ercolanesi* 23: 109–19.

(1993b) "Per una riedizione delle *Tabulae Herculanenses* 11: i *nomina arcaria TH* 70 + 71 e *TH* 74," *Ostraka* 2: 197–209.

(1993c) "Novità sulle tavolette cerate di Pompei ed Ercolano," in L. Franchi dell'Orto, ed., *Ercolano 1738–1988: 250 anni di ricerca archeologica. Atti del convegno internazionale Ravello-Ercolano-Napoli-Pompei*, 521–7. Rome.

(1993d) "Nuovi dati dagli archivi campani sulla datazione e applicazione del 's.c. neronianum'," *Index* 21: 353–64.

(1993e) "Archivi privati e storia sociale della città campane: Puteoli ed Herculaneum," in W. Eck, ed., *Prosopographie und Sozialgeschichte: Studien zur Methodik und Erkenntnismöglichkeit der kaiserzeitlichen Prosopographie*, 339–50. Cologne.

306 *References*

(1994) "Riedizione del trittico Ercolanese *TH* 77 + 78 + 80 + 53 + 92 del 26 gennaio 69," *Cronache Ercolanesi* 24: 137–46.

(1995a) "Nuovi dati sulla struttura e funzione documentale delle *tabulae ceratae* nella prassi campana," in H. Solin, O. Salomies, and U.-M. Liertz, eds., *Acta colloquii epigraphici Latini: Helsingiae 3.–6. Sept. 1991 habiti* (*Societas Scientiarum Fennica, Commentationes Humanarum Litterarum* 104), 59–77. Helsinki.

(1995b) "Nuovi documenti dell'archivio puteolano dei Sulpicii," *Studia et Documenta Historiae et Iuris* 61: 693–705.

(1999a) *Tabulae Pompeianae Sulpiciorum* (*TPSulp.*): *edizione critica dell'archivio puteolano dei Sulpicii* (*Vetera* 12). Rome.

(1999b) "Nuovi dati dalla riedizione delle *tabulae ceratae* della Campania," in (no editor) *XI congresso internazionale di epigrafia greca e latina (Roma)*, 521–44. Rome.

(2000) "*Tabulae Herculanenses*: riedizione delle *emptiones* di schiavi," in U. Manthe and C. Krampe, eds., *Quaestiones Iuris: Festschrift für Joseph Georg Wolf zum 70. Geburtstag* (*Freiburger rechtsgeschichtliche Abhandlungen* n.s. 36), 53–67. Berlin.

(2002a) "Per una riedizione dell'archivo ercolanese di L. Venidius Ennychus," *Cronache Ercolanesi* 32: 257–80.

(2002b) "I consoli del 43 egli Antistii Veteres d'età Claudia dalla riedizione della *Tabulae Herculanenses*," *Zeitschrift für Papyrologie und Epigraphik* 140: 227–36.

Camodeca, G. and G. Del Mastro (2002) "I papiri documentari ercolanesi (*PHerc. Man*): relazione preliminare," *Cronache Ercolanesi* 32: 281–96.

Campbell, B. (1996) "Shaping the Rural Environment: Surveyors in Ancient Rome," *Journal of Roman Studies* 86: 74–99.

(2000) *The Writings of the Roman Land Surveyors: Introduction, Text, Translation and Commentary* (*Journal of Roman Studies Monograph* no. 9). London.

Capasso, M. (1997 [1990]) "Le tavolette della Villa Ercolanese dei Papiri," in M. Capasso, *Volumen: aspetti della tipologia del rotolo librario antico*, 111–17 (previously published in *Cronache Ercolanesi* 20 [1990]: 83–6). Naples.

Caruana, I. D. (1992) "Carlisle: Excavation of a Section of the Annexe Ditch of the First Flavian Fort, 1990," *Britannia* 23: 45–109.

Castello, C. (1938) "Lo strumento dotale come prova del matrimonio," *Studia et Documenta Historiae et Iuris* 4: 208–24.

Cavallo, G. (1992) "Le tavolette come supporto della scrittura: qualche testimonianza indiretta," in É. Lalou, ed., *Les Tablettes à écrire de l'antiquité à l'époque moderne* (*Bibliologia* 12), 97–105. Turnhout.

Cavenaile, R. (1953) "Le *P.Mich.* VII 432 et l'*honesta missio* des légionnaires," in (no editor) *Studi in onore di Aristide Calderini e Roberto Paribeni*, 243–51. Milan.

Cencetti, G. (1950) "Note paleografiche sulla scrittura dei papiri latini dal I al III secolo d.C.," *Memorie dell'accademia delle scienze dell'istituto di Bologna, classe di scienze morali* (fifth series) 1: 3–54.

Champlin, E. (1987) "The Testament of the Piglet," *Phoenix* 41: 174–83.

(1991) *Final Judgments: Duty and Emotion in Roman Wills, 200 BC–AD 250*. Berkeley.

References 307

Chapman, H. (1977) "Wood," in T. R. Blurton, "Excavations at Angel Court, Walbrook," *Transactions of the London and Middlesex Archaeological Society* 28: 67–9.

(1978) "Writing Tablets," in (no editor) *Southwark Excavations 1972–1974 (Joint Publication No. 1*, London and Middlesex Archaeological Society, Surrey Archaeological Society), 397–401.

Chapman, H. and V. Straker (1986) "Writing Tablets," in T. Dyson, ed., *The Roman Quay at St. Magnus House, London (London and Middlesex Archaeological Society Special Paper* 8), 227–9. London.

Charrow, V. R., J. A. Crandall, and R. P. Charrow (1982) "Characteristics and Functions of Legal Language," in R. Kittredge and J. Lehrberger, eds., *Sublanguage: Studies of Language in Restricted Semantic Domains*, 175–90. Berlin and New York.

Ciulei, G. (1983) *Les Triptyques de Transylvanie: études juridiques (Studia Amstelodamensia ad epigraphicam, ius antiquum et papyrologicam pertinentia* 23). Zutphen.

Classen, P. (1977) *Kaiserreskript und Königsurkunde: Diplomatischen Studien zum Problem der Kontinuität zwischen Altertum und Mittelalter* (Byzantine Texts and Studies 15). Thessalonica.

Cloud, J. D. "A *LEX DE PONDERIBUS* (Festus, p. 288L)," *Athenaeum* 63: 405–18.

(1989) "Satirists and the Law," in S. H. Braund, ed., *Satire and Society in Ancient Rome (Exeter Studies in History* 23), 49–67. Exeter.

(2002) "The Pompeian Tablets and Some Literary Texts," in P. McKechnie, ed., *Thinking Like a Lawyer: Essays on Legal History and General History for John Crook on his Eightieth Birthday*, 231–46. Leiden.

Cockle, W. E. H. (1984) "State Archives in Graeco-Roman Egypt from 30 BC to the Reign of Septimius Severus," *Journal of Egyptian Archaeology* 70: 106–22.

Cohen, D. (2003) "Writing, Law, and Legal Practice in the Athenian Courts," in H. Yunis, ed., *Written Texts and the Rise of Literate Culture in Ancient Greece*, 78–96. Cambridge.

Cole, T. (1969) "The Saturnian Verse," *Yale Classical Studies* 21: 3–73.

Coles, R. A. (1966) *Reports of Proceedings in Papyri (Papyrologica Bruxellensia* 4). Brussels.

Collinet, P. (1912) *Études historiques sur le droit de Justinien 1: le caractère oriental de l'oeuvre législative de Justinien et les destinées des institutions classiques en Occident.* Paris.

(1925) *Histoire de l'école de droit de Beyrouth.* Paris.

Collingwood, R. G. (1930) *London in Roman Times.* London.

Collins, A. Y. (1992) "Revelation, Book of," in D. N. Freedman, ed., *The Anchor Bible Dictionary* v: 694–708. New York.

Corbier, M. (1987) "L'Écriture dans l'espace public romain," in *L'Urbs: espace urbain et histoire (Ier siècle av. J.-C. – IIIe siècle ap. J.-C.). Actes du colloque international organisé par le centre national de la recherche scientifique et l'école française de Rome (Collection de l'école française de Rome* 98), 27–60. Rome.

Corcoran, S. (1996) *The Empire of the Tetrarchs: Imperial Pronouncements and Government, AD 284–324.* Oxford.

308 References

Cormack, S. (1997) "Funerary Monuments and Mortuary Practice in Roman Asia Minor," in S. E. Alcock, ed., *The Early Roman Empire in the East* (*Oxbow Monograph* 95), 137–56. Exeter.

Costa, E. (1890) *Il diritto privato romano nelle comedie di Plauto*. Turin.

(1927) and (1928) *Cicerone giureconsulto*. Rome.

Cotton, H. M. (1981) *Documentary Letters of Recommendation in Latin from the Roman Empire* (*Beiträge zur klassischen Philologie* 132). Königstein.

(1993) "The Guardianship of Jesus son of Babatha: Roman and Local Law in the Province of Arabia," *Journal of Roman Studies* 83: 94–108.

(1995) "Subscriptions and Signatures in the Papyri from the Judaean Desert: The ΧΕΙΡΟΧΡΗΣΤΗΣ," *The Journal of Juristic Papyrology* 25: 29–40.

(1997) "Η ΝΕΑ ΕΠΑΡΧΕΙΑ ΑΡΑΒΙΑ: The New Province of Arabia in the Papyri from the Judaean Desert," *Zeitschrift für Papyrologie und Epigraphik* 116: 204–8.

(1998) "The Rabbis and the Documents," in M. Goodman, ed., *Jews in a Graeco-Roman World*, 167–79, 269–71. Oxford.

(1999) "The Languages of the Legal and Administrative Documents from the Judaean Desert," *Zeitschrift für Papyrologie und Epigraphik* 125: 219–31.

Cotton, H. M., W. E. H. Cockle, and F. G. B. Millar (1995) "The Papyrology of the Roman Near East: A Survey," *Journal of Roman Studies* 85: 214–35.

Cotton, H. M. and A. Yardeni (1997) *Discoveries in the Judaean Desert 27: Aramaic, Hebrew and Greek Documentary Texts from Naḥal Ḥever and Other Sites*. Oxford.

Coudry, M. (1994) "Sénatus-consultes et *acta senatus*: rédaction, conservation et archivage des documents émanant du sénat, de l'époque de César à celle des Sévères," in S. Demougin, ed., *La Mémoire perdue: à la recherche des archives oubliées, publiques et privées, de la Rome antique* (CNRS, série histoire ancienne et médiévale 30), 65–102. Paris.

Courtney, E. (1999) *Archaic Latin Prose* (*American Classical Studies* 42). Atlanta.

Courtois, C., L. Leschi, C. Perrat, and C. Saumagne (1952) *Les Tablettes Albertini: actes privés de l'époque vandale*. Paris.

Crake, J. E. A. (1939) "Archival Material in Livy 218–167 BC" (unpublished dissertation, Johns Hopkins).

Crawford, M. H. (1973) "*Foedus* and *Sponsio*," *Papers of the British School at Rome* 41: 1–7.

(1988) "The Laws of the Romans: Knowledge and Diffusion," in J. Gonzalez and X. Arele, eds., *Estudios sobre la Tabula Siarensis* (Anejos de AEA IX CSIC Madrid), 127–40. Madrid.

(1996) *Roman Statutes* (*Bulletin of the Institute of Classical Studies* supplement 64). London.

Cribiore, R. (1996) *Writing, Teachers, and Students in Graeco-Roman Egypt* (*American Studies in Papyrology* 36). Atlanta.

Croke, B. (1990) "City Chronicles of Late Antiquity," in G. Clark, ed., *Reading the Past in Late Antiquity*, 165–203. Elmsford, NY.

Crook, J. A. (1967) *Law and Life of Rome 90 BC–AD 212*. London.

(1978) "Working Notes on Some of the New Pompeii Tablets," *Zeitschrift für Papyrologie und Epigraphik* 29: 229–39.

(1992) "The Development of Roman Private Law," *CAH*² IX: 531–59.

(1995) *Legal Advocacy in the Roman World*. Ithaca.

(1996) "Legal History and General History," *Bulletin of the Institute of Classical Studies* 41: 31–6.

Culham, P. (1984) "Tablets and Temples: Documents in Republican Rome," *Provenance: Journal of the Society of Georgia Archivists* 2: 15–31.

(1989) "Archives and Alternatives in Republican Rome," *Classical Philology* 84: 100–15.

(1991) "Documents and *Domus* in Republican Rome," *Libraries & Culture* 26: 119–34.

(1996) "Fraud, Fakery and Forgery: The Limits of Roman Information Technology," *The Ancient World* 27: 172–83.

D'Arms, J. H. (1970) *Romans on the Bay of Naples: A Social and Cultural Study of the Villas and their Owners from 150 BC to AD 400*. Cambridge, MA.

(1981) *Commerce and Social Standing in Ancient Rome*. Cambridge, MA.

D'Ors, A. (1951) "Πιττάκιον – *pittaciarium*," *Aegyptus* 30: 339–43.

(1953) "*Testamentum porcelli*: introduccion, texto, traduccion y notas," *Suplementos de 'Estudios Clasicos*' 3: 74–83. Madrid.

(1955) "El 'Testamentum Porcelli' y su interés para la historia jurídica," *Revue internationale des droits de l'antiquité* (third series) 2: 219–36.

D'Ors, A. and F. Martin (1979) "*Propositio libellorum*," *American Journal of Philology* 100: 111–24.

Dahlheim, W. (1968) *Struktur und Entwicklung des römischen Völkerrechts im dritten und zweiten Jahrhundert v. Chr. (Vestigia* 8). Munich.

Daly, L. (1973) "*Rotuli*: Liturgy Rolls and Formal Documents," *Greek, Roman, and Byzantine Studies* 14: 333–38.

Daube, D. (1946) "Two Early Patterns of Manumission," *Journal of Roman Studies* 36: 57–75.

(1956) *Forms of Roman Legislation*. Oxford.

(1961) "Texts and Interpretation in Roman and Jewish Law," *Jewish Journal of Sociology* 3: 3–28.

David, J. M. (1999) "Les Procès-verbaux des *judicia publica* de la fin de la république romaine," in R. G. Khoury, ed., *Urkunden und Urkundenformulare im klassischen Altertum und in den orientalischen Kulturen*, 113–25. Heidelberg.

De Meo, C. (1986) *Lingue tecniche del Latino*, 2nd edn. Bologna.

Degni, P. (1998) *Usi delle tavolette lignee e cerate nel mondo greco e romano (Ricerca papirologia* 4). Messina.

Degrassi, A. (1934) "ΟΥΕΤΡΑΝΟΙ ΟΙ ΧΩΡΙΣ ΧΑΛΚΩΝ," *Rivista di filologia e d'istruzione classica* (no volume): 194–200.

Dekkers, E. (1952) "Les Autographes des pères latins," in B. Fischer and V. Fiala, eds., *Colligere Fragmenta: Festschrift Alban Dold zum 70. Geburtstag am 7.7.1952*, 127–39. Beuron.

310 *References*

Del Mastro, G. (1999) "Novità sulle tavolette della Villa dei Papiri," *Cronache Ercolanesi* 29: 53–4.

Della Corte, M. (1951) "Tabelle cerate ercolanesi," *La Parola del Passato* 6: 224–30.

Detienne, M. (1989) "Une écriture inventive, la voix d'Orphée, les jeux de Palamède," in his *L'Écriture d'Orphée*, 101–15. Mayenne.

Digges, D. and J. Rappaport (1993) "Literacy, Orality, and Ritual Practice in Highland Colombia," in J. Boyarin, ed., *The Ethnography of Reading*, 138–55. Berkeley.

Dilke, O. A. W. (1971) *The Roman Land Surveyors: An Introduction to the* Agrimensores. New York.

Dionisotti, A. C. (1982) "From Ausonius' Schooldays? A Schoolbook and its Relatives," *Journal of Roman Studies* 72: 83–125.

Diósdi, G. (1971) "Giustiniano e la 'Stipulatio'," *Labeo* 17: 39–51.

(1981) *Contract in Roman Law from the Twelve Tables to the Glossators*. Budapest.

Doppelfeld, O. (1970) *Rom am Dom: Ausgrabungen des römisch-germanischen Museums (Schriftenreihe der archäologischen Gesellschaft Köln 16)*. Cologne.

Drews, R. (1988) "Pontiffs, Prodigies, and the Disappearance of the *Annales Maximi*," *Classical Philology* 83: 289–99.

Drummond, A. (1989) "Rome in the Fifth Century 1: The Social and Economic Framework," *CAH*[2] VII.2: 113–71.

Düll, R. (1951) "Zur römischen *Stipulatio*," *Zeitschrift der Savigny-Stiftung für Rechtsgeschichte, romanistische Abteilung* 68: 191–216.

Dumézil, G. (1943) *Servius et la fortune*. Paris.

Dunant, C. (1978) "Sus aux voleurs! Une tablette en bronze à inscription grecque du Musée de Genève," *Museum Helveticum* 35: 241–4.

Dunn, W. R. (1984) "Formal Language in Plautus" (unpublished dissertation, Harvard).

Durrbach, F. and P. Roussel (1935) *Inscriptions de Délos: actes des fonctionnaires athéniens préposés à l'administration des sanctuaires après 166 av. J.-C.* Paris.

Dušanic, S. (1984) "*Loci Constitutionum Fixarum*," *Epigraphica* 46: 91–115.

(1984–5) "The Witnesses to the Early 'Diplomata Militaria'," in (no editor) *Sodalitas: scritti in onore di Antonio Guarino (Biblioteca di Labeo 8)* 1: 271–86. Naples.

Dziatzko, K. (1900) *Untersuchungen über ausgewählte Kapitel des antiken Buchwesens*. Leipzig.

Eck, W. (1998) "Inschriften auf Holz: Ein unterschätztes Phänomen der epigraphischen Kultur Roms," in P. Kneissl and V. Losemann, eds., *Imperium Romanum: Studien zu Geschichte und Rezeption: Festschrift für Karl Christ zum 75. Geburtstag*, 203–17. Stuttgart.

(1999) "Öffentlichkeit, Monument und Inschrift," in (no editor) *XI congresso internazionale di epigrafia greca e latina (Roma)*, II: 55–75. Rome.

(2000) "Bronzeinschriften von Ehrendenkmälern aus Rom: Zu dem neuen Militärdiplom von der unteren Sava," *Zeitschrift für Papyrologie und Epigraphik* 133: 275–82.

References

Eck, W., A. Caballos, and F. Fernández (1996) *Das senatus consultum de Cn. Pisone Patre* (*Vestigia* 48). Munich.

Eck, W. and M. M. Roxan (1998) "Zwei Entlassungsurkunden – *tabulae honestae missionis* – für Soldaten der römischen Auxilien," *Archäologisches Korrespondenzblatt* 28: 95–112.

Eckstein, A. M. (1995) "Glabrio and the Aetolians: A Note on *Deditio*," *Transactions of the American Philological Association* 125: 271–89.

(1999) "Pharos and the Question of Roman Treaties of Alliance in the Greek East in the Third Century B.C.E.," *Classical Philology* 94: 395–418.

Edmondson, J. (1993) "*Instrumenta Imperii*: Law and Imperialism in Republican Rome," in B. Halpern and D. W. Hobson, eds., *Law, Politics and Society in the Ancient Mediterranean World*, 156–92. Sheffield.

Eger, O. (1921) "Eine Wachstafel aus Ravenna aus dem zweiten Jahrhundert nach Chr.," *Zeitschrift der Savigny-Stiftung für Rechtsgeschichte, romanistische Abteilung* 42: 452–68.

Eisenhut, W. (1974) "*Votum*," *RE* Supplement 14: cols. 964–73.

El-Mosallamy, A. H. S. (1970) "Revocation of Wills in Roman Egypt," *Aegyptus* 50: 59–73.

Erman, H. (1899) "Die pompejanischen Wachstafeln," *Zeitschrift der Savigny-Stiftung für Rechtsgeschichte, romanistische Abteilung* 20: 172–211.

(1905a) "La Falsification des actes dans l'antiquité," in (no editor) *Mélange Nicole: recueil de mémoires de philologie classique et d'archéologie offerts à Jules Nicole, professeur à l'Université de Genève à l'occasion du xxxᵉ anniversaire de son professorat*, 111–34. Geneva.

(1905b) "Zum antiken Urkundenwesen," *Zeitschrift der Savigny-Stiftung für Rechtsgeschichte, romanistische Abteilung* 26: 456–78.

Evans-Jones, R. and G. MacCormack (1998) "Obligations," in E. Metzger, ed., *A Companion to Justinian's Institutes*, 127–207. London.

Faraone, C. A. (1991a) "The Agonistic Context of Early Greek Binding Spells," in C. A. Faraone and D. Obbink, eds., Magika Hiera: *Ancient Greek Magic and Religion*, 3–32. Oxford.

(1991b) "Binding and Burying the Forces of Evil: The Defensive Use of 'Voodoo Dolls' in Ancient Greece," *Classical Antiquity* 10: 165–205.

(2000) "Handbooks and Anthologies: The Collection of Greek and Egyptian Incantations in Late Hellenistic Egypt," *Archiv für Religionsgeschichte* 2: 195–214.

Feeney, D. (1998) *Literature and Religion at Rome: Culture, Contexts, and Beliefs*. Oxford.

Feissel, D. and J. Gascou (1989) "Documents d'archives romains inédits du moyen Euphrate (IIIᵉ siècle après J.-C.)," *Comptes rendus de l'académie des inscriptions & belles-lettres* (no volume): 535–61.

(1995) "Documents d'archives romains inédits du moyen Euphrate (IIIᵉ siècle après J.-C.) 1. Les Pétitions (*P.Euphr.* 1 à 5)," *Journal des Savants* (no volume): 65–119.

(2000) "Documents d'archives romains inédits du moyen Euphrate (IIIe siècle après J.-C.) III. Actes divers et lettres (*P.Euphr.* II à 17)," *Journal des Savants* (no volume): 157–208.

Feissel, D., J. Gascou, and J. Teixidor (1997) "Documents d'archives romains inédits du moyen Euphrate (IIIe siècle après J.-C.) II. Les Actes de vente-achat (*P.Euphr.* 6 à 10)," *Journal des Savants* (no volume): 3–57.

Fellman, R. (1991) "Hölzerne Kleinfunde aus dem Vicus Vitudurum-Oberwinterthur," *Vitudurum: Beiträge zum römischen Oberwinterthur-Vitudurum* 5: 17–40.

Finley, M. I. (1952) *Studies in Land and Credit in Ancient Athens, 500–200 BC: The Horos-Inscriptions.* New Brunswick, NJ.

Fischer, J. E. (2002) "*Sanides* and *Sanidia*," in G. W. Bakewell and J. P. Sickinger, eds., *Gestures: Essays in Ancient History, Literature, and Philosophy Presented to Alan L. Boegehold on the Occasion of his Retirement and his Seventy-fifth Birthday*, 273–50. Oxford.

Flower, H. I. (1998) "Rethinking *Damnatio Memoriae*: The Case of Cn. Calpurnius Piso Pater in AD 20," *Classical Antiquity* 17: 155–86.

Fordyce, C. J. (1938) "'The Whole Truth' in Roman Procedure," *Classical Review* 52: 59.

Foresti, L. A. (1979) "Zur Zeremonie der Nagelschlagung in Rom und in Etrurien," *American Journal of Ancient History* 4: 144–56.

Fox, W. S. (1912) "III. – Submerged *Tabellae Defixionum*," *American Journal of Philology* 33: 301–10.

Fraenkel, E. (1960) *Elementi plautini in Plauto.* Florence.

France, J. and A. Hesnard (1995) "Une *statio* du quarantième des Gaules et les opérations commerciales dans le port romain de Marseille (place Jules-Verne)," *Journal of Roman Archaeology* 8: 78–93.

Frankfurter, D. (1994) "The Magic of Writing and the Writing of Magic: The Power of the Word in Egyptian and Greek Traditions," *Helios* 21: 189–221.

(1995) "Narrating Power: The Theory and Practice of the Magical *Historiola* in Ritual Spells," in M. Meyer and P. Mirecki, eds., *Ancient Magic and Ritual Power*, 457–76. Leiden and New York.

(1997) "Ritual Expertise in Roman Egypt and the Problem of the Category 'Magician'," in P. Schäfer and H. G. Kippenberg, eds., *Envisioning Magic: A Princeton Seminar and Symposium*, 115–35. Leiden.

Fraser, P. and T. Rönne (1957) *Boeotian and West Greek Tombstones* (Skrifter Utgivna av Svenska Institutet 1 Athen 4°, VI). Lund.

Frederiksen, M. W. (1965) "The Republican Municipal Laws: Errors and Drafts," *Journal of Roman Studies* 55: 183–98.

Frend, W. H. C. (1956) "A Third-Century Inscription Relating to *Angareia* in Phrygia," *Journal of Roman Studies* 46: 46–56.

Frere, S. S. and R. Tomlin (1992) *The Roman Inscriptions of Britain 2: Instrumentum domesticum.* Oxford.

Freundt, C. (1910) *Wertpapiere im antiken und frühmittelalterlichen Rechte* I. Leipzig.

References

313

Frier, B. W. (1979) *Libri Annales Pontificum Maximorum: The Origins of the Annalistic Tradition (Papers and Monographs of the American Academy in Rome, 27).* Ann Arbor.

(1985) *The Rise of the Roman Jurists: Studies in Cicero's* Pro Caecina. Princeton.

(1996) "Early Classical Private Law," in *CAH*[2] x: 959–78.

Gager, J. G., ed. (1992) *Curse Tablets and Binding Spells from the Ancient World.* Oxford.

Gagos, T. and P. Heilporn (2001) "A New *Agnitio Bonorum Possessionis*," in T. Gagos and R. S. Bagnall, eds., *Essays and Texts in Honor of J. David Thomas (American Studies in Papyrology* 42), 175–85.

Gallo, F. (1957) "La pretesa pubblicità dei trasferimenti nel diritto romano arcaico e classico," *Studia et Documenta Historiae et Iuris* 23: 174–264.

Galsterer, B. (1986) "Römische Wachstafeln aus Köln (Vorbericht)," in D. Planck, ed., *Studien zu den Militärgrenzen Roms III: 13. Internationaler Limeskongress, Aalen,* 152–4. Stuttgart.

Garcia Ruiz, E. (1967) "Estudio linguistico de las *defixiones* latinas no incluidas en el corpus de Audollent," *Emerita* 35: 55–89.

Gardner, J. F. (1986) *Women in Roman Law and Society.* London.

(1999) "Women in Business Life: Some Evidence from Puteoli," in P. Setälä and L. Savunen, eds., *Female Networks and the Public Sphere in Roman Society (Acta Instituti Romani Finlandiae* 22), 11–27. Rome.

Gardthausen, V. (1911) "Amtliche Zitate in römischen Urkunden," *Archiv für Urkundenforschung* 3: 1–22.

Gargola, D. (1995) *Lands, Laws and Gods: Magistrates and Ceremony in the Regulation of Public Lands in Republican Rome.* Chapel Hill.

Garner, R. (1987) *Law and Society in Classical Athens.* London.

Garnsey, P. (1970) *Social Status and Legal Privilege in the Roman Empire.* Oxford.

Garnsey, P. and C. Humfress (2001) *The Evolution of the Late Antique World.* Cambridge.

Gavrilov, A. K. (1997) "Techniques of Reading in Classical Antiquity," *Classical Quarterly* 47: 56–73.

Gerhard, G. A. (1904) "*Scriptura interior* und *exterior*," *Zeitschrift der Savigny-Stiftung für Rechtsgeschichte, romanistische Abteilung* 25: 382–9.

Gernet, L. (1955) *Droit et société dans la Grèce ancienne.* Paris.

Gilliam, J. F. (1971) "The Sale of a Slave Through a Greek Diploma," *Journal of Juristic Papyrology* 16–17: 63–70.

Gioffredi, C. (1978) "Su Gai 4.30," *Studia et Documenta Historiae et Iuris* 44: 429–38.

Giovè Marchioli, N. (1993) *Alle origini delle abbreviature latine.* Messina.

Glasbergen, W. (1965–6) "42 n.C. – Het eerste jaartal in de geschiedenis van West-Nederland," *Jaarboek der koninklijke Nederlandse Akademie van Wetenschappen* (no volume): 102–21.

Gleason, M. (1986) "Festive Satire: Julian's *Misopogon* and the New Year at Antioch," *Journal of Roman Studies* 76: 106–19.

Gneist, H. R. (1845) *Die formellen Verträge des neueren römischen Obligationenrechts in Vergleichung mit den Geschäftsformen des griechischen Rechts.* Berlin.

References

Goffart, W. (1980) *Barbarians and Romans AD 418–594: The Techniques of Accommodation.* Princeton.

Gonzenbach, V. von (1984) "Achillesplatte," in H. A. Cahn and A. Kaufmann-Heinimann, eds., *Der spätrömische Silberschatz von Kaiseraugst* (*Basler Beiträge zur Ur- und Frühgeschichte* 9), 1: 225–307. Derendingen.

Goody, J. (1961) "Religion and Ritual: the Definitional Problem," *British Journal of Sociology* 12: 142–64.

(1968) "Introduction," in J. Goody, ed., *Literacy in Traditional Societies,* 1–26. Cambridge.

(1977) "Against 'Ritual': Loosely Structured Thoughts on a Loosely Defined Topic," in S. F. Moore and B. G. Myerhoff, eds., *Secular Ritual,* 25–35. Assen.

Gordon, A. E. (1983) *Illustrated Introduction to Latin Epigraphy.* Berkeley.

Gordon, R. (1990) "From Republic to Principate: Priesthood, Religion, and Ideology," in M. Beard and J. A. North, eds., *Pagan Priests: Religion and Power in the Ancient World,* 179–98. Ithaca.

Graf, F. (1991) "Prayer in Magical and Religious Ritual," in C. A. Faraone and D. Obbink, eds., Magika Hiera: *Ancient Greek Magic and Religion,* 188–213. Oxford.

Greenidge, A. H. J. (1901) *The Legal Procedure of Cicero's Time.* Oxford.

(1977 [1894]) *Infamia: Its Place in Roman Public and Private Law.* Aalen (Oxford).

Grenfell, B. P. (1917–19) "A Latin-Greek Diptych of AD 198," *The Bodleian Quarterly Record* 2: 258–62.

Grewe, S. (1993) "Parodien mündlicher Rechtsformeln bei Petron," in G. Vogt-Spira, ed., *Beiträge zur mündlichen Kultur der Römer* (*Scriptoralia* 47), 37–58. Tübingen.

Gröschler, P. (1997) *Die* tabellae-*Urkunden aus den pompejanischen und herkulanensischen Urkundenfunden.* Berlin.

Gruen, E. S. (1992) *Culture and National Identity in Republican Rome.* Ithaca.

Guarino, A. (1955) "La scrittura nel 'testamentum per aes et libram'," in (no editor) *Studi in onore di Ugo Enrico Paoli,* 377–84. Florence.

(1956) "La forma orale e la forma scritta del testamento romano," in (no editor) *Studi in onore di Pietro de Francisci* II: 55–71. Milan.

Guéraud, O. (1940) "Une déclaration de naissance du 17 Mars 242 après J.-C.," *Études de papyrologie* 6: 21–35.

Habinek, T. N. (1985) *The Colometry of Latin Prose* (*University of California Classical Studies* 25). Berkeley.

Haensch, R. (1992) "Das Statthalterarchiv," *Zeitschrift der Savigny-Stiftung für Rechtsgeschichte, romanistische Abteilung* 109: 209–317.

(1994) "Die Bearbeitungsweisen von Petitionen in der Provinz Aegyptus," *Zeitschrift für Papyrologie und Epigraphik* 100: 487–546.

(1995) "*A commentariis* und *commentariensis*: Geschichte und Aufgaben eines Amtes im Spiegel seiner Titulaturen," in Y. Le Bohec, ed., *La Hiérarchie de l'armée romaine sous le haut-empire: actes du congrès de Lyon,* 267–284. Lyon.

References 315

(1996) "Die Verwendung von Siegeln bei Dokumenten der kaiserzeitlichen Reichsadministration," in M.-F. Boussac and A. Invernizzi, eds., *Archives et sceaux du monde hellénistique/Archivi e sigilli nel mondo ellenistico: Torino, Villa Gualino* (*Bulletin de correspondance hellénique* supplément 29), 449–96. Paris.

(1997) "Zur Konventsordnung in Aegyptus und den übrigen Provinzen des römischen Reiches," in B. Kramer *et al.*, eds., *Akten des 21. internationalen Papyrologenkongresses Berlin* (*Archiv für Papyrusforschung Beiheft* 3), 320–91. Munich.

(2001) "Zum Verständnis von *P.Jericho* 16 gr.," *Scripta Classica Israelica* 20: 155–67.

Hägerström, A. (1929) *Das magistratische Ius in seinem Zusammenhang mit dem römischen Sakralrechte*. Uppsala.

Hanson, A. E. (1984) "*P.Mich*. inv. 6554: An Expanded Affidavit Formula for an Authenticated Copy of a Prefectural *Subscriptio*," *Zeitschrift für Papyrologie und Epigraphik* 55: 191–9.

(1991) "Ancient Illiteracy," in M. Beard *et al.*, eds., *Literacy in the Roman World* (*Journal of Roman Archaeology* supplement 3), 159–98. Ann Arbor.

Haran, M. (1996) "Codex, *Pinax* and Writing Slat," *Scripta Classica Israelica* 15: 212–22.

Harries, J. (1988) "The Roman Imperial Quaestor from Constantine to Theodosius II," *Journal of Roman Studies* 78: 148–72.

(1999) *Law and Empire in Late Antiquity*. Cambridge.

Harris, W. V. (1989) *Ancient Literacy*. Cambridge, MA.

Harrison, A. R. W. (1968) *The Law of Athens: I. The Family and Property*. Oxford.

(1971) *The Law of Athens: II. Procedure*. Oxford.

Hässler, M. (1960) *Die Bedeutung der* Kyria-*Klausel in den Papyrusurkunden*. Berlin.

Hauken, T. (1998) *Petition and Response: An Epigraphic Study of Petitions to Roman Emperors 181–249* (*Monographs from the Norwegian Institute at Athens 2*). Bergen.

Heintz, F. (1998) "Circus Curses and their Archaeological Contexts," *Journal of Roman Archaeology* 11: 337–42.

Hellegouarc'h, J. (1963) *Le Vocabulaire latin des relations et des partis politiques sous la république*. Paris.

Henig, M. (1984) *Religion in Roman Britain*. London.

Hennig, D. (1977) "Der Bericht des Polybios über Boiotien und die Lage von Orchomenos in der 2. Hälfte des 3. Jahrhunderts v. Chr.," *Chiron* 7: 119–48.

Herrmann, L. (1958) "L'Épitaphe de Sergius," *Latomus* 17: 97–101.

Herrmann, P. (1985) "Sühn- und Grabinschriften aus der Katakekaumene im archäologischen Museum von Izmir," *Anzeiger der österreichischen Akademie der Wissenschaften, philosophisch-historische Klasse* 122: 248–61.

(1989) "Rom und die Asylie griechischer Heiligtümer: Eine Urkunde des Dictators Caesar aus Sardeis," *Chiron* 19: 127–64.

316 References

Heuß, A. (1934) "Abschluß und Beurkundung des griechischen und römischen Staatsvertrages," *Klio* 27: 14–53, 218–57.

Hickson, F. V. (1993) *Roman Prayer Language: Livy and the Aneid* [sic] *of Vergil.* Stuttgart.

Hinard, F. (1985) *Les Proscriptions de la Rome républicaine (Collection de l'école française de Rome* 83). Rome.

Hirschfeld, B. (1904) *Die* Gesta Municipalia *in römischer und frühgermanischer Zeit.* Marburg.

Hirschfeld, O. (1975) *Die kaiserlichen Verwaltungsbeamten bis auf Diocletian,* 2nd edn. Berlin.

Hitzig, H. (1909) *"Falsum," RE* 6.2: cols. 1973–6.

Hölkeskamp, K.-J. (2000) *"Fides – deditio in fidem – dextra data et accepta*: Recht, Religion und Ritual in Rom," in C. Bruun, ed., *The Roman Middle Republic: Politics, Religion, and Historiography c. 400–133 BC* (*Acta Instituti Romani Finlandiae* 23), 223–49. Rome.

Honig, R. M. (1960) *Humanitas und Rhetorik in spätrömischen Kaisergesetzen* (*Göttinger rechtswissenschaftliche Studien* 30). Göttingen.

Honoré, A. M. (1962) *Gaius.* Oxford.

Honoré, T. (1979) "'Imperial' Rescripts AD 193–305: Authorship and Authenticity," *Journal of Roman Studies* 69: 51–64.

 (1981) "The Primacy of Oral Evidence?" in C. F. H. Tapper, ed., *Crime, Proof and Punishment: Essays in Memory of Sir Rupert Cross,* 172–92. London.

 (1982) *Ulpian.* Oxford.

 (1984) "Ausonius and Vulgar Law," *Iura* 35: 75–85.

 (1986) "The Making of the Theodosian Code," *Zeitschrift der Savigny-Stiftung für Rechtsgeschichte, romanistische Abteilung* 103: 133–222.

 (1989) "Conveyances of Land and Professional Standards in the Later Empire," in P. Birks, ed., *New Perspectives in the Roman Law of Property: Essays for Barry Nicholas,* 137–52. Oxford.

 (1994) *Emperors and Lawyers,* 2nd edn. Oxford.

 (1998) *Law in the Crisis of Empire 379–455 AD: The Theodosian Dynasty and its Quaestors.* Oxford.

Hoogendijk, F. A. J. and P. van Minnen (1991) *Papyri, Ostraca, Parchments and Waxed Tablets in the Leiden Papyrological Institute* (*P.L. Bat.* 25). Leiden.

Hopkins, K. (1991) "From Violence to Blessing: Symbols and Rituals in Ancient Rome," in A. Molho, K. Raaflaub, and J. Emlen, eds., *City States in Classical Antiquity and Medieval Italy,* 479–98. Stuttgart.

Horst, P. W. van der (1994) "Silent Prayer in Antiquity," *Numen* 41: 1–25.

Humbert, M. (1993) "Droit et religion dans la Rome antique," in J. A. Ankum *et al.,* eds., *Mélanges Felix Wubbe,* 191–206. Fribourg.

Humphrey, C. and J. Laidlaw (1994) *The Archetypal Actions of Ritual: A Theory of Ritual Illustrated by the Jain Rite of Worship.* Oxford.

Husselman, E. (1970) "Procedures of the Record Office of Tebtunis in the First Century AD," in D. H. Samuel, ed., *Proceedings of the Twelfth International Congress of Papyrology* (*American Studies in Papyrology* 7), 223–38. Toronto.

References   317

Huvelin, M. (1904) "Les Tablettes magiques et le droit romain," *Annales internationales d'histoire, congrès de Paris 1900*, 15–81. Paris.

Ilan, T. (1992) "Julia Crispina, Daughter of Berenicianus, a Herodian Princess in the Babatha Archive: A Case Study in Historical Identification," *Jewish Quarterly Review* 82: 361–81.

(2001) "Witnesses in the Judaean Desert Documents: Prosopographical Observations," *Scripta Classica Israelica* 20: 169–78.

Invernizzi, A. (1996) "Gli archivi pubblici di Seleucia sul Tigri," in M.-F. Boussac and A. Invernizzi, eds., *Archives et sceaux du monde hellénistique/Archivi e sigilli nel mondo ellenistico: Torino, Villa Gualino (Bulletin de correspondance hellénique* supplément 29), 131–43. Paris.

Irvine, J. T. (1979) "Formality and Informality in Communicative Events," *American Anthropologist* 81: 773–90.

Isaac, B. (1994) "Tax Collection in Roman Arabia: A New Interpretation of the Evidence from the Babatha Archive," *Mediterranean Historical Review* 9: 256–66.

Isager, S. and M. H. Hansen (1975) *Aspects of Athenian Society in the Fourth Century BC*. Odense.

Jahr, G. (1960) Litis Contestatio: *Streitbezeugung und Prozeßbegründung im Legisaktionen- und im Formularverfahren*. Cologne.

(1963) "Zur *iusta causa traditionis*," *Zeitschrift der Savigny-Stiftung für Rechtsgeschichte, romanistische Abteilung* 80: 141–74.

(1965) "*Testatio*," *RE* Supplement 10: cols. 927–30.

Jakab, É. (1997) Praedicere *und* cavere *beim Marktkauf: Sachmängel im griechischen und römischen Recht (Münchener Beiträge zur Papyrusforschung und antiken Rechtsgeschichte* 87). Munich.

Jhering, R. von (1891 [1875]) *Geist des Römischen Rechts*, 5th edn. Leipzig.

Jocelyn, H. D. (1966) "The Roman Nobility and the Religion of the Republican State," *The Journal of Religious History* 4: 89–104.

Johnston, D. (1988) *The Roman Law of Trusts*. Oxford.

(1999) *Roman Law in Context*. Cambridge.

Jolowicz, H. F. (1937) "Case Law in Roman Egypt," *The Journal of the Society of Public Teachers of Law* 14: 1–15.

Jolowicz, H. F. and B. Nicholas (1972) *Historical Introduction to the Study of Roman Law*, 3rd edn. Cambridge.

Jones, A. H. M. (1972) *The Criminal Courts of the Roman Republic and Principate*. Oxford.

Jongmann, W. (1991) *The Economy and Society of Pompeii*. Amsterdam.

Jordan, D. R. (1976) "*CIL* VIII 19525(B).2 QPVVLVA = Q(UEM) P(EPERIT) V(VLVA)," *Philologus* 120: 127–32.

(1985) "*Defixiones* from a Well near the Southwest Corner of the Athenian Agora," *Hesperia* 54: 205–55.

(1988) "New Archaeological Evidence for the Practice of Magic in Classical Athens," *Praktika of the Twelfth International Congress of Classical Archaeology, Athens*, IV: 273–7. Athens.

References

Jouanique, P. (1968) "Le 'Codex accepti et expensi' chez Ciceron: étude d'histoire de la comptabilité," *Revue historique de droit français et étranger* (series 4) 46: 5–31.

Kaimio, J. (1979) *The Romans and the Greek Language* (*Societas Scientiarum Fennica, Commentationes Humanarum Litterarum* 64). Helsinki.

Kajava, M. (1995) "Some Remarks on the Erasure of Inscriptions in the Roman World (with Special Reference to the Case of Cn. Piso, cos. 7 BC)," in H. Solin, O. Salomies, and U. Liertz, eds., *Acta colloquii epigraphici Latini: Helsingiae 3.-6. Sept. 1991 habiti* (*Societas Scientiarum Fennica, Commentationes Humanarum Litterarum* 104), 201–10. Helsinki.

Karabélias, E. (1984) "La Forme de la *testatio* (*ekmartyrion*) matrimoniale en droit romain classique et post-classique," *Revue historique de droit français et étranger* (fourth series) 62: 599–603.

Kaser, M. (1934) "*Testimonium*," *RE* 5A.1: cols. 1021–61.

(1949) *Das altrömische Ius.* Göttingen.

(1951) "Zum Ediktsstil," in (no editor) *Festschrift Fritz Schulz* II: 21–70. Weimar.

(1955) *Das römische Privatrecht 1: Das altrömische, das vorklassische und klassische Recht* (*Handbuch der Altertumswissenschaft* 10.3.3.1). Munich.

(1959) *Das römische Privatrecht 2: Die nachklassischen Entwicklungen* (*Handbuch der Altertumswissenschaft* 10.3.3.2). Munich.

(1971) *Römisches Privatrecht 1: Das altrömische, das vorklassische und klassische Recht,* 2nd edn. (*Handbuch der Altertumswissenschaft* 10.3.3.1). Munich.

(1972) *Zur Methodologie der römischen Rechtsquellen-Forschung.* Vienna.

Kaser, M. and K. Hackl (1996) *Das römische Zivilprozessrecht,* 2nd edn. (*Handbuch der Altertumswissenschaft,* 10.3.4). Munich.

Katzoff, R. (1980) "Sources of Law in Roman Egypt: The Role of the Prefect," *ANRW* 2.13: 807–44.

(1981) "On the Intended Use of *P.Col.* 123," in R. S. Bagnall *et al.*, eds., *Proceedings of the Sixteenth International Congress of Papyrology* (*American Studies in Papyrology* 23), 559–73. Chico, CA.

(1982a) "Prefectural Edicts and Letters," *Zeitschrift für Papyrologie und Epigraphik* 48: 209–17.

(1982b) "'Responsa prudentium' in Roman Egypt," in (no editor) *Studi in onore di Arnoldo Biscardi* II: 523–35. Milan.

Kaygusuz, I. (1986) "Neue Inschriften aus Ainos (Enez)," *Epigraphica Anatolica* 8: 65–70.

Kenney, E. J. (1969) "Ovid and the Law," *Yale Classical Studies* 21: 243–63.

Kittel, E. (1970) *Siegel.* Brunswick.

Kleinknecht, H. (1937) *Die Gebetsparodie in der Antike* (*Tübinger Beiträge zur Altertumswissenschaft* 28). Stuttgart and Berlin.

Klose, D. (1984) "Nikopolis und Doliche: Neue Tonsiegel aus dem ἀρχεῖον des syrischen Nikopolis," *Jahrbuch für Numismatik und Geldgeschichte* 34: 63–76.

Knütel, R. (1971) "Zum Prinzip der formalen Korrespondenz im römischen Recht," *Zeitschrift der Savigny-Stiftung für Rechtsgeschichte, romanistische Abteilung* 88: 67–104.

References

(1976) "*Stipulatio* und *Pacta*," in D. Medicus and H. H. Seiler, eds., *Festschrift für Max Kaser zum 70. Geburtstag*, 201–28. Munich.

Köhn, J. (1977) "Zur Privatrechtsgeschichte der römischen Spätzeit," *Klio* 59: 503–8.

Körber, K. (1900) *Inschriften des Mainzer Museums*, 3rd edn. Mainz.

Kortenbeutel, H. (1932) "Ein Kaisereid," *Aegyptus* 12: 129–40.

Kotansky, R. (1983) "A Silver Phylactery for Pain," *J. Paul Getty Museum Journal* 11: 169–78.

(1991) "Incantations and Prayers for Salvation on Inscribed Greek Amulets," in C. A. Faraone and D. Obbink, eds., Magika Hiera: *Ancient Greek Magic and Religion*, 107–37. Oxford.

Kreller, H. (1919) *Erbrechtliche Untersuchungen auf Grund der graeco-aegyptischen Papyrusurkunden*. Leipzig and Berlin.

Kroell, M. (1906) *Du role de l'écrit dans la preuve des contrats en droit romain*. Nancy.

Kruse, H. (1934) *Studien zur offiziellen Geltung des Kaiserbildes im römischen Reiche* (*Studien zur Geschichte und Kultur des Altertums* 19.3). Paderborn.

Kübler, B. (1931) "*Subscriptio*," *RE* 4A.1: cols. 490–501.

(1934) "Testament (juristisch)," *RE* 5A.1: cols. 966–1010.

Kunkel, W. (1928) "*Mancipatio*," *RE* 14.1: cols. 998–1009.

(1932) "Συγγραφή, *Syngrapha*," *RE* 4A.2: cols. 1376–87.

(1933) "*P.Berol.* 13877, *PSI* VIII 901 und das Vorkommen der Doppelurkunde im römischen Ägypten," *Aegyptus* 13: 253–9.

(1936) "Zur gräko-ägyptischen Doppelurkunde," in (no editor) *Studi in onore di Salvatore Riccobono nel XL anno del suo insegnamento* 1: 414–33. Palermo.

(1967) *Herkunft und soziale Stellung der römischen Juristen*, 2nd edn. (*Forschungen zum römischen Recht* 4). Graz.

(1973) "Epigraphik und Geschichte des römischen Privatrechts," in (no editor) *Akten des VI. internationalen Kongresses für griechische und lateinische Epigraphik* (*Vestigia* 17), 193–242. Munich.

Kurzon, D. (1986) *It is Hereby Performed: Legal Speech Acts*. Amsterdam and Philadelphia.

Kußmaul, P. (1969) Synthekai: *Beiträge zur Geschichte des attischen Obligationenrechtes*. Basle.

Kuttner, A. (1991) "A Third Century BC Latin Census on a Praenestine Cist," *Römische Mitteilungen* 98: 141–61.

(1993) "Some New Grounds for Narrative: Marcus Antonius's Base (The *Ara Domitii Ahenobarbi*) and Republican Biographies," in P. J. Holliday, ed., *Narrative and Event in Ancient Art*, 198–229. Cambridge.

Lambrinudakis, W. and M. Wörrle (1983) "Ein hellenistisches Reformgesetz über das öffentliche Urkundenwesen," *Chiron* 13: 283–368.

Lane Fox, R. (1994) "Literacy and Power in Early Christianity," in A. K. Bowman and G. Woolf, eds., *Literacy and Power in the Ancient World*, 126–48. Cambridge.

Latte, K. (1960) *Römische Religionsgeschichte* (*Handbücher der Altertumswissenschaft* 5.4). Munich.

References

Lauffer, S. (1971) *Diokletians Preisedikt (Texte und Kommentare* 5). Berlin.

Laughton, E. (1938) "Cato's Charm for Dislocations," *Classical Review* 52: 52–4.

Laurence, R. (1993) "Emperors, Nature and the City: Rome's Ritual Landscape," *Accordia Research Papers* 4: 79–87.

Lemosse, M. (1949) "L'Affranchisement par le cens," *Revue historique de droit français et étranger* (fourth series) 27: 161–203.

Lendon, J. E. (1997) *Empire of Honour: The Art of Government in the Roman World*. Oxford.

Lenel, O. (1956) *Das Edictum Perpetuum*, 3rd edn. Leipzig.

Lentz, T. M. (1983) "Spoken versus Written Inartistic Proof in Athenian Courts," *Philosophy and Rhetoric* 16: 242–61.

—— (1989) *Orality and Literacy in Hellenic Greece*. Carbondale, IL.

Leuregans, P. (1975) "*Testamenti factio non privati sed publici iuris est*," *Revue historique de droit français et étranger* (fourth series) 53: 225–57.

Levy, E. (1929) "Westen und Osten in der nachklassischen Entwicklung des römischen Rechts," *Zeitschrift der Savigny-Stiftung für Rechtsgeschichte, romanistische Abteilung* 49: 230–59.

—— (1943) "Vulgarization of Roman Law in the Early Middle Ages as Illustrated by Successive Versions of *Pauli Sententiae*," *Medievalia et Humanistica* 1: 14–40.

—— (1951) *West Roman Vulgar Law: The Law of Property*. Philadelphia.

—— (1956) *Weströmisches Vulgarrecht: Das Obligationenrecht*. Weimar.

Lévy, J.-P. (1952) "Les Actes d'état civil romains," *Revue historique de droit français et étranger* (fourth series) 30: 449–86.

—— (1954) "Réflexions sur l'importance et l'intérêt des questions de preuves," *Travaux juridiques et économiques de l'Université de Rennes* 18: 95–137.

—— (1959a) "La Fonction dispositive de l'écriture dans le droit grec," *Revue historique de droit français et étranger* (fourth series) 37: 454–5.

—— (1959b) "Cicéron et le preuve judiciaire," in (no editor) *Droits de l'antiquité et sociologie juridique: mélanges Henri Lévy-Bruhl*, 187–97. Paris.

—— (1964) "The Evolution of Written Proof," *American University Law Review* 13: 133–53.

—— (1982) "Sur trois textes bibliques concernant des actes écrits," in (no editor) *Mélanges à la mémoire de Marcel-Henri Prévost*, 23–48. Paris.

—— (1998) "La «Litis denuntiatio» et sa place dans l'évolution de la procédure extraordinaire," in M. Humbert and Y. Thomas, eds., *Mélanges de droit romain et d'histoire ancienne. Hommage à la mémoire de André Magdelain*, 247–57. Paris.

Lévy-Bruhl, H. (1910) *Le Témoignage instrumentaire en droit romain*. Paris.

Lewis, N. (1970) "'Greco-Roman' Egypt: Fact or Fiction?" in D. H. Samuel, ed., *Proceedings of the Twelfth International Congress of Papyrology (American Studies in Papyrology* 7), 3–14. Toronto.

—— (1974) "*Notationes Legentes*," *Bulletin of the American Society of Papyrologists* 11: 44–59.

—— (1975) "A Petition of AD 212," *Bulletin of the American Society of Papyrologists* 12: 159–64.

References

321

(1981) "The Prefect's *Conventus:* Proceedings and Procedures," *Bulletin of the American Society of Papyrologists* 18: 119–29.

(1983) *Life in Egypt Under Roman Rule.* Oxford.

(1989) *The Documents from the Bar Kokhba Period in the Cave of Letters: Greek Papyri.* Jerusalem.

(1996) "On Roman Imperial Promulgations in Greek," *Scripta Classica Israelica* 15: 208–11.

(2000) "Judiciary Routines in Roman Egypt," *Bulletin of the American Society of Papyrologists* 37: 83–93.

(2001) "The Demise of the Aramaic Document in the Dead Sea Region," *Scripta Classica Israelica* 20: 179–81.

Lewis, N., R. Katzoff, and J. Greenfield (1987) "Papyrus Yadin 18," *Israel Exploration Journal* 37: 229–50.

Lewis, S. (1996) *News and Society in the Greek Polis.* Chapel Hill.

Lieberman, S. (1944–5) "Roman Legal Institutions in Early Rabbinics in the *Acta Martyrum*," *Jewish Quarterly Review* 35: 1–55.

Liebeschuetz, J. H. W. G. (1979) *Continuity and Change in Roman Religion.* Oxford.

Liebs, D. (1970) "*Contrarius Actus*: Zur Entstehung des römischen Erlaßvertrags," in D. Liebs, ed., *Sympotica Franz Wieacker sexagenario Sasbachwaldeni a suis libata*, 111–53. Göttingen.

Linderski, J. (1985) "The *Libri Reconditi*," *Harvard Studies in Classical Philology* 89: 207–34.

Lintott, A. (1986) "*Acta Antiquissima*: A Week in the History of the Roman Republic," *Papers of the British School at Rome* 54: 213–28.

(1992) *Judicial Reform and Land Reform in the Roman Republic.* Cambridge.

Löhken, H. (1982) Ordines Dignitatum: *Untersuchungen zur formalen Konstituierung der spätantiken Führungsschicht.* Cologne and Vienna.

Lonis, R. (1980) "La Valeur du serment dans les accords internationaux en Grèce classique," *Dialogues d'histoire ancienne* 6: 267–86.

Łukaszewicz, A. (1981) "A Petition from Priests to Hadrian with his Subscription," in R. S. Bagnall *et al.*, eds., *Proceedings of the XVI International Congress of Papyrology (American Studies in Papyrology* 23), 357–61. Chico, CA.

Lyne, R. O. A. M. (1980) *The Latin Love Poets from Catullus to Horace.* Oxford.

Ma, J. (2000) "Seleukids and Speech-Acts: Performative Utterances, Legitimacy and Negotiation in the World of the Maccabees," *Scripta Classica Israelica* 19: 71–112.

MacCormack, G. (1969a) "Formalism, Symbolism and Magic in Early Roman Law," *Tijdschrift voor Rechtsgeschiedenis/Revue d'histoire du droit* 37: 439–68.

(1969b) "Haegerstroem's Magical Interpretation of Roman Law," *The Irish Jurist* n.s. 4: 153–67.

(1983) "The Oral and Written Stipulation in the *Institutes*," in P. G. Stein and A. D. E. Lewis, eds., *Studies in Justinian's Institutes in Memory of J. A. C. Thomas*, 96–108. London.

MacCormack, S. G. (1981) *Art and Ceremony in Late Antiquity.* Berkeley.

MacCormick, N. and Z. Bankowski (1986) "Speech Acts, Legal Institutions, and Real Laws," in N. MacCormick and P. Birks, eds., *The Legal Mind: Essays for Tony Honoré*, 121–33. Oxford.

MacDowell, D. M. (1978) *The Law in Classical Athens*. Ithaca.

MacMullen, R. (1981) *Paganism in the Roman Empire*. New Haven.

(1988) *Corruption and the Decline of Rome*. New Haven.

(1997) "Tracking Value Changes," in H. W. Pleket and A. M. F. W. Verhoogt, eds., *Aspects of the Fourth Century AD: Proceedings of the Symposium Power & Possession: State, Society, and Church in the Fourth Century AD, Leiden*, 115–34. Leiden.

Macqueron, J. (1982) Contractus Scripturae: *Contrats et quittances dans la pratique romaine*. Camerino.

Maehler, H. (1974) "Ein römischer Veteran und seine Matrikel," in E. Kießling and H.-A. Rupprecht, eds., *Akten des XIII. internationalen Papyrologenkongresses* (*Münchener Beiträge zur Papyrusforschung und antiken Rechtsgeschichte* 66), 241–50. Munich.

(1981) "Lucius the Donkey and Roman Law," *Museum Philologum Londiniense* 4: 161–77.

Maffi, A. (1988) "Écriture et pratique juridique dans la Grèce classique," in M. Detienne, ed., *Les Savoirs de l'écriture: en Grèce ancienne* (*Cahiers de philologie* 14), 188–210. Lille.

Magdelain, A. (1943) *Essai sur les origines de la* sponsio. Paris.

(1978) *La Loi à Rome: histoire d'un concept*. Paris.

(1990) Jus Imperium Auctoritas: *études de droit romain*. Paris.

(1995) *De la royauté et du droit de Romulus à Sabinus*. Rome.

Maier, J.-L. (1987) *Le Dossier du donatisme 1: des origines à la mort de Constance II* (*303–361*). Berlin.

Maiuri, A. (1946) "*Tabulae ceratae herculanenses*," *La Parola del Passato* 3: 373–9.

Maloney, J. (1987) "Writing on the Walls of the Roman City," *Lloyd's Log* (September): 49–50.

Mann, J. C. (1972) "The Development of Auxiliary and Fleet Diplomas," *Epigraphische Studien* 9: 233–40.

(2000) "*Honesta Missio* from the Legions," in G. Alföldy, B. Dobson, and W. Eck, eds., *Kaiser, Heer und Gesellschaft in der römischen Kaiserzeit: Gedenkschrift für Eric Birley*, 153–61. Stuttgart.

Mann, J. C. and M. M. Roxan (1988) "Discharge Certificates of the Roman Army," *Britannia* 19: 341–7.

Maraval, P. (1990) *La Passion inédite de S. Athénogène de Pédachthoé en Cappadoce* (*BGH 1976*) (*Subsidia Hagiographica* 75). Brussels.

Maresch, K. and Z. M. Packman (1990) *Papyri from the Washington University Collection, St. Louis, Missouri Part II* (*P. Wash. Univ.* 2; *Papyrologica Coloniensia* 18). Opladen.

Marichal, R. (1950) "L'Écriture latine du i[er] au viie siècle: les sources," *Scriptorium* 4: 116–42.

(1952) "L'Écriture latine de la chancellerie impériale," *Aegyptus* 32: 336–50.

References   323

(1955) "Bibliographie," *Scriptorium* 9: 127–49.

(1972–3) "Rapports sur les conférences: paléographie latine et française," *Annuaire, école pratique des hautes études, ive section: sciences historiques et philologiques* 105: 363–80.

(1992a) "Les Tablettes à écrire dans le monde romain," in É. Lalou, ed., *Les Tablettes à écrire de l'antiquité à l'époque moderne (Bibliologia* 12), 165–85. Turnhout.

(1992b) *Les Ostraca de Bu Njem (Suppléments de 'Libya Antica'* 7). Tripoli.

Marin, D. St. (1948) "Il *foedus* romano con Callatis," *Epigraphica* 10: 104–30.

Marouzeau, J. (1959) "Sur deux aspects de la langue du droit," in (no editor) *Droits de l'antiquité et sociologie juridique: mélanges Henri Lévy-Bruhl*, 435–44. Paris.

Marrou, H. (1964) ΜΟΥΣΙΚΟΣ ΑΝΗΡ: *étude sur les scènes de la vie intellectuelle figurant sur les monuments funéraires romains*. Rome.

Marshall, A. J. (1984) "Symbols and Showmanship in Roman Public Life: The Fasces," *Phoenix* 38: 120–41.

(1989) "Ladies at Law: The Role of Women in the Roman Civil Courts," in C. Deroux, ed., *Studies in Latin Literature and Roman History* 5 (*Collection Latomus* 206), 35–54.

Martinez, D. G. (1991) *P.Michigan* XVI: *A Greek Love Charm from Egypt (P.Mich. 757) (American Studies in Papyrology 30)*. Atlanta.

Marx, F. (1884) "*Animadversiones criticae in Scipionis Aemiliani historiam et C. Gracchi orationem adversus Scipionem*," *Rheinisches Museum für Philologie* 39: 65–72.

Mashi, C. (1937) "La solennità della 'heredis institutio' nel diritto romano," *Aegyptus* 17: 197–232.

Massow, W. von (1932) *Die Grabmäler von Neumagen*. Berlin and Leipzig.

Mathisen, R. (1998) "*Et Manu Papae*: Papal Subscriptions Written *Sua Manu* in Late Antiquity," in G. Schmeling, ed., Qui Miscuit Utile Dulci: *Festschrift Essays for Paul Lachlan MacKendrick*, 243–51. Wauconda, IL.

Matthews, J. (1993) "The Making of the Code," in J. Harries and I. Wood, eds., *The Theodosian Code*, 19–44. Ithaca, NY.

(1998) "Eternity in Perishable Materials: Law-Making and Literate Communication in the Roman Empire," in T. W. Hillard, R. A. Kearsley, C. E. V. Nixon, and A. M. Nobbs, eds., *Ancient History in a Modern University* II: 253–65. Grand Rapids, MI.

(2000) *Laying Down the Law: A Study of the Theodosian Code*. New Haven.

McDonnell, M. (1996) "Writing, Copying, and Autograph Manuscripts in Ancient Rome," *Classical Quarterly* 46: 469–91.

Mélèze-Modrzejewski, J. (1984) "Le Document grec dans l'Égypte ptolémaïque," in (no editor) *Atti del XVII congresso internazionale di papirologia*, III: 1173–87. Naples.

Menkman, A. (1946) "The Edict of Valerius Eudaimon, Prefect of Egypt," in M. David, B. A. Van Groningen, and E. M. Meijers, eds., *Symbolae ad ius et historiam antiquitatis pertinentes Julio Christiano Van Oven dedicatae (Symbolae Van Oven)*, 191–210. Leiden.

324 *References*

Merten, J. A. (1983) "Schreibtafel und Buchrolle auf treverischen Denkmälern," *Funde und Ausgrabungen im Bezirk Trier* 15: 27–34.

Messick, B. (1983) "Legal Documents and the Concept of 'Restricted Literacy' in a Traditional Society," *International Journal of the Sociology of Language* 42: 41–52.

Meyer, E. (2001) "Wooden Wit: *Tabellae* in Latin Poetry," in E. Tylawsky and C. Weiss, eds., *Essays in Honor of Gordon Williams: Twenty-five Years at Yale*, 201–12. New Haven.

Meyer, M. and R. Smith (1994) *Ancient Christian Magic: Coptic Texts of Ritual Power*. San Francisco.

Millar, F. G. B. (1977) *The Emperor in the Roman World (31 BC – AD 337)*. London.

(1986) "A New Approach to the Roman Jurists," *Journal of Roman Studies* 76: 272–80.

(1995) "Latin in the Epigraphy of the Roman Near East," in H. Solin, O. Salomies, and U. Liertz, eds., *Acta colloquii epigraphici Latini: Helsingiae 3.-6. Sept. 1991 habiti (Societas Scientiarum Fennica, Commentationes Humanarum Litterarum* 104), 403–19. Helsinki.

(1998) *The Crowd in Rome in the Late Republic* (Jerome Lectures 22). Ann Arbor.

Millett, P. (1982) "The Attic *horoi* Reconsidered in the Light of Recent Discoveries," *Opus* 1: 219–49.

Minns, E. H. (1915) "Parchments of the Parthian Period from Avroman in Kurdistan," *Journal of Hellenic Studies* 35: 22–65.

Mitchell, R. E. (1984) "Roman History, Roman Law, and Roman Priests: The Common Ground," *University of Illinois Law Review* (no volume): 541–60.

(1990) *Patricians and Plebeians: The Origin of the Roman State*. Ithaca.

Mitchell, S. (1976) "Requisitioned Transport in the Roman Empire: A New Inscription from Pisidia," *Journal of Roman Studies* 66: 106–31.

Mitteis, L. (1891) *Reichsrecht und Volksrecht in den östlichen Provinzen des römischen Kaiserreichs*. Leipzig.

(1908) *Römisches Privatrecht bis auf die Zeit Diokletians*. Leipzig.

(1912) *Grundzüge und Chrestomathie der Papyruskunde 2: Juristischer Teil 1: Grundzüge*. Leipzig and Berlin.

Moatti, C. (1993) *Archives et partage de la terre dans le monde romain (IIe siècle avant-Ier siècle après J.-C.) (Collection de l'école française de Rome* 173). Rome.

Modrzejewski, J. (1970) "La Règle de droit dans l'Egypte romaine," in D. H. Samuel, ed., *Proceedings of the Twelfth International Congress of Papyrology (American Studies in Papyrology* 7), 317–77. Toronto.

(1974) "À propos de la tutelle dative des femmes dans l'Égypte romaine," in E. Kießling and H.-A. Rupprecht, eds., *Akten des XIII. internationalen Papyrologenkongresses (Münchener Beiträge zur Papyrusforschung und antiken Rechtsgeschichte* 66), 263–92. Munich.

Momigliano, A. (1989) "The Origins of Rome," in *CAH²* vii.2: 52–112.

Mommsen, T. (1885) "Der Rechtsstreit zwischen Oropos und den römischen Steuerpächtern," *Hermes* 20: 268–87.

(1899) *Römisches Strafrecht*. Leipzig.

References

(1904) "Das Verhältniss des Tacitus zu den Acten des Senats," *Sitzungsberichte der königlich preussischen Akademie der Wissenschaften zu Berlin* 35: 1146–55.

(1905 [1895]) "Aegyptische Papyri," in his *Juristische Schriften* I: 181–96 (first published in *Zeitschrift der Savigny-Stiftung für Rechtsgeschichte, romanistische Abteilung* 16: 181–98). Berlin.

(1907 [1877]) "Die pompeianischen Quittungstafeln des L. Caecilius Jucundus," in his *Juristische Schriften* III: 221–74 (first published in *Hermes* 12: 88–141). Berlin.

(1969 [1887]) *Römisches Staatsrecht*, 3rd edn. Graz (Leipzig).

Mommsen, T. and H. Nesselhauf (1936) *Corpvs Inscriptionvm Latinarvm 16: Diplomata militaria ex constitvtionibvs imperatorvm de civitate et convbio militvm veteranorvmqve expressa.* Berlin.

Mommsen, T. and K. Zangemeister (1873) *Corpvs Inscriptionvm Latinarvm 3: Inscriptiones Asiae Provinciarvm Evropae Graecarvm Illyrici Latinae.* Berlin.

Moore, S. F. (1978) *Law as Process: An Anthropological Approach.* London.

Mor, C. G. (1976) "Simbologia e simboli nella vita giuridica," *Simboli e simbologia nell'alto medioevo (Settimane* 23), I: 17–29. Spoleto.

Móra, M. (1968) "Die vulgarrechtliche Forschungseinrichtung," *Gesellschaft und Recht im griechisch-römischen Altertum* I: 133–49.

Mourgues, J.-L. (1987) "The So-Called Letter of Domitian at the End of the *Lex Irnitana*," *Journal of Roman Studies* 77: 78–87.

(1995a) "Les Formules «rescripsi» «recognovi» et les étapes de la rédaction des souscriptions impériales sous le haut-empire romain," *Mélanges d'archéologie et d'histoire de l'école française de Rome* 107: 255–300.

(1995b) "Écrire en deux langues: bilinguisme et pratique de chancellerie sous le haut-empire romain," *Dialogues d'histoire ancienne* 21: 105–29.

(1998) "Forme diplomatique et pratique institutionnelle des *commentarii Augustorum*," in (no editor) *La Mémoire perdue: recherches sur l'administration romaine (Collection de l'école française de Rome* 243), 123–74. Paris and Rome.

Mrsich, T. Q. (1979) "Manzipationsgestus und Altertumswissenschaft," *Zeitschrift der Savigny-Stiftung für Rechtsgeschichte, romanistische Abteilung* 96: 272–89.

Muecke, F. (1993) *Horace: Satires II.* Warminster.

Muir, E. (1997) *Ritual in Early Modern Europe.* Cambridge.

Müller, R. W. (1964) *Rhetorische und syntaktische Interpunktion: Untersuchungen zur Pausenbezeichnung im antiken Latein.* Tübingen.

Musurillo, H. (1954) *The Acts of the Pagan Martyrs:* Acta Alexandrinorum. Oxford.

(1972) *The Acts of the Christian Martyrs.* Oxford.

Nappo, S. C. (1989) "Fregio dipinto dal 'praedium' di Giulia Felice con rappresentazione del foro di Pompei," *Rivista di Studi Pompeiani* 3: 79–96.

Nelson, C. A. (1979) *Status Declarations in Roman Egypt (American Studies in Papyrology* 19). Amsterdam.

Nicholas, B. (1953) "The Form of the Stipulation in Roman Law," *The Law Quarterly Review* 69: 63–79, 233–52.

(1987) *An Introduction to Roman Law*, 3rd edn. Oxford.

(1992) "Verbal Forms in Roman Law," *Tulane Law Review* 66: 1605–13.

References

Nicolet, C. (1980) *The World of the Citizen in Republican Rome* (trans. P. S. Falla). Berkeley.

Niedermeyer, H. (1918) *Über antike Protokoll-Literatur.* Göttingen.

Nisoli, E. (1949) *Die Testamentseröffnung im römischen Recht.* Bern.

Nock, A. D. (1972) "Greek Magical Papyri," in his *Essays on Religion and the Ancient World* I: 176–94. Cambridge, MA.

Nollé, J. (1982) Nundinas instituere et habere: *Epigraphische Zeugnisse zur Einrichtung und Gestaltung von ländlichen Märkten in Afrika und in der Provinz Asia.* Hildesheim, Zurich, and New York.

Norden, E. (1939) *Aus altrömischen Priesterbüchern.* Lund and Leipzig.

Nörr, D. (1981) "Zur Reskriptenpraxis in der hohen Prinzipatszeit," *Zeitschrift der Savigny-Stiftung für Rechtsgeschichte, romanistische Abteilung* 98: 1–46.

(1989) *Aspekte des römischen Völkerrechts: Die Bronzetafel von Alcántara (Bayerische Akademie der Wissenschaften, philosophisch-historische Klasse, Abhandlungen* new series 101). Munich.

North, J. A. (1976) "Conservatism and Change in Roman Religion," *Papers of the British School at Rome* 44: 1–12.

(1986) "Religion and Politics, from Republic to Principate," *Journal of Roman Studies* 76: 251–8.

(1989) "Religion in Republican Rome," *CAH*[2] VII.2: 573–624.

(1998) "The Books of the *pontifices,*" in (no editor) *La Mémoire perdue: recherches sur l'administration romaine* (*Collection de l'école française de Rome* 243), 45–63. Paris and Rome.

Nuber, H. U. (1979–80) "Ein stratigraphischer Aufschluß im Bereich 'Wiesbadener Moorschicht'," in F. Maier, ed., *Ulrich Fischer zum 65. Geburtstag am 3. Juli 1980 (Fundberichte aus Hessen* 19–20), 645–77.

Nyberg, H. S. (1923) "The Pahlavi Documents from Avroman," *Le Monde oriental* 17: 182–230.

Odum, M. (1992) "If It Talks Like a Lawyer, There May Yet Be a Cure," *New York Times* 141 no. 48988 (June 5): B8.

Ogilvie, R. M. (1961) "'Lustrum Condere'," *Journal of Roman Studies* 51: 31–9.

(1965) *A Commentary on Livy Books 1–5.* Oxford.

(1969) *The Romans and their Gods in the Age of Augustus.* London.

Ogilvie, R. M. and A. Drummond (1989) "The Sources for Early Roman History," *CAH*[2] VII.2: 1–29.

Oliver, J. H. (1989) *Greek Constitutions of Early Roman Emperors from Inscriptions and Papyri* (*American Philosophical Society Monographs* 178). Philadelphia.

Ong, W. (1982) *Orality and Literacy: The Technologizing of the Word.* London and New York.

Palazzolo, N. (1987) "L'*edictum* 'de albo corrupto' e il problema della pubblicità delle norme edittali in età postadrianea," in (no editor) *Studi in onore di Cesare Sanfilippo* VII: 593–622. Milan.

Palmer, R. E. A. (1974) *Roman Religion and Roman Empire: Five Essays.* Philadelphia.

References

Pani, G. G. (1986) "Segno e immagine di scrittura: la *tabula ansata* e il suo significato simbolico," *Miscellanea greca e romana* 10: 429–41.

(1988) "Forma, linguaggio e contenuti delle dediche epigrafiche nei *tituli ansati* (iv–ix sec. d.C.)," in A. Donati, ed., *La terza età dell'epigrafia*, 169–94. Faenza.

Paoli, J. (1950) "'VERBA PRAEIRE' dans la 'LEGIS ACTIO'," in (no editor) *Mélanges Fernand de Visscher* (*Revue internationale des droits de l'antiquité* 3) III: 281–324. Brussels.

Paoli, U. (1922) "'Legere' e 'recitare'," *Atene e Roma* 25: 205–7.

Parássoglou, G. M. (1974) "Four Official Documents from Roman Egypt," *Chronique d'Égypte* 49: 332–41.

(1979) "ΔΕΞΙΑ ΧΕΙΡ ΚΑΙ ΓΟΝΥ: Some Thoughts on the Postures of the Ancient Greeks and Romans When Writing on Papyrus Rolls," *Scrittura e civiltà* 3: 5–21.

Partsch, J. (1921) "Die griechische Publizität der Grundstückverträge im Ptolemäerrechte," in (no editor) *Festschrift für Otto Lenel zum fünfzigjährigen Doctorjubiläum am 16. Dezember 1921, überreicht von der rechts- und staatswissenschaftlichen Fakultät der Universität Freiburg i. Br.*, 77–203. Leipzig.

Peachin, M. (1996) *Iudex vice Caesaris: Deputy Emperors and the Administration of Justice during the Principate* (*Heidelberger althistorische Beiträge und epigraphische Studien* 21). Stuttgart.

Pearl, O. M. (1970) "Excerpts from the Minutes of Judicial Proceedings," *Zeitschrift für Papyrologie und Epigraphik* 6: 271–7.

Peruzzi, E. (1973) *Le origini di Roma*. Bologna.

Pescani, P. (1961) "Osservazioni su alcune sigle ricorrenti nelle 'professiones liberorum'," *Aegyptus* 41: 129–40.

Petrucci, A. (1984) "Lire au Moyen Âge," *Mélanges de l'école française de Rome* 96: 603–16.

Petsas, P. M., M. B. Hatzopoulos, L. Gounaropoulou, and P. Paschidis (2000) *Inscriptions du sanctuaire de la mère des dieux autochthone de Leukopétra (Macédoine)* (ΜΕΛΕΤΗΜΑΤΑ 28). Paris and Athens.

Petzl, G. (1994) "Die Beichtinschriften Westkleinasiens," *Epigraphica Anatolica* 22: 1–174.

Pfaff, I. (1905) Tabellio *und* Tabularius. Vienna.

Pflaum, H.-G. (1940) *Essai sur le* cursus publicus *sous le haut-empire romain*. Paris.

(1971) "Une lettre de promotion de l'empereur Marc Aurèle pour un procurateur ducénaire de Gaule Narbonnaise," *Bonner Jahrbücher* 171: 349–66.

Piazza, M. P. (1980) "'Tabulae novae': osservazioni sul problema dei debiti negli ultimi decenni della repubblica," in (no editor) *Atti del II. seminario romanistico Gardesano*, 37–107. Milan.

Piccaluga, G. (1983) "La scrittura coercitiva," *Cultura e scuola* 85: 117–24.

(1994) "La specificità dei *libri lintei romani*," *Scrittura e civiltà* 18: 5–22.

Pierce, R. H. (1968) "*Grapheion*, Catalogue, and Library in Roman Egypt," *Symbolae Osloenses* 43: 68–83.

Pieri, G. (1968) *L'Histoire du cens jusqu'à la fin de la république romaine*. Sirey.

References

Piper, D. J. (1987) "Latins and the Roman Citizenship in Roman Colonies: Livy 34,42,5–6; Revisited," *Historia* 36: 38–50.

Piva, R. (1993) "Neue Wege zur Interpretation des CARMEN ARVALE: Ein Zeugnis fingierter Mündlichkeit?" in G. Vogt-Spira, ed., *Beiträge zur mündlichen Kultur der Römer (Scriptoralia* 47), 59–85. Tübingen.

Poccetti, P. (1999) "Il metallo come supporto di iscrizioni nell'Italia antica: aree, lingue e tipologie testuali," in F. Villar and F. Beltrán, eds., *Pueblos, lenguas y escrituras en la Hispania prerromana: Actas del vii coloquio sobre lenguas y culturas paleohispánicas*, 545–61. Salamanca.

Pólay, E. (1962) "Sklaven-Kaufverträge auf Wachstafeln aus Herculaneum und Dakien," *Acta Antiqua* 16: 385–97.

   (1971) "Die Formalitäten der Urkunden der siebenbürger Wachstafeln," *Klio* 53: 223–38.

   (1980) *The Contracts in the Triptychs Found in Transylvania and their Hellenistic Features (Studia Historica Academiae Scientiarum Hungaricae* 133). Budapest.

Posner, E. (1972) *Archives in the Ancient World*. Cambridge, MA.

Poucet, J. (1988) "Réflexions sur l'écrit et l'écriture dans la Rome des premiers siècles," *Latomus* 48: 285–311.

Powell, J. G. F. (1992) review of J. G. Wolf and J. A. Crook (1989), in *Journal of Roman Studies* 82: 262–3.

Préaux, C. (1964) "La Preuve à l'époque hellénistique principalement dans l'Égypte grecque," in (no editor) *La Preuve 1ᵉ partie: antiquité (Recueils de la société Jean Bodin pour l'histoire comparative des institutions* 16), 161–222. Brussels.

Preisendanz, K. (1972) "Fluchtafel (Defixion)," in *Reallexikon für Antike und Christentum* 8: cols. 1–29. Stuttgart.

Preisigke, F. (1927) *Wörterbuch der griechischen Papyrusurkunden mit Einschluß der griechischen Inschriften, Aufschriften, Ostraka, Mummienschilder usw. aus Ägypten*. Berlin.

Premerstein, A. von (1900) "*Commentarii*," *RE* 4.1: cols. 726–59.

   (1926) "*Libellus*," *RE* 13.1: cols. 26–61.

Prichard, A. M. (1960) "Terminology in *Mancipatio*," *The Law Quarterly Review* 76: 412–28.

   (1974) "*Auctoritas* in Early Roman Law," *The Law Quarterly Review* 90: 378–95.

Priest, N. (1983) "A Loan of Money with Some Notes on the *Ala Mauretana*," *Zeitschrift für Papyrologie und Epigraphik* 51: 65–70.

Pringsheim, F. (1950) *The Greek Law of Sale*. Weimar.

   (1955) "The Transition from Witnessed to Written Transactions in Athens," in (no editor) Aequitas et Bona Fides: *Festgabe zum 70. Geburtstag von August Simonius*, 287–97. Basle.

   (1960) "Griechischer Einfluss auf das römische Recht," *Bollettino dell'istituto di diritto romano* 63: 1–17.

   (1961) "Le Témoignage dans la Grèce et Rome archaïque," in his *Gesammelte Abhandlungen* ii: 330–8. Heidelberg.

Pugliese Carratelli, G. (1948) "*Tabulae Herculanenses* ii," *La Parola del Passato* 3: 165–84.

References

329

(1950) "L'*instrumentum scriptorium* nei monumenti pompeiani ed ercolanesi," in (no editor) *Pompeiana: raccolta di studi per il secondo centenario degli scavi di Pompei*, 266–78. Naples.

Purcell, N. (1993) "*Atrium Libertatis*," *Papers of the British School at Rome* 61: 125–55.

Rabel, E. (1907) "Nachgeformte Rechtsgeschäfte: Mit Beiträgen zu den Lehren von der Injurezession und vom Pfandrecht," *Zeitschrift der Savigny-Stiftung für Rechtsgeschichte, romanistische Abteilung* 28: 290–397.

Raepsaet-Charlier, M.-T. (1986) "Acceptus, *tabularius* à Treves (*CIL* XIII 4208; *AE* 1967, 320)," *Zeitschrift für Papyrologie und Epigraphik* 64: 223–9.

Rathbone, D. W. (1993) "Egypt, Augustus and Roman Taxation," *Cahiers du Centre G. Glotz* 4: 81–112.

(2001) "*PSI* XI 1183: Record of a Roman Census Declaration of AD 47/8," in T. Gagos and R. S. Bagnall, eds., *Essays and Texts in Honor of J. David Thomas* (*American Studies in Papyrology* 42), 99–113.

Rauh, N. (1989) "Finance and Estate Sales in Republican Rome," *Aevum* 63: 45–76.

Rawson, E. (1985) *Intellectual Life in the Late Roman Republic.* Baltimore.

Rea, J. (1971) "Notes on Some III^d and IVth Century Documents," *Chronique d'Égypte* 46: 142–57.

(1977) "A New Version of *P.Yale* inv. 299," *Zeitschrift für Papyrologie und Epigraphik* 27: 151–6.

Reinach, T. (1906) "Inscriptions d'Aphrodisias," *Revue des études grecques* 19: 205–98.

Reinhold, M. (1971) "Usurpation of Status and Status Symbols in the Roman Empire," *Historia* 20: 275–302.

Reuter, M. (1999) "Ein hölzernes Schreibtäfelchen mit Quittung vom 5. April 130 n.Chr. aus dem *vicus* von Hanau-Salisberg," *Germania* 77: 283–93.

Reynolds, J. (1982) *Aphrodisias and Rome* (*Journal of Roman Studies Monographs* 1). London.

Rhodes, P. J. (1980) "Athenian Democracy after 403 BC," *Classical Journal* 75: 305–23.

(2001a) "Public Documents in the Greek States: Archives and Inscriptions Part I," *Greece and Rome* 48: 33–44.

(2001b) "Public Documents in the Greek States: Archives and Inscriptions Part II," *Greece and Rome* 48: 136–53.

Riccobono, S., J. K. Wylie, and B. Beinart (1957) *Stipulation and the Theory of Contract.* Amsterdam.

Richardson, J. S. (1983) "The *Tabula Contrebiensis*: Roman Law in Spain in the Early First Century BC," *Journal of Roman Studies* 73: 33–41.

Ricl, M. (1991) "Meonski πιττάκιον u Ženevi?" *Živa Antika* (special issue 9): 201–6.

(1995) *Svest o Grehu u Maloazijskim Kultovima Rimskog Doba.* Belgrade.

Riepl, W. (1913) *Das Nachrichtenwesen des Altertums, mit besonderer Rücksicht auf die Römer.* Leipzig and Berlin.

330 References

Ritner, R. K. (1995) "Egyptian Magical Practice under the Roman Empire," *ANRW* 2.18.5: 3333–79.

Robert, L. (1966) "Inscriptions d'Aphrodisias," *L'Antiquité Classique* 35: 397–432.

Roberts, A. (1999) *Salisbury: Victorian Titan*. London.

Rodríguez Neila, J. F. (1991–2) "Archivos municipales en las provincias occidentales del imperio romano," *Veleia* 8–9: 145–74.

Rohde, G. (1936) *Die Kultsatzungen der römischen Pontifices*. Berlin.

Rosén, H. (1980) "Die Sprachsituation im römischen Palästina," in G. Neumann, ed., *Die Sprachen im römischen Reich der Kaiserzeit* (*Bonner Jahrbücher Beiheft* 40), 220–39. Cologne and Bonn.

Rosen, L. (1989) *The Anthropology of Justice: Law as Culture in Islamic Society*. Cambridge.

Rotondi, G. (1922 [1912]) *Leges Publicae Populi Romani*. Milan.

Rouse, R. H. and M. A. Rouse (1989) "Wax Tablets," *Language & Communication* 9: 175–91.

Rowe, G. (2001) "Trimalchio's World," *Scripta Classica Israelica* 20: 225–45.

Roxan, M. M. (1978) *Roman Military Diplomas 1954–1977* (*Institute of Archaeology Occasional Publication* no. 2). London.

(1985) *Roman Military Diplomas, 1978 to 1984* (*Institute of Archaeology Occasional Publication* no. 9). London.

(1986) "Observations on the Reasons for Changes in Formula in Diplomas circa AD 140," in W. Eck and H. Wolff, eds., *Heer und Integrationspolitik: Die römischen Militärdiplome als historische Quelle*, 265–92. Cologne and Vienna.

(1994) *Roman Military Diplomas 1985–1993* (*Institute of Archaeology Occasional Publication* no. 14). London.

(1996) "An Emperor Rewards his Supporters: The Earliest Extant Diploma Issued by Vespasian," *Journal of Roman Archaeology* 9: 248–56.

Roxan, M. M. and W. Eck (1993) "A Military Diploma of AD 85 for the Rome Cohorts," *Zeitschrift für Papyrologie und Epigraphik* 96: 67–74.

Rüpke, J. (1992) "Wer las Caesars *bella* als *commentarii*?" *Gymnasium* 99: 201–26.

Ruschenbusch, E. (1989) "Drei Beiträge zur öffentlichen *Diaita* in Athen," in F. J. Fernández Nieto, ed., *Symposion 1982: Vorträge zur griechischen und hellenistischen Rechtsgeschichte (Santander)*, 31–40. Cologne.

Russell, D. (1998) "The Panegyrists and their Teachers," in M. Whitby, ed., *The Propaganda of Power: The Role of Panegyric in Late Antiquity*, 17–50. Leiden.

Russu, I. (1975) *Inscripţiile Daciei Romane* I. Bucharest.

Sachers, E. (1932) "*Tabula*," *RE* 4A.2: cols. 1881–6.

Şahin, S. and D. H. French (1987) "Ein Dokument aus Takina," *Epigraphica Anatolica* 10: 133–42.

Saint-Simon, C. H. Comte de (1985 [1714–16]), *Mémoires (1714–1716): Additions au Journal de Dangeau*. Paris.

Salway, B. (2000) "Prefects, *patroni*, and Decurions: A New Perspective on the Album of Canusium," in A. E. Cooley, ed., *The Epigraphic Landscape of Roman Italy* (*Bulletin of the Institute of Classical Studies Supplement* 73), 115–71.

References 331

Salzmann, D. (1984) "Porträtsiegel aus dem *Nomophylakeion* in Kyrene," *Bonner Jahrbücher* 194: 141–66.

Sanders, H. A. (1938) "A Latin Marriage Contract," *Transactions of the American Philological Association* 69: 104–16.

(1939) "A Soldier's Marriage Certificate in Diploma Form," *Proceedings of the American Philosophical Society* 81: 581–90.

(1947) *Latin Papyri in the University of Michigan Collection (P.Mich* VII). Ann Arbor.

Santifaller, L. (1953) *Beiträge zur Geschichte der Beschreibstoffe im Mittelalter mit besonderer Berücksichtigung der päpstlichen Kanzlei 1: Untersuchungen (Mitteilungen des Instituts für österreichische Geschichtsforschung* 16.1). Graz and Cologne.

Saradi-Mendelovici, H. (1988) "L'Enregistrement des actes privés (*insinuatio*) et la disparition des institutions municipales au VIe siècle," *Cahiers des études anciennes* 21: 117–30.

Scheid, J. (1984) "Le Prêtre et le magistrat: réflexions sur les sacerdotes et le droit public à la fin de la République," in C. Nicolet, ed., *Des ordres à Rome*, 243–80. Paris.

(1994) "Les Archives de la piété: réflexions sur les livres sacerdotaux," in S. Demougin, ed., *La Mémoire perdue: à la recherche des archives oubliées, publiques et privées, de la Rome antique* (CNRS, série histoire ancienne et médiévale 30), 173–85.

Schiller, A. A. (1949) "Bureaucracy and the Roman Law," *Seminar* 7: 26–48.

(1978) *Roman Law: Mechanisms of Development*. The Hague.

Schillinger-Häfele, U. (1980) "Ein halbes hölzernes Schreibtäfelchen aus Mainz," *Mainzer Zeitschrift* 75: 215–18.

Schlossmann, S. (1907) Praescriptiones *und* Praescripta Verba: *Wider die Schriftformel des römischen Formularprozesses*. Leipzig.

(1972 [1905]) Litis Contestatio: *Studien zum römischen Zivilprozeß*. Aalen (Leipzig).

Schmidt, J. (1893) *"Album," RE* 1.1: cols. 1332–6.

Schulz, F. (1942) and (1943) "Roman Registers of Births and Birth Certificates," *Journal of Roman Studies* 32: 78–91 and 33: 55–64.

(1946) *History of Roman Legal Science*. Oxford.

Schwind, F. von (1973) *Zur Frage der Publikation im römischen Recht, mit Ausblicken in das altgriechische und ptolemäische Rechtsgebiet*, 2nd edn. (*Münchener Beiträge zur Papyrusforschung und antiken Rechtsgeschichte* 31). Munich.

Searle, J. R. (1969) *Speech Acts: An Essay in the Philosophy of Language*. Cambridge.

Seeck, O. (1900) *"Codicilli," RE* 4.1: cols. 174–83.

Seidl, C. (1996) "Die finanziellen Schwierigkeiten eines Getreidehändlers und der Profit, den die Linguistik daraus ziehen kann," in H. Rosén, ed., *Aspects of Latin: Papers from the Seventh International Colloquium on Latin Linguistics, Jerusalem*, 99–115. Innsbruck.

Seidl, E. (1973) *Rechtsgeschichte Ägyptens als römischer Provinz*. Sankt Augustin.

Serangeli, S. (1982) *Studi sulla revoca del testamento in diritto romano*. Milan.

References

Serfass, A. (2001) "Petition to the Epistrategos Vedius Faustus," *Zeitschrift für Papyrologie und Epigraphik* 134: 183–90.

Seston, W. (1933) "Les Vétérans sans diplômes des légions romains," *Revue de Philologie* (third series) 7: 375–95.

Seyler, H. (1894) *Geschichte der Siegel*. Leipzig.

Sharpe, J. L. (1992) "The Dakhleh Tablets and Some Codicological Considerations," in É. Lalou, ed., *Les Tablettes à écrire de l'antiquité à l'époque moderne (Bibliologia* 12), 127–48. Turnhout.

Sherk, R. K. (1969) *Roman Documents from the Greek East:* Senatus Consulta *and* Epistulae *to the Age of Augustus*. Baltimore.

Sherwin-White, A. N. (1973) "The *Tabula* of Banasa and the *Constitutio Antoniniana*," *Journal of Roman Studies* 63: 86–98.

Shipley, G. and A. Spawforth (1995) "New Imperial Subscripts to the Spartans," *Annual of the British School at Athens* 90: 429–34.

Sickinger, J. (1994) review of R. Thomas (1992), in *Classical Philology* 89: 273–8.
(1999) *Public Records and Archives in Classical Athens*. Chapel Hill.

Simon, D. (1964) *Studien zur Praxis der Stipulationsklausel*. Munich.

Sirat, C. (1992) "Les Tablettes à écrire dans le monde juif," in É. Lalou, ed., *Les Tablettes à écrire de l'antiquité à l'époque moderne (Bibliologia* 12), 53–8. Turnhout.

Sittl, C. (1890) *Die Gebärden der Griechen und Römer*. Leipzig.

Skeat, T. C. and E. P. Wegener (1935) "A Trial Before the Prefect of Egypt Appius Sabinus, *c.* 250 AD," *Journal of Egyptian Archaeology* 21: 224–47.

Slater, N. (1992) "Plautine Negotiations: The *Poenulus* Prologue Unpacked," *Yale Classical Studies* 29: 131–46.

Small, J. P. (1997) *Wax Tablets of the Mind: Cognitive Studies of Memory and Literacy in Classical Antiquity*. London.

Smallwood, E. M. (1967) *Documents Illustrating the Principates of Gaius Claudius and Nero*. Cambridge.

Smith, J. Z. (1987) *To Take Place: Toward Theory in Ritual*. Chicago and London.
(1995) "Trading Places," in M. Meyer and P. Mirecki, eds., *Ancient Magic and Ritual Power*, 13–27. Leiden and New York.

Smith, R. A. (1934–5) "Relics of Londinium," *The British Museum Quarterly* 9: 95–6.

Smith, R. E. (1954) "Latins and the Roman Citizenship in Roman Colonies: Livy 34,42,5–6," *Journal of Roman Studies* 44: 18–20.

Smith, R. R. R. (1999) "Late Antique Portraits in a Public Context: Honorific Statuary at Aphrodisias in Caria, AD 300–600," *Journal of Roman Studies* 89: 155–89.

Smith, W., W. Wayte, and G. E. Marindin (1901) *A Dictionary of Greek and Roman Antiquities*, 3rd edn. London.

Solin, H. (1968) *Eine neue Fluchtafel aus Ostia (Societas Scientiarum Fennica, Commentationes Humanarum Litterarum* 42.3). Helsinki.

Söllner, A. (2001) "Der Kauf einer Sklavin, beurkundet in Ravenna um die Mitte des 2. Jahrhunderts n. Chr.," in H. Bellen and H. Heinen, eds., *Fünfzig*

References

333

Jahre Forschungen zur antiken Sklaverei an der Mainzer Akademie 1950–2000: Miscellanea zum Jubiläum, 83–96. Stuttgart.

Soubie, A. (1973) "Les Preuves dans les plaidoyers des orateurs attiques," *Revue international des droits de l'antiquité* (third series) 20: 171–253.

(1974) "Les Preuves dans les plaidoyers des orateurs attiques (ii)," *Revue international des droits de l'antiquité* (third series) 21: 77–134.

Speidel, M. A. (1996) *Die römischen Schreibtafeln von Vindonissa (Veröffentlichungen der Gesellschaft Pro Vindonissa* 12). Brugg.

Spier, J. (1992) *Ancient Gems and Finger Rings*. Malibu.

Stanojević, O. (1989) Gaius Noster: *Plaidoyer pour Gaius*. Amsterdam.

Ste. Croix, G. E. M. de (1956) "Greek and Roman Accounting," in A. C. Littleton and B. S. Yamey, eds., *Studies in the History of Accounting*, 14–74. Homewood, IL.

Stein, P. (1971) "The Relations Between Grammar and Law in the Early Principate: The Beginnings of Analogy," *La Critica del Testo* 2: 757–69.

Steinacker, H. (1902) "Zum Zusammenhang zwischen antikem und frühmittelalterlichem Registerwesen," *Wiener Studien* 24: 301–8.

(1927) *Die antiken Grundlagen der frühmittelalterlichen Privaturkunde*. Leipzig and Berlin.

Steiner, D. T. (1994) *The Tyrant's Writ: Myths and Images of Writing in Ancient Greece*. Princeton.

Steinwenter, A. (1915) *Beiträge zum öffentlichen Urkundenwesen der Römer*. Graz.

Strachan-Davidson, J. L. (1912) *Problems of the Roman Criminal Law*. Oxford.

Stühff, G. (1966) *Vulgarrecht im Kaiserrecht unter besonderer Berücksichtigung der Gesetzgebung Konstantins des Großen (Forschungen zum römischen Recht* 21). Weimar.

Suolahti, J. (1963) *The Roman Censors: A Study on Social Structure*. Helsinki.

(1975) "Unknown Source on Ancient Stenography," *Arctos* 9: 109–10.

Svenbro, J. (1993), *Phrasikleia: An Anthropology of Reading in Ancient Greece* (trans. J. Lloyd). Ithaca.

Swarney, P. R. (1993) "Social Status and Social Behaviour as Criteria in Judicial Proceedings in the Late Republic," in B. Halpern and D. W. Hobson, eds., *Law, Politics and Society in the Ancient Mediterranean World*, 137–55. Sheffield.

Szegedy-Maszak, A. (1981) *The Nomoi of Theophrastus*. New York.

Talamanca, M. (1964) "Documentazione e documento (diritto romano)," *Enciclopedia del diritto* 13: 548–78. Milan.

Talbert, R. J. A. (1984) *The Senate of Imperial Rome*. Princeton.

(1988) "Commodus as Diplomat in an Extract from the *Acta Senatus*," *Zeitschrift für Papyrologie und Epigraphik* 71: 137–47.

Tambiah, S. (1968) "The Magical Power of Words," *Man* n.s. 3: 175–208.

(1985) "A Performative Approach to Ritual," in his *Culture, Thought and Social Action: An Anthropological Perspective*, 123–66. Cambridge, MA.

Taubenschlag, R. (1951) "Les Publications officielles du stratège dans l'Egypte greco-romain," *The Journal of Juristic Papyrology* 5: 155–60.

334   *References*

(1955) *The Law of Greco-Roman Egypt in the Light of the Papyri 322 BC–640 AD*, 2nd edn. Warsaw.

Täubler, E. (1913) *Imperium Romanum: Studien zur Entwicklungsgeschichte des römischen Reichs.* Leipzig.

Taylor, L. R. (1966) *Roman Voting Assemblies from the Hannibalic War to the Dictatorship of Caesar* (Jerome Lectures 8). Ann Arbor.

Teitler, H. (1985) Notarii and Exceptores: *An Inquiry into Role and Significance of Shorthand Writers in the Imperial and Ecclesiastical Bureaucracy of the Roman Empire (from the Early Principate to c. 450 AD).* Amsterdam.

Teixidor, J. (1990) "Deux documents syriaques du IIIe siècle après J.-C, provenant du moyen Euphrate," *Comptes rendus de l'académie des inscriptions et belles-lettres* (no volume): 145–66.

Tellegen-Couperus, O. E. (1982) *Testamentary Succession in the Constitutions of Diocletian.* Zutphen.

Tengström, E. (1962) *Die Protokollierung der* Collatio Carthaginensis (*Studia Graeca et Latina Gothoburgensia* 14). Göteborg.

Thielmann, G. (1961) *Die römische Privatauktion* (*Berliner juristische Abhandlungen* 4). Berlin.

Thilo, R. M. (1980) *Der* Codex accepti et expensi *im römischen Recht: Ein Beitrag zur Lehre von der Litteralobligation.* Göttingen.

Thomas, J. A. C. (1976) *Textbook of Roman Law.* Amsterdam, New York, and London.

Thomas, J. D. (1983) "Subscriptions to Petitions to Officials in Roman Egypt," in E. Van't Dack, ed., *Egypt and the Hellenistic World: Proceedings of the International Colloquium, Leuven* (*Studia Hellenistica* 27), 369–82. Louvain.

Thomas, R. (1989) *Oral Tradition and Written Record in Classical Athens.* Cambridge.

(1992) *Literacy and Orality in Ancient Greece.* Cambridge.

Thür, G. (1987) "Neuere Untersuchungen zum Prozeßrecht der griechischen Poleis," in D. Simon, ed., *Akten des 26. deutschen Rechtshistorikertages* (Ius Commune: *Veröffentlichungen des Max-Planck-Instituts für europäische Rechtsgeschichte* Sonderheft 30), 467–84. Frankfurt.

Tiersma, P. M. (1999) *Legal Language.* Chicago and London.

Timpanaro, S. (1988) "Alcuni tipi di sinonimi in asindeto in latino arcaico e loro sopravvivenze in latino classico," *Rivista di filologia e di istruzione classica* 116: 257–97.

Timpe, D. (1988) "Mündlichkeit und Schriftlichkeit als Basis der frührömischen Überlieferung," in J. von Ungern-Sternberg and H. Reinau, eds., *Vergangenheit in mündlicher Überlieferung* (*Colloquium Rauricum* 1), 266–86. Stuttgart.

Tjäder, J.-O. (1955) *Die nichtliterarischen lateinischen Papyri Italiens aus der Zeit 445–700* I. Uppsala.

(1982) *Die nichtliterarischen lateinischen Papyri Italiens aus der Zeit 445–700* II. Stockholm.

References

(1985) "Alcune osservazioni sulla prassi documentaria a Ravenna nel vi. secolo," in G. G. Archi, ed., *Il mondo del diritto nell'epoca giustinianea: caratteri e problematiche*, 23–42. Bologna and Ravenna.

Todd, S. C. (1990) "The Purpose of Evidence in Athenian Courts," in P. Cartledge *et al.* eds., *Nomos: Essays in Athenian Law, Politics and Society*, 19–39. Cambridge.

(1993) *The Shape of Athenian Law*. Oxford.

(1996) "Lysias Against Nikomachos: The Fate of the Expert in Athenian Law," in L. Foxhall and A. D. E. Lewis, eds., *Greek Law in its Political Setting: Justifications Not Justice*, 101–31. Cambridge.

Tomlin, R. S. O. (1988) "The Curse Tablets," in B. Cunliffe, ed., *The Temple of Sulis Minerva at Bath 2: The Finds from the Sacred Spring (Oxford University Committee for Archaeology Monograph* no. 16), 59–277. Oxford.

(1991) "The Writing Tablets," in T. G. Padley and S. Winterbottom, eds., *The Wooden, Leather and Bone Objects from Castle Street, Carlisle: Excavations 1981–2 (Cumberland and Westmorland Antiquarian and Archaeological Society Research Series* 5 fasc. 3), 209–18. Carlisle.

(1992) "The Twentieth Legion at Wroxeter and Carlisle in the First Century: The Epigraphic Evidence," *Britannia* 23: 141–58.

(1996a) "A Five-Acre Wood in Roman Kent," in J. Bird *et al.*, eds., *Interpreting Roman London: Papers in Memory of Hugh Chapman (Oxbow Monograph* 58), 209–15. Oakville, CT.

(1996b) "The Vindolanda Tablets [review article]," *Britannia* 27: 459–63.

(1998) "Roman Manuscripts from Carlisle: The Ink-Written Tablets," *Britannia* 29: 31–84.

(1999) "Curse Tablets in Roman Britain," in (no editor) *XI congresso internazionale di Epigrafia Greca e Latin (Roma)* 1: 553–65. Rome.

Tomulescu, C. (1983) "Éléments vulgaires romains dans la pratique juridique de la Dacie," *Journal of Juristic Papyrology* 19: 13–20.

Torelli, M. (1982) *Typology and Structure of Roman Historical Reliefs* (Jerome Lectures 14). Ann Arbor.

Toutain, J. (1900) "*Votum*," in C. Daremberg and E. Saglio, eds., *Dictionnaire des antiquités grecques et romaines d'après les textes et les monuments* 5: 969–78. Paris.

Treggiari, S. M. (1991) *Roman Marriage*: Iusti Coniuges *from the Time of Cicero to the Time of Ulpian*. Oxford.

Tupet, A.-M. (1986) "Rites magiques dans l'antiquité romaine," *ANRW* 2.16.3: 2591–675.

Turner, E. G. (1968) *Greek Papyri: An Introduction*. Oxford.

(1978) "The Terms Recto and Verso: The Anatomy of the Papyrus Roll," *Actes du XVᵉ congrès international de papyrologie 1 (Papyrologica Bruxellensis* 16). Brussels.

Turpin, W. (1981) "*Apokrimata, Decreta*, and the Roman Legal Procedure," *Bulletin of the American Society of Papyrologists* 18: 145–60.

References

(1991) "Imperial Subscriptions and the Administration of Justice," *Journal of Roman Studies* 81: 101–18.

Valette-Cagnac, E. (1997) *La Lecture à Rome: rites et pratiques.* Paris.

Van Oven, J. C. (1958) "La Stipulation a-t-elle dégénéré?" *Tijdschrift voor Rechtsgeschiedenis/Revue d'histoire du droit* 26: 409–36.

Vandorpe, K. (1995) *Breaking the Seal of Secrecy: Sealing Practices in Greco-Roman and Byzantine Egypt Based on Greek, Demotic and Latin Papyrological Evidence (Uitgaven vanwege de Stichting 'Het Leids Papyrologisch Instituut'* 18). Leiden.

Versnel, H. S.(1991a) "Beyond Cursing: The Appeal to Justice in Judicial Prayers," in C. A. Faraone and D. Obbink, eds., Magika Hiera: *Ancient Greek Magic and Religion*, 60–106. Oxford.

(1991b) "Some Reflections on the Relationship Magic – Religion," *Numen* 38: 177–97.

Vetter, E. (1953) *Handbuch der italischen Dialekte 1.* Heidelberg.

Veyne, P. (1983) "'Titulus praelatus': offrande, solennisation et publicité dans les ex-voto gréco-romains," *Revue Archéologique* (no volume): 281–300.

Vial, C. (1988) "La Conservation des contrats à Délos pendant l'indépendance," in D. Knoepfler, ed., *Comptes et inventaires dans le cité grecque: actes du colloque international d'épigraphie tenu à Neuchâtel du 23 au 26 septembre 1986 en l'honneur de J. Tréheux*, 49–60. Neuchâtel.

Vidal, H. (1965) "Le Dépôt *in aede*," *Revue historique de droit français et étranger* (fourth series) 43: 545–87.

Viereck, P. (1888) *Sermo graecus quo senatus populusque Romanus magistratusque populi Romani usque ad Tiberii Caesaris aetatem in scriptis publicis usi sunt examinatur.* Göttingen.

Vinogradoff, P. (1922) *Outlines of Historical Jurisprudence 2: The Jurisprudence of the Greek City.* Oxford.

Vittinghoff, F. (1936) *Der Staatsfeind in der römischen Kaiserzeit: Untersuchungen zur 'damnatio memoriae'.* Berlin.

Voigt, M. (1888) "Ueber die Bankiers, die Buchführung und die Litteralobligation der Römer," *Abhandlungen der königlich sächsischen Gesellschaft der Wissenschaften, philologisch-historische Klasse* 10: 515–77.

Volkmann, H. (1967) "Kritische Bemerkungen zu den Inschriften des vatikanischen Obelisken," *Gymnasium* 74: 501–8.

Vollgraf, G. (1917) "*De tabella emptionis aetatis Traiani nuper in Frisia reperta*," *Mnemosyne* 45: 341–52.

Voß, W. E. (1982) *Recht und Rhetorik in den Kaisergesetzen der Spätantike: Eine Untersuchung zum nachklassischen Kauf- und Übereignungsrecht.* Frankfurt.

Wachsmuth, D. (1967) ΠΟΜΠΙΜΟΣ Ο ΔΑΙΜΩΝ. Berlin.

Walbank, F. W. (1957) *A Historical Commentary on Polybius* II. Oxford.

(1979) *A Historical Commentary on Polybius* III. Oxford.

Wallace, S. L. (1938) *Taxation in Egypt from Augustus to Diocletian.* Princeton.

Watson, A. (1965) *The Law of Obligations in the Later Roman Republic.* Oxford.

(1968) *The Law of Property in the Later Roman Republic.* Oxford.

References   337

(1971) *Roman Private Law Around 200 BC.* Edinburgh.

(1974) *Law Making in the Later Roman Republic.* Oxford.

ed. (1985) *The Digest of Justinian.* Philadelphia.

(1991a [1960]) "The Form and Nature of *acceptilatio* in Classical Roman Law," in his *Studies in Roman Private Law*, 193–218 (first published in *Revue international des droits de l'antiquité* [third series] 7: 391–416). London.

(1991b [1964]) "*Apochatum pro uncis duabus*," in his *Studies in Roman Private Law*, 185–92 (first published in *Revue internationale des droits de l'antiquité* [third series] 10: 248–54). London.

(1992) *The State, Law and Religion: Pagan Rome.* Athens, GA.

(1993) *International Law in Archaic Rome: War and Religion.* Baltimore.

Weinstock, S. (1934) "*Templum*," *RE* 5A.1: cols. 480–5.

Weiß, E. (1912) "*Recitatio* und *responsum* im römischen Provinzialprozeß, ein Beitrag zum Gerichtsgebrauch," *Zeitschrift der Savigny-Stiftung für Rechtsgeschichte, romanistische Abteilung* 33: 212–39.

(1916) "Peregrinische Manzipationsakte," *Zeitschrift der Savigny-Stiftung für Rechtsgeschichte, romanistische Abteilung* 37: 136–76.

(1929) "*Stipulatio*," *RE* 3A.2: cols. 2540–8.

(1948) "*Professio* und *testatio* nach der *Lex Aelia Sentia* und der *Lex Papia Poppaea*," ΠΡΑΓΜΑΤΕΙΑΙ ΤΗΣ ΑΚΑΔΗΜΙΑΣ ΑΘΗΝΩΝ 14: 1–9.

(1953) "Schriftlichkeit und Mündlichkeit in der römischen Rechtsbildung," in G. Moschetti, ed., *Atti del congresso internazionale di diritto romano e di storia del diritto, Verona*, II: 51–60. Milan.

Welles, C. B. (1938) "The *Immunitas* of the Roman Legionaries in Egypt," *Journal of Roman Studies* 28: 41–9.

Welles, C. B., R. O. Fink, and J. F. Gilliam (1959) *The Excavations at Dura-Europus 5.1: The Parchments and Papyri.* New Haven.

Wenger, L. (1923) "*Signum*," *RE* 2A.2: cols. 2361–448.

(1953) *Die Quellen des römischen Rechts.* Vienna.

Wesener, G. (1962) "*Promulgatio*," *RE* suppl. 9: cols. 1239–41.

Westermann, W. L. and A. A. Schiller (1954) Apokrimata: *Decisions of Septimius Severus on Legal Matter*s. New York.

White, P. (1997) "Julius Caesar and the Publication of *Acta* in Late Republican Rome," *Chiron* 27: 73–84.

Wieacker, F. (1955) *Vulgarismus und Klassizismus im Recht der Spätantike (Sitzungsberichte der Heidelberger Akademie der Wissenschaften, philosophisch-historische Klasse 1955.3).* Heidelberg.

(1956) "Zum Ritual der *adoptio*," *Eos* 48: 579–89.

(1964) "*Furtum Tabularum*," in A. Guarino and L. Labruna, eds., *Synteleia Vincenzo Arangio-Ruiz (Biblioteca de Labeo 2)* I: 562–76. Naples.

(1988) *Römische Rechtsgeschichte (Handbuch der Altertumswissenschaft 3.1.1).* Munich.

Wiedemann, T. (1986) "The *Fetiales*: A Reconsideration," *Classical Quarterly* 36: 478–90.

338 *References*

Wiegels, R. (1982) "Drei römische Kleinschriften aus Sulz, Gomadingen und Riegel," *Fundberichte aus Baden-Württemberg* 7: 347–55.

Wilcken, U. (1894) "ΥΠΟΜΝΗΜΑΤΙΣΜΟΙ," *Philologus* 53: 80–126.

——— (1908) "Papyrus-Urkunden," *Archiv für Papyrusforschung* 4: 526–68.

——— (1920) "Zu den Kaiserreskripten," *Hermes* 55: 1–42.

——— (1930) "Zur *Propositio Libellorum*," *Archiv für Papyrusforschung* 9: 15–23.

Wilhelm, A. (1909) *Beiträge zur griechischen Inschriftenkunde*. Vienna.

Wilkins, J. B. (1994) "The Iguvine Tablets: Problems in the Interpretation of Ritual Text," in C. Malone and S. Stoddart, eds., *Territory, Time and State: The Archaeological Development of the Great Basin*, 152–72. Cambridge.

——— (1996) "Urban Language Ritual," in J. B. Wilkins, ed., *Approaches to the Study of Ritual: Italy and the Ancient Mediterranean (Accordia Specialist Studies on the Mediterranean* 2), 123–41. London.

Williams, G. W. (1982) "The Genesis of Poetry in Rome," in E. J. Kenney and W. V. Clausen, eds., *The Cambridge History of Classical Literature 2.1: The Early Republic*, 53–9. Cambridge.

Williams, W. (1974) "The *Libellus* Procedure and the Severan Papyri," *Journal of Roman Studies* 64: 86–103.

——— (1975) "Formal and Historical Aspects of Two New Documents of Marcus Aurelius," *Zeitschrift für Papyrologie und Epigraphik* 17: 37–78.

——— (1976) "Two Imperial Pronouncements Reclassified," *Zeitschrift für Papyrologie und Epigraphik* 22: 235–45.

——— (1980) "The Publication of Imperial Subscripts," *Zeitschrift für Papyrologie und Epigraphik* 40: 283–94.

——— (1986) "Epigraphic Texts of Imperial Subscripts: A Survey," *Zeitschrift für Papyrologie und Epigraphik* 66: 181–207.

Williamson, C. H. (1983) "Law-Making in the *Comitia* of Republican Rome: The Processes of Drafting and Disseminating, Recording and Retrieving Laws and Plebiscites" (unpublished dissertation, University of London).

——— (1987a) "Monuments of Bronze: Roman Legal Documents on Bronze Tablets," *Classical Antiquity* 6: 160–83.

——— (1987b) "A Roman Law from Narbonne," *Athenaeum* 65: 173–89.

——— (1995) "The Display of Law and Archival Practice in Rome," in H. Solin, O. Salomies, and U. Liertz, eds., *Acta colloquii epigraphici Latini: Helsingiae 3.–6. Sept. 1991 habiti (Societas Scientiarum Fennica, Commentationes Humanarum Litterarum* 104), 239–51. Helsinki.

Wilmanns, J. C. (1981) "Die Doppelurkunde von Rottweil und ihr Beitrag zum Städtewesen in Obergermanien," *Epigraphische Studien* 12: 1–182.

Wilson, J.-P. (1997–8) "The 'Illiterate Trader'?" *Bulletin of the Institute of Classical Studies* 42: 29–53.

Wingo, E. O. (1972) *Latin Punctuation in the Classical Age (Janua Linguarum, Series Practica* 133). The Hague.

Winkler, A. (1958) "Gaius iii.92 anlässlich der These von B. Nicholas: Nur die hier genannten Stipulationsformen seien bis zum Jahre 472 zugelassen gewesen," *Revue internationale des droits de l'antiquité* (third series) 5: 603–36.

References

339

Wiseman, T. P. (1969) "The Census in the First Century BC," *Journal of Roman Studies* 59: 59–75.

Wissowa, G. (1902) *Religion und Kultus der Römer* (*Handbuch der Altertumswissenschaft* 5.4). Munich.

Wolf, J. G. (1984) "Die *mancipatio:* Roms ältestes Rechtsgeschäft," *Jahrbuch der Heidelberger Akademie der Wissenschaften* (no volume): 41.

Wolf, J. G. and J. A. Crook (1989) *Rechtsurkunden in Vulgärlatein aus den Jahren 37–39 n. Chr. (Abhandlungen der Heidelberger Akademie der Wissenschaften, philosophisch-historische Klasse* 3). Heidelberg.

Wolff, H. J. (1937) "Zwei Juristische Papyri der University of Michigan," *Aegyptus* 17: 463–78.

(1978) *Das Recht der griechischen Papyri Ägyptens in der Zeit der Ptolemaeer und des Prinzipats 2: Organisation und Kontrolle des privaten Rechtsverkehrs (Handbuch der Altertumswissenschaft* 10.5.2). Munich.

(1980) "Römisches Provinzialrecht in der Provinz Arabia (Rechtspolitik als Instrument der Beherrschung)," *ANRW* 2.13: 763–806.

Wolters, P. (1903) "*Loco Sigilli*," in (no editor) *Mélanges Perrot: recueil de mémoires concernant l'archéologie classique la littérature et l'histoire anciennes*, 333–40. Paris.

Woolf, G. (1998) *Becoming Roman: The Origins of Provincial Civilization in Gaul.* Cambridge.

Wörrle, M. (1975) "Zwei neue griechische Inschriften aus Myra zur Verwaltung Lykiens in der Kaiserzeit," in J. Borchhardt *et al., Myra: Eine lykische Metropole in antiker und byzantinischer Zeit (Istanbuler Forschungen* 30), 254–300. Berlin.

Wright, R. P. (1958) "Roman Britain in 1957: Inscriptions," *Journal of Roman Studies* 48: 130–55.

Yadin, Y. (1978) *Bar-Kokhba: The Rediscovery of the Legendary Hero of the Second Jewish Revolt Against Rome.* New York.

Yadin, Y., J. Greenfield, and A. Yardeni (1994) "Babatha's Ketubba," *Israel Exporation Journal* 44: 75–99.

Yardeni, A. (2000a) *Textbook of Aramaic, Hebrew and Nabataean Documentary Texts from the Judaean Desert and Related Material B. Translation – Palaeography – Concordance.* Jerusalem.

(2000b) "Notes on Two Unpublished Nabataean Deeds from Naḥal Ḥever – P.Yadin 2 and 3," in L. H. Schiffman, E. Tov, and J. C. VanderKam, eds., *The Dead Sea Scrolls Fifty Years After their Discovery: Proceedings of the Jerusalem Congress*, 862–74. Jerusalem.

(2001) "The Decipherment and Restoration of Legal Texts from the Judaean Desert: A Reexamination of *Papyrus Starcky* (*P.Yadin* 36)," *Scripta Classica Israelica* 20: 121–37.

Youtie, H. C. (1975) "ΥΠΟΓΡΑΦΕΥΣ: The Social Impact of Illiteracy in Graeco-Roman Egypt," *Zeitschrift für Papyrologie und Epigraphik* 17: 201–21.

Zangemeister, K. (1898) *Corpvs Inscriptionvm Latinarvm 4: Inscriptionvm parietariarvm pompeianarvm supplementvm. Pars I: Tabvlae Ceratae Pompeiis repertae annis MDCCCLXXV et MDCCCLXXXVII.* Berlin.

340 *References*

Zanker, P. (1995) *The Mask of Socrates: The Image of the Intellectual in Antiquity.* Berkeley.

Zimmermann, R. (1996) *The Law of Obligations: Roman Foundations of the Civilian Tradition.* Oxford.

Zorzetti, N. (1990) "The *Carmina Convivalia,*" in O. Murray, ed., *Sympotica: A Symposium on the Symposion,* 289–307. Oxford.

Zulueta, F. de (1945) *The Roman Law of Sale.* Oxford.

   (1953) *The Institutes of Gaius Part 2: Commentary.* Oxford.

Index

abbreviation, as characteristic of *tabula*-language 30, 44, 63, 64, 65, 66; in inscriptions 65; in legal language 65, 82; in *senatusconsulta* 111; *see also publicae notationes*

abstract conceptualization, as juristic argument, *see* essence

accensus ("clerk") 98

acceptilationes ("discharges of obligation") 126, 142, 144, 146, 150, 157, 159, 183, 208; Campanian, akin to "unitary acts" 145; receipts modelled on 134, 144

accounts, Roman, financial 107, 134, 137; language in 61, 138; recitation of 86; style 52; written 39

acta ("record") 32, 243, 244, 245, 246, 247, 248, 252, 277, 282, 287; entering documents and testimony into, 241–9; municipal 285, 292; of magistrates, *see also gesta* and *hypomnemata*

acta diurna 30, 31, 32, 33

acta publica 30

acta senatus 31

acta urbis 30

actio auctoritatis (in mancipation) 42

adnotatio 280

adoption (of children) 114, 265

adversaria ("day-books") 33; *see also ephemerides*

Aelius Paetus (S. Aelius Paetus, jurist) 81

aerarium, as depository for *senatusconsulta* 110, 111

Aeschines, on written agreements 14, 21

agreement (*conventum*), written 39

alba, see tablets, Roman, whitened

Albius 220

Albucilla 228

Alfius Caecilian, *see* Caecilian

alliteration, as element of *carmen*-style 45, 46, 47, 49, 52, 53, 55, 69

Allobroges 222

altar of Domitius Ahenobarbus (so-called) 94

altars, labelled as fulfilling vows 101

amicitia 97

Ammianus Marcellinus, on Dura 203

anaglypha Traiani 110

annales ("annals") 32

annales maximi 32

antestatus ("chief witness") 160, 181

Antoninus Pius (T. Aelius Antoninus Caesar Pius, emperor), on *promissio* of interest 260

Antony (M. Antonius) 31

apographe (ἀπογραφή, Egyptian census-registration) 233

Apuleius, on proconsul reading decision 88; on similarity of priests and magicians 79; story of Telephron 69; trial for magic 238

Arabia, documents from, 188–93

arbitration, Roman, documents of 136, 177; on bronze tablet 26

archaic language, on Roman tablets 44, 60, 61, 62, 63, 70; *see also certa verba*

archaizing language, on Roman tablets 44, 47, 61, 62, 63, 70; *see also concepta verba*

archives, Andros 18; Dura-Europos 204; Egypt 18, 186, 212, and *see also* library of Hadrian, Nanaion, and Patrica; Greek, under Roman rule 186; Myra 184, 185; Nikopolis 18; Paros 18; Priene 18; Roman provincial in general, 176; Seleucia 18; Tenos 18

Aristotle, on importance of those guarding the contract 15

Arval Brethren 31, 60, 61, 77

assonance, as element of *carmen*-style 45

asyndeton 7; as characterizing an artistic depiction 94; as element of *carmen*-style 45, 52, 55, 59

Ataecina Proserpina of Turibriga 54

Ateius Capito (C. Ateius Capito, jurist), on rings and sealing 154

atrium Libertatis 29

atrium magnum (Alexandria) 172

341

342   *Index*

attestation of birth, *see* tablets, Roman, of attestation of illegitimate birth
auction 137
auctor (in mancipation) 42
auctoritas 10, 33, 34, 36, 90; imperial 5, 289; in mancipation 42
augurs 24, 76
Augustus (C. Imperator Julius Caesar Octavianus Augustus, emperor), denounces Julia 87; plans to read vow 102; pronounces sentence on Claudius 88
Aurelius, Marcus (M. [Aelius] Aurelius Verus Caesar, emperor), recites *oratio* 89; recites prayer from memory 77
auspices 24, 98
Aulus Gellius, see Gellius
Austin, J. L. 73
authority 5, 10, 12; through archaic or archaizing language 59
autograph 5, 172, 179, 180, 204, 231, 238, 274, 292, 295
Avroman (Kurdistan) 188

Babatha 94, 176, 192, 202
Balbutius 224
bankers 27, 124, 126
basilica 172
Baths of Trajan (Rome), as place for posting 201
biblidia (βιβλίδια, "petitions") 196, 211, 212, 237
biblion (βιβλίον, "book"), as papyrus double-document 201; in court 237
bibliophylax (βιβλιοφύλαξ) 235, 236
bibloi (βίβλοι, "books") 13
Bloch, M. 44
bona fides ("good faith") legal acts 5, 122, 132, 133, 140, 148, 150, 154, 287, 295; written, 151, 154, 168, 177, 248, 278
bonorum possessio ("possession of goods") 165, 175, 212, 268, 269, 273; *see also* tablets, Roman, of request for *bonorum possessio*
books, *see biblion, bibloi,* and *libri*
boundary-disputes, decisions in 88
bronze, favored medium for laws, dedications, edicts 102; for *senatusconsulta* 111; *see also* tablets, Roman, bronze
Brutus (M. Junius Brutus = Q. Servilius Caepio Junianus Brutus) 226

Caecilian (Alfius Caecilian) 244, 245, 246
Caecilius Jucundus (L. Caecilius Jucundus) 126; tablets of, *see* chapter six *passim*
Caesar (C. Julius Caesar), enrolls "foreigners" in senate 66; publishes *acta* 31; recites *carmen* 71; refuses title of king 31; writes Pompey into will 41

Calpurnius Piso (Cn. Calpurnius Piso) 229
Camodeca, G. 132
Campania 7, 121, 124, 125, 126, 127, 134; *see also* Herculaneum, Murecine, Pompeii, and Puteoli
Campanian tablets, *see* chapter six *passim*
Capitolium 27, 28, 54, 97
Capua 135
Carlisle, tablets from 178
carmen 44, 71, 72, 73, 77, 98, 106, 297
carmen-style 45, 54, 56, 115; *see also* alliteration; assonance; asyndeton; end-rhyme; figura etymologica; pleonasm; precision; repetition
Cassiodorus (Magnus Aurelius Cassiodorus Senator), on delay caused by writing on tablets 30
Catiline (L. Sergius Catilina) 111
Cato the Elder (M. Porcius Cato), gives example of prayer 45, 46; his social position 90; on tablet of pontifex maximus 25; paradigms for contracts, 38; records speeches on (and reads from) *tabulae* 89
Catullus (C. Valerius Catullus), on marriage as *foedus* 71
cautiones (written stipulations), in court 237; on tablets 41, 109
"celestial letters" 292
Celsus (P. Iuventius Celsus Titus Aufidius Hoenius Severianus, jurist), on stipulation 256, 257
censors, prayer for lustration from *tabulae* 77; *see also* tablets, Roman, censors'
census 92; as "unitary act" 94; tablets in 92, 94, 95; visual depiction of, *see* altar of Domitius Ahenobarbus
census-return, from Egypt 190
centumviral court 81
ceremonial, in cursing 77; lack of in Greek legal documents 13, 17
ceremonial act 6, 9, 10, 11, 24, 37, 74, 76, 90, 91; recitation in 74, 76
ceremonial act (legal) 84, 112, 118, 120, 121, 168, 216, 254; becomes petitionary 213
certa verba ("fixed words") 38, 62, 63, 75, 80, 81, 83, 84, 121, 207, 254, 269
Cethegus (C. Cornelius Cethegus) 222
Charisius (Flavius Sosipater Charisius, grammarian), on verses and hymns on *libri lintei* 54
charta, see papyrus
cheirographon (χειρόγραφον, "note of hand") 17
chirograph-style 133, 140, 148, 152, 159, 208
chirographs, documentary forms in Campania 148
chirographum 133, 145, 151

Index 343

Christian martyr-acts, 243; decisions in 88
Chrysostom, John, on reading Bible aloud 90
Cicero (M. Tullius Cicero), denunciation of
Verres's financial accounts 30, 52; description
of jurisconsult 82, 83; has *senatusconsultum
ultimum* 111; on Albius's accounts 220; on
archaic language 61; on archaic language in
censors' tablets 60; on archaic language in
financial accounts 61; on bad faith of
Catilinarian conspirators 222; on census 93,
94, 96, 254; on *commentarii* 33; on *ephemerides*
226; on dedication of shrine to *Libertas* 62, 76;
on financial tablets in Gaul 109; on learning
Twelve Tables 68, 71; on letters in court 226;
on Lucceius's testimony 223; on Numidicus's
accounts 221; on parallels *lex*/testament 71; on
psephismata in court 226; on Pythius's sale of
country property 109; on Q. Roscius's
accounts 33, 34, 221; on Quintus's sealing-ring
155, 162; on reading his own speeches in court
227; on reciting one's own *codex* and
day-books in court 220; on style of treaties
and *leges* 49; on tablet sealed by disreputable
person 224; on tablets as proxies for authors
220; on tablets grasping *fides* 221; on tablets in
court 219, 226; on tablets of pontifex maximus
31; on testimony written on papyrus 227; on
Verres's accounts 221; on writing in legal
business 38, 39, 40; recites Verres's provincial
edict 86; use of word *tabula* 30
Cincius (L. Cincius, jurist and grammarian), on
nuncupated vows 28
civil procedure, Roman, *see* formulary procedure
and *legis actio* procedure
Classicus (Caecilius Classicus) 231
Claudius (Tiberius Claudius Nero Germanicus,
emperor), judgment passed on 88;
pronounces judgments 89
Claudius Caecus (Ap. Claudius Caecus) 81
Claudius Pulcher (C. Claudius Pulcher, brother
of Clodius Pulcher) 99
Clodius Pulcher (P. Clodius Pulcher) 62, 99
codex 22; *senatusconsulta* bundled in 111
codex of Justinian 119; on nuptial tablets 119; on
birth-registration tablets 119
codicilli ("little *codices*") 1, 22, 77; as markers of
magisterial status in art 77; of appointment
77, 292; to wills 271
coemptio (a form of fictitious sale), marriage or
divorce by 114
cognitio procedure 122; evidence in 217
Cologne, tablets from 177
combinational acts 125, 133, 139, 147, 157, 180,
181, 208
combinational documents 139, 142, 145,
284

comitia centuriata, procedure for making laws in
97; words used to summon 62
commendationes ("recommendations") 224;
see also laudationes
commentarii ("commentaries" or "book
commentaries," *libri commentarii*) 30, 32, 33;
of augurs 33; of emperor 170; used in court
228
compensatory reasoning, in formal acts, *see*
formality, compensation for failures in; in
informal acts 279
compromissa ("compromises") 135, 278, 279
concepta verba ("modulated words") 38, 62, 63,
69, 70, 81, 83, 84, 121, 267, 269
conceptio (as definition of stipulation) 254,
257
condere ("to establish," used of *leges*) 111
concilium plebis 97
conficere ("to set down carefully") 43
consilium ("council") 218
Constantine (Flavius Valerius Constantinus,
emperor), on donation 281, 282, 283; on sale
284, 285, 286
constituitive acts 108, 112; tablet in 108; *see also*
accounts, Roman, financial and
senatusconsulta
continuus actus ("uninterrupted act") 116, 117,
255, 285
contio (pre-*comitia* meeting) 86, 97
contract, Athenian 13, 14, 15; Roman 6; Roman,
parodied 66
contract *litteris* 108, 110, 112, 259; tablet in 108,
110, 112
contractus (used for legal documents) 167, 168
contrarius actus ("opposing act") 42, 144
conventio ("agreement") 149, 152, 180
copies, attested 134, 136, 170; in Egypt 196; in
Judaea and Arabia 196
court-records, as proof 243; *see also acta* and
hypomnemata
courts, Athenian, 13; Roman, 3, 6, and *see*
chapter eight *passim*; Roman, governors'
192
Crassus (M. Licinius Crassus) 226
cretio (acceptance of inheritance) 175; *see also*
tablets, Roman, of *cretio*
criminal procedure, Roman 84; *see also*
cognitio-procedure
curse-tablet, to Ataecina Proserpina of Turibriga
54
curse-tablets, Athenian 78; Roman, 28, 43, 55,
70, 78, 105; Roman, as accretive 105; Roman,
as legalistic 106, 107; Roman, ceremonial in
77, 105; Roman, physical contexts of 55;
Roman, style and syntax 54, 55, 103,
105

344   *Index*

cursing, as "unitary act" 103, 105, 106; figural representations in 103, 104; tablets in 103, 104, 105

custodes, for prayers 119

Dacia, tablets from 177, 179

damnatio memoriae ("condemnation of memory") 34

debt, in double-document form 193; informal 278

debt-removal 36

declaration, entered into *acta* 246; in double-document form 193; of status, from Egypt 190

dedication 101; as "unitary act" 101, 103, 106; necessity of *pontifice praeeunte* 77; of L. Gemenio(s), son of Lucius 53; of M. and P. Vertuleius, sons of Gaius 53; of shrine to *Libertas* 60, 76; tablets in 101, 102; writing in 102

deditio ("surrender"), on bronze tablet 26

deferre in aerario, terminology for senatusconsulta 111

defigere ("to nail up") 27, 43

definition, in Roman law 254

deisidaimonia (δεισιδαιμονία, "fear of the gods") 37

Delos 16, 17

deltos chalke (δέλτος χαλκῆ, "bronze tablet"), *see* diploma, veterans'

Demosthenes, quotes *syngraphe* 14; on legal documents 21

demonstratio (plaintiff's specification of facts) 82

denuntio (giving of legal notice) 134, 135

deposita ("belongings on deposit," of soldier) 193

depositaries, Athenian 15; Hellenistic 17

devotio ("vowing of one's self") 52

dike emporike (δίκη ἐμπορική, "mercantile charge") 16

Dionysius of Halicarnassus, on Roman census 29

diploma "of a boxer" 204; of marriage 235; veterans' 27, 136, 137, 166, 197, 198, 204, 233

diploma (δίπλωμα), *see also* double-document, papyrus

diptych, curse-tablet as 78; doubled 128; legal document as, 125, 127, 132, and *see* chapter six *passim*

directus ("strict") 263

dispositive document 2, 18, 19, 297

divisions of property, written 278

documents, valuation of in court, *see* chapter eight *passim*

dominium ("ownership") 268, 277

Domitius Ahenobarbus (Cn. Domitius Ahenobarbus) 84; altar of, *see* altar of Domitius Ahenobarbus

Domitius Balbus (Domitius Balbus), will forged 166

donation 280, 286, 287, 290, 291; documents in 281, 282, 283; entered into *acta* 246, 282, 283; incorporating mancipation by late antiquity 265, 282, 283, 290; writing emphasized in 277

double-document 7, 22; papyrus 170, and *see* 187–205 *passim*

dowry-contracts, writing emphasized in 276; and see tablets, Roman, of dowry

Dura-Europos (and environs), documents from, *see* 202–205 *passim*

edict, aediles' 52, 59, 139; aediles', parodied 66; assigning provinces, parodied 66; Egyptian prefect's 52; of Caesar, parodied 66; of Vitellius, parodied 67; praetor's 26, 51, 59, 61, 82, 100; praetor's, as *carmen magistri* 71; provincial governor's 26, 86

edicts 6, 51, 70; archived in Egypt 172; copied 136, 137; granting citizenship or legal privilege 27, 99; imperial 89; making of 97, 100; on bronze 102; posting of 170, 174; written 39, 100

efficacy 5, 11, 108, 121; bestowed by emperor 252; of formality 250; of law, 3; of legal documents 159; of tablets, 2, 163, 287; and *see* chapter five *passim*; of unitary acts 5, 11

Egypt, 7; and *see* archives, Egypt; for record-keeping in, *see also* 171–5 *passim*

"*ego vos testor*" 118

emancipation (of children) 114, 175, 213, 265, 277, 291; writing emphasized in 276; *see also* tablets, Roman, of emancipation

emperor, role in legal change 169, 287, 296

emphyteusis (long-term contract) 288

emptio (informal sale) 39, 149, 284, 286; *tabellae* of 40, and *see also* tablets, Roman, of sale

end-rhyme, as element of *carmen*-style 46, 49, 50, 57

Ennius (Q. Ennius), on Saturnians sung by fauns and seers 54

ephemerides ("day-books") 33; *see also adversaria*

epikrisis (prefect's hearing on status) 175, 232, 233, 234, 235; copy of 233

epistulae ("letters"), entered into *acta* 245, 246; in court 225, 229, 231, 234, 237, 238, 239, 240; in jurists 280, 281, 288

erasure, in Greek legal documents 185, 186, 187; in Roman census-tablets 93; of tablets 34, 43, 89, 110, 185, 236

Index

345

essence, as juristic argument 250, 251, 253, 254, 255, 256, 259, 260, 264, 265, 275, 276
estate-inventory, entered into *acta* 246
existimatio ("reputation") 34

familiae emptor (in wills) 114, 164, 272
Felix of Aptunga, bishop 244
Festus (S. Pompeius Festus, scholar) 71
fideiussio (giving of surety) 138
fidepromissio (form of stipulation) 182
fides ("good faith"), and tablets, 245, and *see* chapter six *passim*; in court 216, 217, 250, and *see* chapter eight *passim*; in handwriting 231, 274; in legal acts 133, 151, 158; *see also bona fides* legal acts; in seals 134, 155, 158, 160, 162, 163, 165, 180, 198, 204, 295; in witnesses to donation 282; of individuals 5, 6, 21, 34, 121, 125, 158, 214, 289, 295; symbol of 117
fiducia (surety) 126; *see also* manicipation, fiduciary
figura ("physical expression") 259
figura etymologica, as element of *carmen*-style 49, 53
flamen dialis 1, 2
Flavius (Cn. Flavius), thief of *legis actiones* 80; vows a temple to Concord 102
Florentinus (jurist), on stipulation 256, 257
Florus (L. Annaeus Florus), on census 29
foedus, *see* treaties, treaty, and tablets, Roman, of treaties
forgery 15, 34, 35, 43, 166, 239, 244, 280
formal acts 132, 133, 134, 287; arguments about validity 250; *see also* ceremonial acts
formal process 21
formal words 10, 38, 64, 115, 118, 268, 290, 291; *see also certa* and *concepta verba*
formalism 38, 63, 80, 263, 276
formality 5, 6, 10, 194, 250, 256, 290; compensation for failures in 165, 250, 253, 258, 259, 260, 261, 262, 265, 268, 269, 270, 276, 277, 297
"formalized" language 73; "formalized" language, anthropological definition of 44, 60
formido ("dread") 264
formula, as component of Roman tablet 44, 63, 64; as legal charge 82; in Roman census 93; in Roman treaties 67
formulae, granting judges 134, 136; in Roman legal acts 38, 39, 40, 61, 63, 68, 84, 106; in Roman legal acts, relationship to praetor's edict 59; in Roman legal procedure 79, 81, 82, 84; in Roman magical and religious ceremonial 79; in Roman wills 69; praetor's control of 82

formularies (templates, form-books), for letters 183; for petitions 183; for Roman legal tablets 115, 183
formulary procedure 82, 83, 84; evidence in 217
forum Augusti, Alexandria 172; Rome 127
Frankfurter, D. 77
fraud 2, 5

Gaius (C. Julius Caesar Germanicus "Caligula," emperor) 231
Gaius (jurist), indifference to writing 40; on *acceptilatio* 144; on contract *litteris* 108; on correct wording in legal procedure 80; on obligation 255; on relationship of *actiones* and *leges* 59; on *sponsio* and stipulation 115, 117, 255; on supersession of *legis actio* procedure 81; on *testamentum per aes et libram* 114, 115, 265; on witnesses for mancipatory acts 118
Gellius, Aulus, as *iudex* in trial 228; on *flamen dialis* 2; wording for supreme fine 83
Germanicus (Nero Claudius Drusus Germanicus = Germanicus Julius Caesar) 229
gesta, of magistrate 243; *see also acta* and *hypomnemata*
gesture 10, 113, 266, 267, 287, 290, 291
glossaries, of legal abbrevations 65
Gneist, H. R. 18
gnosteres (γνωστῆρες, "witnesses") 233
governors, Roman, *see* magistrates, Roman
Gracchus (Ti. Sempronius Gracchus, cos. 177) 87
Graf, F. 77
grammata (γράμματα, "letters"), in court 231, 237, 238
grammateidion (γραμματείδιον, "little wood tablet") 13
grammateion (γραμματεῖον, "wood tablet") 13, 237
Guéraud, O. 208

Hadrian (P. Aelius Hadrianus, emperor) 61; remission of back taxes by 110; visit to Egypt 199
Hadrian's wall 1
Hanau, tablet from 177
handwriting, *see* autograph
Harris, W. 17
heir, institution of 266, 268, 269
Herculaneum 124, 126, 134, 137, 138, 139, 146, 222, 223
Hercules, dedications to 53; temple of 67
Hermogenianus (Aurelius Hermogenianus, jurist) 279
Heuß, A. 96

346   *Index*

holograph, *see* autograph
holographic will 274, 275
honesta missio ("honorable discharge"), certificates of 27, 172, 176, 210, 278
Horace (Q. Horatius Flaccus), on Roman schoolboys 22; on dedicating tablets 28; on poet imitating censor 34
horos-stones 14
hypomnemata (ὑπομνήματα, "memoranda") 33, 212, 213, 217, 242, 243, 244, 245, 246
hypomnematismos (ὑπομνηματισμός), in court 231

Iamblichus 75
idios logos 234, 236
ignominia ("bad *nomen*") 93
illiteracy, of magic-users 78
imperial communication, weight in court 229
incerta, antonym of *certa* and *concepta verba* 62
infamia ("bad reputation") 225
ink 127
Institutes of Justinian, on Leo's constitution on stipulation 263; on sale 286; on stipulation 261
institutio heredis, *see* heir, institution of
instrumenta ("equipment" or "instruments") 157; as documents 39, 119, 234, 260, 261, 275, 277, 278, 281, 297; used generically in late-antique compilations 251
instrumenta publica 288
instrumentum testationis 284
intentio (plaintiff's statement of claims) 82
interpolations, in Greek legal documents 185, 186, 187
interpunctuation, as an aid to reading aloud 83
interrogationes in iure ("legal examinations") 134, 135
intertium (formal passing to giving of sentence) 134, 135
iudex and *iudices*, *see* judges
iudicia ("judgments"), written 39; *see also sententiae*
iuridicus 137
ius actorum conficiendorum 247
ius commercii 182
ius Latii 182
ius respondendi 123

Janiculum (hill), red flag on 98
Jerome (Eusebius Hieronymus), on will of the piglet 68, 70
Jhering, R. von 10
John Chrysostom, *see* Chrysostom, John
Jucundus, *see* Caecilius Jucundus
Judaea, documents from, *see* 187–202 *passim*

judges 3, 80, 124
Julia Crispina 192
Julian (Flavius Claudius Julianus, emperor), on *grammatia* 280
Julius Bassus (C. Julius Bassus) 228
Jupiter 1, 47
jurisconsults, described as singing 82; *see also* jurists
jurists 3, 4, 5, 6, 11, 251; as drafters of laws 252, 296; role in valuation of legal documents 123, 124; *see also* Aelius Paetus, Ateius Capito, Celsus, Cincius, Florentinus, Gaius, Hermogenianus, Manilius, Modestinus, Paulus, Pomponius, Sabinus, Ulpian, and chapter nine *passim*
justice 2, 3, 122
Justinian 6, 110, 114; on donations 283; on formality 264; on "public documents" 288; on sale 286; on stipulation 263
Justinianic code 65, 252
Juvenal (Decimus Iunius Iuvenalis), on fall of Sejanus 229; on marriage-*tabellae* 117

kalendarium (papyrus day-book) 172
koine (κοινή) 17

Latin, as necessary in Roman acts 60
laudationes ("letters of praise") 224; *see also commendationes*
law, anthropological studies of 4; Athenian 16; Greek 16, 18; Roman 2, 3, 7; Roman, in cultural context 3, 4; Roman, late antique 2; written 2, 3; and, for Roman, *see also lex*
laws, Roman 5; and *see also leges*
lease-inscriptions, Athenian 14
legal documents, Athenian, 12, 13, 14, 15, 295; Athenian, form, language, and style 13, 14; Greek, 6, 11, 12, 20; Greek, emendations in 185; Greek, lack of formality in 13, 18, 20; Hellenistic 17, 18, 19, 185, 295; preservation 5; Ptolemaic 12, 16; Ptolemaic, form, language, and style 16, 17; registration or deposition in Greek archives 15, 17, 18, 185; Roman 2, 4, 6, 11, 12, 21; Roman, as part of "unitary act" 112; Roman, characteristics similar to those of other tablets 37; Roman, dating formulae in 187, 195, 202; Roman, form, language, and style 21, and *see* chapter three *passim*; Roman, in court, 162, and *see* chapter eight *passim*; Roman, use of non-Latin languages in 187, 191; Roman, valuation of 122, 123, 124, 151, 159, 169, 277, 284; Roman, written by late Republic 38; Roman, *see also contractus, instrumenta*, and tablets, Roman
legal procedure 4
leges Iuliae (on procedure) 81, 85

Index

347

legis actio procedure 80, 82, 83, 84
legitima auctoritas ("legitimate authority")
252
legitimae tabellae ("legitimate little tablets," of
dowry) 118
legitimacy 2, 4, 5, 10; bestowed by emperors and
jurists in late antiquity 252; emperor as source
of in late antiquity 293
Leo (emperor), on donation 282; on stipulation
263, 290; on writing in contracts 288
letters, *see epistulae*
Lévy, J.-P. 12
lex (law), archaic language of 61; as collective
term 49, 71, 72; as formulaic paradigm for
legal act 38; as formulaic paradigm for prayer
46, 47; as terms of contract 66; as terms of
treaty 47, 71, 95; as terms of vow 53;
cancellation of 99; making of 97; making of a
"unitary act" 101, 266; on bronze 102; on
imperium of Vespasian 49; on sealing wills 165;
style 49; written 39, 99; *see also* Twelve Tables
lex Aebutia 81
lex Aelia Sentia 172, 175
lex Clodia on Cicero's exile 99
lex Cornelia on forgery 165; extended 166
lex Cornelia Baebia, parodied 66
lex Iulia de vicesima hereditatium 165, 172
lex Iulia on adultery 85
lex Iulia Titia 172, 212
lex Papia Poppaea 172
lex Rubria 151
lex Tappula (parody) 67
Libanius, on tablets and memory 6
libellary procedure 86
libellus ("little book") 22, 66, 67, 77, 231, 233;
announcing auction 137; bringing a legal
charge through 82, 85, 106; of Piso 229; used
to denounce Julia 87; Vitellius uses in
attempted abdication 87
libellus ("petition") 196; posting of when
answered 201; posting of, see also petitions,
answered, posting of
liberalitas, in donation 281, 287
Libertas, shrine to 60
Libo (M. Scribonius Libo Drusus) 231
libraries, burned in AD 23, 294
library of Hadrian (archive in Alexandria) 186
libri ("books") 22, 77; as formularies 81
libri commentarii, see commentarii
libripens ("scale-holder"), in mancipatory acts
113, 114, 118, 181, 272
linen 24, 25; for books 25, 54
linum ("string") 2, 22, 128, 129, 130, 143, 162, 166,
240
literacy, Greek 13; Roman Republican 37; *see also*
illiteracy

litterae ("letters") 225, 228, 229; and *epistulae*,
lack of intrinsic authority 225, 239, 248
Livy (T. Livius), on being moved to *tabula
aerarii* 86, 93; on treaty Rome/Aetolians 97;
on treaty Rome/Alba Longa 71, 95
loans, fictive 18
locatio (lease) 149
Lollia Paulina, her jewels 40, 41
Louis XIV 9
Lucceius (L. Lucceius) 223
Lucian, on forgery 167
lustration, in census 93, 94

Macro (Q. Naevius Cordus Sutorius
Macro) 228
Macrobius (Ambrosius Theodosius Macrobius),
on judges and evidence in early trial 218; on
media for consulting oracles 1
magic 2, 4, 7, 10; and law 294
magicians, as similar to priests 77, 78, 79; write
out curses 78
magistrates, Roman 5, 21–24, 25, 27, 79, 80, 122,
124, 184; and archival practice, *see* 184–7
passim; impact on legal change 1, 169, 296
mancipation 113, 134, 136, 265; as "unitary act"
115, 265; Campanian documentation of 139,
146; fiduciary 126, 139, 140; formal words in
115, 283, 290, 291; in Dacia 56, 181, 182;
qualities of 42; on *tabulae* 40, 112, 120, 248;
references to removed from late antique codes
251, 272; *tabulae* in 115, 164; warranty clauses
with 59, 139
mancipation and mancipatory acts, ceremonial
in 113, 114, 115; witnesses in 118
mancipatory will 114, 164, 175, 213, and *see*
265–76 *passim*; as continuous act 116; as
"unitary act" 115, 271, 275; *institutio heredis* in
266; nuncupation in 118, 266; of Antonius
Silvanus 57, 207; of M. Sempronius Priscus
207; on *tabulae* 40, 175, 220, 240, 274, 276;
parody of 67; parody of, *see also testamentum
porcelli*; qualities of 43; regulated by legislation
165, 168; tablet in 266, 272; witnessing of 273;
see also Gaius (jurist), on *testamentum per aes
et libram, testamentum per aes et libram*, and
will-opening
mandata (imperial) 229
mandatum (mandate, a contract) 149, 245, 246
Manilius (M.' Manilius, jurist), *leges* of 59
"*manum de tabula*" (Roman proverb) 36
manumission, as part of act of emancipation 291;
of slaves 175, 207, 213, 277, 288; of slaves, in
churches 287
marriage contract, in double-document form
193; writing emphasized in 276

348   *Index*

Mars 54; with the Lares, and the Senones, prayer to 60

martyr-acts, *see* Christian martyr-acts

martyres (μάρτυρες, "witnesses") 195, 203

martyropoiemata (μαρτυροποιήματα, "attestations") 193

matrix (μάτριξ, "register") 172

memory 6, 101, 112, 116

Metellus Numidicus (Q. Caecilius Metellus Numidicus) 221

Mitteis, L. 18, 19

Modestinus (Herennius Modestinus, jurist) 85; on requests for tutors 212; on wills 267

Mommsen, T. 3; on *acceptilationes* 144

mos maiorum ("way of the ancestors") 83

Mourgues, J.-L. 210

Murecine (tablets), 126, 138; and *see* chapter six *passim*

mutuum (loan) 149, 150

Myra (city), archives 184, 185

nails 43, 93, 103, 104; *see also defigere*

Nanaion (archive in Alexandria) 173, 186

Nero (Nero Claudius Caesar, emperor) 27, 32, 35

nexum (obligation created *per aes et libram*) 114

Nikareta 17, 18

nomen ("name"), as component of Roman tablet 44, 63, 64, 69, 70

nomen deferre ("to bring an accusation") 84, 106

nomikoi (νομικοί, scribes and legal consultants) 183, 195, 200, 235, 236

nomina (entries in account-books) 39, 64, 108

nomina arcaria 108, 134, 136, 137, 138, 140, 146

nomina transscripticia 108, 109; *see also* contract *litteris*

nota, in Roman census 93

notaries 17, 182, 275; *see also nomikoi*

novae tabulae ("new tablets" as eradicating debt) 36

noxal surrender (handing-over of offender) 114

Nukulaelae people 74

nuncupare ("to announce") 61, 64

nuncupation 28, 64, 118; in mancipatory will 266, 267, 268, 269, 270, 273, 274

nuncupative will 273, 275; see also *testamentum per nuncupationem* (AD 439)

oaths 134, 135

observatio ("punctiliousness") 264, 266, 271, 272, 273, 281, 282, 284, 290, 291, 292

officials (Hellenistic) 17

officials, Roman, *see* magistrates, Roman

Olympia, posting treaties at 97

orality, in juristic arguments, *see* chapter nine *passim*

ordo, as component of Roman tablet 44, 63, 64

orthographos (ὀρθογράφος, "correct writer," clerk) 200

Otacilia 108

Ovid (P. Ovidius Naso), plays with image of recording testimony 224

pactio ("settlement"), written 39

pactum ("agreement," a contract), written 39, 140, 278, 280

pagina ("page") 128

palimpsest 185, 187

papyrus, as Greek writing material 1, 9; for learning to write 23; for Roman legal documents 22, 203; for Roman legal documents, replacing wood 206, 211, 214; in Roman world 1, 5, 7; legal documents from Athens 13; legal documents from Ptolemaic Egypt 16; legal documents from Roman Egypt 175, 191, 298; used for *ephemera* by Romans 176, 247, 248

paradigm, of balancing *fides* and *tabulae* in court 250; of Roman documentary practice 206

paradigms, for Roman legal acts 38; for Roman prayers 38

parchment, Roman legal documents 22, 202

parody, as characteristic of *tabula*-documents 44, 63, 66, 70

pascua ("pastures"), archaic terminology for income 60

patria potestas ("paternal power"), sons under 33, 107

Patrica (archive in Alexandria) 173

Paulus (Julius Paulus, jurist), on *libelli* of adultery 85; on stipulation 257, 258, 259; on *senatusconsultum Neronianum* 167; on *tabularium* 39

Paulus's *Sententiae*, on stipulation 261

pen 1

performative, language 73, 74, 103; power 6, 73

petitions, Ptolemaic 16; Roman 252; Roman, answered, archiving of 199; Roman, answered, changing legal value of 198; Roman, answered, copies of 197, 198, 199, 234; Roman, answered, from Egypt 196, 197; Roman, answered, from Judaea and Arabia 196, 197, 198; Roman, answered, imperial posting of 199, 200, 201, 209; Roman, answered, posting of 176, 199, 200

Petronia Justa 223

"phase-three documents" 135, 138, 140, 142, 152

Philip V (of Macedon) 97

Philostratus, on defects in magic 103

pignus (pledge) 149, 279

pittacia ("wood tablets"), in Spain, late-Roman west, late antiquity 176, 285

Index

349

pittakion (πιττάκιον, "tablet") 106, 173, 174, 176, 184, 198; as wood tablet 184

Plautus (T. Maccius Plautus), on banker and *tabellae* 120; on schoolboy with *tabula* 23; parodies of formal language in 66

plebiscitum, making of 97; on Cicero's exile 99; on weights and measures 51

pleonasm, as element of *carmen*-style 45, 50

Pliny the Elder (C. Plinius Secundus), on absence of sealing in East 158; on *carmina* 297; on income listed as *pascua* 60; on Lollia Paulina's jewelry 40; on prayer in *obsecratio* 75; on sealing-rings and crime 157, 167; on sealing-rings and *sponsiones* 157; on spells (*carmina*) for safe travel 72

Pliny the Younger (C. Plinius Caecilius Secundus), on trial of Julius Bassus 228

Plutarch, on *flamen dialis* 2

poets 24, 66

Polybius, on Romans' *deisidamonia* 37; on Romans' *fides* 21; on Roman magistrates' good behavior 151

polyptychs 176

Pompeius Reginus (Pompeius Reginus) 41

Pompeii 124, 134, 139, 146, 222

Pompey (Cn. Pompeius Magnus) 41, 226

Pomponius (S. Pomponius, jurist), on damage to praetor's edict 100; on history of Roman law 81; on stipulation 254, 257

pontifex 25, 31, 102; and jurisprudence 38

postulatio (request for granting of legal action) 82, 83, 85

praeire verba ("to speak words before") 25, 46, 76, 77, 79, 102

praeiudicia ("previous judgments") 241

praeteritio 89

prayer, as necessary part or religious ritual 75; for dedication of altar 46, 60; for purification of fields 45; of Arval brethren 60, 61; read from *libri* or *tabulae* 33, 77; style and syntax 45, 46, 70

precision, as an element of *carmen*-style 48, 51, 52, 55, 57, 58, 115; in legal language 83, 84, 115

prefect (of Egypt) 137, 187

prestige, in court 216; of personal documents in court 228, 230

priests, Roman 24, 25, 60, 71; calendar of 81; see also augur and *pontifex*

professio ("profession") of legitimate birth 137, 207, 276, 277, 278; treated as a petition 210, 211; writing emphasized in 276; see also tablets, Roman, of *professio* of legitimate birth

promulgari ("to make known"), a law 97

proof 5, 15, 19, 151, 159, 259, 278, 279; see also chapter eight *passim*

prostagma (πρόσταγμα, "ordinance"), of prefect of Egypt 230

provinces and provincials, 5, 6, 28, 123; and see chapter seven *passim*

"public documents," see *instrumenta publica*

publicae notationes ("notations known to public," abbreviations) 65

Pudentilla, wife of Apuleius 238, 239, 240, 241

pugillares ("small writing tablets") 22

purchase, Roman, formulae in 38

Puteoli 127, 135

quaestio (board of inquiry or court) 84, 85; *de repetundis*, procedure in 84

quaestor, as drafter of law 252

Quintilian (M. Fabius Quintilianus), on archaic words 61; on danger in challenging sealed tablets 225; on intent vs. words 267; on lightening impact of tablets 227; on *praeiudicia* 241; on tablets capturing *voluntas* 222; on testimony 224

reading from tablets, see *recitatio*

receipt, attested 193; see also *acceptilationes*

reciprocity 5

recitatio ("recitation") 73, 74, 75, 76; as like singing 87; as serious, final, and authoritative 87, 88, 89; in formulary procedure 83; in legal procedure 74, 80, 86; in *legis actio* procedure 80; of decree 88; of imperial edicts 89; of judicial decisions 88, 89; of *leges* 86, 98; of prayers 74, 76, 77, 79; of *senatusconsulta* 86; of speeches 89; of spells on curse-tablets 74, 78, 79, 103, 105; of tablet-lists 86; of wills 86

recognovi ("I have read through and acknowledged"), used in subscriptions 207

registration of birth, see *professio* of legitimate birth; tablets, Roman, of attestation of illegitimate birth and tablets, Roman, of *professio* of legitimate birth

relatum in tabulas (used of *senatusconsultum*) 111

religio ("religious scruple") 34

religion, Roman 4, 7, 10

religious acts 10

repetition, as element of *carmen*-style 45, 46, 47, 48, 50, 51, 55, 58, 59

res mancipi ("things owned through mancipation") 40, 193, 194

restipulatio (demand for counter-guarantee) 39; see also stipulation

reus, as debtor/person bound over 106; as defendant 242

Revelation, book of 201

rings 2; Roman, for sealing 158

ritual 5, 9, 10, 107; in magical acts 77; see also ceremonial

350   *Index*

Rome (city) 135
Romanists (scholars of Roman law) 3, 4, 7
romanization 5, 6, 205, 296
Roscius (Q. Roscius) 221
Rottweil, tablet from 177

Sabinus (Masurius Sabinus, jurist) 254
sagmen (special herb) 95
sale, Aramaic, from Arabia 192; Greek, from Arabia 192; in double-document form 193; Roman, documents in 285; Roman, entered into *acta* 246, 285; Roman, formulae in 38; Roman, incorporating mancipation by late antiquity 265; Roman, in late antiquity 278, 280, 284, 286, 287; Roman, writing emphasized in 277, 285
Sallust (C. Sallustius Crispus), on *fides* 162
Salona (Dalmatia), inscribed prayer from 46, 49, 60
Saturnian verse 28, 53, 54; as rhythmical rather than quantitative 54
Saturnus 54
Scaevola (Q. Mucius Scaevola "pontifex") 39
Scaevola (Q. Mucius Scaevola "augur") 220
Scaurus (M. Aemilius Scaurus) 31
scheda ("sheet") 248
Schiller, A. A. 200
Scipio Aemilianus (P. Cornelius Scipio Aemilianus Africanus Numantinus) 62
Scipio Africanus (P. Cornelius Scipio Africanus) 86
Scipio, Lucius (L. Cornelius Scipio, brother of Africanus the Elder) 88
scribes 24; use of formularies by 183; writing interior versions of *acceptilationes* 183; writing exterior versions of documents 150, 183; writing legal documents in East 202, 205; *see also nomikoi*, notaries, *orthographos*, *tabellio*, and *tabularius*
sealers, *see signatores*
sealing 5, 22, 125, 156, 158, 159, 160, 162; at end of document 155; by slaves 155; in Dacia 179; in Egypt 195; in formal *testatio*-style documents 133; in informal chirograph-style documents 150; of letters 160; of wills 164, 274, 275
seals, Delos 17, 159; Greek 21; Roman 125, 128, 130, 143, 154, 158, 179, 240; Roman, as expressions of *fides* 154, 155, 160; Roman, as expressions of *fides*, ranked by status 156
Searle, J. R. 73
Sejanus (L. Aelius Sejanus) 229
senatusconsulta 31, 39; making of 97, 107, 110, 119; with instructions for inscribing treaties 96; tablet in 110, 111, 112

senatusconsultum de Cn. Pisone patre 61
senatusconsultum Neronianum (AD 61) 125, 130, 131, 163, 167, 178, 269
senatusconsultum on the assigning of tutors 172
senatusconsultum ultimum 111
Seneca the Elder (L. Annaeus Seneca), combination of stipulation and mancipation in his time 140
Seneca the Younger (L. Annaeus Seneca), Augustus's judgment on Claudius 88; on *chirographum* and *signatores* 156; on creditors' desires 157; on priests and *carmina* 71
sententiae (legal decisions) 134, 136
Septimius Severus (L. Septimius Severus, emperor), visit to Egypt 200
Servinius Gallus (L. Servinius Gallus), edict of 137
Servius (commentator on Vergil) 54
Servius (king) 29
sestertius, purchase with 118
shorthand-writers 247
signatores ("sealers") 125, 133, 159, 162, 223; different from *testes* 160, 161; of wills 164; ranked by status 156
Silanus (M. Junius Silanus) 84
Smith, J. Z. 77
societas (partnership) 150
sollemnia ("formal requirements") 85, 268, 285, 286, 287, 296
sollemnitas ("solemnity") 250, 258, 261, 262, 263, 266, 269, 270, 271, 272, 284, 285; *see also* 287–93 *passim*
solutio per aes et libram (dissolution of an act *per aes et libram*) 42
Soxis, petition of priests of 199, 209
speech-act 44
sponsio ("solemn promise") 39, 115; references to removed from late-antique codes 251; *see also* stipulation
statio vicesimaria (office of inheritance tax) 172
stipula ("reed") 117, 118
stipulation 115; and *fides* 133; as "unitary act" 118, 253, 254, 261, 264; ceremony or gesture in 117, 118; combined with *bona fides* legal acts 151; formal words in 118; in donation 281; juristic discussion of, *see* 253–65 *passim*; of warranty of slaves 139; on *tabulae* 40, 41, 61, 112, 117, 151, 248; style and syntax of 58; tablets in 117, 118, 253; written 39; *see also fidepromissio* and *sponsio*
stria ("groove") 128, 166
string, *see linum*
stylus 1, 22, 34, 127
subscribing 5

Index

351

subscription, adding value 210; of author-protagonist 206, 207, 208, 210, 211, 289, 295; of donation 281; of emperor 289; of marriage document 277; of "public documents" 288; of slave-sales 290; of tablets 209, 214; of will 274, 275, 289; to "diploma of a boxer" 204; to letters 210, 238; to petitions 198, 199; to petitions, imperial, 199, 201, 209, 210; and *see also* petitions, answered; written by guardian or tutor 208, 209, 211

Suetonius (C. Suetonius Tranquillus), on direction of writing for reports to senate 190; on mock edict 66; on *senatusconsultum Neronianum* 165, 166, 167; portent about king 110

sulcus ("deep groove") 128, 129, 130, 133, 135, 136, 150, 154, 166, 178

Sulpicii (family of bankers in Puteoli) 126

summons, to court 191; *see also denuntiones*

suovetaurilia ("purificatory sacrifice") 45

superstites, see testes

symbolic objects or signs 10

Symmachus (Q. Aurelius Symmachus), judge in trial 245, 246

syngraphe (συγγραφή) 14, 16; Gaius on 18; Pseudo-Asconius on 18; six-witness 17; see also contract (Greek or Athenian)

tabellae ("little tablets") 1, 22, 24; for voting 98; major differences from *tabulae* 24

tabellio ("scribe") 273, 288, 292

tablae (τάβλαι) 106

tablet of the *aerarii* (Roman census) 93

tablets, Egyptian, of bouleutic membership 174; in Athenian courts 13; in Athens 13

tablets, Roman, as embodiments of acts 22, 28, 73, 91, 101, 103, 105, 107, 113, 120, 125, 137, 157; as embodiments of *fides* 156, 157, 225; as final and authoritative 30, 33, 34, 35, 36, 37, 42, 43, 87, 88, 89, 219, 225, 241, 245; as markers of magisterial status in art 77; as proof 216, 218, 219, 220, 227, 234, 296; as templates for reading 74, 91, and *see* chapter four *passim*; bankers' 221; basic meaning 24; believed early use 39; bronze 9, 22, 26, 27, 35, 67, 95, 96, 99, 102; burning of 110; calendar 25; censors' 25, 27, 29, 34, 36, 60, 210, 220; copies of grants of citizenship, 27, 171; and *see also* diploma; copies of nominations of tutors 173, 207, 211; copy of act of dissolution 178; emperor uses to consult oracle 1; financial, 27, 28, 30, 33, 109, 120, 178, and *see also* accounts, Roman, financial; contract *litteris*; *nomina arcaria*; *nomina transscripticia*; financial, in court 219; for Cato's speeches 89; for cursing *see*

curse-tablets, Roman; for drafting 24; for legal charge 82, 209; for lists of *iudices* 26, 36; for lists of decurions 26, 36; for lists of members of associations 26, 36; for lists of senators 26, 36; for prayers 25; for shorthand writing 247; from North Africa 264; in general 1, 2, 3, 4, 5, 6, 7, 9, 10, 11; in legal acts 113, 114, 115, 119, 153; in legal procedure 83, 84, 85, 106, 107, 173; legal, in general 6; longevity 35; multiple 22, and *see also* diptych, triptych, polyptych, and *codex* (*codices*); no public/private distinction 29, 30, 37, 41, 42, 43; of appointment to office, *see codicilli*, of appointment; of arbitration 177; of Arval brethren 32; of attestation of illegitimate birth 175, 207, 233; of boys assuming the toga 172; of contract 177; of *cretio* 175, 207; of customs-officials 176; of debt 41, 177; of discharge of obligation, 178, and *see also acceptilatio*; of donation 281, 283; of dowry 41, 117; of emancipation (of children) 175; of governors, 241, 246, and *see also hypomnemata*; of grants of citizenship 27, 170, 171; of guarantees of crop-shares 176; of *honesta missio* 172, 174, 176, 210; of imperial benefaction 171; of imperial constitutions 292; of judicial decisions 88, 89; of *leges* 26, 97, 220; of marriage 41, 119, 240, 277; of mining privileges 176; of plebiscites 26, 27, 51; of *professio* of legitimate birth 119, 172, 198, 210, 211, 233, 240; of request for *bonorum possessio* 175; of restipulation 220; of sale 177, 231, 241, 278, 285; of *senatusconsulta* 26, 27, 97, 220; of *senatusconsulta*, style of 50; of slave-manumission 175, 233, 235, 236; of stipulation 41, 61, and *see also cautiones*; of the *pontifices* 25, 30, 31, 32, 33, 35; of the praetor 34, 220, 242; of the praetor's edict 35, 51, 82, 100; of treaties 26, 27, 47, 95; of vow 53, 102; of wills, *see* mancipatory will, on tablets; of witness-statement 177, 224; on sacrificial animals 101; posting of 176, and *see also* edicts, posting of; preservation of 30, 33, 42, 240; reused, for letters 177; revered qualities of 33; schoolboy 22, 23; similarities between 21, 295; substitute of papyrus double-documents for 194; surveyors' 26; syntax of 45, 47, 48, 49, 50, 51, 52, 53, 54, 55, 56, 57, 69; Verres's 242; whitened 25, 26, 31, 35; with wax coating 2, 6, 9, 22, 71, 114; wood 26, 30; wood, physical description 22; and *see tabula*

tablia (ταβλία), Egyptian tablets with tax-lists 174

tablinum 27, 28, 33; derivation from *tabulae* 27; in Egypt 171

tabula ansata ("eared tablet") 28

352

Index

tabula pertusa ("perforated tablet") 127, 130, 166, 168, 179

tabulae publicae ("public tablets") 29, 30, 62, 77, 217, 242, 247

tabulae sistendi (attestations of appearance) 134, 135

tabulae triumphatores ("triumphal tablets") 28, 53, 54

tabularium, Africa 240; Caesarea 172; Egypt 171; Ephesus 172; imagined contents of 39; Roman forum 29

tabularius ("scribe") 172, 176, 233, 244, 288

Tacitus (P. Cornelius Tacitus), on annals vs. *acta diurna* 32; on *libelli* at Libo's trial 231; on will-forgery (AD 61) 166

templa (inaugurated spaces) 21–24, 27, 29; created through *concepta verba* 62

temple, of Ceres 111; of Concord 102; of the Nymphs 29

temples, Roman 27, 28, 42, 43, 93, 95; *see also atrium Libertatis*; Capitolium; Flavius; Hercules, temple of; *Libertas*, shrine of; and temple

testamentum, of Julius Caesar 41; recited 86; written 39, 70; and *see also* mancipatory will

testamentum per aes et libram ("testament with bronze and balance") 114; and *see* mancipatory will

testamentum per nuncupationem ("nuncupatory testament," AD 439) 274

testamentum porcelli ("testament of the piglet") 68

testamentum scriptum ("written will," AD 439) 274

testatio ("attestation") 133, 134, 135, 237; *see also* witness-statements, Roman

testatio-style 133, 134, 135, 136, 137, 138, 140, 142, 143, 223; and *see* chapter six *passim*

testes (witnesses as judges) 96, 118, 119, 159; of wills 163, 165, 168; not same as *signatores* 160, 161, 168; seals as 155, 162

"*testes estote*" 118

testimony, as proof 227; written 149, 150; *see also* witness-statements

Tiberius (Tiberius Julius Caesar Augustus, emperor) 228, 231

Titius (C. Titius) 218

Todd, S. C. 16

toga 172

Torelli, M. 94

traditio ("handing-over") 181, 281, 282, 283, 285

traditionalism 5; *see also mos maiorum*

Trajan (M. Ulpius Traianus, emperor) 1; remission of back taxes by 110

transversa writing (writing across the fibers) 128, 135, 188, 190, 213

treaties 95; archaic language of 61; as "unitary acts" 96; nine epigraphically preserved 96; parodies of 67; written 39, 95, 96; *see also* tablets, Roman, of treaties

treaty, with Aetolians (211 BC) 97; with Alba Longa 47, 95; with Callatis 48

tribunal 80

Trimalchio 41, 67

"tripartite" will 274, 290

"tripled writing" 128

triptych, legal document as 125, 129, 132, 179; to protect seals 154, 156; and *see* chapter six *passim*

triumph 28

tutor, abdication of 190; nomination of 137, 207, 211; request for, treated as petition 212

Twelve Tables 26, 37, 49, 61, 65, 68, 80, 84, 86; as *carmen necessarium* 71

Ulpian (Domitius Ulpianus, jurist), on defacing praetor's edict 100; on institution of heir 269; on praetor's manumission of a slave 123; on recompense in theft of account-books 109; on stipulation 116, 256, 257; on vowing and dedicating 101; on wills 42

undersealing, *see* sealing, at end of document

"unitary act" 4, 5, 91, 92, 105, 106, 112, 115, 120, 133, 134, 145, 150, 258, 266, 276, 290; tablet in 92, 101, 103, 107, 112, 115, 120, 295; legal tablet in 92, 112, 119, 276

vadimonium (promise to appear in court) 41, 134, 135

Valens (emperor), conspiracy against 295

Valentinian (emperor), on sale 285

Valerius Maximus, on evidence in Metellus Numidicus's trial 221

Valerius Probus (M. Valerius Probus, grammarian) 65, 66, 81

Valkenburg 177

Varro (M. Terentius Varro), dedications made *pontifice praeeunte* 77; on acceptable formulae in sale of sheep 61; on antiquity of Saturnians 54; on creating *templa* through *concepta verba* 62; on language in mancipation 113; on language of stipulations 58, on variations in words used to summon *comitia centuriata* 62; dedications made *pontifice praeeunte* 77; provides ancient formulae 38

Venidius Ennychus (L. Venidius Ennychus), edict about citizenship of 137

Veranius (Q. Veranius), governor of Lycia and Pamphilia 184, 185, 187

verba ("words"), as both written and spoken 260; for contrast with intent, *see voluntas*

veritas ("truth" or "reality") 120, 121, 279, 281

Index

353

Verres (C. Verres) 30, 52, 86, 220, 221, 242

Versnel, H. 104

Vespasian (T. Flavius Vespasianus, emperor) 27, 49

Vindolanda, account-keeping at 30; leaf-tablets at 176; rubbish at 179

Vindonissa, fragmentary tablets from 177, 179

Visellius Varus (L. Visellius Varus) 108

Vitellius (A. Vitellius, emperor), attempted abdication 87; edict against astrologers 67

Vitrasius (C. Vitrasius, magician) 78

Vitruvius (Vitruvius Pollio, architect), on *tablinum* 28

volumen ("papyrus roll") 226

voluntas ("will" or "intent") 265, 267, 268, 269, 270, 273, 274, 275; *voluntas* vs. *verba*, discussion 267

votum ("vow") 28, 52, 53, 62, 70, 101; as act of legally independent person 107; legalistic language of 106; on bronze 102; parody of 67; *see also devotio*

vow, *see votum*

wax 1, 2, 22, 23, 34, 35, 115, 244; for ancestor-masks 35; on wood, for imperial portraits 35; shape of letters on 61

will, Athenian 13, 14, 15; Roman, *see* holographic will, mancipatory will, nuncupatory will, *testamentum*, *testamentum per aes et libram*, *testamentum per nuncupationem*, *testamentum scriptum*, and "tripartite" will

will-openings 41, 165, 180, 240, 245

witnesses 70; Athenian 13, 14, 15; in Egypt, *see gnosteres*; Hellenistic 17, 18, 21; Roman, of ceremonial acts 118; Roman, *see testes*

witnessing, Roman 159, 160, 162, 289; and sealing 158, 159, 180, 289; and sealing, late equivalence 160; of Roman donations 282, 283; of Roman wills 164

witness-statements, Athenian 14; Roman, 177, 222, 228, 229; Roman, entered into *acta* 245, 246; Roman, from Herculaneum 223

Wolff, H.-J. 12, 17, 19

writing, as *sollemnis* 291; late-antique emphasis on, *see* chapter nine *passim*

Yemen (before 1962) 19

Zeno (emperor), on donation 282; on *emphyteusis* 288

For EU product safety concerns, contact us at Calle de José Abascal, 56–1°, 28003 Madrid, Spain or eugpsr@cambridge.org.

www.ingramcontent.com/pod-product-compliance
Ingram Content Group UK Ltd.
Pitfield, Milton Keynes, MK11 3LW, UK
UKHW011326060825
461487UK00005B/364